HUMAN EVOLUTION AND CULTURE

HIGHLIGHTS OF ANTHROPOLOGY

SIXTH EDITION

Carol R. Ember
Human Relations Area Files

Melvin Ember
Human Relations Area Files

Peter N. Peregrine
Lawrence University

PEARSON
Prentice
Hall

UPPER SADDLE RIVER, NEW JERSEY 07458

Library of Congress Cataloging-in-Publication Data

Ember, Carol R.
   Human evolution and culture: highlights of anthropology/Carol R. Ember, Melvin Ember, Peter N. Peregrine—6th ed.
     p. cm.
   Rev. ed. of: Anthropology: a brief introduction/Carol R. Ember, Melvin Ember. 5th ed.
   Includes bibliographical references and index.
   ISBN 978-0-13-603635-7
   1. Anthropology.   I. Ember, Melvin.   II. Peregrine, Peter N. (Peter Neal).   III. Ember, Carol R. Anthropology.
IV. Title.
   GN25.E46 2009
   301—dc22
                                                       2008005965

Editorial Director: Leah Jewell
Publisher: Nancy Roberts
Editorial Assistant: Nart Varoqua
Director of Marketing: Brandy Dawson
Marketing Manager: Lindsey Prudhomme
Production Liaison: Barbara Reilly
Operations Specialist: Ben Smith
Director, Image Resource Center: Melinda Patelli
Manager, Rights and Permissions: Zina Arabia
Manager, Visual Research: Beth Brenzel
Manager, Cover Visual Research and Permissions: Karen Sanatar
Image Permission Coordinator: Fran Toepfer
Cover Art Director: Jayne Conte
Cover Design: Maureen Eide
Cover Photo: Walter Bibikow/Corbis
Composition/Full-Service Project Management: Kari Callaghan Mazzola and John P. Mazzola/Big Sky Composition
Printer/Binder: Edwards Brothers, Inc.
Cover Printer: Phoenix Color Corp.

This book was set in 10/12 Adobe Garamond.

Pearson Education Ltd., London
Pearson Education Singapore, Pte. Ltd
Pearson Education Canada, Inc.
Pearson Education—Japan
Pearson Education Australia PTY, Limited

Pearson Education North Asia, Ltd., Hong Kong
Pearson Educación de Mexico, S.A. de C.V.
Pearson Education Malaysia, Pte. Ltd
Pearson Education Upper Saddle River, New Jersey

10 9 8 7 6 5 4 3 2
ISBN 13: 978-0-13-603635-7
ISBN 10:   0-13-603635-X

CONTENTS

Chapter 6   The First Hominids and the Emergence of *Homo*   122

Chapter 7   The Emergence of *Homo sapiens*   153

Chapter 11   Economics   258

Chapter 12   Social Stratification: Class, Ethnicity, and Racism   284

Chapter 13   Sex and Gender   305

Chapter 19   Applied and Practicing Anthropology   435

PREFACE

This book presents the highlights of the twelfth edition of our *Anthropology*. The size of the book makes it useful for quarter courses, as well as for courses that encourage a lot of supplemental reading.

The human species may be the most widespread species in the world today. Humans have been moving tremendous distances ever since *Homo erectus* moved out of Africa. In the past 100 years or so, the number of migrants has grown enormously. For example, between the 1880s and 1920s, 20 million people left China for other parts of Asia, the Americas, and many other places around the world. And the migrations continue today. With jet planes, cell phones, and the Internet, people can live global lives, and often move back and forth from one country to another. Anthropology increasingly studies immigrant populations and the flow of people and ideas across the globe. We have included feature boxes in several chapters to highlight this growing interest in migrants and immigrants—for example, why some immigrant groups retained their "mother tongues" longer than others and how foods have spread in recent times.

In preparing this book we try to go beyond descriptions, as always. We are interested not only in *what* humans are and were like, but also in *why* they got to be that way, in all their variety. To help students appreciate what it means to understand, we include an extended discussion of explanation and evidence in the first chapter. When alternative explanations are discussed subsequently, we try to communicate the necessity of evaluating them logically as well as on the basis of the available evidence. Throughout the book, we try to communicate that no idea, including ideas put forward in textbooks, should be accepted even tentatively without supporting tests that could have gone the other way.

Organization of the Text

Part I: Introduction

Chapter 1: The Importance of Anthropology Chapter 1 introduces the student to anthropology. We discuss what we think is distinctive about anthropology in general, and about each of its subfields in particular. We show how each of the subfields is related to other disciplines such as biology, psychology, and sociology. We point out the increasing importance of applied anthropology and the importance of understanding others in today's globalized world. We discuss what it means to understand scientifically. The feature box explains the differences between scientific and humanistic understanding, and points out that the two approaches are not incompatible.

Chapter 2: How We Discover the Past   This chapter gives an overview of archaeological and paleoan-thropological research. We discuss the types of evidence archaeologists and paleoanthropologists use to reconstruct the past, the methods they use to collect the evidence, and how they go about analyzing and interpreting the evidence of the past. We describe the many techniques used by archaeologists and pale-oanthropologists to determine the age of archaeological materials and fossils. We also discuss ethics in archaeology. The chapter's feature box provides an example of how gender is studied by archaeologists.

Part II: Human Evolution: Biological and Cultural

Chapter 3: Genetics and Evolution   This chapter discusses evolutionary theory as it applies to all forms of life, including humans. Following an extensive review of genetics and the processes of evolution, in-cluding natural selection and what it means, we discuss how natural selection may operate on behavioral traits and how cultural evolution differs from biological evolution. We consider ethical issues posed by the possibility of genetic engineering. We discuss creationism and intelligent design. We consider hybridiza-tion as a potentially important process of evolution. The feature box examines the evidence suggesting that evolution proceeds abruptly rather than slowly and steadily.

Chapter 4: Human Variation and Adaptation   Here we bring the discussion of human genetics and evolution into the present, dealing with physical variation in living human populations and how physi-cal anthropologists study and explain such variation. We examine how both the physical environment and the cultural environment play important roles in human physical variation. In a section on "race" and racism we discuss why many anthropologists think the concept of "race" as applied to humans is not scientifically useful. We discuss the myths of racism and how "race" is largely a social category in humans. The feature box deals with differences in average I.Q. scores and what they mean.

Chapter 5: Primates: Present and Past   This chapter describes common primate traits, the various liv-ing primates, the distinctive hominid traits, the emergence of primates, the emergence of anthropoids, and the divergence of hominids from the other hominoids. The chapter's feature box describes how a pa-leontologist has reexamined his theory of primate origins.

Chapter 6: The First Hominids and the Emergence of *Homo*   Chapter 6 begins with a discussion of the evolution of bipedalism. Then we discuss the transition from hominoids to hominids, early hominid tools and lifestyles, trends in hominid evolution, early *Homo* species, and Lower Paleolithic cultures. The feature box discusses how we know something was a tool.

Chapter 7: The Emergence of *Homo sapiens*   This chapter discusses the transition from *Homo erectus* to *Homo sapiens,* Middle Paleolithic cultures, the emergence of modern humans, what happened to the Neandertals, and the Upper Paleolithic in Europe, Africa, Asia, and the New World. The feature box dis-cusses how paleontologists put faces on fossil skulls.

Chapter 8: Food Production and the Rise of States   Here we discuss the domestication of plants and animals, consequences of the rise of food production, the rise and fall of cities and states, and what may explain those developments. The chapter's feature box discusses how chemical analyses of bones and teeth can tell us what ancient people ate.

Part III: Cultural Variation

In most of the chapters that follow, we try to convey the range of cultural variation with ethnographic ex-amples from all over the world. Wherever we can, we discuss possible explanations of why societies may be similar or different in regard to some aspect of culture. If anthropologists have no explanation as yet for the variation, we say so. If we have some idea of the conditions that may be related to a particular kind of variation, even if we do not know yet why they are related, we discuss that, too. If we are to train students to go beyond what we know now, we have to tell them what we do not know, as well as what we think we know.

Chapter 9: The Study of Culture   This chapter introduces the concept of culture and includes an expanded discussion of the concept of society. We first try to convey a feeling for what culture is before dealing more explicitly with the concept and some assumptions about it. A section on cultural relativism puts the concept in its historical context and covers recent thinking on the subject. We discuss the fact that individual behavior varies in all societies and how such variation may be the beginning of new cultural patterns. The chapter's feature box discusses the increasing cultural diversity within the countries of the world because of immigration and migration.

Chapter 10: Language and Communication   Here we discuss communication in humans and other animals. We look at the debate over the degree of difference between human and nonhuman primate language abilities. We discuss the origins of language and how creoles and children's language acquisition can help us understand the origins, and we cover new research on infant understanding of language. We describe the fundamentals of descriptive linguistics and the processes of linguistic divergence. After discussing the interrelationships between language and other aspects of culture, we discuss the ethnography of speaking and the differences in speech according to status, gender, and ethnicity. We discuss interethnic or intercultural communication, indicating how linguists can play a role in helping people improve their cross-cultural communication, and we touch on the history of writing and literacy. The feature box discusses why some immigrant groups retain their "mother tongues" longer than others.

Chapter 11: Economics   Chapter 11 discusses how societies vary in getting their food, how they have changed over time, and how that variation seems to affect other kinds of cultural variation—including variation in social stratification and political life. We discuss how societies vary in the ways they allocate resources (what is "property" and what ownership may mean), convert or transform resources through labor into usable goods, and distribute and perhaps exchange goods and services. We describe recent experimental evidence on sharing and cooperation. The chapter's feature box explores where particular foods came from and how different foods and cuisines spread around the world as people migrated.

Chapter 12: Social Stratification: Class, Ethnicity, and Racism   This chapter explores the variation in degree of social stratification and how various forms of social inequality may develop. We discuss how egalitarian societies work hard to prevent dominance. We show how people in the United States often deny the existence of class. We end with an extensive discussion of "race," racism, and ethnicity and how they often relate to the inequitable distribution of resources. The feature box discusses social stratification on the global level: how the gap between rich and poor countries has been widening, and what may account for that trend.

Chapter 13: Sex and Gender   The first part of Chapter 13 focuses on gender concepts and how and why they vary cross-culturally. We discuss the gender division of labor in primary and secondary subsistence, and why females generally work harder. We include material on female hunting and discuss its impact on theories about the gender division of labor, and we discuss gender roles in warfare. In the second part of the chapter we discuss variation in sexual attitudes and practices, including marital sex and extramarital sex. We also discuss homosexuality, including female-female relationships. The feature box describes cross-cultural research on why some societies allow women to participate in combat.

Chapter 14: Marriage, Family, and Kinship   After discussing various theories about why marriage might be universal, we discuss variation in marriage and restrictions on marriage: how one marries, whom one marries, and how many one marries. We explain variation in family form, including the phenomenon of couples choosing to live together without marriage. The chapter's feature box discusses why one-parent families are on the increase in the United States and other countries. In discussing variation in marital residence and kinship structure, we emphasize how understanding residence is important for understanding social life in all societies.

Chapter 15: Political Life   Here we look at how societies have varied in their levels of political organization, the various ways people become leaders, the degree to which they participate in the political process, and the peaceful and violent methods of resolving conflict. We discuss how colonialization has transformed legal systems and ways of making decisions, and we expand our discussion of states as empires. The feature box discusses the role of migrants in the growth of cities around the world.

Chapter 16: Religion and Magic   In this chapter, we focus on variation in religious belief and practice, including the character and hierarchy of supernatural beings and the intervention of gods in human affairs. We discuss religious change and the rise of fundamentalism. The feature box discusses research on New England fishermen that suggests how their taboos may reduce anxiety.

Chapter 17: Culture Change and Globalization   After discussing the ultimate sources of culture change—discovery and innovation—we explore some of what is known about the conditions under which people are likely to accept innovations. We discuss the costs and benefits of innovations, and types of external and internal pressures for culture change. We draw particular attention to processes of change in the modern world, including colonialization, commercialization, industrialization, and globalization. We also discuss the rise of new cultures, or ethnogenesis. We close with a discussion of the likelihood of cultural diversity in the future. We point out that globalization does not always result in similarity (e.g., McDonald's in Japan has become very Japanese). We discuss how worldwide communication can sometimes allow the less powerful to be heard. To convey that culture change often has biological consequences, the feature box discusses obesity, hypertension, and diabetes as health consequences of modernization.

Part IV: Using Anthropology

Chapter 18: Global Issues   In this chapter we discuss the relationship between basic and applied research, and how research may suggest possible solutions to various global social problems, including natural disasters and famines, homelessness, crime, family violence, war, and terrorism. One feature box discusses global warming and our dependence on oil. A second feature box is on ethnic conflicts.

Chapter 19: Applied and Practicing Anthropology   This chapter looks at anthropological work outside of academia, the ethical issues involved in trying to improve people's lives, and the difficulties in evaluating whether a program is beneficial. We point out how applied anthropologists are playing more of a role in planning, rather than serving only as peripheral advisers to those programs already in place. The feature box discusses how medical anthropology views eating disorders and their relation to conceptions of beauty.

Features of This Book

Feature Boxes   Feature boxes appear in each chapter. These boxes focus on migrants and immigrants in recent times and on current issues in cultural anthropology.

Readability   We derive a lot of pleasure from trying to describe research findings, especially complicated ones, in ways that introductory students can understand. Thus, we try to minimize technical jargon, using only those terms that students must know to appreciate the achievements of anthropology and to take advanced courses. We think readability is important, not only because it may enhance the reader's understanding of what we write, but also because it should make learning about anthropology more enjoyable. When new terms are introduced, which of course must happen sometimes, they are set in boldface type and defined in the text (and in the Glossary at the end of the book).

Glossary   At the end of each chapter we list the new terms that have been introduced. These terms are set in boldface type and defined in the text. We deliberately do not repeat the definitions at the end of the chapter to allow students to ask themselves if they know the terms; however, we do provide page numbers to find the definitions and we also provide all the definitions again in the Glossary at the end of the book.

Outlines and Summaries   In addition to the outline provided at the beginning of each chapter, there is a detailed summary at the end of each chapter that will help students review the major concepts and findings discussed in the chapter.

Critical Questions   At the end of each chapter we provide three or four questions that may stimulate thinking about the implications of the chapter. The questions do not ask for repetition of what is in the text. We want students to imagine, to go beyond what we know or think we know.

End-of-Book Notes   Because we believe in the importance of documentation, we think it is essential to tell our readers, both professionals and students, what our conclusions are based on. Usually the basis is published research. The abbreviated notes at the end of the book provide information for finding the complete citation in the References section at the end of the book.

Supplements

This textbook is part of a complete teaching and learning package that has been carefully created to enhance the topics discussed in the text.

Instructor's Resource Manual with Tests   (0-13-603766-6) For each chapter in the text, this valuable resource provides a detailed outline, a list of objectives, discussion questions, and classroom activities. In addition, test questions in multiple-choice, true-false, and short-answer formats are available for each chapter; the answers to all questions are page-referenced to the text.

TestGEN-EQ   (0-13-603767-4) This computerized software allows instructors to create their own personalized exams, to edit any or all of the existing test questions, and to add new questions. Other special features of this program include random generation of test questions, creation of alternate versions of the same test, scrambling question sequence, and test preview before printing.

Prentice Hall Anthropology PowerPoint® Slides   (0-13-603768-2) These PowerPoint slides combine graphics and text for each chapter in a colorful format to help instructors convey anthropological principles in a new and exciting way. For easy access, they are available in the Instructor's Resource Center at <www.prenhall.com/anthropology>.

Strategies in Teaching Anthropology, Fifth Edition   (0-13-603466-7) Unique in focus and content, this book focuses on the "how" of teaching Anthropology across all of its sub-fields—Cultural Anthropology, Biological Anthropology, Archaeology, and Linguistics—to provide a wide array of associated learning outcomes and student activities. It is a valuable single-source compendium of strategies and "tricks of the trade" from a group of seasoned teaching anthropologists who are working in a variety of teaching settings and who share their pedagogical techniques, knowledge, and observations. Please see your local Pearson sales representative for more information.

MyAnthroKit (0-13-603765-8) MyAnthroKit is an online resource that contains book-specific practice tests, chapter summaries, learning objectives, flashcards, Weblinks, Research Navigator, and media-rich activities that enhance topics covered in your textbook. For more information, please contact your local Pearson sales representative.

Discovering Anthropology: Researchers at Work—Cultural Anthropology (0-13-227762-X) This collection of case studies provides examples of anthropologists working in a variety of settings. Please see your local Pearson sales representative for information about packaging this supplement with *Human Evolution and Culture*.

Research Navigator™ Research Navigator™ can help students complete research assignments efficiently and with confidence by providing three exclusive databases of high-quality, scholarly, and popular articles accessed by easy-to-use search engines.

- **EBSCO's ContentSelect™ Academic Journal Database**, organized by subject, contains many of the leading academic journals for anthropology. Instructors and students can search the online journals by keyword, topic, or multiple topics. Articles include abstract and citation information and can be cut, pasted, e-mailed, or saved for later use.
- *The New York Times* **Search-by-Subject Archive** provides articles specific to Anthropology and is searchable by keyword or multiple keywords. Instructors and students can view full-text articles from the world's leading journalists writing for *The New York Times*.
- **Link Library** offers editorially selected "best of the Web" sites for Anthropology. Link Libraries are continually scanned and kept up-to-date, providing the most relevant and accurate links for research assignments.

Gain access to Research Navigator™ by using the access code found in the front of the brief guide called *The Prentice Hall Guide to Research Navigator™* (0-13-600863-1).

The Dorling Kindersley/Prentice Hall Atlas of Anthropology (0-13-191879-6) Beautifully illustrated by Dorling Kindersley, with narrative by leading archaeological author Brian M. Fagan, this striking atlas features 30 full-color maps, timelines, and illustrations to offer a highly visual but explanatory geographical overview of topics from all four fields of Anthropology. Please contact your Pearson representative for ordering information.

Acknowledgments

We thank the people at Prentice Hall for all of their help, particularly Nancy Roberts, Publisher for the Social Sciences, and we thank Kari Callaghan Mazzola and John P. Mazzola of Big Sky Composition for seeing the manuscript through the production process.

We also thank the following reviewers, whose comments directly influenced the creation of this new edition: Garrett Cook, Baylor University; Daniel R. Maher, University of Arkansas–Fort Smith; and Sheperd Jenks, Albuquerque TVI Community College.

Thank you all, named and unnamed, who gave us advice.

Carol R. Ember
Melvin Ember
Peter N. Peregrine

ABOUT THE AUTHORS

Carol R. Ember started at Antioch College as a chemistry major. She began taking social science courses because some were required, and she soon found herself intrigued with the subject matter. There were a lot of questions without answers, and she became excited about the possibility of a research career in social science. She spent a year in graduate school at Cornell studying sociology before continuing on to Harvard, where she studied anthropology primarily with John and Beatrice Whiting.

For her Ph.D. dissertation she worked among the Luo of Kenya. While she was there she noticed that many boys were assigned "girls' work," such as babysitting and household chores, because their mothers (who did most of the agriculture) did not have enough girls to help out. She decided to study the possible effects of task assignment on the social behavior of boys. Using systematic behavior observations, she compared girls, boys who did a great deal of "girls' work," and boys who did little such work. She found that boys assigned "girls' work" were intermediate in many social behaviors compared with the other boys and girls. Later, she did cross-cultural research on variation in marriage, family, descent groups, and war and peace, mainly in collaboration with Melvin Ember, whom she married in 1970. All of these cross-cultural studies tested theories on data for worldwide samples of societies.

From 1970 to 1996, she taught at Hunter College of the City University of New York. She has served as president of the Society of Cross-Cultural Research and was one of the directors of the Summer Institutes in Comparative Anthropological Research, which were funded by the National Science Foundation. Since 1996 she has served as executive director of the Human Relations Area Files, Inc., a nonprofit research agency at Yale University.

After graduating from Columbia College, Melvin Ember went to Yale University for his Ph.D. His mentor at Yale was George Peter Murdock, an anthropologist who was instrumental in promoting cross-cultural research and building a full-text database on the cultures of the world to facilitate cross-cultural hypothesis testing. This database came to be known as the Human Relations Area Files (HRAF) because it was originally sponsored by the Institute of Human

Relations at Yale. Growing in annual installments and now distributed in electronic format, the HRAF database currently covers approximately 400 cultures, past and present, all over the world. HRAF also now produces and distributes a Web-based database on archaeology.

Melvin Ember did fieldwork for his dissertation in American Samoa, where he conducted a comparison of three villages to study the effects of commercialization on political life. In addition, he did research on descent groups and how they changed with the increase of buying and selling. His cross-cultural studies focused originally on variation in marital residence and descent groups. He has also done cross-cultural research on the relationship between economic and political development, the origin and extension of the incest taboo, the causes of polygyny, and how archaeological correlates of social customs can help us draw inferences about the past.

After four years of research at the National Institute of Mental Health, he taught at Antioch College and then Hunter College of the City University of New York. He has served as president of the Society for Cross-Cultural Research. Since 1987 he has been president of the Human Relations Area Files, Inc., a nonprofit research agency at Yale University.

Peter N. Peregrine came to anthropology after completing an undergraduate degree in English. He found anthropology's social scientific approach to understanding humans more appealing than the humanistic approach he had learned as an English major. He undertook an ethnohistorical study of the relationship between Jesuit missionaries and Native American peoples for his master's degree and realized that he needed to study archaeology to understand the cultural interactions experienced by Native Americans prior to contact with the Jesuits.

While working on his Ph.D. at Purdue University, Peter Peregrine did research on the prehistoric Mississippian cultures of the eastern United States. He found that interactions between groups were common and had been shaping Native American cultures for centuries. Native Americans approached contact with the Jesuits simply as another in a long string of intercultural exchanges. He also found that relatively little research had been done on Native American interactions and decided that comparative research was a good place to begin examining the topic. In 1990 he participated in the Summer Institute in Comparative Anthropological Research, where he met Carol R. Ember and Melvin Ember.

Peter Peregrine taught at Juniata College and is currently professor and chair of the anthropology department at Lawrence University in Appleton, Wisconsin. He serves as research associate for the eHRAF Collection of Archaeology and is co-editor with Melvin Ember of the 9-volume *Encyclopedia of Prehistory*. He continues to do archaeological research, and to teach anthropology and archaeology to undergraduate students.

CHAPTER 1

THE IMPORTANCE OF ANTHROPOLOGY

Chapter Outline

- The Scope of Anthropology
- The Holistic Approach
- The Anthropological Curiosity
- Fields of Anthropology
- Explanation and Evidence
- The Relevance of Anthropology

What is **anthropology** and what can it do? By definition, anthropology is a discipline of infinite curiosity about human beings. The term comes from the Greek *anthropos* for "man, human" and *logos* for "study." Anthropologists seek answers to an enormous variety of questions about humans. They are interested in discovering when, where, and why humans appeared on the earth, how and why they have changed since then, and how and why modern human populations vary in certain physical features. Anthropologists are also interested in how and why societies in the past and present have varied in their customary ideas and practices. There is a practical side to anthropology, too. Applied and practicing anthropologists put anthropological methods, information, and results to use in efforts to solve practical problems.

But defining anthropology as the study of human beings is not completely satisfactory, for such a definition would appear to incorporate a whole catalog of disciplines: sociology, psychology, political science, economics, history, human biology, and perhaps even the humanistic disciplines of philosophy and literature. Needless to say, practitioners of the many other disciplines concerned with humans would not be happy to be regarded as being in subbranches of anthropology. After all, most of those disciplines have existed longer than anthropology, and each is somewhat distinctive. There must, then, be something unique about anthropology—a reason for its having developed as a separate discipline and for its having retained a separate identity over the last 100 years.

The Scope of Anthropology

Anthropologists are generally thought of as individuals who travel to little-known corners of the world to study exotic peoples or who dig deep into the earth to uncover the fossil remains or the tools and pots of people who lived long ago. These views, though clearly stereotyped, do indicate how anthropology differs from other disciplines concerned with humans. Anthropology is broader in scope, both geographically and historically. Anthropology is concerned explicitly and directly with all varieties of people throughout the world, not just those close at hand or within a limited area. It is also interested in people of all periods. Beginning with the immediate ancestors of humans, who lived a few million years ago, anthropology traces the development of humans until the present. Every part of the world that has ever contained a human population is of interest to anthropologists.

Anthropologists have not always been as global and comprehensive in their concerns as they are today. Traditionally, they concentrated on non-Western cultures and left the study of Western civilization and other complex societies to other disciplines. In recent years, however, this division of labor among the disciplines has begun to disappear. Now anthropologists work in their own and other complex societies.

What induces anthropologists to choose so broad a subject for study? In part, they are motivated by the belief that any suggested generalization about human beings, any possible explanation of some characteristic of human culture or biology, should be shown to apply to many times and places of human existence. If a generalization or explanation does not prove to apply widely, we are entitled or even obliged to be skeptical about it. The skeptical attitude, in the absence of persuasive evidence, is our best protection against accepting invalid ideas about humans.

For example, when American educators discovered in the 1960s that African-American schoolchildren rarely drank milk, they assumed that lack of money or education was the cause. But evidence from anthropology suggested a different explanation. Anthropologists had known for years that in many parts of the world where milking animals are kept, people do not drink fresh milk; rather, they sour it before they drink it, or they make it into cheese. Why they do so is now clear. Many people lack an enzyme, lactase, that is necessary for breaking down lactose, the sugar in milk. When such people drink regular milk, it actually interferes with digestion. Not only is the lactose in milk not digested but other nutrients are less likely to be digested as well; in many cases, drinking milk will cause cramps, stomach gas, diarrhea, and nausea. Studies indicate that milk intolerance is found in many parts of the world.[1] The condition is common in adulthood among Asians, southern Europeans, Arabs and Jews, West Africans, Inuit (Eskimos), North American Indians, and South American Indians, as well as African Americans. Because anthropologists are acquainted with human life in an enormous variety of geographic and historical settings, they are often able to correct mistaken beliefs about people.

The Holistic Approach

In addition to the worldwide as well as the historical scope of anthropology, another distinguishing feature of the discipline is its **holistic**, or multifaceted, approach to the study of human beings. Anthropologists study not only all varieties of people but many aspects of human experience as well. For example, when describing a group of people, an anthropologist might discuss the history of the area in which the people live, the physical environment, the organization of family life, the general features of their language, the group's settlement patterns, political and economic systems, religion, and styles of art and dress.

In the past, individual anthropologists tried to be holistic and cover many subjects. Today, as in many other disciplines, so much information has been accumulated that anthropologists tend to specialize in one topic or area. Thus, one anthropologist may investigate the physical characteristics of some of our prehistoric ancestors. Another may study the biological effect of the environment on a human population over time. Still another will concentrate on many customs of a particular group of people. Despite this specialization, however, the discipline of anthropology retains its holistic orientation in that its many different specialties, taken together, describe many aspects of human existence, both past and present.

The Anthropological Curiosity

Thus far we have described anthropology as being broader in scope, both historically and geographically, and more holistic in approach than other disciplines concerned with human beings. But this statement again implies that anthropology is the all-inclusive human science. How, then, is anthropology really different from those other disciplines? We suggest that anthropology's distinctiveness lies principally in the kind of curiosity it arouses.

In studying a human population anthropologists tend to focus on *typical* characteristics (traits, customs) of that population: People in many societies depend on agriculture. Why? And where, when, and why did people first start to farm? Why do some populations have lighter skin than others? Why do some languages contain more terms for color than others? Why do some societies have more political participation than others? The anthropological curiosity mostly focuses on the typical characteristics of human groups and how to explain them. Economists take a monetary system for granted and study how it operates. Anthropologists ask how frequently monetary systems are found, why they vary, and why only some societies during the last few thousand years used money. In short, anthropologists are curious about the typical characteristics of human groups—how and why populations and their characteristics have varied around the globe and throughout the ages.

Fields of Anthropology

Different anthropologists concentrate on different typical characteristics of societies. Some are concerned primarily with *biological* or *physical characteristics* of human populations; others are interested principally in what we call *cultural characteristics*. Hence, there are two broad classifications of subject matter in anthropology: **biological (physical) anthropology** and **cultural anthropology**. Biological anthropology is one major field of anthropology. Cultural anthropology is divided into three major subfields—archaeology, linguistics, and ethnology. Ethnology, the study of recent cultures, is now usually referred to by the parent name, cultural anthropology (see Figure 1.1). Crosscutting these four fields is a fifth, applied or practicing anthropology.

Biological Anthropology

Biological (physical) anthropology seeks to answer two distinct sets of questions. The first set includes questions about the emergence of humans and their later evolution (this focus is called **human paleontology** or **paleoanthropology**). The second set includes questions about how and why contemporary human populations vary biologically (this focus is called **human variation**).

In order to reconstruct human evolution, human paleontologists search for and study the buried, hardened remains or impressions—known as **fossils**—of humans, prehumans, and related animals. Paleontologists working in East Africa, for instance, have excavated the fossil remains of human-like beings who lived more than 3 million years ago. These findings have suggested the approximate dates when our ancestors began to develop two-legged walking, very flexible hands, and a larger brain.

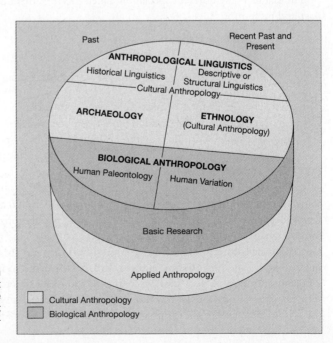

Figure 1.1   The Subdivisions of Anthropology

The four major subdisciplines of anthropology (in bold type) may be classified according to subject matter (biological or cultural) and according to the period with which each is concerned (distant past versus recent past and present). There are applications of anthropology in all four subdisciplines.

In attempting to clarify evolutionary relationships, human paleontologists may use not only the fossil record but also geological information on the succession of climates, environments, and plant and animal populations. Moreover, when reconstructing the past of humans, paleontologists are also interested in the behavior and evolution of our closest relatives among the mammals—the prosimians, monkeys, and apes, which, like ourselves, are members of the order of **Primates**. Anthropologists, psychologists, and biologists who specialize in the study of primates are called **primatologists**. The various species of primates are observed in the wild and in the laboratory. One especially popular subject of study is the chimpanzee, which bears a close resemblance to humans in behavior and physical appearance, has a similar blood chemistry, and is susceptible to many of the same diseases. It now appears that chimpanzees share as much as 99 percent of their genes with humans.[2]

From primate studies, biological anthropologists try to discover characteristics that are distinctly human, as opposed to those that might be part of the primate heritage. With this information, they may be able to infer what our prehistoric ancestors were like. The inferences from primate studies are checked against the fossil record. The evidence from the earth, collected in bits and pieces, is correlated with scientific observations of our closest living relatives. In short, biological anthropologists piece together bits of information obtained from different sources. They construct theories that explain the changes observed in the fossil record and then attempt to evaluate their theories by checking one kind of evidence against another. Human paleontology thus overlaps with disciplines such as geology, general vertebrate (and particularly primate) paleontology, comparative anatomy, and the study of comparative primate behavior.

The second major focus of biological anthropology, the study of human variation, investigates how and why contemporary human populations differ in biological or physical characteristics. All living people belong to one species, *Homo sapiens*, for all can successfully interbreed. Yet there is much that varies among human populations. Investigators of human variation ask such questions as: Why are some peoples taller than others? How have human populations adapted physically to their environmental conditions? Are some peoples, such as Inuit (Eskimos), better equipped than other peoples to endure cold? Does darker skin pigmentation offer special protection against the tropical sun?

Birute Galdikas works with two orangutans in Borneo.

To understand the biological variations observable among contemporary human populations, biological anthropologists use the principles, concepts, and techniques of at least three other disciplines: human genetics (the study of human traits that are inherited), population biology (the study of environmental effects on, and interaction with, population characteristics), and epidemiology (the study of how and why diseases affect different populations in different ways). Research on human variation, therefore, overlaps research in other fields.

Cultural Anthropology

Cultural anthropology focuses on universals and variation in culture in the past and present. But what is culture? Because the concept of culture is so central to anthropology, we devote a whole chapter to it. To an anthropologist, the term *culture* refers to the customary ways of thinking and behaving of a particular population or society. The culture of a social group includes many things—its language, religious beliefs, food preferences, music, work habits, gender roles, how they rear their children, how they construct their houses, and many other learned behaviors and ideas that have come to be widely shared or customary among the group. The three main branches of cultural anthropology are **archaeology** (the study of past cultures, primarily through their material remains), **anthropological linguistics** (the anthropological study of languages), and **ethnology** (the study of existing and recent cultures), now usually referred to by the parent name, cultural anthropology.

Archaeology   The archaeologist seeks not only to reconstruct the daily life and customs of peoples who lived in the past but also to trace cultural changes and to offer possible explanations for those changes. This concern is similar to that of the historian, but the archaeologist reaches much farther back in time. The historian deals only with societies that left written records and is therefore limited to the last 5,000 years of human history. Human societies, however, have existed for more than a million years, and only a small proportion in the last 5,000 years had writing. For all those past societies lacking a written record, the archaeologist serves as historian. Lacking written records for study, archaeologists must try to reconstruct history from the remains of human cultures. Some of these remains are as grand as the Mayan temples discovered at Chichén Itzá in Yucatán, Mexico. More often they are as ordinary as bits of broken pottery, stone tools, and garbage heaps.

Most archaeologists deal with **prehistory**, the time before written records. But there is a specialty within archaeology, called **historical archaeology**, that studies the remains of recent peoples who left written records. This specialty, as its name implies, employs the methods of both archaeologists and historians to study recent societies for which there is both archaeological and historical information.

In trying to understand how and why ways of life have changed through time in different parts of the world, archaeologists collect materials from sites of human occupation. Usually, these sites must be unearthed. On the basis of materials they have excavated and otherwise collected, archaeologists ask various questions: Where, when, and why did the distinctive human characteristic of toolmaking first emerge? Where, when, and why did agriculture first develop? Where, when, and why did people first begin to live in cities?

To collect the data they need to suggest answers to these and other questions, archaeologists use techniques and findings borrowed from other disciplines, as well as what they can infer from anthropological studies of recent and contemporary cultures. For example, to guess where to dig for evidence of early toolmaking, archaeologists rely on geology to tell them where sites of early human occupation are likely to be found, because of erosion and uplifting, near the surface of the earth. To infer when agriculture first developed, archaeologists date the relevant excavated materials by a process originally developed by chemists. And to try to understand why cities first emerged, archaeologists may use information from historians, geographers, and others about how recent and contemporary cities are related economically and politically to their hinterlands. If we can discover what recent and contemporary cities have in common, we can speculate on why cities developed originally. Thus, archaeologists use information from the present and recent past in trying to understand the distant past.

Anthropological Linguistics   Anthropological linguistics is another branch of cultural anthropology. Linguistics, or the study of languages, is a somewhat older discipline than anthropology, but the early linguists concentrated on the study of languages that had been written for a long time—languages such as English that had been written for nearly a thousand years. Anthropological linguists began to do fieldwork in places where the language was not yet written. This meant that anthropologists could not consult a dictionary or grammar to help them learn the language. Instead, they first had to construct a dictionary and grammar, after which they could study the structure and history of the language.

Like biological anthropologists, linguists study changes that have taken place over time, as well as contemporary variation. Some anthropological linguists are concerned with the emergence of language and also with the divergence of languages over thousands of years. The study of how languages change over time and how they may be related is known as **historical linguistics**. Anthropological linguists are also interested in how contemporary languages differ, especially in how they construct words, phrases, and other features. This focus of linguistics is generally called **descriptive** or **structural linguistics**. The study of how language is used in social contexts is called **sociolinguistics**.

In contrast with the human paleontologist and archaeologist, who have physical remains to help them reconstruct change over time, the historical linguist deals only with languages—and usually unwritten ones at that. (Remember that writing is only about 5,000 years old, and most languages since then have not been written.) Because an unwritten language must be heard in order to be studied, it does not leave any trace once its speakers have died. Linguists interested in reconstructing the history of unwritten languages must begin in the present, with comparisons of contemporary languages. On the basis of these comparisons, they draw inferences about the kinds of change in language that may have occurred in the past and that may account for similarities and differences observed in the present. The historical linguist typically asks such questions as these: Did two or more contemporary languages diverge from a common ancestral language? If they are related, how far back in time did they begin to differ?

Unlike the historical linguist, the descriptive (or structural) linguist is typically concerned with discovering and recording the principles that determine how sounds and words are put together in speech. For example, a structural description of a particular language might tell us that the sounds *t* and *k* are interchangeable in a word without causing a difference in meaning. In American Samoa, one could say *Tutuila* or *Kukuila* as the name of the largest island, and everyone, except perhaps the tourist or the newly arrived anthropologist, would understand that the same island was being mentioned.

The sociolinguist is interested in the social aspects of language, including what people speak about and how they interact conversationally, their attitudes toward speakers of other dialects or languages, and how people speak differently in different social contexts. In English, for example, we do not address everyone we meet in the same way. "Hi, Sandy" may be the customary way a person greets a friend. But we would probably feel uncomfortable addressing a doctor by her or his first name; instead, we would probably say, "Good morning, Dr. Brown." Such variations in language use, which are determined by the social status of the persons being addressed, are significant for the sociolinguist.

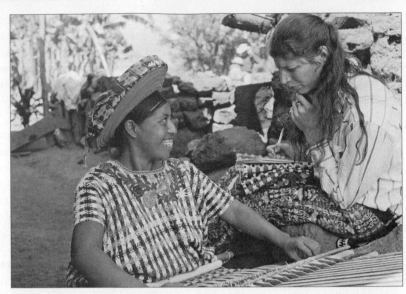

Anthropologist Margaret Kieffer interviews a Mayan woman in Guatemala.

Ethnology (Cultural Anthropology)   Ethnologists seek to understand how and why peoples today and in the recent past differ in their customary ways of thinking and acting. Ethnology—now usually called *cultural anthropology*—is concerned with patterns of thought and behavior, such as marriage customs, kinship organization, political and economic systems, religion, folk art, and music, and with the ways in which these patterns differ in contemporary societies. Ethnologists also study the dynamics of culture—that is, how various cultures develop and change. In addition, they are interested in the relationship between beliefs and practices within a culture. Thus, the aim of ethnologists is largely the same as that of archaeologists. Ethnologists, however, generally use data collected through observation and interviewing of living peoples. Archaeologists, on the other hand, must work with fragmentary remains of past cultures, on the basis of which they can only make inferences about the customs of prehistoric peoples.

One type of ethnologist, the **ethnographer,** usually spends a year or so living with, talking to, and observing the people whose customs he or she is studying. This fieldwork provides the data for a detailed description (an **ethnography**) of customary behavior and thought. Ethnographers vary in the degree to which they strive for completeness in their coverage of cultural and social life. Earlier ethnographers tended to strive for holistic coverage; more recent ethnographers have tended to specialize or focus on narrower realms such as ritual healing or curing, interaction with the environment, effects of modernization or globalization, or gender issues. Ethnographies often go beyond description; they may address current anthropological issues or try to explain some aspect of a culture.

Because so many cultures have undergone extensive change in the recent past, it is fortunate that another type of ethnologist, the **ethnohistorian,** is prepared to study how the ways of life of a particular group of people have changed over time. Ethnohistorians investigate written documents (which may or may not have been produced by anthropologists). They may spend many years going through documents, such as missionary accounts, reports by traders and explorers, and government records, to try to establish the cultural changes that have occurred. Unlike ethnographers, who rely mostly on their own observations, ethnohistorians rely on the reports of others. Often they must attempt to piece together and make sense of widely scattered, and even apparently contradictory, information. Thus, the ethnohistorian's research is very much like that of the historian, except that the ethnohistorian is usually concerned with the history of a people who did not themselves leave written records. The ethnohistorian tries to reconstruct the recent history of a people and may also suggest why certain changes in their way of life took place.

With the data collected and analyzed by the ethnographer and ethnohistorian, the work of a third type of ethnologist, the **cross-cultural researcher,** can be done. The cross-cultural researcher is interested in discovering general patterns about cultural traits—what is universal, what is variable, why traits vary, and what the consequences of the variability might be. Why, for example, is there more gender inequality in some societies than in others? Is family violence related to aggression in other areas of life? What are the effects of living in a very unpredictable environment? In testing possible answers to such questions, cross-cultural researchers use data from samples of cultures to try to arrive at explanations or relationships that hold across cultures. Archaeologists may find the results of cross-cultural research useful for making inferences about the past, particularly if researchers have discovered material indicators of cultural variation.

Because ethnologists may be interested in many aspects of customary behavior and thought—from economic behavior to political behavior to styles of art, music, and religion—ethnology overlaps with disciplines that concentrate on some particular aspect of human existence, such as sociology, psychology, economics, political science, art, music, and comparative religion. But the distinctive feature of cultural anthropology is its interest in how all these aspects of human existence vary from society to society, in all historical periods, and in all parts of the world.

Applied Anthropology

All knowledge may turn out to be useful. In the physical and biological sciences it is well understood that technological breakthroughs like DNA splicing, spacecraft docking in outer space, and the development of minuscule computer chips could not have taken place without an enormous amount of basic research to uncover the laws of nature in the physical and biological worlds. If we did not understand fundamental principles, the technological achievements we are so proud of would not be possible. Researchers are often simply driven by curiosity, with no thought as to where the research might lead, which is why such research is sometimes called *basic research.* The same is true of the social sciences. If a researcher finds out that societies with combative sports tend to have more wars, it may lead to other inquiries about the relationships between one kind of aggression and another. The knowledge acquired may ultimately lead to discovering ways to reduce social problems, such as family violence and war.

Whereas basic research may ultimately help to solve practical problems, applied research is more explicit in its practical goals. Today about half of all professional anthropologists are applied, or practicing, anthropologists. **Applied** or **practicing anthropology** is explicit in its concern with making anthropological knowledge useful.[3] Applied anthropologists may be trained in any or all of the subfields of anthropology. In contrast to basic researchers, who are almost always employed in colleges, universities, and museums, applied anthropologists are usually employed in settings outside traditional academia, including government agencies, international development agencies, private consulting firms, businesses, public health organizations, medical schools, law offices, community development agencies, and charitable foundations.

In urban areas before new construction begins, archaeologists may be called upon to excavate and record information on historical sites, as shown here in New York City.

Biological anthropologists may be called upon to give forensic evidence in court, or they may work in public health, or design clothes and equipment to fit human anatomy. Archaeologists may be involved in preserving and exhibiting artifacts for museums and in doing contract work to find and preserve cultural sites that might be damaged by construction or excavation. Linguists may work in bilingual educational training programs or may work on ways to improve communication. Ethnologists may work in a wide variety of applied projects ranging from community development, urban planning, health care, and agricultural improvement, to personnel and organizational management, and assessment of the impact of change programs on people's lives.[4] We discuss applied and practicing anthropology more fully in the final chapter of the book.

Explanation and Evidence

Anthropologists in the field try to arrive at accurate answers to descriptive questions. How do the people make a living? How do they marry? What gods do they believe in? But as important as accurate description is, it is not the ultimate goal of anthropology. Anthropologists want to *understand*—to know *why* people have certain customs or beliefs, not just to see that they *do* have them. As difficult as the *how* and *what* questions are to answer, the *why* questions are even harder. *Why* questions deal with explanations, which are harder to generate and harder to evaluate. In science, to understand is to explain, and so the major goal of science is to arrive at trustworthy explanations.[5]

For many anthropologists, the plausibility or persuasiveness of an explanation cannot be considered a sufficient reason to accept it. The explanation must also be tested and supported by objective evidence that could have falsified it. And even when it is supported, there still may be grounds for skepticism. According to the scientific orientation, all knowledge is uncertain and therefore subject to increasing or decreasing confirmation as new tests are made. This means that we will never arrive at absolute truth. On the other hand, and this is encouraging, we should be able to achieve more and more reliable understanding if we keep testing our theories.

But what is scientific understanding—what does it mean to explain, and what kinds of evidence are needed to evaluate an explanation?

Explanations

An **explanation** is an answer to a *why* question. There are many types of explanations, some more satisfying than others. For example, suppose we ask why a society thinks that a couple should abstain from sex for a year or so after the birth of a baby. If we say their tradition is to practice a long postpartum sex taboo, is this a satisfactory explanation? We would have to say no, because the thing to be explained (the taboo) is being explained by itself, by its prior existence. To explain something in terms of tradition is to say that people do it because they already do it, which is not informative. What kinds of explanations are more satisfactory, then? In science, there are two kinds of explanations that are sought: associations and theories.

Associations or Relationships

One way of explaining something (an observation, an action, a custom) is to say how it conforms to a general principle or relationship. So to explain why the water left outside in the basin froze, we say that it was cold last night and that water freezes at 32°F. The statement that water solidifies (becomes ice) at 32° is a statement of a relationship or association between two **variables**—things or quantities that vary. In this case, variation in the state of water (liquid versus solid) is related to variation in the temperature of the air (above versus below 32°F). The truth of the relationship is suggested by repeated observations. In the physical sciences, such relationships are called **laws** when they are accepted by almost all scientists. We find such explanations satisfactory because they allow us to predict what will happen in the future or to understand something that has happened regularly in the past.

In the social sciences, associations are usually stated *probabilistically*; that is, we say that two or more variables tend to be related in a predictable way, which means that there are usually some exceptions. For example, to explain why a society has a long postpartum sex taboo, we can point to the association (or correlation) that John Whiting found in a worldwide sample of societies: Societies with apparently low-protein diets tend to have long postpartum sex taboos.[6] We call the relationship between low-protein diets and the sex taboo a **statistical association**, which means that the observed relationship is unlikely to be due to chance. Why this association exists is a theoretical issue.

Theories

Even though laws and statistical associations explain by relating what is to be explained to other things, we want to know more: why those laws or associations exist. Why does water freeze at 32°F? Why do societies with low-protein diets tend to have long postpartum sex taboos? Therefore, scientists try to formulate theories that will explain the observed relationships (laws and statistical associations).[7] **Theories** are explanations of laws and statistical associations.

By way of example, let us consider why some societies have long postpartum sex taboos. We have already noted that an observed statistical association can be used to help explain it. In general (but not

SCIENCE AND HUMANISM

Some people question whether the scientific approach is desirable or possible when it comes to humans. They often describe themselves as humanists because they use the human capacity to intuit, empathize, evoke, interpret, and illuminate as ways to understand. This orientation offers a very different kind of understanding because, compared with that offered by science, it does not insist on objectivity, nor does it insist on putting insights to empirical tests as science does. This is not to say that scientists do not intuit or interpret. They often do in the process of deriving theories, which involves a creative leap of imagination. And scientists, like anyone else, may empathize with the plight of the people they study. But the crucial difference between the humanistic and scientific orientations lies in the end result. For humanists, interpretation or evocation is the goal; for scientists, the goal is testing interpretations to see if they may be wrong.

Is objectivity possible? Or, because we are humans observing other humans, can we only be subjective? Objectivity requires trying to get at the truth despite the observer's subjective desires or needs. Is that possible? Can any human be unbiased? In an absolute sense, no one can be completely free of bias. But science has ways to strive for objectivity; it does not need to assume that every human is completely unbiased. Remember that even when humans engage in physical science, they are often the observers or the creators of the instruments that do the observation. When an instrument points to a number, two persons may get slightly different readings because they look at the instrument from different angles. But neither person will be far off the mark, and the average of readings by two or more individuals will be very close to the "true" score.

But do we see other people objectively? Undoubtedly, some things about them are harder to "see" than others. It is easier to know objectively that wives and husbands usually sit down to dinner together, harder to "see" how they feel about one another. Suppose you are in a society where you never observe any obvious expression of affection between husbands and wives. At first, your own cultural bias might lead you to think that such couples don't care for each other much. Such an observation might indeed be biased (and not objective) if it turned out that couples privately express affection to each other but avoid public expressions. Or it might be that couples communicate their affection for each other in ways you didn't notice. But that doesn't mean that you wouldn't be able to figure this out eventually. In trying to understand the meaning of female-male relationships, you might very well try to establish close, personal relationships with some families. You might then ask people to tell you stories to try to see how they portrayed relations between husband and wife. In short, a humanistic approach might help you understand how couples really feel about each other. But a scientist might go through the same procedure too in order to come to a tentative understanding.

As this example illustrates, humanistic understanding and science are really not incompatible. Both the scientist and the humanist would agree on the need to convey what a culture is like (e.g., with regard to how couples feel about each other). But scientists would insist on more. First, they would try to verify, perhaps by systematic interviewing, how commonly a feeling is shared in the culture; second, they would want to explain why this feeling is common in some cultures but not in others. Therefore, they would have to create a theory to explain the variation and then collect evidence to test the theory to see if it might be wrong.

The poet Marianne Moore wrote that poetry gives us "imaginary gardens with real toads in them." Can imagination, humanistic or scientific, be meaningful without at least some real toads?

Sources: James Lett, "Scientific Anthropology," in David Levinson and Melvin Ember, eds., *Encyclopedia of Cultural Anthropology,* 4 vols. (New York: Henry Holt, 1996). The quote from Marianne Moore is from John Timpane, "Essay: The Poetry of Science," *Scientific American* (July 1991): 128.

always), if a society has a low-protein diet, it will have a long postpartum sex taboo. But most people would ask additional questions: Why does a low-protein diet explain the taboo? What is the mechanism by which a society with such a diet develops the custom of a long postpartum sex taboo? A theory is intended to answer such questions.

John Whiting's theory is that a long postpartum sex taboo may be an adaptation to certain conditions. Particularly in tropical areas, where the major food staples are low in protein, babies are vulnerable to the protein-deficiency disease called *kwashiorkor*. But if a baby could continue to nurse for a long time, it might have a better chance of surviving. The postpartum sex taboo might be adaptive, Whiting's theory suggests, because it increases the likelihood of a baby's survival. If a mother puts off having another baby for a while, the first baby might have a better chance to survive because it can be fed mother's milk for a longer time. Whiting suggests that parents may be aware, whether unconsciously or consciously, that having another baby too soon might jeopardize the survival of the first baby, and so they might decide that it would be a good idea to abstain from intercourse for more than a year after the birth of the first baby.

As this example of a theory illustrates, there are differences between a theory and an association. A theory is more complicated, containing a series of statements. An association usually states quite simply that there is a relationship between two or more measured variables. Another difference is that, although a theory may mention some things that are observable, such as the presence of a long postpartum sex taboo, parts of it are difficult or impossible to observe directly. For example, with regard to Whiting's theory, it would be difficult to find out if people had deliberately or unconsciously decided to practice a long postpartum sex taboo because they recognized that babies would thereby have a better chance to survive. Then, too, the concept of adaptation—that some characteristic promotes greater reproductive success—is difficult to verify because it is difficult to find out whether different individuals or groups have different rates of reproduction because they do or do not practice the supposedly adaptive custom. Thus, some concepts or implications in a theory are unobservable (at least at the present time), and only some aspects may be observable. In contrast, statistical associations or laws are based entirely on observations.[8]

Why Theories Cannot Be Proved

Many people think that the theories they learned in physics or chemistry courses have been proved. Unfortunately, many students get that impression because their teachers present "lessons" in an authoritative manner. It is now generally agreed by scientists and philosophers of science that although some theories may have considerable evidence supporting them, no theory can be said to be proved or unquestionably true. This is because many of the concepts and ideas in theories are not directly observable and therefore not directly verifiable. For example, scientists may try to explain how light behaves by postulating that it consists of particles called photons, but photons cannot be observed, even with the most powerful microscope. So exactly what a photon looks like and exactly how it works remain in the realm of the unprovable. The photon is a **theoretical construct**, something that cannot be observed or verified directly. Because all theories contain such constructs, theories cannot be proved entirely or with absolute certainty.[9]

Why should we bother with theories, then, if we cannot prove that they are true? Perhaps the main advantage of a theory as a kind of explanation is that it may lead to new understanding or knowledge. A theory can suggest new relationships or imply new predictions that might be supported or confirmed by new research. For example, Whiting's theory about long postpartum sex taboos has implications that could be investigated by researchers. Because the theory discusses how a long postpartum sex taboo might be adaptive, we would expect that certain changes would result in the taboo's disappearance. For example, suppose people adopted either mechanical birth-control devices or began to give supplementary high-protein foods to babies. With birth control, a family could space births without abstaining from sex, so we would expect the custom of postpartum abstinence to disappear. So, too, we would expect it to disappear with protein supplements for babies, because kwashiorkor would then be less likely to afflict the babies. Whiting's ideas might also prompt investigators to try to find out whether parents are consciously or unconsciously aware of the problem of close birth spacing in areas with low supplies of protein.

Although theories cannot be proved, they are rejectable. The method of *falsification,* which shows that a theory seems to be wrong, is mainly how theories are judged.[10] Scientists derive implications or predictions that should be true if the theory is correct. So, for example, Whiting predicted that societies with long postpartum sex taboos would be found more often in the tropics than in temperate regions and that they would be likely to have low-protein food supplies. Such predictions of what might be found are called **hypotheses**. If the predictions turn out not to be correct, the researcher is obliged to conclude that there may be something wrong with the theory or something wrong with the test of the theory. Theories that are not falsified are accepted for the time being because the available evidence seems to be consistent with them. But remember that no matter how much the available evidence seems to support a theory, we can never be certain it is true. There is always the possibility that some implication of it, some hypothesis derivable from it, will not be confirmed in the future.

Evidence: Testing Explanations

In any field of investigation, theories are generally the most plentiful commodity, apparently because of the human predisposition to try to make sense of the world. It is necessary, then, for us to have procedures that enable us to select from among the many available theories those that are more likely to be correct. "Just as mutations arise naturally but are not all beneficial, so hypotheses [theories] emerge naturally but are not all correct. If progress is to occur, therefore, we require a superfluity of hypotheses and also a mechanism of selection."[11] In other words, generating a theory or interpretation is not enough. We need some reliable method of testing whether or not that interpretation is likely to be correct. If an interpretation is not correct, it may detract from our efforts to achieve understanding by misleading us into thinking the problem is already solved.

The strategy in all kinds of testing in science is to predict what one would expect to find if a particular interpretation were correct, and then to conduct an investigation to see if the prediction is generally consistent with the data. If the prediction is not supported, the investigator is obliged to accept the possibility that the interpretation is wrong. If, however, the prediction holds true, then the investigator is entitled to say that there is evidence to support the theory. Thus, conducting research designed to test expectations derived from theory allows researchers to eliminate some interpretations and to accept others, at least tentatively.

Operationalization and Measurement

To transform theoretical predictions into statements that might be verified, a researcher provides an **operational definition** of each of the concepts or variables mentioned in the prediction. An operational definition is a description of the procedure that is followed to measure the variable.[12]

Whiting predicted that societies with a low-protein diet would have a long postpartum sex taboo. Amount of protein in the diet is a variable; some societies have more, others have less. Length of the

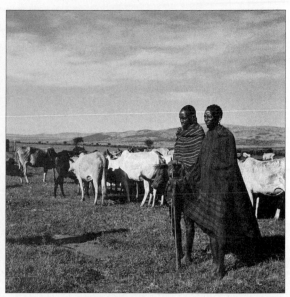

The Yanomamö Indians of Brazil (*left*) depend on root crops. The Masai pastoralists of Kenya (*right*) depend largely on milk and other products of their cattle.

postpartum sex taboo is a variable; a society may have a short taboo or a long taboo. Whiting operationally defined the first variable, *amount of protein,* in terms of staple foods.[13] If a society depended mostly on root and tree crops (cassava, bananas), Whiting rated the society as having low protein. If the society depended mostly on cereal crops (wheat, barley, corn, oats), he rated it as having moderate protein, because cereal crops have more protein by weight than root and tree crops. If the society depended mostly on hunting, fishing, or herding for food, he rated it as having high protein. The other variable in Whiting's prediction, *length of postpartum sex taboo,* was operationalized as follows: A society was rated as having a long taboo if couples customarily abstained from sex for more than a year after the birth of a baby; abstention for a year or less was considered a short taboo.

Specifying an operational definition for each variable is extremely important because it allows other investigators to check a researcher's results.[14] Science depends on *replication,* the repetition of results. Only when many researchers observe a particular association can we call that association or relationship a law. Providing operational definitions is also extremely important because it allows others to evaluate whether a measure is appropriate. Only when we are told exactly how something was measured can we judge whether the measure reflects what it is supposed to reflect. Specifying measures publicly is so important in science that we are obliged to be skeptical of any conclusions that involve variables that were not measured.

To **measure** something is to say how it compares with other things on some scale of variation.[15] People often assume that a measuring device is always a physical instrument, such as a scale or a ruler, but physical devices are not the only way to measure something. *Classification* is also a form of measurement. When we classify persons as male or female or employed versus unemployed, we are dividing them into *sets.* Deciding which set they belong to is a kind of measurement because doing so allows us to compare them. We can also measure things by deciding which cases or examples have more or less of something (e.g., more or less protein in the diet). The measures employed in physical science are usually based on

A thermometer provides a way of comparing or measuring the "heat" of different locations or over different time periods. While the physical sciences often use physical instruments and the social sciences often use humans to observe, all measurements compare things on some scale of variation.

scales that allow us to assign numbers to each case; we measure height in meters and weight in grams, for example. However we measure our variables, the fact that we can measure them means that we can test our hypotheses to see if the predicted relationships actually exist, at least most of the time.

Sampling

After deciding how to measure the variables in some predicted relationship, the investigator must decide how to select which cases to study to see if the predicted relationship holds. If the prediction is about the behavior of people, the sampling decision involves which people to observe. If the prediction is about an association between societal customs, the sampling decision involves which societies to study. Investigators must decide not only which cases to choose but also how many to choose. No researcher can investigate all the possible cases, so choices must be made. Some choices are better than others. The best is some kind of random sample. A random sample is one in which all cases selected had an equal chance of being included in the sample. Almost all statistical tests used to evaluate the results of research require random sampling, because only results based on a random sample can be assumed to be probably true for some larger set or universe of cases.

Statistical Evaluation

When researchers have measured the variables of interest for all the sample cases, they are ready to see if the predicted relationship actually exists in the data. Remember, the results may not turn out to be what the theory predicts. Sometimes researchers construct a *contingency table,* like that shown in Table 1.1, to

Table 1.1	Association between Availability of Protein and Duration of Postpartum Sex Taboo		
	Duration of Postpartum Sex Taboo		
Availability of Protein	**Short (0–1 Year)**	**Long (More Than 1 Year)**	**Total**
High	47	15	62
Medium	38	25	63
Low	20	27	47
Total	105	67	172

Source: Adapted from John W. M. Whiting, "Effects of Climate on Certain Cultural Practices," in Ward H. Goodenough, ed., *Explorations in Cultural Anthropology* (New York: McGraw-Hill, 1964), p. 520.

see if the variables are associated as predicted. In Whiting's sample of 172 societies, each case is assigned to a box, or cell, in the table, depending on how the society is measured on the two variables of interest. For example, a society that has a long postpartum sex taboo and a low-protein diet is placed in the third row of the Long Duration column. (In Whiting's sample [see Table 1.1] there are 27 such societies.) A society that has a short postpartum sex taboo and a low-protein diet is placed in the third row in the Short Duration column. (There are 20 such societies in the sample.) The statistical question is: Does the way the cases are distributed in the six cells of the table generally support Whiting's prediction? If we looked just at the table, we might not know what to answer. Many cases appear to be in the expected places. For example, most of the high-protein cases (47 of 62) have short taboos, and most of the low-protein cases (27 of 47) have long taboos. But there are also many exceptions (e.g., 20 cases have low protein and a short taboo). So, although many cases appear to be in the expected places, there are also many exceptions. Do the exceptions invalidate the prediction? How many exceptions would compel us to reject the hypothesis? Here is where we resort to *statistical tests of significance*.

Statisticians have devised various tests that tell us how "perfect" a result has to be for us to believe that there is probably an association between the variables of interest, that one variable generally predicts the other. Essentially, every statistical result is evaluated in the same objective way. We ask: What is the chance that this result (the numbers in the cells of the table) is purely accidental, that there is no association at all between the two variables? Although some of the mathematical ways of answering this question are complicated, the answer always involves a *probability value* (or *p-value*)—the likelihood that the observed result or a stronger one could have occurred by chance. The statistical test used by Whiting gives a *p*-value of less than .01 ($p < .01$) for the table. In other words, there is less than 1 chance out of 100 that the cell numbers are purely accidental. A *p*-value of less than .01 is a fairly low probability; most social scientists conventionally agree to call any result with a *p*-value of .05 or less (5 or fewer chances out of 100) a *statistically significant*, or probably true, result. When we describe relationships or associations in the rest of this book, we are almost always referring to results that have been found to be statistically significant.

But why should a probably true relationship have any exceptions? If a theory is really correct, shouldn't *all* the cases fit? There are many reasons why we can never expect a perfect result. First, even if a theory is correct (e.g., if a low-protein diet really does favor the adoption of a long postpartum sex taboo), there may still be other causes that we have not investigated. Some of the societies could have a long taboo even though they have high protein. For example, societies that depend mostly on hunting for their food, and would therefore be classified as having a high-protein diet, may have a problem carrying infants from one campsite to another and may practice a long postpartum sex taboo so that two infants will not have to be carried at the same time.

Exceptions to the predicted relationship might also occur because of *cultural lag*.[16] Culture lag occurs when change in one aspect of culture takes time to produce change in another aspect. Suppose that a society recently changed crops and is now no longer a low-protein society but still practices the taboo. This society would be an exception to the predicted relationship, but it might fit the theory if it stopped practicing the taboo in a few years. Measurement inaccuracy is another source of exceptions. Whiting's measure of protein, which is based on the major sources of food, is not a very precise measure of protein in the diet. It does not take into account the possibility that a "tree-crop" society might get a lot of protein from fishing or raising pigs. So it might turn out that some supposedly low-protein societies have been misclassified, which may be one reason why there are 20 cases in the lowest cell in the left-hand column of Table 1.1. Measurement error usually produces exceptions.

Significant statistical associations that are predictable from a theory offer tentative support for the theory. But much more is needed before we can be fairly confident about the theory. Replication is needed to confirm whether the predictions can be reproduced by other researchers using other samples. Other predictions should be derived from the theory to see if they too are supported. The theory should be pitted against alternative explanations to see which theory works better. The research process in science thus requires time and patience. Perhaps most important, it requires that researchers be humble. No matter how wonderful one's own theory seems, it is important to acknowledge that it may be wrong.

The Relevance of Anthropology

The idea that it is impossible to account for human behavior scientifically, either because our actions and beliefs are too individualistic and complex or because human beings are understandable only in other-worldly terms, is a self-fulfilling notion. We cannot discover principles explaining human behavior if we neither believe such principles exist nor bother to look for them. If we are to increase our understanding of human beings, we first have to believe it is possible to do so.

If we aim to understand humans, it is essential that we study humans in all times and places. We must study ancient humans and modern humans. We must study their cultures and their biology. How else can we understand what is true of humans generally or how they are capable of varying? If we study just our own society, we may come up only with explanations that are culture-bound, not general or applicable to most or all humans. Anthropology is useful, then, to the degree that it contributes to our understanding of human beings everywhere.

In addition, anthropology is relevant because it helps us avoid misunderstandings between peoples. If we can understand why other groups are different from ourselves, we might have less reason to condemn them for behavior that appears strange to us. We may then come to realize that many differences between peoples are products of physical and cultural adaptations to different environments. For example, someone who first finds out about the !Kung as they lived in the Kalahari Desert of southern Africa in the 1950s might assume that the !Kung were "backward." (The exclamation point in the name !Kung

A large number of emigrants from the former Soviet Union, particularly from Black Sea cities and towns such as Odessa, live in the Brighton Beach neighborhood of Brooklyn. Migrant and immigrant communities such as "Little Odessa" are an increasing focus of anthropological study.

signifies one of the clicking sounds made with the tongue by speakers of the !Kung language.) The !Kung wore little clothing, had few possessions, lived in meager shelters, and enjoyed none of our technological niceties like radio and computers. But let us reflect on how a typical North American community might react if it awoke to find itself in an environment similar to that in which the !Kung lived. The people would find that the arid land makes both agriculture and animal husbandry impossible, and they might have to think about adopting a nomadic existence. They might then discard many of their material possessions so that they could travel easily, in order to take advantage of changing water and food supplies. Because of the extreme heat and the lack of extra water for laundry, they might find it more practical to be almost naked than to wear clothes. They would undoubtedly find it impossible to build elaborate homes. For social security, they might start to share the food brought into the group. Thus, if they survived at all, they might end up looking and acting far more like the !Kung looked than like typical North Americans.

As the world becomes increasingly interconnected or globalized, the importance of understanding and trying to respect cultural and physical differences becomes necessary. Misunderstandings can cause people to go to war, and war with modern weapons of mass destruction can kill more people than ever before. The gap between rich and poor countries has widened and anthropologists have been increasingly concerned with the effects of inequality. Even when the powerful countries want to help others, they often try to impose their ways of life, which they consider superior. But anthropologists may not think that particular ways of life are generally superior. What's good for some may not be good for other people in different circumstances.

Knowledge of our past may bring both a feeling of humility and a sense of accomplishment. If we are to attempt to deal with the problems of our world, we must be aware of our vulnerability so we do not think that problems will solve themselves. But we also have to think enough of our accomplishments to believe that we can find solutions to problems. Much of the trouble we get into may be a result of feelings of self-importance and invulnerability—in short, our lack of humility. Knowing something about our evolutionary past may help us to understand and accept our place in the biological world. Just as for any other form of life, there is no guarantee that any particular human population, or even the entire human species, will perpetuate itself indefinitely. The earth changes, the environment changes, and humanity itself changes. What survives and flourishes in the present might not do so in the future.

Yet our vulnerability should not make us feel powerless. There are many reasons to feel confident about the future. Consider what we have accomplished so far. By means of tools and weapons fashioned from sticks and stones, we were able to hunt animals larger and more powerful than ourselves. We discovered how to make fire, and we learned to use it to keep ourselves warm and to cook our food. As we domesticated plants and animals, we gained greater control over our food supply and were able to establish more permanent settlements. We mined and smelted ores to fashion more durable tools. We built cities and irrigation systems, monuments and ships. We made it possible to travel from one continent to another in a single day. We conquered some illnesses and prolonged human life.

In short, human beings and their cultures have changed considerably over the course of history. Human populations have often been able to adapt to changing circumstances. Let us hope that humans continue to adapt to the challenges of the present and future.

Summary

1. Anthropology is literally the study of human beings. It differs from other disciplines concerned with people in that anthropology is: (a) concerned with humans in all places of the world and it traces human evolution and cultural development from millions of years ago to the present day; (b) holistic, that is, studies all aspects of peoples' experiences; (c) concerned with identifying and explaining typical characteristics (traits, customs) of particular human populations.

2. Biological anthropology, one of the major fields of anthropology, studies the emergence of humans and their later physical evolution (human paleontology) and how and why contemporary human populations vary biologically (human variation).

3. Cultural anthropology has three subfields—archaeology, anthropological linguistics, and ethnology (now usually referred to by the parent name, cultural anthropology). All the subfields deal with aspects of human culture, that is, with the customary ways of thinking and behaving of particular societies.

4. Archaeologists seek to reconstruct and explain the daily life and customs of prehistoric peoples from the remains of human cultures.

5. Anthropological linguists are concerned with the emergence of language and with the divergence of languages over time (historical linguistics) as well as how contemporary languages differ, both in construction (descriptive or structural linguistics) and in actual speech (sociolinguistics).

6. The ethnologist (now often called a cultural anthropologist) seeks to understand how and why peoples of today and the recent past differ in their customary ways of thinking and acting. There are three major types of cultural anthropologists: ethnographers, ethnohistorians, and cross-cultural researchers.

7. In all four major subdisciplines of anthropology, there are applied anthropologists, people who apply anthropological knowledge to achieve more practical goals.

8. Scientists try to achieve two kinds of explanations—associations and theories. Theories are falsified by deriving hypotheses or predictions that should be true if the theory is correct.

9. By showing us why other people are the way they are, both culturally and physically, anthropology may make us more tolerant. Knowledge of our past may bring us both a feeling of humility and a sense of accomplishment.

Glossary Terms

anthropological linguistics (p. 6)
anthropology (p. 2)
applied (practicing) anthropology (p. 9)
archaeology (p. 6)
biological (physical) anthropology (p. 4)
cross-cultural researcher (p. 9)
cultural anthropology (p. 4)
descriptive (structural) linguistics (p. 7)
ethnographer (p. 8)
ethnography (p. 8)
ethnohistorian (p. 8)
ethnology (p. 6)
explanation (p. 11)
fossils (p. 4)
historical archaeology (p. 6)
historical linguistics (p. 7)
holistic (p. 3)

Homo sapiens (p. 5)
human paleontology (p. 4)
human variation (p. 4)
hypotheses (p. 14)
laws (p. 11)
measure (p. 15)
operational definition (p. 14)
paleoanthropology (p. 4)
prehistory (p. 6)
Primates (p. 5)
primatologists (p. 5)
sociolinguistics (p. 7)
statistical association (p. 11)
theoretical construct (p. 13)
theories (p. 11)
variables (p. 11)

Critical Questions

1. Why study anthropology? What are its goals and how is it useful?

2. How does anthropology differ from other fields of study you've encountered that deal with humans? (Compare with psychology, sociology, political science, history, or biology, among others.)

3. Can a unique event be explained? Explain your answer.

4. Why is scientific understanding always uncertain?

CHAPTER 2

HOW WE DISCOVER THE PAST

Chapter Outline

- The Evidence of the Past
- Finding the Evidence
- Analyzing the Evidence
- Dating the Evidence
- The Results of Archaeological Research
- Ethics in Archaeological Research

How can archaeologists and **paleoanthropologists** (anthropologists who study human evolution) know about what may have happened thousands or even millions of years ago? There are no written records from those periods from which to draw inferences. But we do have other kinds of "record," other kinds of evidence from the past. And we have ways of "reading" this evidence, which tells us a lot about how our human ancestors evolved and how they lived long ago.

The Evidence of the Past

Archaeologists and paleoanthropologists rely on four kinds of evidence to learn about the past: *artifacts, ecofacts, fossils,* and *features.* As we will see, each provides unique information about the past. Together, artifacts, ecofacts, fossils, and features provide a story about human life long ago. However, we need to be trained to "read" this story.

Artifacts

Anything made or modified by humans is an **artifact**. The book you are reading now, the chair you are sitting in, the pen you are taking notes with are all artifacts. In fact, we are surrounded by artifacts, most of which we will lose or throw away. And that is exactly how things enter what we call the "archaeological record." Think about it: How much garbage do you produce in a day? What kinds of things do you throw away? Mostly paper, probably, but also wood (from the ice cream bar you had at lunch), plastic (like the pen that ran out of ink last night), and even metal (the dull blade on your razor). Into the garbage they go and out to the dump or landfill. Under the right conditions many of those items will survive for future archaeologists to find. Most of the artifacts that make up the archaeological record are just this kind of mundane waste—the accumulated garbage of daily life that archaeologists may recover and examine to reconstruct what daily life was like long ago.

By far the most common artifacts from the past are stone tools, which archaeologists call **lithics**. Indeed, lithics are the only kind of artifact available for 99 percent of human history. Humans first started using stone tools more than 2.5 million years ago, and some tools of stone (grinding and polishing stones, for example) are still used today. Stone has been used for almost any purpose you can think of, from cutting tools to oil lamps, although their most common use has probably been for hunting, butchering, and hide-processing tools. Another common kind of artifact is **ceramics** (pots and other items made from baked clay). Humans first started making ceramics about 10,000 years ago, and ceramic objects such as storage and cooking vessels quickly came to be used widely. Because they are both fragile and relatively easy to make, ceramics show up frequently in the garbage that makes up the archaeological record. Wood and bone artifacts are common too, and were used to make hide-working, cooking, hunting, and even butchering tools. Wood and bone tools have been used by humans at least as long as stone tools, but unlike stone tools they tend not to survive well in the archaeological record. In some places metals and glass are also common artifacts. These survive well in the archaeological record, and hence they are often found where they were used.

Ecofacts

Ecofacts are natural objects that have been used or affected by humans. A good example is the bone from animals that people have eaten. These bones are somewhat like artifacts, but they haven't been made or modified by humans, just used and discarded by them. Another example is pollen found at archaeological sites. Because humans bring plants back to their houses to use, pollens from many plants are commonly found. These pollens may not have come from the same location. The only reason they are together is that they have been brought together by human use. Other examples are the remains of insect and animal pests that associate with humans, such as cockroaches and mice. Their remains are found in sites because they take advantage of the conditions that humans create. Their presence is in part caused by the human presence, and thus they are considered ecofacts too.

Fossils

And then there are fossils, which are rare but particularly informative about human biological evolution. A fossil may be an impression of an insect or leaf on a muddy surface that now is stone. Or it may consist of the actual hardened remains of an animal's skeletal structure. When an animal dies, the organic matter that made up its body begins to deteriorate. The teeth and skeletal structure consist largely of inorganic mineral salts, and soon they are all that remains. Under most conditions, these parts eventually deteriorate too. But once in a great while conditions are favorable for preservation—for instance, when volcanic ash, limestone, or highly mineralized groundwater is present to create a high-mineral environment. If the remains are buried under such circumstances, the minerals in the ground may become bound into the structure of the teeth or bone, hardening the remains and thus making them less likely to deteriorate.

But we don't have fossil remains of everything that lived in the past, and sometimes we only have fragments from one or a few individuals. So the fossil record is very incomplete. For example, Robert Martin estimates that the earth has probably seen 6,000 primate species; remains of only 3 percent of those species have been found. It is hardly surprising then that primate paleontologists cannot identify most of the evolutionary connections between early and later forms. The task is particularly difficult with small mammals, such as the early primates, which are less likely than large animals to be preserved in the fossil record.[1]

Features

Features are a kind of artifact, but archaeologists distinguish them from other artifacts because they cannot be easily removed from an archaeological site. Hearths are good examples. When humans build a fire on bare ground the soil becomes heated and is changed—all the water is driven out of it and its crystalline structure is broken down and reformed. It becomes hard, redder, and even slightly magnetic (as we discuss later). When an archaeologist finds a hearth, what exactly is found? An area of hard, reddish soil,

Shown here is the fossilized skeleton of an Ornithopod dinosaur.

often surrounded by charcoal and ash. Here, then, is an artifact—an object of human manufacture. But it would be very difficult, if not impossible, for the archaeologist to pick the hearth up and take it back to the lab for study like a lithic or ceramic. A hearth is really an intrinsic feature of a site—hence the name *feature*.

Hearths are common features, but by far the most common features are called *pits*. Pits are simply holes dug by humans that are later filled with garbage or eroded soil. They are usually fairly easy to distinguish because the garbage or soil they are filled with is often different in color and texture from the soil into which the pit was dug. *Living floors* are another common type of feature. These are the places where humans lived and worked. The soils in these locations are often compacted through human activity and are full of minute pieces of garbage—seeds, small stone flakes, beads, and the like—that became embedded in the floor. A large or very deep area of such debris is called a *midden*. Middens are often the remains of garbage dumps or areas repeatedly used over long periods of time, such as caves. Finally, *buildings* are a common feature on archaeological sites. These can range from the remains of stone rings that once held down the sides of tents to palaces built of stones that had been shaped and fitted together. Even the remains of wooden houses (or parts of them) have been preserved under some conditions. Features are a diverse array of things that can provide lots of information about the past.

Finding the Evidence

Evidence of the past is all around us, but finding it is not always easy or productive. Archaeologists and paleoanthropologists usually restrict their search to what are called *sites*. **Sites** are known or suspected locations of human activity in the past that contain a record of that activity. Sites can range from places where humans camped for perhaps only one night to large ancient cities. Regardless of their size or complexity, sites can reveal many things about life in the past.

How Are Sites Created?

Sites are created when the remnants of human activity are covered or buried by some natural process. The most dramatic one is volcanic activity; the record of human behavior (and even the humans themselves) can be totally buried within seconds. The most impressive example of this must be Pompeii, an entire city that was buried in the eruption of Mount Vesuvius in A.D. 79. Today archaeologists are digging out the city and finding the remains of ancient life just as it was left in the moments before the eruption.[2] Less dramatic means of burying the record of human behavior are the natural processes of dirt accumulation and erosion. Wind- or water-borne soil and debris can cover a site either quickly (as in a flood) or over a long period of time, preserving intact the artifacts, ecofacts, fossils, and features left by humans. Finally, the processes through which soils are built up can also bury artifacts, ecofacts, fossils, and features in a way that allows archaeologists to uncover them later. In forests, for example, falling leaves cover the locations where humans camped. Over time the leaves decay and build up soil, covering the remains of the human encampment slowly but completely over many years.

Since good locations to live and work in are often reused by humans, many sites contain the remains of numerous human occupations. The most valuable sites to archaeologists and paleoanthropologists are those in which the burial processes worked quickly enough that each use of the site is clearly separated from the previous one. Such sites are called **stratified**; each layer, or *stratum,* of human occupation is separate like a layer in a layer cake. Not only do stratified sites allow the archaeologist or paleoanthropologist to distinguish the sequence of site occupations, but the strata themselves provide a way to know the relative ages of the occupations—earlier occupations will always be below later ones.

Taphonomy

It is important to note that the very processes that create sites can often damage or destroy them. The study of the processes of site disturbance and destruction is called **taphonomy**. Some archaeologists and paleoanthropologists argue that natural processes such as wind and water erosion not only bury the materials left by humans but may affect them so significantly that we need to be very cautious when interpreting what is found in an archaeological site. For example, Harold Dibble and his colleagues have argued that the Lower Paleolithic site of Cagny-L'Epinette in France does not actually contain locations where Lower Paleolithic peoples lived and worked, as previous excavators suggested. Rather, Dibble and his colleagues argue that what looks like locations of human activity were created by water running across the site and accumulating artifacts in low-lying places.[3] This doesn't mean that nothing can be learned from such a site, even one that has been subjected to considerable disturbance, but rather that archaeologists and paleoanthropologists must use caution when interpreting the site. An understanding of site taphonomy can help an archaeologist make an informed and cautious interpretation of the past.[4]

How Are Sites Found?

There is no single method of finding sites, and indeed many sites are found by happenstance—someone digs into the ground and discovers a lot of artifacts or perhaps a feature. But when archaeologists and paleoanthropologists want to go out and find sites, they typically employ one of two basic methods: pedestrian survey and remote sensing.

Pedestrian survey is what the name suggests—walking around and looking for sites. But there are a number of techniques that archaeologists and paleoanthropologists use to enhance the effectiveness of pedestrian survey beyond simply walking around. These include the use of sampling and systematic surveying methods to reduce the area to be covered on foot. Another way archaeologists reduce the area to be examined is by focusing their search on places humans are likely to have occupied. Paleoanthropologists,

A site is a location where archaeological materials are found in context. Here Vietnamese archaeologists expose the remains of the ancient citadel of Hanoi, preserved below the modern city.

for example, typically focus only on those locations where there are exposed fossil beds dating to the time period of the early humans or apes they are interested in finding. Pedestrian survey, while very low tech, can be an extremely effective way of finding sites.

Remote sensing is a much more high-tech way of finding sites. With remote sensing techniques, archaeologists and paleoanthropologists find archaeological deposits by sensing their presence from a remote location, usually the current surface of the ground beneath which the archaeological deposits are buried. Most remote sensing techniques are borrowed from exploration geology, and are the same ones geologists use to find mineral or oil deposits. They typically involve the measurement of minute variations in phenomena like the earth's magnetic or gravitational field, or changes in an electric current or pulse of energy directed into the ground. When these subtle changes, called *anomalies,* are located, more detailed exploration can map the extent and depth of the buried archaeological deposits.

One of the most common remote sensing techniques used in archaeology is *geomagnetics.* Geomagnetic sensing is based on the fact that the earth has a strong magnetic field that varies locally depending on what is beneath the ground. Features such as hearths, stone walls, and pits filled with organic material can alter the earth's magnetic field, as can metal and ceramic artifacts. By carefully measuring the earth's magnetic field, an archaeologist can often locate these features and artifacts. The archaeologist uses a highly sensitive instrument called a magnetometer to map the earth's magnetic field over a large area. When the map is complete, areas with anomalously high or low readings point to locations where buried features or artifacts may be present. In many cases, these anomalies form patterns that can be easily interpreted. For example, the remains of a buried house may be "seen."

Geomagnetic sensing is called a "passive" technique because the archaeologist simply measures the existing magnetic field. There are also "active" remote sensing techniques by which the archaeologist sends a pulse of energy into the ground and records how it is affected by whatever is buried. One of the most commonly used active techniques is *soil interface radar* (SIR), sometimes also called *ground penetrating radar* (GPR). This technique is based on the fact that different soils reflect radar energy differently. By sending a radar pulse into the ground and recording how the soils reflect it, the archaeologist can map the various soils below the ground. More importantly, if there are features such as walls and pits below the ground, those can be mapped as well. To conduct a radar survey, the archaeologist pulls an antenna along the ground, the size of which depends on the depth of penetration the archaeologist wants and the features expected. The antenna both sends and receives the radar pulses, and the received radar reflections are recorded on a paper strip or in a computer file. These recordings give the archaeologist a picture of what is below the ground.

How Are Artifacts, Ecofacts, and Features Recovered from Sites?

Whether they are identified by pedestrian survey or remote sensing, once archaeological deposits are found there is only one way to recover them—by excavation. Excavation itself is a complex process with two goals: (1) to find every scrap of evidence (or a statistically representative sample) about the past that a given site holds, and (2) to record the horizontal and vertical location of that evidence with precision. Archaeologists and paleoanthropologists have developed many excavation strategies and techniques to accomplish these goals, but all of them involve the careful removal of the archaeological deposits; the recovery of artifacts, ecofacts, fossils, and features from the soil in which those deposits have been buried; and the detailed recording of where each artifact, ecofact, fossil, and feature was located on the site.

Few sites can ever be fully excavated. The cost involved would be tremendous, and most archaeologists feel it is important to leave some archaeological deposits undisturbed for future archaeologists using new techniques. And so archaeological excavations usually use some method of sampling, which allows

Paleoanthropologists excavate an early human site in northwestern Kenya. The exposed fossils are those of an elephant that may have been butchered by humans.

archaeologists to recover a full range of artifacts, ecofacts, fossils, and features from only a small portion of a site. Sampling, however, requires that the archaeologist carefully plan where excavations will be conducted so that all areas of the site have an equal likelihood of being examined.

To date, no one has figured out a way to recover artifacts, ecofacts, fossils, and features from a site without destroying the site in the process, and this is one of the strange ironies of archaeological research. As we discuss shortly, it is the relationships between and among artifacts, ecofacts, fossils, and features that are of most interest to archaeologists, and it is precisely these relationships that are destroyed when archaeologists remove them from a site. For this reason most excavation by professional archaeologists today is done only when a site is threatened with destruction, and then only by highly trained personnel using rigorous techniques. Archaeologists and paleoanthropologists collect data in basically the same ways, with one important difference. Archaeologists are most concerned with recovering intact features, whereas paleoanthropologists are most concerned with recovering intact fossils. This leads to some differences in approaches to collecting data, particularly where to look. So archaeologists tend to seek out undisturbed sites where intact features can be found. In contrast, disturbances are a plus for paleoanthropologists, because disturbed sites may make finding fossils easier—they may be eroding out of the surface of the ground and be easily visible without digging. This doesn't mean archaeologists never excavate disturbed sites, because they do. And paleoanthropologists have sometimes made important discoveries by excavating undisturbed sites.[5]

Analyzing the Evidence

Once archaeologists and paleoanthropologists have found a site and recovered artifacts and other materials from it, they are ready to begin "reading" what they've found to learn the story of the past. This "reading" of the archaeological record is called *analysis*. Like excavation, archaeological analysis is a varied and sophisticated process that we will touch on only briefly here.

It should be obvious from our discussion of the archaeological record that much of what is lost or discarded by humans never survives. It is also the case that much of what does survive comes to us in fragments and in a fragile, deteriorated state. Before doing analysis, then, archaeologists and paleoanthropologists must first conserve and reconstruct the materials they have found.

Conservation and Reconstruction

Conservation is the process of treating artifacts, ecofacts, and in some cases even features, to stop decay and, if possible, reverse the deterioration process. Some conservation is very simple, involving only cleaning and drying the item. Some conservation is highly complex, involving long-term chemical treatments and long-term storage under controlled conditions. The so-called "Ice Man," for example, the 5,000-year-old individual found in 1993 in the Italian Alps, is kept in permanently glacial-like conditions after investigators found to their dismay that warming the remains for study induced the growth of mold. The archaeologists removed the mold, but decided that his remains would have to be kept under the same conditions that preserved them in the first place, and so a complex storage facility had to be built to recreate the glacial environment in which he was originally found.[6]

Reconstruction is like building a three-dimensional puzzle when you're not sure which pieces belong and you know not all of the pieces are there. First, materials have to be sorted into similar types. For example, to reconstruct ceramics from a site, all the ceramics have to be sorted into types with similar color, decoration, and shapes. Then pieces are compared to see if any may come from the same vessel. Once all the pieces thought to be from the same vessel are located, they can be assembled. Reconstruction is a long, difficult process—in some cases taking years.

Shown here is a conservator applying preservative to a decaying Alaskan totem pole.

What Can We Learn from Artifacts?

Once conservation and reconstruction are complete, the archaeologist or paleoanthropologist can begin to analyze the artifacts they've found. Archaeologists have developed specific and often unique ways to analyze the many different types of artifacts. Stone tools are examined in different ways from ceramics, and both are examined differently from bone. But there are some commonalities in the way artifacts are analyzed, regardless of what they are made of.

First, archaeologists typically examine the *form* or shape of an artifact. For most common artifacts, such as lithics and ceramics, possible forms are known well enough to be grouped into a **typology** or set of types, which is often the primary purpose of *formal analysis*. This is because typologies allow archaeologists to place a particular artifact into context with other artifacts found at the site or at other sites. Typologies often provide a lot of information about an artifact, including its age, the species or culture with which it is affiliated, and in some cases even how it was made, used, or exchanged in the past. Figure 2.1 shows a projectile point typology for a site in Tennessee from the time period between about 7300 and 5000 B.C. Over time the forms of the projectile points changed. The bases of points (f) and (g) are very different in their form from those of (c), (d), and (e), and all of them are different from (a). With this sort of typology, an archaeologist can estimate the age of a projectile point just by looking at the form of its base.

Second, archaeologists often measure artifacts, recording their size in various, often strictly defined, dimensions. Such *metric analysis,* as this activity is called, is used much like formal analysis to group artifacts into a typology. Figure 2.2 shows the standard measurements taken from projectile points. With these measurements one can create a typology similar to that in Figure 2.1. Instead of looking at the form of the projectile points, one looks at their sizes. Clearly, the base widths of points (a), (d), and

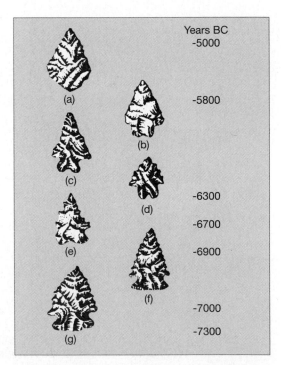

Figure 2.1   A Projectile Point Chronology from the Icehouse Bottom Site in Tennessee

Source: Jefferson Chapman, *Tellico Archaeology* (Knoxville: Tennessee Valley Authority, 1985), figure 1.15.

Distal

Maximum length

Maximum width

Neck width

Base width

Proximal

Figure 2.2   Standard Metrical Measurements of Chipped Stone Tools

(f) in Figure 2.1 are going to differ in a manner similar to the way their base forms differ. The value of metric analysis, however, is that the typology created is less subjective than a typology using forms. In addition, many measurements can be taken from broken or partial artifacts that might not be classifiable by formal analysis.

Third, archaeologists often attempt to understand how an artifact was made. By examining the material the artifact is made from and how that material was manipulated, archaeologists can learn about the technology, economy, and exchange systems of the peoples who made the artifact. For example, if the material is not locally available, that means the people traded for it. Archaeologists can also study present-day peoples and how they make similar artifacts in order to understand how ancient artifacts were made. Anne Underhill was interested in understanding how ceramics were produced during the Longshan period in China—a time known for its elegant, thin-walled pottery. In addition to studying the Longshan ceramics and the sites they came from, Underhill also visited living potters who make similar vessels today. She found that both full-time and part-time potters produce ceramics today, but was this the case in the past? Underhill measured ceramics being produced by these potters and performed a metric analysis. She found, to her surprise, that both full-time and part-time potters produce high-quality and highly uniform ceramics, difficult to distinguish from one another.[7]

Finally, archaeologists attempt to understand how an artifact was used. Knowing how an artifact was used gives the archaeologist a direct window onto ancient life. A number of sophisticated techniques have been developed to determine use. For stone, bone, and wood tools, there is a technique called *use-wear analysis,* which can determine how a tool was used through the careful examination of the kind of wear on its edges. We discuss use-wear analysis in more detail in later chapters. For ceramic vessels, techniques have been developed to extract residues trapped in the clay and determine what the vessel held.

Shown here is a Longshan thin-walled ceramic of the type studied by Anne Underhill.

Archaeologist Patrick McGovern and chemist Rudolf Michel, for example, took samples of a pale yellow residue found in grooves inside ceramic vessels from Grodin Tepe in Turkey. Their analysis determined that the residue was from barley beer, providing the earliest evidence of brewing in the world (the ceramics date from 3500 to 3100 B.C.).[8]

So what can archaeologists learn by placing artifacts in typologies through formal and metric analysis, and by learning how an artifact was manufactured and used? A lot. Typologies allow archaeologists to use relative dating (which we discuss later) to determine the age of an artifact or site by locating it in a sequence involving other artifacts and sites with known ages. Typologies thus allow archaeologists to determine which human groups were related to one another in the distant past, how information was shared among those groups, and in some cases even what social behavior was like (how labor was organized, who traded with whom).

For example, Carla Sinopoli examined the ceramics from the Iron Age site of Vijayanagara, in southern India. Previous excavations had identified distinct residential areas of the site, including a "Noblemen's Quarter," elite residences of high-caste Hindus, the "East Valley," thought to contain residences of lower-caste Hindus, and the "Islamic Quarter," which is thought to house Muslim mercenaries. When Sinopoli compared ceramics across the three areas, she found distinct differences: The "Islamic Quarter" had significantly more eating vessels than either of the two other areas, a difference that Sinopoli interpreted as being related to Hindu restrictions on the use of ceramics for holding food (some Hindus will not reuse food containers, so they are often made of disposable materials, such as leaves). So ceramics not only can inform the archaeologist about the social organization of a site, they can also reveal religious beliefs![9] Even gender roles can be revealed archaeologically (see the box "Women in the Shell Mound Archaic").

One of the main issues addressed by archaeologists interested in gender is how we can learn about and understand gender roles in prehistoric cultures. Gender roles might seem impossible to study in archaeological contexts. How is gender preserved in the archaeological record? How can knowledge about gender roles be recovered? Information about gender roles can be recovered if one is aware of how particular kinds of material culture are associated ethnographically with particular gender roles, and changes in them over time. Archaeologists argue that such an awareness leads not only to a better understanding of gender in prehistory but can also lead to a fuller understanding of prehistoric cultures overall.

An example is Cheryl Claassen's work on the Shell Mound Archaic culture of the Tennessee River valley. The Shell Mound Archaic represents the remains of people who lived in Tennessee and Kentucky between about 5,500 and 3,000 years ago. They were hunters and gatherers who lived in small villages, and probably moved seasonally between summer and winter communities. The most distinctive feature of the Shell Mound Archaic is the large mounds of mollusk shells they constructed for burying their dead. Tens of thousands of shells were piled together to create these mounds. Yet, around 3,000 years ago, shellfishing and thus the creation of shell burial mounds stopped abruptly. Claassen wondered why.

Suggested explanations include climate change, overexploitation of shellfish, and the migration of shellfishing peoples out of the area. None has proven wholly satisfactory. In contemporary cultures shellfishing is typically done by women and children, and Claassen wondered whether an approach that considered gender roles might be more productive. She decided to approach the problem through the perspective of women's workloads, since it would have been women who would most likely have been the ones shellfishing. The end of shellfishing would have meant that women would have had a lot of free time—free time that could have been put to use in some other way. What might have changed to lead women to stop shellfishing? Did some other activities become more important, so that women's labor was needed more for those other tasks?

Women's labor might have been redirected toward domesticated crops. There is archaeological evidence that about 3,000 years ago several productive crops that required intensive labor came into wide use. For example, *chenopodium,* one of the more plentiful and nutritious of these new crops, has tiny seeds that require considerable labor to harvest, clean, and process. Women were likely the ones burdened with such work. They not only would have harvested these crops but also would have been the ones to process and prepare meals from them. Thus the emergence of agricultural economies would have required women to undertake new labor in food production and processing that may well have forced them to stop engaging in other tasks, like shellfishing, especially if the new tasks produced a larger food supply.

The development of agricultural activities might also have brought about changes in ritual and ceremonialism. The shell burial mounds were clearly central to Shell Mound Archaic death ceremonies. Considerable labor, mostly by women, would have been required to collect the shells and build these mounds. Later societies in the region buried their dead in earthen mounds. Could this be a reflection of the new importance dirt had in an emerging agricultural economy? If so, what role did women play in ceremonies of death and burial? If they were no longer the providers of the raw materials needed for burial, does that mean their status in society as a whole changed?

We may never know exactly why the Shell Mound Archaic disappeared, or how women's work and women's roles in society changed. But as Claassen points out, taking a gender perspective provides new avenues along which to pursue answers to these questions, and interesting new questions to pursue.

Sources: Cheryl Claassen, "Gender and Archaeology," in P. N. Peregrine, C. R. Ember, and M. Ember, eds., *Archaeology: Original Readings in Method and Practice* (Upper Saddle River, NJ: Prentice Hall, 2002), pp. 210–24; also in C. R. Ember, M. Ember, and P. N. Peregrine, eds., *Research Frontiers,* in *New Directions in Anthropology* (Upper Saddle River, NJ: Prentice Hall, CD-ROM, 2004); Cheryl Claassen, "Gender, Shellfishing, and the Shell Mound Archaic," in J. Gero and M. Conkey, eds., *Engendering Archaeology* (Oxford: Blackwell, 1991), pp. 276–300.

Knowing how an artifact was made allows the archaeologist to understand the technology and technical abilities of peoples in the past. For example, Thomas Wynn analyzed both the final forms and the methods used by early humans—*Homo erectus*—to make stone tools roughly 300,000 years ago. He found that manufacturing these tools was a multistage process, involving several distinct steps and several distinct stone-working techniques to arrive at the finished product. He then took this information and evaluated it in terms of a measure of human cognitive ability developed by Jean Piaget, and concluded that the people who made these tools probably had organizational abilities similar to those of modern humans.[10]

Finally, knowing how an artifact was used allows the archaeologist to know something of people's behavior and activities. Lawrence Keeley conducted detailed use-wear analyses on Acheulian hand axes made by *Homo erectus* peoples and found that they had a variety of uses. Some apparently cut meat, others cut wood, and others were used to dig in the ground (probably for edible roots). On some hand axes, one edge was apparently used for one activity and the other for a different activity. Thus hand axes appear to have been multipurpose tools for our *Homo erectus* ancestors—something like a Swiss Army knife that they carried along with them. This knowledge gives us an interesting picture of these people: They used a fairly sophisticated manufacturing technique to make multipurpose tools that they carried with them and used for whatever job was at hand. This is a picture of the behavior of our ancient ancestors that is unavailable from any other source.[11]

What Can We Learn from Ecofacts and Fossils?

Ecofacts are diverse, and what archaeologists and paleoanthropologists can learn from them is highly diverse as well. Here we will focus on fossils. Later, in discussing the Upper Paleolithic world, we will discuss how archaeologists use ecofacts to reconstruct ancient environments. And later, when we discuss the

Shown here is an Acheulian hand axe. Lawrence Keeley examined the edge wear on hand axes to determine how they were used.

origins of domesticated plants and animals, we will learn how archaeologists use ecofacts to distinguish wild plants and animals from domestic plants and animals and to reconstruct how these plants and animals were domesticated.

Paleontologists (studying humans or other species) can tell a great deal about an extinct animal from its fossilized bones or teeth, but that knowledge is based on much more than just the fossil record itself. Paleontologists rely on comparative anatomy to help reconstruct missing skeletal pieces, as well as the soft tissues attached to bone. New techniques, such as electron microscopy, CAT scans, and computer-assisted biomechanical modeling, provide much information about how the organism may have moved about, the microstructure of bone and teeth, and how the organism developed. Chemical analysis of fossilized bone can suggest what the animal typically ate. Paleontologists are also interested in the surroundings of the fossil finds. With methods developed in geology, chemistry, and physics, paleontologists use the surrounding rocks to identify the time period in which the organism died. In addition, the study of associated fauna and flora can suggest what the ancient climate and habitat were like.

Much of the evidence for primate evolution comes from teeth, which are the most common animal parts (along with jaws) to be preserved as fossils. Animals vary in *dentition*—the number and kinds of teeth they have, their size, and their arrangement in the mouth. Dentition provides clues to evolutionary relationships because animals with similar evolutionary histories often have similar teeth. For example, no primate, living or extinct, has more than two incisors in each quarter of the jaw. That feature, along with others, distinguishes the primates from earlier mammals, which had three incisors in each quarter. Dentition also suggests the relative size of an animal and often offers clues about its diet. For example, comparisons of living primates suggest that fruit-eaters have flattened, rounded tooth cusps, unlike leaf- and insect-eaters, which have more pointed cusps.[12] CAT scan methodology has helped paleontologists image the internal parts of teeth, such as the thickness of enamel, which can also suggest the diet (seed- and nut-eaters have thicker enamel). Electron microscopy has revealed different patterns of growth in bones and teeth; different species have different patterns.[13]

Paleontologists can tell much about an animal's posture and locomotion from fragments of its skeleton. Arboreal quadrupeds have front and back limbs of about the same length; because their limbs tend to be short, their center of gravity is close to the branches on which they move. They also tend to have long grasping fingers and toes. Terrestrial quadrupeds are more adapted for speed, so they have longer limbs and shorter fingers and toes. Disproportionate limbs are more characteristic of vertical clingers and leapers and *brachiators* (species that swing through the branches). Vertical clingers and leapers have longer, more powerful hind limbs; brachiators have longer forelimbs.[14] Even though soft tissues are not preserved, much can be inferred from the fossils themselves. For example, the form and size of muscles can be estimated by marks found on the bones to which the muscles were attached. And the underside of the cranium may provide information about the proportions of the brain devoted to vision, smell, or memory. The skull also reveals information about characteristics of smell and vision. For example, animals that rely more on smell than on vision tend to have large snouts. Nocturnal animals tend to have large eye sockets.

What Can We Learn from Features?

The analysis of features is a little bit different from the analysis of artifacts, ecofacts, and fossils. Because we cannot remove features to the lab (see our earlier discussion of hearths), we cannot subject them to the same range of analyses as artifacts, ecofacts, and fossils. However, archaeologists have developed a number of powerful tools to analyze features in the field. The primary one is detailed mapping, usually using a surveyor's transit. Extensive records about each feature describe not only what the feature is, but also what archaeological materials were found associated with it. These kinds of information can be combined using a *geographic information system* (GIS). A GIS allows the archaeologist to produce a map of the features on a site and combine that map with information about other archaeological materials found there. Combining these kinds of information can reveal patterns in the archaeological record that tell us about human behaviors in the past.

A good example of how patterns of features can reveal past human behavior comes from the Range Site in west-central Illinois. Humans lived on the Range Site for over a thousand years, and during that time the ways they organized their settlement changed. About 2,300 years ago the people at the Range Site lived in small houses arranged around a circular courtyard. This pattern continued with some elaboration for almost 700 years; the courtyard area was a focus of activity and perhaps ritual. About 1,000 years ago the pattern changed. Houses became more substantial and were arranged linearly, in rows. This change suggests a radical alteration in social organization. From cross-cultural research (comparative studies using ethnographic data), we know that a circular community commonly functions as a single political and economic unit, whereas a community arranged linearly often consists of more than one political and economic unit. What the changes in the Range Site seem to show is an attenuation or reduction of the basic social and economic unit, from the community to the individual household. This change seems to have occurred because a large, centralized polity developed at Cahokia, only 15 kilometers away. The circular community, and the sociopolitical system it reflected, had persisted at the Range Site for almost a millennium, and then was transformed with the rise of Cahokia.[15]

Putting It All in Context

You might have gained the impression from our discussion that archaeologists and paleoanthropologists analyze artifacts, ecofacts, fossils, and features as individual objects, separate from one another. Nothing could be further from the truth. In fact, the analysis of the Range Site just described is much more like a typical archaeological analysis. It combines information about features across time to come to a generalization about how the social and economic organization of the people living there changed. We call this putting the material in context. **Context** is how and why the artifacts and other materials are related. This is really what archaeology and paleoanthropology are all about. Artifacts, ecofacts, fossils, and features in

Archaeologists examine the wall of an excavation at Nippur, Iraq. The thick white line in the wall is the plastered floor of a building. Items found on the floor can all be assumed to date from the same time, while items found below it can be assumed to date from an earlier time. This is a simple example of using stratigraphy for relative dating.

isolation may be beautiful or interesting by themselves, but it is only when they are placed in context with the other materials found on a site that we are able to "read" and tell the story of the past.

To illustrate this point, let's consider a set of letters that were found separately: A E G I M N N. They are arranged here in alphabetical order, the way a set of beautiful artifacts might be arranged in a museum display in order of size. But do these arrangements tell us anything? No. What if we knew something about the relationships between and among these letters—their context? What if, for example, we knew that the *M* was the first letter found, and that the *A* and *E* were found next to the *M,* but in reverse order, that one *N* was found between the *E* and *I,* and that the other *N* was found between the *I* and the *G?* Knowing in what context the letters were found would tell us that the letters should be arranged like this: *M E A N I N G.* And meaning is exactly what context gives to artifacts, ecofacts, fossils, and features.

Dating the Evidence

An important, indeed vital, part of putting artifacts and other materials into context is putting them in chronological order. To reconstruct the evolutionary history of the primates, for example, one must know how old primate fossils are. For some time, relative dating methods were the only methods available. The last half century has seen important advances in absolute dating, including techniques that allow the dating of the earliest phases of primate evolution. **Relative dating** is used to determine the age of a specimen or deposit relative to another specimen or deposit. **Absolute dating**, or **chronometric dating**, is used to measure how old a specimen or deposit is in years.

Relative Dating Methods

The earliest, and still the most commonly used, method of relative dating is based on **stratigraphy**, the study of how different rock or soil formations are laid down in successive layers or strata (see Figure 2.3 on page 38). Older layers are generally deeper or lower than more recent layers. Indicator artifacts or ecofacts are used to establish a stratigraphic sequence for the relative dating of new finds. These **indicator artifacts** or **ecofacts** are items of human manufacture or remains from animals and plants that spread widely over short periods of time, or that disappeared fairly rapidly, or that changed rapidly. Different artifacts and ecofacts are used as indicators of relative age in different areas of the world. In Africa, elephants, pigs, and horses have been particularly important in establishing stratigraphic sequences. Figure 2.3 shows the stratigraphy of Olduvai Gorge, an important site where early human fossils have been found. The stratigraphy here was established in part on the basis of fossil pigs.[16] The various species of pig in the successive strata are different, allowing the archaeologist or paleoanthropologist to differentiate the strata based on the species found within them. Once the stratigraphy of an area is established, the relative ages of two different fossils, or features, in the same or different sites are indicated by the associated indicator artifacts or ecofacts. Major transitions in indicator artifacts or ecofacts define the epochs and larger units of geologic time. The dates of the boundaries between such units are estimated by absolute dating, described in the next section.

If a site has been disturbed, stratigraphy will not be a satisfactory way to determine relative age. As noted earlier, remains from different periods may be washed or blown together by water or wind. Or a landslide may superimpose an earlier layer on a later layer. Still, it may be possible using absolute, or chronometric, dating methods to estimate the relative age of the different fossils found together in a disturbed site.

Figure 2.3 Stratigraphy of Beds I-IV along Olduvai Main Gorge

Notice how complex the four stratigraphic layers are. Each has numerous layers of soil and rock within them. Index fossils, particularly pigs, along with a series of potassium-argon dates, allowed the researchers to identify the four major strata of the site, which correspond to four major periods of human occupation.

Source: Louis S. B. Leakey, *Olduvai Gorge*, vol. I (New York: Cambridge University Press, 1951–1961). figure 2, p. 96. Copyright © 1965. Reprinted with the permission of Cambridge University Press.

Absolute, or Chronometric, Dating Methods

Many of the absolute dating methods are based on the decay of a radioactive isotope. Because the rate of decay is known, the age of the specimen can be estimated, within a range of possible error.

Radiocarbon Dating **Radiocarbon**, or **carbon-14 (^{14}C)**, **dating** is perhaps the most widely known method of determining the absolute age of a specimen. It is based on the principle that all living matter possesses a certain amount of a radioactive form of carbon (carbon-14, or ^{14}C). Radioactive carbon, produced when nitrogen-14 is bombarded by cosmic rays, is absorbed from the air by plants and then ingested by animals that eat the plants (see Figure 2.4). After an organism dies, it no longer takes in any of the radioactive carbon. Carbon-14 decays at a slow but steady pace and reverts to nitrogen-14. (By *decays,* we mean that the ^{14}C gives off a certain number of beta radiations per minute.) The rate at which the

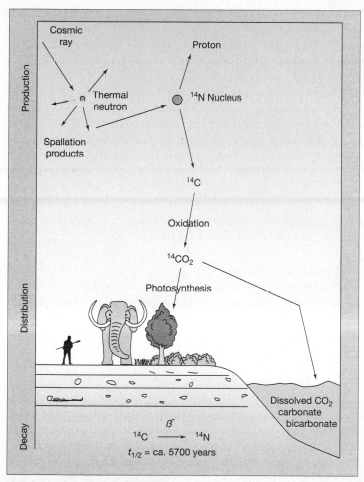

Figure 2.4   The Carbon-14 Cycle

Source: R. E. Taylor, "Radiocarbon Dating," in R. E. Taylor and M. J. Aitken, eds., *Chronometric Dating in Archaeology* (New York: Plenum, 1997), figure 3.1, p. 67. Copyright © 1997. Reprinted by permission of Springer Science and Business Media.

carbon decays—its **half-life**—is known: ^{14}C has a half-life of 5,730 years. In other words, half of the original amount of ^{14}C in organic matter will have disintegrated 5,730 years after the organism's death; half of the remaining ^{14}C will have disintegrated after another 5,730 years; and so on. After about 50,000 years, the amount of ^{14}C remaining in the organic matter is too small to permit reliable dating.

To discover how long an organism has been dead—that is, to determine how much ^{14}C is left in the organism and therefore how old it is—we either count the number of beta radiations given off per minute per gram of material, or use a particle accelerator to measure the actual amount of ^{14}C in a sample. Modern ^{14}C emits about 15 beta radiations per minute per gram of material, and ^{14}C that is 5,730 years old emits only half that amount (the half-life of ^{14}C) per minute per gram. So if a sample of some organism gives off 7.5 radiations a minute per gram, which is only half the amount given off by modern ^{14}C, the organism must be 5,730 years old. Similarly, because the amount of ^{14}C in a sample slowly declines over time, the atoms in a sample can be sent through a particle accelerator to separate them by weight (the lighter ^{12}C accelerates faster than the heavier ^{14}C) and measure the actual amount of each. This method, called AMS (accelerator mass spectrometry), is more accurate than the beta radiation method, requires only a very small sample of material, and provides a way to date specimens that are up to 80,000 years old.[17]

Thermoluminescence Dating   Many minerals emit light when they are heated (*thermoluminescence*), even before they become red hot. This cold light comes from the release, under heat, of "outside" electrons trapped in the crystal structure. **Thermoluminescence dating** makes use of the principle that if an object is heated at some point to a high temperature, as when clay is baked to form a pot, it will release all the trapped electrons it held previously. Over time, the object will continue to trap electrons from radioactive elements (potassium, thorium, uranium) around it. The amount of thermoluminescence emitted when the object is heated during testing allows researchers to calculate the age of the object, if it is known what kind of radiation the object has been exposed to in its surroundings (e.g., the surrounding soil in which a clay pot is found).

Thermoluminescence dating is well suited to samples of ancient pottery, brick, tile, terra cotta, and other objects that are made at high temperatures. This method can also be applied to burnt flint tools, hearth stones, lava or lava-covered objects, meteorites, and meteor craters.[18]

Electron Spin Resonance Dating   **Electron spin resonance dating** is a technique that, like thermoluminescence dating, measures trapped electrons from surrounding radioactive material. But the method in this case is different. The material to be dated is exposed to varying magnetic fields, and a spectrum of the microwaves absorbed by the tested material is obtained. Because no heating is required for this technique, electron spin resonance is especially useful for dating organic material such as bone and shell, which decompose if heated.[19]

Paleomagnetic Dating   When rock of any kind forms, it records the ancient magnetic field of the earth. When this knowledge is put together with the fact that the earth's magnetic field has reversed itself many times, the geomagnetic patterns in rocks can be used to date the fossils within those rocks. **Paleomagnetic dating** dates rocks in terms of the sequence of geomagnetic patterns in them. Strictly speaking, paleomagnetic dating is not an absolute dating method, but geomagnetic time periods have been dated absolutely in conjunction with potassium-argon dating (described later). Paleomagnetic dating has dated primate fossil finds from the Eocene through the Miocene, from 55 million to 5 million years ago.[20]

Not only does the earth's magnetic field reverse itself, but the locations of its poles move constantly (albeit very slowly) over time. The wanderings of the North Pole have been determined for the recent past, and this knowledge allows archaeologists to date some archaeological features. When soil, rock, or metal is heated to a high temperature, it liquifies and its constituent molecules align themselves to the earth's magnetic field. When cooled, the molecules retain their alignment, and thus create something of an arrow pointing to the earth's magnetic poles. When an archaeologist finds a hearth, pottery kiln, metal workshop, or something else in which earth, rock, or metal was heated to its melting point and cooled in place, the archaeologist can take a sample of that material, record its location in terms of the earth's present-day magnetic field, and then measure the material's magnetic field in the laboratory. The difference between the direction of the earth's current magnetic field and that recorded in the material can be used to date when the material melted and cooled.

Potassium-Argon Dating and Argon-Argon Dating   Potassium-40 (^{40}K), a radioactive form of potassium, decays at an established rate and forms argon-40 (^{40}Ar). The half-life of ^{40}K is a known quantity, so the age of a material containing potassium can be measured by the amount of ^{40}K compared with the amount of ^{40}Ar it contains.[21] Radioactive potassium's (^{40}K's) half-life is very long—1,330 million years. This means that **potassium-argon (K-Ar) dating** may be used to date samples from 5,000 years up to 3 billion years old.

The K-Ar method is used to date potassium-rich minerals in rock, not the fossils that may be found in the rock. A very high temperature, such as occurs in a volcanic event, drives off any original argon in the material. The amount of argon that accumulates afterward from the decay of radioactive potassium is directly related to the amount of time since the volcanic event. This type of dating has been extremely useful in East Africa, where volcanic events have occurred frequently since the Miocene, which began 24 million years ago. If the material to be dated is not rich in potassium, or the area did not experience any high-temperature events, other methods of absolute dating are required.

One problem with the K-Ar method is that the amounts of potassium and argon must be measured on different rock samples; researchers must assume that the potassium and argon are evenly distributed in all the rock samples from a particular stratum. Researchers got around this problem by developing the **^{40}Ar-^{39}Ar dating** method. After measuring the amount of ^{40}Ar, a nuclear reactor is used to convert another kind of argon, ^{39}Ar, to potassium so that the potassium-argon ratio can be measured from the same sample.[22]

Uranium-Series Dating   The decay of two kinds of uranium, ^{235}U and ^{238}U, into other isotopes (such as ^{230}Th, thorium) has also proved useful for dating sites, particularly in caves where stalagmites and other calcite formations form. Because water that seeps into caves usually contains uranium but not thorium, the calcite formations trap uranium. Uranium starts decaying at a known rate into other isotopes (such as thorium-230, or ^{230}Th), and the ratio of those isotopes to uranium isotopes can be used to estimate the time elapsed. The thorium-uranium ratio is useful for dating cave sites less than 300,000 years old where there are no volcanic rocks suitable for the potassium-argon method. Early *Homo sapiens* (modern-looking humans) from European cave sites in Germany, Hungary, and Wales were dated this way.[23] There are different varieties of **uranium-series dating**, depending on the specific isotope ratios used.

Fission-Track Dating   **Fission-track dating** is another way to determine the absolute age of fossil deposits. Like the K-Ar method, it dates minerals contemporaneous with the deposit in which fossils are found and it also requires the prior occurrence of a high-temperature event, such as a volcanic eruption. But the kinds of samples it can date, such as crystal, glass, and many uranium-rich minerals, include a much wider variety than those that can be dated by the K-Ar method. The age range of fission-track dating, like that of K-Ar dating, is extensive—20 years to 5 billion years.[24]

How does fission-track dating work? This method is basically the simplest of all the methods discussed here. It entails counting the number of paths or tracks etched in the sample by the fission—explosive division—of uranium atoms as they disintegrate. Scientists know that ^{238}U, the most common uranium isotope, decays at a slow, steady rate. This decay takes the form of spontaneous fission, and each separate fission leaves a scar or track on the sample, which can be seen, when chemically treated, through a microscope. To find out how old a sample is, one counts the tracks, then measures their ratio to the uranium content of the sample.

The fission-track method was used to date Bed I at Olduvai Gorge in Tanzania, East Africa, where some early human ancestors were found.[25] It was able to corroborate earlier K-Ar estimates that the site dated back close to 2 million years. That the K-Ar and fission-track methods use different techniques and have different sources of error makes them effective as checks on each other. When the two methods support each other, they provide very reliable evidence.

Other Techniques   The dating techniques outlined above are the most commonly used in archaeology and paleoanthropology, but there are many others, and new techniques are being developed all the time. For example, stone tools made from obsidian can be dated in some cases because a thin layer of stone, called an hydration layer, builds up on the obsidian over time when it is exposed to air. Similarly, rock art is sometimes dated by measuring the buildup of a patina over the art after it has been painted or carved on a piece of stone. Bones can sometimes be dated by measuring the breakdown of DNA, which occurs in a regular manner (similar to radioisotope decay) when heat and humidity are stable. These and many other techniques add a wide range of choices to the tool-kit that archaeologists and paleoanthropologists can use to date their finds.

The Results of Archaeological Research

When archaeologists and paleoanthropologists finish a research project, what is the result? What are the goals of archaeological research?

One goal is the description or reconstruction of what happened in the past. Much of what archaeologists do, and much of what we do in this book, has this goal. Archaeologists attempt to determine how people lived in a particular place at a particular time, and when and how their lifestyles changed. Also of interest, of course, is whether new populations carrying new cultures arrived, or whether people with a particular culture moved out of a given area. Creating histories of cultures and their changes over time is called, simply enough, **culture history**. Doing culture history was the primary goal of archaeology until the 1950s.[26]

A second major goal of archaeological research, and one that has become the primary goal since the 1950s, is testing specific explanations about human evolution and behavior. In part this change in focus results from our increased knowledge about the past—the culture history of many areas is well known today. But this change is also due to changes going on in anthropology as a whole. Until the 1950s a school of thought called historical particularism was dominant in American anthropology. It suggested that variation in human cultures was best explained by considering the specific historical developments of particular cultures. Like the purpose of historical particularism, the purpose of culture history was to trace historical developments.

After the 1950s a variety of new approaches arose in anthropology, most of them sharing the idea that the environment and how humans use it actively shapes cultures and mostly explains cultural variability. Archaeology became a key tool for anthropologists attempting to understand how changes in the ways humans used the environment explained variation in human cultures. One of the results of this focus on hypothesis testing and human use of the environment was research on agricultural origins, which we discuss in a later chapter. That chapter also discusses the rise of cities and states, which further transformed human use of the environment.

In addition to testing explanations, archaeology has a primary role within anthropology in its attempt to identify and understand general trends and patterns in human biological and cultural evolution. As we discussed in the first chapter, cross-cultural research (comparative ethnography) has this goal as well. But only archaeology is able to look through long stretches of time and directly examine evolutionary trends. In later chapters in this book we trace the evolution of humans and human cultures from their beginnings. As we shall see, a major emphasis in paleoanthropology is demonstrating long-term trends and patterns in the biological evolution of humans. These trends and patterns help us understand how and why we have come to be the way we are. In this pursuit, both archaeology and paleoanthropology help us answer what may be the fundamental question of anthropology: What does it mean to be human?

Ethics in Archaeological Research

Archaeologists must always be concerned with the ethics of their work when undertaking or reporting the results of their research. Archaeology does not simply describe past cultures; it can also have a profound effect on living peoples. For example, many people find the idea of archaeologists excavating, cleaning, and preserving the remains of ancestors to be offensive. Therefore, archaeologists must be sensitive to the desires and beliefs of the populations that descend from the ones they are researching. In addition, artifacts from some ancient cultures are in great demand by art and antiquities collectors, and archaeological finds can lead to uncontrolled looting if archaeologists are not careful about how and to whom they report their discoveries. Wholesale ransacking of ancient cemeteries in some parts of China, for example, started because new archaeological discoveries led Chinese antiquities to become increasingly popular among collectors, and hence increasingly valuable to those able to discover them.[27]

While it is the ethical responsibility of archaeologists to consult with descendant populations and to be careful about how archaeological finds are reported, it is also an ethical responsibility of archaeologists to present the results of their work to the general public. Publishing archaeological results increases public awareness about the past and the importance of historic preservation. If people know how much can be learned from the archaeological record, they may be less likely to destroy it or to support those who destroy it for personal gain. Of course, when archaeologists excavate sites, they also destroy some of the context of the artifacts, ecofacts, fossils, and features found in the sites. But if they leave some of the sites unexcavated, they are preserving them (at least partially) for future investigation. To offset their partial destruction, archaeologists are ethically obligated to publish the results of their work. Reporting the results of archaeological research, therefore, plays a central role in both archaeological research and archaeological ethics.

Summary

1.   Archaeologists and paleoanthropologists have four basic sources of evidence about the past: artifacts, ecofacts, fossils, and features. Artifacts are any objects made by humans. Ecofacts are natural objects used or modified by humans. Fossils are the preserved remains of ancient plants and animals. And features are artifacts that cannot be removed from archaeological sites.

2. Archaeological sites are locations where the evidence of the past has been buried and preserved. Sites are found through pedestrian survey or remote sensing, and artifacts, ecofacts, fossils, and features are recovered from sites through excavation. Key to excavation is the preservation of context; that is, the relationships between and among artifacts, ecofacts, fossils, and features.

3. Information about the past is obtained by analyzing the evidence recovered from sites. Much information can be gained through the analysis of the forms, sizes, and composition of archaeological materials, but the materials themselves are not the primary focus of analysis. Rather, it is the context between and among artifacts, ecofacts, fossils, and features that allows the archaeologist or paleoanthropologist to gain insights about the past.

4. A key aspect of putting archaeological material into context is being able to date material accurately. Many kinds of dating techniques are used. Relative dating techniques determine the age of archaeological materials relative to other materials of known ages. Absolute dating techniques determine the age of the archaeological deposits or materials themselves.

5. Archaeology allows for cultural histories to be developed and explanations about cultural change to be tested. Its primary goal is to provide insights into human physical and cultural evolution—the central concern of this book.

Glossary Terms

absolute dating (p. 37)
^{40}Ar-^{39}Ar dating (p. 41)
artifact (p. 23)
ceramics (p. 23)
chronometric dating (p. 37)
conservation (p. 29)
context (p. 36)
culture history (p. 42)
ecofacts (p. 23)
electron spin resonance dating (p. 40)
features (p. 24)
fission-track dating (p. 41)
half-life (p. 40)
indicator artifacts or ecofacts (p. 37)

lithics (p. 23)
paleoanthropologists (p. 23)
paleomagnetic dating (p. 40)
potassium-argon (K-Ar) dating (p. 41)
radiocarbon, or carbon-14 (^{14}C), dating (p. 39)
relative dating (p. 37)
sites (p. 25)
stratified (p. 25)
stratigraphy (p. 37)
taphonomy (p. 26)
thermoluminescence dating (p. 40)
typology (p. 30)
uranium-series dating (p. 41)

Critical Questions

1. Why is context so important in archaeological research?

2. What kinds of information can be learned from a stone projectile point?

3. What factors have to be considered when choosing a dating technique?

GENETICS AND EVOLUTION

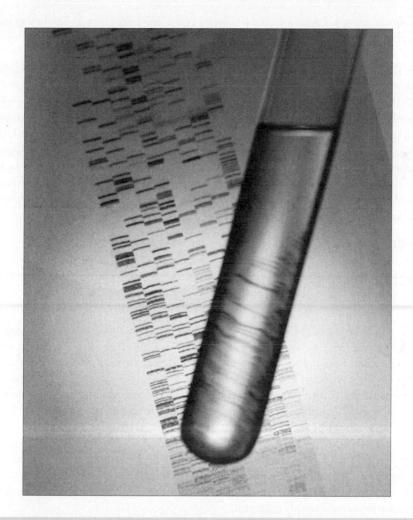

Chapter Outline

- The Evolution of Evolution
- Principles of Natural Selection
- Heredity
- Sources of Variability

- Origin of Species
- Natural Selection of Behavioral Traits

Astronomers estimate that the universe has been in existence for some 15 billion years, plus or minus a few billion. To make this awesome history more understandable, Carl Sagan devised a calendar that condenses this span into a single year.[1] Using as a scale 24 days for every billion years and 1 second for every 475 years, Sagan moves from the "Big Bang," or beginning of the universe, on January 1 to the origin of the Milky Way on May 1. September 9 marks the beginning of our solar system, and September 25 the origin of life on earth. At 10:30 in the evening of December 31, the first human-like primates appear. Sagan's compression of history provides us with a manageable way to compare the short span of human existence with the total time span of the universe. Human-like beings have been around for only about 90 minutes out of a 12-month period! In this book we are concerned with what has happened in the last few hours of that year.

Some 55 million to 65 million years ago, the first primates appeared. They were ancestral to all living primates, including monkeys, apes, and humans. The early primates may or may not have lived in trees, but they had flexible digits and could grasp things. Later, about 35 million years ago, the first monkeys and apes appeared. About 15 million years ago, some 20 million years after the appearance of monkeys and apes, the immediate ape-like ancestors of humans probably emerged. About 4 million years ago the first human-like beings appeared. Modern-looking humans evolved only about 100,000 years ago.

How do we account for the biological and cultural evolution of humans? The details of the emergence of primates and the evolution of humans and their cultures are covered in subsequent chapters. In this chapter we focus on how the modern theory of evolution developed and how it accounts for change over time.

The Evolution of Evolution

Traditional Western ideas about nature's creatures were very different from Charles Darwin's theory of *evolution,* which suggested that different species developed, one from another, over long periods of time. In the fifth millennium B.C., the Greek philosophers Plato and Aristotle believed that animals and plants form a single, graded continuum going from more perfection to less perfection. Humans, of course, were at the top of this scale. Later Greek philosophers added the idea that the creator gave life or "radiance" first to humans, but at each subsequent creation some of that essence was lost.[2] Macrobius, summarizing the thinking of Plotinus, used an image that was to persist for centuries, the image of what came to be called the "chain of being": "The attentive observer will discover a connection of parts, from the Supreme God down to the last dregs of things, mutually linked together and without a break. And this is Homer's golden chain, which God, he says, bade hand down from heaven to earth."[3] Belief in the chain of being was accompanied by the conviction that an animal or plant species could not become extinct. The notion of extinction threatened people's trust in God; it was unthinkable that a whole group of God's creations could simply disappear.

The idea of the chain of being persisted through the years, but it was not discussed extensively by philosophers, scientists, poets, and theologians until the eighteenth century. Those discussions prepared the way for evolutionary theory. It is ironic that, although the chain of being did not allow for evolution, its idea that there was an order of things in nature encouraged studies of natural history and comparative anatomical studies, which stimulated the development of the idea of evolution. People were also now motivated to look for previously unknown creatures. Moreover, humans were not shocked when naturalists suggested that humans were close to apes. This notion was perfectly consistent with the idea of a chain of being; apes were simply thought to have been created with less perfection.

Charles Robert Darwin.

Source: Gemalde von John Collier, 1883, "Charles Robert Darwin." Ol auf Leinwand, 125.7 x 96.5 cm. London, National Portrait Gallery/1024. Bildarchiv Preussischer Kulturbesitz. Photo: Jochen Remmer.

Early in the eighteenth century, an influential scientist, Carolus Linnaeus (1707–1778), classified plants and animals in a *systema naturae*, which placed humans in the same order (Primates) as apes and monkeys. Linnaeus did not suggest an evolutionary relationship between humans and apes; he mostly accepted the notion that all species were created by God and fixed in their form. Not surprisingly, then, Linnaeus is often viewed as an anti-evolutionist. But Linnaeus's hierarchical classification scheme, in descending order going from kingdom to class, order, **genus** (a group of related species), and species, provided a framework for the idea that humans, apes, and monkeys had a common ancestor.[4]

Others did not believe that species were fixed in their form. According to Jean Baptiste Lamarck (1744–1829), acquired characteristics could be inherited and therefore species could evolve; individuals who in their lifetime developed characteristics helpful to survival would pass those characteristics on to future generations, thereby changing the physical makeup of the species. For example, Lamarck explained the long neck of the giraffe as the result of successive generations of giraffes stretching their necks to reach the high leaves of trees. The stretched muscles and bones of the necks were somehow transmitted to the offspring of the neck-stretching giraffes, and eventually all giraffes came to have long necks. But because Lamarck and later biologists failed to produce evidence to support the hypothesis that acquired characteristics can be inherited, this explanation of evolution is now generally dismissed.[5]

By the nineteenth century, some thinkers were beginning to accept evolution while others were trying to refute it. For example, Georges Cuvier (1769–1832) was a leading opponent of evolution. Cuvier's theory of catastrophism proposed that a quick series of catastrophes accounted for changes in the earth and the fossil record. Cataclysms and upheavals such as Noah's flood had killed off previous sets of living creatures, which each time were replaced by new creations.

Major changes in geological thinking occurred in the nineteenth century. Earlier, geologist James Hutton (1726–1797) had questioned catastrophism, but his work was largely ignored. In contrast, Sir Charles Lyell's (1797–1875) volumes of the *Principles of Geology* (1830–1833), which built on Hutton's earlier work, received immediate acclaim. Their concept of *uniformitarianism* suggested that the earth is constantly being shaped and reshaped by natural forces that have operated over a vast stretch of time. Lyell also discussed the formation of geological strata and paleontology. He used fossilized fauna to define different geological epochs. Lyell's works were read avidly by Charles Darwin before and during Darwin's now-famous voyage on the *Beagle*. The two corresponded and subsequently became friends.

After studying changes in plants, fossil animals, and varieties of domestic and wild pigeons, Charles Darwin (1809–1882) rejected the notion that each species was created at one time in a fixed form. The results of his investigations pointed clearly, he thought, to the evolution of species through the mechanism of natural selection. While Darwin was completing his book on the subject, Alfred Russel Wallace (1823–1913), a naturalist, sent him a manuscript that came to conclusions about the evolution of species that matched Darwin's own.[6] In 1858, the two men presented the astonishing theory of natural selection to their colleagues at a meeting of the Linnaean Society of London.[7]

In 1859, when Darwin published *The Origin of Species by Means of Natural Selection,*[8] he wrote, "I am fully convinced that species are not immutable; but that those belonging to what are called the same genera are lineal descendants of some other and generally extinct species, in the same manner as the acknowledged varieties of any one species."[9] His conclusions outraged those who believed in the biblical account of creation, and the result was bitter controversy that continues to this day.[10]

Until 1871, when his *The Descent of Man* was published, Darwin avoided stating categorically that humans were descended from nonhuman forms, but the implications of his theory were clear. People immediately began to take sides. In June 1860, at the annual meeting of the British Association for the Advancement of Science, Bishop Wilberforce saw an opportunity to attack the Darwinists. Concluding his speech, he faced Thomas Huxley, one of the Darwinists' chief advocates, and inquired, "Was it through his grandfather or his grandmother that he claimed descent from a monkey?" Huxley responded,

> If . . . the question is put to me would I rather have a miserable ape for a grandfather than a man highly endowed by nature and possessing great means and influence and yet who employs those faculties and that influence for the mere purpose of introducing ridicule into a grave scientific discussion—I unhesitatingly affirm my preference for the ape.[11]

While Huxley's retort to Bishop Wilberforce displays both humor and quick wit, it does not answer the Bishop's question very well. A better answer, and one we pursue later, is that Darwinists would claim that we descended from monkeys neither through our grandmother or our grandfather, but that both we and monkeys are descended from a common ancestor who lived long ago. Darwinists would further argue that natural selection was the process through which the physical and genetic form of that common ancestor diverged to become both monkey and human.

Natural selection is a process we can see at work in the world today. It is a process that has been studied in both the laboratory and in nature, and it is a process that most scientists would argue is very well understood. However, as in all scientific endeavors, understanding grows and changes as new information is obtained. The understanding of natural selection we have today is quite different from that originally put forward by Darwin. A century and a half of research has added tremendously to the information Darwin had to work with, and entirely new fields, like population genetics, have emerged. With this new information we know that Darwin was wrong about some things. For example, it seems clear that natural selection is not always a uniform process, but can act in jumps and starts (see the box titled "Is Evolution Slow and Steady or Fast and Abrupt?" on pages 50–51). As we will see, different types of natural selection occur—some that make particular traits more common in a population, others that limit overall variation.

The fact that the ideas put forward by Darwin have changed, and are changing as new research is done, does not mean they were wrong. Darwin's ideas were simply incomplete. Each day as we add to our knowledge base we move closer to an even more complete understanding of natural selection. The development and transformation of ideas as new information is discovered is one of the hallmarks of science. Indeed, this is a central facet of science that proponents of "creation science" and "intelligent design theory" ignore. What physical evidence could be put forward to demonstrate that God (or some intelligent force) created the diversity of life on earth? In the absence of objective evidence supporting creationism or intelligent design, scientists conclude that natural selection, which *is* supported by objective evidence, better explains the diversity of life. We discuss creationist ideas further in the section on the origin of species on pages 62–63.

Principles of Natural Selection

Darwin was not the first person to view the creation of new species in evolutionary terms, but he was the first to provide a comprehensive, well-documented explanation—natural selection—for the way evolution had occurred. **Natural selection** is the main process that increases the frequency of adaptive traits through time. The operation of natural selection involves three conditions or principles.[12] The first is *variation:* Every species is composed of a great variety of individuals, some of which are better adapted to their environment than others. The existence of variety is important. Without it, natural selection has nothing on which to operate; without variation, one kind of characteristic could not be favored over another. The second principle of natural selection is *heritability:* Offspring inherit traits from their parents, at least to some degree and in some way. The third principle of natural selection is *differential reproductive success:* Since better adapted individuals generally produce more offspring over the generations than the poorer adapted, the frequency of adaptive traits gradually increases in subsequent generations. A new species emerges when changes in traits or geographic barriers result in the reproductive isolation of the population.

When we say that certain traits are adaptive or advantageous, we mean that they result in greater reproductive success in a particular environment. The phrase "particular environment" is very important. Even though a species may become more adapted to a particular environment over time, we cannot say that one species adapted to its environment is "better" than another species adapted to a different environment. For example, we may like to think of ourselves as "better" than other animals, but humans are clearly less adapted than fish for living under water, than bats for catching flying insects, or than raccoons for living on suburban garbage.

Although the theory of natural selection suggests that disadvantageous or maladaptive traits will generally decline in frequency or even disappear eventually, it does not necessarily follow that all such traits will do so. After all, species derive from prior forms that have certain structures. This means that not all changes are possible; it also means that some traits are linked to others that might have advantages that outweigh the disadvantages. Choking may be very maladaptive for any animal, yet all vertebrates are capable of choking because their digestive and respiratory tubes cross in the throat. This trait is a genetic legacy, probably from the time when the respiratory system developed from tissue in the digestive system of some ancestral organism. Apparently, the propensity to choke has not been correctable evolutionarily.[13] Our food tube can catch some air just as our air tube can catch some food.

Changes in a species can be expected to occur as the environment changes or as some members of the species move into a new environment. With environmental change, different traits become adaptive. The forms of the species that possess the more adaptive traits will become more frequent, whereas those forms whose characteristics make continued existence more difficult or impossible in the modified environment will eventually become extinct.

IS EVOLUTION SLOW AND STEADY OR FAST AND ABRUPT?

Darwin's evolutionary theory suggested that new species emerge gradually over time. Through the process of natural selection, frequencies of traits would slowly change, and eventually a new species would appear. But Darwin did not explain why so much speciation has occurred. If trait frequencies change only gradually over time, wouldn't descendant populations retain their ability to interbreed and wouldn't they, therefore, continue to belong to the same species?

In the 1930s and 1940s, biologists and geneticists advanced what came to be called the "modern synthesis" in evolutionary theory, adding what was known from genetics about heredity. Mutation and the recombination of genes now provided for genetic variety. The driving force of change was still adaptation to environments through natural selection; gene frequencies of a population presumably changed slowly as adaptive traits (because of existing genes or mutations) increased in prevalence and maladaptive traits decreased. As for speciation, the development and divergence of different species, the modern synthesis postulated that it would occur when subpopulations became isolated by geographic barriers or when different subpopulations encountered different climatic conditions or moved into new ecological niches; those environmental isolating processes would eventually result in the development of reproductive isolation and therefore new species.

This gradualist view of evolution was challenged in 1972 by Niles Eldredge and Stephen Jay Gould. Their alternative model of evolution is referred to as "punctuated equilibrium." They still assume that natural selection is the primary mechanism of evolutionary change, but they see the pace of evolution quite differently. In their view, new species evolve quickly; but once a successful species emerges, its characteristics are likely to change very little over long periods of time. Thus, in contrast to the modern synthesis, Eldredge and Gould do not think it is common for the world's species to change gradually into descendant species. Rather, species are born more or less abruptly, they have lifetimes during which they do not change much, and they become extinct. As examples, Eldredge and Gould cite the history of North-American trilobites and Bermudan land snails. In both groups of animals, it looks as if the different species did not change for a long period of time—millions of years for some species—but then certain species seem to have been quickly replaced by related species from nearby areas. In short, Eldredge and Gould believe that the succession of one species after another involves replacement from outside more often than gradual change over time.

Evolution may or may not occur as the model of punctuated equilibrium specifies, but most evolutionists today agree that change could occur relatively quickly. Recent research suggests that some relatively quick climate changes in the earth's history helped bring about massive extinctions of species and families of species and exponential increases in the subsequent number of new families. For example, there is considerable evidence that a large meteorite collided with the earth at the end of the Cretaceous geological period, about 65 million years ago. Louis Alvarez and his colleagues proposed that so much dust was sent into the atmosphere by the collision that the earth was shrouded in darkness for months, if not longer. Some investigators now think that the meteorite impact may have also triggered a great deal of volcanic activity, even on the opposite side of the world, which would also have reduced solar radiation to the earth's surface. Not only the dinosaurs disappeared about 65 million years ago, so also did many sea animals and plants. Afterward, the earth saw the proliferation of many other kinds of animals, such as fish, lizards, birds, and mammals, as well as flowering trees. As we shall see in the chapter on primates, our own biological order, the Primates, is believed to have emerged around that time.

Peter Grant recently studied the same finches on the Galápagos Islands that partially inspired Darwin's theory. But, unlike Darwin, Grant had the chance to see natural selection in action. And it was surprisingly quick. Central to the project was the attachment of colored bands to each individual bird, which allowed each bird to be identified at a distance. In the midst of the project, in 1977, when half the birds had been banded, there was a serious drought. There were two main species of finch on one island, the cactus finch (*Geospiza scandens*) and the medium ground finch (*Geospiza fortis*). During the next 18 months, 85 percent of the adult medium ground finches disappeared. Those finches that survived tended to be larger and to have larger beaks than the ones that died. Why larger beaks? Both species of finch eat seeds, but small seeds produced by grasses and herbs are scarce in a drought; bigger seeds are more available. So it seems that natural selection under conditions of drought favored finches with bigger beaks, which are better at cracking the husks of large seeds.

If it were not for the fact that wet years, which favor smaller finches, occur between years of drought, we might see the quick evolution of new finch species. It is estimated that 20 drought episodes would be sufficient to produce a new species of finch. Galápagos finches do not really provide an example of punctuated equilibrium (no replacement from outside occurred), but they do suggest that evolutionary change could be a lot quicker than Darwin imagined.

Controversy continues over whether evolution is slow and steady or fast and abrupt. But many scholars, including Gould, pointed out that there is no need to pit one model against the other. Both may be correct in different instances. In any case much more investigation of evolutionary sequences is needed to help us evaluate the competing theoretical models.

Sources: Ian Tattersall, "Paleoanthropology and Evolutionary Theory," in Peter N. Peregrine, Carol R. Ember, and Melvin Ember, eds., *Physical Anthropology: Original Readings in Method and Practice* (Upper Saddle River, NJ: Prentice Hall, 2002), pp. 29–41; also in Carol R. Ember, Melvin Ember, and Peter N. Peregrine, eds., *New Directions in Anthropology* (Upper Saddle River, NJ: Prentice Hall, CD-ROM, 2004); Charles Devillers and Jean Chaline, *Evolution: An Evolving Theory* (New York: Springer-Verlag, 1993); Peter R. Grant, "Natural Selection and Darwin's Finches," *Scientific American* (October 1991): 82–87; Jonathan Weiner, *Beak of the Finch* (New York: Vintage, 1994).

Consider how the theory of natural selection would explain why giraffes became long-necked. Originally, the necks of giraffes varied in length, as happens with virtually any physical characteristic in a population. During a period when food was scarce, those giraffes with longer necks, who could reach higher tree leaves, might be better able to survive and suckle their offspring, and thus they would leave more offspring than shorter-necked giraffes. Because of heredity, the offspring of long-necked giraffes are more likely to have long necks. Eventually, the shorter-necked giraffes would diminish in number and the longer-necked giraffes would increase. The resultant population of giraffes would still have variation in neck length but on the average would be longer necked than earlier forms.

Natural selection does not account for all variation in the frequencies of traits. In particular, it does not account for variation in the frequencies of neutral traits—that is, those traits that do not seem to confer any advantages or disadvantages on their carriers. Changes in the frequencies of neutral traits may result rather from random processes that affect gene frequencies in isolated populations—*genetic drift*—or from matings between populations—*gene flow*. We discuss these other processes later in the chapter.

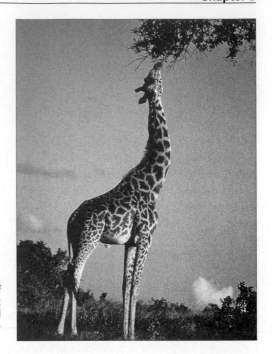

The giraffe's long neck is adaptive for eating tree leaves high off the ground. If food were scarce, longer-necked giraffes would get more food and reproduce more successfully than shorter-necked giraffes; in this environment, natural selection would favor giraffes with longer necks.

Observed Examples of Natural Selection

Because the process of natural selection may involve nearly imperceptible gradations over generations, it is often difficult to observe directly. Nevertheless, because some life forms reproduce rapidly, some examples of natural selection have been observed over relatively short periods in changing environments. Darwin's finches are not the only life forms to show quick evolution.

For example, scientists think they have observed natural selection in action in British moths. In 1850, an almost black moth was spotted for the first time in Manchester. That was quite unusual, for most of the moths were speckled gray. A century later, 95 percent of the moths in industrial parts of Britain were black; only in the rural areas were the moths mostly gray. How is this to be explained? It seems that in the rural areas, the gray-speckled moth is hard to spot by bird predators against the lichen growing on the bark of trees. But in industrial areas, lichen is killed by pollution. The gray-speckled moths, formerly well adapted to blend into their environment, became clearly visible against the darker background of the lichen-free trees and were easier prey for birds. In contrast, the black moths, which previously would have had a disadvantage against the lighter bark, were now better adapted for survival. Their dark color was an advantage, and subsequently the darker moths became the predominant variety in industrial regions.

How can we be sure that natural selection was the mechanism accounting for the change? Consistent evidence comes from a series of experiments performed by H. B. D. Kettlewell. He deliberately released specially marked moths, black and gray, into two areas of England—one urban industrial and one rural—and then set light traps to recapture them subsequently. The proportions of the two kinds of moths recovered tell us about differential survival. Kettlewell found that proportionately more black moths compared with gray moths were recovered in the urban industrial area. Just the reverse happened in the rural area; proportionately more gray-speckled moths were recovered.[14] Questions have been raised recently about whether the Kettlewell experiments were properly conducted.[15] However, the basic conclusion has been replicated by subsequent research.[16] The same transformation—the switch to darker color—has occurred

The changes that occurred in the moth population in different areas of England show natural selection in action. Before industrialization, tree trunks were lighter and light-colored moths predominated. (Rural areas today, with little or no industrial air pollution, show that natural selection in unpolluted areas still favors light-colored moths.) But with industrial pollution and the darkening of tree trunks, light-colored moths became more visible to predators. Darker-colored moths quickly increased in number in the new industrial environment.

in 70 other species of moth, as well as in a beetle and a millipede. And the transformation did not just occur in Britain; it also happened in other highly polluted areas, including the Ruhr area of Germany and the Pittsburgh area of the United States. Moreover, in the Pittsburgh area, antipollution measures in the last 50 years have apparently caused the black moth to dwindle in number once again.[17]

The type of natural selection in the moth example is called **directional selection** because a particular trait seems to be positively favored and the average value shifts over time toward the adaptive trait. But there can also be **normalizing selection**. In this type of selection the average value does not change, but natural selection removes the extremes. An example is the birthweight of babies. Both very low birthweights and very high birthweights are disadvantageous and would be selected against. Directional and normalizing selection both assume that natural selection will either favor or disfavor genes, but there is a third possibility—balancing selection. **Balancing selection** occurs when a *heterozygous* (varied) combination of *alleles* (genes) is positively favored even though a *homozygous* (genes in the pairs are the same) combination is disfavored. In the next chapter, we discuss a trait that apparently involves balancing selection—sickle-cell anemia—which is found in persons of West African ancestry, among other populations.

Another well-known example of observed natural selection is the acquired resistance of houseflies to the insecticide DDT. When DDT was first used to kill insects, beginning in the 1940s, several new, DDT-resistant strains of housefly evolved. In the early DDT environment, many houseflies were killed, but the few that survived were the ones that reproduced, and their resistant characteristics became common to the housefly populations. To the chagrin of medical practitioners, similar resistances develop in bacteria. A particular antibiotic may lose its effectiveness after it comes into wide use because new, resistant bacterial strains emerge. These new strains will become more frequent than the original ones because of natural selection. In the United States now, a few strains are resistant to all antibiotics on the market, a fact that worries medical practitioners. One possible way to deal with the problem is to stop using antibiotics for a few years, so resistance to those antibiotics might not develop or develop only slowly.

The theory of natural selection answered many questions, but it also raised at least one whose answer eluded Darwin and others. The appearance of a beneficial trait may assist the survival of an organism, but what happens when the organism reproduces by mating with members that do not possess this new variation? Will not the new adaptive trait eventually disappear if subsequent generations mate with individuals that lack this trait? Darwin knew variations were transmitted through heredity, but he did not have a clear model of the mode of inheritance. Gregor Mendel's pioneering studies in the science of genetics provided the foundation for such a model, but his discoveries did not become widely known until 1900.

Heredity

Gregor Mendel's Experiments

Mendel (1822–1884), a monk and amateur botanist who lived in what is now the Czech Republic, bred several varieties of pea plants and made detailed observations of their offspring. He chose as breeding partners plants that differed by only one observable trait. Tall plants were crossed with short ones, and yellow ones with green, for example.

When the pollen from a yellow pea plant was transferred to a green pea plant, Mendel observed a curious phenomenon: All of the first-generation offspring bore yellow peas. It seemed that the green trait had disappeared. But when seeds from this first generation were crossed, they produced both yellow and green pea plants in a ratio of three yellow to one green pea plant. Apparently, Mendel reasoned, the green trait had not been lost or altered; the yellow trait was simply **dominant** and the green trait was **recessive**. Mendel observed similar results with other traits. Tallness dominated shortness, and the factor for smooth-skinned peas dominated the factor for wrinkled ones. In each cross, the 3-to-1 ratio appeared in the second generation. Self-fertilization, however, produced different results. Green pea plants always yielded green pea plants, and short plants always produced short plants.

From his numerical results, Mendel concluded that some yellow pea plants were pure (*homozygous*) for that trait, whereas others also possessed a green factor (the plants were *heterozygous*). That is, although two plants might both have yellow peas, one of them might produce offspring with green peas. In such cases, the genetic makeup, the **genotype**, differed from the observable appearance, or **phenotype**.

Genes: The Conveyors of Inherited Traits

Mendel's units of heredity were what we now call **genes**. He concluded that these units occurred in pairs for each trait and that offspring inherited one unit of the pair from each parent. Each member of a gene pair or group is called an **allele**. If the two genes, or alleles, for a trait are the same, the organism is

Gregor Mendel.

homozygous for that trait; if the two genes for a characteristic differ, the organism is **heterozygous** for that trait. A pea plant that contains a pair of genes for yellow is homozygous for the trait. A yellow pea plant with a dominant gene for yellow and a recessive gene for green, although phenotypically yellow, has a heterozygous genotype. As Mendel demonstrated, the recessive green gene can reappear in subsequent generations. But Mendel knew nothing of the composition of genes or the processes that transmit them from parent to offspring. Many years of scientific research have yielded much of the missing information.

The genes of higher organisms (not including bacteria and primitive plants such as green-blue algae) are located on rope-like bodies called **chromosomes** within the nucleus of every one of the organism's cells. Chromosomes, like genes, usually occur in pairs. Each allele for a given trait is carried in the identical position on corresponding chromosomes. The two genes that determined the color of Mendel's peas, for example, were opposite each other on a pair of chromosomes.

Mitosis and Meiosis   The body cells of every plant or animal carry chromosome pairs in a number appropriate for its species. Humans have 23 pairs, or a total of 46 chromosomes, each carrying many times that number of genes. Each new body cell receives this number of chromosomes during cellular reproduction, or **mitosis**, as each pair of chromosomes duplicates itself.

But what happens when a sperm cell and an egg cell unite to form a new organism? What prevents the human baby from receiving twice the number of chromosomes characteristic of its species—23 pairs from the sperm and 23 pairs from the egg? The process by which the reproductive cells are formed, **meiosis**, ensures that this will not happen (see Figure 3.1 on page 56). Each reproductive cell contains half the number of chromosomes appropriate for the species. Only one member of each chromosome pair is carried in every egg or sperm. At fertilization, the human embryo normally receives 23 separate chromosomes from its mother and the same number from its father, which add up to the 23 pairs.

DNA   Each gene carries a set of instructions encoded in its chemical structure. It is from this coded information carried in genes that a cell makes all the rest of its structural parts and chemical machinery. It appears that in most living organisms, heredity is controlled by the same chemical substance, **DNA**—deoxyribonucleic acid. An enormous amount of research has been directed toward understanding DNA—what its structure is, how it duplicates itself in reproduction, and how it conveys or instructs the formation of a complete organism.

Here we see meiosis in a plant cell. The left image shows the metaphase stage. Note how the chromosomes lie against and even on top of one another. The right image shows the anaphase stage, when the chromosomes separate and the cell is ready to divide.

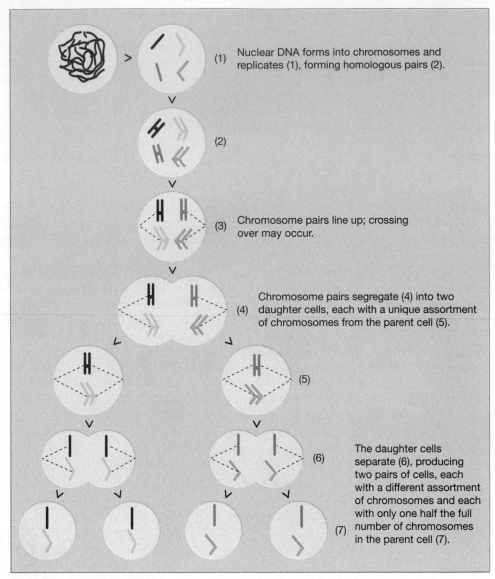

(1) Nuclear DNA forms into chromosomes and replicates (1), forming homologous pairs (2).

(2)

(3) Chromosome pairs line up; crossing over may occur.

(4) Chromosome pairs segregate (4) into two daughter cells, each with a unique assortment of chromosomes from the parent cell (5).

(5)

(6) The daughter cells separate (6), producing two pairs of cells, each with a different assortment of chromosomes and each with only one half the full number of chromosomes in the parent cell (7).

(7)

Figure 3.1   Meiosis (Sex Cells)

One of the most important keys to understanding human development and genetics is the structure and function of DNA. In 1953, American biologist James Watson, with British molecular biologist Francis Crick, proposed that DNA is a long, two-stranded molecule shaped like a double helix (see Figure 3.2). Genetic information is stored in the linear sequences of the bases; different species have different sequences, and every individual is slightly different from every other individual. Notice that in the DNA molecule each base always has the same opposite base; adenine and thymine are paired, as are cytosine and guanine. The importance of this pattern is that the two strands carry the same information, so that when the double helix unwinds each strand can form a template for a new strand of complementary bases. Because DNA stores the information required to make up the cells of an organism, it has been called the language of life. As George and Muriel Beadle put it,

> the deciphering of the DNA code has revealed our possession of a language much older than hieroglyphics, a language as old as life itself, a language that is the most living language of all—even if its letters are invisible and its words are buried deep in the cells of our bodies.[18]

Once it was understood that genes are made of DNA, concerted efforts were begun to map DNA sequences and their locations on the chromosomes of different organisms. A project known as the Human Genome Project set out to assemble a complete genetic map for humans. In July 2000, the initial mapping of the human genome was completed.[19] This was a significant achievement and has already led to several breakthroughs in our understanding of how the genetic code functions.[20] For example, researchers recently reported finding two new genes that appear to provide partial resistance to malaria. These newly found genes appear to have evolved recently, perhaps only a few thousand years ago. If researchers can discover how these genes help to defend their carriers against malaria, that may help medical science discover how to prevent or treat this devastating disease.[21]

Messenger RNA   DNA stores the information to make cells, but it does not directly affect the formation of cells. One type of ribonucleic acid (RNA), **messenger RNA (mRNA)**, is copied from a portion of DNA and moves outside the cell nucleus to direct the formation of proteins. Proteins have so many functions that they are considered to be responsible for most of the characteristics of an organism. They act as catalysts for synthesizing DNA and RNA and for the activities of cells; they also contribute many structural elements that determine the shape and movement of cells. Messenger RNA is like DNA in that it has a linear sequence of bases attached to a sugar-phosphate backbone, but it is slightly different chemically. One difference is that messenger RNA has the base uracil instead of the base thymine. Messenger RNA also has a different sugar-phosphate backbone and is single- rather

Figure 3.2   DNA
Chromosomes are built of DNA (A), which consists of two spiral sugar-phosphate strands (B) linked by the nitrogenous bases adenine, guanine, thymine, and cytosine (C). When the DNA molecule reproduces, the bases separate and the spiral strands unwind (D). Because adenine can only bond to thymine, and cytosine can only bond to guanine, each original strand serves as a mold along which a new complementary chain is formed.

than double-stranded. Messenger RNA is formed when a double-stranded DNA molecule unwinds and forms a template for the mRNA. After a section of DNA is copied, the mRNA releases from the DNA and leaves the nucleus, and the double helix of the DNA is reformed.

Protein Synthesis   Once the mRNA is released from the DNA, it travels out of the cell nucleus and into the body of the cell. There it attaches to a structure in the cell called a **ribosome**, which uses the information on the mRNA to make proteins. The ribosome essentially "reads" the chemical bases on the mRNA in commands that tell the ribosome the specific amino acids to join together to form a protein (see Figure 3.3). For example, the mRNA sequence adenine, adenine, guanine (AAG) tells the ribosome to place the amino acid lysine in that location, whereas the sequence adenine, adenine, cytosine (AAC) calls for the amino acid histidine. There are also mRNA commands that tell the ribosome when to begin and when to stop constructing a protein. Thus, the DNA code copied onto mRNA provides all the information necessary for ribosomes to build the proteins that make up the structures of organisms and drive the processes of life.

Figure 3.3   Translation and Protein Synthesis
The mRNA copy of the cellular DNA is "read" by a ribosome that attaches the amino acid with the corresponding transfer RNA (tRNA) to a growing chain of amino acids (called a polypeptide chain because the amino acids are linked together by peptide bonds). A chain more than 100 amino acids long is called a protein.

Sources of Variability

Natural selection proceeds only when individuals within a population vary. There are two genetic sources of new variation: genetic recombination and mutation. There are also two processes through which variations are shuffled through populations: gene flow and genetic drift. Scholars have recently begun to consider one other potential source of variability: hybridization.

Genetic Recombination

The distribution of traits from parents to children varies from one offspring to another. Brothers and sisters, after all, do not look exactly alike, nor does each child resemble 50 percent of the mother and 50 percent of the father. This variation occurs because when a sperm cell or an egg is formed, the single member of each chromosome pair it receives is a matter of chance. Each reproductive cell, then, carries a random assortment of chromosomes and their respective genes. At fertilization, the egg and sperm that unite are different from every other egg carried by the mother and every other sperm carried by the father. A unique offspring is thus produced by a shuffling of the parents' genes. One cause of this shuffling is the random **segregation**, or sorting, of chromosomes in meiosis. Conceivably, an individual could get any of the possible assortments of the paternal and maternal chromosomes. Another cause of the shuffling of parental genes is **crossing-over**, the exchange of sections of chromosomes between one chromosome and another (see Figure 3.4). Thus, after meiosis, the egg and sperm do not receive just

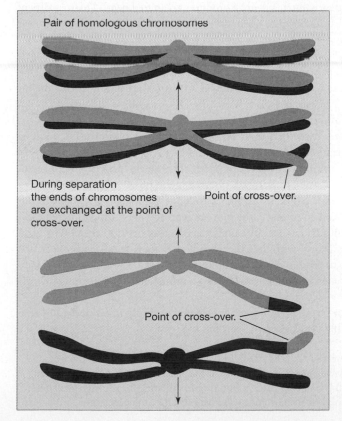

Figure 3.4   Crossing-Over

Source: From Noel T. Boaz and Alan J. Almquist, *Biological Anthropology: A Synthetic Approach to Human Evolution,* 2nd ed. (Upper Saddle River, NJ: Prentice Hall, 2001).

a random mixture of complete paternal and maternal chromosomes; because of crossing-over they also receive chromosomes in which some of the sections may have been replaced.

The traits displayed by each organism are not simply the result of combinations of dominant and recessive genes, as Mendel had hypothesized. In humans, most traits are influenced by the activity of many genes. Skin color, for example, is the result of several inherited characteristics. A brownish shade results from the presence of a pigment known as *melanin;* the degree of darkness in the hue depends largely on the amount of melanin present and how it is distributed in the layers of the skin. Another factor contributing to the color of all human skin is the blood that flows in blood vessels located in the outer layers of the skin. Humans carry at least five different genes for the manufacture of melanin and many other genes for the other components of skin hue. In fact, almost all physical characteristics in humans are the result of the concerted action of many genes. Some traits are sex-linked. The X chromosome, which together with the presence or absence of a Y chromosome determines sex, may also carry the gene for hemophilia or the gene for color blindness. The expression of these two characteristics depends on the sex of the organism.

Genetic recombination produces variety, which is essential for the operation of natural selection. Ultimately, however, the major source of variability is mutation. This is because mutation replenishes the supply of variability, which is constantly being reduced by the selective elimination of less fit variants. Mutation also produces variety in organisms that reproduce asexually.

Mutation

A **mutation** is a change in the DNA sequence. Such a change produces an altered gene. The majority of mutations are thought to occur because of occasional mismating of the chemical bases that make up DNA. Just as a typist will make errors in copying a manuscript, so will DNA, in duplicating itself, occasionally change its code. A mutation will result from such an error. Some mutations have more drastic consequences than others. Suppose the error is in one base on a DNA strand. The effect depends on what that portion of the DNA controls. The effect may be minimal if the product hardly affects the organism. On the other hand, if the change occurs at a place where the DNA regulates the production of many proteins, the effect on the organism can be serious.

Although it is very difficult to estimate the proportions of mutations that are harmful, neutral, or beneficial, there is no doubt that some mutations have lethal consequences. We can discuss the relative merits or disadvantages of a mutant gene only in terms of the physical, cultural, and genetic environment of that gene. Galactosemia, for example, is caused by a recessive mutant gene and usually results in mental retardation and blindness. But it can be prevented by dietary restrictions begun at an early age. In this instance, the intervention of human culture counteracts the mutant gene and allows the afflicted individual to lead a normal life. Thus, some cultural factors can modify the effects of natural selection by helping to perpetuate a harmful mutant gene. People with the galactosemia trait who are enabled to function normally can reproduce and pass on one of the recessive genes to their children. Without cultural interference, natural selection would prevent such reproduction. Usually, natural selection acts to retain only those mutations that aid survival.

Even though most mutations may not be adaptive, those that are will multiply in a population relatively quickly, by natural selection. As Theodosius Dobzhansky has suggested:

> Consistently useful mutants are like needles in a haystack of harmful ones. A needle in a haystack is hard to find, even though one may be sure it is there. But if the needle is valuable, the task of finding it is facilitated by setting the haystack on fire and looking for the needle among the ashes. The role of the fire in this parable is played in biological evolution by natural selection.[22]

The black moth that was spotted in Manchester in 1850 probably resulted from a mutation. If the tree trunks had been light colored, that moth or its offspring probably would have died out. But as industrialization increased and the tree trunks became darker, a trait that was once maladaptive became adaptive.

Genetic recombination and mutation are the sources of new variations, but evolutionary biologists have identified two other processes that are important in distributing those variations through populations: genetic drift and gene flow.

Genetic Drift

The term **genetic drift** refers to various random processes that affect gene frequencies in small, relatively isolated populations. Genetic drift is also known as the *Wright effect,* after geneticist Sewall Wright, who first directed attention to this process. Over time in a small population, genetic drift may result in a neutral or nearly neutral gene becoming more or less frequent just by chance.

One variety of genetic drift, called the *founder effect,* occurs when a small group of organisms recently derived from a larger population migrates to a relatively isolated location. If a particular gene is absent just by chance in the migrant group, the descendants are also likely to lack that gene, assuming that the group remains isolated. Similarly, if all members of the original migrant group just by chance carried a particular gene, their descendants would also be likely to share that gene. Isolation can occur for physical reasons, such as when a group moves to a previously uninhabited place and does not return. The populations that traveled over land when the Bering land bridge connected Asia to North America could not readily return when the sea level rose. This may explain why Native Americans have a higher proportion of individuals with type O blood than other populations—the first migrants may have had, by chance, a predominance of individuals with type O blood.

Or the isolation can occur for social reasons. A religious sect of Dunkers emigrated from Germany to the United States in the early 1700s. The fact that the 50 original families kept to themselves probably explains why some of their gene frequencies differ from what is found in both the German and general U.S. populations.[23]

Gene Flow

Gene flow is the process whereby genes pass from one population to another through mating and reproduction. Unlike the other processes of natural selection and genetic drift, which generally increase the differences between populations in different environments, gene flow tends to work in the opposite direction—it *decreases* differences between populations. Two populations at opposite ends of a region may have different frequencies of a particular gene, but the populations located between them have an intermediate gene frequency because of gene flow between them. The variation in gene frequency from one end of the region to the other is called a **cline**. In Europe, for example, there is a cline in the distribution of blood type B, which gradually diminishes in frequency from east to west.[24]

Most genetically determined characteristics in humans have gradually or clinally varying frequencies as one moves from one area to another. Neighboring regions have more similar gene frequencies than regions widely separated. But these clines do not always coincide, which makes the concept of "race" as applied to humans not very useful for understanding human biological variation.[25] We discuss this situation in more detail in the chapter on human variation and adaptation.

Gene flow may occur between distant as well as close populations. Long-range movements of people, to trade or raid or settle, may result in gene flow. But they do not always do so.

Hybridization

A **species** is a population that consists of organisms able to interbreed and produce fertile and viable off-spring. In general, individuals from one species do not successfully mate with members of a different species because of genetic and behavioral differences. If members of different species do mate, fertilization usu-ally does not occur and, if it does, the embryo usually does not survive. In the cases where offspring are born, they are usually infertile. However, recent studies have suggested that **hybridization**, the creation of a viable offspring from two different species, may be more possible than once thought. Hybridization may be an important source of new variation in some populations.

The finches of the Galápagos Islands that Darwin used as evidence for natural selection and that we refer to in the box titled "Is Evolution Slow and Steady or Fast and Abrupt?" (on pages 50–51) also pro-vide an example of hybridization in action. Many female cactus finches (*Geospiza scandens*) died during a period of severe drought, leaving an abundance of males. High competition for mates led a few female ground finches (*Geospiza fortis*) to mate with the abundant male cactus finches, something that would not normally occur. The result was hybrid offspring with unique characteristics. These hybrids, both male and female, went on to mate only with cactus finches, because they imprinted on the male cactus finch song as infants. The end result was a one-time influx of ground finch genes into the cactus finch population, adding new variations upon which natural selection could work.[26]

Origin of Species

One of the most controversial aspects of Darwin's theory was the suggestion that one species could, over time, evolve into another. How could one species evolve into another? What is the explanation for this differentiation? How does one group of organisms become so unlike another group with the same an-cestry that it forms a totally new species? **Speciation**, or the development of a new species, may occur if one subgroup of a species finds itself in a radically different environment. In adapting to their separate environments, the two subgroups may each undergo enough genetic changes to prevent them from in-terbreeding, should they renew contact. Numerous factors can prevent the exchange of genes. Two species living in the same area may breed at different times of the year, or their behavior during breeding—their courtship rituals—may be distinct. The difference in body structure of closely related forms may in it-self bar interbreeding. Geographic barriers may be the most common barriers to interbreeding.

Speciation versus Creation

But some people, particularly those who call themselves "scientific creationists," argue that while natu-ral selection can produce variation within species (often referred to as *microevolution*), it cannot produce new species (often referred to as *macroevolution*). Creationists argue that God created all living things, and that evolution has only changed those living things in minor ways and has not created new kinds of liv-ing things. The major problem with the creationist view is that there is solid empirical evidence for spe-ciation. For example, William Rice and George Salt demonstrated that if they sorted fruit flies by their environmental preferences (such as light intensity and temperature) and then bred the sorted groups sep-arately, they could produce flies incapable of interbreeding—separate species—in as little as 35 generations.[27] The fossil record contains numerous examples of speciation and even the development of entirely new kinds of creatures. For example, the evolution of birds from terrestrial creatures is clearly ev-idenced in the fossil record.[28] While many creationists downplay the evidence for speciation, the evi-dence is plentiful, and can be seen by the public in museums all over the world.

With the abundant evidence for speciation found in both the fossil record and in experimental observations, creationists have recently developed a new argument to discount the role of natural selection in the process of speciation. The new argument is that life in general, and species in particular, are so complex that a random, undirected process like natural selection could never have created them. The complexity of life, these creationists argue, must stem from "intelligent design." This new appeal to intelligent design in the origin of species is actually an old, and widely discredited, one. In his 1802 book *Natural Theology,* William Paley wrote, "Suppose I had found a watch upon the ground, and it should be enquired how the watch happened to be in that place . . . the inference, we think, is inevitable; that the watch must have had a maker . . .".[29] By this Paley implied that if we find a complex mechanism at work in the world, like a watch, we must conclude that a maker exists. Paley extended the argument to the complexity of life, and concluded that life must stem from an intelligent designer—God.

Darwin wrote *On the Origin of Species* in part as a response to Paley, and Darwinists have been responding ever since. But in recent years the "intelligent design" movement, or as proponents call it, the "wedge," has brought Paley's ideas back with force. Indeed the force is an active political one, with the explicit purpose "to reverse the stifling dominance of the materialist world view, and to replace it with a science consonant with Christian and theistic convictions."[30] Intelligent design is, at the core, a political movement.

Does being a political, rather than scientific, movement mean intelligent design ideas have no value in understanding speciation? Of course not. The problem is that intelligent design cannot explain speciation in a scientific way. The central argument made by proponents of intelligent design is simply that what we see in the world is too complex to be accounted for by natural selection, but they offer no alternative natural mechanism. They argue that if natural selection may not account for all cases of speciation, then the only alternative is divine intervention. Clearly this reasoning is flawed. Just because we do not understand something today does not mean we should toss out all we do know. Rather, the scientific approach is to continue to examine unexplained phenomena in order to learn more about them.

Intelligent design proponents also fail to answer critics who point out that natural selection can and has accounted for even the most complex of features—such as wings and eyes. If the key facts that intelligent design and other creationist scholars appeal to are biblical ones, it is important to point out that most biblical scholars do not agree with creationist arguments. As theologian Ernan McMullin suggests, the Bible "ought to be understood as conveying fundamental theological truths about dependence of the natural and human worlds on their Creator, rather than explaining how exactly these worlds first took shape."[31] On the other hand, there is nothing in science that can absolutely rule out supernatural intervention in the natural world, because supernatural activities are beyond the realm of scientific explanation. For example, while we now know that people with a condition called hypertrichosis grow hair all over their faces because of a single mutation on the X chromosome, science cannot rule out the possibility that the mutation was caused by the "curse of the werewolf" or a divine punishment for sin.[32] Science cannot rule out such possibilities because they cannot be observed, measured, or experimentally tested. Science and religion should be regarded as different ways of understanding the world, the former relying on evidence, the latter relying on faith.

Natural Selection of Behavioral Traits

Until now we have discussed how natural selection might operate to change a population's physical traits, such as the color of moths or the neck length of giraffes. But natural selection can also operate on the behavioral characteristics of populations. Although this idea is not new, it is now receiving more attention. The approaches called **sociobiology,**[33] **behavioral ecology,**[34] and **evolutionary psychology**[35] involve the application of evolutionary principles to the behavior of animals and humans. Behavioral ecology is interested in how all kinds of behavior are related to the environment; sociobiology is particularly interested in social organization and social behavior; and evolutionary psychology is interested in how evolution may have produced lasting variation in the way humans behave, interact, and perceive the world. The typical behaviors of a species are assumed to be adaptive and to have evolved by natural selection. For example, why do related species exhibit different social behaviors even though they derive from a common ancestral species?

Consider the lion, as compared with other cats. Although members of the cat family are normally solitary creatures, lions live in social groups called *prides.* Why? George Schaller has suggested that lion social groups may have evolved primarily because group hunting is a more successful way to catch large mammals in open terrain. He has observed that not only are several lions more successful in catching prey than are solitary lions, but several lions are more likely to catch and kill large and dangerous prey such as giraffes. Then, too, cubs are generally safer from predators when in a social group than when alone with their mothers. Thus, the social behavior of lions may have evolved primarily because it provided selective advantages in the lions' open-country environment.[36]

It is important to remember that natural selection operates on expressed characteristics, or the phenotype, of an individual. In the moth example, the color of the moth is part of its *phenotype,* subject to natural selection. Behavior is also an expressed characteristic. If hunting in groups, a behavioral trait gets you more food, then individuals who hunt in groups will do better. But we must also remember that natural selection requires traits to be heritable. Can the concept of heritability be applied to learned behavior, not just genetically transmitted behavior? And, even more controversially, if the concept of heritability can include learning, can it also include cultural learning? Recent research on domesticated dogs suggests it may. Domesticated dogs appear to understand social cues used by humans, such as pointing, while wolves do not. These findings suggest that some aspects of cultural learning in animals may be heritable.[37]

Early theorizing in sociobiology and behavioral ecology appeared to emphasize the genetic component of behavior. For example, Edward O. Wilson, in his book *Sociobiology,* defined sociobiology as "the systematic study of the biological causes of behavior."[38] But Bobbi Low points out that, although the term *biological* may have been interpreted to mean "genetic," most biologists understand that expressed or observable characteristics are the results of genes, environment, and life history, all interacting. Behavior is a product of all three. If we say that some behavior is heritable, we mean that the child's behavior is more likely to resemble the parents' behavior than the behavior of others.[39] Learning from a

Prides of lions that live in open country are more successful in catching large animals than are solitary lions. This social behavior may have evolved because it provided selective advantages in the lions' open-country environment.

Mountain lions live in wooded environments and hunt individually. Here we see one chasing down a snowshoe rabbit.

parent could be an important part of why the offspring is like the parent. If the child is more like the parent than like others, then the likeness is heritable, even if it is entirely learned from the parent.

The sociobiological approach has aroused considerable controversy in anthropology, probably because of its apparent emphasis on genes, rather than experience and learning, as determinants of human behavior. Anthropologists have argued that the customs of a society may be more or less adaptive because cultural behaviors also have reproductive consequences. It is not just an individual's behavior that may have reproductive consequences. So does natural selection also operate in the evolution of culture? Many biologists think not. They say there are substantial differences between biological and cultural evolution. But are the two kinds of evolution that different? To answer this question, we must remember that the operation of natural selection requires three conditions, as we already noted: variation, heritability or mechanisms that duplicate traits in offspring, and differential reproduction because of heritable differences. Do these three requirements apply to cultural behavior?

In biological evolution, variability comes from genetic recombination and mutation. In cultural evolution, it comes from recombination of learned behaviors and from invention.[40] Cultures are not closed or reproductively isolated, as species are. A species cannot borrow genetic traits from another species, but a culture can borrow new things and behaviors from other cultures. The custom of growing corn, which has spread from the New World to many other areas, is an example of this phenomenon. As for the requirement of heritability, although learned traits obviously are not passed to offspring through purely genetic inheritance, parents who exhibit adaptive behavioral traits are more likely to "reproduce" those traits in their children, who may learn them by imitation or by parental instruction. Children and adults may also copy adaptive traits they see in people outside the family. Finally, as for the requirement of differential reproduction, it does not matter whether the trait in question is genetic or learned or both. As Henry Nissen emphasized, "behavioral incompetence leads to extinction as surely as does morphological disproportion or deficiency in any vital organ. Behavior is subject to selection as much as bodily size or resistance to disease."[41]

Many theorists are comfortable with the idea of applying the theory of natural selection to cultural evolution, but others prefer to use different terminology when dealing with traits that do not depend on purely genetic transmission from one generation to the next. For example, Robert Boyd and Peter

Richerson discuss human behavior as involving "dual inheritance." They distinguish cultural transmission, by learning and imitation, from genetic transmission, but they emphasize the importance of understanding both and the interaction between them.[42] William Durham also deals separately with cultural transmission, using the term *meme* (analogous to the term *gene*) for the unit of cultural transmission. He directs our attention to the interaction between genes and culture, calling that interaction "coevolution," and provides examples of how genetic evolution and cultural evolution may lead to changes in each other, how they may enhance each other, and how they may even oppose each other.[43]

So biological and cultural evolution in humans may not be completely different processes. As we will discuss later, some of the most important biological features of humans—such as our relatively large brains—may have been favored by natural selection because our ancestors made tools, a cultural trait. Conversely, the cultural trait of informal and formal education may have been favored by natural selection because humans have a long period of immaturity, a biological trait.

As long as the human species continues to exist and the social and physical environment continues to change, there is reason to think that natural selection of biological and cultural traits will also continue. However, as humans learn more and more about genetic structure they will become more and more capable of curing genetically caused disorders and even altering the way evolution proceeds. Today, genetic researchers are capable of diagnosing genetic defects in developing fetuses, and parents can and do decide often whether to terminate a pregnancy. Soon genetic engineering will probably allow humans to fix defects and even try to "improve" the genetic code of a growing fetus. Whether and to what extent humans should alter genes will undoubtedly be the subject of continuing debate. Whatever the decisions we eventually make about genetic engineering, they will affect the course of human biological and cultural evolution.

Summary

1. If we think of the history of the universe in terms of 12 months, the history of human-like primates would take up only about one and a half hours. The universe is some 15 billion years old; modern-looking humans have existed for about 100,000 years.

2. Ideas about evolution took a long time to take hold because they contradicted the biblical view of events; species were viewed as fixed in their form by the creator. But in the eighteenth and early nineteenth centuries increasing evidence suggested that evolution was a viable theory. In geology, the concept of uniformitarianism suggested that the earth is constantly subject to shaping and reshaping by natural forces working over vast stretches of time. A number of thinkers during this period began to discuss evolution and how it might occur.

3. Charles Darwin and Alfred Wallace proposed the mechanism of natural selection to account for the evolution of species. Basic principles of the theory of natural selection are that (1) every species is composed of a great variety of individuals, some of which are better adapted to their environment than others; (2) offspring inherit traits from their parents at least to some degree and in some way; and (3) since better adapted individuals generally produce more offspring over the generations than the more poorly adapted, the frequency of adaptive traits increases in subsequent generations. In this way, natural selection results in increasing proportions of individuals with advantageous traits.

4. Mendel's and subsequent research in genetics and our understanding of the structure and function of DNA and mRNA help us to understand the biological mechanisms by which traits may be passed from one generation to the next.

5. Natural selection depends on variation within a population. The primary sources of biological variation are genetic recombination, mutation, genetic drift, gene flow, and hybridization.

6. Speciation, the development of a new species, may occur if one subgroup becomes separated from other subgroups. In adapting to different environments, these subpopulations may undergo enough genetic changes to prevent interbreeding, even if they reestablish contact. Once species differentiation occurs, it is believed that the evolutionary process cannot be reversed.

7. So-called "creation scientists" and proponents of "intelligent design" theory argue that the origin of species cannot be accounted for through natural selection. This argument ignores the enormous body of evidence—experimental, fossil, and field data—that demonstrates how natural selection works to create new species.

8. Natural selection can also operate on the behavioral characteristics of populations. The approaches called sociobiology and behavioral ecology involve the application of evolutionary principles to the behavior of animals. Much controversy surrounds the degree to which the theory of natural selection can be applied to human behavior, particularly cultural behavior. There is more agreement that biological and cultural evolution in humans may influence each other.

Glossary Terms

allele (p. 54)
balancing selection (p. 53)
behavioral ecology (p. 63)
chromosome (p. 55)
cline (p. 61)
crossing-over (p. 59)
directional selection (p. 53)
DNA (p. 55)
dominant (p. 54)
evolutionary psychology (p. 63)
genes (p. 54)
gene flow (p. 61)
genetic drift (p. 61)
genotype (p. 54)
genus (p. 47)
heterozygous (p. 55)

homozygous (p. 55)
hybridization (p. 62)
meiosis (p. 55)
messenger RNA (mRNA) (p. 57)
mitosis (p. 55)
mutation (p. 60)
natural selection (p. 49)
normalizing selection (p. 53)
phenotype (p. 54)
recessive (p. 54)
ribosome (p. 58)
segregation (p. 59)
sociobiology (p. 63)
speciation (p. 62)
species (p. 62)

Critical Questions

1. Do you think the theory of natural selection is compatible with religious beliefs? Explain your reasoning.

2. How might the discovery of genetic cures and the use of genetic engineering affect the future of evolution?

3. Why do you think humans have remained one species?

HUMAN VARIATION AND ADAPTATION

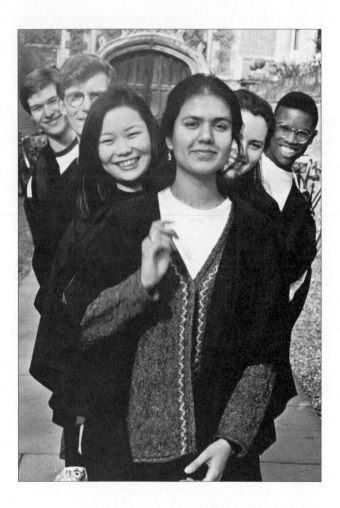

Chapter Outline

- Processes in Human Variation and Adaptation
- Physical Variation in Human Populations
- Race and Racism
- The Future of Human Variation

In any given human population, individuals vary in external features such as skin color or height and in internal features such as blood type or susceptibility to a disease. If you measure the frequencies of such features in different populations, you will typically find differences on average from one population to another. So, for example, some populations are typically darker in skin color than other populations.

Why do these physical differences exist? They may be largely the product of differences in genes. Or they may be largely due to growing up in a particular environment, physical and cultural. Or they may be the result of an interaction between environmental factors and genes.

We turn first to the processes that may singly or jointly produce the varying frequencies of physical traits in different human populations. Then we discuss specific differences in external and internal characteristics and how they might be explained. Then we discuss whether racial classification helps or hinders the study of human variation. We close with some brief remarks about the future of human variation.

Processes in Human Variation and Adaptation

Mutations—changes in the structure of a gene—are the ultimate source of all genetic variation. Because different genes make for greater or lesser chances of survival and reproduction, natural selection results in more favorable genes becoming more frequent in a population over time. We call this process **adaptation**. Adaptations are genetic changes that give their carriers a better chance to survive and reproduce than individuals without the genetic change who live in the same environment. It is the environment, of course, that favors the reproductive success of some traits rather than others.

How adaptive a gene or trait is depends on the specific environment; what is adaptive in one environment may not be adaptive in another. For example, in the chapter on genetics and evolution, we discussed the advantage that dark moths had over light moths when certain areas of England became industrialized. Predators could not easily see the darker moths against the newly darkened trees, and these moths soon outnumbered the lighter variety. Similarly, human populations live in a great variety of environments, so we would expect natural selection to favor different genes and traits in those different environments. As we shall see, variations in skin color and body build are among the many features that may be at least partly explainable by how natural selection works in different environments.

Acclimatization

Natural selection may favor certain genes because of certain physical environmental conditions, as in the case of the moths in England. But the physical environment can sometimes produce variation even in the absence of genetic change. As we shall see, climate may influence the way the human body grows and develops, and therefore some kinds of human variation may be explainable largely as a function of environmental variation. We call this process *acclimatization*. **Acclimatization** involves physiological adjustments in individuals to environmental conditions. Acclimatizations may have underlying genetic factors, but they are not themselves genetic. Individuals develop them during their lifetimes, rather than being born with them.

Many acclimatizations are simple physiological changes in the body that appear and disappear as the environment changes. For example, when we are chilled, our bodies attempt to create heat by making our muscles work, a physiological response to the environment that we experience as shivering. Longer exposure to cold weather leads our bodies to increase our metabolic rates so that we generate more internal heat. Both these physiological changes are acclimatizations, one short term (shivering), one longer term (increased metabolic rate).

As we discuss later in this chapter, some long-term acclimatizations are difficult to distinguish from adaptations because they become established as normal operating processes, and they may persist even after the individual moves into an environment that is different from the one that originally fostered the acclimatization. It also appears that some acclimatizations are closely related to genetic adaptations. For example, tanning, an acclimatization among light-skinned people when exposed to high levels of solar radiation, is related to the adaptation of light skin color to environments with low solar radiation.

Influence of the Cultural Environment

Humans are not only influenced by their environments through adaptations and acclimatizations, but humans can also dramatically affect their environments. Culture allows humans to modify their environments, and such modifications may lessen the likelihood of genetic adaptations and physiological acclimitizations. For example, the effects of cold may be modified by the culture traits of living in houses, harnessing energy to create heat, and clothing the body to insulate it. In these cultural ways, we alter our "microenvironments." Iron deficiency may be overcome by the culture trait of cooking in iron pots. If a physical environment lacks certain nutrients, people may get them by the culture trait of trading for them; trading for salt has been common in world history. Culture can also influence the direction of natural selection. As we shall see, the culture of dairying seems to have increased the frequency of genes that allow adults to digest milk.[1]

In addition, individual cultures sometimes practice behaviors that lead to physical variations among their members and between members of one culture and another. For example, elites in many highland Andean societies (the Inca, for example) practiced head binding. The heads of elite children were tightly bound with cloth. As the child grew, the binding forced the skull to take on an elongated, almost conical shape. This cultural practice, then, created physical variations among individuals that were intended to identify members of elite groups.[2] Many cultures have practices that are intended to create physical variations that distinguish members of their culture from members of other cultures. The Hebrew Bible, for example, tells the story of how Abraham was instructed by God to circumcise himself and all his male descendants as a sign of the covenant between them.[3] Thus male descendants of Abraham traditionally share a culturally induced physical variation (lack of a foreskin) to identify themselves as a group.

Physical Variation in Human Populations

The most noticeable physical variations among populations are those that are external, on the surface— body build, facial features, skin color, and height. No less important are those variations that are internal, such as variation in susceptibility to different diseases and differences in the ability to produce certain enzymes.

We begin our survey with some physical features that appear to be strongly linked to variation in climate, particularly variation in temperature, sunlight, and altitude.

Body Build and Facial Construction

Scientists have suggested that the body build of many birds and mammals may vary according to the temperature of the environment in which they live. Bergmann and Allen, two nineteenth century naturalists, suggested some general rules for animals, but it was not until the 1950s that researchers began

Those Samburu people from Kenya illustrate Bergmann's rule. They have the long-limbed, lean body type that is often found in equatorial regions. Such a body type provides more surface area in relation to body mass and thus may facilitate the dissipation of body heat.

to examine whether these rules applied to human populations.[4] **Bergmann's rule** describes what seems to be a general relationship between body size and temperature: The slenderer populations of a species inhabit the warmer parts of its geographic range, and the more robust populations inhabit the cooler areas.

D. F. Roberts's studies of variation in mean body weight of human populations in regions with widely differing temperatures have provided support for Bergmann's rule.[5] Roberts discovered that the lowest body weights were found among residents of areas with the highest mean annual temperatures, and vice versa. Figure 4.1 (on page 72) shows the relationship between body weight of males and average annual temperature for four different geographic populations. Although the slope of the relationship is slightly different for each group, the trend is the same—with colder temperatures, weight is greater. Looking at the general trend across populations (see the "Total" line), we see that where the mean annual temperatures are about freezing (0°C; 32°F), the average weight for males is about 65 kilograms (143 pounds); where the mean annual temperatures are about 25°C (77°F), men weigh, on the average, about 50 kilograms (110 pounds).

Allen's rule refers to another kind of variation in body build among birds and mammals: Protruding body parts (e.g., limbs) are relatively shorter in the cooler areas of a species' range than in the warmer areas. Research comparing human populations tends to support Allen's rule.[6]

The rationale behind these theories is that the long-limbed, lean body type often found in equatorial regions provides more surface area in relation to body mass and thus facilitates the dissipation of body heat. In contrast, the chunkier, shorter-limbed body type found among residents of cold regions promotes retention of body heat because the amount of surface area relative to body mass is lessened. The build of the Inuit (Eskimo) appears to exemplify Bergmann's and Allen's rules. The relatively large bodies and short legs of the Inuit may be adapted to the cold temperatures in which they live.

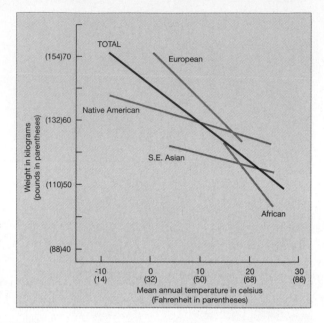

Figure 4.1 Relationship between Body Weight of Males and Average Annual Temperature for Four Major Population Groups

Source: D. F. Roberts, "Body Weight, Race, and Climate," *American Journal of Physical Anthropology,* 11 (1953), figure 2. Copyright 1953. Reprinted by permission of John Wiley & Sons, Inc.

It is not clear whether differences in body build among populations are due solely to natural selection of different genes under different conditions of cold or heat. Some of the variations may be acclimatizations induced during the life span of individuals.[7] Alphonse Riesenfeld provided experimental evidence that extreme cold can affect body proportions during growth and development. Rats raised under conditions of extreme cold generally showed changes that resemble characteristics of humans in cold environments. These cold-related changes included shortening of the long bones, consistent with Allen's rule.[8]

Like body build, facial structure may also be affected by environment. Riesenfeld found experimentally that the facial width of rats increased in cold temperatures and their nasal openings grew smaller.[9] Because the rats raised in cold environments were genetically similar to those raised in warmer environments, we can confidently conclude that the environment, not genes, brought about these changes in the rats. How much the environment directly affects variation in the human face is not clear. We do know that variation in climate is associated with facial variation. For example, people living in the humid tropics tend to have broad, short, flat noses, whereas people living in climates with low humidity (with cold or hot temperatures) tend to have long, thin noses. A narrow nose may be a more efficient humidifier of drier air than a broad nose.[10]

Skin Color

Human populations obviously differ in average skin color. Many people consider skin color the most important indicator of "race," and they sometimes treat others differently solely on this basis. But anthropologists, in addition to being critical of prejudice, also note that skin color is not a good indicator of ancestry. For example, dark skin is commonly found in sub-Saharan Africa. However, there are natives of southern India whose skin is as dark as or darker than that of many Africans. Yet these people are not closely related to Africans, either genetically or historically.

This Inuit father and his son illustrate Allen's rule. Both have relatively large bodies and short limbs, which help them maintain body heat in the cold climate they inhabit.

How can we explain the wide range of skin colors among the peoples of the world? The color of a person's skin depends on both the amount of dark pigment, or melanin, in the skin and the amount of blood in the small blood vessels of the skin.[11] Despite the fact that there is still much to understand about the genetics of skin color, we can explain much of the variation.

The amount of melanin in the skin seems to be related to the climate in which a person lives. **Gloger's rule** states that populations of birds and mammals living in warmer climates have more melanin and, therefore, darker skin, fur, or feathers, than do populations of the same species living in cooler areas. On the whole, this association with climate holds true for people as well as for other mammals and birds.

The populations of darker-skinned humans do live mostly in warm climates, particularly sunny climates (see Figure 4.2 on page 74). Dark pigmentation seems to have at least one specific advantage in sunny climates. Melanin protects the sensitive inner layers of the skin from the sun's damaging ultraviolet rays; therefore, dark-skinned people living in sunny areas are safer from sunburn and skin cancers than are light-skinned people. Dark skin may also confer other important biological advantages in tropical environments, such as greater resistance to tropical diseases.[12]

What, then, might be the advantages of light-colored skin? Presumably, there must be some benefits in some environments; otherwise, all human populations would tend to have relatively dark skin. Although light-skinned people are more susceptible to sunburn and skin cancers, the ultraviolet radiation that light skin absorbs also facilitates the body's production of vitamin D. Vitamin D helps the body incorporate calcium and thus is necessary for the proper growth and maintenance of bones. Too much vitamin D, however, can cause illness. Thus, the light-colored skin of people in temperate latitudes maximizes ultraviolet penetration, perhaps ensuring production of sufficient amounts of vitamin D for good health, whereas the darker skin of people in tropical latitudes minimizes ultraviolet penetration, perhaps preventing illness from too much vitamin D.[13] Light skin may also confer another advantage in colder environments: It is less likely to be damaged by frostbite.[14]

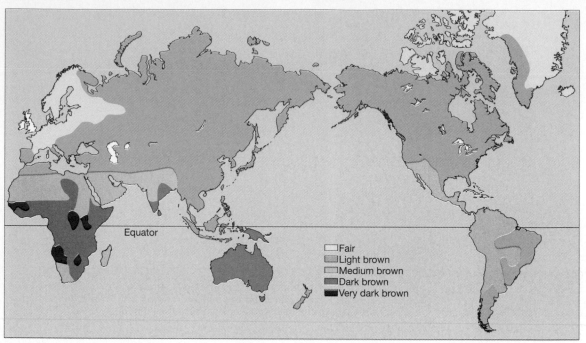

Figure 4.2   Variation in Skin Color

Source: Ashley H. Robins, *Biological Perspectives on Human Pigmentation* (Cambridge: Cambridge University Press, 1991). Copyright © by Cambridge University Press. Reprinted by permission of Cambridge University Press.

We now have direct evidence that confirms the connection between solar radiation and skin pigmentation. Anthropologists Nina Jablonski and George Chaplin used data from NASA satellites to determine the average amount of ultraviolet radiation people were exposed to in different parts of the world. They compared these average radiation amounts to data on skin reflectance (the lighter one's skin, the more light it reflects) and found that dark skin is more prevalent where ultraviolet radiation is more intense. Interestingly, there seems to be one notable exception—Native Americans tend to be lighter-skinned than expected. Jablonski and Chaplin suggest that this is because they are recent migrants to the New World, and their skin colors have not adapted to the varying levels of ultraviolet radiation they encountered in the Americas, just as the skin colors of European colonizers have not.[15]

Adaptation to High Altitude

Oxygen constitutes 21 percent of the air we breathe at sea level. At high altitudes, the percentage of oxygen in the air is the same, but because the barometric pressure is lower, we take in less oxygen with each breath.[16] We breathe more rapidly, our hearts beat faster, and all activity is more difficult. The net effects are discomfort and a condition known as **hypoxia**, or oxygen deficiency.

If high altitude presents such difficulties for many human beings, how is it that populations numbering in the millions can live out their lives, healthy and productive, at altitudes of 6,000, 12,000, or even 17,000 feet? Populations in the Himalayas and the Andes have adapted to their environments and do not display the symptoms suffered by low-altitude dwellers when they are exposed to high altitudes. Moreover, high-altitude dwellers have come to terms physiologically with extreme cold, deficient nutrition, strong winds, rough countryside, and intense solar radiation.[17]

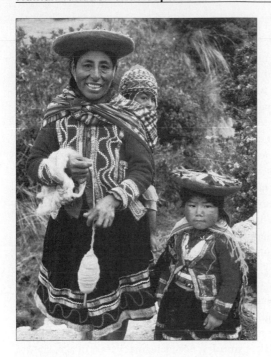

Highland Andean peoples, like this Quechua woman and her children, have larger chests and greater lung capacity than people living at low altitude. These differences are thought to be acclimatizations to life at high altitude and the problem of hypoxia, or oxygen deficiency.

Early studies of Andean high-altitude dwellers found that they differed in certain physical ways from low-altitude dwellers. Compared with low-altitude dwellers, high-altitude Andean Indians had larger chests and greater lung capacity, as well as more surface area in the capillaries of the lungs (which was believed to facilitate the transfer of oxygen to the blood).[18] Early researchers thought that genetic changes had allowed the Andeans to maximize their ability to take in oxygen at the lower barometric pressure of their high-altitude environment. Recent research, however, has cast some doubt on this conclusion. It appears now that other populations living at high altitudes do not show the Andean pattern of physical differences. In the Himalayas, for example, low-altitude dwellers and high-altitude dwellers do not differ in chest size or lung size, even though both groups show adequate lung functioning.[19]

Thus, current research does not suggest that high-altitude living requires biological adaptations that are purely genetic. In fact, some evidence suggests that humans who grow up in a high-altitude environment may adapt to hypoxia during their lifetimes, as they mature. For example, Peruvians who were born at sea level but who grew up at high altitudes developed the same amount of lung capacity as people who spent their entire lives at high altitudes.[20] Consistent with a presumed environmental effect, the children of high-altitude Peruvians who grow up in the lowlands do not develop larger chests. What appeared to earlier researchers to be a genetic adaptation among highland Andean populations appears in fact to be an acclimatization that develops early in childhood and persists for the lifetime of an individual. As with other traits that have been studied, it appears that life experiences can have profound effects on how the body grows.

Height

Studies of identical twins and comparisons of the height of parents and children suggest that heredity plays a considerable role in determining height,[21] so genetic differences must at least partly explain differences between populations in average height. But if average height can increase dramatically in a few decades, as in Japan between 1950 and 1980 and in many other countries in recent times,[22] then environmental influences are also likely to be important.

The considerable variation in average height among human populations may be partly explained by temperature differences. The Dutch, in Europe, are among the tallest populations in the world on average, and the Mbuti of Zaire, in central Africa, are among the shortest.[23] We already know that weight is related to mean annual temperature (Bergmann's rule). Weight is also related to height (taller people are likely to be heavier). So, since the taller (heavier) Dutch live in a cooler climate, some of the population variation in height would appear to involve adaptation to heat and cold.[24] Other factors besides heat and cold must also be operating, however, because tall and short peoples can be found in most areas of the world.

Many researchers think that poor nutrition and disease lead to reduced height and weight. In many parts of the world, children in higher social classes are taller on the average than children in lower social classes,[25] and this difference is more marked in economically poorer countries,[26] where the wealth and health differences between the classes are particularly large. During times of war and poor nutrition, children's stature often decreases. For example, in Germany during World War II, the stature of children 7 to 17 years of age declined as compared with previous time periods, despite the fact that stature had generally increased over time.[27]

More persuasive evidence for the effects of poor nutrition and disease comes out of longitudinal studies of the same individuals over time. For example, Reynaldo Martorell found that children in Guatemala who had frequent bouts of diarrhea were on the average over an inch shorter at age seven than children without frequent diarrhea.[28] Although malnourished or diseased children can catch up in their growth, follow-up research on Guatemalan children suggests that if stunting occurs before 3 years of age, stature at age 18 will still be reduced.[29]

A controversial set of studies links a very different environmental factor to variation in height in human populations. The factor at issue is stress, physical and emotional, in infancy.[30] Contrary to the view that any kind of stress is harmful, it appears that some presumably stressful experiences in infancy are associated with greater height and weight. Experimental studies with rats provided the original stimulus for the studies investigating the possible effect of stress on height. The experiments showed that rats that were physically handled ("petted") by the experimenters grew to be longer and heavier than rats not petted. Researchers originally thought that this was because the petted rats had received "tender loving care." But someone noticed that the petted rats seemed terrified (they urinated and defecated) when petted by humans, which suggested that the petting might have been stressful. It turned out in subsequent studies that even more obviously stressful experiences such as electric shock, vibration, and temperature extremes also produced rats with longer skeletons as compared with unstressed rats.

Thomas Landauer and John Whiting thought that stress in human infants might similarly produce greater adult height. Many cultures have customs for treating infants that could be physically stressful, including circumcision, branding of the skin with sharp objects, piercing the nose, ears, or lips for the insertion of ornaments, molding and stretching the head and limbs for cosmetic purposes, and vaccination. In addition, Shulamith Gunders and John Whiting suggested that separating the baby from its mother right after birth is another kind of stress. In cross-cultural comparisons by Whiting and his colleagues,[31] it seems that *both* physical stress and mother-infant separation, *if practiced before two years of age,* predict greater adult height; males are on the average two inches taller in such societies. (It is important to note that the stresses being discussed are short in duration, often a one-time occurrence, and do not constitute prolonged stress or abuse, which can have opposite effects.)

Because the cross-cultural evidence is associational, not experimental, it is possible that the results are due to some factor confounded with infant stress. Perhaps societies with infant stress have better nutrition or have climates that favor tallness. Recently, using new cross-cultural comparisons, J. Patrick Gray

In recent times there has been a dramatic increase in average height, which may be due to one or more environmental factors. Here we see a Chinese-American girl who is taller than her mother and almost as tall as her father.

and Linda Wolfe attempted to assess different possible predictors of height variation between populations. The predictors compared were nutrition, climate, geography, physical stress, and mother-infant separation. Gray and Wolfe's analysis indicated which of those factors predicted adult height independently of the others. It turned out that geographic region, climatic zone, and customs of infant stress were all significant independent predictors of height.[32] So the results now available clearly show that the effect of infant stress cannot be discounted.

Persuasive evidence for the stress hypothesis also comes from an experimental study conducted in Kenya.[33] Landauer and Whiting arranged for a randomly selected sample of children to be vaccinated before they were two years old. Other children were vaccinated soon after they were two. A few years later the two groups were compared with respect to height. Consistent with the cross-cultural evidence on the possible effect of stress on height, the children vaccinated before the age of two were significantly taller than the children vaccinated later. The children vaccinated before the age of two were selected randomly for early vaccination, so it is unlikely that nutritional or other differences between the two groups account for their difference in height.

As we noted earlier, in several areas of the world, people have been getting taller. What accounts for this recent trend toward greater height? Several factors may be involved. Some researchers think that it may be the result of improved nutrition and lower incidence of infectious diseases.[34] But it might also be that infant stress has increased as a result of giving birth in hospitals, which usually separate babies from mothers and also subject the newborns to medical tests, including the taking of blood. And various kinds of vaccinations have also become more common in infancy.[35]

In short, differences in human size seem to be the result of both adaptations and acclimatizations, with both of these, in turn, affected by cultural factors such as nutrition and stress.

Susceptibility to Infectious Diseases

Certain populations seem to have developed inherited resistances to particular infectious diseases. That is, populations repeatedly decimated by certain diseases in the past now have a high frequency of genetic characteristics that ameliorate the effects of these diseases. As Arno Motulsky pointed out, if there are genes that protect people from dying when they are infected by one of the diseases prevalent in their area, these genes will tend to become more common in succeeding generations.[36]

A field study of the infectious disease myxomatosis in rabbits supports this theory. When the virus responsible for the disease was first introduced into the Australian rabbit population, more than 95 percent of the infected animals died. But among the offspring of animals exposed to successive epidemics of myxomatosis, the percentage of animals that died from the disease decreased from year to year. The more epidemics the animals' ancestors had lived through, the smaller the percentage of current animals that died of the disease. Thus, the data suggested that the rabbits had developed a genetic resistance to myxomatosis.[37]

Infectious diseases seem to follow a similar pattern among human populations. When tuberculosis first strikes a population that has had no previous contact with it, the disease is usually fatal. But some populations seem to have inherited a resistance to death from tuberculosis. For example, the Ashkenazi Jews in America (those whose ancestors came from central and eastern Europe) are one of several populations whose ancestors survived many years of exposure to tuberculosis in the crowded European ghettos where they had previously lived. Although the rate of tuberculosis infection is identical among American Jews and non-Jews, the rate of tuberculosis mortality is significantly lower among Jews than among non-Jews in the United States.[38] After reviewing other data on this subject, Motulsky thought it likely "that the present relatively high resistance of Western populations to tuberculosis is genetically conditioned through natural selection during long contact with the disease."[39]

We tend to think of measles as a childhood disease that kills virtually no one, and we now have a vaccine against it. But when first introduced into populations, the measles virus can kill large numbers of people. In 1949, the Tupari Indians of Brazil numbered about 200 people. By 1955, two-thirds of the Tupari had died of measles introduced into the tribe by rubber gatherers in the area.[40] Large numbers of people died of measles in epidemics in the Faeroe Islands in 1846, in Hawaii in 1848, in the Fiji Islands in 1874, and among the Canadian Inuit very recently. It seems that where mortality rates from measles are low, populations have acquired a genetic resistance to death from this disease.[41]

But why is a population susceptible to a disease in the first place? Epidemiologist Francis Black suggests that lack of genes for resistance is not the whole answer. A high degree of genetic homogeneity in the population may also increase susceptibility.[42] A virus grown in one host is preadapted to a genetically similar new host and is therefore likely to be more virulent in the new host. For example, the measles virus adapts to a host individual; when it replicates, the viral forms that the host cannot kill are those most likely to survive and continue replicating. When the virus passes to a new host with similar genes, the preadapted virus is likely to kill the new host. If, on the other hand, the next host is very different genetically, the adaptation process starts over again; the virus is not so virulent at first because the host can kill it.

Populations that recently came to an area, and that had a small group of founders (as was probably true for the first Native Americans and the Polynesian seafarers who first settled many islands in the Pacific), tended to have a high degree of genetic homogeneity. Therefore, epidemic diseases introduced by Europeans (such as measles) would be likely to kill many of the natives within the first few years after contact. It is estimated that up to 56 million people died in the New World after contact with Europeans, mostly because of introduced diseases such as smallpox and measles. Similarly caused depopulation occurred widely in the Pacific.[43]

Some researchers suggest that nongenetic factors may also partly explain differential resistance to infectious disease. For example, cultural practices may partly explain the epidemics of measles among the Yanomamö Indians of Venezuela and Brazil. The Yanomamö frequently visit other villages, and that, together with the nonisolation of sick individuals, promoted a very rapid spread of the disease. Because many

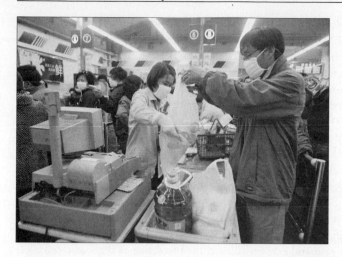

Permanent settlements and high population densities allow diseases to spread rapidly and produce epidemics. Here shoppers at a supermarket in China wear masks in hopes of preventing the spread of SARS.

individuals were sick at the same time, there were not enough healthy people to feed and care for the sick; mothers down with measles could not even nurse their babies. Thus, cultural factors may increase exposure to a disease and worsen its effect on a population.[44]

Epidemics of infectious disease may occur only if many people live near each other. Food collectors, who usually live in small dispersed bands, do not have enough people in and near the community to keep an epidemic going. Without enough people to infect, short-lived microorganisms that cause or carry diseases die out. In contrast, among agriculturalists, there are larger numbers of people in and around the community to whom a disease can spread. Permanent settlements, particularly urban settlements, also are likely to have poor sanitation and contaminated water.[45] Tuberculosis is an example of an infectious disease that, although very old, began to kill large numbers of people only after the emergence of sedentary, larger communities.[46]

Sickle-Cell Anemia

Another biological variation is an abnormality of the red blood cells known as **sickle-cell anemia**, or **sicklemia**. This is a condition in which normal, disk-shaped red blood cells assume a crescent (sickle) shape when deprived of oxygen. The sickle-shaped red blood cells do not move through the body as readily as normal cells, and thus cause more oxygen deficiency and damage to the heart, lungs, brain, and other vital organs. In addition, the red blood cells tend to "die" more rapidly, and the anemia worsens still more.[47]

Sickle-cell anemia is caused by a variant form of the genetic instructions for hemoglobin, the protein that carries oxygen in the red blood cells.[48] Individuals who have sickle-cell anemia have inherited the same allele (Hb^S) from both parents and are therefore homozygous for that gene. Individuals who receive this allele from only one parent are heterozygous; they have one Hb^S allele and one allele for normal hemoglobin (Hb^A). Heterozygotes generally will not show the full-blown symptoms of sickle-cell disease, although in some cases a heterozygous individual may have a mild case of anemia. A heterozygous person has a 50 percent chance of passing on the sickle-cell allele to a child. And if the child later mates with another person who is also a carrier of the sickle-cell allele, the statistical probability is that 25 percent of their children will develop sickle-cell anemia. Without advanced medical care, most individuals with two Hb^S alleles are unlikely to live more than a few years.[49]

Why has the allele for sickle-cell persisted in various populations? If people with sickle-cell anemia do not usually live to reproduce, we would expect a reduction in the frequency of Hb^S to near zero through the process of *normalizing selection.* But the sickle-cell allele occurs fairly often in some parts of the world, particularly in the wet tropical belt of Africa, where frequencies may be between 20 and 30 percent, and in Greece, Sicily, and southern India.[50]

Because the sickle-cell gene occurs in these places much more often than expected, researchers in the 1940s and the 1950s began to suspect that heterozygous individuals (who carry one Hb^S allele) might have a reproductive advantage in a malarial environment.[51] If the heterozygotes were more resistant to attacks of malaria than the homozygotes for normal hemoglobin (who get the Hb^A allele from both parents), the heterozygotes would be more likely to survive and reproduce, and therefore the recessive Hb^S allele would persist at a higher than expected frequency in the population. This kind of outcome is an example of *balancing selection.*[52]

A number of pieces of evidence support the "malaria theory." First, geographic comparisons show that the sickle-cell allele tends to be found where the incidence of malaria is high (see Figure 4.3). Second, as land in the tropics is opened to yam and rice agriculture, the incidence of the sickle-cell allele also increases. Indeed, recent studies suggest malaria may have evolved alongside agriculture in these regions.[53] The reason seems to be that malaria, carried principally by the *Anopheles gambiae* mosquito, becomes more prevalent as tropical forest gives way to more open land where mosquitoes can thrive in warm, sunlit ponds. Indeed, even among peoples of similar cultural backgrounds, the incidence of the

Figure 4.3   Geographic Distribution of Sicklemia and Its Relationship to the Distribution of Malaria
Source: John Buettner-Janusch, *Physical Anthropology: A Perspective* (New York: Wiley, 1973).

sickle-cell allele increases with greater rainfall and surpluses of water. Third, children who are heterozygous for the sickle-cell trait tend to have fewer malarial parasites in their bodies than do homozygous normal individuals, and they are more likely to survive.[54] The sickling trait does not necessarily keep people from contracting malaria, but it greatly decreases the rate of mortality from malaria—and in evolutionary terms, the overall effect is the same.[55] Fourth, if there is no balancing selection because malaria is no longer present, we should find a rapid decline in the incidence of the sickle-cell allele. Indeed, we find such a decline in populations with African ancestry. Those who live in malaria-free zones of the New World have a much lower incidence of sicklemia than do those who live in malarial regions of the New World.[56]

Hb^S is not the only abnormal hemoglobin to have a distribution related to malaria. It seems that a number of abnormal hemoglobins may be widespread because of the advantage heterozygotes have against the disease. For example, another abnormal hemoglobin, Hb^E, occurs in populations from India through Southeast Asia and New Guinea where malaria occurs, but Hb^S is not that common. Why should Hb^E heterozygotes have resistance to malaria? One possibility is that malarial parasites are less able to survive in an individual's blood with some normal and some abnormal hemoglobin. Abnormal hemoglobin cells are more delicate and live less long, so they may not readily support malarial parasites.[57]

Lactase Deficiency

When American educators discovered that African-American schoolchildren very often did not drink milk, they assumed that lack of money or education was the reason. These assumptions provided the impetus for establishing the school milk programs prevalent around the country. However, it now appears that after infancy many people lack an enzyme, lactase I, which is necessary for breaking down the sugar in milk, lactose, into simpler sugars that can be absorbed into the bloodstream.[58] Thus, a person without lactase cannot digest milk properly, and drinking it may cause bloating, cramps, stomach gas, and diarrhea. A study conducted in Baltimore among 312 African-American and 221 European-American children in grades 1 through 6 in 2 elementary schools indicated that 85 percent of the African-American children and 17 percent of the European-American children were milk-intolerant.[59]

More recent studies indicate that lactose intolerance occurs frequently in adults in many parts of the world.[60] The condition is common in Southeast and East Asia, India, the Mediterranean and the Near East, sub-Saharan Africa, and among Native North and South Americans. The widespread incidence of lactose intolerance should not be surprising. After infancy, mammals normally stop producing lactase.[61]

If lactose intolerance in adulthood in mammals is normal, we need to understand why only some human populations have the ability to make lactase I in adulthood and digest lactose. Why would selection favor this genetic ability in some populations but not in others? In the late 1960s, F. J. Simoons and Robert McCracken noted a relationship between lactose absorption and dairying (raising cows for milk). They suggested that with the advent of dairying, individuals with the genetic ability to produce lactase in adulthood would have greater reproductive success, and hence dairying populations would come to have a high proportion of individuals with the ability to break down lactose.[62]

But people in some dairying societies do not produce lactase in adulthood. Rather, they seem to have developed a cultural solution to the problem of lactase deficiency; they transform their milk into cheese, yogurt, sour cream, and other milk products that are low in lactose. To make these low-lactose products, people separate the lactose-rich whey from the curds or treat the milk with a bacterium (*Lactobacillus*) that breaks down the lactose, thus making the milk product digestible by a lactase-deficient person.[63]

Left: A girl milks a cow in Barnstable, Massachusetts. Natural selection may favor production of the enzyme lactase, a genetic way of making milk digestible in dairying populations far from the equator. Right: A Masai woman milks a cow in Kenya. Natural selection may favor the souring of milk, a cultural way of making it digestible in dairying populations close to the equator.

So why in some dairying societies did natural selection favor a biological solution (the production in adulthood of the enzyme lactase) rather than the cultural solution? William Durham has collected evidence that natural selection may favor the biological solution in dairying societies farther from the equator. The theory is that lactose behaves biochemically like vitamin D, facilitating the absorption of calcium—but only in people who produce lactase so that they can absorb the lactose. Because people in more temperate latitudes are not exposed to that much sunlight, particularly in the winter, and therefore make less vitamin D in their skin, natural selection may have favored the lactase way of absorbing dietary calcium.[64] In other words, natural selection may favor lactase production in adulthood, as well as lighter skin, at higher latitudes (where there is less sunlight).

This is an example of how culture may influence the way natural selection favors some genes over others. Without dairying, natural selection may not have favored the genetic propensity to produce lactase. This propensity is yet another example of the complex ways in which genes, environment, and culture interact to create human variation.

Race and Racism

Fortunately, internal variations such as lactase deficiency have never been associated with intergroup tensions—perhaps because such differences are not immediately obvious. Unfortunately, the same cannot be said for some of the more obvious external human differences such as skin color.

For as long as any of us can remember, countless aggressive actions—from fistfights to large-scale riots and civil wars—have stemmed from tensions and misunderstandings between various groups commonly referred to by many as "races." *Race* has become such a common term that most of us take the concept for granted, not bothering to consider what it does, and does not, mean. We may talk about the "human race," which means that all humans belong to the same breeding population. Yet we are often asked to check a box to identify our particular "race." We discuss first how biologists sometimes use the term *race;* then we turn to why many biological anthropologists and others now conclude that the concept of race does not usefully apply to humans. We discuss how racial classifications are largely social constructions that have been used to justify discrimination, exploitation, and even the extermination of certain categories of people.

Race as a Construct in Biology

Biological variation is not uniformly distributed in any species. While all members of a species can potentially interbreed with others, most matings take place within smaller groups or breeding populations. Through the processes of natural selection and genetic drift, populations inhabiting different geographic regions will come to exhibit some differences in biological traits. When differences within a species become sufficiently noticeable, biologists may classify different populations into different *varieties,* or *races.* If the term race is understood to be just a shorthand or classificatory way that biologists describe slight population variants within a species, the concept of race would probably not be controversial. Unfortunately, as applied to humans, racial classifications have often been confounded with racism, the belief that some "races" are innately inferior to others. The misuse and misunderstanding of the term *race* and its association with racist thinking is one reason why many biological anthropologists and others have suggested that the term should not be applied to human biological differences.

A second reason for not applying racial classification to humans is that humans have exhibited so much interbreeding that different populations are not clearly classifiable into discrete groups that can be defined in terms of the presence or absence of particular biological traits.[65] Therefore, many argue that "race" is not scientifically useful for describing human biological variation. The difficulty in employing racial classification is evident by comparing the number of "races" that classifiers come up with. The number of "racial" categories in humans has varied from as few as 3 to more than 37.[66]

How can human groups be clearly divided into "races" if most adaptive biological traits show clines or gradual differences from one region to another?[67] Skin color is a good example of clinal variation. In the area around Egypt, there is a gradient of skin color as one moves from north to south in the Nile Valley. Skin generally becomes darker closer to the equator (south) and lighter closer to the Mediterranean. But other adaptive traits may not have north-south clines, because the environmental predictors may be distributed differently. Nose shape varies with humidity, but clines in humidity do not particularly correspond to variation in latitude. So the gradient for skin color would not be the same as the gradient for nose shape. Because adaptive traits tend to be clinally distributed, there is no line you could draw on a world map that would separate "white" from "black" people or "whites" from "Asians."[68] Only traits that are neutral in terms of natural selection will tend (because of genetic drift) to cluster in regions.[69]

Racial classification is problematic also because there is sometimes more physical, physiological, and genetic diversity *within* a single geographic group that might be called a "race" (e.g., Africans) than there is *between* supposed "racial" groups. Africans vary more among themselves than they do in comparison with people elsewhere.[70] Analyses of all human populations have demonstrated that 93 to 95 percent of genetic variation is due to individual differences within populations, while only 3 to 5 percent of genetic variation is due to differences among major human population groups.[71] "Race" when applied to humans is a social category, not a scientific one.

African metal workers created magnificent works of art like this golden head from Ghana long before Europeans arrived.

Race and Civilization

Many persons hold the racist viewpoint that the biological inferiority of certain groups, which they call "races," is reflected in the supposedly "primitive" quality of their cultures. They will argue that the "developed" nations are "white" and the "underdeveloped" nations are not. (We put terms like "white," which are used as racial categories, in quotes to indicate the problematic nature of the categories.) But to make such an argument ignores much of history. Many of today's so-called underdeveloped nations—primarily in Asia, Africa, and South America—had developed complex and sophisticated civilizations long before European nations expanded and acquired considerable power. The advanced societies of the Shang dynasty in China, the Mayans in Mesoamerica, and the African empire of Ghana were all founded and developed by "nonwhites."

Between 1523 and 1028 B.C., China had a complex form of government, armies, metal tools and weapons, and production and storage facilities for large quantities of grain. The early Chinese civilization also had writing and elaborate religious rituals.[72] From A.D. 300 to 900, the Mayans were a large population with a thriving economy. They built many large and beautiful cities in which were centered great pyramids and luxurious palaces.[73] According to legend, the West African civilization of Ghana was founded during the second century A.D. By A.D. 770, the time of the Soninke rulers, Ghana had developed two capital cities—one Muslim and the other non-Muslim—each with its own ruler and both supported largely by Ghana's lucrative gold market.[74]

Considering how recently northern Europeans developed cities and central governments, it seems odd that some "whites" should label Africans, Native Americans, and others backward in terms of historical achievement, or biologically inferior in terms of capacity for civilization. But racists, both "white" and "nonwhite," choose to ignore the fact that many populations have achieved remarkable advances in civilization. Most significant, racists refuse to believe that they can acknowledge the achievements of another group without in any way downgrading the achievements of their own.

Race, Conquest, and the Role of Infectious Disease

There are those who would argue that Europeans' superiority accounted for their ability to colonize much of the world during the last few hundred years. But it now appears that Europeans were able to dominate at least partly because many native peoples were susceptible to diseases introduced by the Europeans.[75] Earlier, we discussed how continued exposure to epidemics of infectious diseases, such as tuberculosis and measles, can cause succeeding generations to acquire a genetic resistance to death from such diseases. Smallpox had a long history in Europe and Africa; genetic resistance eventually made it mostly a survivable childhood disease. But in the New World it was quite another story. Cortez and the conquistadores were inadvertently aided by smallpox in their attempt to defeat the Aztecs of Mexico. In 1520, a member of Cortez's army unwittingly transmitted smallpox to the natives. The disease spread rapidly, killing at least 50 percent of the population, and so the Aztecs were at a considerable disadvantage in their battling with the Spanish.[76]

Outbreaks of smallpox repeatedly decimated many Native American populations in North America a century or two later. In the early seventeenth century, the Massachusett and Narragansett Indians, with populations of 30,000 and 9,000, respectively, were reduced by smallpox to a few hundred members. Extremely high mortality rates were also noted among the Crow, the Blackfoot, and other Native American groups during the nineteenth century. The germ theory alone may not completely explain these epidemics; Europeans may have deliberately encouraged the spread of one new disease, smallpox, by purposely distributing infected blankets to the natives. Motulsky calls the spread of smallpox "one of the first examples of biological warfare."[77]

Race and Behavior

As an outgrowth of earlier attempts to show that inferior "races" have "primitive" cultures, some scholars have attempted to demonstrate behavioral differences between "races." One of the most active has been psychologist J. Philippe Rushton, whose 1995 book *Race, Evolution, and Behavior* purports to demonstrate behavioral differences between the "Negroid," "Caucasoid," and "Mongoloid" "races" in terms of sexual practices, parenting, social deviance, and family structure, among others.

Rushton argues that these behaviors have a genetic basis rooted in adaptations to particular environments. He suggests that "Negroids" are adapted to the warm environments of East Africa, where humans first evolved, through a reproductive strategy in which individuals have many offspring but put little energy into their children's upbringing and care. This strategy is known in evolutionary theory as *r-selected,* and is well documented among creatures such as fish, reptiles, and even some mammals (rabbits, for example).[78] Rushton further suggests that as humans left Africa they adapted to the "colder" climates of Asia by adopting a more *K-selected* reproductive strategy, which involves having few offspring but putting lots of energy into their upbringing and care. K-selected strategies are also well documented in the animal world, and it is interesting to note that apes (and humans) are often presented as examples of highly K-selected species.[79]

The data Rushton uses to support his argument come almost entirely from modern nations, many with a history of racial discrimination (such as South Africa, Japan, and the United States). But if genetic differences in behavior do exist among these three "races," differences that have their origins in the exodus of modern humans from Africa more than 100,000 years ago, then those differences should be apparent both between and among all the cultures of the world. That is, "Negroid" cultures should all share behaviors that are clearly different from those of "Caucasoid" cultures, "Caucasoid" cultures should all share behaviors that are different from those of "Mongoloid" cultures, and so on. Do such differences exist?

DIFFERENCES IN AVERAGE IQ SCORES—WHAT DO THEY MEAN?

In late 1994, a new book reignited controversy about the relationship between "race" and intelligence. Once again people thought they had evidence of African-American "inferiority." But once again there were problems with the evidence. The book was *The Bell Curve,* by Richard Herrnstein and Charles Murray. It purported to show that the intelligence of an individual was largely inherited and unchangeable throughout the life span, that an individual's success was largely based on intelligence, and that African Americans were likely to remain at the bottom of society because they had less intelligence than European Americans. Herrnstein and Murray appealed to a lot of studies to buttress their argument. But their argument was still faulty.

If you look at the average scores on many standard intelligence tests, you might conclude, as racists have, that African Americans are less intelligent than European Americans. The averages are different between the two groups; African Americans typically have lower scores. But what does this average difference mean? Herrnstein and Murray, like many before them, fail to distinguish between a measure, such as a particular IQ test, and what is supposedly being measured, intelligence. If a test only imperfectly measures what it purports to measure, lower average IQ scores merely mean lower scores on that particular IQ test; they do not necessarily reflect lower intelligence. There are many reasons why some smart people might not do well on particular kinds of IQ tests. For example, the way the tests are administered may affect performance, as may lack of familiarity with the format or the experiences and objects referred to. The test might also not measure particular kinds of intelligence such as social "smarts" and creativity.

If African Americans were really less intelligent, more than their average IQ scores would be lower. The whole frequency distribution of their individual scores should also be lower—they should have fewer geniuses and more retarded individuals. That is, the bell-shaped curve showing how their scores are distributed should range lower than the curve for other Americans, and African Americans should also have proportionately fewer scores at the very high end of the scale. But neither expectation is confirmed. According to research by Henry Grubb, the proportion of African Americans at the low end of the scale is not significantly different from the proportion of European Americans. And Grubb and Andrea Barthwell report that, on the basis of IQ tests administered by Mensa (a high-IQ society), the proportion of African Americans at the high end of the scale is not different from the proportion of European Americans. So the available evidence suggests that African Americans have lower average test scores, but not fewer very high scores or more very low scores (proportionately). Why, then, might their average scores be lower?

Grubb and Barthwell point out that the average scores are not lower on all IQ tests. One test that shows no significant difference is an untimed version of an intelligence test using pictures (the pictorial reasoning test). You can administer the pictorial reasoning test in one of two ways—timed or untimed. A person must finish the test by the end of a prescribed, relatively short time period; or the test-taker can respond to the questions without any time limit. African Americans have lower average scores than European Americans on the timed version of the pictorial reasoning test (although not as much lower as on other tests) but not on the untimed version. This finding suggests that a timed test measures or reflects more than just intelligence. What else besides intelligence might affect performance on a timed IQ test?

Familiarity with a particular format or the content could increase performance on a timed test. So could familiarity or comfort with speed. Although they do not have evidence for how African Americans feel about speed, Grubb and Barthwell cite a study that shows that discomfort with speed can affect performance on an IQ test. The study, conducted by A. Lieblich and S. Kugelmass, compared Jewish and Arab children in

Israel. The Arab children scored lower than the Jewish children on the parts of a standard Wechsler intelligence test that were timed, but the Arab children scored the same or even higher on the parts that were untimed. Lieblich and Kugelmass concluded that the Arabs' poorer performance on the timed tests may reflect a cultural abhorrence of speed; "Time is of the Devil" is an Arab saying. Speed is not highly valued in some cultures. If unfamiliarity or discomfort with speed can affect performance on an IQ test, then clearly the test is not measuring intelligence only.

Critics have pointed to many other problems with the evidence presented in *The Bell Curve*. But the fundamental problem is the same as with all attempts to use differences in average IQ scores to make judgments about the capability of different groups. IQ tests may not adequately measure what they purport to measure. If they do not—and there are good reasons to think they do not—it is scientifically and morally incorrect to conclude that differences in average scores are caused by genetic differences in intelligence.

Sources: Richard J. Herrnstein and Charles Murray, *The Bell Curve: Intelligence and Class Structure in American Life* (New York: Free Press, 1994); Henry J. Grubb and Andrea G. Barthwell, "Superior Intelligence and Racial Equivalence: A Look at Mensa," paper presented at the 1996 annual meeting of the Society for Cross-Cultural Research; Henry J. Grubb, "Intelligence at the Low End of the Curve: Where Are the Racial Differences?" *Journal of Black Psychology*, 14 (1987): 25–34; Leon J. Kamin, "Behind the Curve," *Scientific American* (February 1995): 99–103.

The authors of this text used information about the 186 cultures composing the Standard Cross-Cultural Sample to test whether Rushton's ideas hold up.[80] We examined 26 separate behaviors that Rushton predicted would differ among the "races." Contrary to Rushton's predictions, most of them showed no differences between the supposed "racial" groups. Only one of them showed the differences that Rushton predicted, and five of them demonstrated a pattern that was the *opposite* of what Rushton predicted. So Rushton's gross division of humans into three "races" does not generally predict variation in human behavior. His ideas appear plainly wrong and do not support the belief that it is scientifically useful to distinguish human "races."[81]

Race and Intelligence

Attempts to document differences in intelligence among the so-called races have a fairly long history. One of the latest attempts was a 1994 book, titled *The Bell Curve*, by Richard J. Herrnstein and Charles Murray (see the feature box titled "Differences in Average IQ Scores").

In the nineteenth century, European white supremacists tried to find scientific justification for what they felt was the genetically inherited mental inferiority of "blacks." They did this by measuring skulls. It was believed that the larger the skull, the greater the cranial capacity and the bigger (hence, also better) the brain. Although the skull-measuring mania quickly disappeared and is no longer considered seriously as a way to measure intelligence, other "facts" may be used to demonstrate the presumed intellectual superiority of "white" people—namely, statistics from intelligence tests.

The first large-scale intelligence testing in the United States began with the nation's entry into World War I, in 1917. Thousands of draftees were given the so-called Alpha and Beta IQ tests to determine military assignments. Later, psychologists arranged the test results according to the "racial" categories of "white" and "black" and found what they had expected—"blacks" scored consistently lower than "whites." This result was viewed as scientific proof of the innate intellectual inferiority of "blacks" and was used to justify further discrimination against them, both in and out of the army.[82]

Otto Klineberg's subsequent statistical analyses of IQ-test results demonstrated that "blacks" from northern states scored higher than "blacks" from the South. Although dedicated racists explained that this difference was due to the northward migration of innately intelligent "blacks," most academics attributed the result to the influence of superior education and more stimulating environments in the North. When further studies showed that northern "blacks" scored higher than southern "whites," the better-education-in-the-North theory gained support, but again racists insisted such results were due to northward migration by more intelligent "whites."

As a further test of his conclusions, Klineberg gave IQ tests to "black" schoolgirls born and partly raised in the South who had spent varying lengths of time in New York City. He found that the longer the girls had been in the North, the higher their average IQ. In addition to providing support for the belief that "blacks" are not inherently inferior to "whites," these findings suggested that cultural factors can and do influence IQ scores, and that IQ is not a fixed quantity.

The controversy about race and intelligence was fueled again in 1969 by Arthur Jensen.[83] He suggested that although the IQ scores of American "blacks" overlapped considerably with the IQ scores of "whites," the average score for "blacks" was 15 points lower than the average for "whites." IQ scores presumably have a large genetic component, so the lower average score for "blacks" implied to Jensen that "blacks" were genetically inferior to "whites." But others contend that the evidence presented by Jensen and more recently by Murray and Herrnstein implies no such thing.

The critics of the genetic interpretation point to at least two problems. First, there is widespread recognition now that IQ tests are probably not accurate measures of "intelligence" because they are probably biased in favor of the subculture of those who construct the tests. That is, many of the questions on the test refer to things that "white," middle-class children are familiar with, thus giving such children an advantage.[84] So far, no one has come up with a "culture-fair," or bias-free, test. There is more agreement that, although the IQ test may not measure "intelligence" well, it may predict scholastic success or how well a child will do in the primarily "white"-oriented school system.[85]

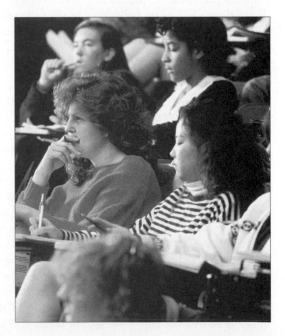

Until all people have an equal education and opportunities to achieve, there is no way we can be sure that some people are smarter than others.

A second major problem with a purely genetic interpretation of the IQ difference is that many studies show that IQ scores can be influenced by the social environment. Economically deprived children, whether "black" or "white," will generally score lower than affluent "white" or "black" children. And training of children with low IQ scores clearly improves their test scores.[86] More dramatic evidence is provided by Sandra Scarr and her colleagues. "Black" children adopted by well-off "white" families have IQ scores above the average for "whites." And those "blacks" with more European ancestry do not have higher IQ scores.[87] So the average difference between "blacks" and "whites" in IQ cannot be attributed to a presumed genetic difference. For all we know, the 15-point average difference may be due completely to differences in environment or to test bias.

Geneticist Theodosius Dobzhansky reminded us that conclusions about the causes of different levels of achievement on IQ tests cannot be drawn until all people have equal opportunities to develop their potentials. He stressed the need for an open society operating under the democratic ideal, where all persons are given an equal opportunity to develop whatever gifts or aptitudes they possess and choose to develop.[88]

The Future of Human Variation

Laboratory fertilization, subsequent transplantation of the embryo, and successful birth have been accomplished with humans and nonhumans. *Cloning*—the exact reproduction of an individual from cellular tissue—has been achieved with frogs, sheep, and other animals. And *genetic engineering*—the substitution of some genes for others—is increasingly practiced in nonhuman organisms. Indeed, as we discussed in the chapter on genetics and evolution, genetic engineering is now used in humans to eliminate certain disorders that are produced by defective genes. What are the implications of such practices for the genetic future of humans? Will it really be possible someday to control the genetic makeup of our species? If so, will the effects be positive or negative?

It is interesting to speculate on the development of a "perfect human." Aside from the serious ethical question of who would decide what the perfect human should be like, there is the serious biological question of whether such a development might in the long run be detrimental to the human species, for what is perfectly suited to one physical or social environment may be totally unsuited to another. The collection of physical, emotional, and intellectual attributes that might be "perfect" in the early twenty-first century might be inappropriate in the twenty-second century.[89] Even defects such as the sickle-cell trait may confer advantages under certain conditions, as we have seen.

In the long run, the perpetuation of genetic variability is probably more advantageous than the creation of a "perfect" and invariable human being. In the event of dramatic changes in the world environment, absolute uniformity in the human species might be an evolutionary dead end. Such uniformity might lead to the extinction of the human species if new conditions favored genetic or cultural variations that were no longer present in the species. Perhaps our best hope for maximizing our chances of survival is to tolerate, and even encourage, the persistence of many aspects of human variation, both biological and cultural.[90]

Summary

1. Physical variation—variation in the frequencies of physical traits—from one human population to another is the result of one or more of the following factors: adaptation, acclimatization, and the influence of the social or cultural environment.

2. Some physical variations in human populations involve genetic variation; other variations, including body build, facial construction, and skin color, may be adapted to variation in climate. Still other variations, such as the ability to make lactase, may be adapted partially to variation in cultural environment.

3. Most biological anthropologists today agree that "race" is not a useful way of referring to human biological variation because human populations do not unambiguously fall into discrete groups defined by a particular set of biological traits. Physical traits that are adaptive vary clinally, which makes it meaningless to divide humans into discrete "racial" entities. Rather, it is suggested that "racial" classifications are mostly social categories that are presumed to have a biological basis.

4. Perhaps the most controversial aspect of racial discrimination is the supposed relationship between "racial" categories and intelligence. Attempts have been made to show, by IQ tests and other means, the innate intellectual superiority of one "racial" category over another. But there is doubt that IQ tests measure intelligence fairly. Because evidence indicates that IQ scores are influenced by both genes and environment, conclusions about the causes of differences in IQ scores cannot be drawn until all the people being compared have equal opportunities to develop their potentials.

Glossary Terms

acclimatization (p. 69)   Gloger's rule (p. 73)
adaptation (p. 69)   hypoxia (p. 74)
Allen's rule (p. 71)   sickle-cell anemia (sicklemia) (p. 79)
Bergmann's rule (p. 71)

Critical Questions

1. Why is skin color used more often than hair or eye color or body proportions in "racial" classifications?

2. If Europeans had been more susceptible to New World and Pacific diseases, would the world be different today?

3. How might studies of natural selection help increase tolerance of other populations?

PRIMATES: PRESENT AND PAST

Chapter Outline

- Common Primate Traits
- The Various Living Primates
- Distinctive Hominid Traits
- The Emergence of Primates
- The Emergence of Anthropoids
- The Miocene Anthropoids
- The Divergence of Hominids from the Other Hominoids

Humans belong to the order of *Primates*. How do primates differ from other mammals? And what distinguishes humans from the other primates? After discussing these questions, we turn to the evolution of the primates: When, where, and why did the early primates emerge, and how and why did they diverge? Our overview covers the period from about 65 million years ago to the end of the Miocene, a little over 5 million years ago.

But how can living primates such as chimpanzees tell us anything about humans or the primates that were our ancestors? After all, each living primate species has its own history of evolutionary divergence from the earliest primate forms. All living primates, including humans, evolved from earlier primates that are now extinct. Nonetheless, by observing how humans and other primates differ from and resemble each other, we may be able to infer how and why humans diverged from the other primates.

Common Primate Traits

All primates belong to the class Mammalia, and they share all the common features of mammals. Except for humans, the bodies of primates are covered with dense hair or fur, which provides insulation. Even humans have hair in various places, though perhaps not always for insulation. Mammals are *warm-blooded;* that is, their body temperature is more or less constantly warm and usually higher than that of the air around them. Almost all mammals give birth to live young that develop to a considerable size within the mother and are nourished by suckling from the mother's mammary glands. The young have a relatively long period of dependence on adults after birth. This period is also a time of learning, for a great deal of adult mammal behavior is learned rather than instinctive. Play is a learning technique common to mammal young and is especially important to primates.

The primates have a number of physical and social traits that set them apart from other mammals. No one of the primates' physical features is unique to primates; animals from other orders share one or more of the characteristics described below. But the complex of all these physical traits is unique to primates.[1]

Many skeletal features of the primates reflect an **arboreal** (tree-living) existence. All primate hind limbs are structured principally to provide support, but the "feet" in most primates can also grasp things (see Figure 5.1). Some primates—orangutans, for instance—can suspend themselves from their hind limbs. The forelimbs are especially flexible, built to withstand both pushing and pulling forces. Each of the hind limbs and forelimbs has one bone in the upper portion and two bones in the lower portion (with the exception of the tarsier). This feature has changed little since the time of the earliest primate ancestors. It has remained in modern primates (although many other mammals have lost it) because the double bones give great mobility for rotating arms and legs.

Another characteristic structure of primates is the clavicle, or collarbone. The clavicle also gives primates great freedom of movement, allowing them to move the shoulders both up and down and back and forth. Although humans obviously do not use this flexibility for arboreal activity, they do use it for other activities. Without a clavicle we could not throw a spear or a ball; no fine tools could be made and no doorknobs turned if we did not have rotatable forearms.

Primates generally are **omnivorous**; that is, they eat all kinds of food, including insects and small animals, as well as fruits, seeds, leaves, and roots. The teeth of primates reflect this omnivorous diet. The chewing teeth—the **molars** and **premolars**—are unspecialized, particularly in comparison with those of other groups of animals, such as the grazers. The front teeth—the **incisors** and **canines**—are often very specialized, principally in the lower primates. For example, in many prosimians the slender, tightly packed lower incisors and canines form a "dental comb" the animals use in grooming or for scraping hardened tree gum (which is a food for them) from tree trunks.[2]

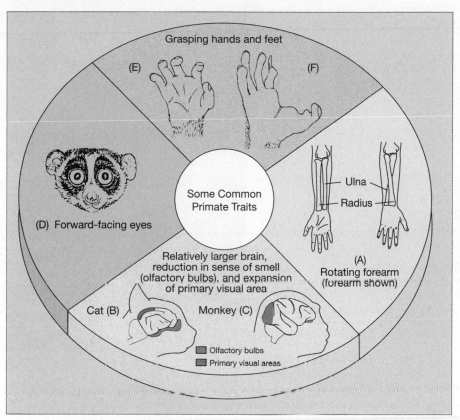

Figure 5.1 Some Common Primate Traits

Sources: (B) and (C) from Terrence Deacon, "Primate Brains and Senses," in Stephen Jones, Robert Martin, and David Pilbeam, eds., *The Cambridge Encyclopedia of Human Evolution* (New York: Cambridge University Press, 1992), figure on p. 110. Copyright © 1992. Reprinted by permission of Cambridge University Press; (D), (E), and (F) from Matt Cartmill, "Non-Human Primates," in Stephen Jones, Robert Martin, and David Pilbeam, eds., *The Cambridge Encyclopedia of Human Evolution*, figures from pp. 24–25. Copyright © 1992. Reprinted by permission of Cambridge University Press.

Primate hands are extremely flexible. All primates have prehensile—grasping—hands, which can be wrapped around an object. Primates have five digits on both hands and feet (in some cases, one digit may be reduced to a stub), and their nails, with few exceptions, are broad and flat, not claw-like. This structure allows them to grip objects; the hairless, sensitive pads on their fingers, toes, heels, and palms also help them to grip. Most primates have **opposable thumbs**, a feature that allows an even more precise and powerful grip.

Vision is very important to primate life. Compared with other mammals, primates have a relatively larger portion of the brain devoted to vision rather than smell. Primates are characterized by stereoscopic, or depth, vision. Their eyes are directed forward rather than sideways, as in other animals—a trait that allows them to focus on an object (insects or other food or a distant branch) with both eyes at once. Most primates also have color vision, perhaps to recognize when plant foods are ready to eat.

Another important primate feature is a large brain relative to body size. That is, primates generally have larger brains than animals of similar size, perhaps because their survival depends on an enormous amount of learning, as we discuss later. In general, animals with large brains seem to mature more slowly and to live longer than animals with small brains.[3] The more slowly an animal matures and the longer it lives, the more it can learn.

A baby Macaque clings to its wire-and-cloth "surrogate mother" during the Harry Harlow experiment. Harlow demonstrated that social interaction was necessary for primates to develop normally.

For the most part, primates are social animals. For most primates, particularly those that are **diurnal**—that is, active during the day—group life may be crucial to survival. Social relationships begin with the mother and other adults during the fairly long dependency period of primates. The prolonged dependency allows infants more time to observe and learn the complex behaviors essential to survival while enjoying the care and protection of mature adults.

The Various Living Primates

The order Primates is often divided into two suborders: the *prosimians*—literally, premonkeys—and the *anthropoids.* The prosimians include lemurs, lorises, and tarsiers. The anthropoid suborder includes New World monkeys, Old World monkeys, the lesser apes (gibbons, siamangs), the great apes (orangutans, gorillas, chimpanzees), and humans.

Prosimians

The **prosimians** resemble other mammals more than the anthropoid primates do. For example, the prosimians depend much more on smell for information and typically have more mobile ears, whiskers, longer snouts, and relatively fixed facial expressions. The prosimians also exhibit many traits shared by all primates, including grasping hands, stereoscopic vision, and enlarged visual centers in the brain.

Lemur-Like Forms   Lemurs and their relatives, the indris and the aye-ayes, are found only on two island areas off the southeastern coast of Africa, Madagascar and the Comoro Islands. These primates range in size from the mouse lemur to the 4-foot-long indri. Many of the species in this group are **quadrupeds**—

Shown here is a ringtailed lemur mother with its baby holding on. Prosimians such as ringtailed lemurs depend much more on smell than do anthropoids. Prosimians also have more mobile ears and whiskers, longer snouts, and relatively fixed facial expressions.

animals that move on all fours—in the trees as well as on the ground. Some species, such as the indris, use their hind limbs alone to push off from one vertical position to another in a mode of locomotion called **vertical clinging and leaping**. Lemurs are mostly vegetarians, eating fruit, leaves, bark, and flowers. Many lemur species, particularly those that are **nocturnal** (active during the night), are solitary during their active hours. Others are much more social, living in groups ranging in size from a small family to as many as 60 members.[4] An unusual feature of the lemur-like primates is that females often dominate males, particularly over access to food. In most primates, and in most other mammals, female dominance is rarely observed.[5]

Loris-Like Forms Members of the loris group, found in both Southeast Asia and sub-Saharan Africa, are all nocturnal and arboreal. They eat fruit, tree gum, and insects, and usually give birth to single infants.[6] There are two major subfamilies, the lorises and the bushbabies (galagos). Bushbabies are quick, active animals that hop between branches and tree trunks in the vertical-clinging-and-leaping pattern. On the ground they often resort to a kangaroo-like hop. Lorises are much slower, walking sedately along branches hand over hand in the quadrupedal fashion.

Tarsiers The nocturnal, tree-living tarsiers, found now only on the islands of the Philippines and Indonesia, are the only primates that depend completely on animal foods. They are usually insect-eaters, but they sometimes capture and eat other small animals. They are well equipped for night vision, possessing enormous

Nocturnal tree-living tarsiers, like this one in the Philippines, are the only primates that depend completely on animal foods. Their enormous eyes equip them to find insects and other prey in the night. Their elongated ankle bones (tarsals) make them very good at vertical clinging and leaping.

eyes, extraordinary eyesight, and enlarged visual centers in the brain. The tarsiers get their name from their elongated tarsal bones (the bones of the ankle), which give them tremendous leverage for their long jumps. Tarsiers are very skilled at vertical clinging and leaping. They live in family groups composed of a mated pair and their offspring. Like some higher primates, male and female tarsiers sing together each evening to advertise their territories.[7]

The classification of tarsiers is somewhat controversial. Some classifiers group tarsiers with anthropoids. In this other classification scheme the suborders of primates are labeled *strepsirhines* (which includes lemurs and lorises) and *haplorhines* (which includes tarsiers and anthropoids). Tarsiers have chromosomes similar to those of other prosimians; they also have claws for grooming on some of their toes, more than two nipples, and a uterus shaped like that of other prosimians (two-horned). Like bushbabies, tarsiers move about through vertical clinging and leaping. In other respects tarsiers are more like the anthropoids. They have a reduced dependence on smell; not only are their noses smaller, but they lack the wet, dog-like snout of lemurs. In common with the anthropoids, their eyes are closer together and are protected by bony orbits.[8]

Anthropoids

The anthropoid suborder includes humans, apes, and monkeys. Most **anthropoids** have rounded braincases; reduced, nonmobile outer ears; and relatively small, flat faces instead of muzzles. They also have highly dextrous hands.[9] The anthropoid order is divided into two main groups: **platyrrhines** and **catarrhines** (see Figure 5.2). Platyrrhines have broad, flat-bridged noses, with nostrils facing outward; these monkeys are found only in the New World, in Central and South America. Catarrhines have narrow noses with nostrils facing downward. Catarrhines include monkeys of the Old World (Africa, Asia, and Europe), as well as apes and humans.

The squirrel monkey, like all platyrrhines, almost never leaves the trees. It is well suited to an arboreal lifestyle; note how it uses both hands and feet to grasp branches.

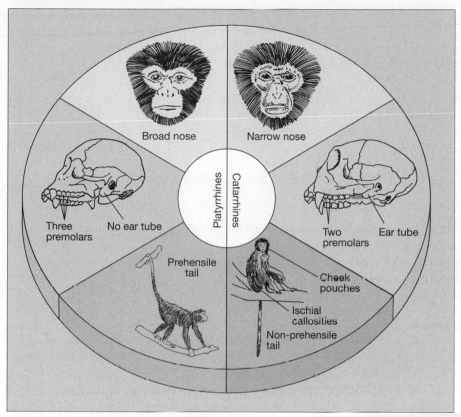

Figure 5.2   Features of Platyrrhines and Catarrhines

Source: Based on Noel T. Boaz and Alan J. Almquist, *Biological Anthropology: A Synthetic Approach to Human Evolution* (Upper Saddle River, NJ: Prentice Hall, 1997).

New World Monkeys   Besides the shape of the nose and the position of the nostrils, other anatomical features distinguish the New World monkeys (platyrrhines) from the catarrhine anthropoids. The New World species have three premolars, whereas the Old World species have two. Some New World monkeys have a **prehensile** (grasping) tail; no Old World monkeys do. All the New World monkeys are completely arboreal; they vary a lot in the size of their groups; and their food ranges from insects to nectar and sap to fruits and leaves.[10]

Two main families of New World monkeys have traditionally been defined. One family, the *callitrichids,* contains marmosets and tamarins; the other family, the *cebids,* contains all the other New World monkeys. The callitrichids are very small, have claws instead of fingernails, and give birth to twins who mature in about two years. Perhaps because twinning is so common and the infants have to be carried, callitrichid fathers and older siblings have often been observed carrying infants. Callitrichid groups may contain a mated pair (monogamy) or a female mated to more than one male (polyandry). The callitrichids eat a lot of fruit and tree sap, but like other very small primates, they obtain a large portion of their protein requirements from insects.[11]

Cebids are generally larger than callitrichids, take about twice as long to mature, and tend to bear only one offspring at a time.[12] The cebids vary widely in size, group composition, and diet. For example, squirrel monkeys weigh about 2 pounds, whereas woolly spider monkeys weigh more than 16 pounds. Some cebids have small groups with one male-female pair, others have groups of up to 50 individuals. Some of the smallest cebids have a diet of leaves, insects, flowers, and fruits, whereas others are mostly fruit-eaters with lesser dependence on seeds, leaves, or insects.[13]

Old World Monkeys   The Old World monkeys, or **cercopithecoids**, are related more closely to humans than to New World monkeys. They have the same number of teeth as apes and humans. The Old World monkey species are not as diverse as their New World cousins, but they live in a greater variety of habitats. Some live both in trees and on the ground; others, such as the gelada baboon, are completely **terrestrial**, or ground-living. Macaques are found both in tropical jungles and on snow-covered mountains, and they range from the Rock of Gibraltar to Africa to northern India, Pakistan, and Japan. There are two major subfamilies of Old World monkeys.

COLOBINE MONKEYS   The colobines live mostly in trees, and their diet consists principally of leaves and seeds. Their digestive tracts are equipped to obtain maximum nutrition from a high-cellulose diet; they have pouched stomachs, which provide a large surface area for breaking down plant food, and very large intestinal tracts. One of the most noticeable features of colobines is the flamboyant color typical of newborns. For example, in one species dusky gray mothers give birth to brilliant orange babies.[14]

CERCOPITHECINE MONKEYS   The cercopithecine subfamily of monkeys includes more terrestrial species than any other subfamily of Old World monkeys. Many of these species are characterized by a great deal of **sexual dimorphism** (the sexes look very different); the males are larger, have longer canines, and are more aggressive than the females. Cercopithecines depend more on fruit than do colobines. They are also more capable of surviving in arid and seasonal environments.[15] An unusual physical feature of these monkeys is the ischial callosities, or callouses, on their bottoms—an adaptation that enables them to sit comfortably in trees or on the ground for long periods of time.[16]

The Hominoids: Apes and Humans

The **hominoid** group includes three separate families: the lesser apes, or **hylobates** (gibbons and siamangs); the great apes, or **pongids** (orangutans, gorillas, and chimpanzees); and humans, or **hominids**. Several characteristics distinguish the hominoids from the other primates. Their brains are relatively

Grooming is an important activity among Old World primates. Here two macaques groom each other.

A troop of baboons in Kenya spends most of its time on the ground.

large, especially the areas of the cerebral cortex associated with the ability to integrate data. All hominoids have fairly long arms, short, broad trunks, and no tails. The wrist, elbow, and shoulder joints of hominoids allow a greater range of movement than in other primates. Hominoid hands are longer and stronger than those of other primates. Unlike other anthropoids, who move quadrupedally along the ground or along tops of tree branches, hominoids often suspend themselves from below the branches and swing or climb hand over hand from branch to branch.[17] All hominoids, at least occasionally, move bipedally, as we discuss in more detail in the chapter on the first hominids and the emergence of *Homo*.

The dentition of hominoids demonstrates some unique features as well (see Figure 5.3). Hominoid molars are flat and rounded compared to those of other anthropoids, and have what is called a

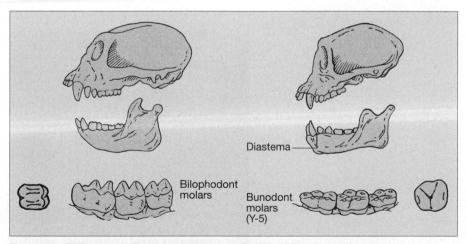

Figure 5.3 Difference in Dentition between an Old World Monkey and an Ape

In Old World monkeys (left), the cusps of the lower molars form two parallel ridges; in apes (right), the five cusps form a Y-shaped pattern. Apes also have a space between the lower canine and first premolar, called a diastema.

Source: Adapted from Noel T. Boaz and Alan J. Almquist, *Essentials of Biological Anthropology* (Upper Saddle River; NJ: Prentice Hall, 1999), p. 164.

"Y-5" pattern on the lower molars—that is, the lower molars have five cusps with a Y-shaped groove opening toward the cheek running between them. Other anthropoids have what is called a **bilophodont** pattern—their molars have two ridges or "loafs" running perpendicular to the cheeks. All hominoids except for humans also have long canine teeth that project beyond the tops of the other teeth, and a corresponding space on the opposite jaw, called a **diastema**, where the canine sits when the jaws are closed. The contact of the upper canine and the lower third premolar creates a sharp cutting edge, in part due to the premolar being elongated to accommodate the canine.[18] These dental features are related to the hominoids' diets, which often include both fibrous plant materials, which can be efficiently cut with sharp canines against elongated premolars, and soft fruits, which can be efficiently chewed with wide, flat molars.

The skeletal and dental features shared by the hominoids point toward their common ancestry. Their blood proteins show many similarities, too. This blood likeness is particularly strong among chimpanzees, gorillas, and humans. For this reason, primatologists think chimpanzees and gorillas are evolutionarily closer to humans than are the lesser apes and orangutans, which probably branched off at some earlier point. We discuss the fossil evidence that supports an early split for the orangutans later in this chapter.

Gibbons and Siamangs   The agile gibbons and their close relatives the siamangs are found in the jungles of Southeast Asia. The gibbons are small, weighing only about 11–15 pounds. The siamangs are somewhat larger, but no more than 25 pounds. Both are mostly fruit-eaters, although they also eat leaves and insects. They are spectacular **brachiators**; their long arms and fingers let them swing hand over hand through the trees.[19] A gibbon can move more than 30 feet in a single forward swing.

Gibbons and siamangs live in small family groups consisting of an adult pair, who appear to mate for life, and one or two immature offspring. When the young reach adulthood, they are driven from home by the adults. There is little sexual dimorphism—males and females do not differ in size or appearance— nor is there any clear pattern of dominance by either sex. These lesser apes are also highly territorial; an adult pair advertises their territory by singing and defends it by chasing others away.[20]

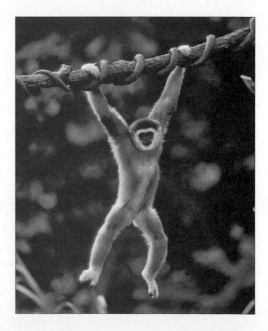

A white-handed gibbon demonstrates its ability as a brachiator.

Orangutans   Orangutans survive only on the islands of Borneo and Sumatra. Unlike gibbons and sia-mangs, they are clearly recognizable as males or females. Males not only weigh almost twice as much as females (up to 200 pounds), but they also have large cheek pads, throat pouches, beards, and long hair.[21] Like gibbons and siamangs, orangutans are primarily fruit-eaters and arboreal. They are the heaviest of the arboreal primates, and perhaps for this reason they move slowly and laboriously through the trees. Orangutans are unusual among the higher primates in that, except for mothers and their young, adults spend much of their time alone.

Gorillas   Gorillas are found in the lowland areas of western equatorial Africa and in the mountain areas of Congo, Uganda, and Rwanda.[22] Unlike the other apes, who are mostly fruit-eaters, gorillas mostly eat other parts of plants—stems, shoots (e.g., bamboo), pith, leaves, roots, and flowers. In many populations fruit-eating is rare; in some, however, fruit is a common part of the diet.[23]

Gorillas are by far the largest of the surviving apes. In their natural habitats, adult males weigh up to 450 pounds and females up to 250 pounds. To support the weight of massive chests, gorillas travel mostly on the ground on all fours in a form of locomotion known as **knuckle walking**: They walk on the thickly padded middle joints of their fingers. As adults, their heavier bodies make climbing more precarious.[24] They sleep on the ground or in tub-shaped nests they make from nonfood plants each time they bed down.[25]

Gorillas tend to live in groups consisting of a dominant male, called a silverback, other adult males, adult females, and immature offspring. Both males and females, when mature, seem to leave the groups into which they were born to join other groups. The dominant male is very much the center of attention; he acts as the main protector of the group and the leader in deciding where the group will go next.[26]

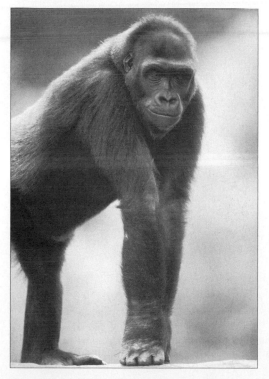

A young gorilla shows how it knuckle-walks. The back feet are flat on the ground, and only the knuckles of the "hands" touch the ground.

Chimpanzees Chimpanzees live in the forested areas of Africa, from Sierra Leone in the west to Tanzania in the east. There are two distinct species of chimpanzee—the common chimpanzee (*Pan troglodytes*) and the bonobo, or pygmy, chimpanzee (*Pan paniscus*). Bonobos tend to be more slender than common chimpanzees, with longer limbs and digits, smaller heads, darker faces, and a distinct part in their hair. Unlike common chimpanzees, bonobos show almost no sexual dimorphism in dentition or skeletal structure. More significant seem to be differences in social behavior. Bonobos are more gregarious than common chimpanzees, and groups tend to be more stable. Groups also tend to be centered around females rather than males.[27]

Although they are primarily fruit-eaters, chimpanzees show many similarities to their close relatives, the gorillas. Both are arboreal and terrestrial. Like gorillas, chimpanzees move best on the ground, and when they want to cover long distances they come down from the trees and move by knuckle walking. Occasionally, they stand and walk upright, usually when they are traveling through tall grass or are trying to see long distances. Chimpanzees sleep in tree nests that they carefully prepare anew, complete with a bunch of leaves as a pillow, each time they bed down.[28]

Chimpanzees (including bonobos) are less sexually dimorphic than the other great apes. Males weigh a little more than 100 pounds on the average, females somewhat less. But males have longer canines.

After three decades of studies at Gombe Park in Tanzania and elsewhere, researchers have found that common chimpanzees not only eat insects, small lizards, and birds, but they also actively hunt and kill larger animals.[29] At Gombe, the red colobus monkey is by far the most often hunted animal. Hunting appears to be undertaken more often during the dry season when food is scarce.[30] Prey is caught mostly by the males, which hunt either alone or in small groups. It is then shared with—or, perhaps more accurately, begged by—as many as 15 other chimpanzees in friendly social gatherings that may last up to nine hours.[31]

A bonobo's slender limbs, dark face, and parted hair are some of the traits that distinguish it from common chimpanzees.

It appears that chimpanzees come together and drift apart depending on circumstances such as the availability of food and the risk of predation.[32] Scholars have recently compared information from nine long-term studies of chimpanzee social organization and behavior, and have come to the conclusion that there are behaviors specific to particular groups. These behaviors, which include customary tool use, grooming, and mating displays, do not appear to be determined by the environment, and hence have been interpreted by some scholars as being cultural.[33]

Hominids   According to the classification we use here, the hominoids we call hominids include only one living species—modern humans. Humans have many distinctive characteristics that set them apart from other anthropoids and other hominoids, which lead many to place humans in a category separate from the pongids. However, others believe that the differences are not so great as to justify a separate hominid category for humans. For example, humans, chimpanzees, and gorillas are very similar in their proteins and DNA. And it is widely agreed that the lines leading to humans, chimpanzees, and gorillas diverged from a common ancestor perhaps 5–6 million years ago.[34]

Distinctive Hominid Traits

We turn now to some of the features that distinguish us—the hominids—from the other primates. Although we like to think of ourselves as unique, many of the traits we discuss here are at the extreme of a continuum that can be traced from the prosimians through the apes.

Physical Traits

Of all the primates, only hominids consistently walk erect on two feet. All other primates require thick, heavy musculature to hold their heads erect; this structure is missing in hominids, for our heads are more or less balanced on top of our spinal columns. A dish-shaped pelvis (peculiar to hominids), a lumbar curve in the spine, straight lower limbs, and arched, nonprehensile feet are all related to **bipedalism**. Because hominids are fully bipedal, we can carry objects without impairing our locomotor efficiency.

Although many primates have an opposable thumb, which enables them to grasp and examine objects, the greater length and flexibility of the hominid thumb allow us to handle objects with greater dexterity. We are capable of both a power grip, to hold large or heavy objects firmly, and a precision grip, to hold small or delicate objects without dropping or breaking them. We also have remarkable hand-eye coordination, as well as a remarkably sophisticated brain.

The hominid brain is large and complex, particularly the **cerebral cortex**, the center of speech and other higher mental activities. The brain of the average adult modern human measures more than 1,300 cubic centimeters, compared with 525 cubic centimeters for the gorilla, the primate with the next largest brain. The frontal areas of the hominid brain are also larger than those of other primates, so that hominids have more prominent foreheads than monkeys or gorillas. Hominids have special areas of the brain that are dedicated to speech and language. The large hominid brain requires an enormous amount of blood, and the way blood is carried to and from the brain is also unique.[35] We'll say more about the hominid brain and its evolution in the chapter on the first hominids and the emergence of *Homo*.

Hominid teeth reflect our completely omnivorous diet, and they are not very specialized, which may reflect the fact that we use tools and cooking to prepare our food. As discussed earlier, other hominoids have long canines and a diastema, whereas hominid canines do not usually project beyond the tops of the other teeth. This allows hominids to move their jaws both vertically and horizontally when chewing;

horizontal movement would be prevented by the long upper canines of the other hominoids. Hominid molars have thicker enamel than the molars of other hominoids, and both horizontal movement and thickened molars may be related to a dietary emphasis on coarse grains and seeds, something we'll discuss further in the chapter on the first hominids and the emergence of *Homo*. The hominid jaw is shaped like a parabolic arch, rather than a U-shape, as in the apes, and is composed of relatively thin bones and light muscles. Modern humans have chins; other primates do not.

One other distinctive hominid trait is the sexuality of hominid females, who may engage in intercourse at any time throughout the year; most other primate females engage in sex only periodically, just around the time they can conceive.[36] Hominids are also unusual among the primates in having female-male bonding.[37]

Why does hominid female sexuality differ from that of most other primates? One suggestion is that more or less continuous female sexuality became selectively advantageous in hominids after female-male bonding developed in conjunction with local groups consisting of at least several adult males and adult females.[38] More specifically, the combination of group living and male-female bonding—a combination unique to hominids among the primates—may have favored a switch from the common higher-primate pattern of periodic female sexuality to the pattern of more or less continuous female sexuality. Such a switch may have been favored in hominids because periodic rather than continuous female sexuality would undermine female-male bonding in multimale-multifemale groups.

Field research on nonhuman primates strongly suggests that males usually attempt to mate with any females ready to mate. If the female (or females) a male was bonded to was not interested in sex at certain times, but other females in the group were, it seems likely that the male would try to mate with those other females. Frequent "extramarital affairs" might jeopardize the male-female bond and thereby presumably reduce the reproductive success of both males and females. Hence natural selection may have favored more or less continuous sexuality in hominid females if hominids already had the combination of group living (and the possibility of "extramarital affairs") and marriage. If bonded adults lived alone, as do gibbons, noncontinuous female sexuality would not threaten bonding, because "extramarital" sex would not be likely to occur. Similarly, seasonal breeding would also pose little threat to male-female bonds, because all females would be sexually active at more or less the same time.[39] So the fact that the combination of group living and male-female bonding occurs only in hominids may explain why continuous female sexuality developed in hominids. The bonobo, or pygmy chimpanzee, female does engage in intercourse throughout the year, but bonobos do not have male-female bonding and the females are not interested in sex quite as often as hominid females.[40]

Behavioral Abilities

In comparison with other primates, a much greater proportion of hominid behavior is learned and culturally patterned. As with many physical traits, we can trace a continuum in the learning abilities of all primates. The great apes, including orangutans, gorillas, and chimpanzees, are probably about equal in learning ability.[41] Old and New World monkeys do much less well in learning tests, and, surprisingly, gibbons perform more poorly than most monkeys.

Toolmaking   The same kind of continuum is evident in inventiveness and toolmaking. There is no evidence that any nonhuman primates except great apes use tools, although several species of monkeys use "weapons"—branches, stones, or fruit dropped onto predators below them on the ground. Chimpanzees both fashion and use tools in the wild. For example, they strip leaves from sticks and then use the sticks to "fish" termites from their mound-shaped nests. They use leaves to mop up termites, to sponge up

Chimps in the wild use tools—in this case, a stone to crack palm nuts. As far as we know, though, they don't use tools to make other tools, as humans do.

water, or to wipe themselves clean. Indeed, tool use varies enough in chimpanzees that primatologist Christophe Boesch has suggested that local chimpanzee groups have cultural differences in terms of the tools they employ.[42]

One example of chimpanzee tool use suggests planning. In Guinea, West Africa, observers watched a number of chimpanzees crack oil palm nuts with two stones. The "platform" stone had a hollow depression; the other stone was used for pounding. The observers assumed that the stones had been brought by the chimpanzees to the palm trees, because no stones like them were nearby and the chimps were observed to leave the pounding stone on top of or near the platform stone when they were finished.[43] Observers in other areas of West Africa have also reported that chimpanzees use stones to crack nuts. In one location in Liberia, an innovative female appeared to have started the practice; it seems to have been imitated within a few months by 13 others who previously showed no interest in the practice.[44]

In captivity, chimpanzees have also been observed to be inventive toolmakers. One mother chimpanzee was seen examining and cleaning her son's teeth, using tools she had fashioned from twigs. She even extracted a baby tooth he was about to lose.[45]

Hominids have usually been considered the only toolmaking animal, but observations such as these call for modification of the definition of toolmaking. If we define toolmaking as adapting a natural object for a specific purpose, then at least some of the great apes are toolmakers too. Perhaps it would be more accurate to say hominids are the only habitual toolmaking animal, just as we say hominids are the only habitual bipedal hominoid, even though the other hominoids all can and do walk bipedally sometimes. As far as we know, though, hominids are unique in their ability to use one tool to make another.

Language   Only modern humans have spoken, symbolic language. But, as with toolmaking abilities, the line between modern human language and the communications of other primates is not as sharp as we once thought. In the wild, vervet monkeys make different alarm calls to warn of different predators. Observers playing tape recordings of these calls found that monkeys responded to them differently, depending on the call. If the monkeys heard an "eagle" call, they looked up; if they heard a "leopard" call, they ran high into the trees.[46]

Common chimpanzees are also communicative, using gestures and many vocalizations in the wild. Researchers have used this "natural talent" to teach chimpanzees symbolic language in experimental settings. In their pioneering work, Beatrice T. Gardner and R. Allen Gardner raised a female chimpanzee named

Washoe and trained her to communicate with startling effectiveness by means of American Sign Language hand gestures.[47] After a year of training, she was able to associate gestures with specific activities. For example, if thirsty, Washoe would make the signal for "give me" followed by the one for "drink." As she learned, the instructions grew more detailed. If all she wanted was water, she would merely signal for "drink." But if she craved soda pop, as she did more and more, she prefaced the drink signal with the sweet signal—a quick touching of the tongue with her fingers. Later, the Gardners had even more success in training four other common chimpanzees, who were taught by fluent deaf users of American Sign Language.[48]

Bonobos have provided strong evidence that they understand simple grammatical "rules," very much like two-year-old humans. Pointing to graphic symbols for different particular meanings, a bonobo named Kanzi regularly communicated sequences of types of symbols; for example, he would point to a symbol for a verb ("bite") and then point to a symbol for an object ("ball," "cherry," "food").[49]

Other Hominid Traits   Although many primates are omnivores, eating insects and small reptiles in addition to plants—some even hunt small mammals—only hominids hunt very large animals. Also, hominids are one of the few primates that are completely terrestrial. We do not even sleep in trees, as many other ground-living primates do. Perhaps our ancestors lost their perches when the forests receded, or cultural advances such as weapons or fire may have eliminated the need to seek nightly shelter in the trees. In addition, we have the longest dependency period of any of the primates, requiring extensive parental care and support for up to 20 years or so.

Finally, hominids are unlike almost all other primates in having a division of labor by gender in food-getting and food sharing in adulthood. Among nonhuman primates, both females and males forage for themselves after infancy. Hominids have more gender-role specialization, perhaps because men, unencumbered by infants and small children, were freer to hunt and chase large animals.

Having examined our distinctive traits, those traits we share with other primates, now we turn to the fossil evidence about primate evolution, from the earliest forms to apes.

The Emergence of Primates

When did the primates first emerge? This question turns out to be hard to answer with the current fossil record. Some paleoanthropologists have suggested that fossil finds from the **Paleocene** epoch, which began about 65 million years ago, are from archaic primates. These are the *plesiadapiforms*. They have been found in both Europe and North America, which in the Paleocene were one landmass. The most well known of the plesiadipiforms is ***Plesiadipis***. This squirrel-like animal had a large snout and large incisors. It also had a large nasal cavity and eye orbits located on the sides of the skull, suggesting a well-developed sense of smell and little or no stereoscopic vision (depth perception). The fingers of *Plesiadipis* had claws, and its hands and feet did not appear to allow for grasping. These features suggest that *Plesiadipis* was not a primate. However, the elbow and ankle joints suggest great mobility, and despite the large incisors the teeth suggest a primate-like omnivorous diet. The structure of their inner ears also resembled that of modern primates. Because it had these primate-like features, some scholars believe that the plesiadipiforms were archaic primates.[50]

Other paleoanthropologists find so few similarities between the plesiadapiforms and later obvious primates that they do not include the plesiadapiforms in the order Primates.[51] There is no dispute, however, about fossils dating from the early **Eocene**, about 55 million years ago. These oldest definite

Shown here is a reconstruction of *Carpolestes simpsoni*, an arboreal creature from the late Paleocene that may be the common ancestor of the primates.

primates appear in two major groups of prosimians—*adapids* and *omomyids*. Because these two kinds of primate are different from each other in major ways, and because they both appeared rather abruptly at the border of the Paleocene and Eocene, there presumably was an earlier common primate ancestor. One strong candidate for the common primate ancestor is *Carpolestes simpsoni*, a mouse-sized arboreal creature from Wyoming dating to about 56 million years ago. **Carpolestes** has an interesting mix of primate and nonprimate characteristics. While it lacks stereoscopic vision, *Carpolestes* has nails instead of claws on its big toes, and it has grasping hands and feet.[52] Not all scholars are convinced that *Caropolestes* is the common ancestor of all primates, and in Figure 5.4 (on page 108) the circled P represents where paleontologist Robert D. Martin placed the common ancestor of primates, in the late Cretaceous.

Now we turn to the conditions that may have favored the emergence of the primates.

The Environment

It is generally agreed that the earliest primate may have emerged by the Paleocene, 65 million to 55 million years ago, and perhaps earlier, in the late **Cretaceous**. The beginning of the Paleocene marked a major geological transition, what geologists call the transition from the Mesozoic to the Cenozoic era. About 75 percent of all animal and plant life that lived in the last part of the Cenozoic (the late Cretaceous) vanished by the early Paleocene. The extinction of the dinosaurs is the most famous of these disappearances.[53]

The climate of the Cretaceous period was almost uniformly damp and mild, but temperatures began falling at the end of the Cretaceous. Around the beginning of the Paleocene epoch, both seasonal and geographic fluctuations in temperature began to develop. The climate became much drier in many areas, and vast swamplands disappeared. The climate of the Paleocene was generally somewhat cooler than in the late Cretaceous, but by no means cold. Forests and savannas thrived in fairly high latitudes. Subtropical climates existed as far north as latitude 62 in Alaska.[54]

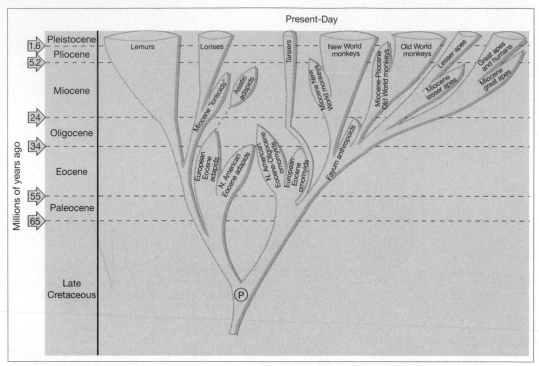

Figure 5.4   A View of the Evolutionary Relationships between Early Primates and Living Primates

This view is adapted from one suggested by R. D. Martin. The primate lineages that do not extend to the present day indicate presumed extinctions. Branching from a common "stalk" suggests divergence from a common ancestor. The circled P represents the unknown common ancestor of all primates.

Sources: From Robert D. Martin, *Primate Origins and Evolution: A Phylogenetic Reconstruction* (Princeton, NJ: Princeton University Press, 1990). The dates for the Paleocene, Eocene, Oligocene, and the beginning of the Miocene are from William A. Berggren, Dennis V. Kent, John D. Obradovich, and Carl C. Swisher III, "Toward a Revised Paleogene Geochronology," in Donald R. Prothero and William A. Berggren, eds., *Eocene-Oligocene Climatic and Biotic Evolution* (Princeton, NJ: Princeton University Press, 1992), pp. 29–45. The dates for the end of the Miocene, Pliocene, and Pleistocene are from Steve Jones, Robert Martin, and David Pilbeam, eds., *The Cambridge Encyclopedia of Human Evolution* (New York: Cambridge University Press, 1992).

One important reason for the very different climates of the past is **continental drift** (Figure 5.5). In the early Cretaceous (ca. 135 million years ago), the continents were clumped into two large landmasses or "supercontinents"—*Laurasia,* which included North America and Eurasia, and *Gondwanaland,* which included Africa, South America, India, Australia, and Antarctica. By the beginning of the Paleocene (ca. 65 million years ago) Gondwanaland had broken apart, with South America drifting west away from Africa, India drifting east, and Australia and Antarctica drifting south. As the continents changed position, they moved into locations with different climatic conditions. More importantly, the movement of the continents affected the global climate.[55]

With changes in climate come changes in vegetation. Although the first deciduous trees (that lose their leaves in winter) and flowering plants (called *angiosperms*) arose during the Cretaceous, it was during the late Paleocene and early Eocene that large trees with large fruits and seeds became common.[56] Although some mammals date from the Cretaceous, the Paleocene saw the evolution and diversification of many different types of mammals probably as a result of the expansion and diversification of

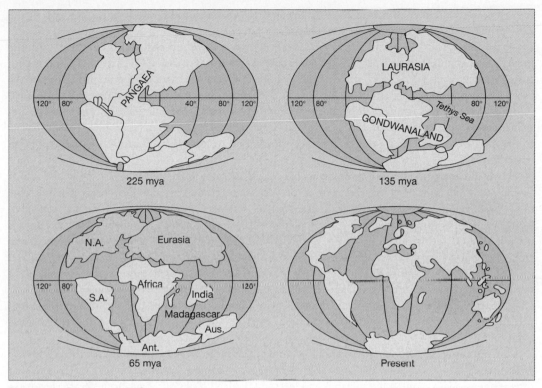

Figure 5.5   Continental Drift

The supercontinent Pangea split into Laurasia and Gondwanaland 135 million years ago (mya). These further divided into the continents as we know them today.

Source: Noel T. Boaz and Alan J. Almquist, *Biological Anthropology: A Synthetic Approach to Human Evolution* (Upper Saddle River, NJ: Prentice Hall, 1997).

deciduous trees and flowering plants. Indeed, primate paleontologists think primates evolved from the **insectivore** order of mammals, including modern shrews and moles, that is adapted to eating insects—insects that would have lived off the new deciduous trees and flowering plants. The insectivores were very adaptable and were able to take advantage of many different habitats—under the ground, in water, on the ground, and above the ground, including the woody habitat of bushes, shrubs, vines, and trees. It was the last kind of adaptation, above the ground, that may have been the most important for primate evolution. The woody habitat had been exploited only partially in earlier periods. But then several different kinds, or taxa, of small animals, one of which may have been the archaic primate, began to take advantage of the woody habitat.

What in Particular May Have Favored the Emergence of Primates?

The traditional explanation of primate origins suggests that the primates evolved from insectivores that took to the trees (*arboreal* life). Different paleoanthropologists emphasized different possible adaptations to life in the trees. In 1912, G. Elliot Smith suggested that taking to the trees favored vision over smell. Vision would be more useful in an animal that searched for food in the maze of tree branches. With smaller snouts and the declining importance of the sense of smell, the eyes of the early primates would have come to face forward. In 1916, Frederic Wood Jones emphasized changes in the hand and foot. He thought that tree climbing would favor grasping hands and feet, with the hind limbs becoming more specialized for support and propulsion. In 1921, Treacher Collins suggested that the eyes of the early primates came to face forward not just because the snout got smaller. Rather, he thought that three-dimensional binocular vision would be favored because an animal jumping from branch to branch would be more likely to survive if it could accurately judge distances across open space.[57] In 1968, Frederick Szalay suggested that a shift in diet—from insects to seeds, fruits, and leaves—might have been important in the differentiation of primates from insectivores.[58]

Arboreal theory still has some proponents, but Matt Cartmill highlighted some crucial weaknesses.[59] Living mammals that dwell in trees seem to do very well without primate-like characteristics. One of the best examples, Cartmill says, is the tree squirrel. Its eyes are not front-facing, its sense of smell is not reduced in comparison with other rodents, it has claws rather than nails, and it lacks an opposable thumb. Yet these squirrels are very successful in trees. They can leap accurately from tree to tree, they can walk over or under small branches, they can go up and down vertical surfaces, and they can even hang from their hind legs to get food below them. Furthermore, other animals have some primate traits but do not live in trees or do not move around in trees as primates do. For example, carnivores, such as cats, hawks, and owls, have forward-facing eyes, and the chameleon, a reptile, and some Australian marsupial mammals that prey on insects in bushes and shrubs have grasping hands and feet.

Cartmill thinks that some factor other than moving about in trees may account for the emergence of the primates. He proposes that the early primates may have been basically insect-eaters, and that three-dimensional vision, grasping hands and feet, and reduced claws may have been selectively advantageous for hunting insects on the slender vines and branches that filled the undergrowth of tropical forests. Three-dimensional vision would allow the insect hunter to gauge the prey's distance accurately. Grasping feet would allow the predator to move quietly up narrow supports to reach the prey, which could then be grabbed with the hands. Claws, Cartmill argues, would make it difficult to grasp very slender branches. And the sense of smell would have become reduced, not so much because it was no longer useful, but because the location of the eyes at the front of the face would leave less room for a snout. (See the feature box titled "Cartmill Reexamines His Theory of Primate Origins" for a discussion of Cartmill's recent revision in response to criticisms.)

Robert Sussman's theory builds on Cartmill's *visual predation theory* and on Szalay's idea about a dietary shift.[60] Sussman accepts Cartmill's point that the early primates were likely to eat and move about mostly on small branches, not on large trunks and branches (as do squirrels). If they did, grasping hands and feet and nails rather than claws (as squirrels have) would have been advantageous. Sussman also accepts Szalay's point that the early primates probably ate the new types of plant foods (flowers, seeds, and fruits) that were beginning to become abundant, as flowering trees and plants spread throughout the world. But Sussman asks an important question: If the early primates ate mostly plant foods rather than quick-moving insects, why did they become more reliant on vision than on smell? Sussman suggests it was because the early primates were probably nocturnal (as many prosimians still are): If they were to locate and manipulate small food items at the ends of slender branches in dim light, they would need improved vision.

We still have very little fossil evidence of the earliest primates. *Carpolestes* suggests that grasping hands and feet evolved first, sometime in the late Paleocene, and stereoscopic vision evolved somewhat later. When more fossils become available, we may be better able to evaluate the various explanations that have been suggested for the emergence of primates.

CARTMILL REEXAMINES HIS THEORY OF PRIMATE ORIGINS

Matt Cartmill originally conceived his visual predation theory to explain primate origins because he thought that the arboreal theory did not explain enough. Cartmill's theory attracted some criticism.

One criticism, by J. Allman, is that if visual predation is such an important predictor of forward-facing eyes, then why don't some visual predators have such eyes? Cats and owls have forward-facing eyes, but mongooses and robins do not. A second criticism, by Paul Garber, is that if claws were disadvantageous for moving on slender branches, why does at least one small primate—the Panamanian tamarin—feed on insects among small twigs and vines but have claws on four of its five digits? And Robert Sussman pointed out that most small nocturnal prosimians eat more fruit than insects. Sussman suggests that the need for precise finger manipulation to grasp small fruits and flowers at the ends of small branches, while hanging on by the hind feet, might favor both clawless digits and grasping extremities.

How did he respond? Cartmill acknowledged these problems and responded to them by revising his theory. He also suggested how new research could test some of the implications of his revisions.

In regard to the problem of forward-facing eyes, Cartmill says that Allman's own research suggests a solution: namely, that forward-facing eyes are advantageous for seeing something in front more clearly in dim light. Daytime predators have eye pupils that constrict to see ahead more clearly, so fully forward-facing eyes are not necessary for daytime predation. Nocturnal predators relying on sight are more likely to have forward-facing eyes because constricting pupils would be disadvantageous at night. So Cartmill now believes that the earliest primates were probably nocturnal. And he now thinks that they also probably ate fruit (in addition to insects), as Sussman suggests, just as many contemporary nocturnal prosimians do. If they ate fruit and insects at the ends of small branches and twigs, claws may have been disadvantageous. The Panamanian tamarin is not a case to the contrary; it has claws, to be sure, but it also eats tree gum on the tree trunks to which it clings, using its claws as a tree squirrel does.

Cartmill thinks that his modified theory explains the changes in primate vision better than Sussman's theory. For example, how can we explain stereoscopic, forward-facing eyes in the early primates? Sussman says that the early primates were fruit-eaters, but Cartmill points out that, although stereoscopic, forward-facing eyes are not necessary for getting nonmoving fruit. Rather, forward-facing eyes might be essential for catching insects.

Cartmill suggests how future research on other arboreal mammals may help us answer some of the remaining questions about the origins of primates. Arboreal marsupials, for instance, tend to have grasping hind feet with clawless divergent first toes, and many have reduced claws on some other toes and fingers. The eyes of arboreal marsupials are also somewhat convergent (not as much, of course, as the eyes of primates). One genus of marsupial, an opossum in South America (*Caluromys*), has many additional primate-like features, including a relatively large brain, more forward-facing eyes, a short snout, and a small number of offspring at one time. Studies by Tab Rasmussen suggest that *Caluromys* fits both Cartmill's and Sussman's theories because it eats fruit on terminal branches and catches insect prey with its hands. More field research on marsupials and other animals with some primate-like habits or features could tell us a lot more. So would new fossil finds.

Sources: Matt Cartmill, "Explaining Primate Origins." In Peter N. Peregrine, Carol R. Ember, and Melvin Ember, eds., *Physical Anthropology: Original Readings in Method and Practice* (Upper Saddle River, NJ: Prentice Hall, 2002), pp. 42–52, also in Carol R. Ember, Melvin Ember, and Peter N. Peregrine eds., *Research Frontiers in New Directions in Anthropology* (Upper Saddle River, NJ: Prentice Hall, CD-ROM, 2004); Matt Cartmill, "New Views on Primate Origins," *Evolutionary Anthropology,* 1 (1992): 105–11; Robert Sussman, "Primate Origins and the Evolution of Angiosperms," *American Journal of Primatology,* 23 (1991): 209–23; D. Tab Rasmussen, "Primate Origins: Lessons from a Neotropical Marsupial," *American Journal of Primatology,* 22 (1990): 263–77.

Early Eocene Primates: Omomyids and Adapids

Two groups of prosimians appear in the early Eocene. One group, called **omomyids**, had many tarsier-like features; the other group, **adapids**, had many lemur-like features. The omomyids were very small, no bigger than squirrels; the adapids were cat-sized.

Omomyids are considered tarsier-like because of their large eyes, long tarsal bones, and very small size. The large eyes suggest that they were active at night; the smaller-sized omomyids may have been insect-eaters and the larger ones may have relied more on fruit.[61] Most of the omomyids had dental formulas characteristic of modern prosimians: two incisors and three premolars on each side of the lower jaw rather than the three incisors and four premolars of early mammals.[62] The importance of vision is apparent in a fossilized skull of the Eocene omomyid *Tetonius.* Imprints in the skull show that the brain had large occipital and temporal lobes, the regions associated with perception and the integration of visual memory.[63]

The lemur-like adapids were more active during the day and relied more on leaf and fruit vegetation. In contrast to the omomyids, adapid remains show considerable sexual dimorphism in the canines. And they retain the four premolars characteristic of earlier mammals (although with fewer incisors).[64] One adapid known from its abundant fossil finds is *Notharctus.* It had a small, broad face with full stereoscopic vision and a reduced muzzle. It appears to have lived in the forest and had long, powerful hind legs for leaping from tree to tree.[65]

There was a great deal of diversity among all mammals during the Eocene epoch, and the primates were no exception. Evolution seems to have proceeded rapidly during those years. Both the omomyids and adapids had a few features that suggest links between them and the anthropoids that appear later, in the Oligocene, but there is no agreement that either group gave rise to the anthropoids.[66] Although the omomyids had some resemblances to modern tarsiers and the adapids had some resemblances to lemurs and lorises, paleoanthropologists are not sure that either group was ancestral to modern prosimians. But it is generally thought that the populations ancestral to lemurs and lorises as well as tarsiers did emerge in the Eocene or even earlier, in the late Paleocene.[67]

The Emergence of Anthropoids

The anthropoids of today—monkeys, apes, and humans—are the most successful living primates and include well over 150 species. Unfortunately, the fossil record documenting the emergence of the anthropoids is extremely spotty, and there is no clear fossil record of the Old World forms (the catarrhines) in the two areas where they are most abundant today—the rain forests of sub-Saharan Africa and Southeast Asia.[68] Some paleoanthropologists think that recent Eocene primate finds from China, Southeast Asia, and Algeria have anthropoid affinities, but there is no clear agreement on their evolutionary status.[69]

Undisputed remains of early anthropoids date from a somewhat later period, the late Eocene and early Oligocene, about 34 million years ago, in the **Fayum** area, southwest of Cairo, Egypt. One of the earliest fossil primates at Fayum is *Catopithecus,* dating to around 35 million years ago. Several recent finds have made it one of the best-known late Eocene primates. *Catopithecus* was about the size of a modern marmoset or squirrel monkey. Its dentition suggests a mixed diet of fruit and insects. Its eyes were small, suggesting it was active during the day (diurnal). The few skeletal remains of *Catopithecus* suggest it was an agile arboreal quadruped. It may be the best candidate for the earliest anthropoid, though how it was related to other primates is still debated.[70]

Oligocene Anthropoids

The Fayum is an uninviting area of desert, but it has yielded a remarkable array of early anthropoid fossils. During the **Oligocene** epoch, 34 million to 24 million years ago, the Fayum was a tropical rain forest very close to the shores of the Mediterranean Sea. The area had a warm climate, and it contained many rivers and lakes. The Fayum, in fact, was far more inviting than the northern continents then, for the climates of both North America and Eurasia were beginning to cool during the Oligocene. The general cooling seems to have resulted in the virtual disappearance of primates from the northern areas, at least for a time.

Oligocene anthropoids from the Fayum are grouped into two main types: the monkey-like **parapithecids** and the ape-like **propliopithecids**. Dating from 35 million to 31 million years ago, the parapithecids and the propliopithecids had enough features to be unquestionably classified as anthropoids.

Parapithecids   The monkey-like parapithecids had three premolars (in each quarter), as do most prosimians and the New World monkeys. They were similar to modern anthropoids, with a bony partition behind the eye sockets, broad incisors, projecting canines, and low, rounded cusps on their molars. But they had prosimian-like premolars and relatively small brains. The parapithecids were small, generally weighing under 3 pounds, and resembled the squirrel monkeys living now in South and Central America.[71] Their relatively small eye sockets suggest that they were not nocturnal. Their teeth suggest that they ate mostly fruits and seeds. Locomotion is best known from one of the parapithecids, *Apidium,* an arboreal quadruped that also did a considerable amount of leaping.[72] The parapithecids are the earliest definite anthropoid group, and although there is still disagreement among paleoanthropologists, most believe that the emergence of the anthropoids preceded the split between the New World monkeys (platyrrhines) and the Old World monkeys (catarrhines).[73]

That parapithecids may be ancestral to New World monkeys (platyrrhines) raises an interesting puzzle in primate evolution: the origin of the New World monkeys. Anthropoidal primates such as

Shown here is a reconstruction of what two Oligocene primates might have looked like. In the foreground is a group of *Aegyptopithecus*; in the background are two individuals of *Apidium*. Some of the fauna that shared the Fayum region with these early primates are also shown.

Dolichocebus, a small fruit-eating monkey similar to the modern squirrel monkey,[74] appear suddenly and without any apparent ancestors in South America around 25 million years ago. Since the parapithecids predate the appearance of anthropoids in South America, and resemble them in many ways, it seems reasonable to view them as part of the population ancestral to the New World monkeys.[75]

But how did anthropoidal primates get from Africa to South America? Although the continents were closer together in the late Oligocene, when primates first appear in South America, at least 3,000 kilometers separated South America and Africa. An extended continental shelf and islands created by lower sea levels in the late Oligocene may have made it possible to "island-hop" from Africa to South America over ocean stretches as short as 200 kilometers, but that is still a long distance for an arboreal primate.

Going from Africa to Europe and North America, which were still joined in the late Oligocene, is not a likely route either. North America and South America were not joined until some 5 million years ago, so even if the ancestors of the New World monkeys made it to North America, they would still have needed to make a long ocean crossing to reach South America. One suggestion is that the ancestors of the New World monkeys "rafted" across the Atlantic on large mats of vegetation. Such "rafts," of matted plants, roots, and soil, break away from the mouths of major rivers today, and they can be quite large. It seems an unlikely scenario, but many scholars believe such drifting vegetation must have been the means of bringing anthropoids to South America.[76]

Propliopithecids   The other type of anthropoid found in the Fayum, the propliopithecids, had the dental formula of modern catarrhines. This trait clearly places the propliopithecids with the catarrhines.[77] In contrast with the parapithecids, which had three premolars (in each quarter of the jaw), the propliopithecids had only two premolars, as do modern apes, humans, and Old World monkeys. Propliopithecids shared with the parapithecids the anthropoid dental characteristics of broad lower incisors, projecting canines, and lower molars with low, rounded cusps. And, like parapithecids, propliopithecids had a bony partition behind the eye socket.

Aegyptopithecus, the best-known propliopithecid, probably moved around quadrupedally in the trees, and weighed about 13 pounds. Its molars were low with large cusps, and it had relatively large incisors, suggesting that *Aegyptopithecus* ate mostly fruit. Its eyes were relatively small, and thus it was probably active during the day. It had a long muzzle and a relatively small brain. Endocasts of the brain cavity suggest *Aegyptopithecus* had a relatively large area of the brain dedicated to vision and a relatively small area dedicated to smell. The skulls of *Aegyptopithecus* show considerable sexual dimorphism, and individuals also changed dramatically as they aged, developing bony ridges along the top and across the back of the

Shown here is the fossil skull of an *Aegyptopithecus* from the Fayum. Its dentition, its small, bony eye sockets, and its relatively large brain make it an unambiguous ancestor of Old World monkeys and apes.

skull, much like modern great apes. Although its teeth, jaws, and some aspects of the skull were ape-like, the rest of *Aegyptopithecus's* skeleton was monkey-like,[78] and they are classified by most scholars as primitive catarrhines. Because the propliopithecids lack the specialized characteristics of living Old World monkeys and apes (catarrhines), but share the dental formula of the catarrhines, some paleoanthropologists think that the propliopithecids included the ancestor of both the Old World monkeys and the hominoids (apes and humans).[79]

The Miocene Anthropoids

During the **Miocene** epoch, 24 million to 5.2 million years ago, monkeys and apes clearly diverged in appearance, and numerous kinds of apes appeared in Europe, Asia, and Africa. In the early Miocene, the temperatures were considerably warmer than in the Oligocene. From early to late Miocene, conditions became drier, particularly in East Africa. By about 18 million years ago, Africa came into contact with Eurasia, ending the moderating effect that the Tethys Sea, which separated Africa from Eurasia, had on the climates of both continents. The contact of Africa and, more significantly, India with the Eurasian continent also initiated mountain building, changing established weather patterns. The overall effect was that southern Eurasia and eastern Africa became considerably drier than they had been. Once again, these changes appear to have significantly influenced primate evolution.

We can infer that late in the Miocene, between about 8 million and 5 million years ago, the direct ancestor of humans—the first hominid—may have emerged in Africa. The inference about where hominids emerged is based on the fact that undisputed hominids lived in East Africa after about 5 million years ago. The inference about when hominids emerged is based not as much on fossil evidence as it is on comparative molecular and biochemical analyses of modern apes and humans. As we will see in the next chapter, the effect of a drier climate and the creation of more open, grassland environments may have directly influenced the evolution of the hominids.

One of the Miocene apes (known or unknown) was ancestral to hominids, so our discussion here deals mostly with the *proto-apes*—anthropoids with some ape-like characteristics—of the early Miocene and the definite apes of the middle and late Miocene. We know relatively little about monkeys and prosimians in the early Miocene because monkey fossils are rare from this time period. The situation is different for the middle and late Miocene: Old World monkey fossils become much more abundant than ape fossils.[80] As for prosimians, fossils from the Miocene are scarce, but we know that at least some adapids survived into the middle Miocene in India and the late Miocene in China.[81] Some loris-like prosimians appear in East Africa, Pakistan, and India during the Miocene.[82]

Early Miocene Proto-Apes

Most of the fossils from the early Miocene are described as proto-apes. They have been found mostly in Africa. The best-known genus is ***Proconsul***, found in sites in Kenya and Uganda that are about 20 million years old.[83]

All of the various *Proconsul* species that have been found were much bigger than any of the anthropoids of the Oligocene, ranging from about the size of a gibbon to that of a female gorilla.[84] They lacked a tail. That lack is one of the most definitive features of hominoids, and most paleoanthropologists now agree that *Proconsul* was definitely hominoid, but quite unlike any ape living today. Modern hominoids have many anatomical features of the shoulder, elbow, wrists, and fingers that are adapted for locomotion by suspension (brachiation). Suspension was apparently not *Proconsul's* method of getting around.

Its elbows, wrists, and fingers may have permitted brachiation,[85] but, like the Oligocene anthropoids, *Proconsul* was primarily an arboreal quadruped (see Figure 5.6). Some of the larger forms may have sometimes moved on the ground. Judging by teeth, most *Proconsul* species appear to have been fruit-eaters, but larger species may have also consumed leaves.[86]

Some recent finds from East Africa suggest that other types of proto-ape were also on the scene in the early Miocene. But these other finds are fragmentary and not clearly classifiable. *Proconsul* may or may not have been ancestral to later apes and humans, but given its combination of monkey-like and ape-like features, it may have looked a lot like the common ancestor of apes and humans.

Middle Miocene Apes

The first definitely ape-like finds come from the middle Miocene, 16 million to 10 million years ago. The oldest, dating to about 13 million years ago, is **Pierolapithecus**, and was recently found near Barcelona, Spain.[87] Another hominoid, **Kenyapithecus**, was found on Maboko Island and nearby locations in Kenya.[88]

Both *Pierolapithecus* and *Kenyapithecus* have many of *Proconsul's* features, but have teeth and faces that resemble those of more modern hominoids. And, in contrast to *Proconsul, Kenyapithecus* was probably more terrestrial. It also had very thickly enameled teeth and robust jaws, suggesting a diet of hard, tough foods, or possibly a great deal of grit in the food because *Kenyapithecus* lived mostly on the ground. Whether *Kenyapithecus* is ancestral to the later apes and humans is something of a puzzle because its limbs do not show the capacity for brachiation that is characteristic of all the later apes.[89] *Pierolapithecus,* however, has wrists and vertebrae that would have made it capable of brachiation, but also has relatively short fingers like modern monkeys. *Pierolapithecus* probably spent most of its time in trees, walking along larger branches as monkeys do, and also brachiating among smaller branches, as apes do.[90] Thus, *Pierolapithecus* is a good candidate for the ancestor of later forest-dwelling apes.

Figure 5.6 The Forelimbs and Hindlimbs of *Proconsul africanus*

These forelimbs and hind limbs (dating from about 20 million years ago) are about the same length, suggesting that *Proconsul africanus* moved on all fours on the tops of branches. *Proconsul africanus* was the smallest of the *Proconsul* species, weighing about 22 to 26 pounds.

Source: R. Ciochon and R. Corruccini, eds., *New Interpretation of Ape and Human Ancestry.* Copyright © 1983. Reprinted by permission of Springer Science and Business Media.

Late Miocene Apes

From the end of the middle Miocene into the late Miocene, the apes diversified and moved into many areas. Fossils are abundant in Europe and Asia, less so in Africa. This does not mean that apes were more numerous than monkeys. In fact, the fossil record suggests that monkeys in the Old World became more numerous than apes toward the end of the Miocene, and this trend continues to the present day.

One well-known late Miocene ape from Europe is *Oreopithecus,* which dates from about 8 million years ago. Despite being well represented by fossils, including nearly complete ones preserved in beds of hard coal, its classification is enigmatic. *Oreopithecus* was clearly adapted to life in thickly forested marshlands. It had extremely long arms and hands and mobile joints, and was likely an agile brachiator. Its dentition suggests it had a diet that consisted mostly of leaves. However, the dentition and skull of *Oreopithecus* also had a number of unique features that suggest affinity to some Old World monkeys. *Oreopithecus* had an ape-like body and a monkey-like head. Because of its suspensory locomotion and other ape-like features, most scholars today consider it an early, albeit specialized, ape.[91]

Most paleoanthropologists divide the later Miocene apes into at least two main groups: the sivapithecids, represented primarily by the genus *Sivapithecus* and found primarily in western and southern Asia, and the dryopithecids, represented primarily by the genus *Dryopithecus* and found primarily in Europe.

Sivapithecids   At one time ***Sivapithecus***, which dates from roughly 13 million to 8 million years ago, was thought to be ancestral to hominids. It had flat and thickly enameled molars, smaller canines, and less sexual dimorphism than other Miocene apes, and in some reconstructions (now considered faulty) had a parabolic dental arcade—all hominid features. It also lived in a mixed woodland-grassland environment, and the wear on its teeth suggested a diet of coarse grasses and seeds, much like the diet of the later early hominids. However, as more fossil material was uncovered, scholars recognized that *Sivapithecus* was remarkably similar to the modern orangutan in the face, and it is now thought to be ancestral to the orangutan.[92]

Dryopithecids   ***Dryopithecus***, which appears about 15 million years ago, was a chimpanzee-sized ape that lived in the forests of Eurasia. It was mainly arboreal and apparently omnivorous. *Dryopithecus* had thinner tooth enamel than *Sivapithecus,* lighter jaws, and pointed molar cusps. In the palate, jaw, and midface, *Dryopithecus* looked like the African apes and humans. In contrast to later hominoids, however, *Dryopithecus* had a very short face and a relatively small brow ridge.[93]

The reconstructed skull of a *Dryopithecus* strongly resembles that of modern African apes.

The fingers and elbows of *Dryopithecus* and *Sivapithecus* suggest that they were much more capable of suspending themselves than were earlier hominoids. *Sivapithecus* may have moved about more on the ground than *Dryopithecus,* but both were probably mostly arboreal.[94] Indeed, recent finds of *Dryopithecus* hand, arm, shoulder, and leg bones strongly suggest that *Dryopithecus* was highly efficient at suspensory locomotion and probably moved through the trees like modern orangutans do.

It is still very difficult to identify the particular evolutionary lines leading from the Miocene apes to modern apes and humans. Only the orangutans have been linked to a late Miocene ape genus, *Sivapithecus,* so presumably that lineage continued into modern times.[95] *Dryopithecus* disappears from the fossil record after about 10 million years ago, leaving no descendants, perhaps because less rainfall and more seasonality reduced the forests where they lived.[96]

The Divergence of Hominids from the Other Hominoids

The later Miocene apes are best known from Europe and Asia. Until recently there has been an almost complete lack of African fossil hominoids dating between 13.5 million and 5 million years ago.[97] Recently, two species, *Orrorin tugenensis,* from Kenya and dated to about 6 million years ago, and *Sahelanthropus tchadensis,* from Chad and dated to perhaps 7 million years ago, have provided a glimpse of hominoid evolution during this time period, which we discuss in the next chapter. Still, this scarcity of fossils from 13.5 to 5 million years ago is unfortunate for our understanding of human evolution because the earliest unambiguous bipedal primates (hominids) appear in Africa near the beginning of the Pliocene, after 5 million years ago. To understand the evolutionary links between the apes of the Miocene and the hominids of Africa, we need more fossil evidence from late Miocene times in Africa.

However, we do have some idea about the transition to hominids beyond the few fossil remains. The molecular biology of the various modern primates suggests when the last common ancestor of humans and our closest primate relatives, chimpanzees, probably lived.

The Molecular Clock

In 1966, on the basis of biochemical comparisons of blood proteins in the different surviving primates, Vincent Sarich and Allan Wilson estimated that gibbons diverged from the other hominoids about 12 million years ago, orangutans 10 million years ago, and the other apes (gorillas and chimps) from hominids only 4.5 million years ago. These estimates depended on the assumption that the more similar in chemistry the blood proteins of different primates are—for instance, comparing chimpanzees and humans—the closer those primates are in evolutionary time. In other words, the more similar the blood proteins of related species, the more recently they diverged.[98]

But knowing that species are close molecularly does not translate into evolutionary time unless it is assumed that molecular changes occur at a constant rate. After all, a reliable "molecular clock" should not slow down or speed up from one period of time to another. To maximize the likelihood of molecular change at a constant rate, researchers try to examine molecular characteristics that are probably neutral in terms of adaptation. (Natural selection can speed up the rate of molecular change in the case of a characteristic that is very advantageous or very disadvantageous.) The rate of change in a neutral characteristic is calculated from the time of some divergence that is absolutely dated. For example, if we know that two lineages split 20 million years ago, and we know the degree of molecular difference between a contemporary representative of each, we can estimate the rate of change that produced that degree of difference. Given such an estimated rate of change (in a particular characteristic), we can estimate the amount of time that has elapsed since other pairs of related species diverged from each other.[99]

Subsequent comparative studies of the living primates have employed a variety of techniques, including comparisons of amino acid sequences, chromosomal structures, and the degree of matching of DNA strands from different species.[100] These studies have confirmed the probable recency of the hominid divergence from chimpanzees and gorillas. Although the different techniques yield slightly different estimates, the results are not that divergent. Most of the recent comparisons place the split somewhat earlier than the Sarich and Wilson estimates, but not by much. The common ancestor of chimpanzees and hominids is estimated to have lived 5 million to 6 million years ago, the common ancestor of gorillas and hominids a little further back.[101]

So what does the fossil evidence tell us about where and when hominids first emerged? *Sahelanthropus tchadensis* and *Orrorin tugenensis* appear to support the molecular data. Both show mixed hominid and hominoid traits, both are from Africa, and both date to 6–7 million years ago. We turn to the early hominids in the next chapter.

Summary

1. Although no living primate can be a direct ancestor of humans, we do share a common evolutionary history with the other surviving primates. Studying the behavioral and anatomical features of our closest living relatives may help us make inferences about primate evolution. Studying distinctive human traits may help us understand why the line of primates that led to humans branched away from the line leading to chimpanzees and gorillas.

2. No one trait is unique to primates. However, primates do share the following features: two bones in the lower part of the leg and in the forearm, a collarbone, flexible prehensile (grasping) hands, stereoscopic vision, a relatively large brain, only one (or sometimes two) offspring at a time, long maturation of the young, and a high degree of dependence on social life and learning.

3. The order Primates is divided into two suborders: the prosimians and the anthropoids. Compared with the anthropoids, prosimians depend more on smell for information. They have mobile ears, whiskers, longer snouts typically, and relatively fixed facial expressions. Anthropoids have rounded braincases; reduced, nonmobile outer ears; and relatively small, flat faces instead of muzzles. They have highly dextrous hands.

4. The anthropoid order is divided into two main groups: platyrrhines (monkeys of the New World) and catarrhines. The catarrhines are subdivided into cercopithecoids (Old World monkeys) and hominoids (apes and humans). The anthropoid apes consist of the hylobates, or lesser apes (gibbons and siamangs), and the pongids, or great apes (orangutans, gorillas, and chimpanzees).

5. Along with the gorilla, the chimpanzee has proteins and DNA remarkably similar to those of humans, as well as anatomical and behavioral similarities to humans. Wild chimpanzees have been seen to create and use tools, modifying a natural object to fulfill a specific purpose. High conceptual ability is also demonstrated by both the chimpanzee's and the gorilla's facility in learning sign language.

6. The differences between hominids and the other anthropoids show us what makes humans distinctive as a species. Hominids are totally bipedal; they walk on two legs and do not need the arms for locomotion. The hominid brain, particularly the cerebral cortex, is the largest and most complex. Hominid offspring have a proportionately longer dependency stage. And in comparison with other primates, more hominid behavior is learned and culturally patterned. Spoken, symbolic language and the use of tools to make other tools are uniquely modern human behavioral traits. Hominids also generally have a division of labor in food-getting and food sharing in adulthood.

7. The surviving primates are thought to be descendants of small, originally terrestrial insectivores (the order, or major grouping, of mammals, including modern shrews and moles, that is adapted to feeding on insects). However, exactly who the common ancestor was and when it emerged are not yet known.

8. The earliest definite primate fossils date from the early Eocene, about 55 million years ago. They are classified into two major groups of prosimians—adapids and omomyids. These two kinds of primates have major differences so their common ancestor would have had to emerge earlier, probably in the Paleocene.

9. The traditional view of primate evolution was that arboreal (tree) life would have favored many of the common primate features, including distinctive dentition, greater reliance on vision over smell, three-dimensional binocular vision, and grasping hands and feet. A second theory proposes that some of the distinctive primate characteristics were selectively advantageous for hunting insects on the slender vines and branches that filled the undergrowth of forests. A third theory suggests that the distinctive features of primates (including reliance more on vision than on smell) were favored because the early primates were nocturnal and ate flowers, fruits, and seeds, which they had to locate on slender branches in dim light.

10. Undisputed remains of early anthropoids unearthed in Egypt date from the early Oligocene (after 34 million years ago). They include the monkey-like parapithecids and the propliopithecids with ape-like teeth.

11. During the Miocene epoch (24 million to 5.2 million years ago), monkeys and apes clearly diverged in appearance, and numerous kinds of apes appeared in Europe, Asia, and Africa. Most of the fossils from the early Miocene are described as proto-apes. From the end of the middle Miocene into the late Miocene, the apes diversified and spread geographically. Most paleoanthropologists divide the later Miocene apes into at least two main groups: dryopithecids, found primarily in Europe, and sivapithecids, found primarily in western and southern Asia.

12. The fossil record does not tell us much about the first hominids, but biochemical and genetic analyses of modern apes and humans suggest that the hominid-ape split occurred during the late Miocene (after about 6 million years ago). Because undisputed hominids lived in East Africa after about 4 million years ago, the first hominid probably emerged in Africa.

Glossary Terms

adapid (p. 112)
Aegyptopithecus (p. 114)
anthropoids (p. 96)
arboreal (p. 92)
bilophodont (p. 100)
bipedalism (p. 103)
brachiators (p. 100)
canines (p. 92)
Carpolestes (p. 107)
catarrhines (p. 96)
cercopithecoids (p. 98)

cerebral cortex (p. 103)
continental drift (p. 108)
Cretaceous (p. 107)
diastema (p. 100)
diurnal (p. 94)
Dryopithecus (p. 117)
Eocene (p. 106)
Fayum (p. 112)
hominids (p. 98)
hominoids (p. 98)
hylobates (p. 98)

incisors (p. 92)

insectivore (p. 109)

Kenyapithecus (p. 116)

knuckle walking (p. 101)

Miocene (p. 115)

molars (p. 92)

nocturnal (p. 95)

Oligocene (p. 113)

omnivorous (p. 92)

omomyid (p. 112)

opposable thumb (p. 93)

Paleocene (p. 106)

Parapithecids (p. 113)

Pierolapithecus (p. 116)

platyrrhines (p. 96)

Plesiadipis (p. 106)

pongids (p. 98)

prehensile (p. 97)

premolars (p. 92)

Proconsul (p. 115)

propliopithecids (p. 113)

prosimians (p. 94)

quadrupeds (p. 94)

sexual dimorphism (p. 98)

Sivapithecus (p. 117)

terrestrial (p. 98)

vertical clinging and leaping (p. 95)

"Y-5" pattern (p. 100)

Critical Questions

1. How could you infer that a fossil primate lived in the trees?

2. Under what conditions would the ability to communicate be adaptive?

3. We like to think of the human lineage as biologically unique, which of course it is (like all evolutionary lineages). But some paleoanthropologists say that humans, chimpanzees, and gorillas are so similar that all three should be grouped as hominids. What do you think, and why do you think so?

CHAPTER 6

THE FIRST HOMINIDS
AND THE EMERGENCE OF HOMO

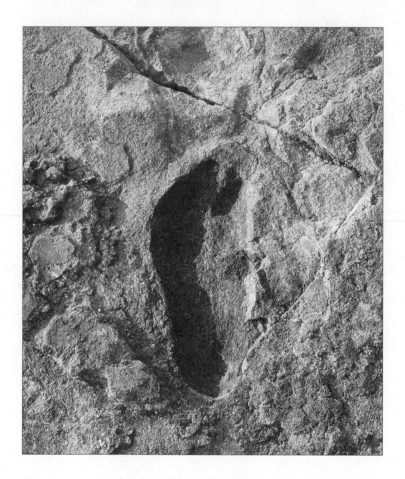

Chapter Outline

- The Evolution of Bipedal Locomotion
- The Transition from Hominoids to Hominids
- *Australopithecus:* The First Definite Hominid

- Early Hominid Tools and Lifestyles
- Trends in Hominid Evolution
- Early *Homo* Species
- *Homo erectus*
- Lower Paleolithic Cultures

Bipedal locomotion is a defining feature of the hominids. Undisputed bipedal hominids lived in East Africa about 4 million years ago. These hominids, and some others who lived later in eastern and southern Africa, are generally classified in the genus *Australopithecus*. In this chapter we discuss what we know or suspect about the transition from hominoids to hominids, the emergence of australopithecines, and their relationship to later hominids, including ourselves. We also discuss early hominid tools and lifestyles.

The Evolution of Bipedal Locomotion

Perhaps the most crucial change in early hominid evolution was the development of *bipedal locomotion,* or walking on two legs. We know from the fossil record that other important physical changes—including the expansion of the brain, modification of the female pelvis to allow bigger-brained babies to be born, and reduction of the face, teeth, and jaws—did not occur until about 2 million years after the emergence of bipedalism. Other human characteristics, such as an extended period of infant and child dependency and increased meat-eating, may also have developed after that time.

We do not know whether bipedalism developed quickly or gradually, because the fossil record for the period between 8 million and 4 million years ago is very skimpy. We do know, on the basis of their skeletal anatomy, that many of the Miocene anthropoids were capable of assuming an upright posture. For example, *brachiation,* swinging by the arms through the trees, puts an animal in an upright position; so does climbing up and down trees with the use of grasping hands and feet. It is also likely that the protohominids were capable of occasional bipedalism, just as many modern monkeys and apes are.[1]

Judging by the available fossil record, definitely bipedal hominids first emerged in Africa. Their emergence coincides with a change from extensive tropical forest cover to more discontinuous patches of forest and open country.[2] About 16 million to 11 million years ago, a drying trend set in that continued into the Pliocene. Gradually, the African rain forests, deprived of intense humidity and rainfall, dwindled in extent; areas of **savanna** (grasslands) and scattered deciduous woodlands became more common. The tree-dwelling primates did not completely lose their customary habitats, because some tropical forests remained in wetter regions, and natural selection continued to favor the better adapted tree dwellers in those forested areas. But the new, more open country probably favored characteristics adapted to ground living in some primates as well as other animals. In the evolutionary line leading to humans, these adaptations included bipedalism.

Theories for the Evolution of Bipedalism

What in particular may have favored the emergence of bipedal hominids? One idea is that bipedalism was adaptive for life amid the tall grasses of the savannas because an erect posture may have made it easier to spot ground predators as well as potential prey.[3] However, this theory does not adequately account for why baboons and some other Old World monkeys also live in savanna environments, yet, although they can occasionally stand erect, they have not evolved to fully bipedal locomotion. Also recent evidence suggests that the area where early hominids lived in East Africa was not predominantly savanna; rather, it seems to have been a mix of woodland and open country.[4]

Other theories stress the importance of freeing the hands to perform other activities at the same time as the protohominid was moving about. Gordon Hewes emphasized the importance of carrying hunted or scavenged meat,[5] but many paleoanthropologists now question whether early hominids hunted or even scavenged.[6] However, the ability to carry any food to a place safe from predators may have been one of the more important advantages of bipedalism. C. Owen Lovejoy has suggested that food carrying might have been important for another reason. If males provisioned females and their babies by carrying food back to a home base, the females would have been able to conserve energy by not traveling and therefore might have been able to produce and care for more babies.[7] Thus, whatever the advantages of carrying food, the more bipedal a protohominid was, the more it might reproduce.

But carrying food or provisioning families might not have been the only benefit of freeing the hands; feeding itself may have been more efficient. Clifford Jolly has argued that bipedalism would have allowed early hominids to efficiently harvest small seeds and nuts because both hands could be used to pick up food and move it directly to the mouth.[8] In the changing environments of East Africa, where forests were giving way to more open woodlands and savannas, an advantage in foraging for small seeds and nuts might have been favored by natural selection.

Bipedalism might also have been favored by natural selection because the freeing of the hands would allow protohominids to use, and perhaps even make, tools that they could carry with them as they moved about. Consider how advantageous such tool use might have been. Sherwood Washburn noted that some contemporary ground-living primates dig for roots to eat, "and if they could use a stone or a stick they might easily double their food supply."[9] David Pilbeam also suggests why tool use by the more open-country primates may have appreciably increased the number and amount of plant foods they could eat: In order to be eaten, many of the plant foods in the grassy areas probably had to be chopped, crushed, or otherwise prepared with the aid of tools.[10] Tools may also have been used to kill and butcher animals for food. Without tools, primates in general are not well equipped physically for regular hunting or even scavenging. Their teeth and jaws are not sharp and strong enough, and their speed afoot is not fast enough. So the use of tools to kill and butcher game might have enlarged even further their ability to exploit the available food supply.

Finally, tools may have been used as weapons against predators, which would have been a great threat to the relatively defenseless ground-dwelling protohominids. In Milford Wolpoff's opinion, it was the advantage of carrying weapons *continuously* that was responsible for transforming occasional bipedalism to

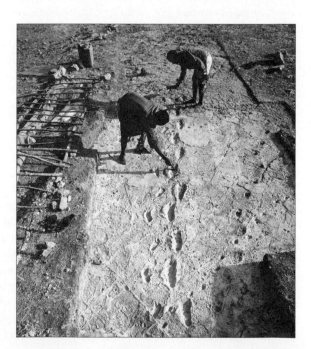

Mary Leakey's expedition discovered a trail approximately 70 yards long of 3.8-million-year-old fossilized footprints at Laetoli, Tanzania. Shown here are footprints that were left by two adults who were clearly upright walkers. The footprints show a well-developed arch and forward-facing big toe.

completely bipedal locomotion.[11] In particular, Sue Savage-Rumbaugh has suggested that the ability to abduct or snap the wrist would have permitted early humans "to perfect both throwing and rock-striking skills [for toolmaking] and consequently to develop throwing as a much more effective predator defense system than apes could ever manage."[12]

But some anthropologists question the idea that tool use and toolmaking favored bipedalism. They point out that the first clear evidence of stone tools appears more than 2 million years *after* the emergence of bipedalism. So how could toolmaking be responsible for bipedalism? Wolpoff suggests an answer. Even though bipedalism appears to be at least 2 million years older than stone tools, it is not unlikely that protohominids used tools made of wood and bone, neither of which would be as likely as stone to survive in the archaeological record. Moreover, unmodified stone tools present in the archaeological record might not be recognizable as tools.[13]

Some researchers have taken a closer look at the mechanics of bipedal locomotion to see if it might be a more efficient form of locomotion in the savanna-woodland environment, where resources are likely to be scattered. Compared with the quadrupedal locomotion of primates such as chimpanzees, bipedalism appears to be more efficient for long-distance travel.[14] But why travel long distances? If the ancestors of humans had the manipulative ability and tool-using capability of modern chimpanzees (e.g., using stones to crack nuts), and those ancestors had to move around in a more open environment, then those individuals who could efficiently travel longer distances to exploit those resources might do better.[15]

Finally, bipedalism might have been favored by natural selection as a way of regulating body temperature, particularly in the increasingly hot and dry environments of East Africa at the end of the Miocene and the beginning of the Pliocene. Peter Wheeler has argued that a bipedal posture limits the area of the body directly exposed to the sun, especially when the sun is at its hottest, at midday.[16] Bipedal posture would also facilitate convective heat loss by allowing heat to rise up and away from the body rather than being trapped underneath it. (We radiate a lot of body heat through the head.) Cooling through the evaporation of sweat would also be facilitated by a bipedal posture, as more skin area would be exposed to cooling winds. Thus, natural selection may have favored bipedalism because it reduced heat stress in the warming environments of East Africa.

All of the theories about the origin of bipedalism are still speculative. We do not yet have direct evidence that any of the factors we have discussed were actually responsible for bipedalism. Any or all of the factors may explain the transformation of an occasionally bipedal protohominid to a completely bipedal hominid.

The "Costs" of Bipedalism

We must remember that there are also "costs" to bipedal walking. Bipedalism makes it harder to overcome gravity to supply the brain with sufficient blood,[17] and the weight of the body above the pelvis and lower limbs puts greater stress on the hips, lower back, knees, and feet. As Adrienne Zihlman points out, the stresses on the lower body are even greater for females.[18] Females have to support extra weight during pregnancy, and as mothers they usually are responsible for carrying nursing infants. So whatever the advantages of bipedalism, they must be greater than the disadvantages—or our ancestors never would have become bipedal.

We must also remember that the evolution of bipedalism required some dramatic changes in the ancestral ape skeleton. While apes today can and do walk bipedally, they cannot do so efficiently or for long periods of time. To be habitually bipedal, the ancestral ape skeleton had to be modified, and the major changes that allowed the early hominids to become fully bipedal occurred primarily in the skull, pelvis, knees, and feet.[19] Let's take a look at each of these changes.

In both ancient and modern apes, the spinal column enters the skull toward the back, which makes sense because apes generally walk on all fours, with the spine roughly parallel to the ground. In bipedal hominids, the spinal column enters the skull at the bottom, through a hole called the **foramen magnum**. Thus, when hominids became bipedal, the skull ended up on top of the spinal column.

The shape of ancient and modern ape pelvises is considerably different from that of a bipedal hominid. Ape pelvises are long and flat, forming a bony plate in the lower back to which the leg muscles attach. In bipedal hominids the pelvis is bowl-shaped, which supports the internal organs and also lowers the body's center of gravity, allowing better balance on the legs. The hominid pelvis also provides a different set of muscle attachments and shifts the orientation of the femurs (the upper leg bones) from the side of the pelvis to the front. These changes allow hominids to move their legs forward in a bipedal stride (and do things like kick a soccer ball). Apes, in comparison, move their legs forward (when they walk bipedally) by shifting their pelvis from side to side, not by kicking each leg forward alternately as we do.[20]

Another change associated with the hominid ability to kick the leg forward is our "knock-kneed" posture. Ape legs hang straight down from the pelvis. Bipedal hominid legs, on the other hand, angle inward toward one another. This configuration not only helps us move our legs forward but also helps us maintain a center of gravity in the midline of our bodies, so that our center of gravity does not shift from side to side when we walk or run.

Finally, the feet of bipedal hominids have two major changes compared to those of apes. First, hominid feet have an enlarged group of ankle bones forming a robust heel that can withstand the substantial forces experienced as a result of habitual bipedalism. Second, hominid feet have an arch, which also aids in absorbing the forces endured by the feet during bipedal locomotion. We know this arch is vital to our ability to be habitually bipedal because "flat-footed" people who lack it have chronic problems in their feet, ankles, knees, and back.[21]

When did these changes take place? We don't know for sure, but fossils from East Africa—Ethiopia, Tanzania, and Kenya—clearly show that bipedal hominids lived there between 4 million and 5 million years ago, perhaps even earlier.

The Transition from Hominoids to Hominids

Western Chad, in north-central Africa with its windswept deserts, does not seem a likely place to find fossil apes or hominids, but paleoanthropologist Michel Brunet thinks it might be.[22] Western Chad was covered by an ancient lake, and for several million years was a location where forest-dwelling mammals, including primates, congregated. Around 7 million years ago a primate called ***Sahelanthropus tchadensis*** lived on the shores of the lake, where its bones were fossilized and recovered by Brunet and his colleagues in 2001. *Sahelanthropus,* represented by an almost complete skull, has a unique mix of hominid and hominoid traits. While the skull itself is hominoid, with a small brain, large brow ridges, and wide face, the teeth seem more hominid-like, especially the canines, which do not project below the tooth row.[23] There is no evidence that *Sahelanthropus* was bipedal. So for now, we have to wait for additional evidence to know whether *Sahelanthropus* was the first bipedal ape.

There is, however, tantalizing evidence that another possible early hominid, ***Orrorin tugenensis***, was bipedal. Discovered in western Kenya by Brigitte Senut and colleagues in 1998, *Orrorin tugenensis* consists of 19 specimens of jaw, teeth, finger, arm, and leg bones, including the top of a femur.[24] The femur in *Orrorin,* according to Senut, shows adaptations to bipedalism, including a long, angled "head" (or top). Other scholars are not convinced. *Orrorin* dates between 5.8 and 6 million years.

Shown here is a reconstructed skull of *Sahelanthropus tchadensis*, possibly the earliest hominid, dating to almost seven million years ago.

In 1992, a team of researchers led by anthropologist Tim White began surveying a 4.4-million-year-old fossil deposit at Aramis, in the Middle Awash region of Ethiopia. There they discovered 17 fossils of what may be the earliest hominid (more have been found since, including some fragments dating perhaps as early as 5.8 million years ago): *Ardipithecus ramidus*.[25] What makes ***Ardipithecus ramidus*** unique is the combination of ape-like dentition along with evidence of bipedal locomotion and an overall hominid-like skeleton. Like apes, *Ardipithecus* has relatively small cheek teeth with thin enamel and relatively large canines. However, its arm bones seem hominid-like, and the base of its skull shows the foramen magnum positioned underneath the skull, just as in definitely bipedal hominids.[26] The feet of *Ardipithecus* also seem adapted to bipedalism.[27]

Australopithecus: The First Definite Hominid

Although some doubt remains about the status of *Ardipithecus* and others as hominids, there is no doubt that the australopithecines (members of the genus ***Australopithecus***) were hominids. Their teeth share the basic hominid characteristics of small canines, flat and thickly enameled molars, and a parabolic dental arch, and there is unambiguous evidence that even the earliest australopithecines were fully bipedal. Not only do their skeletons reflect bipedal locomotion, but at Laetoli, Tanzania, more than 50 hardened human-like footprints about 3.6 million years old give striking confirmation that the hominids there were fully bipedal. The bipedalism of the australopithecines does not mean that these earliest definite hominids were terrestrial all of the time. All of the australopithecines, including the later ones, seem to have been capable of climbing and moving in trees, judging by arm versus leg length and other skeletal features.[28]

Most scholars divide the various australopithecine species into two groups, the "gracile" australopithecines and the "robust" australopithecines.[29] The **gracile australopithecines** include *A. anamensis*, *A. afarensis*, and *A. africanus*. All of them have smaller dentition and lighter facial and dental musculature than the robust australopithecines. The **robust australopithecines** have larger dentition than the gracile species, and massive faces and jaws. Some robust individuals had a ridge of bone called a **sagittal crest** on the top of their heads; the ridge anchored the heavy musculature for their large teeth and jaws.

Gracile Australopithecines

Australopithecus anamensis   The earliest australopithecine species is ***Australopithecus anamensis***, which has been found in several locations in northern Kenya and is dated between 3.9 and 4.2 million years ago.[30] The general picture is that it was a small bipedal hominid with teeth similar to those of the later *A. afarensis*.[31] The more controversial specimens have long bones suggesting well-developed bipedalism. Curiously, elbow and knee joints look more like those of the later *Homo* genus than like those of any other species of *Australopithecus*. It has been said that *A. anamensis* is "*afarensis*-like from the neck up and *Homo*-like from the neck down."[32]

Australopithecus afarensis   *Australopithecus afarensis* is perhaps the most well-represented australopithecine species. Remains from at least two dozen individuals were unearthed at Laetoli, Tanzania.[33] Although the remains there consisted largely of teeth and jaws, there is no question that the Laetoli hominids were bipedal, because it was at the Laetoli site that the now-famous trail of footprints was found. Two hominids walking erect and side by side left their tracks in the ground 3.6 million years ago. The remains of at least 35 individuals have been found at another site, Hadar, in Ethiopia. The Hadar finds are remarkable for their completeness. Whereas paleoanthropologists often find just parts of the cranium and jaws, many parts of the skeleton were also found at Hadar. For example, paleoanthropologist Donald Johanson found 40 percent of the skeleton of a female hominid he named Lucy, after the Beatles' song "Lucy in the Sky with Diamonds."[34]

Dating of the hominid remains at Laetoli suggests that the hominids there lived between 3.8 million and 3.6 million years ago.[35] Although Lucy and the other hominids at Hadar were once thought to be about as old as those at Laetoli, recent dating suggests that they are somewhat younger—less than 3.2 million years old. Lucy probably lived 2.9 million years ago.[36] The environment Lucy lived in was semiarid, upland savanna with rainy and dry seasons.[37]

Shown here is a reconstruction of a female *Australopithecus afarensis* skeleton. Note the long fingers and how long the arms are relative to the legs. Both suggest that *A. afarensis* was at least partially arboreal.

A. afarensis was a small hominid, but, like most of the living great apes, was sexually dimorphic. Females weighed perhaps 65 pounds and stood a little more than 3 feet tall; males weighed more than 90 pounds and stood about 5 feet tall.[38] *A. afarensis* teeth were large compared to their body size, and they had thick molar enamel. They also had large, ape-like canines, which, on some specimens, projected beyond the adjacent teeth. However, even the longer canines did not rub against the lower teeth or fit into a diastema (a space between the teeth), and thus did not prevent side-to-side movement of the lower jaw.[39] This is important, because side-to-side movement of the lower jaw allowed *A. afarensis* to efficiently chew small seeds and nuts. The thick enamel on the molars and wear patterns on the molar crowns suggest that such small, hard materials made up a significant part of the diet of *A. afarensis*.[40] The cranium of *A. afarensis* reflects its dentition. The face juts forward because of the large teeth and jaws, and the base of the skull flares out to provide attachment areas for large neck muscles to support the heavy face. The brain is small, about 400 cubic centimeters (cc), but relatively large for an animal this size.[41]

The arms and legs of *A. afarensis* were about the same length, and the fingers and toe bones are curved, suggesting they were heavily muscled. Most scholars believe these limb proportions and strong hands and feet point to a partially arboreal lifestyle.[42] In other words, *A. afarensis* may have spent a lot of time in the trees, feeding, sleeping, and avoiding terrestrial predators. The pelvis and leg bones of *A. afarensis,* however, demonstrate that it moved bipedally when on the ground. The pelvis is wide and flaring, and has the bowl-like shape of all later hominids. The legs angle inward, and the feet have an arch and an ankle much like later hominids.[43] Detailed analyses of the Laetoli footprints suggest that *A. afarensis* may have had a shorter and less efficient stride than modern humans.[44]

While *A. afarensis* is the most well-represented australopithecine species, it was not the first one discovered. That distinction rests with *Australopithecus africanus.*

Australopithecus africanus   In 1925, Raymond Dart, Professor of Anatomy at the University of Witwatersrand in Johannesburg, South Africa, presented the first evidence that an erect bipedal hominid existed in the Pliocene epoch. As he separated bones from a matrix of material found in the Taung cave on the edge of the Kalahari Desert, Dart realized he was looking at more than the remains of an ape. He described the experience:

> On December 23, [1924,] the rock parted. I could view the face from the front, although the right side was still embedded. The creature that had contained this massive brain was no giant anthropoid such as a gorilla. What emerged was a baby's face, an infant with a full set of milk teeth and its permanent molars just in the process of erupting.[45]

By the teeth Dart identified the fossil as the remains of a five- to seven-year-old child (although recent analysis by electron microscope suggests that the child was no more than three and a half[46]). He named the specimen ***Australopithecus africanus***, which means "southern ape of Africa." Dart was certain the skull was that of a bipedal animal. He based his conclusion on the fact that the foramen magnum faced downward, indicating that the head was carried directly over the spine. Furthermore, the Taung child's incisors and canine teeth were short, and therefore definitely more human-like than ape-like. Dart's conclusion met with widespread skepticism and opposition. Not the least of the problems was that scientists at the time believed hominids had originated in Asia. Other australopithecines were not discovered until the 1930s, when Robert Broom recovered some fossils from the Sterkfontein cave near Johannesburg. Dart's and Broom's conclusions did not begin to be accepted until after 1945, when Wilfred Le Gros Clark, a Professor of Anatomy at Oxford, supported the hominid status of their finds.[47]

Shown here is a fossil skull of an *Australopithecus africanus* (STS 5), nicknamed "Mrs. Ples," found by Robert Broom at Sterkfontein cave in 1947.

Since the Taung child's discovery more than 80 years ago, the remains of hundreds of other similar australopithecines have been unearthed from caves at Sterkfontein and Makapansgat in South Africa. From this abundant evidence a fairly complete picture of *A. africanus* can be drawn: "The brain case is rounded with a relatively well-developed forehead. Moderate brow ridges surmount a rather projecting face."[48] The estimated cranial capacity for the various finds from Taung and Sterkfontein is between 428 and 485 cc.[49]

Like *A. afarensis, A. africanus* was very small; the adults were three and a half to four and a half feet tall, weighed 60 to 90 pounds, and were sexually dimorphic.[50] The large, chinless jaw of *A. africanus*

Here is a reconstruction of an *Australopithecus africanus* mother and child picking berries in a tree. Like *A. afarensis, A. africanus* probably spent time in trees both feeding and avoiding predators.

resembles that of *A. afarensis,* but some of the dental features of *A. africanus* are similar to those of modern humans—broad incisors and small, short canines. And, although the premolars and molars were larger than in modern humans, their form was very similar.

Dating of the australopithecine finds from the South African limestone caves is somewhat difficult because none of the absolute dating techniques can be applied. But relative dating is possible. Comparisons of the fauna found in the strata with fauna found elsewhere suggest that the South African *A. africanus* lived between 3 million and 2 million years ago. The climate was probably semiarid, not too different from the climate of today.[51]

Other Gracile Australopithecines   New fossils from Eastern Africa found in the last decade suggest there may have been other species of gracile australopithecine as well. Two groups of fossils in particular are considered by most scholars to represent new australopithecine species, named ***Australopithecus bahrelghazali*** and ***Australopithecus garhi***. *A. bahrelghazali* is currently represented by a single, fragmentary jaw, and only a handful of skull and limb fragments represent *A. garhi*.

Australopithecus garhi, found in rock dating to approximately 2.5 million years ago, is particularly interesting. *A. garhi* has larger molars than *A. afarensis,* yet does not have the huge face and jaws of the robust australopithecines. It also lacks the enlarged brain of early *Homo.* Several limb bones were found in the same rock layers, and these do resemble *A. afarensis. A. garhi,* then, looks to be an *afarensis*-like creature but with greatly enlarged molars.[52]

It is interesting, however, that the remains of butchered animals were found in the same rock layer as the *A. garhi* remains. Several bones found near the *A. garhi* fossils show unambiguous cut marks and signs of having been broken with a stone tool. Unfortunately, no stone tools have been found, but the evidence for butchery suggests they must have been used. And since no other species of hominid have been found in the area, it is reasonable to think that *A. garhi* was the toolmaker and butcher. The fossil's discoverer, Berhane Asfaw, suggests that *A. garhi* is in the right place, at the right time, and has the right physical and behavioral traits to be the direct ancestor of early *Homo.*[53]

Equally intriguing is *Australopithecus bahrelghazali,* not so much because of its physical features, but because it was found further west, in what is now central Chad. *A. bahrelghazali* is the first early hominid to be found outside of the Rift Valley (a long valley in East Africa where the earth is pulling apart, exposing fossils from millions of years ago), and until *A. bahrelghazali* surfaced, few thought definite early hominids were present anywhere else. *A. bahrelghazali* dates to about 3 million years ago, and is very

Shown here is a reconstructed skull of *Australopithecus garhi*. Note the large molars but relatively small face.

similar to contemporary *A. afarensis* fossils from the Rift Valley. It differs from *A. afarensis* in some distinct ways (its premolars, for example, have thinner enamel and more well-defined roots), but the important difference is where *A. bahrelghazali* lived. Most scholars assume the early hominids represent a specific adaptation to the Rift Valley. The discovery of an early australopithecine some 2,500 kilometers west of the Rift Valley calls this assumption into question.[54]

A related hominid genus, ***Kenyanthropus platyops***, is thought by some scholars to be yet another australopithecine (and hence should not be regarded as a separate genus). The nearly complete 3.5-million-year-old skull of *Kenyanthropus platyops* from western Kenya shows traits that Meave Leakey and her colleagues think separate it from the australopithecines that lived at the same time. Its face is smaller and flatter, and its molars are smaller than those of the australopithecines. Leakey believes *Kenyanthropus* may be a direct link to *Homo,* but others are not convinced that its features lie outside the range of the australopithecines.[55]

Robust Australopithecines

The robust australopithecines lived in eastern Africa and in southern Africa from about 2.7 million to 1 million years ago, and are quite distinct from the gracile australopithecines. Indeed, some paleoanthropologists think these fossils are so different that they deserve to be classified in a different genus, which they call *Paranthropus,* literally, "beside humans." Robust australopithecines were found first in South African caves, in Kromdraai and in Swartkrans, and later in East Africa, in the Omo Basin in Ethiopia, on the east and west sides of Lake Turkana in Kenya, and Olduvai Gorge in Tanzania.[56] Most paleoanthropologists classify the South African robust australopithecines from about 1.8 million to 1 million years ago as *A. robustus* and the East African robust forms from 2.3 million to 1.3 million years ago as *A. boisei.*[57] The third robust species, *A. aethiopicus,* is even earlier, dating back more than 2.5 million years ago, and may have been ancestral to *A. boisei.*

In contrast to the gracile australopithecines, the robust australopithecines had thicker jaws, with larger molars and premolars but smaller incisors, more massive muscle attachments for chewing, and well-developed sagittal crests and ridges to support heavy chewing.[58] In addition, *A. robustus* and *A. boisei* have somewhat larger cranial capacities (about 490–530 cc) than any of the gracile species.

It used to be thought that the robust australopithecines were substantially bigger than the other australopithecines—hence the term *robust.* But recent calculations suggest that these australopithecines were not substantially different in body weight or height from the other australopithecines. The robustness is primarily in the skull and jaw, most strikingly in the teeth. If the robust forms were larger in body size, their slightly bigger brain capacity would not be surprising, since larger animals generally have larger brains. However, the body of the robust forms is similar to that of *A. africanus,* so the brain of the robust australopithecines was relatively larger than the brain of *A. africanus.*[59]

Australopithecus aethiopicus *Australopithecus aethiopicus* is the earliest and also the least known of the robust australopithecines. *Australopithecus aethiopicus* is represented by a small group of fossils found in northern Kenya and southern Ethiopia dating between 2.3 million and 2.7 million years ago, including one spectacular find—a nearly complete skull (known as the "Black Skull" because of its dark color) found in 1985.[60] Even though we have only a few fossils, it seems clear that *A. aethiopicus* was quite different from other australopithecines. *A. aethiopicus* had much larger dentition, particularly the molars, huge cheekbones, projecting and dish-shaped (round and flat) faces, and large sagittal crests. But they are similar to *A. afarensis* in most other ways. Overall, *A. aethiopicus* resembles *A. afarensis* with a massively "scaled-up" dental apparatus.[61]

Australopithecus robustus   In 1936, Robert Broom, then curator of vertebrate paleontology at the Transvaal museum in South Africa, began visiting quarries seeking fossils for the museum, particularly hominids that might support Raymond Dart's earlier discovery of the Taung child. In 1938, a quarry manager gave Broom a hominid jaw that had been found in a nearby cave called Kromdraai. Broom immediately began excavating in the cave, and within days was able to piece together the skull of what would prove to be a new australopithecine species—***Australopithecus robustus***.[62] While Broom had expected another example of *Australopithecus africanus* (he had found an *A. africanus* skull in 1936), this one had larger teeth, a massive jaw, and a flatter face than *A. africanus*.[63] Many scholars since Broom believe the robust australopithecines are unique enough to warrant classification in a separate *Paranthropus* genus.

During the 1940s Broom added many new fossils of *A. robustus* and *A. africanus* to the collections of the Transvaal Museum. But his discoveries also raised a problem. How did two strikingly different hominid species evolve in the same environment? In 1954, John T. Robinson proposed that *A. africanus* and *A. robustus* had different dietary adaptations—*A. africanus* being an omnivore (dependent on meat and plants) and *A. robustus* a vegetarian, with a need for heavy chewing. Robinson's view was hotly debated for many years. Later evidence from electron microscopy supported Robinson's view that *A. robustus* ate mostly small, hard objects such as seeds, nuts, and tubers. But how different was *A. africanus* in this respect? Recent analyses suggest that *A. africanus* also engaged in fairly heavy chewing.[64]

The idea that *A. robustus* was just a vegetarian is also questioned by a relatively new chemical technique that analyzes strontium-calcium ratios in teeth and bones to estimate the proportion of plant versus animal food in the diet. This new kind of analysis suggests that *A. robustus* was an omnivore.[65] Thus *A. robustus* may have needed large teeth and jaws to chew seeds, nuts, and tubers, but that doesn't mean that it didn't eat other things too. Most paleoanthropologists think that *A. robustus* died out shortly after 1 million years ago[66] and is not ancestral to our own genus, *Homo*.[67]

Australopithecus boisei   Legendary paleoanthropologist Louis Leakey began his search for a human ancestor in 1931 at Olduvai Gorge in western Tanzania. It was not until 1959 that his efforts paid off with the discovery of what he called ***Australopithecus boisei*** (named after a benefactor, Charles Boise). Leakey, his wife, Mary Leakey, and their children (including paleoanthropologist Richard Leakey) assembled a rich collection of nonhominid fossils and also amassed a remarkable collection of ancient stone tools.

Shown here is a fossil skull of *Australopithecus boisei* found by Louis and Mary Leakey in 1959. Note its huge face and teeth and its sagittal crest.

The discovery of *A. boisei* was particularly important because it demonstrated that early hominids were present in East Africa. Until the Leakeys found *A. boisei,* it was thought that South Africa was the homeland of the hominids. Indeed, Leakey initially assigned *A. boisei* to a new genus—*Zinjanthropus*—to highlight its location (*Zinj* means "East Africa" in Arabic). Today we know that the most ancient fossil hominids are all found in East Africa, but in 1959 simply finding a fossil hominid in East Africa was remarkable.

What did *A. boisei* look like? Compared with *A. robustus, A. boisei* had even more extreme features that reflected a huge chewing apparatus—enormous molar teeth and expanded premolars that look like molars; a massive, thick and deep jaw; thick cheekbones; and a more pronounced sagittal crest.[68] Indeed, *A. boisei* has been called a "hyperrobust" australopithecine—a name that definitely captures the species.

A. boisei lived between about 2.3 and 1.3 million years ago. Like *A. robustus,* it seems to have lived in a dry, open environment and ate a lot of coarse seeds, nuts, and roots. And, like *A. robustus,* most paleoanthropologists think *A. boisei* is not ancestral to our genus, *Homo.*[69] We don't know whether *A. boisei* was the maker of the stone tools the Leakeys found at Olduvai. After all, at least two other hominid species—*Homo habilis* and *Homo erectus*—lived at the same time there and could have been the toolmakers.

One Model of Human Evolution

The picture that emerges from our overview of the australopithecines is one of diversity. There seem to have been many different species of australopithecine, and even within species there seems to be a relatively high level of variation.[70] All lived in eastern and southern Africa, where the environments were diverse and changing. Forests were giving way to open woodlands and grasslands. Large lakes formed and then broke apart through uplifting and volcanic activity in the rift valley of eastern Africa. And the climate continued to warm until the end of the **Pliocene**, some 1.6 million years ago.

At this point you may well be wondering how all these species fit together. Figure 6.1 shows one model entertained by paleoanthropologists about how the known fossils may be related. The main disagreement among paleontologists concerns which species of *Australopithecus* were ancestral to the line leading to modern humans. For example, the model shown in Figure 6.1 suggests that *A. africanus* is not ancestral to *Homo,* only to one line of robust australopithecines. *Australopithecus afarensis* is viewed as ancestral to both lines of robust australopithecines and to the line leading to modern humans. Those who think that *A. afarensis* was the last common ancestor of all the hominid lines shown in Figure 6.2 think the split to *Homo* occurred over 3 million years ago.[71]

Despite the uncertainty and disagreements about what species was ancestral to the *Homo* line, there is widespread agreement among paleoanthropologists about other aspects of early hominid evolution: (1) there were at least two separate hominid lines between 3 million and 1 million years ago; (2) the robust australopithecines were not ancestral to modern humans but became extinct about 1 million years ago; and (3) *Homo habilis* (and successive *Homo* species) were in the direct ancestral line to modern humans. Let us turn now to these direct ancestors, the first members of the genus *Homo.*

Early Hominid Tools and Lifestyles

In the beginning of this chapter we discussed the origins of bipedalism and how that fundamental hominid means of locomotion first appeared and was refined in the australopithecines. Now we will consider a number of other trends in hominid evolution, including the routine use of patterned or nearly standardized stone tools, which is considered one sign of the emergence of culture. It is usually assumed,

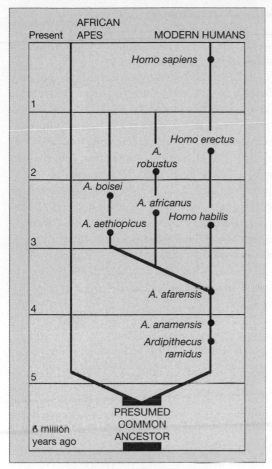

Figure 6.1   One Model of Human Evolution

Source: Adapted from "The Fossil Trail" by New York Times Graphics, *The New York Times,* September 5, 1995, p. C9. Copyright © 1995 by The New York Times Company. Reprinted by permission of New York Times Graphics. Dates changed slightly to reflect recent redating.

Figure 6.2   The Production of a Simple Oldowan Chopper Core and the Resultant Flakes

Source: From R. Freyman, "The First Technology," in *Scientific American* (April 1987): 112. Reprinted by permission of the artist, Ed Hanson.

but not known for sure of course, that patterned stone tools were made by the first members of our own genus, *Homo,* for it is in the genus *Homo* that we first see a number of trends that probably started because of habitual stone toolmaking and use—expansion of the brain, modification of the female pelvis to accommodate bigger-brained babies, and reduction in the teeth, face, and jaws.

Even though stone tools are found at various sites in East Africa before the time early *Homo* appeared, most anthropologists surmise that members of early *Homo* species, rather than the australopithecines, made those tools. After all, early *Homo* had a brain capacity almost one-third larger than the australopithecines'. But the fact is that none of the earliest stone tools is clearly associated with early *Homo,* so it is impossible as yet to know who made them.[72] We turn now to a discussion of those earliest stone tools and what archaeologists and paleoanthropologists infer about the lifestyles of their makers, the hominids (whoever they were) who lived between about 2.5 million and 1.5 million years ago.

The earliest identifiable stone tools found so far come from various sites in East Africa and date from about 2.5 million years ago,[73] and maybe earlier. They range from very small flakes (thumb-size) to cobble or core tools that are fist-size.[74] These early tools were apparently made by striking a stone with another stone, a technique called **percussion flaking**. Both the sharp-edged flakes and the sharp-edged cores (the pieces of stone left after flakes are removed) were probably used as tools. Unfortunately, little can be inferred about lifestyles from the earliest tool sites because little else was found with the tools. In contrast, finds of later tool assemblages at Olduvai Gorge in Tanzania have yielded a rich harvest of cultural information. Louis Leakey described the site as follows:

> [It] is a fossil hunter's dream, for it shears 300 feet through stratum after stratum of earth's history as through a gigantic layer cake. Here, within reach, lie countless fossils and artifacts which but for the faulting and erosion would have remained sealed under thick layers of consolidated rock.[75]

The oldest cultural materials from Olduvai (Bed I) date from Lower Pleistocene times (about 1.6 million years ago). The stone artifacts include mostly sharp-edged flakes and core tools such as choppers and scrapers. Choppers are cores that have been partially flaked and have a side that might have been used for chopping; scrapers have flaking along one side and a flat edge. Whenever a stone has facets removed from only one side of the cutting edge, we call it a **unifacial tool**. If the stone has facets removed from both sides, we call it a **bifacial tool**. Bifacial tools in early stone tool assemblages are not as plentiful or as elaborated as in later tool traditions. The kind of tool assemblage found in Bed I and to some extent in later (higher) layers is referred to as **Oldowan** (see Figure 6.2 on page 135).[76]

Archaeologists have experimented with what can be done with Oldowan tools. The flakes appear to be very versatile; they can be used for slitting the hides of animals, dismembering animals, and whittling wood into sharp-pointed sticks (wooden spears or digging sticks). The larger stone tools (choppers and scrapers) can be used to hack off branches or cut and chop tough animal joints.[77] Those who have made and tried to use stone tools for various purposes are so impressed by the sharpness and versatility of flakes that they wonder whether most of the core tools were really used as tools. The cores could mainly be what remained after the wanted flakes were struck off.[78] Archaeologists surmise that many early tools were also made of wood and bone, but these do not survive in the archaeological record. Stone flakes are very effective for sharpening wood to a very fine point.[79] None of the early flaked stone tools can plausibly be thought of as weapons. So, if the toolmaking hominids were hunting or defending themselves with weapons, they had to have used wooden spears, clubs, or unmodified stones as missiles. Later Oldowan tool assemblages also include stones that were flaked and battered into a rounded shape. The unmodified stones and the shaped stones might have been lethal projectiles.[80]

Experiments may indicate what can be done with tools, but they cannot tell us what was *actually* done with them. Microscopic analysis of the wear on tools, are more informative. Scratches parallel to the edge

A replica of an Oldowan stone tool is used to chop into a large bone to extract the nutrient-rich marrow. Few animals have jaws powerful enough to break open the bones of large mammals, but stone tools would have allowed early humans to do so.

of a tool often occur when a tool is used in a sawing motion; perpendicular scratches suggest whittling or scraping.[81] Lawrence Keeley used high-powered microscopes in his experimental investigations of tools and found that different kinds of "polish" develop on tools when they are used on different materials. The polish on tools used for cutting meat is different from the polish on tools used for woodworking. On the basis of microscopic investigation of the 1.5-million-year-old tools from the eastern side of Lake Turkana, Keeley and his colleagues concluded that at least some of the early tools were probably used for cutting meat, others for cutting or whittling wood, and still others for cutting plant stems.[82]

For many years it seemed plausible to assume that hominids were the hunters and the animals the prey. But archaeologists had to reexamine this assumption with the emergence of the field of *taphonomy,* which studies the processes that can alter and distort an assemblage of bones. So, for example, flowing water can bring bones and artifacts together, which may have happened at Olduvai Gorge about 1.8 million years ago. (The area of what is now the gorge bordered the shores of a shallow lake at that time.) And other animals such as hyenas could have brought carcasses to some of the same places that hominids spent time.[83]

But there is little doubt that shortly after 2 million years ago hominids were cutting up animal carcasses for meat either obtained by scavenging meat (taking meat from the kills of other animals) or actually hunting the animals. Pat Shipman suggested that scavenging, not hunting, was the major meat-getting activity of the hominids living in Olduvai Gorge between 2 million and 1.7 million years ago because the cut marks made by the stone tools usually overlie teeth marks made by carnivores. The fact that the cut marks were sometimes made first, however, suggested to Shipman that the hominids were also sometimes the hunters.[84]

It seems that the hominids moved around during the year; most of the sites in what is now the Olduvai Gorge appear to have been used only in the dry season, as indicated by an analysis of the kinds of animal bones found there.[85] The early Olduvai hominids were hunters or scavengers; they apparently exploited a wide range of animals. Although most of the bones are from medium-sized antelopes and wild pigs, even large animals such as elephants and giraffes seem to have been eaten.[86] It is clear, then, that the Olduvai hominids scavenged or hunted for meat, but we cannot tell yet how important meat was in their diet.

There is also no consensus about how to characterize the Olduvai sites that contain concentrations of stone tools and animal bones. In the 1970s, there was a tendency to think of them as home bases to which hominids (presumably male) brought meat to share with others (presumably nursing mothers and young children). Indeed, Mary Leakey identified two locations where she thought early hominids had built simple structures. One was a stone circle that she suggested formed the base of a small brush windbreak. The

HOW DO YOU KNOW SOMETHING IS A TOOL?

When you look at photographs or drawings of early stone tools, do you ever wonder how paleoanthropologists can distinguish them from ordinary rocks? It is not always easy. Paleoanthropologists mainly look for flakes or rocks with flakes removed, but rocks can be flaked by knocking against other rocks in a riverbed or rolling down a craggy hill. To tell that a core tool is not a naturally flaked rock, paleoanthropologists typically look for three distinct features.

First, the tool has to be made of the *right kind of rock.* The rock must be both flakable and durable. You can flake shale, for example, but it is not durable. Many metamorphic rocks are durable, but you cannot flake them because there are too many flaws in the rock. Most stone tools are made from obsidian, quartz, flint, or chert.

Second, paleoanthropologists look for *bilateral flaking.* Bilateral flaking occurs when flakes are struck from two sides of a stone to form a cutting edge. Natural processes may knock a couple of flakes from one side of a stone but will rarely knock them off from opposite sides.

Third, paleoanthropologists look for *retouching.* Retouching occurs when additional flakes are removed from an existing tool in order to resharpen it. Again, natural processes may knock a series of flakes from one side of a rock but will rarely create something resembling a retouched cutting edge.

Paleoanthropologists may also look for a distinct *striking platform* on flakes. A striking platform is the place where the blow landed that knocked the flake from the core. When a flake is struck from a core, it leaves a clean scar that can be used as a striking platform to knock a flake from the opposite side of the core. On flakes made by humans, the striking platform is often the scar left by a previous flake. Just as bilateral flaking is rare in nature, so too is a flake scar with a clearly prepared striking platform.

With these features, paleoanthropologists can usually distinguish naturally flaked rocks from stone tools. But this is not always the case, and many paleoanthropologists have made mistakes. Indeed, one of the most famous mistakes was made by Louis Leakey, one of the first paleoanthropologists to identify early hominid tools. In the late 1960s, Leakey claimed that a site in California called Calico Hills contained early human tools. This claim was met with disbelief, as no evidence of premodern humans has ever been found in North America, and, as we discuss in the next chapter, there is good evidence that modern-looking humans were the continent's first inhabitants. However, because it was Leakey who made the claim, it had to be taken seriously. A group of respected paleoanthropologists met at the site upon Leakey's request to make a determination. Their finding? The alleged stone tools were natural objects, not made by humans.

Calico Hills is an important cautionary tale. How do you know something is a tool? In addition to the tool's physical features, paleoanthropologists must also consider the context in which it is found. When alleged tools are found in the absence of hominids or with no other clear evidence of stone tool use, as in the case of Calico Hills, and the context does not suggest the possibility of tools, paleoanthropologists should question their presence.

Sources: Vance Haynes, "The Calico Site: Artifacts or Geofacts?" *Science,* 181 (1973): 305–10; Leland Patterson, "Criteria for Determining the Attributes of Man-Made Lithics," *Journal of Field Archaeology,* 10 (1983): 297–307.

other was a circular area of dense debris surrounded by an area virtually without debris. Leakey suggested that the area lacking debris may represent the location of a ring of thorny brush with which early hominids surrounded their campsite in order to keep out predators—much like pastoralists living in the region do today.[87] But archaeologists today are not so sure that these sites were home bases. Places with meaty bones lying around may not have been so safe for hominids to use as home bases. Second, the animal remains at the sites had not been completely dismembered and butchered. If the sites had been hominid home bases, we would expect more complete processing of carcasses.[88] Third, natural process-es as simple as trees growing through a site can create circular areas of debris such as the ones Leakey identified as structures, and without better evidence that early hominids made them, one cannot be sure that the circles of debris were indeed structures.[89]

Alternatively, some archaeologists think that these early sites with many animal bones and tools may just have been places where hominids processed food but did not live. Why would the hominids return repeatedly to a particular site? Richard Potts suggests one possible reason—that hominids left caches of stone tools and stones for toolmaking at various locations to facilitate recurrent food-collecting and pro-cessing activities.[90]

Stone Tools and Culture

The presence of patterned stone tools means that these early hominids had probably developed culture. Archaeologists consider a pattern of behavior, such as a particular way to make a tool that is shared and learned by a group of individuals, to be a sign of cultural behavior. To be sure, toolmaking does not imply that early humans had anything like the complex cultures of humans today. Chimpanzees also have patterns of tool use and toolmaking that appear to be shared and learned, but they do not have that much in the way of cultural behavior.

It seems clear that the early hominids, like most other primates, were social beings. It also seems clear from the archaeological record that early hominids were making and using stone tools on a regular basis. Tools are frequently found in discrete concentrations often in association with a large number of animal bones and other debris from human activity suggesting, as we have already noted, campsites or even small shelters used by groups of individuals over periods of time. In such a situation, sharing of food is very likely. It seems counterintuitive to think that individuals would have purposely brought food to a common location only to keep it to themselves. It does seem reasonable to speculate that closely related individuals, like parents, children, and siblings, would be more likely to associate and share food with one another than more distantly related individuals. Even when food sharing takes place among chimpanzees it is usually among closely related individuals.[91] Thus, the ancient locations of early hominid social ac-tivity may be evidence of family groups. How would such a system of social behavior—the creation of a common meeting, resting, and living place for a group of related individuals to share food—have evolved? Let's consider one model.

One Model for the Evolution of Culture

Early *Homo* had a brain almost one-third larger than that of the australopithecines. As we discuss later in the section on trends in hominid evolution, one of the possible consequences of brain expansion was the lessening of maturity at birth. That babies were born more immature may at least partly explain the lengthening of the period of infant and child dependency in hominids. Compared with other animals, we spend not only a longer proportion of our life span, but also the longest absolute period, in a depend-ent state. Prolonged infant dependency has probably been of great significance in human cultural evo-lution. According to Theodosius Dobzhansky,

> it is this helplessness and prolonged dependence on the ministrations of the parents and other per-sons that favors . . . the socialization and learning process on which the transmission of culture wholly depends. This may have been an overwhelming advantage of the human growth pattern in the process of evolution.[92]

It used to be thought that the australopithecines had a long period of infant dependency, just as modern humans do, but the way their teeth apparently developed suggests that the early australopithecines followed an ape-like pattern of development. Thus, prolonged maturation may be relatively recent, but just how recent is not yet known.[93]

Although some use of tools for digging, defense, or scavenging may have influenced the development of bipedalism, full bipedalism may have made possible more efficient toolmaking and consequently more efficient foraging and scavenging. As we have seen, there are archaeological signs that early hominids may have been scavenging (and perhaps even hunting) animals as far back as the late Pliocene. Indeed, we have fairly good evidence that early hominids were butchering and presumably eating big game some 2 million years ago.

Whenever it was that hominids began to scavenge for game and perhaps hunt regularly, the development of scavenging would require individuals to travel long distances frequently in search of suitable carcasses. Among groups of early *Homo,* longer infant and child dependency may have fostered the creation of home bases or at least established meeting places. The demands of childbirth and caring for a newborn might have made it difficult for early *Homo* mothers to travel for some time after the birth. Certainly, it would have been awkward for a mother carrying a nursing child to travel long distances in order to hunt. While carrying an infant might be possible with a sling, successful hunting might not be so likely with a needy and potentially noisy child along. Because early *Homo* males (and perhaps females without young children) would have been freer to roam farther from home, they probably became the scavengers or hunters. Women with young children may have gathered wild plants within a small area that could be covered without traveling far from the home base or meeting place.

The creation of home bases or meeting places among early *Homo* groups may have increased the likelihood of food sharing. If mothers with young children were limited to gathered plant foods in a relatively small area, the only way to ensure that they and their children could obtain a complete diet would have been to share the other foods obtained elsewhere. Sharing with close relations would have made it more likely that their offspring would survive to have offspring. Thus, if early *Homo* had home bases and families, those characteristics could have encouraged the development of the learned and shared behaviors we call culture.

Obviously this is a "just-so" story—a tale that we may never be able to prove really happened. However, it is a tale that is consistent with the archaeological record. Patterned stone tools do not appear until early *Homo* comes on the scene. And with early *Homo* we see the start of several trends in hominid evolution that appear to reflect the manufacture and use of patterned stone tools—the expansion of the brain, the modification of the female pelvis to accommodate bigger-brained babies, and a general reduction in the size of teeth, face, and jaws.

Trends in Hominid Evolution

Expansion of the Brain

The australopithecines had relatively small cranial capacities, about 380–530 cubic centimeters (cc)—not much larger than that of chimpanzees. But around 2.3 million years ago, close to the time that patterned stone tools first appeared, some hominids show evidence of enlarged brain capacity. These hominids, early *Homo,* had cranial capacities averaging about 630–640 cc, which is about 50 percent of the brain capacity of modern humans (which averages slightly more than 1,300 cc). (See Figure 6.3.)

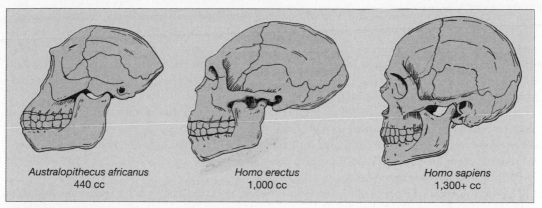

Figure 6.3   Comparison of the Estimated Cranial Capacities of *Australopithecus africanus*, *Homo erectus*, and *Homo sapiens*

Source: Estimated cranial capacities from Ian Tattersall, Eric Delson, and John van Couvering, eds., *Encyclopedia of Human Evolution and Prehistory* (New York: Garland, 2000). Reproduced by permission of Routledge, Inc., part of The Taylor & Francis Group.

The australopithecines were small, and the earliest *Homo* finds were hardly bigger, so much of the increase in brain size over time might have been a result of later hominids' bigger bodies. When we correct for body size, however, it turns out that brain size increased not only absolutely but also relatively after 2 million years ago. Between about 4 million and 2 million years ago, relative brain size remained just about the same. Only in the last 2 million years has the hominid brain doubled in relative size and tripled in absolute size.[94] Many anthropologists think that the increase is linked to the emergence of stone toolmaking about 2.5 million years ago. The reasoning is that stone toolmaking was important for the survival of our ancestors, and therefore natural selection would have favored bigger-brained individuals because they had motor and conceptual skills that enabled them to be better toolmakers. Other anthropologists think that the expansion of the brain may have been favored by other factors, such as warfare, hunting, longer life, and language.[95] Whatever the factors favoring bigger brains, they also provided humans with an expanded capacity for culture. Thus, along with bipedalism, the expansion of the brain marks a watershed in human evolution.

As the hominid brain expanded, natural selection also favored the widening of the female pelvis to allow larger-brained babies to be born. But there was probably a limit to how far the pelvis could widen and still be adapted to bipedalism. Something had to give, and that something was the degree of physical development of the human infant at birth—for instance, the human infant is born with cranial bones so plastic that they can overlap. Because birth takes place before the cranial bones have hardened, the human infant with its relatively large brain can pass through the opening in the mother's pelvis. Human infants are born at a relatively early stage of development, and are wholly dependent on their parents for many years. As we have noted, this lengthy period of infant dependency may have been an important factor in the evolution of culture.

Reduction of the Face, Teeth, and Jaws

As in the case of the brain, substantial changes in the face, teeth, and jaws do not appear in hominid evolution until after about 2 million years ago. The australopithecines all have cheek teeth that are very large relative to their estimated body weight, perhaps because the diet of the australopithecines was especially high in plant foods,[96] including small, tough objects such as seeds, nuts, and tubers. The australopithecines have thick jawbones, probably also related to their chewing needs. The australopithecines have relatively large faces that project forward below the eyes. But when we get to the *Homo* forms, we see reduction in the size of the face, cheek teeth, and jaws (see Figure 6.4). It would seem that natural selection in favor of a bigger and stronger chewing apparatus was relaxed. One reason might be that members of the *Homo* genus started to eat foods that were easier to chew, such as roots, fruits, and meat. Or, as we discuss later, it may have been the development of habitual tool use and the control of fire that allowed members of the *Homo* genus to change their diet to include easier to chew foods, including meat. If food is cooked and easy to chew, individual humans with smaller jaws and teeth would not be disadvantaged, and therefore the face, cheek teeth, and jaw would get smaller on average over time.[97]

The expansion of the brain and reduction of the face occurred at about the same time, and were probably related. A recent discovery in human genetics appears to provide direct evidence of a connection. Researchers studying muscle diseases in modern humans discovered that humans have a unique myosin gene called MYH16 (myosin is a protein in muscle tissue) that is only present in jaw muscles. Comparing MYH16 to related genes in primates, the researchers determined that MYH16 evolved about 2.4 million years ago—around the time the brain began to enlarge and the face and jaw began to shrink. So, the expansion of the brain appears to have been aided by a mutation in myosin that caused jaw muscles to shrink.[98]

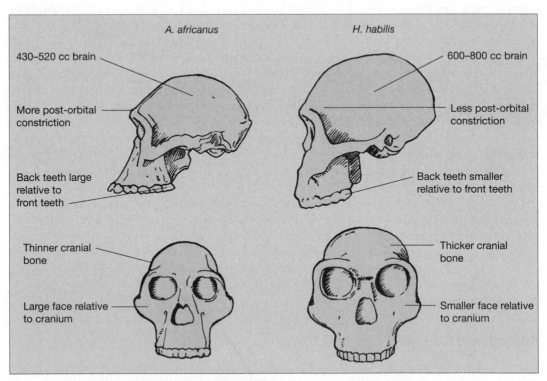

Figure 6.4   Comparison of *A. africanus* and *H. habilis*

Early *Homo* Species

Hominids with a brain absolutely and relatively larger than that of the australopithecines appear about 2.3 million years ago. These hominids, classified in our own genus, *Homo,* are generally divided into two species: **Homo habilis** and **Homo rudolfensis**. Both are known primarily from the western parts of Kenya and Tanzania, but remains have been found elsewhere in eastern and southern Africa, including the Omo Basin of Ethiopia and Sterkfontein cave in South Africa. Both lived in the same place and time as the robust australopithecine, *Australopithecus boisei,* and may later have lived at the same time as *Homo erectus.*

Homo habilis appears to be the earlier of these two species, appearing around 2.3 million years ago. Compared with the australopithecines, *H. habilis* had a significantly larger brain, averaging 630–640 cc,[99] and reduced molars and premolars.[100] The rest of the skeleton is reminiscent of the australopithecines, including the presence of powerful hands and relatively long arms, suggesting that *H. habilis* was at least partially arboreal. *H. habilis* may also have been sexually dimorphic like the australopithecines, as individuals seem to have greatly differed in size.

Homo rudolfensis is roughly contemporary with *Homo habilis,* and shares many of its features. Indeed, many paleoanthropologists make no distinction between the two species, putting *H. rudolfensis* into *H. habilis.* Those who do see them as distinct species point to the larger and more thickly enameled cheek teeth of *H. rudolfensis,* its flatter and broader face, and its more modern-like limb proportions. Even with its larger teeth and broader face, the dentition of *H. rudolfensis* is considerably reduced over the australopithecines and, as in *H. habilis,* its brain is at least a third larger. We have little postcranial skeletal material for either early *Homo* species, so it is impossible to tell whether the female pelvis had changed. But, with brains averaging a third larger than the australopithecines', it seems likely that some modifications must have developed to allow bigger-brained babies to be born. We do know that changes in the female pelvis to accommodate bigger-brained babies can be seen in *Homo erectus,* which spread to many parts of the Old World, and it is this species that we turn to next.

Homo erectus

Homo erectus was the first hominid species to be widely distributed in the Old World. Until recently, it was thought that *Homo erectus* lived in East Africa about 1.6 million years ago but not until after about 1 million years ago in Asia.[101] Recent redating, however, suggests that *H. erectus* in Java may be somewhat older, dating to perhaps 1.8 million years ago.[102] And newer *H. erectus* fossils from Dmanisi, in the southeastern European nation of Georgia, have recently been dated to at least 1.7 million years ago.[103] If this last dating is accurate, hominids may have moved out of Africa earlier. Indeed, one well-preserved skull found at Dmanisi in 2001 has some features that are reminiscent of *H. habilis*—a brain only about 600 cc, relatively large canines, and a relatively thin brow ridge.[104]

Some scholars see enough differences between Asian and African populations of *H. erectus* to argue that they should be separated into two distinct species, *Homo erectus* for the Asian populations and *Homo ergaster* for the African ones. *Homo erectus* (or *Homo ergaster*) fossils are also found in Europe. But some paleoanthropologists think that the finds in Europe typically classified as *H. erectus* are actually early examples of *H. sapiens.*[105] Others think that the European fossils and similar ones found in southern Africa and the Near East should be grouped into a distinct species, *Homo heidelbergensis.* There is also *Homo floresiensis,* a diminutive hominid that appears to be a miniature form of *Homo erectus* that evolved only on the isolated island of Flores, Indonesia. It is all a bit confusing. Later we will try to sort it all out.

The Discovery of *Homo erectus*

In 1891, Eugene Dubois, a Dutch anatomist digging in Java, found what he called *Pithecanthropus erectus,* meaning "erect ape man." (We now refer to this hominid as *Homo erectus.*) The discovery was not the first human-like fossil found; Neandertals, which we discuss in the next chapter, were known many years earlier. But no one was certain, not even Dubois himself, whether the fossil he found in Java was an ape or a human.

The actual find consisted of a cranium and a thighbone. For many years it was thought that the fragments were not even from the same animal. The skull was too large to be that of a modern ape but was smaller than that of an average human, having a cranial capacity between the average ape's 500 cc and the average modern human's 1,300 cc. The thighbone, however, matched that of a modern human. Did the two fragments in fact belong together? The question was resolved many years later by fluorine analysis. If fossils from the same deposit contain the same amount of fluorine, they are the same age. The skull fragment and thighbone found by Dubois were tested for fluorine content and found to be the same age. A discovery by G. H. R. von Koenigswald in the mid-1930s, also in Java, not only confirmed Dubois's earlier speculations and extended our knowledge of the physical characteristics of *Homo erectus* but also gave us a better understanding of this early human's place in time. Since then, many more *H. erectus* fossils have been found in Java. These *H. erectus* in Java were thought not to be more than 1 million years old.[106] Now, however, argon-argon dating puts some of the Java specimens back to perhaps 1.8 million years ago.[107]

Physical Characteristics of *Homo erectus*

The *Homo erectus* skull generally was long, low, and thickly walled, with a flat frontal area and prominent brow ridges. It had a unique pentagonal shape when looked at from the back, formed in part by a rounded ridge, called a **sagittal keel**, running along the crest of the skull. There was also a ridge of bone running horizontally along the back of the skull, called an **occipital torus**, which added to the skull's overall long shape (see Figure 6.5).[108]

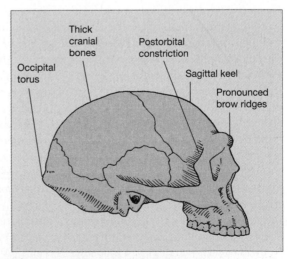

Figure 6.5   *Homo erectus* Features

Compared with early *Homo*, *H. erectus* had relatively small teeth. *H. erectus* was the first hominid to have third molars that were smaller than the second or first molars, as in modern humans. The molars also had an enlarged pulp cavity, called **taurodontism**, which may have allowed the teeth to withstand harder use and wear than the teeth of modern humans. But the *H. erectus* jaw was lighter and thinner than in either early *Homo* or the australopithecines, and the face was less **prognathic**, or forward thrusting, in the upper and lower jaw. The brain, averaging 895–1,040 cc, was larger than that found in any of the australopithecines or early *Homo* species, smaller than the average brain of a modern human.[109] Endocasts, which provide a picture of the surface of the brain, suggest that it was organized more like the brain of modern humans than like that of australopithecines.

Homo erectus had a prominent, projecting nose, in contrast to the australopithecines' flat, nonprojecting nose.[110] From the neck down, *H. erectus* was practically indistinguishable from *H. sapiens*. In contrast to the smaller australopithecines and early *Homo* species who lived in East Africa around the same time, *H. erectus* was comparable to modern humans in size. The almost complete skeleton of the boy at Nariokotome, Kenya suggests that he was about five-and-a-half feet tall and about eleven years of age when he died; researchers estimate that he would have been over six feet tall had he lived to maturity. About 1.6 million years ago, the Nariokotome region was probably open grassland, with trees mostly along rivers.[111] *Homo erectus* in East Africa was similar in size to Africans today who live in a similarly open, dry environment.[112] *H. erectus* was also less sexually dimorphic than either the australopithecines or early *Homo*. The degree of sexual dimorphism in *H. erectus* was comparable to that in modern humans.

Homo floresiensis

Whether or not there are distinct African and Asian species of *Homo erectus*, most scholars agree that **Homo floresiensis** is a distinct species that is closely related to *Homo erectus*. *H. floresiensis* has only been found on the Indonesian island of Flores, and only a handful of individuals have been located to date. All are tiny (they stood perhaps three feet tall), and have very small brains, on the order of 380 cc.[113] The structure of the brain, however, seems closely related to that of *H. erectus*, as do the structures of the skull.[114] In other words, *H. floresiensis* appears to be a tiny version of *H. erectus*. *H. floresiensis* made tools that look similar to those made by *H. erectus*, and in some cases the tools look even more sophisticated.[115]

Shown here is a skull of the dwarf species *Homo floriensis* next to that of a modern human. Note how small it is in comparison.

How might a miniature version of *H. erectus* have evolved? Dwarfism appears to be an adaptation that occurs when there are few predators—a species in isolation can become smaller, and have a large population, if there are no predators threatening them. This may be what happened on Flores.[116] The island also hosted a number of dwarf species in addition to *H. floresiensis,* including a dwarf elephant that appears to have been one of the favorite foods of *H. floresiensis. H. floresiensis* may have survived until as recently as 12,000 years ago—well into the time period when modern humans were living in Indonesia.

The Evolution of *Homo erectus*

The evolution of *Homo erectus* reflects a continuation of the general evolutionary trends we discussed previously. The brain continued to expand, increasing more than a third over early *Homo* (just as early *Homo* had increased more than a third over the australopithecines). The face, teeth, and jaws continued to shrink, taking on an almost modern form. An increasing use and variety of tools may have led to a further development of the brain. *Homo erectus* was eating and probably cooking meat, and this may have led to further reduction in the teeth and jaws.

One additional change in *Homo erectus* is an apparent reduction in the extent of sexual dimorphism to almost modern levels. Recall that the australopithecines and early *Homo* were quite sexually dimorphic. What might have caused this change? In other primates, sexual dimorphism appears to be linked to social systems in which males are at the top of dominance hierarchies and dominant males control sexual access to multiple females. In contrast, lack of sexual dimorphism seems most pronounced in the animals where *pair bonding* exists—that is, where one male and one female form a breeding pair that lasts for a long period of time.[117] Could pair bonding have developed in *Homo erectus?* It seems possible.

In animal species where females can feed themselves and their babies after birth, pair bonding is rare. But in species where females cannot feed both themselves and their babies, pair bonding is common. Why? The Embers have suggested that a pair bond provides the best solution to the problem of incompatibility between a mother's feeding requirements and tending a newborn baby. A male partner can bring food and/or watch the newborn while the mother gets food.[118] But most primates lack pair bonding. This may be because primate infants are able to cling to their mother's fur soon after birth, so that the mother's hands are free to forage. Human infants demonstrate a residual form of this innate ability to cling during their first few weeks of life. This is called the *Moro reflex.*[119]

We have no way of knowing if *Homo erectus* had fur like other primates, but we think probably not because, as we discuss below, we think they may have worn clothing. The brain in *Homo erectus* may also have already expanded enough that *Homo erectus* infants, like modern human infants, could not adequately support their heads even if they could hold onto their mother's fur. In any case, when early hominids began to depend on scavenging and hunting for food (and for skins to be used in clothing), it would have been difficult and hazardous for a parent with a newborn baby to engage in these activities with a baby along. Pair bonding ("marriage") would have been an effective solution to this problem because each parent could help protect the baby while the other was away getting food. (For further discussion of this theory, see the chapter on marriage, family, and kinship.)

Another important aspect of the evolution of *Homo erectus* was the movement of populations out of eastern and southern Africa. As with the lessening of sexual dimorphism, it seems likely that cultural innovations were the key to allowing *Homo erectus* to move into new environments. All animals adapt to such changes through natural selection, but natural selection typically takes a relatively long time and requires physical changes in the adapting organisms. *Homo erectus* was able to adapt to new environments very quickly and without apparent physical changes. This suggests that the primary mechanisms of adaptation for *Homo erectus* were cultural rather than biological.

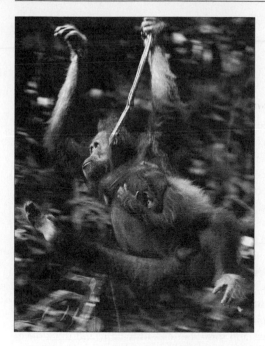

This orangutan mother has no problem traveling with her infant, as it can cling tightly to her fur. *Homo erectus* mothers probably had no fur to hold on to and had to carry their infants.

What cultural adaptations might *Homo erectus* have made? Fire may have been the crucial one because it would make it possible to move to and live in colder climates. As we discuss below, there is tantalizing evidence that *Homo erectus* used fire. But fire can only warm people when they are stationary; it doesn't help when people are out collecting food. To be mobile in colder climates, *Homo erectus* may have begun to wear animal furs for warmth. Some *Homo erectus* tools look like the hide-processing tools used by more recent human groups,[120] and it seems unlikely that *Homo erectus* could have survived in the colder locations where they have been found, in eastern Europe and Asia, without some form of clothing. If *Homo erectus* was wearing furs for warmth, they must have been hunting. *Homo erectus* could not have depended on scavenging to acquire skins—the skin is the first thing predators destroy when they dismember a carcass.

Lower Paleolithic Cultures

The stone tool traditions of *Homo erectus* are traditionally called **Lower Paleolithic**. These stone tool traditions involve "core" tool techniques, in which a core of stone, rather than a flake, is used as the basic raw material for finished tools. Since stone tools are the most common cultural material in the archaeological record of these ancient peoples, the entire culture of *Homo erectus* is often termed *Lower Paleolithic*, a practice we follow here.

The archaeological finds of tools and other cultural artifacts dating from 1.5 million years to about 200,000 years ago are assumed to have been produced by *Homo erectus*. But hominid fossils are not usually associated with these materials. Therefore it is possible that some of the tools during this period were produced by hominids other than *H. erectus*, such as australopithecines earlier and *H. sapiens* later. But the so-called *Acheulian* tool assemblages dating from 1.5 million years ago to more than a million years later are very similar to each other, and *H. erectus* is the only hominid that spans the entire period. Thus it is conventionally assumed that *H. erectus* was responsible for most if not all of the Acheulian tool assemblages we now describe.[121]

The Acheulian Tool Tradition

The stone toolmaking tradition known as the **Acheulian** was named after the site at St. Acheul, France, where the first examples were found. But the oldest Acheulian tools recovered are from East Africa, on the Peninj River, Tanzania, dating back about 1.5 million years.[122] In contrast to Oldowan, Acheulian assemblages have more large tools created according to standardized designs or shapes. Oldowan tools have sharp edges made by a few blows. Acheulian toolmakers shaped the stone by knocking more flakes off most of the edges. Many of these tools were made from very large flakes that had first been struck from very large cores or boulders.

One of the most characteristic and common tools in the Acheulian tool kit is the so-called **hand axe**, which is a teardrop-shaped, bifacially flaked tool with a thinned sharp tip. Other large tools resemble cleavers and picks. There were also many kinds of flake tools, such as scrapers with a wide edge.

Early Acheulian tools appeared to have been made by blows with a hard stone, but later tools are wider and flatter and may have been made with a **soft hammer** of bone or antler.[123] This soft hammer technique of making stone tools was an important innovation. Tools made by a **hard hammer** technique, rock against rock, have limits in terms of their sharpness and form, because only large and thick flakes can be easily made with a hard hammer technique. Flakes created by soft hammer flaking are much thinner and longer than hard hammer flakes, and the flintknapper generally has better control over their size and shape. This means that thinner and sharper tools can be made, as well as tools with complex shapes.[124]

Were hand axes made for chopping trees, as their name suggests? Experiments suggest that they are not good for cutting trees; they seem more suited for butchering large animals.[125] Lawrence Keeley microscopically examined some Acheulian hand axes, and the wear on them is more consistent with animal butchery. They may also have been used for woodworking, particularly hollowing and shaping wood, and they are also good for digging.[126] William Calvin has even suggested that a hand axe could be used as a projectile thrown like a discus into a herd of animals in the hope of injuring or killing an animal.[127]

Acheulian tools are found widely in Africa, Europe, and western Asia, but bifacial hand axes, cleavers, and picks are not found as commonly in eastern and southeastern Asia.[128] Because *H. erectus* has been found in all areas of the Old World, it is puzzling that the tool traditions seem to differ from west to east. Some archaeologists have suggested that large bifacial tools may be lacking in eastern and southeastern Asia because *H. erectus* in Asia had a better material to make tools out of—bamboo. Bamboo has been used recently in Southeast Asia for many purposes, including incredibly sharp arrows and sticks for digging and cutting. Geoffrey Pope has shown that bamboo is found precisely in those areas of Asia where hand axes and other large bifacial tools are largely missing.[129]

Big-Game Eating

Some of the Acheulian sites have produced evidence of big-game eating. F. Clark Howell, who excavated sites at Torralba and Ambrona, Spain, found a substantial number of elephant remains and unmistakable evidence of human presence in the form of tools. Howell suggests that the humans at those sites used fire to frighten elephants into muddy bogs from which they would be unable to escape.[130] To hunt elephants in this way, the humans would have had to plan and work cooperatively in fairly large groups.

But do these finds of bones of large and medium-sized animals, in association with tools, tell us that the humans definitely were big-game hunters? Some archaeologists who have reanalyzed the evidence from Torralba think that the big game may have been scavenged. Because the Torralba and Ambrona sites are near ancient streams, many of the elephants could have died naturally, their bones accumulating in certain spots because of the flow of water.[131] What seems fairly clear is that the humans did deliberately butcher different kinds of game—different types of tools are found with different types of animals.[132] Thus, whether the humans hunted big game at Torralba and Ambrona is debatable; all we can be sure of, as of now, is that they probably consumed big game and hunted smaller game.

Control of Fire

One way in which *H. erectus* is thought to have hunted is by using *fire drives*—a technique still used by hunting and gathering peoples in recent times. It is highly effective: Animals are driven out of their hiding places and homes by fire and dispatched by hunters positioned downwind of the oncoming flames. Most peoples who use this technique today set fires deliberately, but fires caused by lightning strikes may have also been utilized. Did *H. erectus* set these fires? Because *H. erectus* was the first hominid to be found throughout the Old World and in areas with freezing winters, most anthropologists presume that *H. erectus* had learned to control fire, at least for warmth. There is archaeological evidence of fire in some early sites, but fires can be natural events.[133]

Suggestive but not conclusive evidence of the deliberate use of fire comes from Kenya in East Africa and is over 1.4 million years old.[134] More persuasive evidence of human control of fire, dating from nearly 800,000 years ago, comes from the site of Gesher Benot Ya'aqov in Israel. Here researchers found evidence of burned seeds, wood, and stone, as well as concentrations of burned items suggestive of hearths.[135] Evidence of the deliberate use of fire comes from Europe somewhat later. The evidence of control of fire at Gesher Benot Ya'aqov and European sites is not associated with *H. erectus* fossils, so the link between deliberate use of fire and *H. erectus* cannot definitely be established yet.[136] The lack of clear evidence does not, of course, mean that *H. erectus* did not use fire. After all, *H. erectus* did move into cold areas of

Homo erectus probably hunted large game animals, and they probably learned how to control fire.

the world, and it is hard to imagine how that could have happened without the deliberate use of fire. Such a move is also hard to imagine if *H. erectus* were relatively hairless and did not get warm skins and furs from hunting.

Clothing, therefore, may have been necessary, but fire might have been even more important, and not only for warmth. Cooking would now be possible. The control of fire was a major step in increasing the energy under human control. Cooking would have made all kinds of food (not just meat) more safely digestible and therefore more usable.[137] Fires would also have kept predators away, a not inconsiderable advantage given that there were many.

Campsites

Acheulian sites were usually located close to water sources, lush vegetation, and large stocks of herbivorous animals. Some camps have been found in caves, but most were in open areas surrounded by rudimentary fortifications or windbreaks. Several African sites are marked by stony rubble brought there by *H. erectus,* possibly for the dual purpose of securing the windbreaks and providing ammunition in case of a sudden attack.[138]

The presumed base campsites display a wide variety of tools, indicating that the camp was the center of many group functions. More specialized sites away from camp have also been found. For example, a butchering site in Tanzania contained dismembered hippopotamus carcasses and rare heavy-duty smashing and cutting tools. Workshops are characterized by tool debris and are located close to a source of natural stone suitable for toolmaking.[139]

A camp has been excavated at the Terra Amata site near Nice, on the French Riviera. The camp appears to have been occupied in the late spring or early summer, judging by the pollen found in fossilized human feces. The excavator describes stake holes driven into the sand, paralleled by lines of stones, presumably marking the spots where the people constructed huts of roughly 30 by 15 feet (Figure 6.6). A

Figure 6.6   A Reconstruction of the Oval Huts Built at Terra Amata
These huts were approximately 30 feet by 15 feet.
Source: Copyright © 1969 by Eric Mose. Reprinted by permission of Eric Mose, Jr.

basic feature of each hut was a central hearth that seems to have been protected from drafts by a small wall built just outside the northeast corner of the hearth. The evidence suggests that the Terra Amata occupants gathered seafood such as oysters and mussels, did some fishing, and hunted in the surrounding area. The animal remains suggest that they obtained both small and large animals but mostly got the young of larger animals such as stags, elephants, boars, rhinoceroses, and wild oxen. Some of the huts contain recognizable toolmakers' areas, scattered with tool debris; occasionally, the impression of an animal skin shows where the toolmaker actually sat.[140]

Summary

1. The drying trend in climate that began about 16 million to 11 million years ago diminished the African rain forests and gave rise to areas of savanna and scattered woodlands. The more open country probably favored characteristics adapted to ground living in some primates. In the evolutionary line leading to humans, these adaptations included bipedalism.

2. One of the crucial changes in early hominid evolution was the development of bipedalism. There are several theories for this development: Bipedalism may have increased the ability to see predators and potential prey while moving through the tall grasses of the savanna; by freeing the hands for carrying, it may have facilitated transferring food from one place to another; freeing the hands may have made at easier to gather seeds; tool use, which requires free hands to carry tools and weapons, may have favored two-legged walking; and bipedalism may have made long-distance traveling more efficient. Two-legged walking may also have helped to cool the body.

3. *Sahelanthropus, Orrorin,* and *Ardipithecus* are likely candidates for the first hominid. They date as early as 6 million years ago, and may have walked bipedally. Undisputed hominids dating before 4 million years ago have been found in East Africa. These definitely bipedal hominids are now generally classified in the genus *Australopithecus*.

4. At least six species of australopithecine have been identified, and these are generally divided into two types: gracile and robust. The gracile australopithecines have relatively smaller teeth and jaws, and include *A. anamensis, A. afarensis,* and *A. africanus.* The robust australopithecines have relatively larger teeth and jaws, and are more muscular than the gracile australopithecines. They include *A. aethiopicus, A. robustus,* and *A. boisei.*

5. The earliest identifiable stone tools found so far come from various sites in East Africa and date from about 2.5 million years ago. Flake tools predominate, but choppers are also common. These early stone tools are referred to as Oldowan. Experimental research suggests that flakes can be used for slitting the hides of animals, dismembering animals, and whittling wood. Choppers can be used to hack off branches or cut and chop tough animal joints. Hominids shortly after 2 million years ago were cutting up animal carcasses for meat, mostly obtained through scavenging rather than hunting.

6. The presence of stone tools and perhaps home bases suggests that early hominids had culture.

7. Important physical changes in early hominids that led to the evolution of our genus, *Homo,* include the expansion of the brain, the modification of the female pelvis to allow bigger-brained babies to be born, and the reduction of the face, teeth, and jaws. These physical changes are seen in the species *Homo habilis* and *Homo rudolfensis,* both of which date to around 2.3 million years ago. Early *Homo* appears to have used tools and scavenged or possibly hunted meat, so culture, or the evolution of cultural behavior, seems to have played a role in these physical changes as well.

8.   *Homo erectus* emerged about 1.8 million to 1.6 million years ago and was the first hominid species to be widely distributed in the Old World. It had a larger brain capacity than *Homo habilis* and an essentially modern postcranial skeleton. What differentiates *Homo erectus* most from modern humans is the shape of the skull, which is long, low, and has prominent brow ridges. Some of the locations where *Homo erectus* lived in eastern Europe and Asia were quite cold. *Homo erectus* may have learned to use fire to survive the cold.

9.   Lower Paleolithic tools and other cultural artifacts from about 1.6 million to about 200,000 years ago were probably produced by *H. erectus*. Acheulian is the name given to the most well-known tool tradition of this period. Acheulian tools include both small flake tools and large tools, but hand axes and other large bifacial tools are characteristic.

Glossary Terms

Acheulian (p. 148)
Ardipithecus ramidus (p. 127)
Australopithecus (p. 127)
Australopithecus aethiopicus (p. 132)
Australopithecus afarensis (p. 128)
Australopithecus africanus (p. 129)
Australopithecus anamensis (p. 128)
Australopithecus bahrelghazali (p. 131)
Australopithecus boisei (p. 133)
Australopithecus garhi (p. 131)
Australopithecus robustus (p. 133)
bifacial tool (p. 136)
foramen magnum (p. 126)
gracile australopithecines (p. 127)
hand axe (p. 148)
hard hammer (p. 148)
Homo erectus (p. 143)
Homo floresiensis (p. 145)

Homo habilis (p. 143)
Homo rudolfensis (p. 143)
Kenyanthropus platyops (p. 132)
Lower Paleolithic (p. 147)
occipital torus (p. 144)
Oldowan (p. 136)
Orrorin tugenensis (p. 126)
percussion flaking (p. 136)
Pliocene (p. 134)
prognathic (p. 145)
robust australopithecines (p. 127)
sagittal crest (p. 127)
sagittal keel (p. 144)
Sahelanthropus tchadensis (p. 126)
savanna (p. 123)
soft hammer (p. 148)
taurodontism (p. 145)
unifacial tool (p. 136)

Critical Questions

1.   How could there have been more than one species of hominid living in East Africa at the same time?

2.   Why might early hominids have begun to make stone tools? How would stone tools have been more useful than wood or bone tools?

3.   When compared to earlier hominids, *Homo erectus* is larger, has a larger brain, and smaller teeth. How might these physical changes correlate with apparent behavioral changes in *Homo erectus*?

4.   *Homo erectus* lived in many places in the Old World. What may have enabled them to spread so widely?

CHAPTER 7

THE EMERGENCE OF HOMO SAPIENS

Chapter Outline

- The Transition from *Homo erectus* to *Homo sapiens*
- Middle Paleolithic Cultures
- The Emergence of Modern Humans
- What Happened to the Neandertals?
- The Upper Paleolithic World

Recent finds in Africa indicate the presence of *Homo sapiens* at least 100,000 years ago. Completely modern-looking humans, ***Homo sapiens sapiens***, appeared by 50,000 years ago. One paleoanthropologist, Christopher Stringer, characterizes the modern human, *Homo sapiens sapiens,* as having "a domed skull, a chin, small eyebrows, brow ridges, and a rather puny skeleton."[1] Some of us might not like to be called puny, but except for our larger brain, most modern humans definitely are puny compared with *Homo erectus* and even with earlier forms of our own species, *H. sapiens.* We are relatively puny in several respects, including our thinner and lighter bones, as well as our smaller teeth and jaws.

In this chapter we discuss the fossil evidence, as well as the controversies, about the transition from *H. erectus* to modern humans, which may have begun 500,000 years ago. We then discuss what we know archaeologically about the Middle Paleolithic cultures between about 300,000 and 40,000 years ago. And then we discuss what the Upper Paleolithic world was like 40,000 to 10,000 years ago.

The Transition from *Homo erectus* to *Homo sapiens*

Most paleoanthropologists agree that *H. erectus* evolved into *H. sapiens,* but they disagree about how and where the transition occurred. There is also disagreement about how to classify some fossils from about 500,000 to 200,000 years ago that have a mix of *H. erectus* and *H. sapiens* traits.[2] A particular fossil might be called *H. erectus* by some anthropologists and "archaic" *Homo sapiens* by others. And, as we shall see, still other anthropologists see so much continuity between *H. erectus* and *H. sapiens* that they think it is completely arbitrary to call them different species. According to these anthropologists, *H. erectus* and *H. sapiens* may just be earlier and later varieties of the same species and therefore all should be called *H. sapiens.* (*H. erectus* would then be *H. sapiens erectus.*)

Homo heidelbergensis

In recent years some scholars have suggested that the "transitional" fossils share common traits and may actually represent a separate species—***Homo heidelbergensis***, named after a jaw found in 1907 in the village of Mauer near Heidelberg, Germany.[3] Other specimens that have been suggested as members of this species have been found in many parts of the Old World. *Homo heidelbergensis* differs from *Homo erectus* in having smaller teeth and jaws, a much larger brain (on the order of 1,300 cc), a skull that lacks a sagittal keel and occipital torus, a brow ridge that divides into separate arches above each eye, and a more robust skeleton (see Figure 7.1). *Homo heidelbergensis* differs also from *Homo sapiens: H. heidelbergensis* had a large and more prognathic face with relatively large teeth and jaws, a brow ridge, a long, low cranial vault with a sloping forehead, and a more robust skeleton.[4]

Neandertals: *Homo sapiens* or *Homo neandertalensis*?

There may be disagreement about how to classify the mixed-trait fossils from 500,000 to 200,000 years ago, but recently an outright battle has emerged about many of the fossils that are less than 200,000 years old. Some anthropologists argue that they were definitely *Homo sapiens* and classify them as *Homo sapiens neandertalensis.* Others say that they were part of a distinct species, ***Homo neandertalensis***, more commonly referred to as the **Neandertals**. The Neandertals have been a confusing hominid fossil group since the first specimen was found in 1856. Somehow through the years, the Neandertals have become the victims of their cartoon image, which usually misrepresents them as burly and more ape than human.

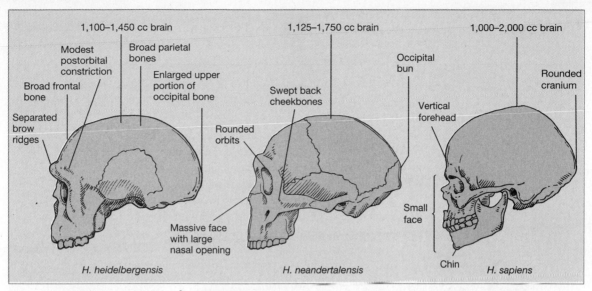

Figure 7.1   Comparison of the crania of *Homo heidelbergensis*, *Homo neandertalensis*, and *Homo sapiens*

Actually, they might go unnoticed in a cross-section of the world's population today. Were they members of our species? For a while the answer seemed to be yes. But newer archaeological and genetic evidence has led many to question the relationship between Neandertals and modern humans, and today the tide seems to have turned against those who would group them together. Let's take a look at some of the history of research on the Neandertals.

In 1856, three years before Darwin's publication of *The Origin of Species,* a skullcap and other fossilized bones were discovered in a cave in the Neander Valley (*tal* is the German word for "valley"), near Düsseldorf, Germany. The fossils in the Neander Valley were the first that scholars could tentatively consider as early hominid. (The fossils classified as *Homo erectus* were not found until later in the nineteenth century, and the fossils belonging to the genus *Australopithecus* not until the twentieth century.) After Darwin's revolutionary work was published, the Neandertal find aroused considerable controversy. Some dismissed the Neandertal as irrelevant to human evolution; they saw it as a freak or as a peculiar, disease-ridden individual. However, similar fossils turned up later in Belgium, Yugoslavia, France, and elsewhere in Europe, which meant that the original Neandertal find could not be dismissed as an oddity.[5]

The predominant reaction to the original and subsequent Neandertal-like finds was that the Neandertals were too "brutish" and "primitive" to have been ancestral to modern humans. This view prevailed in the scholarly community until well into the 1950s. It is now universally agreed, however, that the skeletal traits of the Neandertals are completely consistent with bipedalism.

Perhaps more important, when the much more ancient australopithecine and *H. erectus* fossils were accepted as hominids in the 1940s and 1950s, anthropologists realized that the Neandertals did not look that different from modern humans—despite their sloping foreheads, large brow ridges, flattened braincases, large jaws, and nearly absent chins.[6] After all, they did have larger brains (averaging more than 1,450 cc) than modern humans (slightly more than 1,300 cc).[7] Some scholars believe that the large brain capacity of Neandertals suggests that they were capable of the full range of behaviors characteristic of modern humans. Their skeletons did, however, attest to one behavioral trait that differed from what we usually see in modern humans: Judging by their robust bones, Neandertals made very strenuous use of their bodies.[8]

PUTTING FACES ON FOSSILS

Have you wondered how we know what early humans looked like? How did the artists who have made images of early humans determine what to sculpt or draw? The answer lies in the field of forensic anthropology and more particularly in the field of facial reconstruction.

Facial reconstruction is based on knowledge of skull musculature and the thickness of soft tissue, determined over many years (the first such analysis was done in 1895) from cadavers and, more recently, magnetic resonance images of living people. From these measurements, forensic anthropologists have established a standard set of 21 to 34 locations on the skull where the average soft tissue thicknesses are known. The

Boule's reconstruction of a Neandertal, displayed at Chicago's Field Museum in 1929, illustrates how subjective fossil reconstructions can be. It falsely implies that Neandertals could not stand upright or straighten their knees, and that they were more primitive than they actually were.

first step in facial reconstruction is to mark these locations on a cast of the skull to be reconstructed, using pegs that are the same length as the thickness of muscle and soft tissue at that location. Clay is then used to cover the skull cast to the depth of these pegs (the musculature of the face is first modeled in more sophisticated reconstructions, then clay is used to represent the soft tissues, up to the depth of the pegs).

The size and shape of the nose are reconstructed based on the size and shape of the nasal opening. The size and shape of lips and ears are more difficult to determine, and the skull itself can tell the forensic anthropologist almost nothing about hair or eye color, whether the person had facial hair, or how the person's hair was cut. Those aspects of facial reconstruction require some artistic intuition, and it is helpful to know something about the person, such as sex, age, and ethnicity.

But what about ancient humans? The standard measurements used to reconstruct faces from modern human skulls cannot be assumed to work for ancient skulls. For those, the forensic anthropologists have to go back to the basis of facial reconstruction—muscle and soft tissue. When reconstructing the faces of ancient humans, forensic anthropologists begin with a careful reconstruction of skull musculature, often aided by the comparative anatomy of modern great apes. Once the muscles are in place, glands, fatty tissue, and skin are added, and the face begins to take shape. Just as for modern human reconstructions, the size and shape of the nose are determined from the size and shape of the nasal opening. Lips, ears, eyes, and hair are, however, subject to almost pure guesswork—we really have no way of knowing how hairy our ancestors were, whether they had full lips like ours or thin lips like other great apes, or whether their ears were large or small.

Though based on study of the likely muscular anatomy in fossils and the comparative anatomy of modern humans and great apes, it is important to remember that the reconstruction of an ancient face is in part an artistic exercise. This is why different reconstructions vary in how they depict ancient humans. They may be educated guesses, but they are not necessarily accurate.

Sources: John Prag and Richard Neave, *Making Faces: Using Forensic and Archaeological Evidence* (College Station: Texas A&M University Press, 1997); Stephanie Moser, *Ancestral Images: The Iconography of Human Origins* (Ithaca, NY: Cornell University Press, 1998).

It took almost 100 years for scholars to accept the idea that Neandertals were not that different from modern humans and perhaps should be classified as *Homo sapiens neandertalensis.* But there has been a growing debate over whether the Neandertals in western Europe were ancestral to modern-looking people who lived later in western Europe, after about 40,000 years ago.

In 1997, a group of researchers from the United States and Germany published findings that forced a reconsideration of the Neandertals and their relationship to modern humans. These scholars reported that they had been able to extract DNA from the original Neandertal specimen found in Germany in 1856.[9] The DNA they extracted was not nuclear DNA—the material that makes up the human genome. Rather, it came from tiny structures found in all eukaryotic cells (i.e., cells with a membrane-bound nucleus and DNA in the chromosomes) called *mitochondria.* Mitochondria produce enzymes needed for energy production, and they have their own DNA, which replicates when a cell replicates but is not thought to be under any pressure from natural selection.[10]

So the only source of change in mitochondrial DNA (usually referred to as *mt*DNA) is random mutation. Mitochondrial DNA is inherited only from mothers in animals; it is not carried into an egg cell by sperm, but is left with the sperm's tail on the outside of the egg. These unique characteristics make it possible to use mtDNA to measure the degree of relatedness between two species, and even to say how long ago those species diverged.[11] The longer two species have been separated, the more differences there will be in their mtDNA, which is thought to mutate at a fairly constant rate of about 2 percent per million years. Thus, the number of differences between the mtDNA of two organisms can be converted into an estimated date in the past when those organisms stopped being part of the same breeding population. While controversy remains over many of the details of how and why mtDNA mutates and about its accuracy for determining absolute dates of divergence, most scholars agree that it is a powerful tool for examining relative degrees of relatedness between species.[12]

How similar is Neandertal mtDNA to modern human DNA? Not as similar as many scholars would have expected. Among individual modern humans, there are usually five to ten differences in the sequence of mtDNA examined by the U.S. and German researchers. Between modern humans and the Neandertal specimen, there tend to be about 25 differences—more than three times that among modern humans (see Figure 7.2 on page 158). This suggested to the researchers that the ancestors of modern humans and the Neandertal in Germany must have diverged about 600,000 years ago.[13] If the last common ancestor of ours and the Neandertal lived that long ago, the Neandertal would be a much more distant relative than previously thought. This research has since been replicated with mtDNA from other Neandertal fossils.[14]

Recent archaeological findings from Europe and the Near East may indicate that Neandertals and the modern human were different species. It has been known for decades that both modern human and Neandertal fossils are found in the same locations in parts of the Levant, but recent improvements in dating technology and newly discovered fossils have even more clearly demonstrated that the two kinds of hominid coexisted. In fact, several caves in the Mount Carmel region of Israel contain both modern human and Neandertal occupations. If these two groups of hominids coinhabited the Near East for perhaps as much as 30,000 years and did not interbreed or share much in the way of tool technology, that suggests the two were different species.[15] And finds in Europe seem to corroborate that assessment. As early modern humans began moving into Europe they appear to have displaced populations of Neandertals already living there. Sites with tools thought to be associated with Neandertals disappear throughout Europe as sites with tools thought to be associated with modern humans expand their range.[16] Significantly, the area of Europe (Iberia) last colonized by modern humans contains the most recent Neandertal fossils yet found, dating to some 30,000 years ago.[17]

With all this evidence pointing to Neandertals being a different species from modern humans, why is there an ongoing debate? In part this is because none of the evidence is conclusive, and much of it can

Figure 7.2   Differences in mtDNA Sequences among Humans, the Neandertal, and Chimpanzees
The x-axis shows the number of sequence differences; the y-axis shows the percent of individuals that share that number of sequence differences.
Source: Cell, 90 (1997): 25.

be interpreted in alternate ways. Perhaps more important, however, Neandertal culture, typically referred to as Middle Paleolithic after the predominant tool technology, has some features that resemble the culture of early modern humans.

Middle Paleolithic Cultures

The period of cultural history associated with the Neandertals is traditionally called the **Middle Paleolithic** in Europe and the Near East and dates from about 300,000 years to about 40,000 years ago.[18] For Africa, the term *Middle Stone Age* is used instead of Middle Paleolithic. The tool assemblages from this period are generally referred to as *Mousterian* in Europe and the Near East and as *post-Acheulian* in Africa.

Tool Assemblages

The Mousterian   The Mousterian type of tool complex is named after the tool assemblage found in a rock shelter at Le Moustier in the Dordogne region of southwestern France. Compared with an Acheulian assemblage, a **Mousterian tool assemblage** has a smaller proportion of large core tools such as hand axes and cleavers and a bigger proportion of small flake tools such as scrapers.[19] Although many flakes struck off from a core were used "as is," the Mousterian is also characterized by flakes that were often altered or "retouched" by striking small flakes or chips from one or more edges (see Figure 7.3).[20] Studies of the wear on scrapers suggest that many were used for scraping hides or working wood. The fact that

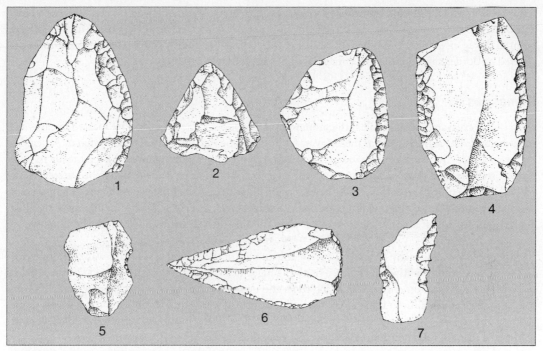

Figure 7.3   A Typical Mousterian Tool Kit

A Mousterian tool kit emphasized sidescrapers (1–4), notches (5), points (6), and saw-toothed denticulates (7). How these stone artifacts were actually used is not known, but the points may have been joined to wood shafts, and denticulates could have been used to work wood. The tools illustrated here are from Mousterian sites in western Europe.

Source: From Richard G. Klein, "Ice-Age Hunters of the Ukraine," *Scientific American* (June 1974): 96–105.

some of the tools, particularly points, were thinned or shaped on one side suggests that they were hafted or attached to a shaft or handle.[21]

Toward the end of the Acheulian period, a technique developed that enabled the toolmaker to produce flake tools of a predetermined size instead of simply chipping flakes away from the core at random. In this **Levalloisian method**, the toolmaker first shaped the core and prepared a "striking platform" at one end. Flakes of predetermined and standard sizes could then be knocked off. Although some Levallois flakes date as far back as 400,000 years ago, they are found more frequently in Mousterian tool kits.[22]

The tool assemblages in particular sites may be characterized as Mousterian, but one site may have more or fewer scrapers, points, and so forth, than another site. A number of archaeologists have suggested possible reasons for this variation. For example, Sally Binford and Lewis Binford suggested that different activities may have occurred in different sites. Some sites may have been used for butchering and other sites may have been base camps; hence the kinds of tools found in different sites should vary.[23] And Paul Fish has suggested that some sites may have more tools produced by the Levalloisian technique because larger pieces of flint were available.[24]

The Post-Acheulian in Africa   Like Mousterian tools, many of the post-Acheulian tools in Africa during the Middle Stone Age were struck off prepared cores in the Levalloisian way. The assemblages consist mostly of various types of flake tools. A well-described sequence of such tools comes from the area around the mouth of the Klasies River on the southern coast of South Africa. This area contains rock shelters and small caves in which early and later *Homo sapiens* lived. The oldest cultural remains in one of the caves may date back 120,000 years.[25] These earliest tools include parallel-sided flake blades (probably used as knives), pointed flakes (possibly spearpoints), burins or gravers (chisel-like tools), and scrapers. Similar tools discovered at Border cave, South Africa, may have been used almost 200,000 years ago.[26]

Homesites

Most of the excavated Middle Paleolithic homesites in Europe and the Near East are located in caves and rock shelters. The same is true for the excavated Middle Stone Age homesites in sub-Saharan Africa. We might conclude, therefore, that Neandertals (as well as many early modern humans) lived mostly in caves or rock shelters. But that conclusion could be incorrect. Caves and rock shelters may be overrepresented in the archaeological record because they are more likely to be found than sites that originally were in the open but now are hidden by thousands of years, and many feet, of sediment. Sediment is the dust, debris, and decay that accumulate over time; when we dust the furniture and vacuum the floor, we are removing sediment.

Still, we know that many Neandertals lived at least part of the year in caves. This was true, for example, along the Dordogne River in France. The river gouged deep valleys in the limestone of that area. Below the cliffs are rock shelters with overhanging roofs and deep caves, many of which were occupied during the Middle Paleolithic. Even if the inhabitants did not stay all year, the sites do seem to have been occupied year after year.[27] Although there is evidence of some use of fire in earlier cultures, Middle Paleolithic humans seem to have relied more on fire. There are thick layers of ash in many rock shelters and caves and evidence that hearths were used to increase the efficiency of the fires.[28]

Quite a few Neandertal homesites were in the open. In Africa, open-air sites were located on floodplains, at the edges of lakes, and near springs.[29] Many open-air sites have been found in Europe, particularly eastern Europe. The occupants of the site at Moldova in western Russia lived in river-valley houses framed with wood and covered with animal skins. Bones of mammoths, huge elephants now extinct, surround the remains of hearths and were apparently used to help hold the animal skins in place. Even though the winter climate near the edge of the glacier nearby was cold at that time, there still would have been animals to hunt because the plant food for the game was not buried under deep snow.

The hunters probably moved away in the summer to higher land between the river valleys. In all likelihood, the higher ground was grazing land for the large herds of animals the Moldova hunters depended on for meat. In the winter river valley sites, archaeologists have found skeletons of wolf, arctic fox, and hare with their paws missing. These animals probably were skinned for pelts that were made into clothing.[30]

Getting Food

How Neandertals and early modern humans got their food probably varied with their environment. In Africa, they lived in savanna and semiarid desert. In western and eastern Europe, they had to adapt to cold; during periods of increased glaciation, much of the environment was steppe grassland and tundra.

The European environment during this time was much richer in animal resources than the tundra of northern countries is today. Indeed, the European environment inhabited by Neandertals abounded in game, both big and small. The tundra and alpine animals included reindeer, bison, wild oxen, horses, mammoths, rhinoceroses, and deer, as well as bears, wolves, and foxes.[31] Some European sites have also yielded bird and fish remains. For example, people in a summer camp in northern Germany apparently hunted swans and ducks and fished for perch and pike.[32] Little, however, is known about the particular plant foods the European Neandertals may have consumed; the remains of plants are unlikely to survive thousands of years in a nonarid environment.

Neandertals appear to have hunted a wide variety of game. In this reconstruction, two Neandertals are shown attacking a mastodon they have trapped in a pit.

In Africa, too, early *Homo sapiens* varied in how they got food. For example, we know that the people living at the mouth of the Klasies River in South Africa ate shellfish as well as meat from small grazers such as antelopes and large grazers such as eland and buffalo.[33] But archaeologists disagree about how the Klasies River people got their meat when they began to occupy the caves in the area.

Richard Klein thinks they hunted both large and small game. Klein speculates that because the remains of eland of all ages have been found in Cave 1 at the Klasies River site, the people there probably hunted the eland by driving them into corrals or other traps, where animals of all ages could be killed. Klein thinks that buffalo were hunted differently. Buffalo tend to charge attackers, which would make it difficult to drive them into traps. Klein believes that, because bones from mostly very young and very old buffalo are found in the cave, the hunters were able to stalk and kill only the most vulnerable animals.[34]

Lewis Binford thinks the Klasies River people hunted only small grazers and scavenged the eland and buffalo meat from the kills of large carnivores. He argues that sites should contain all or almost all of the bones from animals that were hunted. According to Binford, since more or less complete skeletons are found only from small animals, the Klasies River people seem not, at first, to have hunted all the animals they used for food.[35]

But newer evidence suggests that people were hunting big game as much as 400,000 years ago. Wooden spears that old were recently found in Germany in association with stone tools and the butchered remains of more than ten wild horses. The heavy spears resemble modern aerodynamic javelins, which suggests they would have been thrown at large animals such as horses, not at small animals. This evidence strongly suggests that hunting, not just scavenging, may be older than archaeologists once thought.[36]

Rituals

At Drachenloch cave in the Swiss Alps, a stone-lined pit holding the stacked skulls of seven cave bears was found in association with a Neandertal habitation. Why preserve these skulls? One reason might be for rituals intended to placate or control bears. Cave bears were enormous—some nearly nine feet tall—

and competed with Neandertals for prime cave living sites. Perhaps the Neandertals preserved the skulls of bears they killed in the cave as a way of honoring or appeasing either the bears or their spirits. But the evidence is not completely persuasive. In our own society some may hang a deer or moose head on the wall without any associated ritual. So at this point we cannot say for certain whether or not Neandertals engaged in ritual behavior.[37]

The Emergence of Modern Humans

Cro-Magnon humans, who appear in western Europe about 35,000 years ago, were once thought to be the earliest specimens of modern humans, or *Homo sapiens sapiens*. (The Cro-Magnons are named after the rock shelter in France where they were first found, in 1868.[38]) But we now know that modern-looking humans appeared earlier outside of Europe. As of now, the oldest unambiguous fossils classified as *H. sapiens* come from Ethiopia and date to perhaps 160,000 years ago.[39] Additional fossils, discovered in one of the Klasies River mouth caves in South Africa, are possibly as old as 100,000 years.[40] Other *Homo sapiens* fossils of about the same age have been found in Border cave in South Africa.[41] Remains of anatomically modern humans (*Homo sapiens sapiens*) found at two sites in Israel, at Skhul and Qafzeh, which used to be thought to date back 40,000 to 50,000 years, may be 90,000 years old.[42] There are also anatomically modern human finds in Borneo, at Niah, from about 40,000 years ago and in Australia, at Lake Mungo, from about 30,000 years ago.[43]

These modern-looking humans differed from the Neandertals and early *H. sapiens* in that they had higher, more bulging foreheads, thinner and lighter bones, smaller faces and jaws, chins (the bony protuberances that remain after projecting faces recede), and only slight brow ridges (or no ridges at all; see Figure 7.1 on page 155).

Theories about the Origins of Modern Humans

Two theories about the origins of modern humans continue to be debated among anthropologists. One, which can be called the *single-origin theory*, suggests that modern humans emerged in just one part of the Old World and then spread to other parts, replacing Neandertals. (Africa is generally thought to be

This *Homo sapiens* skull from Ethiopia is the oldest member of our species yet found, dating to 160,000 years ago.

the place of modern humans' origin.) The second theory, which has been called the multiregional theory, suggests that modern humans evolved in various parts of the Old World after *Homo erectus* spread out of Africa.[44]

Single-Origin Theory   According to the single-origin theory, the Neandertals did not evolve into modern humans. Rather, Neandertals became extinct after 35,000 years ago because they were replaced by modern humans. Single-origin theorists think that the first *H. sapiens sapiens* had some biological or cultural advantage, or both, that allowed them to spread and replace Neandertals.

The main evidence for the single-origin theory comes from the mtDNA of living peoples. In 1987, Rebecca Cann and her colleagues presented evidence that the mtDNA from people in the United States, New Guinea, Africa, and East Asia showed differences suggesting that their common ancestor lived only 200,000 years ago. Cann and colleagues further claimed that, since the amount of variation among individuals was greatest in African populations, the common ancestor of all lived in Africa.[45] (It is generally the case that people living in a homeland exhibit more variation than any emigrant descendant population.)

There were many problems with early mtDNA studies, but over the years those problems have been addressed and new and better mtDNA analyses have been performed. Most scholars now agree that the mtDNA of modern humans shows a remarkably small amount of variation (in fact, less than half the variation found in most chimpanzee populations), which strongly suggests that we all share a very recent, common ancestry.[46] More detailed analyses of mtDNA diversity in modern humans have allowed scholars to identify the ancestral roots of contemporary populations around the world, and these analyses also point to modern human origins in East Africa and a subsequent spread out of that region.[47]

Evidence for an East African origin of modern humans and the subsequent expansion also comes from research on variation in the Y chromosome. The Y chromosome is the chromosome that determines whether a person is male. A female inherits an X chromosome from both her mother and father, while a male inherits an X chromosome from his mother and a Y chromosome from his father. Only men have a Y chromosome, and since there is only one copy in any given man, the Y chromosome is the only nuclear chromosome that, like mtDNA, does not undergo recombination. While the Y chromosome can be affected by selection, it is thought that most variation in the Y chromosome, like variation in mtDNA, is caused by random mutations. Variation in the Y chromosome can therefore be analyzed in much the same way as variation in mtDNA.[48]

The results of research on variation in the Y chromosome mirror those on variation in mtDNA. Analysis of Y chromosome variation points to Africa as the source of modern humans, and suggests an exodus from Africa of modern humans. One of the major differences between mtDNA studies and Y chromosome studies is in the dating of the most recent common ancestor. As noted earlier, studies of mtDNA suggest the most recent common ancestor lived about 200,000 years ago, while studies of the Y chromosome suggest the most recent ancestor lived only about 100,000 years ago.[49] Additional research, including new research on variation in nuclear DNA, may help to resolve these differences. For now, however, it seems clear that the modern human gene pool has a single, and fairly recent, origin in Africa.[50]

Multiregional Theory   According to the multiregional theory, *Homo erectus* populations in various parts of the Old World gradually evolved into anatomically modern-looking humans. The theorists espousing this view believe that the "transitional" or "archaic" *H. sapiens* and the Neandertals represent phases in the gradual development of more "modern" anatomical features. Indeed, as we have noted, some of these theorists see so much continuity between *Homo erectus* and modern humans that they classify *Homo erectus* as *Homo sapiens erectus*.

Continuity is the main evidence used by the multiregional theorists to support their position. In several parts of the world there seem to be continuities in skeletal features between *Homo erectus* and *Homo sapiens*. For example, *Homo erectus* fossils from China tend to have broader faces with more horizontal cheekbones than specimens from elsewhere in the world, traits that also characterize modern Chinese populations.[51] Southeast Asia provides more compelling evidence, according to multiregional theorists. There, a number of traits—relatively thick cranial bones, a receding forehead, an unbroken brow ridge, facial prognathism, relatively large cheekbones, and relatively large molars—appear to persist from *Homo erectus* through modern populations (see Figure 7.4).[52] But others suggest that these traits cannot be used to establish a unique continuation from *Homo erectus* in Southeast Asia because these traits are found in modern humans all over the world. And still others argue that the traits are not as similar as the multiregional theorists claim.[53]

In support of their position, multiregional theorists argue that the mtDNA and Y chromosome evidence supports multiregional evolution rather than a single-origin of modern humans, that genetic variation in modern humans may reflect the emigration of *Homo erectus* out of Africa rather than the emigration of *Homo sapiens sapiens*. This interpretation would mean that the accepted rates of mutation in both mtDNA and the Y chromosome are wrong, that both actually mutate much more slowly than currently thought.[54] However, this interpretation is contradicted by established correlations between differences in mtDNA among human groups known to have colonized New Guinea and Australia at particular points in time, which seem to fit the accepted rate of mutation, and with the divergence between humans and apes, the date of which also seems to accord with the accepted faster rate of mtDNA mutation.

To explain why human evolution would proceed gradually and in the same direction in various parts of the Old World, multiregional theorists point to cultural improvements in cutting-tool and cooking

Figure 7.4 Fossil Evidence for Regional Continuity

Continuity in southeast Asian and Australian populations: Skulls of (a) *Homo erectus*, (b) early *Homo sapiens*, and (d) modern *Homo sapiens*, all from southeast Asia and Australia, have similar foreheads, brow ridges, and occipital and facial shapes, while skulls from Africa, represented here by (c), an early *Homo sapiens*, have different forms. The similarity in southeast Asian and Australian populations over more than 500,000 years argues for regional continuity rather than replacement.

technology that occurred all over the Old World. These cultural improvements may have relaxed the prior natural selection for heavy bones and musculature in the skull. The argument is that unless many plant and animal foods were cut into small pieces and thoroughly cooked in hearths or pits that were efficient thermally, they would be hard to chew and digest. Thus people would have needed robust jaws and thick skull bones to support the large muscles that enabled them to cut and chew their food. But robust bone and muscle would no longer be needed after people began to cut and cook more effectively.[55]

Intermediate Theories   The single-origin and multiregional theories are not the only possible interpretations of the available fossil record. There is also the intermediate interpretation that there may have been some replacement of one population by another, some local continuous evolution, and some interbreeding between early modern humans, who spread out of Africa, and populations encountered in North Africa, Europe, and Asia.[56] As biologist Alan Templeton has noted, the debates over a single-origin versus multiregional evolution

> are based on the myth that replacement of one physical feature in a fossil series with another feature can only be created by one population replacing another (by exterminating them, for example), but such fossil patterns could be a reflection of one genotype replacing another through gene flow and natural selection. Morphological replacement should not be equated with population replacement when one is dealing with populations that can interbreed.[57]

Interestingly, data on the genetic diversity of human body lice seems to support the intermediate theory of human origins. Humans are plagued by a single species of hair lice, *Pediculus humanus,* which happens to have two distinct genetic lineages. One is found worldwide, the other only in the Americas. These two genetic lineages of lice appear to have diverged over one million years ago. If modern humans evolved less than 200,000 years ago (and the worldwide louse lineage suggests it experienced some dramatic changes about 100,000 years ago, which may relate to modern humans leaving Africa), then how did the other lineage of lice continue? One answer is that they were transferred to modern humans from a previously isolated population of *Homo erectus* in Asia.[58] If that happened, some archaic and some modern humans must have been in very close contact—either body to body or sharing clothing.

What Happened to the Neandertals?

Regardless of which theory (single-origin, multiregional, or intermediate) is correct, it seems clear that Neandertals and modern humans (*H. sapiens sapiens*) coexisted in Europe and the Middle East for at least 20,000 years, and maybe as long as 60,000 years. What happened to the Neandertals? Three answers have generally been considered. First, they interbred with modern humans and the unique Neandertal characteristics slowly disappeared from the interbreeding population. Second, they were killed off by modern humans. Third, they were driven to extinction due to competition with modern humans. Let's take a look at each of these scenarios.

Interbreeding

The interbreeding scenario seems the most probable, yet evidence supporting it is weak. If modern humans and Neandertals interbred, we should be able to find "hybrid" individuals in the fossil record. In fact, a group of scholars has argued that an Upper Paleolithic skeleton from Portugal demonstrates a combination of modern human and Neandertal features.[59] The finding remains controversial, however, because it is a child's skeleton (approximately 4 years old) and its Neandertal-like features have not been corroborated by other scholars. More significantly, if the interbreeding hypothesis is correct, then the mtDNA analysis we have discussed several times in this chapter must be wrong. On the other hand, recent research on Neandertal tools suggests that some Neandertal groups adopted new techniques of tool manufacture (described in detail later) that are thought to be uniquely associated with modern humans.[60] If Neandertals were learning from modern humans, then the idea that they could have interbred and perhaps been absorbed within the modern human population gains credibility.

Genocide

The genocide scenario, that modern humans killed off Neandertals, has appeal as a sensational story, but little evidence. Not a single "murdered" Neandertal has ever been found, and one might wonder, in a fight between the powerful Neandertals and the more gracile modern humans, who might get the better of whom.

Extinction

Finally, the extinction scenario, that Neandertals simply could not compete with modern humans, seems to have the best archaeological support. As we discussed earlier, there appear to be "refugee" populations of Neandertals in Iberia as recently as perhaps 30,000 years ago. The "retreat" of Neandertals from the Middle East, eastern Europe, and finally western Europe following the movement of modern humans into those region seems to support the "refugee" interpretation.[61] More importantly, physical anthropologist Erik Trinkaus has argued, based on both physical characteristics of the Neandertal skeleton and their apparent patterns of behavior, that Neandertals were less efficient hunters and gatherers than modern humans.[62] And not only may Neandertals have been less efficient than modern humans in getting food, they may have needed more of it. Steve Churchill has suggested that Neandertals' stocky bodies and great muscle mass might have required 25 percent more calories than modern humans.[63] If this is true, a modern human group would have been able to live and reproduce more easily than a Neandertal group in the same territory, and this would likely drive the Neandertals away. When there were no new territories to run to, the Neandertals would go extinct—precisely what the archaeological record seems to suggest.[64]

But were modern humans and their cultures really that much more efficient than Middle Paleolithic cultures? As we will see, the Upper Paleolithic world does seem to mark a watershed in the evolution of human culture, with humans expanding their physical horizons throughout the world and their intellectual horizons into the realms of art and ritual.

The Upper Paleolithic World

The period of cultural history in Europe, the Near East, and Asia known as the Upper Paleolithic dates from about 40,000 years ago to the period known as the *Neolithic* (beginning about 10,000 years ago, depending on the area). In Africa, the cultural period comparable to the Upper Paleolithic is known as the *Later Stone Age* and may have begun much earlier. In North and South America the period begins when humans first entered the New World, some time before 12,000 years ago (these colonizers are typically called *Paleo-Indians*) and continues until what are called *Archaic traditions* emerged some 10,000 years ago. To simplify terminology, we use the term Upper Paleolithic to refer to cultural developments in all areas of the world during this period.

In many respects, lifestyles during the **Upper Paleolithic** were similar to lifestyles before. People were still mainly hunters and gatherers and fishers who probably lived in small mobile bands. They made their camps out in the open in skin-covered huts and in caves and rock shelters. And they continued to produce smaller and smaller stone tools.

But the Upper Paleolithic is also characterized by a variety of new developments. One of the most striking is the emergence of art—painting on cave walls and stone slabs, and carving tools, decorative objects, and personal ornaments out of bone, antler, shell, and stone. (Perhaps for this as well as other purposes, people began to obtain materials from distant sources.) Because more archaeological sites date from the Upper Paleolithic than from any previous period and some Upper Paleolithic sites seem larger than any before, many archaeologists think that the human population increased considerably during the Upper Paleolithic.[65] And new inventions, such as the bow and arrow, the spear-thrower, and tiny replaceable blades that could be fitted into handles, appear for the first time.[66]

The Last Ice Age

The Upper Paleolithic world had an environment very different from today's. The earth was gripped by the last ice age, with glaciers covering Europe as far south as Berlin and Warsaw, and North America as far south as Chicago. To the south of these glacial fronts was a tundra zone extending in Europe to the Alps and in North America to the Ozarks, Appalachians, and well out onto the Great Plains. Environmentally, both Europe and North America probably resembled contemporary Siberia and northern Canada. Elsewhere in the world conditions were not as extreme, but were still different from conditions today.[67]

For one thing, the climate was different. Annual temperatures were as much as 10 degrees Celsius below today's, and changes in ocean currents would have made temperature contrasts (i.e., the differences between summer and winter months) more extreme as well. The changing ocean currents also changed weather patterns, and Europe experienced heavy annual snowfall. Not all the world was cold; still, the presence of huge ice sheets in the north changed the climate throughout the world. North Africa, for example, appears to have been much wetter than today, and South Asia was apparently drier. And everywhere the climate seems to have been highly variable.[68]

The plants and animals of the Upper Paleolithic world were adapted to these extreme conditions. Among the most important, and dramatic, were the large game animals collectively known as *Pleistocene megafauna*.[69] These animals, as their name suggests, were huge compared to their contemporary descendants. In North America, for example, giant ground sloths stood some 8–10 feet tall and weighed several thousand pounds. Siberian mammoths were the largest elephants ever to live—some standing more than 14 feet tall. In East Asia, species such as the woolly rhinoceros and giant deer were present.

Upper Paleolithic Europe

With the vast supplies of meat available from megafauna, it is not surprising that many Upper Paleolithic cultures relied on hunting, and this was particularly true of the Upper Paleolithic peoples of Europe, on whom we focus here because we know the archaeology better. Their way of life represents a common pattern throughout the Old World. But as people began to use more diverse resources in their environments, the use of local resources allowed Upper Paleolithic groups in much of the Old World to become more sedentary than their predecessors. They also began to trade with neighboring groups in order to obtain resources not available in their local territories.[70]

As was the case in the known Middle Paleolithic sites, most of the Upper Paleolithic remains that have been excavated were situated in caves and rock shelters. In southwestern France, some groups seem to have paved parts of the shelter floors with stones. Tent-like structures were built in some caves, apparently to keep out the cold.[71] Some open-air sites have also been excavated.

The site at Dolni Vestonice in what is now the Czech Republic, dated to around 25,000 years ago, is one of the first for which there is an entire settlement plan.[72] The settlement seems to have consisted of four tent-like huts, probably made from animal skins, with a great open hearth in the center. Around the outside were mammoth bones, some rammed into the ground, which suggests that the huts were surrounded by a wall. All told, there were bone heaps from about 100 mammoths. Each hut probably housed a group of related families—about 20–25 people. (One hut was approximately 27 by 45 feet and had five hearths distributed inside it, presumably one for each family.) With 20 to 25 people per hut, and assuming that all four huts were occupied at the same time, the population of the settlement would have been 100 to 125 people.

Up a hill from the settlement was a fifth and different kind of hut. It was dug into the ground and contained a bake oven and more than 2,300 small, fired fragments of animal figurines. There were also some hollow bones that may have been musical instruments. Another interesting feature of the settlement was a burial find, of a woman with a disfigured face. She may have been a particularly important personage; her face was found engraved on an ivory plaque near the central hearth of the settlement.

Upper Paleolithic Tools

Upper Paleolithic toolmaking appears to have had its roots in the Mousterian and post-Acheulian traditions, because flake tools are found in many Upper Paleolithic sites. But the Upper Paleolithic is characterized by a preponderance of blades; there were also burins, bone and antler tools, and microliths. In addition, two new techniques of toolmaking appeared—*indirect percussion* and *pressure flaking*. Blades were found in Middle Paleolithic assemblages, but they were not widely used until the Upper Paleolithic. Although blades can be made in a variety of ways, **indirect percussion** using a hammer-struck punch was common in the Upper Paleolithic. After shaping a core into a pyramidal or cylindrical form, the toolmaker put a punch of antler, wood, or other hard material into position and struck it with a hammer. Because the force is readily directed, the toolmaker was able to strike off consistently shaped **blades**, which are more than twice as long as they are wide.[73]

The Upper Paleolithic is also noted for the production of large numbers of bone, antler, and ivory tools; needles, awls, and harpoons made of bone appear for the first time.[74] The manufacture of these implements may have been made easier by the development of many varieties of burins. **Burins** are chisel-like stone tools used for carving; bone and antler needles, awls, and projectile points could be produced with them.[75] Burins have been found in Middle and Lower Paleolithic sites but are present in great number and variety only in the Upper Paleolithic.

Pressure flaking also appeared during the Upper Paleolithic. Rather than using percussion to strike off flakes as in previous technologies, pressure flaking works by employing pressure with a bone, wood, or antler tool at the edge of the tool to remove small flakes. Pressure flaking would usually be used in the final stages of retouching a tool.[76]

As time went on, all over the Old World smaller and smaller blade tools were produced. The very tiny ones, called **microliths**, were often hafted or fitted into handles, one blade at a time or several blades together, to serve as spears, adzes, knives, and sickles. The hafting required inventing a way to trim the blade's back edge so that it would be blunt rather than sharp. In this way the blades would not split the handles into which they might be inserted; the blunting would also prevent the users of an unhafted blade from cutting themselves.[77]

Shown here are an upper Paleolithic bone needle and spear or harpoon points. Upper Paleolithic peoples made a much wider variety of tools than their predecessors.

Some archaeologists think that the blade technique was adopted because it made for more economical use of flint. André Leroi-Gourhan of the Musée de l'Homme in Paris calculated that with the old Acheulian technique, a 2-pound lump of flint yielded 16 inches of working edge and produced only two hand axes. If the more advanced Mousterian technique were used, a lump of equal size would yield 2 yards of working edge. The indirect percussion method of the Upper Paleolithic would yield as much as 25 yards of working edge.[78] With the same amount of material, a significantly greater number of tools could be produced. Getting the most out of a valuable resource may have been particularly important in areas lacking large flint deposits. Then again, if the population were increasing, that by itself would require more tools and more working edges to be produced.

Jacques Bordaz suggested that the evolution of toolmaking techniques, which continually increased the amount of usable edge that could be gotten out of a lump of flint, was significant because people could then spend more time in regions where flint was unavailable. Another reason for adopting the blade toolmaking technique may have been that it made for easy repair of tools. For example, the cutting edge of a tool might consist of a line of razor-like microliths set into a piece of wood. The tool would not be usable if just one of the cutting edge's microliths broke off or was chipped. But if the user carried a small prepared core of flint from which an identical-sized microlith could be struck off, the tool could be repaired easily by replacing the lost or broken microlith. A spear whose point was lost could be repaired similarly. Thus, the main purpose of the blade toolmaking technique may not have been to make more economical use of flint but rather to allow easy replacement of damaged blades.[79]

How Were the Tools Used? One way of suggesting what a particular tool was used for in the past is to observe the manner in which similar tools are used by members of recent or contemporary societies, preferably societies with subsistence activities and environments similar to those of the ancient toolmakers. This method of study is called reasoning from **ethnographic analogy**. The problem with such reasoning is that we cannot be sure that the original use of a tool was the same as the present use. When selecting recent or contemporary cultures that may provide the most informative and accurate comparisons, we should try to choose those that derive from the ancient culture we are interested in. If the cultures being compared are historically related—prehistoric and recent Pueblo cultures in the southwestern United States, for example—there is a greater likelihood that the two groups used a particular kind of tool in similar ways and for similar purposes.[80]

Another way of suggesting what a particular kind of tool was used for is to compare the visible and microscopic wear marks on the prehistoric tools with the wear marks on similar tools made and experimentally used by contemporary researchers. The idea behind this approach is that different uses leave different wear marks. A pioneer in this research was S. A. Semenov, who recreated prehistoric stone tools and used them in a variety of ways to find out which uses left which kinds of wear marks. For example, by cutting into meat with his recreated stone knives, he produced a polish on the edges that was like the polish found on blades from a prehistoric site in Siberia. This finding led Semenov to infer that the Siberian blades were probably also used to cut meat.[81]

The tools made by Upper Paleolithic peoples suggest that they were much more effective hunters and fishers than their predecessors.[82] During the Upper Paleolithic, and probably for the first time, spears were shot from a spear-thrower rather than thrown with the arm. We know this because bone and antler **atlatls** (the Aztec word for "spear-thrower") have been found in some sites. A spear propelled off a grooved board could be sent through the air with increased force, causing it to travel farther and hit harder, and with less effort by the thrower. The bow and arrow was also used in various places during the Upper Paleolithic; and harpoons, used for fishing and perhaps for hunting reindeer, were invented at this time.

These new tools and weapons for more effective hunting and fishing do not rule out the possibility that Upper Paleolithic peoples were still scavenging animal remains. Olga Soffer suggests that Upper Paleolithic peoples may have located their settlements near places where many mammoths died naturally in order to make use of the bones for building (see Figure 7.5). For example, in Moravia the

Figure 7.5 Mammoth-Bone Shelters

Here we see the type of mammoth-bone shelters constructed about 15,000 years ago on the East European Plain. Often mammoth skulls formed part of the foundation for the tusk, long bone, and wooden frame, covered with hide. As many as 95 mammoth mandibles were arranged around the outside in a herring-bone pattern. Ten men and women could have constructed this elaborate shelter of 258 square feet in six days, using 46,000 pounds of bone.

mammoths may have come to lick deposits of calcite and other sources of magnesium and calcium, particularly during the late spring and early summer when resources were short and mortality was high. Consistent with the idea that humans may not have killed so many of the enormous mammoths is the fact that in some places there are few human-made cut marks on mammoth bones. For example, at Dolni Vestonice, where bones of 100 mammoths were found, few bones show cut marks from butchering and few bones were found inside the huts. In contrast, the site is littered with bison, horse, and reindeer bones, suggesting that these other animals were deliberately killed and eaten by humans. If the people had been able to kill all the mammoths we find the remains of, why would they have hunted so many other animals?[83]

Upper Paleolithic Art

The earliest discovered traces of art are beads and carvings, and then paintings, from Upper Paleolithic sites. We might expect that early artistic efforts were crude, but the cave paintings of Spain and southern France show a marked degree of skill. So do the naturalistic paintings on slabs of stone excavated in southern Africa. Some of those slabs appear to have been painted as much as 28,000 years ago, which suggests that painting in Africa is as old as painting in Europe.[84] But painting may be even older than that. The early Australians may have painted on the walls of rock shelters and cliff faces at least 30,000 years ago and maybe as much as 60,000 years ago.[85] And at Blombos Cave in South Africa engraved pieces of red ochre date back to more than 77,000 years ago.[86]

Peter Ucko and Andrée Rosenfeld identified three principal locations of paintings in the caves of western Europe: (1) in obviously inhabited rock shelters and cave entrances—art as decoration or "art for art's sake"; (2) in "galleries" immediately off the inhabited areas of caves; and (3) in the inner reaches of caves, whose difficulty of access has been interpreted by some as a sign that magical-religious activities were performed there.[87]

The subjects of the paintings are mostly animals. The paintings are on bare walls, with no backdrops or environmental trappings. Perhaps, like many contemporary peoples, Upper Paleolithic men and women believed that the drawing of a human image could cause death or injury. If that were indeed their belief,

Shown here are paintings in the "Hall of Bulls" at Lascaux in France. Cave paintings like this demonstrate the remarkable skill of Upper Paleolithic artists.

it might explain why human figures are rarely depicted in cave art. Another explanation for the focus on animals might be that these people sought to improve their luck at hunting. This theory is suggested by evidence of chips in the painted figures, perhaps made by spears thrown at the drawings. But if hunting magic was the chief motivation for the paintings, it is difficult to explain why only a few show signs of having been speared. Perhaps then the paintings were inspired by the need to increase the supply of animals. Cave art seems to have reached a peak toward the end of the Upper Paleolithic period, when the herds of game were decreasing.

The particular symbolic significance of the cave paintings in southwestern France is more explicitly revealed, perhaps, by the results of Patricia Rice and Ann Paterson's statistical study.[88] The data suggest that the animals portrayed in the cave paintings were mostly the ones that the painters preferred for meat and for materials such as hides. For example, wild cattle (bovines) and horses are portrayed more often than we would expect by chance, probably because they were larger and heavier (meatier) than the other animals in the environment. In addition, the paintings mostly portray animals that the painters may have feared the most because of their size, speed, natural weapons such as tusks and horns, and unpredictability of behavior. That is, mammoths, bovines, and horses are portrayed more often than deer and reindeer.[89] The art of the cultural period after the Upper Paleolithic also seems to reflect how people mostly got their food. In that period, when getting food no longer depended on hunting large game (because they were becoming extinct), the art ceased to focus on portrayals of animals.

Upper Paleolithic Cultures in Africa and Asia

Europe was not the only region where Upper Paleolithic peoples thrived. In North Africa, for example, Upper Paleolithic peoples hunted large animals on the grasslands that covered the region during that period. They lived in small communities located within easy access to water and other resources, and moved regularly, probably to follow the animal herds. Trade took place between local groups, particularly for high-quality stone used in making tools.[90] In eastern and southern Africa, a way of life known as the Later Stone Age developed that persisted in some areas until very recently. People lived in small, mobile groups, hunting large animals and collecting a wide variety of plant foods.

In South Asia the Upper Paleolithic saw an increasingly sedentary lifestyle developing along the banks of freshwater streams. The Upper Paleolithic peoples in South Asia combined hunting, fishing, and gathering with seasonal movements to exploit seasonally abundant resources.[91] In East and Southeast Asia ocean resources became vital to coastal-dwelling peoples, while those inland lived primarily in caves, hunting and collecting broadly in the local environment. Many of these sites appear to have been occupied for long periods of time, suggesting some degree of sedentism. During the Upper Paleolithic, peoples from Asia also populated Australia, New Guinea, and some of the islands of western Melanesia, clearly demonstrating the ability of these peoples to navigate on the sea and to use its resources.[92]

The Earliest Humans and Their Cultures in the New World

So far in this chapter we have dealt only with the Old World—Africa, Europe, and Asia. What about the New World—North and South America? How long have humans lived there, and what were their earliest cultures like?

Because only *Homo sapiens sapiens* fossils have been found in North and South America, migrations of humans to the New World had to have taken place some time after the emergence of *H. sapiens sapiens*. But exactly when these migrations occurred is subject to debate, particularly about when people got to areas south of Alaska. On the basis of similarities in biological traits such as tooth forms and blood types, and on possible linguistic relationships, anthropologists agree that Native Americans originally came from Asia. The traditional assumption is that they came to North America from Siberia, walking across a land bridge (Beringia) that is now under water (the Bering Strait) between Siberia and Alaska. The ice sheets or glaciers that periodically covered most of the high latitudes of the world contained so much of the world's water (the ice sheets were thousands of feet thick in some places) that Beringia was dry land in various periods (see Figure 7.6). Until recently, the prevailing view was that humans were not present south of Alaska until after 11,500 years ago. Now it appears from an archaeological site called Monte Verde in Chile that modern humans got to southern South America by at least 12,500 years ago, and maybe as much as 33,000 years ago. The Monte Verde site contains more than 700 stone tools, the remains of hide-covered huts, and a child's footprint next to a hearth.[93] The site suggests that there was at least one wave of human migration into the New World before 11,500 years ago, by walking and/or perhaps in boats. Even when the last glaciers were at their fullest extent, there was a small ice-free corridor through which people could have walked. And there were ice-free corridors earlier.

It was geologically possible then for humans to have walked into the New World at various times, and they could have traveled by boat, too. Parts of the Beringia land bridge were exposed from about 60,000 to 25,000 years ago. It wasn't until between 20,000 and 18,000 years ago that the land bridge was at its maximum. When did the land bridge disappear? It used to be widely believed that the land bridge was flooded around 14,000 years ago, but recent evidence suggests that walking across Beringia was still possible until about 10,000 years ago. An ice-free corridor between the Laurentide and Cordilleran ice sheets may have been present after 25,000 years ago, but that corridor is not likely to have supported big game, and permitted humans to hunt enough for sustenance, until after about 14,000 years ago. So some investigators suggest that moving through the ice-free corridor to what is now south of Canada was not likely until after 14,000 years ago.[94]

Figure 7.6 Beringia and the Ice Sheets

Source: David K. Meltzer, "Pleistocene Peopling of the Americas," *Evolutionary Anthropology,* 1 (1993): 157–69. Copyright © 1993.

The people there may or may not have hunted big game, but just a little while later there were people living in the Amazon jungle of what is now Brazil who were definitely not hunters of mammoths and other big game, as the contemporaneous Clovis people of North America were. In other words, it looks like the earliest inhabitants of the New World—in Chile, Brazil, North America—varied in culture. The people in the Amazon lived by collecting fruits and nuts, fishing, and hunting small game. They lived in caves with painted art on the walls and left 30,000 stone chips from making tips of spears, darts, or harpoons.[95]

There is no disagreement that humans were living south of Canada around 11,000 years ago. The Clovis people, as they are called (after an archaeological site near Clovis, New Mexico), left finely shaped spear points in many locations in North America. And we have human skeletal remains from after 11,000 years ago. Now that the Monte Verde site has been reliably dated, we know that there were people south of Canada before the Clovis people were in New Mexico. And there are other possible sites of pre-Clovis occupation, although many archaeologists do not agree that the presumed tools at these sites were made by humans (these objects could have been made by rockfalls or other natural forces) or that the sites are accurately dated. One site that may be another pre-Clovis site is the Meadowcroft Rockshelter in western Pennsylvania.[96]

In the bottom third of a stratum that seems to date from 19,600 to 8,000 years ago, the Meadowcroft site shows clear signs of human occupation—a small fragment of human bone, a spearpoint, and chipped knives and scrapers. If the dating is accurate, the tools would be about 12,800 years old. William Parry suggests we need to date the human bone found in the site. If the bone turns out to date from before 12,000 years ago, few anthropologists would question the conclusion that humans occupied the Meadowcroft site before the time of the Clovis people.[97]

According to comparative linguists Joseph Greenberg and Merritt Ruhlen, there were three waves of migration into the New World.[98] Comparing hundreds of languages in North and South America, Greenberg and Ruhlen group them into three different language families. Because each of these language families has a closer relationship to an Asian language family than to the other New World language families,

Shown here are Clovis points, the earliest stone weapons in the Americas, dating to more than 11,000 years ago.

Figure 7.7   Population Frequencies of Shovel-Shaped Incisors

Inuit (Eskimos) and Aleuts, speakers of Na-Dené languages, and other Native American language groups differ in the frequency of shovel-shaped incisors. These genetic differences seem to reflect three waves of migration into the New World.

Source: From Christy G. Turner, II, "Telltale Teeth," *Natural History* (January 1987): 8.

it would appear that three different migrations came out of Asia. The first arrivals spoke a language that diverged over time into most of the languages found in the New World, the Amerind family of languages; the speakers of these related languages came to occupy all of South and Central America as well as most of North America. Next came the ancestors of the people who speak languages belonging to the Na-Dené family, which today includes Navajo and Apache in the southwestern United States and the various Athapaskan languages of northern California, coastal Oregon, northwestern Canada, and Alaska. Finally, perhaps 4,000 years ago, came the ancestors of the Inuit (Eskimo) and Aleut (the latter came to occupy the islands southwest of Alaska and the adjacent mainland), who speak languages belonging to the Inuit-Aleut family.

Christy Turner's study of New World teeth supports the Greenberg and Ruhlen proposal of three separate migrations. Turner looked at the proportions of shovel-shaped incisors, a common Asian trait, in New World populations. The varying proportions fall into three distinct groupings, the same three suggested by the linguists[99] (see Figure 7.7). But a recent genetic analysis suggests that Inuit-Aleut may have split from Na-Dené in the New World.[100] The peopling of the New World may have been even more complicated. New evidence suggests there could have been four separate migrations from the Old World, from different regions of Asia.[101]

The Paleo-Indians

Archaeological remains of early New World hunters, called *Paleo-Indians,* have been found in the United States, Mexico, and Canada. Just south of the farthest reaches of the last glaciation, the area east of the Rockies known as the High Plains abounded with mammoths, bison, wild camels, and wild horses. The tools found with mammoth kills are known as the *Clovis complex,* which includes the Clovis projectile point as well as stone scrapers and knives and bone tools. The Clovis projectile point is large and leaf-shaped, flaked on both sides. It has a broad groove in the middle, presumably so that the point could be attached to a wooden spear shaft.[102] Because one mammoth was found with eight Clovis points in it, there is little dispute that Clovis people hunted large game.[103] Recent dating places most Clovis sites between 11,200 and 10,900 years ago.[104]

The mammoth disappeared about 10,000 years ago, and the largest game animal became the now-extinct large, straight-horned bison. The hunters of that bison used a projectile point called the *Folsom point,* which was much smaller than the Clovis point. Tools are also found with many other kinds of animal remains, including wolf, turtle, rabbit, horse, fox, deer, and camel, so the bison hunters obviously depended on other animals as well.[105] In the Rio Grande valley, the Folsom toolmakers characteristically established a base camp on low dune ridges overlooking both a large pond and broad, open grazing areas. If we assume that the pond provided water for the grazing herds, the people in the camp would have been in an excellent position to watch the herds.[106]

As the climate of what is now the American Southwest became drier, the animals and the cultural adaptations changed somewhat. About 9,000 years ago the smaller modern bison replaced the earlier straight-horned variety.[107] Base camps began to be located farther from ponds and grazing areas and closer to streams. If the ponds were no longer reliable sources of water during these drier times, the animals probably no longer frequented them, which would explain why the hunters had to change the sites of their base camps. Not much is known about the plant foods these Paleo-Indian people may have exploited, but on the desert fringes plant gathering may have been vital. In Nevada and Utah, archaeologists have found milling stones and other artifacts for processing plant food.[108]

The Olsen-Chubbuck site, a kill site excavated in Colorado, shows the organization that may have been involved in hunting bison.[109] In a dry gulch dated to 6500 B.C. were the remains of 200 bison. At the bottom were complete skeletons and at the top, completely butchered animals. This find clearly suggests that Paleo-Indian hunters deliberately stampeded the animals into a natural trap—an arroyo, or steep-sided dry gully. The animals in front were probably pushed by the ones behind into the arroyo. Joe Ben Wheat estimated that the hunters may have obtained 55,000 pounds of meat from this one kill. If we judge from nineteenth-century Plains Indians, who could prepare bison meat to last a month, and estimate that each person would eat a pound a day, the kill at the Olsen-Chubbuck site could have fed more than 1,800 people for a month (they probably did not all live together throughout the year). The hunters must have been highly organized not only for the stampede itself but also for butchering. It seems that the enormous carcasses had to be carried to flat ground for that job. In addition, the 55,000 pounds of meat and hides had to be carried back to camp.[110]

Although big game may have been most important on the High Plains, other areas show different adaptations. For example, Paleo-Indian people in woodland regions of what is now the United States seem to have depended more heavily on plant food and smaller game. In some woodland areas, fish and shellfish may have been a vital part of the diet.[111] On the Pacific coast, some Paleo-Indian people developed food-getting strategies more dependent on fish.[112] And in other areas, the lower Illinois River valley being one example, Paleo-Indian people who depended on game and wild vegetable foods managed to get enough food to live in permanent villages of perhaps 100 to 150 people.[113]

Here is the "river of bones" at the Olsen-Chubbuck site. These are the remains of bison that Paleo-Indian hunters stampeded into an arroyo.

The End of the Upper Paleolithic

After about 10,000 years ago, the glaciers began to disappear, and with their disappearance came other environmental changes. The melting of the glacial ice caused the oceans to rise, and, as the seas moved inland, the waters inundated some of the richest fodder-producing coastal plains, creating islands, inlets, and bays. Other areas were opened up for human occupation as the glaciers retreated and the temperatures rose.[114] The cold, treeless plains, tundras, and grasslands eventually gave way to dense mixed forests, mostly birch, oak, and pine, and the Pleistocene megafauna became extinct. The warming waterways began to be filled with fish and other aquatic resources.[115]

Archaeologists believe that these environmental changes induced some populations to alter their food-getting strategies. When the tundras and grasslands disappeared, hunters could no longer obtain large quantities of meat simply by remaining close to large migratory herds of animals, as they probably did during Upper Paleolithic times. Even though deer and other game were available, the number of animals per square mile (density) had decreased, and it became difficult to stalk and kill animals sheltered in the thick woods. Thus, in many areas people seemed to have turned from a reliance on big-game hunting to the intensive collecting of wild plants, mollusks, fish, and small game to make up for the extinction of the large game animals they had once relied upon.

The Maglemosian Culture of Northern Europe   Some adaptations to the changing environment can be seen in the cultural remains of the settlers in northern Europe who are called *Maglemosians* by archaeologists. Their name derives from the peat bogs (*magle mose* in Danish means "great bog") where their remains have been found.

To deal with the new, more forested environment, the Maglemosians made stone axes and adzes to chop down trees and form them into various objects. Large timbers appear to have been split for houses; trees were hollowed out for canoes; and smaller pieces of wood were made into paddles. The canoes presumably were built for travel and perhaps for fishing on the lakes and rivers that abounded in the post-glacial environment.

We do not know to what extent the Maglemosians relied on wild plant foods, but there were a lot of different kinds available, such as hazelnuts. However, we do know many other things about the Maglemosians' way of life. Although fishing was fairly important, as suggested by the frequent occurrence of bones from pike and other fish, as well as fishhooks, these people apparently depended mainly on hunting for food. Game included elk, wild ox, deer, and wild pig. In addition to many fishing implements and the adzes and axes, the Maglemosians' tool kit included the bow and arrow. Some of their tools were ornamented with finely engraved designs. Ornamentation independent of tools also appears in amber and stone pendants and small figurines representing, for example, the head of an elk.[116]

Like the Maglemosian finds, many of the European post–Upper Paleolithic sites are along lakes, rivers, and oceanfronts. But these sites probably were not inhabited year round; there is evidence that at least some groups moved seasonally from one place of settlement to another, perhaps between the coast and inland areas.[117] Finds such as kitchen piles of shells that centuries of post–Upper Paleolithic seafood-eaters had discarded and the remains of fishing equipment, canoes, and boats indicate that these people depended much more heavily on fishing than had their ancestors in Upper Paleolithic times.

The Archaic Cultures of Eastern North America   A related set of adaptations to the changing environment can be seen among the peoples who inhabited eastern North America at the end of the ice age. As the climate became warmer and drier, the flora and fauna of North America changed. Megafauna, as elsewhere in the world, went extinct, and were replaced by smaller mammals, particularly deer. The availability of meat was greatly reduced—hunters could count on coming home with pounds, not tons, of meat. Warmer adapted plants replaced cold adapted plants, and were used for food to replace the meat that was no longer available. Warmer adapted plants had advantages as food resources for humans over cold adapted ones because edible seeds, fruits, and nuts were more common, and often more plentiful and accessible, on the warmer adapted plants. Thus a much greater diversity of plants and animals came to be used by the Archaic peoples.[118]

The Archaic peoples of North America, like the Maglemosian peoples in Europe, began to follow a more sedentary lifestyle. Two forms of Archaic settlement appear to have been typical. One was a residential base camp, which would have been inhabited seasonally by several, probably related, families. The other was a special-purpose camp, which would have been a short-term habitation near a particular resource or perhaps used by a group of hunters for a short period of time.[119] On the Atlantic coast, for example, individual groups apparently moved seasonally along major river valleys, establishing summer base camps in the piedmont and winter camps near the coast. Special-purpose camps were created year-round as groups went out from the base camp to hunt and collect particular resources, such as stone for making tools.[120]

One of the innovations of the Archaic peoples was the development of ground stone woodworking tools. Axes, adzes, and tools for grinding seeds and nuts become more and more common in the tool kit.[121] This probably reflects the emergence of greater areas of forest following the retreat of the glaciers from North America, but it also demonstrates a greater reliance on forest products and, most likely, a greater use of wood and wood products. Fish and shellfish also came to be relied upon in some areas, and this too reflects the adjustment made by the Archaic peoples to the changing conditions they faced at the end of the last ice age.

Here are some examples of Archaic ground stone woodworking tools from eastern North America (wooden handles are reproductions). Archaic peoples apparently used wood more extensively than the Paleo-Indians.

The innovation of most lasting importance in both the New and Old Worlds, however, was the development of domesticated plants and animals. In both parts of the world, peoples at the end of the ice age began to experiment with plants. By around 14,000 years ago in the Old World, and 10,000 years ago in the New World, some species had been domesticated. It is this fundamental change in getting food—the invention of agriculture—to which we turn in the next chapter.

Summary

1. Most anthropologists agree that *Homo erectus* began to evolve into *Homo sapiens* after about 500,000 years ago. But there is disagreement about how and where the transition occurred. The mixed traits of the transitional fossils include large cranial capacities (well within the range of modern humans), together with low foreheads and large brow ridges, which are characteristic of *H. erectus* specimens. The earliest definite *H. sapiens,* who did not look completely like modern humans, appeared at least 100,000 years ago.

2. *Homo sapiens* have been found in many parts of the Old World—in Africa and Asia as well as in Europe. Some of these *H. sapiens* may have lived earlier than the Neandertals of Europe. There is still debate over whether the Neandertals in western Europe became extinct or survived and were ancestral to the modern-looking people who lived in western Europe after about 40,000 years ago.

3. The period of cultural history associated with the Neandertals is traditionally called the Middle Paleolithic in Europe and the Near East and dates from about 300,000 to about 40,000 years ago. For Africa, the term Middle Stone Age is used. The assemblages of flake tools from this period are generally referred to as Mousterian in Europe and the Near East and as post-Acheulian in Africa. Compared with an Acheulian assemblage, a Mousterian tool assemblage has a smaller proportion of large

hand axes and cleavers and a larger proportion of small flake tools such as scrapers. Some Mousterian sites show signs of intentional burial.

4. Fossil remains of fully modern-looking humans, *Homo sapiens sapiens,* have been found in Africa, the Near East, Asia, and Australia, as well as in Europe. The oldest of these fossils have been found in East Africa and may be 160,000 years old.

5. Two theories about the origins of modern humans continue to be debated among anthropologists. One, the *single-origin theory,* suggests that modern humans emerged in just one part of the Old World—the Near East and, more recently, Africa have been the postulated places of origin—and spread to other parts of the Old World, superseding Neandertals. The second theory, the *multiregional theory,* suggests that modern humans emerged in various parts of the Old World, becoming the varieties of humans we see today.

6. The period of cultural history known as the Upper Paleolithic in Europe, the Near East, and Asia or the Later Stone Age in Africa dates from about 40,000 years ago to about 14,000 to 10,000 years ago. During this time the world was locked in an ice age, with glaciers covering much of northern Europe and North America, and annual temperatures as much as 10 degrees Celsius below today's.

7. The Upper Paleolithic tool kit is characterized by the preponderance of blades; there were also burins, bone and antler tools, and (later) microliths. In many respects, lifestyles were similar to lifestyles before. People were still mainly hunters and gatherers and fishers who probably lived in highly mobile bands. They made their camps out in the open and in caves and rock shelters.

8. The Upper Paleolithic is also characterized by a variety of new developments: new techniques of toolmaking, the emergence of art, population growth, and new inventions such as the bow and arrow, the spear-thrower (atlatl), and the harpoon.

9. Only *Homo sapiens sapiens* remains have been found in the New World. The prevailing opinion is that humans migrated to the New World over a land bridge between Siberia and Alaska in the area of what is now the Bering Strait. Until recently it was thought that humans were not present south of Alaska until after 11,500 years ago. Now it appears from an archaeological site called Monte Verde in Chile that modern humans got to southern South America by at least 12,500 years ago and perhaps as much as 33,000 years ago.

10. At the end of the ice age, around 14,000 years ago, the climate began to become more temperate. Many large animals relied upon by Upper Paleolithic peoples for food went extinct, and at the same time new, warmer-adapted plants provided a rich, new food source. Around the world people began to use more plant foods and a broader range of resources overall. In many parts of the world people began experimenting with domesticating plants and animals.

Glossary Terms

atlatl (p. 170)
blade (p. 168)
burin (p. 168)
Cro-Magnon (p. 162)
ethnographic analogy (p. 170)
Homo heidelbergensis (p. 154)
Homo neandertalensis (p. 154)
Homo sapiens sapiens (p. 154)

indirect percussion (p. 168)
Levalloisian method (p. 159)
microlith (p. 168)
Middle Paleolithic (p. 158)
Mousterian tool assemblage (p. 158)
Neandertal (p. 154)
pressure flaking (p. 168)
Upper Paleolithic (p. 167)

Critical Questions

1. If the single-origin or "out-of-Africa" theory were correct, in what ways could *Homo sapiens* have been able to replace *Homo erectus* and *Homo neandertalensis* populations?

2. How do Middle Paleolithic cultures differ from Lower Paleolithic cultures?

3. Upper Paleolithic cave paintings arouse our imaginations. We have described some research that tested ideas about what these paintings might mean. Can you think of other ways to understand the significance of cave art?

CHAPTER 8

FOOD PRODUCTION AND THE RISE OF STATES

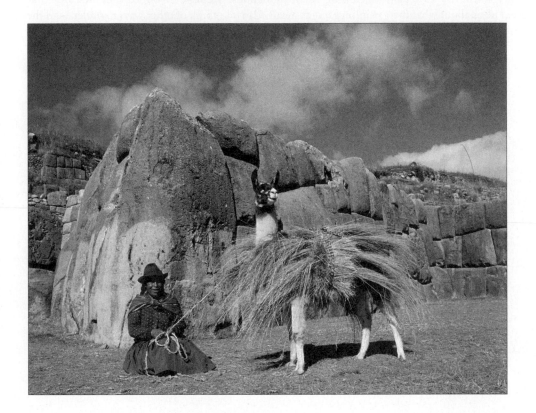

Chapter Outline

- Preagricultural Developments
- The Domestication of Plants and Animals
- Why Did Food Production Develop?
- Consequences of the Rise of Food Production
- The Rise of Cities and States
- The First Cities and States in Other Areas
- The Decline and Collapse of States

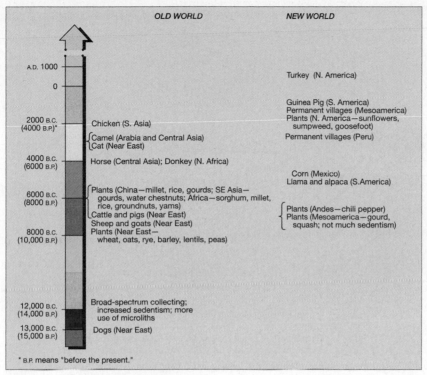

Figure 8.1   The Evolution of Domestication

Source: Dates for animal domestication are from Juliet Clutton-Brock, "Domestication of Animals," in Stephen Jones, Robert Martin, and David Pilbeam, eds., *The Cambridge Encyclopedia of Human Evolution* (New York: Cambridge University Press, 1992), figure from p. 384. Copyright © 1992. Reprinted by permission of Cambridge University Press.

Beginning about 14,000 years ago, people in some regions began to depend less on big-game hunting and more on relatively stationary food resources, such as fish, shellfish, small game, and wild plants (see Figure 8.1). In some areas, particularly Europe and the Middle East, the exploitation of local, relatively permanent resources may account for an increasingly settled way of life. The cultural period in which these developments took place is usually now called the **Epipaleolithic** in the Middle East and the **Mesolithic** in Europe. Other areas of the world generally show a similar switch to what is called *broad-spectrum food-collecting.* In Mesoamerica this period is called the *Archaic.*

We see the first clear evidence of a changeover to food production—the cultivation and domestication of plants and animals—in the Middle East, about 8000 B.C.[1] This kind of shift, often called the *Neolithic Revolution,* occurred, probably independently, in other areas of the Old and New Worlds within the next few thousand years. In the Old World there were independent centers of domestication in China, Southeast Asia (what is now Malaysia, Thailand, Cambodia, and Vietnam), and Africa around 6000 B.C.[2] In the New World there were centers of cultivation and domestication in the highlands of Mesoamerica (about 7000 B.C.), the central Andes around Peru (about 7000 B.C.), and the Eastern Woodlands of North America (about 2000 B.C., but perhaps earlier).[3] Figure 8.2 on page 184 shows the regions of the world that domesticated today's main food crops.

In this chapter we discuss what is believed about the origins of food production and settled life, called **sedentarism**—how and why people in different places may have come to cultivate and domesticate

Figure 8.2 Original Locations of the World's Main Food Crops

The world's main food crops were originally domesticated in different regions.

Source: Frank Hole, "Origins of Agriculture," in Stephen Jones, Robert Martin, and David Pilbeam, eds., *The Cambridge Encyclopedia of Human Evolution* (New York: Cambridge University Press, 1992), figure from p. 376. Copyright © 1992. Reprinted by permission of Cambridge University Press.

plants (referred to as **agriculture**) and animals and to live in permanent villages. We then discuss the rise of cities and states. Much of our discussion focuses on the Middle East and Mesoamerica, the areas we know best archaeologically for the developments leading to food production and the rise of states.

Preagricultural Developments

The Middle East

In the Middle East there seems to have been a shift from mobile big-game hunting to the utilization of a broad spectrum of natural resources at the end of the Upper Paleolithic, similar to those changes that happened in Europe, which we discussed at the end of the previous chapter.[4] There is evidence that people subsisted on a variety of resources, including fish, mollusks, and other water life; wild deer, sheep, and goats; and wild grains, nuts, and legumes.[5] The increased utilization of stationary food sources such as wild grain may partly explain why some people in the Middle East began to lead more sedentary lives during the Epipaleolithic.

Even today, a traveler passing through the Anatolian highlands of Turkey and other mountainous regions in the Middle East may see thick stands of wild wheat and barley growing as densely as if they had been cultivated.[6] Just how productive these resources can be was demonstrated in a field experiment duplicating prehistoric conditions. Using the kind of flint-blade sickle an Epipaleolithic worker would have used, researchers were able to harvest a little over two pounds of wild grain in an hour. A family of four, working only during the few weeks of the harvest season, probably could have reaped more wheat and barley than they needed for the entire year.[7] The amount of wild wheat harvested in the experiment prompted Kent Flannery to conclude, "Such a harvest would almost necessitate some degree of sedentism—after all, where could they go with an estimated metric ton of clean wheat?"[8] Moreover, the stone equipment used for grinding would have been too hard to carry. Part of the harvest would probably have been set aside for immediate consumption, ground, and then cooked either by roasting or boiling. The rest of the harvest would have been stored to supply food for the remainder of the year. A grain diet, then, could have been the impetus for the construction of roasters, grinders, and storage pits by some preagricultural people, as well as for the construction of solid, fairly permanent housing. Once a village was built, people may have been reluctant to abandon it. We can visualize the earliest preagricultural settlements clustered around such naturally rich regions, as archaeological evidence indeed suggests they were.

The Natufians of the Middle East   Eleven thousand years ago the Natufians, a people living in the area that is now Israel and Jordan, inhabited caves and rock shelters and built villages on the slopes of Mount Carmel in Israel. For example, the site of Eynan contains the remains of three villages in sequence, one atop another. Each village consisted of about 50 circular *pit houses*. The floor of each house was sunk a few feet into the ground, so that the walls of the house consisted partly of earth, below ground level, and partly of stone, above ground level. The villages appear to have had stone-paved walks; circular stone pavements ringed what seem to be permanent hearths; and the dead were interred in village cemeteries.

The tools suggest that the Natufians harvested wild grain intensively. Sickles recovered from their villages have a specific sheen, which experiments have shown to be the effect of flint striking grass stems, as the sickles would have been used in the cutting of grain. The Natufians are the earliest Epipaleolithic people known to have stored surplus crops. Beneath the floors of their stone-walled houses they constructed plastered storage pits.[9] The remains of many wild animals are also found in Natufian sites; Natufians appear to have concentrated on hunting gazelle, which they would take by surrounding whole herds.[10]

Natufian food collecting was different from that of earlier food-collecting cultures.[11] Not only was it based on a more intensive use of stationary resources such as wild grain, but the archaeological evidence suggests increasing social complexity. Natufian sites on the average were five times larger than those of their predecessors. Communities were occupied for most of the year, if not year-round. Burial patterns suggest more social differences between people. Although the available wild cereal resources appear to have enabled the Natufians to live in relatively permanent villages, their diet seems to have suffered. Their tooth enamel shows signs of nutritional deficiency, and their stature declined over time.[12]

Mesoamerica

A similar shift toward more broad-spectrum hunting and gathering occurred in the New World at the end of the Paleo-Indian period, about 10,000 years ago. The retreat of glacial ice from North America and overall warmer and wetter climate brought dramatic changes to plant and animal communities throughout North America and Mesoamerica. Pleistocene megafauna, such as mammoths, mastodon, rhinoceros, giant ground sloth, and others, as well as a variety of smaller game animals, such as the horse, all went extinct in a relatively short period of time.[13] Hunting strategies shifted toward a broader range of game species, particularly deer, antelope, bison, and small mammals. At the same time, deciduous woodlands and grasslands expanded, providing a range of new plants to exploit. Ground stone woodworking tools such as axes and adzes first appeared, as did nut-processing tools such as mortars and pestles. Shellfish began to be exploited in some areas. Throughout North America and Mesoamerica people began to expand the range of plants and animals they relied upon.[14]

The Archaic Peoples of Highland Mesoamerica   In Highland Mesoamerica, the mountainous regions of central and southern Mexico, we also see a shift from big-game hunting to a broader use of resources, in part due to a change in climate more like today's. Altitude became an important factor in the hunting and collecting regime, as different altitudes have different plant and animal resources. Valleys tend to have scrubby, grassland vegetation, whereas foothills and mountains have "thorn forests" of cactuses and succulents giving way to oak and pine forests at higher altitudes, where there is more moisture. This vertical zonation means that a wide range of plants and animals were available in relatively close proximity—different environments were close by—and the **Archaic** peoples took advantage of these varied conditions to hunt and collect a broad range of resources.[15]

About 8,000 years ago the Archaic peoples in Mesoamerica appear to have moved seasonally between communities of two different sizes: camps with 15 to 30 residents (*macrobands*) and camps with only 2 to 5 residents (*microbands*). Macroband camps were located near seasonally abundant resources, such as acorns or mesquite pods. Several families would have come together when these resources were in season, both to take advantage of them and to work together to harvest them while they were plentiful, perhaps to perform rituals, and simply to socialize. Remains of these microband camps are often found in caves or rock shelters from which a variety of environments could be exploited by moving either upslope or downslope from the campsite.[16] Unlike the Natufians of the Middle East, there is no evidence of social differences among the Archaic peoples of Highland Mesoamerica.

Other Areas

The still-sparse archaeological record suggests that a change to broad-spectrum collecting also occurred in Southeast Asia. For example, at inland base camps we find the remains of animals from high mountain ridges as well as lowland river valleys, birds and primates from nearby forests, bats from caves, and fish from streams. The few coastal sites indicate that many kinds of fish and shellfish were collected and that animals such as deer, wild cattle, and rhinoceros were hunted.[17] The preagricultural developments

These young Fulbe-Waila girls in Chad are collecting seeds much like preagricultural peoples did.

in Southeast Asia probably were responses to changes in the climate and environment, including a warming trend, more moisture, and a higher sea level.[18]

In Africa, too, the preagricultural period was marked by a warmer, wetter environment. For example, there were lakes in what is now the southern and central Sahara Desert, where people fished and hunted hippopotamuses and crocodiles. This pattern of broad-spectrum food-collecting seems also to have been characteristic of the areas both south and north of the Sahara.[19] One area showing increased sedentism is the Dakhleh Oasis in the Western Desert of Egypt. Between 9,000 and 8,500 years ago, the inhabitants lived in circular stone huts on the shores of rivers and lakes. Bone harpoons and pottery are found there and in other areas from the Nile Valley through the central and southern Sahara westward to what is now Mali. Fishing seems to have allowed people to remain along the rivers and lakes for much of the year.[20]

Why Did Broad-Spectrum Collecting Develop?

It is apparent that the preagricultural switch to broad-spectrum collecting was fairly common throughout the world. Climate change was probably at least partly responsible. For example, the worldwide rise in sea level because of glacial melting may have increased the availability of fish and shellfish. Changes in climate may have also been partly responsible for the decline in the availability of big game, particularly the large herd animals. Another possible cause of the decline in big game was human activity, specifically overkilling of some of these animals.[21] The extinction in the New World of many of the large Pleistocene animals, such as the mammoth, coincided with the movement of humans from the Bering Strait region into the Americas.[22] However, an enormous number of bird species also became extinct during the last few thousand years of the North American Pleistocene, and it is difficult to argue that human hunters caused all of those extinctions. Because the bird and mammal extinctions occurred simultaneously, it is likely that most or nearly all the extinctions were due to climatic and other environmental changes.[23]

Population growth may have also led to the shift to broad-spectrum collecting. As Mark Cohen has noted, hunter-gatherers were "filling up" the world, and they may have had to seek new sources of food.[24] Consistent with the idea that the world was filling up around this time is the fact that not until after 30,000 years ago did hunter-gatherers begin to move into previously uninhabited parts of the world, such as Australia and the New World.[25]

Broad-spectrum collecting does not necessarily mean that people were eating better. A decline in stature often indicates a poorer diet. During the preagricultural period, height apparently declined by as much as two inches in many parts of the Old World (Greece, Israel, India, and northern and western Europe).[26] In other areas of the world, such as Australia and what is now the midwestern United States, skeletal evidence also suggests a decline in the general level of health with the rise of broad-spectrum collecting.[27]

Broad-Spectrum Collecting and Sedentarism

Does the switch to broad-spectrum collecting explain the increasingly sedentary way of life we see in various parts of the world in preagricultural times? The answer seems to be both yes and no. In some areas of the world—some sites in Europe, the Middle East, Africa, and Peru—settlements became more permanent. In other areas, such as the semiarid highlands of Mesoamerica, the switch to broad-spectrum collecting was not associated with increasing sedentarism. Even after the Highland Mesoamericans began to cultivate plants, they still did not live in permanent villages.[28] Why?

It would seem that it is not simply the switch to broad-spectrum collecting that accounts for increasing sedentarism in many areas. Rather, a comparison of settlements on the Peruvian coast suggests that the more permanent settlements were located nearer, within three and a half miles, to most, if not all, of the diverse food resources exploited during the year. The community that did not have a year-round settlement seems to have depended on more widely distributed resources. What accounts for sedentarism may thus be the nearness[29] or the high reliability and yield[30] of the broad-spectrum resources, rather than the broad spectrum itself.

Sedentarism and Population Growth

Although some population growth undoubtedly occurred throughout the hunting and gathering phase of world history, some anthropologists have suggested that populations would have increased dramatically when people began to settle down.

The settling down of a nomadic group may reduce the typical spacing between births.[31] Nomadic !Kung have children spaced four years apart on the average; in contrast, recently sedentarized !Kung have children about three years apart. Why might birth spacing change with settling down? If effective contraceptives are not available, prolonged sexual abstinence after the birth of a child—the postpartum sex taboo—may be the method used to space births. Abortion or infanticide may also be practiced.[32] Carrying one small child is difficult enough; carrying two might be too burdensome. Nomadic groups may be motivated to have children farther apart because of the problem of carrying small children.

Although some nomadic groups may have deliberately spaced births by abstinence or infanticide, there is no evidence that such practices explain why four years separate births among nomadic !Kung. There may be another explanation, involving an unintended effect of how babies are fed. Nancy Howell and Richard Lee have suggested that the presence of baby foods other than mother's milk may be responsible for the decreased birth spacing in sedentary agricultural !Kung groups.[33] It is now well established that the longer a mother nurses her baby without supplementary foods, the longer it is likely to be before she starts ovulating again. Nomadic !Kung women have little to give their babies in the way of soft, digestible

Shown here is a !Kung group moving camp. When hunters and gatherers move, they have to carry their children and all of their possessions with them. Spacing births an average of four years apart helps to ensure that a woman will not have to carry more than two children at a time.

food, and the babies depend largely on mother's milk for two to three years. But sedentary !Kung mothers can give their babies soft foods such as cereal (made from cultivated grain) and milk from domesticated animals. Such changes in feeding practices may shorten birth spacing by shortening the interval between birth and the resumption of ovulation. In preagricultural sedentary communities, it is possible that baby foods made from wild grains might have had the same effect. For this reason alone, therefore, populations may have grown even before people started to farm or herd.

Some investigators suspect that a critical minimum of fat in the body may be necessary for ovulation. A sedentary !Kung woman may have more fatty tissue than a nomadic !Kung woman, who walks many miles daily to gather wild plant foods, often carrying a child with her. Thus, sedentary !Kung women might resume ovulating sooner after the birth of a baby and may be likely to have more closely spaced children. If some critical amount of fat is necessary for ovulation, that would explain why in our own society many women who have little body fat—long-distance runners, gymnasts, and ballet dancers are examples—do not ovulate regularly.[34]

The Domestication of Plants and Animals

Neolithic means "of the new stone age"; the term originally signified the cultural stage in which humans invented pottery and ground-stone tools. We now know, however, that both were present in earlier times, so we cannot define a Neolithic state of culture purely on the basis of the presence of pottery and ground-stone tools. At present, archaeologists generally define the **Neolithic** in terms of the presence of domesticated plants and animals. In this type of culture, people began to produce food rather than merely collect it. The line between food-collecting and food-producing occurs when people begin to plant crops and to keep and breed animals. How do we know when this transition occurred? In fact, archaeologically we do not see the beginning of food production; we can see signs of it only after plants and animals show differences from their wild varieties. When people plant crops, we refer to the process as cultivation. It is only when the crops cultivated and the animals raised are *modified*—different from wild varieties—that we speak of plant and animal **domestication**.

We know, in a particular site, that domestication occurred if plant remains have characteristics different from those of wild plants of the same types. For example, wild grains of barley and wheat have a fragile **rachis**—the seed-bearing part of the stem—which shatters easily, releasing the seeds. Domesticated grains have a tough rachis, which does not shatter easily. In addition, the grain of wild barley and wheat has a tough shell protecting the seed from premature exposure, whereas domesticated grain has a brittle shell that can be easily separated, which facilitates preparing the seed for grinding into flour.

Consider how the rachis of wheat and barley may have changed. When humans arrived with sickles and flails to collect the wild stands of grain, the seeds harvested probably contained a high proportion of tough-rachis mutants, because these could best withstand the rough treatment of harvest processing. If planted, the harvested seeds would be likely to produce tough-rachis plants. If in each successive harvest seeds from tough-rachis plants were the least likely to be lost, tough-rachis plants would come to predominate.[35]

Domesticated species of animals also differ from the wild varieties. For example, the horns of wild goats in the Middle East are shaped differently from those of domesticated goats.[36]

Domestication in the Middle East

For some time most archaeologists have thought that the "Fertile Crescent," the arc of land stretching up from Israel and the Jordan Valley through southern Turkey and then downward to the western slopes of the Zagros Mountains in Iran, was one of the earliest centers of plant and animal domestication. We know that several varieties of domesticated wheat were being grown there after about 8000 B.C., as were oats, rye, barley, lentils, peas, and various fruits and nuts (apricots, pears, pomegranates, dates, figs, olives, almonds, and pistachios).[37] It appears that animals were first domesticated in the Middle East. Dogs were first domesticated before the rise of agriculture, around 13,000 B.C., goats and sheep around 7000 B.C., and cattle and pigs around 6000 B.C.[38]

Let us look at an early Neolithic site in the Middle East to see what life there may have been like after people began to depend on domesticated plants and animals for food.

Ali Kosh   At the stratified site of Ali Kosh in what is now southwestern Iran (see Figure 8.3), we see the remains of a community that started out about 7500 B.C. living mostly on wild plants and animals. Over the next 2,000 years, until about 5500 B.C., agriculture and herding became increasingly important. After 5500 B.C., we see the appearance of two innovations—irrigation and the use of domesticated cattle—that seem to have stimulated a minor population explosion during the following millennium.

From 7500 to 6750 B.C., the people at Ali Kosh cut little slabs of raw clay out of the ground to build small, multiroom structures. There is evidence that the people at Ali Kosh may have moved for the summer (with their goats) to the grassier mountain valleys nearby, which were just a few days' walk away.

Figure 8.3   Early Agricultural Settlements in the Near East

Modern cities are represented by a dot, early settlements by a square. The dark gray tint indicates the area known as the Fertile Crescent.

We have a lot of evidence about what the people at Ali Kosh ate. They got some of their food from cultivated emmer wheat and a kind of barley and a considerable amount from domesticated goats. We know the goats were domesticated because wild goats do not seem to have lived in the area. Also, the fact that virtually no bones from elderly goats were found in the site suggests that the goats were domesticated and herded rather than hunted. Moreover, it would seem from the horn cores found in the site that mostly young male goats were eaten, so the females probably were kept for breeding and milking. But with all these signs of deliberate food production, there is an enormous amount of evidence—literally tens of thousands of seeds and bone fragments—that the people at the beginning of Ali Kosh depended mostly on wild plants (legumes and grasses) and wild animals (including gazelles, wild oxen, and wild pigs). They also collected fish, such as carp and catfish, and shellfish, such as mussels, as well as waterfowl that visited the area during part of the year.

The flint tools used during this earliest phase at Ali Kosh were varied and abundant. Finds from this period include tens of thousands of tiny flint blades, some only a few millimeters wide. About 1 percent of the chipped stone found by archaeologists was **obsidian**, or volcanic glass, which came from what is now eastern Turkey, several hundred miles away. Thus, the people at Ali Kosh during its earliest phase definitely had some kind of contact with people elsewhere. From 6750 to 6000 B.C., the people increased their consumption of cultivated food plants; 40 percent of the seed remains in the hearths and refuse areas were now from emmer wheat and barley. The proportion of the diet coming from wild plants was much reduced, probably because the cultivated plants have the same growing season and grow in the same kind of soil as the wild plants. Grazing by the goats and sheep that were kept may also have contributed to the reduction of wild plant foods in the area and in the diet. The village may or may not have gotten larger, but the multiroom houses definitely had. The rooms were now larger than 10 by 10 feet; the walls were much thicker; and the clay-slab bricks were now held together by a mud mortar. Also, the walls now often had a coat of smooth mud plaster on both sides. There were courtyards with domed brick ovens and brick-lined roasting pits.

Even though the village probably contained no more than 100 individuals, it participated in an extensive trading network. Seashells were probably obtained from the Persian Gulf, which is some distance to the south; copper may have come from what is now central Iran; obsidian was still coming from eastern Turkey; and turquoise somehow made its way from what is now the border between Iran and Afghanistan. Some of these materials were used as ornaments worn by both sexes—or so it seems from the remains of bodies found buried under the floors of houses.

After about 5500 B.C., the area around Ali Kosh begins to show signs of a much larger population, apparently made possible by a more complex agriculture employing irrigation and plows drawn by domesticated cattle. In the next thousand years, by 4500 B.C., the population of the area probably tripled. This population growth was apparently part of the cultural developments that culminated in the rise of urban civilizations in the Middle East.[39]

Domestication in Mesoamerica

In Mesoamerica, people sowed a variety of plants, but after doing so they went on with their seasonal rounds of hunting and gathering, and came back later to harvest what they had sown. Domestication may have been a way for Archaic peoples to make desirable plants more common. For example, one of the first domesticates was the bottle gourd. These were not eaten but were used to carry water. Joyce Marcus and Kent Flannery hypothesize that the bottle gourd was domesticated by people deliberately planting them in areas where they did not grow naturally, so that as groups moved through those areas they always had access to gourds for carrying water.[40]

Other domesticates included tomatoes, cotton, a variety of beans and squashes, and, perhaps most importantly, maize. The earliest domesticated form of maize (corn), dating from about 5000 B.C., has been found in Tehuacán, Mexico. Genetic studies of maize show that it was domesticated from teosinte, a tall wild grass that still grows widely in Mexico.[41] Indeed, these genetic studies suggest that changes occured in only two genes, one related to the kernel glumes (outer casing), and one related to the stalk shape.[42] The genes of modern corn were already established 4,000–6,000 years ago.

Early maize was considerably different from modern maize. The oldest maize cobs—dating to about 7,000 years ago—are tiny, only about an inch long. They have only a half-dozen rows of seeds, and each seed is tiny. Maize is almost completely dependent on humans to reproduce—the shift from seeds with brittle coats to cobs with a tough husk meant that someone had to open the husk without damaging the seeds in order for them to be dispersed and reproduce.[43]

People who lived in Mesoamerica, Mexico and Central America, are often credited with the invention of planting maize, beans, and squash together in the same field. This planting strategy provides some important advantages. Maize takes nitrogen from the soil; beans, like all legumes, put nitrogen back into the soil. The maize stalk provides a natural pole for the bean plant to twine around, and the low-growing squash can grow around the base of the tall maize plant. Beans supply people with the amino acid lysine, which is missing in maize. Thus, maize and beans together provide all the essential amino acids that humans need to obtain from their food. Teosinte may have provided the model for this unique combination, as wild runner beans and wild squash occur naturally where teosinte grows.[44]

Domestication Elsewhere in the World

South America and the Eastern United States   Evidence of independent domestication of plants comes from at least two other areas in the New World: South America and the eastern United States. We can trace more than 200 domesticated plants to the Andes in South America, including potatoes, lima beans, peanuts, amaranth, and quinoa. The first clear domesticates were squashes and gourds, which may date back to 8000 B.C., which makes domestication in the Andes as old as in Mesoamerica, and perhaps even older.[45] The origins of the root crops manioc and sweet potato are less certain, but those crops probably originated in lowland tropical forest regions of South America.[46]

Many of the plants grown in North America, such as corn, beans, and squash, were apparently introduced from Mesoamerica. However, at least three seed plants were probably domesticated independently in North America at an earlier time—sunflowers, sumpweed, and goosefoot. Sunflowers and sumpweed contain seeds that are highly nutritious in terms of protein and fat; goosefoot is high in starch and similar to corn in food value.[47] Sumpweed is an unusually good source of calcium, rivaled only by greens, mussels, and bones. It is also a very good source of iron (better than beef liver) and thiamine.[48] These plants may have been cultivated in the area of Kentucky, Tennessee, and southern Illinois beginning around 2000 B.C. (Corn was introduced about A.D. 200.)

On the whole, domestic animals were less important economically in the New World than they were in many parts of the Old World. The central Andes was the only part of the New World where animals were a significant part of the economy. Used for meat, transportation, and wool, llamas and alpacas (members of the camel family) were domesticated as early as 5000 B.C. in the Andes.[49] Guinea pigs, misnamed because they are neither pigs nor from Guinea, are rodents that were domesticated in the Andes sometime later. They were an important source of food even before domestication.[50] Since they were domesticated, they have been raised in people's dwellings.

Animal domestication in the New World differed from that in the Old World because different wild species were found in the two hemispheres. The Old World plains and forests were the homes for the wild ancestors of the cattle, sheep, goats, pigs, and horses we know today. In the New World, the Pleistocene herds of horses, mastodons, mammoths, and other large animals were long extinct, allowing few opportunities for domestication of large animals.[51]

Asia The earliest clear evidence of cereal cultivation outside the Middle East is from China. Late in the sixth millennium B.C. in North China there were sites where foxtail millet was cultivated. Storage pits, storage pots, and large numbers of grinding stones suggest that millet was an enormously important item in the diet. The wild-animal bones and the hunting and fishing tools that have been found suggest that people still depended on hunting and fishing somewhat, even though domesticated pigs (as well as dogs) were present. In South China, from about the same time, archaeologists have found a village by the edge of a small lake where people cultivated rice, bottle gourds, water chestnuts, and the date-like fruit called jujube. The people in South China also raised water buffalo, pigs, and dogs. And, as in the North China sites, some of their food came from hunting and fishing.[52]

Mainland Southeast Asia may have been a place of domestication as early as the Middle East was. The dating of domestication in Southeast Asia is not yet clear; the dates of the oldest site with probable domesticates—Spirit cave in northwest Thailand—range from about 9500 B.C. to 5500 B.C. Some of the plants found at Spirit cave are not clearly distinguishable from wild varieties, but others, such as gourds, betel nut, betel leaf, and water chestnut, were probably domesticates.[53]

Some early cultivated crops may not have been used for food at all. In particular, bamboo may have been used to make cutting tools and for a variety of building purposes, and gourds were probably used as containers or bowls. We do not know yet exactly when rice was first domesticated, but there is definite evidence of cultivated rice in Thailand after 4000 B.C.

Bananas and taro may have been first domesticated in New Guinea. Recent analyses of soils from archaeological deposits at Kuk Swamp have identified phytoliths (small silica crystals formed between plant cells that are unique to particular species of plants) from bananas and taro dating from almost 7,000 years ago.[54] Archaeologists have known that agricultural fields with soil mounds and irrigation features have a long history in New Guinea, dating back as far as 10,000 years. The new findings of very early taro and banana cultivation suggest that New Guinea may have been the location where these plants were first domesticated. Other major food plants domesticated in Southeast Asia include yams, breadfruit, and coconuts.[55]

Africa Some plants and animals were domesticated first in Africa. Most of the early domestications probably occurred in the wide, broad belt of woodland-savanna country south of the Sahara and north of the equator. Among the cereal grains, sorghum was probably first domesticated in the central or eastern part

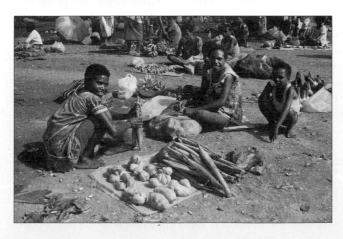

Bananas and taro were domesticated in New Guinea nearly 7,000 years ago.

of this belt, bulrush millet and a kind of rice (different from Asian rice) in the western part, and finger millet in the east. Groundnuts (peanuts) and yams were first domesticated in West Africa.[56] We do know that farming became widespread in the northern half of Africa after 6000 B.C.; investigators continue to debate whether the earliest crops grown there were indigenous or borrowed from the Middle East. There is little doubt, however, that some of the plant foods were first domesticated in sub-Saharan Africa because the wild varieties occur there.[57] Many of the important domestic animals in Africa today, especially sheep and goats, were first domesticated elsewhere in the Old World, but one form of cattle, as well as donkey and guinea fowl, were probably first domesticated in Africa.[58]

Why Did Food Production Develop?

Why did domestication occur? And why did it occur independently in many different places within a period of a few thousand years? Considering that people depended only on wild plants and animals for millions of years, the differences in exactly when domestication first occurred in different parts of the world seem small.

There are many theories of why **food production** developed; most have tried to explain the origin of domestication in the area of the Fertile Crescent. Gordon Childe's theory, popular in the 1950s, was that a drastic change in climate caused domestication in the Middle East.[59] According to Childe, the postglacial period was marked by a decline in summer rainfall in the Middle East and northern Africa. As the rains decreased, people were forced to retreat into shrinking pockets, or oases, of food resources surrounded by desert. The lessened availability of wild resources provided an incentive for people to cultivate grains and to domesticate animals, according to Childe.

However, the climatic changes that occurred in the Middle East after the retreat of the last glaciers had probably occurred at earlier interglacial periods too, but there had never been a similar food-producing revolution before. Hence, according to Braidwood, there must be more to the explanation of why people began to produce food than simply changes in climate.[60]

Binford and Flannery thought that the incentive to domesticate animals and plants may have been a desire to reproduce what was wildly abundant in the most bountiful or optimum hunting and gathering areas. Because of population growth in the optimum areas, people might have moved to surrounding areas containing fewer wild resources. It would have been in those marginal areas that people might have first turned to food production in order to reproduce what they used to have. The Binford-Flannery model seems to fit the archaeological record in the Levant, the southwestern part of the Fertile Crescent, where population increase did precede the first signs of domestication.[61] But, as Flannery admitted, in some regions, such as southwestern Iran, the optimum hunting-gathering areas do not show population increase before the emergence of domestication.[62]

The Binford-Flannery model focuses on population pressure in a small area as the incentive to turn to food production. Mark Cohen theorizes it was population pressure on a global scale that explains why so many of the world's peoples adopted agriculture within the span of a few thousand years.[63] He argues that hunter-gatherers all over the world gradually increased in population so that by about 10,000 years ago the world was more or less filled with food collectors. Thus people could no longer relieve population pressure by moving to uninhabited areas. To support their increasing populations, they would have had to exploit a broader range of less desirable wild foods; that is, they would have had to switch to broad-spectrum collecting, or they would have had to increase the yields of the most desirable wild plants by weeding, protecting them from animal pests, and perhaps deliberately planting the most productive among them. Cohen thinks that people might have tried a variety of these strategies but would generally have ended up depending on cultivation because that would have been the most efficient way to allow more people to live in one place.

Recently, some archaeologists have returned to the idea that climatic change might have played a role in the emergence of agriculture. It seems clear from the evidence now available that the climate of the Middle East about 13,000–12,000 years ago became more seasonal: The summers got hotter and drier than before and the winters became colder. These climatic changes may have favored the emergence of annual species of wild grain, which archaeologically we see proliferating in many areas of the Middle East.[64] People such as the Natufians intensively exploited the seasonal grains, developing an elaborate technology for storing and processing the grains and giving up their previous nomadic existence to do so. The transition to agriculture may have occurred when sedentary foraging no longer provided sufficient resources for the population. This could have happened because sedentarization led to population increase and therefore resource scarcity,[65] or because local wild resources became depleted after people settled down in permanent villages.[66] In the area of Israel and Jordan where the Natufians lived, some of the people apparently turned to agriculture, probably to increase the supply of grain, whereas other people returned to nomadic food collection because of the decreasing availability of wild grain.[67]

Change to a more seasonal climate might also have led to a shortage of certain nutrients for food collectors. In the dry seasons certain nutrients would have been less available. For example, grazing animals get lean when grasses are not plentiful, so meat from hunting would have been in short supply in the dry seasons. Although it may seem surprising, some recent hunter-gatherers have starved when they had to rely on lean meat. If somehow they could have increased their carbohydrate or fat intake, they might have been more likely to get through the periods of lean game.[68] So it is possible that some wild-food collectors in the past thought of planting crops to get them through the dry seasons when hunting, fishing, and gathering did not provide enough carbohydrates and fat for them to avoid starvation.

Mesoamerica presents a very different picture, because the early domesticates were not important to subsistence. Theories about population pressure and nutrient shortage don't seem to fit Mesoamerica well. However, there were apparently shortages of desired plants, such as bottle gourds, and domestication may well have occurred as humans actively sowed these desired plants. The difference between this model and the ones described previously is that humans in Mesoamerica were apparently not forced into domestication by climate change or population pressure, but actively turned to domestication to obtain more of the most desired or useful plant species. The most interesting case is maize, which only became a staple food some 2,500 or more years after it was first domesticated. Why did it become a staple? Probably both because it was a suitable staple crop (especially when intercropped with beans and squash, as discussed earlier) and because people liked it, so they grew it in large quantities. Over time, and perhaps because of conflict, population pressure, and other forces similar to those that apparently led to domestication in the Middle East, people in Mesoamerica and later North and South America came to rely on maize as their dietary mainstay.

Consequences of the Rise of Food Production

We know that intensive agriculture (permanent rather than shifting cultivation) probably developed in response to population pressure, but we do not know for sure that population pressure was even partly responsible for plant and animal domestication in the first place. Still, population growth certainly accelerated after the rise of food production (see Figure 8.4 on page 196), possibly because the spacing between births was reduced further and therefore fertility (the number of births per mother) increased. Increased fertility may have been advantageous because of the greater value of children in farming and herding economies; there is evidence from recent population studies that fertility rates are higher where children contribute more to the economy.[69] The increased workload of mothers may also (but inadvertently) decrease birth spacing. The busier a mother is, the less frequently she may nurse and the more likely her baby will be given

Figure 8.4   Population Growth since 10,000 Years Ago

The rate of population growth accelerated after the emergence of farming and herding 10,000 years ago. The rate of growth has accelerated even more dramatically in recent times.

Source: Adapted from Ansley J. Coale, "The History of the Human Population," *Scientific American* (September 1974): 41–51. Copyright © 1974 by Scientific American, Inc.

supplementary food by other caretakers such as older siblings.[70] Less frequent nursing[71] and greater reliance on food other than mothers' milk may result in an earlier resumption of ovulation after the birth of a baby.

Although the rise of food production may have led to increased fertility, it appears that health declined at least sometimes with the transition to food production. The two trends may seem paradoxical, but rapid population growth can occur if each mother gives birth to a large number of babies, even if many of them die early because of disease or poor nutrition. Nutritional and disease problems are indicated by such features as incomplete formation of tooth enamel, nonaccidental bone lesions (incompletely filled-in bone), reduction in stature, and decreased life expectancy. Many of the studied prehistoric populations that relied heavily on agriculture seem to show less adequate nutrition and higher infection rates than populations living in the same areas before agriculture.[72] Some of the agricultural populations are shorter and had lower life expectancies.

The reasons for a decline in health in those populations are not yet clear. Greater malnutrition can result from an overdependence on a few dietary staples that lack some necessary nutrients. Overdependence on a few sources of food may also increase the risk of famine because the fewer the staple crops, the greater the danger to the food supply posed by a weather-caused crop failure. But some or most nutritional problems may be the result of social and political factors, particularly the rise of different socioeconomic classes of people and unequal access, between and within communities, to food and other resources.[73] (See the box titled "Chemical Analyses of Bones and Teeth" on page 198.)

For the first time, apparel made of woven textiles appeared. This development was not simply the result of the domestication of flax (for linen), cotton, and wool-growing sheep. These sources of fiber alone could not produce cloth. It was the development by Neolithic society of the spindle and loom for spinning and weaving that made textiles possible. True, textiles can be woven by hand without a loom, but to do so is a slow, laborious process, impractical for producing garments.

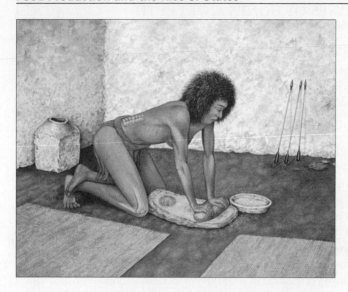

As this reconstruction shows, transforming grain into flour was a "daily grind," putting a great deal of stress on the lower back and knees. Studies of Neolithic skeletons of women show marks of stress on bone and arthritis, probably reflecting their long hours of work at the grinding stone.
Source: Roberto Osti, "The Eloquent Bones of Abu Hureyra," courtesy of *Scientific American* (August 1994), p. 73, top.

There is also evidence of long-distance trade, as we have noted. Obsidian from southern Turkey was being exported to sites in the Zagros Mountains of Iran and to what are now Israel, Jordan, and Syria in the Levant. Great amounts of obsidian were exported to sites about 190 miles from the source of supply; more than 80 percent of the tools used by residents of those areas were made of this material.[74] Marble was being sent from western to eastern Turkey, and seashells from the coast were traded to distant inland regions.

The Rise of Cities and States

From the time agriculture first developed until about 6000 B.C., people in the Middle East lived in fairly small villages. There were few differences in wealth and status from household to household, and apparently there was no governmental authority beyond the village. There is no evidence that these villages had any public buildings or craft specialists or that one community was very different in size from its neighbors. In short, these settlements had none of the characteristics we commonly associate with "civilization."

But sometime around 6000 B.C., in parts of the Middle East—and at later times in other places—a great transformation in the quality and scale of human life seems to have begun. For the first time we can see evidence of differences in status among households. For example, some are much bigger than others. Communities begin to differ in size and to specialize in certain crafts. And there are signs that some political officials had acquired authority over several communities, that what anthropologists call "chiefdoms" had emerged.

Somewhat later, by about 3500 B.C., we can see many, if not all, of the conventional characteristics of **civilization**: cities (the word "civilized" literally means "citified"); the first inscriptions, or writing; many kinds of full-time craft specialists; monumental architecture; great differences in wealth and status; and the kind of strong, hierarchical, centralized political system that we call the **state.**

This type of transformation has occurred many times and in many places in human history (see Figure 8.5 on page 199). The most ancient civilizations arose in the Middle East around 3500 B.C., in northwestern India and in Peru about 2500 B.C., in northern China around 1750 B.C., in Mexico a few hundred years before the time of Christ, and in tropical Africa somewhat later.[75] At least some of these

Archaeologists study ancient diets in several ways, most of them indirect. They can indirectly infer some of what ancient people ate from recovered food wastes. For example, if you find a lot of corncobs, chances are that the people ate a lot of corn. Plant and animal foods can be identified in the charred remains of cooking fires and (when preserved) in the ancient people's feces, or coprolites. Such inferences are usually biased in favor of hard food sources such as seeds, nuts, and grains (which are likely to be preserved); rarely are the remains of soft plants such as bananas or tubers found. Archaeologists can also indirectly infer diet from the artifacts they find, particularly, of course, ones we can be pretty sure were used in obtaining or processing food. So, for example, if you find a stone with a flat or concave surface that looks like what people use in some places to grind corn, it is very likely that the ancient people also ground grain (or other hard things such as seeds) for food. But plant remains or implements do not tell us how much people relied on particular sources of food.

There is a more direct way to study ancient diets. Anthropologists have discovered that in many ways "you are what you eat." In particular, chemical analyses of bones and teeth, the most common remains found in excavations, can reveal distinctive traces of the foods that metabolically went into the bones and teeth.

One kind of informative chemical analysis involves the ratio of strontium to calcium in bone. This analysis can indicate the relative amounts of plant and animal food in the diet. So, for example, we know from strontium analysis of bones that just before the beginnings of cereal agriculture in the Middle East, people were eating a lot of plant food, probably wild cereals that were intensively collected. Then there was a temporary decline in such collecting, suggesting overexploitation of the wild resources or at least their decreasing availability. This problem was presumably solved by the cultivation and domestication (modification) of cereals.

Carbon isotope ratios can tell us what types of plants people were eating. Trees, shrubs, and temperate-zone grasses (such as rice) have carbon isotope ratios that are different from those of tropical and subtropical grasses (such as millet and corn). People in China relied heavily on cereals about 7,000–8,000 years ago, but the cereals were not the same in the north and south. Contrary to what we might expect, the carbon isotope ratios tell us that an originally temperate-zone cereal (rice) was the staple in subtropical southern China; in the more temperate north, an originally tropical or subtropical grass (millet) was most important. There was heavy dependence on millet in the north. It is estimated that 50 to 80 percent of the diet between 5000–500 B.C. came from millet.

In the New World, seed crops such as sunflower, sumpweed, and goosefoot were domesticated in eastern North America long before corn, introduced from Mexico, became the staple. We know this partly from the archaeology; the remains of the early seed crops are older than the remains of corn. Corn, an originally subtropical plant, has a carbon isotope ratio that is different from the ratio for the earlier, temperate-zone seed crops. Thus, the shift in carbon isotope ratios after A.D. 800–900 tells us that corn had become the staple.

Nonchemical analyses of human bones and teeth were traditionally used by physical anthropologists and archaeologists to study similarities and differences between peoples in different geographic regions, between living humans and possible fossil ancestors, and between living humans and other surviving primates. Much of the research involved surface measurements, particularly of the skull (outside and inside). In recent years, physical anthropologists and archaeologists have begun to study the "insides" of bones and teeth. The new kinds of chemical analysis mentioned here are part of that trend. In N. J. van der Merwe's pithy words: "The emphasis in studies of human evolution has . . . shifted from a preoccupation with the brain to an equal interest in the stomach."

Sources: N. J. van der Merwe, "Reconstructing Prehistoric Diet," in Stephen Jones, Robert Martin, and David Pilbeam, eds., *The Cambridge Encyclopedia of Human Evolution* (New York: Cambridge University Press, 1992), pp. 369–72; Clark Spenser Larsen, "Bare Bones Anthropology: The Bioarchaeology of Human Remains," in Peter N. Peregrine, Carol R. Ember, and Melvin Ember, eds., *Archaeology: Original Readings in Method and Practice* (Upper Saddle River, NJ: Prentice Hall, 2002), also in Carol R. Ember, Melvin Ember, and Peter N. Peregrine, eds., *Research Frontiers,* in *New Directions in Anthropology* (Upper Saddle River, NJ: Prentice Hall, CD-ROM, 2004).

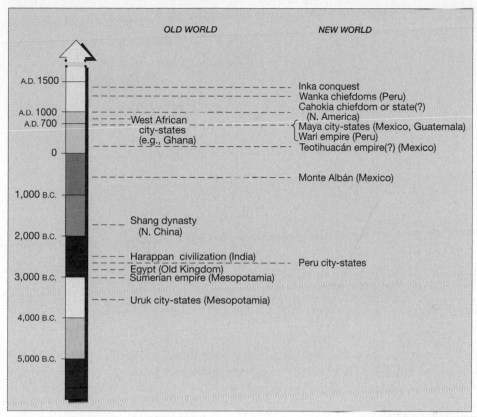

OLD WORLD   NEW WORLD

A.D. 1500 — — — — — — — — — — — — — — — Inka conquest
— — — — — — — — — — — — — — — — — Wanka chiefdoms (Peru)
Cahokia chiefdom or state(?)
A.D. 1000 — (N. America)
A.D. 700 — — — — West African — — — — — — — — Maya city-states (Mexico, Guatemala)
city-states { Wari empire (Peru)
(e.g., Ghana) — — — — — — — — — — Teotihuacán empire(?) (Mexico)
0 —

— — — — — — — — — — — — — — — Monte Albán (Mexico)
1,000 B.C. —

2,000 B.C. — — — — — Shang dynasty
(N. China)

— — — — — Harappan civilization (India) — — — — Peru city-states
— — — — — Egypt (Old Kingdom)
3,000 B.C. — — — — — Sumerian empire (Mesopotamia)

— — — — — Uruk city-states (Mesopotamia)
4,000 B.C. —

5,000 B.C. —

Figure 8.5   The Emergence of Civilization

civilizations evolved independently of the others—for example, those in the New World and those in the Old World. Why did they do so? What conditions favored the emergence of cities and centralized, state-like political systems? In discussing what archaeologists have learned or suspect about the growth of ancient civilizations, we focus primarily on the Middle East and Mexico because archaeologists know the most about the sequences of cultural development in those two areas.

Archaeological Inferences about Civilization

The most ancient civilizations have been studied by archaeologists rather than historians because those civilizations evolved before the advent of writing. How do archaeologists infer that a particular people in the preliterate past had social classes, cities, or a centralized government? It appears that the earliest Neolithic societies were *egalitarian;* that is, people did not differ much in wealth, prestige, or power. Some later societies show signs of social inequality, indicated by burial finds. Archaeologists generally assume that inequality in death reflects inequality in life, at least in status and perhaps also in wealth and power. Thus, we can be fairly sure that a society had differences in status if only some people were buried with special objects, such as jewelry or pots filled with food. And we can be fairly sure that high status was assigned at birth rather than achieved in later life if we find noticeable differences in children's tombs. For example, some (but not all) child burials from as early as 5500 to 5000 B.C. at Tell es-Sawwan in Iraq, and from about

Shown here is a reconstruction of the ornaments found with a royal burial from the Sumerian city of Ur. The headdress is made of gold and the necklaces include gold and lapis lazuli. Archaeologists assume that such special treatment indicates elite status.

800 B.C. at La Venta in Mexico, are filled with statues and ornaments, suggesting that some children had high status from birth[76] But burials indicating differences in status do not necessarily mean a society had significant differences in wealth. It is only when archaeologists find other substantial differences, as in house size and furnishings, that we can be sure the society had different socioeconomic classes of people.

Some archaeologists think that states first evolved around 3500 B.C. in greater Mesopotamia, the area now shared by southern Iraq and southwestern Iran. Archaeologists do not always agree on how a state should be defined, but most think that hierarchical and centralized decision making affecting a substantial population is the key criterion. States usually have cities with a substantial part of the population not involved directly in the collection or production of food (which means that people in cities are heavily dependent on people elsewhere); full-time religious and craft specialists; public buildings; and often an official art style. There is a hierarchical social structure topped by an elite class from which the leaders are drawn. The government tries to claim a monopoly on the use of force. (Our own state society says that citizens do not have the right "to take the law into their own hands.") The state uses its force or threat of force to tax its population and to draft people for work or war.[77]

How can archaeologists tell, from the information provided by material remains, whether a society was a state or not? This depends in part on what is used as the criterion for a state. For example, Henry Wright and Gregory Johnson defined a state as a centralized political hierarchy with at least three levels of administration.[78] But how might archaeologists infer that such a hierarchy existed in some area? Wright and Johnson suggested that the way settlement sites differ in size is one indication of how many levels of administration there were in an area.

During the early Uruk period (just before 3500 B.C.), in what is now southwestern Iran, there were some 50 settlements that seem to fall into three groups in terms of size.[79] There were about 45 small villages, three or four "towns," and one large center, Susa. These three types of settlements seem to have been part of a three-level administration hierarchy, since many small villages could not trade with Susa without passing through a settlement intermediate in size. Because a three-level hierarchy is Wright and Johnson's criterion of a state, they think a state had emerged in the area by early Uruk times.

Evidence from the next period, middle Uruk, suggests more definitely that a state had emerged. This evidence takes the form of clay seals that were apparently used in trading.[80] *Commodity sealings* were used to keep a shipment of goods tightly closed until it reached its destination, and *message sealings* were used to keep track of goods sent and received. The clay seals found in Susa include many message seals and *bullae*, clay containers that served as bills of lading for goods received. The villages, in contrast, had few message seals and bullae. Again, this finding suggests that Susa administered the regional movement of goods and that Susa was the "capital" of the state.

Let us turn now to the major features of the cultural sequences leading to the first states in southern Iraq.

Cities and States in Southern Iraq

Farming communities older than the first states have not been found in the arid lowland plains of southern Iraq—the area known as Sumer, where some of the earliest cities and states developed. Perhaps silt from the Tigris and Euphrates rivers has covered them. Or, as has been suggested, Sumer may not have been settled by agriculturalists until people learned how to drain and irrigate river-valley soils otherwise too wet or too dry for cultivation. At any rate, small communities depending partly on agriculture had emerged in the hilly areas north and east of Sumer early in the Neolithic. Later, by about 6000 B.C., a mixed herding-farming economy developed in those areas.

The Formative Era Elman Service called the period from about 5000 to 3500 B.C. the *formative era*, for it saw the coming together of many changes that seem to have played a part in the development of cities and states. Service suggested that with the development of small-scale irrigation, lowland river areas began to attract settlers. The rivers provided not only water for irrigation but also mollusks, fish, and waterbirds for food. And they provided routes by which to import needed raw materials, such as hardwood and stone, that were lacking in Sumer.

Changes during this period suggest an increasingly complex social and political life. Differences in status are reflected in the burial of statues and ornaments with children. Different villages specialized in the production of different goods—pottery in some, copper and stone tools in others.[81] Temples were built in certain places that may have been centers of political as well as religious authority for several communities.[82] Furthermore, some anthropologists think that chiefdoms, each having authority over several villages, had developed by this time.[83]

Sumerian Civilization By about 3500 B.C., there were quite a few cities and states in the area of Sumer. Most were enclosed in a fortress wall and surrounded by an agricultural area. About 3000 B.C. all of Sumer was unified under a single government. After that time, Sumer became an empire. It had great urban centers. Imposing temples, commonly set on artificial mounds, dominated the cities. In the city of Warka the temple mound was about 150 feet high. The empire was very complex and included an elaborate system for the administration of justice, codified laws, specialized government officials, a professional standing army, and even sewer systems in the cities. Among the many specialized crafts were brickmaking, pottery, carpentry, jewelry making, leatherworking, metallurgy, basketmaking, stonecutting, and sculpture. Sumerians learned to construct and use wheeled wagons, sailboats, horse-drawn chariots, and spears, swords, and armor of bronze.[84]

As economic specialization developed, social stratification became more elaborate. Sumerian documents describe a system of social classes: nobles, priests, merchants, craftworkers, metallurgists, bureaucrats, soldiers, farmers, free citizens, and slaves. Slaves were common in Sumer; they often were captives, brought back as the spoils of war.

Shown here are examples of two of the earliest writing systems on earth. On the left is a cuneiform tablet and on the right is a section of a hieroglyphic panel.

We see the first evidence of writing around 3000 B.C. The earliest Sumerian writings were in the form of ledgers containing inventories of items stored in the temples and records of livestock or other items owned or managed by the temples. Sumerian writing was wedge-shaped, or **cuneiform**, formed by pressing a stylus against a damp clay tablet. For contracts and other important documents, the tablet was fired to create a virtually permanent record. Egyptian writing, or hieroglyphics, appeared about the same time. **Hieroglyphics** were written on rolls woven from papyrus reeds, from which our word *paper* derives.

Cities and States in Mesoamerica

Cities and states emerged in Mesoamerica—Mexico and Central America—later than they did in the Middle East. The later appearance of civilization in Mesoamerica may be linked to the later emergence of agriculture in the New World, as we saw in the previous chapter, and possibly to the near-absence of large animals such as cattle and horses that could be domesticated.[85] We focus primarily on the developments that led to the rise of the city-state of Teotihuacán, which reached its height shortly after the time of Christ. Teotihuacán is located in a valley of the same name, which is the northeastern part of the larger Valley of Mexico.

The Formative Period   The formative period in the area around Teotihuacán (1000–300 B.C.) was characterized initially by small, scattered farming villages on the hilly slopes just south of the Teotihuacán Valley. There were probably a few hundred people in each hamlet, and each of these scattered groups was probably politically autonomous. After about 500 B.C., there seems to have been a population shift to settlements on the valley floor, probably in association with the use of irrigation. Between about 300 and 200 B.C., small "elite" centers emerged in the valley; each had an earthen or stone raised platform. Residences or small temples of poles and thatch originally stood on these platforms. That some individuals, particularly those in the elite centers, were buried in special tombs supplied with ornaments, headdresses, carved bowls, and a good deal of food indicates some social inequality.[86] The various elite centers may indicate the presence of chiefdoms.

The City and State of Teotihuacán   About 150 years before the time of Christ, no more than a few thousand people lived in scattered villages in the Teotihuacán Valley. In A.D. 100, there was a city of 80,000. By A.D. 500, well over 100,000 people, or approximately 90 percent of the entire valley population, seem to have been drawn or coerced into Teotihuacán.[87]

The city of Teotihuacán, which had its peak in 500 A.D., was a planned city built on a grid pattern. At the center was the Pyramid of the Sun, seen here in the background on the left.

The layout of the city of Teotihuacán, which shows a tremendous amount of planning, suggests that from its beginning the valley was politically unified under a centralized state. Mapping has revealed that the streets and most of the buildings are laid out in a grid pattern following a basic modular unit of 57 square meters. Residential structures are often squares of this size, and many streets are spaced according to multiples of the basic unit. Even the river that ran through the center of the city was channeled to conform to the grid pattern. Perhaps the most outstanding feature of the city is the colossal scale of its architecture. Two pyramids dominate the metropolis, the so-called Pyramid of the Moon and the Pyramid of the Sun. At its base the latter is as big as the great Pyramid of Cheops in Egypt.

The thousands of residential structures built after A.D. 300 follow a standard pattern. Narrow streets separate the one-story buildings, each of which has high, windowless walls. Patios and shafts provide interior light. The layout of rooms suggests that each building consisted of several apartments; more than 100 people may have lived in one of these apartment compounds. There is variation from compound to compound in the size of rooms and the elaborateness of interior decoration, suggesting considerable variation in wealth.[88]

At the height of its power (A.D. 200–500), the metropolis of Teotihuacán encompassed an area larger than imperial Rome.[89] Much of Mesoamerica seems to have been influenced by Teotihuacán. Archaeologically, its influence is suggested by the extensive spread of Teotihuacán-style pottery and architectural elements. Undoubtedly, large numbers of people in Teotihuacán were engaged in production for, and the conduct of, long-distance trade. Perhaps 25 percent of the city's population worked at various specialized crafts, including the manufacture of projectile points and cutting and scraping tools from volcanic obsidian. Teotihuacán was close to major deposits of obsidian, which was apparently in some demand over much of Mesoamerica. Materials found in graves indicate that there was an enormous flow of foreign goods into the city, including precious stones, feathers from colorful birds in the tropical lowlands, and cotton.[90]

The First Cities and States in Other Areas

So far we have discussed the emergence of cities and states in southern Iraq and Mesoamerica whose development is best, if only imperfectly, known archaeologically. But other state societies probably arose more or less independently in many other areas of the world as well. We say "independently" because such states seem to have emerged without colonization or conquest by other states.

Almost at the same time as the Sumerian empire, the great dynastic age was beginning in the Nile Valley in Egypt. The Old Kingdom, or early dynastic period, began about 3100 B.C., with a capital at Memphis. The archaeological evidence from the early centuries is limited, but most of the population appears to have lived in largely self-sufficient villages. Many of the great pyramids and palaces were built around 2500 B.C.[91]

Elsewhere in Africa states also arose. In what is present-day Ethiopia the Axum (or Aksum) state evolved beginning sometime early in the first millennium A.D., and ultimately became a center of trade and commerce between Africa and the Arabian Peninsula. Among the unique accomplishments of the Axum state were multistory stone residences built in a singular architectural style. Axum is also notable as being perhaps the first officially Christian state in the world.[92]

In sub-Saharan Africa, by A.D. 800, the savanna and forest zones of western Africa had a succession of city-states. One of them was called Ghana, and it became a major source of gold for the Mediterranean world (as did other states in what came to be known as the "Gold Coast").[93] In the Congo River basin a powerful kingdom had evolved by A.D. 1200, with cities described as having tens of thousands of residences and a king that was recognized as an equal by the Portuguese king in the early 1500s.[94] Farther south, states apparently arose in several areas early in the second millennium A.D. One of these was responsible for the large, circular stone structures known today as the Great Zimbabwe.[95]

In the Indus Valley of northwestern India, a large state society had developed by 2300 B.C. This Harappan civilization did not have much in the way of monumental architecture, such as pyramids and palaces, and it was also unusual in other respects. The state apparently controlled an enormous territory—over a million square kilometers. There was not just one major city but many, each built according to a similar pattern and with a municipal water and sewage system.[96]

The Shang dynasty in northern China (1750 B.C.) has long been cited as the earliest state society in the Far East. But recent research suggests that an even earlier one, the Xia dynasty, may have emerged in the same general area by 2200 B.C.[97] In any case, the Shang dynasty had all the earmarks of statehood: a stratified, specialized society; religious, economic, and administrative unification; and a distinctive art style.[98]

In South America, a group of distinct state societies may have emerged as early as 2500 B.C. in the Supe and Pativilca valleys north of Lima, Peru. Each valley contains a group of large cities that seem to have been interdependent—cities on the coast supplied inland cities with fish, while inland cities served as political and economic centers. The cities contain plaza areas and large pyramids, which are thought to be temple structures.[99] After 200 B.C. the major river valleys leading from the Andes to the sea witnessed the

Shown here is the excavation of an ancient culvert at Harappa. Despite large public works like this water control system, there was little display of grandeur at Harappa. Unlike in many other ancient civilizations, all Harappan cities were laid out according to the same basic plan.

Shown here is an artist's reconstruction of what Cahokia may have looked like during its fluorescence.

development of a complex agricultural system dependent on irrigation. The separate, but similar, states participated in a widespread system of religious symbols and beliefs called Chavín. The various states included the well-known Moche state, creators of some of the most remarkable effigy ceramics ever known, and the Nazca state, the people of which constructed a huge landscape of intaglios (inscribed images and lines) on the hard ground of highland deserts. By A.D. 700, these regional states were integrated into a large, militaristic empire called Wari (or Huari).[100]

And in North America a huge settlement, with over 100 earthen mounds (one of them, Monk's Mound, is the largest pre-Columbian structure north of Mexico), and covering an area of more than 13 square kilometers, developed near present-day St. Louis late in the first millennium A.D. The site is called Cahokia, and it was certainly the center of a large and powerful chiefdom. Whether it had achieved a state level of organization is controversial. There is evidence for religious and craft specialists and there is clear social stratification, but whether or not the leaders of Cahokian society were able to govern by force is still unclear.[101]

Theories about the Origin of the State

We have seen that states developed in many parts of the world. Why did they evolve when and where they did? We consider those theories that have been discussed frequently by archaeologists.[102]

Irrigation Irrigation seems to have been important in many of the areas in which early state societies developed—Mesoamerica, southern Iraq, the Nile Valley, China, and South America. It has been suggested that the labor and management needed for the upkeep of an irrigation system led to the formation of a political elite, the overseers of the system, who eventually became the governors of the society.[103] Proponents of this view believe that both the city and civilization were outgrowths of the administrative requirements of an irrigation system.

Critics note that this theory does not seem to apply to all areas where cities and states may have emerged independently. For example, in southern Iraq, the irrigation systems serving the early cities were generally small and probably did not require extensive labor and management. Large-scale irrigation works were not constructed until after cities had been fully established.[104] Even in China, for which the irrigation theory was first formulated, there is no evidence of large-scale irrigation as early as Shang times.[105]

Although large-scale irrigation may not always have preceded the emergence of the first cities and states, even small-scale irrigation systems could have resulted in unequal access to productive land and so may have contributed to the development of a stratified society.[106] In addition, irrigation systems may have given rise to border and other disputes between adjacent groups, thereby prompting people to concentrate in cities for defense and stimulating the development of military and political controls.[107] Finally, as Robert Adams and Elman Service both suggested, the main significance of irrigation, either large or small scale, may have been its intensification of production, a development that in turn may have indirectly stimulated craft specialization, trade, and administrative bureaucracy.[108]

Population Growth, Circumscription, and War   Robert Carneiro has suggested that states may emerge because of population growth in an area that is physically or socially limited. Competition and warfare in such a situation may lead to the subordination of defeated groups, who are obliged to pay tribute and to submit to the control of a more powerful group.[109] Carneiro illustrated his theory by describing how states may have emerged on the northern coast of Peru.

After the people of that area first settled into an agricultural village life, population grew at a slow, steady rate. Initially, new villages were formed as population grew. But in the narrow coastal valleys—blocked by high mountains, fronted by the sea, and surrounded by desert—this splintering-off process could not continue indefinitely. The result, according to Carneiro, was increasing land shortage and warfare between villages as they competed for land. Since the high mountains, the sea, and the desert blocked any escape for losers, the defeated villagers had no choice but to submit to political domination. In this way, chiefdoms may have become kingdoms as the most powerful villages grew to control entire valleys. As chiefs' power expanded over several valleys, states and empires may have been born.

Marvin Harris suggested a somewhat different form of circumscription. He argued that the first states with their coercive authority could emerge only in areas that supported intensive grain agriculture (and the possibility of high food production) and were surrounded by areas that could not support intensive grain agriculture. So people in such areas might put up with the coercive authority of a state because they would suffer a sharp drop in living standards if they moved away.[110]

Carneiro suggested that his theory applies to many areas besides the northern coast of Peru, including southern Iraq and the Indus and Nile valleys. Although there were no geographic barriers in areas such as northern China or the Mayan lowlands on the Yucatán Peninsula, the development of states in those areas may have been the result of social circumscription. Carneiro's theory seems to be supported for southern Iraq, where there is archaeological evidence of population growth, circumscription, and warfare.[111] And there is evidence of population growth before the emergence of the state in the Teotihuacán Valley.[112]

But population growth does not necessarily mean population pressure. For example, the populations in the Teotihuacán and Oaxaca valleys apparently did increase prior to state development, but there is no evidence that they had even begun to approach the limits of their resources. More people could have lived in both places.[113] Nor is population growth definitely associated with state formation in all areas where early states arose. For example, according to Wright and Johnson, there was population growth long before states emerged in southwestern Iran, but the population apparently declined just before the states emerged.[114]

Also, Carneiro's circumscription theory leaves an important question unanswered: Why would the victors in war let the defeated populations remain and pay tribute? If the victors wanted the land, why wouldn't they try to exterminate the defeated and occupy the land themselves, which has happened often in history?

Local and Long-Distance Trade   It has been suggested that trade was a factor in the emergence of the earliest states.[115] Wright and Johnson theorized that the organizational requirements of producing items for export, redistributing the items imported, and defending trading parties would foster state formation.[116] Does the archaeological evidence support such a theory?

In southern Iraq and the Mayan lowlands, long-distance trade routes may indeed have stimulated bureaucratic growth. In the lowlands of southern Iraq, as we have seen, people needed wood and stone for building, and they traded with highland people for those items. In the Mayan lowlands, the development of civilization seems to have been preceded by long-distance trade. Farmers in the lowland regions traded with faraway places in order to obtain salt, obsidian for cutting blades, and hard stone for grinding tools.[117] In southwestern Iran, long-distance trade did not become very important until after Susa became the center of a state society, but short-distance trade may have played the same kind of role in the formation of states.

Kwang-chih Chang put forward a similar theory for the origin of states in China. He suggested that Neolithic societies in the Yellow River valley developed a long-distance trade network, which he called an *interaction sphere,* by about 4000 B.C. Trade spread cultural elements among the societies in the interaction sphere, so that they came to share some common elements. Over time, these societies came to depend on each other both as trade partners and as cultural partners, and around 2000 B.C. they unified into a single political unit under the Shang dynasty.[118] Thus Chang sees political unification in China as an outgrowth of a preexisting system of trade and cultural interaction.

The Various Theories: An Evaluation   Why do states form? As of now, no one theory seems to fit all the known situations. The reason may be that different conditions in different places may have favored the emergence of centralized government. After all, the state, by definition, implies an ability to organize large populations for a collective purpose. In some areas, this purpose may have been the need to organize trade with local or far-off regions. In other cases, the state may have emerged as a way to control defeated populations in circumscribed areas. In still other instances, a combination of factors may have fostered the development of the state type of political system.[119]

Consequences of State Formation

One of the ways states change the lifestyles of people is by allowing for larger and denser populations.[120] As we have already seen, agriculture itself gives populations the potential to grow, and the development of a state only furthers that potential. Why? Because a state is able to build infrastructure—irrigation systems, roadways, markets—that allows both the production and distribution of agricultural products to become more efficient. States are able to coordinate information as well, and can use that information to manage agricultural production cycles and to anticipate or manage droughts, blights, or other natural disasters. States are also able to control access to land (through laws and a military) and thus can both maintain farmers on the land and prevent others (from either within or outside of the state) from removing the farmers or interfering with their ability to produce food.

With increased efficiency of agricultural production and distribution, states also allow many (if not most) people in the society to be relieved of food production. These people are freed to become craftspeople, merchants, and artists, as well as bureaucrats, soldiers, and political leaders. People may also live apart from agricultural fields, and thus cities with dense populations can arise. Cities can also arise in locations that are not suited to agriculture but that perhaps are suited to trade or defense. Art, music, and literature often flourish in such contexts, and these too are often consequences of the rise of states. Organized religion also often develops after states appear. Thus all the hallmarks we associate with civilization can be seen as resulting from the evolution of states.[121]

The development of states can have many negative impacts as well. When states develop, people become governed by force and are no longer able to say "no" to their leaders. Police and military forces can become instruments of oppression and terror.[122] On a less obvious level, the class stratification of states creates differences in access to resources and an underclass of poor, uneducated, and frequently unhealthy people. Health issues are exacerbated by the concentration of people in cities, an environment in which

Shown here is a street in the old city of Jaipur, India. The rise of states allows cities with dense populations to develop, and, along with them, the many potentials and problems that cities and their populations create.

epidemic diseases can flourish.[123] Without direct access to food supplies, people in cities also face the threat of malnutrition or outright starvation if food production and distribution systems fail.[124]

All states appear to be expansionistic, and the emergence of state warfare and conquest seems one of the most striking negative impacts of the evolution of states. In fact, more human suffering can probably be linked to state expansion than to any other single factor. Why do states expand? One basic reason may be that they are able to. States have standing armies ready to fight or be sent to conquer enemies. Another reason for state expansion might be related to the threat of famine and disease, which is more likely with intensive agriculture.[125] The Embers have found that resource unpredictability is strongly associated with a higher frequency of warfare, and perhaps states fearful of shortfalls in resources may resort to war ahead of time as a means of gaining access to more resources (or of limiting the unpredictability of resources).[126] A third answer to the question of why states tend to expand might be that belligerence is simply part of the nature of states. States often arise through military means, and it may be vital to the continuation of some states that military power be continually demonstrated.[127] Regardless of the causes, war and conquest are the consequences of state formation. Often, too, defeat in war is the fate of states.

The Decline and Collapse of States

When you look over the list of ancient states we have discussed in this chapter—Teotihuacán, Sumer, pharonic Egypt—you will notice one element common to them all: Each eventually collapsed; none maintained its power and influence into historic times. Why? It is an important question because, if collapse is the ultimate fate of many if not all states, then we can anticipate that our own state is likely to collapse eventually

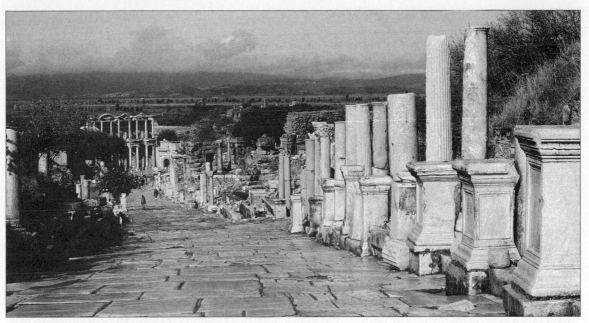

The history of Ephesus, a former city lying in ruins in what is now western Turkey, illustrates the waxing and waning of states and empires. From about 1000 B.C. to 100 B.C., Ephesus was controlled by the Greeks, Lydians, Persians, Macedonians, and Romans, among others.

One suggested explanation for the decline and collapse of states is environmental degradation. If states originally arose where the environment was conducive to intensive agriculture and harvests big enough to support social stratification, political officials, and a state type of political system, then perhaps environmental degradation—declining soil productivity, persistent drought, and the like—contributed to the collapse of ancient states. Harvey Weiss has suggested that persistent drought helped to bring about the fall of the ancient Akkadian empire, in the Middle East. By 2300 B.C., the Akkadians had established an empire stretching 1,300 kilometers from the Persian Gulf in what is now Iraq to the headwaters of the Euphrates River in what is now Turkey. But a century later the empire collapsed. Weiss thinks that a long-term drought brought the empire down, as well as other civilizations around at that time. Many archaeologists doubted there was such a widespread drought, but new evidence indicates that the worst dry spell of the past 10,000 years began just as the Akkadians' northern stronghold was being abandoned.[128] The evidence of the drought, windblown dust in sediment retrieved from the bottom of the Persian Gulf, indicates that the dry spell lasted 300 years. Other geophysical evidence suggests that the drought was worldwide.[129]

Environmental degradation may also have contributed to the collapse of Mayan civilization.[130] Lake sediments show that the region inhabited by the Maya experienced an extended period of drought lasting between roughly A.D. 800 and 1000. The Maya, who depended on rainfall agriculture for subsistence, may not have been able to produce enough food in areas around temple complexes during this long period of drought to feed the resident populations. People would have been forced to move into less populated areas to survive, and the temple complexes would have slowly been abandoned.[131]

The behavior of humans may sometimes be responsible for environmental degradation. Consider the collapse of Cahokia, a city of at least 15,000 people that thrived for a while in the area where the Missouri and Mississippi rivers converge. In the twelfth century A.D., Cahokia had large public plazas, a city wall constructed from some 20,000 logs, and massive mounds. But within 300 years only the mounds were left. Silt from flooding covered former croplands and settled areas. Geographer Bill Woods thinks that overuse of woodlands for fuel, construction, and defense led to deforestation, flooding, and persistent crop failure. The result was the abandonment of Cahokia.[132]

Many other ideas have been put forward to explain collapse, ranging from catastrophes to almost mystical factors such as "social decadence," but, as with theories for the origin of states, no single explanation seems to fit all or even most of the situations. While it is still not clear what specific conditions led to the emergence, or collapse, of the state in each of the early centers of civilization, the question of why states form and decline is a lively focus of research today. More satisfactory answers may come out of ongoing and future investigations.

Summary

1. In the period immediately before plants and animals were domesticated, there seems to have been a shift in many areas of the world to less dependence on big-game hunting and greater dependence on broad-spectrum collecting.

2. In some sites in Europe, the Middle East, Africa, and Peru, the switch to broad-spectrum collecting seems to be associated with the development of more permanent communities. In other areas, such as the semiarid highlands of Mesoamerica, permanent settlements may have emerged only after the domestication of plants and animals.

3. The shift to the cultivation and domestication of plants and animals has been referred to as the Neolithic revolution, and it occurred, probably independently, in a number of areas. To date, the earliest evidence of domestication comes from the Middle East at about 8000 B.C. Dating for the earliest domestication in other areas of the Old World is not so clear, but the presence of different domesticated crops in different regions suggests that there were independent centers of domestication in China, Southeast Asia (what is now Malaysia, Thailand, Cambodia, and Vietnam), New Guinea, and Africa some time around or after 6000 B.C. In the New World, there appear to have been several early areas of cultivation and domestication: the highlands of Mesoamerica (about 7000 B.C.), the central Andes around Peru (about the same time, but perhaps even earlier), and the Eastern Woodlands of North America (about 2000 B.C.).

4. Theories about why food production originated remain controversial, but most archaeologists think that certain conditions must have pushed people to switch from collecting to producing food. Some possible causal factors include (1) population growth causing people to move to marginal areas where they tried to reproduce their former abundance; (2) global population growth; and (3) the emergence of hotter and drier summers and colder winters.

5. Archaeologists do not always agree on how a state should be defined, but most seem to agree that hierarchical and centralized decision making affecting a substantial population is the key criterion. Most states have cities with public buildings, full-time craft and religious specialists, an official art style, and a hierarchical social structure topped by an elite class from which the leaders are drawn. Most states maintain power with a monopoly on the use of force. Force or the threat of force is used by the state to tax its population and to draft people for work or war.

6. Theories about the rise of states suggest the importance of irrigation, circumscription and war, and trade. At this point, no one theory is able to explain the formation of every state. Perhaps different organizational requirements in different areas all favored centralized government.

7. When states arise they have a dramatic impact. Populations grow and become concentrated in cities. Agriculture becomes more efficient, allowing many people to be removed from food production. States provide a context in which what we commonly call civilization—art, music, literature, and organized religion—can develop and flourish. But states also provide a context in which warfare and political terror can flourish. The social differentiation found in states produces an underclass of poor and often unhealthy people. States are prone to epidemic disease and periodic famine.

8. History suggests that all ancient states collapse eventually.

Glossary Terms

agriculture (p. 184)
Archaic (p. 186)
civilization (p. 197)
cuneiform (p. 202)
domestication (p. 189)
Epipaleolithic (p. 183)
food production (p. 194)

hieroglyphics (p. 202)
Mesolithic (p. 183)
Neolithic (p. 189)
obsidian (p. 191)
rachis (p. 189)
sedentarism (p. 183)
state (p. 197)

Critical Questions

1. Do the various theories of the rise of food production explain why domestication occurred in many areas of the world within a few thousand years?

2. Cities and states did not appear until after the emergence of food production. Why might food production be necessary, but not sufficient, for cities and states to develop?

3. Like the emergence of food production, the earliest cities and states developed within a few thousand years of each other. What might be the reasons?

CHAPTER 9

THE STUDY OF CULTURE

Chapter Outline

- Defining Features of Culture
- Attitudes That Hinder
  the Study of Cultures
- Cultural Relativism

- Describing a Culture
- Some Assumptions
  about Culture

212

We all consider ourselves to be unique individuals with our own set of personal opinions, preferences, habits, and quirks. Indeed, all of us are unique; and yet most of us share the feeling that it is wrong to eat dogs, the belief that bacteria or viruses cause illness, the habit of sleeping on a bed. We share many such feelings, beliefs, and habits with most of the people who live in our society. We hardly ever think about the ideas and customs we share, but they constitute what anthropologists refer to as "North American culture."

We tend not to think about our culture because it is so much a part of us that we take it for granted. But when we become aware that other peoples have different feelings from ours, different beliefs, and different habits, we are becoming aware that our culture is different. Most North Americans would never even think of the possibility of eating dog meat if we did not know that people in some other societies commonly do so. We would not realize that our belief in germs was cultural if we were not aware that people in some societies think that illness is caused by witchcraft or evil spirits. We could not become aware that it is our custom to sleep on beds if we were not aware that people in many societies sleep on the floor or on the ground. It is only when we compare ourselves with people in other societies that we become aware of cultural differences and similarities. This is, in fact, the way that anthropology as a profession began. When Europeans began to explore and move to faraway places, they were forced to confront the sometimes striking facts of cultural variation.

Defining Features of Culture

In everyday usage, the word *culture* refers to a desirable quality we can acquire by attending a sufficient number of plays and concerts and visiting art museums and galleries. The anthropologist, however, has a different definition, as Ralph Linton noted:

> *Culture* refers to the total way of life of any society, not simply to those parts of this way which the society regards as higher or more desirable. Thus culture, when applied to our own way of life, has nothing to do with playing the piano or reading Browning. For the social scientist such activities are simply elements within the totality of our culture. This totality also includes such mundane activities as washing dishes or driving an automobile, and for the purposes of cultural studies these stand quite on a par with "the finer things of life." It follows that for the social scientist there are no uncultured societies or even individuals. Every society has a culture, no matter how simple this culture may be, and every human being is cultured, in the sense of participating in some culture or other.[1]

Culture, then, refers to innumerable aspects of life. Some anthropologists think of culture as the rules or ideas behind behavior.[2] Most anthropologists focus on how people behave customarily, including how they interact with others and the habits they share with others. In this view, **culture** is the set of learned behaviors and ideas (including beliefs, attitudes, values, and ideals) that are characteristic of a particular society or other social group. It should be noted that some anthropologists also include *material culture* in culture—things like houses, musical instruments, and tools that are the products of customary behavior.

Different kinds of groups can have cultures. People come to share behaviors and ideas because they communicate with and observe each other. While groups from families to societies share cultural traits, anthropologists have traditionally been concerned with the cultural characteristics of *societies*. Many anthropologists define **society** as a group of people who occupy a particular territory and speak a common language not generally understood by neighboring peoples. By this definition, societies may or may not correspond to countries or nations. There are many countries, particularly the newer ones, that have within their boundaries different peoples speaking mutually unintelligible languages. By our definition of society, such countries are composed of many different societies and therefore many cultures. And most societies have recently become more multicultural because of immigration and migration. Also, by our definition of society, some societies may even include more than one country or nation. For example, we would have to say that Canada and the United States form a single society because the two groups generally speak English, live next to each other, and share many common ideas and behaviors. That is why we refer to "North American culture" in this chapter. Not everyone would agree that Canada and the United States form a single society; some would prefer to consider the United States and Canada two different societies because they are separate political entities.

Culture Is Commonly Shared

If only one person thinks or does a certain thing, that thought or action represents a personal habit, not a pattern of culture. For a thought or action to be considered cultural, it must be commonly shared by some population or group of individuals. Even if some behavior is not commonly practiced, it is cultural if most people think it is appropriate. The idea that marriage should involve only two people is cultural in North American society. Most North Americans share this idea and act accordingly when they marry. The role of president or prime minister is not widely shared—after all, there is only one such person at a time—but the role is cultural because most inhabitants of a country with such a position agree that it should exist, and its occupant is generally expected to exhibit certain behaviors. We usually share many behaviors and ideas with our families and friends (although anthropologists are not particularly concerned with this type of cultural group). We commonly share cultural characteristics with segments of our population whose ethnic or regional origins, religious affiliations, and occupations are the same as or similar to our own. We share certain practices and ideas with most North Americans. And we share some cultural traits with people beyond our society who have similar interests (such as rules for international sporting events) or similar roots (as do the various English-speaking nations).

When we talk about the commonly shared customs of a society, which constitute the central concern of cultural anthropology, we are referring to *a* culture. When we talk about the commonly shared customs of a group within a society, which are a central concern of sociology, we are referring to a **subculture**. And when we study the commonly shared customs of some group that includes different societies, we are talking about a phenomenon for which we do not have a single word—for example, as when we refer to *Western culture* (the cultural characteristics of societies in or derived from Europe) or the *culture of poverty* (the presumed cultural characteristics of poor people the world over).

We must remember that even when anthropologists refer to something as cultural, there is always individual variation, which means that not everyone in a society shares a particular cultural characteristic of that society. For example, it is cultural in North American society for adults to live apart from their parents. But not all adults in our society do so, nor do all adults wish to do so. The custom of living apart from parents is considered cultural because most adults practice that custom. As Edward Sapir noted in the late 1930s, in every society studied by anthropologists—in the simplest as well as the most complex—individuals do not all think and act the same.[3] As we discuss later, individual variation is the source of new culture.[4]

Culture Is Learned

Not all things shared generally by a population are cultural. The typical hair color of a population is not cultural, nor is eating. For something to be considered cultural, it must be learned as well as shared. A typical hair color (unless dyed) is not cultural because it is genetically determined. Humans eat because they must; but what and when and how they eat are learned and vary from culture to culture. Most North Americans do not consider dog meat edible, and indeed the idea of eating dogs horrifies us. But in China, as in some other societies, dog meat is considered delicious. In our society, many people consider a baked ham to be a holiday dish. In several societies of the Middle East, however, including those of Egypt and Israel, eating the meat of a pig is forbidden by sacred writings.

To some extent, all animals exhibit learned behaviors, some of which may be shared by most individuals in a population and may therefore be considered cultural. But different animal species vary in the degree to which their shared behaviors are learned or are instinctive. The sociable ants, for instance, despite all their patterned social behavior, do not appear to have much, if any, culture. They divide their labor, construct their nests, form their raiding columns, and carry off their dead—all without having been taught to do so and without imitating the behavior of other ants. In contrast, much of the behavior of humans appears to be culturally patterned.

We are increasingly discovering that our closest biological relatives, the monkeys and the apes, not only learn a wide variety of behaviors on their own, they also learn from each other. Some of their learned responses are as basic as those involved in maternal care; others are as frivolous as the taste for candy. Frans de Waal reviewed seven long-term studies of chimpanzees and identified at least 39 behaviors that were clearly learned from others.[5] When shared and socially learned, these behaviors could be described as cultural.

Most human learned behavior is probably acquired with the aid of spoken, symbolic language. All people known to anthropologists, regardless of their kind of society, have had a complex system of spoken, symbolic communication, what we call *language*.

Language is *symbolic* in that a word or phrase can represent what it stands for, *whether or not that thing is present*. The symbolic quality of language has tremendous implications for the transmission of culture. It means that a human parent can tell a child that a snake, for example, is dangerous and should be avoided. The parent can then describe the snake in great detail—its length, diameter, color, texture, shape, and means of locomotion. The parent can also predict the kinds of places where the child is likely to encounter snakes and explain how the child can avoid them. Should the child encounter a snake, he or she will probably recall the symbolic word for the animal, remember as well the related information, and so avoid danger.

To sum up, we may say that something is cultural if it is a learned behavior or idea (belief, attitude, value, ideal) that is generally shared by the members of a society or other social group.

Much of culture is learned by children imitating their parents and other role models.

Attitudes That Hinder the Study of Cultures

Many of the Europeans who first traveled to faraway places were revolted or shocked by customs they observed. Such reactions are not surprising. People commonly feel that their own behaviors and attitudes are the correct ones and that people who do not share those patterns are immoral or inferior. The person who judges other cultures solely in terms of his or her own culture is **ethnocentric**—that is, he or she holds an attitude called **ethnocentrism**. Most North Americans would think that eating dogs or insects is disgusting, but they clearly do not feel the same way about eating beef. Similarly, they would react negatively to child betrothal, lip plugs, or digging up the bones of the dead.

Our own customs and ideas may appear bizarre or barbaric to an observer from another society. Hindus in India, for example, would consider our custom of eating beef both primitive and disgusting. In their culture, the cow is a sacred animal and may not be slaughtered for food. In many societies a baby is almost constantly carried by someone, in someone's lap, or asleep next to others.[6] People in such societies may think it is cruel of us to leave babies alone for long periods of time, often in devices that resemble cages (cribs and playpens). Even our most ordinary customs—the daily rituals we take for granted—might seem thoroughly absurd when viewed from an outside perspective. An observer of our society might take notes on certain strange behaviors that seem quite ordinary to us, as the following description shows:

> The daily body ritual performed by everyone includes a mouth-rite. Despite the fact that these people are so punctilious about the care of the mouth, this rite involves a practice which strikes the uninitiated stranger as revolting. It was reported to me that the ritual consists of inserting a small bundle of hog hairs into the mouth, along with certain magical powders, and then moving the bundle in a highly formalized series of gestures. In addition to the private mouth-rite, the people seek out a holy-mouth man once or twice a year. These practitioners have an impressive set of paraphernalia, consisting of a variety of augers, awls, probes, and prods. The use of these objects in the exorcism of the evils of the mouth involves almost unbelievable ritual torture of the client. The holy-mouth man opens the client's mouth and, using the above mentioned tools, enlarges any holes which decay may have created in teeth. Magical materials are put into these holes. If there are no naturally occurring holes in the teeth, large sections of one or more teeth are gouged out so that the supernatural substance can be applied. In the client's view, the purpose of these ministrations is to arrest decay and to draw friends. The extremely sacred and traditional character of the rite is evident in the fact that the natives return to the holy-mouth man year after year, despite the fact that their teeth continue to decay.[7]

We are likely to protest that to understand the behaviors of a particular society—in this case, our own—the observer must try to find out what the people in that society say about why they do things. For example, the observer might find out that periodic visits to the "holy-mouth man" are for medical, not magical, purposes. Indeed, the observer, after some questioning, might discover that the "mouth-rite" has no sacred or religious connotations whatsoever. Actually, Horace Miner, the author in the 1950s of the passage on the "daily mouth ritual," was not a foreigner. An American, he described the "ritual" the way he did to show how the behaviors involved might be interpreted by an outside observer.

Ethnocentrism hinders our understanding of the customs of other people and, at the same time, keeps us from understanding our own customs. If we think that everything we do is best, we are not likely to ask why we do what we do or why "they" do what "they" do.

We may not always glorify our own culture. Other ways of life may sometimes seem more appealing. For instance, a North American who has two or three jobs just to make a living might briefly be attracted to the lifestyle of the !Kung of the Kalahari Desert in the 1950s. The !Kung shared their food and therefore were free to engage in leisure activities during the greater part of the day. They obtained all their food by men hunting animals and women gathering wild plants. They had no facilities for refrigeration, so

Because we are ethnocentric about many things, it is often difficult to criticize our own customs, some of which might seem shocking to a member of another society. The elderly in America often spend their days alone. In contrast, the elderly in Japan often live in a three-generational family.

sharing a large freshly killed animal was clearly more sensible than hoarding meat that would soon rot. Moreover, the sharing provided a kind of social security system for the !Kung. If a hunter was unable to catch an animal on a certain day, he could obtain food for himself and his family from someone else in his band. Then, at some later date the game he caught would provide food for the family of another, unsuccessful hunter. This system of sharing also ensured that persons too young or too old to help with the collecting of food would still be fed.

Could we learn from the !Kung? Perhaps we could in some respects, but we must not glorify their way of life either or think that their way of life might be easily imported into our own society. Other aspects of !Kung life would not appeal to many North Americans. For example, when the nomadic !Kung decided to move their camps, they had to carry all the family possessions, substantial amounts of food and water, and all young children below age four or five. This is a sizable burden to carry for any distance. The !Kung traveled about 1,500 miles in a single year.[8] Thus, for them being nomadic meant that families could not have many possessions. It is unlikely that most North Americans would find the !Kung way of life enviable in this respect.

Both ethnocentrism and its opposite, the glorification of other cultures, hinder effective anthropological study.

Cultural Relativism

A hundred years ago, some evolutionists thought of Western cultures as being at the highest or most progressive stage of evolution, and non-Western cultures were often believed to represent earlier stages of evolution. Not only were these early ideas based on very poor evidence of the details of world ethnography, they were also based on a good deal of ethnocentrism.

INCREASING CULTURAL DIVERSITY
WITHIN THE COUNTRIES OF THE WORLD

The modern world is culturally diverse in two ways. There are native cultures in every part of the world, and there are migrant or immigrant cultures in most countries. (Migrants are people who have left one place to settle in another, often because they are forced by persecution or genocide to migrate; immigrants are people who have come into a new country, often because they have chosen to.) Parts of populations have moved away from their native places since the dawn of humanity. The first modern-looking humans moved out of Africa only in the last 100,000 years. People have been moving ever since. The people we call Native Americans were actually the first migrants to the New World; most anthropologists think they came from northeast Asia. In the last 200 years the United States and Canada have experienced more extensive immigration. As is commonly said, they have become nations of migrants and immigrants, and Native Americans are now vastly outnumbered by the people and their descendants who came from Europe, Africa, Asia, Latin America, and elsewhere. North America not only has native and regional subcultures, but also ethnic, religious, and occupational subcultures, each with its own distinctive set of culture traits. Thus, North American culture is partly a "melting pot" and partly a mosaic of cultural diversity. Many of us, not just anthropologists, like this diversity. We like to go to ethnic restaurants regularly. We like salsa, sushi, and spaghetti. We compare and enjoy the different geographic varieties of coffee. We like music and artists from other countries. We often choose to wear clothing that may have been manufactured halfway around the world. We like all of these things not only because they may be affordable. We like them mostly, perhaps, because they are different.

Many of the population movements in the world today, as in the past, are responses to persecution and war. The word *diaspora* is often used nowadays to refer to these major dispersions. Most were and are involuntary: people fleeing danger and death. But not always. Scholars distinguish different types of diaspora, including "victim," "labor," "trade," and "imperial" diasporas. The Africans who were sold into slavery, the Armenians who fled genocide in the early twentieth century, the Jews who fled persecution and genocide in various places over the centuries, the Palestinians who fled to the West Bank, Gaza, Jordan, and Lebanon in the mid-twentieth century, and the Rwandans who fled genocide toward the end of the twentieth century were mostly victims. The Chinese, Italians, and the Poles may have mostly moved to take advantage of job opportunities, the Lebanese to trade, and the British to extend and service their empire. Often these categories overlap; population movements can and have occurred for more than one reason. Some of the recent diasporas are less one-way than in the past. People are more "transnational," just as economics and politics are more "globalized." The new global communications have facilitated the retention of homeland connections—socially, economically, and politically. Some diasporic communities play an active role in the politics of their homelands, and some nation-states have begun to recognize their far-flung emigrants as important constituencies.

As cultural anthropologists increasingly study migrant and immigrant groups, they focus on how the groups have adapted their cultures to new surroundings, what they have retained, how they relate to the homeland, how they have developed an ethnic consciousness, and how they relate to other minority groups and the majority culture.

Sources: Melvin Ember, Carol R. Ember, and Ian Skoggard, eds., *Encyclopedia of Diasporas: Immigrant and Refugee Cultures around the World,* 2 vols. (New York: Kluwer Academic/Plenum Publishers, 2004); David Levinson and Melvin Ember, eds., *American Immigrant Cultures: Builders of a Nation,* 2 vols. (New York: Macmillan Reference, 1997).

Franz Boas and many of his students—like Ruth Benedict, Melville Herskovits, and Margaret Mead—challenged the attitude that Western cultures were obviously superior. The anthropological attitude that a society's customs and ideas should be described objectively and understood in the context of that society's problems and opportunities became known as **cultural relativism**. Does cultural relativism mean that the actions of another society, or of our own, should not be judged? Does our insistence on objectivity mean that anthropologists should not make moral judgments about the cultural phenomena they observe and try to explain? Does it mean that anthropologists should not try to bring about change? Not necessarily. While the concept of cultural relativism remains an important anthropological tenet, anthropologists differ in their interpretation of the principle of cultural relativism.

Many anthropologists are now uncomfortable with the strong form of cultural relativism advocated by Benedict and Herskovits in the 1930s and 1940s, that all patterns of culture are equally valid. What if the people practice slavery, torture, or genocide? If the strong doctrine of relativism is adhered to, then cultural practices such as these are not to be judged, and we should not try to eliminate them. A weaker form of cultural relativism asserts that anthropologists should strive for objectivity in describing a people, and in their attempts to understand the reasons for cultural behavior they should be wary of superficial or quick judgment. Tolerance should be the basic mode unless there is strong reason to behave otherwise.[9] The weak version of cultural relativity does not preclude anthropologists from making judgments or from trying to change behavior they think is harmful. But judgments need not, and should not, preclude accurate description and explanation in spite of any judgments we might have.

But now that we have defined what is cultural, we must ask a further question: How does an anthropologist go about deciding which particular behaviors, values, and beliefs of individuals are cultural?

Describing a Culture

Individual Variation

Describing a particular culture might seem relatively uncomplicated at first. You simply observe what the people in that society do and then record their behavior. But consider the substantial difficulties you might encounter. How would you decide which people to observe? And what would you conclude if each of the first dozen people you observed or talked to behaved quite differently in the same situation?

To understand better how an anthropologist might make sense of diverse behaviors, let us examine the diversity at a professional football game in the United States. When people attend a football game, various members of the crowd behave differently while "The Star-Spangled Banner" is being played. As they stand and listen, some people remove their hats; a child munches popcorn; a veteran of the armed forces stands at attention; a teenager searches the crowd for a friend; and the coaches take a final opportunity to intone secret chants and spells designed to sap the strength of the opposing team. Yet, despite these individual variations, most of the people at the game respond in a basically similar manner: Nearly everyone stands silently, facing the flag. Moreover, if you go to several football games, you will observe that many aspects of the event are similar. Although the plays will vary from game to game, the rules of the game are never different, and although the colors of the uniforms of the teams are different, the players never appear on the field dressed in swimsuits.

Although the variations in individual reactions to a given stimulus are theoretically limitless, they tend to fall within socially acceptable limits. The child listening to the anthem may continue to eat popcorn but will probably not do a rain dance. Similarly, it is unlikely that the coaches will run onto the field and embrace the singer. It is part of the anthropologist's goal to find out what those limits are. She or he may note, for example, that some limitations on behavior have a practical purpose: A spectator who disrupts the game by wandering onto the field would be required to leave. Other limitations are purely traditional. In our society it is considered proper for a man to remove his overcoat if he becomes overheated, but others would undoubtedly frown upon his removing his trousers even if the weather were quite warm. Using such observations, the anthropologist discovers the customs and the ranges of acceptable behavior that characterize the society under study.

By focusing on the range of customary behavior, discovered by observing or asking about individual variation, the anthropologist is able to describe cultural characteristics of a group. An anthropologist interested in describing courtship and marriage in our society would initially encounter variety. The anthropologist may note that one couple prefers to go to a movie on a first date, whereas another couple chooses to go bowling; some couples have very long engagements, and others never become engaged at all; some couples emphasize religious rituals in the marriage ceremony, but others are married by civil authorities; and so on. Despite this variability, the anthropologist might begin to detect certain regularities in courting practices. Couples nearly always arrange the dates by themselves; they try to avoid their parents when on dates; they often manage to find themselves alone at the end of a date; they put their lips together frequently; and so forth. After a series of more and more closely spaced encounters, a man and woman may decide to declare themselves publicly as a couple, either by announcing that they are engaged or by revealing that they are living together or intend to do so. Finally, if the two of them decide to marry, they must in some way have their union recorded by the civil authorities.

In our society a person who wishes to marry cannot disregard the customary patterns of courtship. If a man saw a woman on the street and decided he wanted to marry her, he could conceivably choose a quicker and more direct form of action than the usual dating procedure. He could get on a horse, ride to the woman's home, snatch her up in his arms, and gallop away with her. In Sicily, until the last few decades such a couple would have been considered legally married, even if the woman had never met the man before or had no intention of marrying. But in our society, any man who acted in such a fashion would be arrested and jailed for kidnapping and would probably have his sanity challenged. Such behavior would not be acceptable in our society. Although individual behaviors may vary, most social behavior falls within culturally acceptable limits.

In deciding what is cultural behavior, anthropologists look for commonalities, understanding that there is always considerable variation. In North American culture, unmarried couples are allowed and even encouraged to spend time with each other, but how they spend their time may vary from activities such as eating in restaurants to activities such as bike riding.

Cultural Constraints

The French sociologist Emile Durkheim stressed that culture is something *outside* us exerting a strong coercive power on us. We do not always feel the constraints of our culture because we generally conform to the types of conduct and thought it requires. Standards or rules about what is acceptable behavior are referred to by social scientists as **norms**. The importance of a norm usually can be judged by how members of a society respond when the norm is violated.

Cultural constraints are of two basic types, *direct* and *indirect*. Naturally, the direct constraints are the more obvious. If you choose to wear a casual shorts outfit to a wedding, you will probably be subject to some ridicule and a certain amount of social isolation. But if you choose to wear nothing, you may be exposed to a stronger, more direct cultural constraint—arrest for indecent exposure.

Although indirect forms of cultural constraint are less obvious than direct ones, they are no less effective. Durkheim illustrated this point when he wrote, "I am not obliged to speak French with my fellow-countrymen, nor to use the legal currency, but I cannot possibly do otherwise. If I tried to escape this necessity, my attempt would fail miserably."[10] In other words, if Durkheim had decided he would rather speak Serbo-Croatian than French, nobody would have tried to stop him. But no one may have understood him either. And although he would not have been put into prison for trying to buy groceries with Icelandic money, he would have had difficulty convincing the local merchants to sell him food.

In a series of classic experiments on conformity, Solomon Asch revealed how strong cultural constraints can be. Asch coached the majority of a group of college students to give deliberately incorrect answers to questions involving visual stimuli. A "critical subject," the one student in the room who was not so coached, had no idea that the other participants would purposely misinterpret the evidence presented to them. Asch found that in one-third of the experiments, the critical subjects consistently allowed their own correct perceptions to be distorted by the obviously incorrect statements of the others. And in another 40 percent of the experiments, the critical subject yielded to the opinion of the group some of the time.[11]

The existence of social or cultural constraints, however, is not necessarily incompatible with individuality. Cultural constraints are usually exercised most forcefully around the limits of acceptable behavior. Thus, there is often a broad range of behavior within which individuals can exercise their uniqueness. And individuals do not always give in to the wishes of the majority. In the Asch experiments, many individuals, about one-fourth of the critical subjects, consistently retained their independent opinions in the face of complete disagreement with the majority.

Ideal versus Actual Cultural Patterns

Every society has ideas (values and norms) about how people in particular situations ought to feel and behave. In everyday terms we speak of these ideas as *ideals;* in anthropology we refer to them as *ideal cultural patterns.* These patterns tend to be reinforced through cultural constraints. But we all know that people do not always behave according to the standards they express. If they did, there would be no need for direct or indirect constraints. Some of our ideal patterns differ from actual behavior because the ideal is outmoded—that is, it is based on the way society used to be. (Consider the ideal of "free enterprise," that industry should be totally free of governmental regulation.) Other ideal patterns may never have been actual patterns and may represent merely what people would like to see as correct behavior.

To illustrate the difference between ideal and actual culture, consider the idealized belief, long cherished in North America, that everybody is "equal before the law," that everybody should be treated in the same way by the police and courts. Of course, we know that this is not always true. The rich, for example, may receive less jail time and be sent to nicer prisons. Nevertheless, the ideal is still part of our culture; most of us continue to believe that the law should be applied equally to all.

How to Discover Cultural Patterns

There are two basic ways in which an anthropologist can discover cultural patterns. When dealing with customs that are overt or highly visible within a society—for example, our custom of sending children to school—the investigator can determine the existence of such practices by direct observation and by interviewing some knowledgeable people. When dealing with a particular sphere of behavior that encompasses many individual variations, or when the people studied are unaware of their pattern of behavior, the anthropologist should collect information from a sample of individuals in order to establish what the cultural pattern is.

One example of a cultural pattern that most people in a society are not aware of is how far apart people stand when they are having a conversation. Yet there is considerable reason to believe that unconscious cultural rules govern such behavior. These rules become obvious when we interact with people who have different rules. We may experience considerable discomfort when another person stands too close (indicating too much intimacy) or too far (indicating unfriendliness). Edward Hall reported that Arabs customarily stand quite close to others, close enough to be able to smell the other person. In interactions between Arabs and North Americans, then, the Arabs will move closer at the same time that the North Americans back away.[12]

If we wanted to arrive at the cultural rule for conversational distance between casual acquaintances, we could study a sample of individuals from a society and determine the *modal response,* or *mode.* The mode is a statistical term that refers to the most frequently encountered response in a given series of responses. So, for the North American pattern of casual conversational distance, we would plot the actual distance for many observed pairs of people. Some pairs may be 2 feet apart, some 2.5, and some 4 feet apart. If we count the number of times every particular distance is observed, these counts provide what we call a *frequency distribution.* The distance with the highest frequency is the *modal pattern.* Very often the frequency distribution takes the form of a *bell-shaped curve,* as shown in Figure 9.1.

There the characteristic being measured is plotted on the horizontal axis (in this case, the distance between conversational pairs), and the number of times each distance is observed (its frequency) is plotted

Distance between people conversing varies cross-culturally. The faces of the Rajput Indian men on the left are much closer than the faces of the American women on the right.

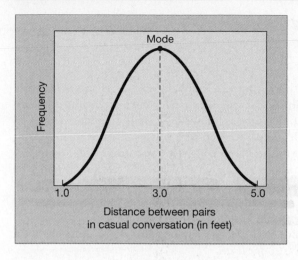

Mode

Frequency

1.0   3.0   5.0

Distance between pairs
in casual conversation (in feet)

Figure 9.1   Frequency Distribution Curve

on the vertical axis. If we were to plot how a sample of North American casual conversational pairs is distributed, we would probably get a bell-shaped curve that peaks at around 3 feet.[13] Is it any wonder, then, that we sometimes speak of keeping others "at arm's length"?

Frequency distributions may be calculated on the basis of behaviors exhibited or responses given by all the members of a particular population. But studying everybody is rarely necessary. Instead, most social scientists rely on a subset, or sample, that is believed to be representative of the larger population. As we noted in the first chapter, the best way to ensure that a sample is representative is to choose a *random sample*.

Because it is relatively easy to make generalizations about public aspects of a culture, such as the existence of executive, legislative, and judicial branches in the U.S. government, or about widely shared norms or behaviors, which almost anyone can identify correctly, random sampling is often not necessary. But in dealing with aspects of culture that are more private, difficult to put into words, or unconscious, the investigator may have to observe or interview a sample of people in order to generalize correctly about whether or not there are cultural patterns. The reason is that most people may not be aware of others' private behavior and thoughts, such as sexual attitudes and behavior, nor are they aware of unconscious cultural patterns, such as conversational distance. The fact that something is less readily observed publicly or harder to put into words does not imply that it is less likely to be shared. However, it is harder to discover those aspects of culture.

Although we may be able to discover by interviews and observation that a behavior, thought, or feeling is widely shared within a society, how do we establish that something commonly shared is learned, so that we can call it cultural? Establishing that something is or is not learned may be difficult. Because children are not reared apart from adult caretakers, the behaviors they exhibit as part of their genetic inheritance are not clearly separated from those they learn from others around them. We suspect that particular behaviors and ideas are learned if they vary from society to society. And we suspect purely genetic determinism when particular behaviors or ideas are found in all societies. For example, as we will see in the chapter on language and communication, children the world over seem to acquire language at about the same age, and the structure of their early utterances seems to be similar. These facts suggest that human children are born with an innate grammar. However, although early childhood language seems similar the world over, the particular languages spoken by adults in different societies show considerable variability. This variability suggests that particular languages have to be learned.

Some Assumptions about Culture

Culture Is Generally Adaptive

There are some cultural behaviors that, if carried to an extreme, would decrease the chances of survival of a particular society. For example, certain tribes in New Guinea view women as unclean and dangerous individuals with whom physical contact should be as limited as possible. Suppose the men in one such tribe decided to avoid contact, including sexual contact, with women. Clearly, we would not expect such a society to survive for long. Either the people clinging to those customs will become extinct, taking the customs with them, or the customs will be replaced, thereby possibly helping the people to survive. By either process, **maladaptive customs**—those that diminish the chances of survival and reproduction—are likely to disappear. The customs of a society that enhance survival and reproductive success are **adaptive** and are likely to persist. Hence, we assume that if a society has survived long enough to be described in the annals of anthropology (the "ethnographic record"), much, if not most, of its cultural repertoire is adaptive, or was at one time.

When we say that a custom is adaptive, we mean it is adaptive only with respect to a specific physical and social environment. What may be adaptive in one environment may not be adaptive in another. Therefore, when we ask why a society may have a particular custom, we really are asking if that custom makes sense as an adaptation to that society's particular environmental conditions. Many cultural behaviors that would otherwise appear incomprehensible to us may be understandable as a society's response to its environment. Witness the long postpartum sex taboo we discussed in the first chapter.

Just as culture may be an adjustment to the physical environment and to biological demands, it may also represent an adjustment to the social environment. For example, we do not know for sure why the Hopi Indians of what is now the state of Arizona began building their settlements on the tops of mesas. They must have had strong reasons for doing so, because there are many difficulties in building on such sites, not the least of which is the problem of hauling water long distances. It is possible that the Hopi chose to locate their villages on mesa tops for defensive reasons when Athapaskan-speaking groups of Indians (the Navajo and Apache) moved into the Hopi area.

A given custom represents one society's adaptation to its environment; it does not represent all possible adaptations. Different societies may choose different means of adjusting to the same situation. Thus, among some South American Indian societies where people's diets are low in protein, there is no long postpartum sex taboo, but induced abortion is reported to be a common practice. This practice may serve the same function of spacing out live births and thereby preventing too early weaning of children.

Although we may assume that societies surviving long enough to be described have had many more adaptive culture traits than maladaptive traits, that does not mean that all culture traits are adaptive. Some, if not many, traits may be neutral in terms of adaptation. That is, they may have no direct relationship to reproductive success. Consider, for example, rules about what to wear at weddings and funerals, how to set the table, and how far to stand from someone. Perhaps someone will uncover survival and reproductive consequences of these shared behaviors, but probably they are neutral in terms of survival. Such neutral traits may once have had adaptive consequences, or they may never have had any.

We must remember that a society is not forced to adapt its culture to changing environmental circumstances. Even in the face of changed circumstances, people may choose not to change their customs. For example, the Tapirapé of central Brazil did not alter their custom of limiting the number of births, even though they suffered severe population losses after contact with Europeans and their diseases. The Tapirapé population fell to fewer than 100 people from over 1,000. Clearly they were on the way to extinction, yet they continued to value small families. Not only did they believe that a woman should have no more than three children, but they took specific steps to achieve this limitation. They practiced infanticide if twins were born, if the third child was of the same sex as the first two children, and if the possible fathers broke certain taboos during pregnancy or in the child's infancy.[14]

Of course, it is also possible that a people will behave maladaptively even if they try to alter their behavior. After all, although people may alter their behavior according to what they perceive will be helpful to them, what they perceive to be helpful may not prove to be adaptive.

Culture Is Mostly Integrated

When we hear of an unfamiliar cultural pattern, our natural response is to try to imagine how that pattern would work in our own society. We might wonder, for example, what would happen if North American women adopted a long postpartum sex taboo—say, one year of abstinence after the birth of a baby. Such a question is purely whimsical, for the customs of one culture cannot easily be grafted onto another culture. A long postpartum sex taboo presupposes a lack of effective birth-control methods, but our society already has many such methods. Moreover, a long postpartum sex taboo could conceivably affect important aspects of our culture, such as the idea that a happy marriage is a sexy one. The point is that with such a taboo imposed on it, our culture would no longer be the same. Too many aspects of the culture would have to be changed to accommodate the new behavior. This is so because our culture is mostly integrated.

In saying that a culture is mostly *integrated*, we mean that the elements or traits that make up that culture are not just a random assortment of customs but are mostly adjusted to or consistent with one another. One reason anthropologists believe that culture tends to be integrated is that culture is generally adaptive. If certain customs are more adaptive in particular settings, then those "bundles" of traits will generally be found together under similar conditions. For example, the !Kung, as we have mentioned, subsisted by hunting wild animals and gathering wild plants. They were also nomadic, had very small communities, had few material possessions, and shared food within their bands. As we will see, these cultural traits usually occur together when people depend on hunting and gathering for their food.

A culture may also tend to be integrated for psychological reasons. The ideas of a culture—attitudes, values, ideals, and rules for behavior—are stored, after all, in the brains of individuals. Research in social psychology has suggested that people tend to modify beliefs or behaviors that are not cognitively or conceptually consistent with other information.[15] We do not expect cultures to be completely integrated, just as we do not expect individuals to be completely consistent. But if a tendency toward cognitive consistency is found in humans, we might expect that at least some aspects of a culture would tend to be integrated for that reason.

Humans are also capable of rational decision making; they can usually figure out that certain things are not easy to do because of other things they do. For example, if a society has a long postpartum sex taboo, we might expect that most people in the society could figure out that it would be easier to observe the taboo if husband and wife did not sleep in the same bed. Or if people drive on the left side of the road, as in England, it is easier and less dangerous to drive a car with a steering wheel on the right because that placement allows you to judge more accurately how close you are to cars coming at you from the opposite direction.

The tendency for a culture to be integrated, then, may be cognitively and emotionally, as well as adaptively, induced.

Culture Is Always Changing

When you examine the history of a society, it is obvious that its culture has changed over time. Some of the shared behaviors, beliefs, and values that were common at one time are modified or replaced at another time. In North American society, we only have to consider our attitudes toward sex and marriage to realize that a lot of our culture has changed recently. The impetus for change may come from within the society or from without. From within, the unconscious or conscious pressure for consistency will produce culture change if enough people adjust old behavior and thinking to new. Change can also occur if people try to invent better ways of doing things.

A good deal of culture change may be stimulated by changes in the external environment. If agricultural people move into an arid area, they will either have to give up farming or develop a system of irrigation. In the modern world, changes in the social environment may be stimuli for culture change, not just changes in the physical environment. Many North Americans, for example, started to think seriously about conserving energy and about using sources of energy other than oil only after oil supplies from the Middle East were curtailed in 1973 and 1974. Different societies have often affected each other, and a significant amount of the radical and rapid culture change that has occurred in the last few hundred years has been due to the imperial expansion of Western societies into other areas of the world. Native Americans, for instance, were forced to alter their lifestyles drastically when they were driven off their lands and confined to reservations. In the chapter on culture change and globalization, we discuss the major patterns of culture change in the modern world, much of it affected by the expansion of the West.

If we assume that cultures are more than random collections of behaviors, beliefs, and values—that they tend to be adaptive, integrated, and changing—then the similarities and differences between them should be understandable. That is, we can expect that similar circumstances within or outside the culture will give rise to, or favor, similar cultural responses. In the chapters that follow, we hope to convey the highlights of what anthropologists know about aspects of cultural variation and what they do not know.

External — has to be environment changes.

This painting of a beach scene in the early 1900s reminds us of how much cultural ideas about modesty have changed over time.

We frequently describe particular cultures to illustrate aspects of cultural variation. When we do so, the reader should understand that the description of a particular culture or cultural trait always pertains to a particular time period and sometimes to a specific subgroup. For example, the !Kung of the 1950s were mostly dependent on the collection of wild plants and animals and moved their camp sites frequently, but later they became more sedentary and engaged in wage labor.

Types of Research in Cultural Anthropology

Cultural anthropologists use several methods to conduct research. The types of research in cultural anthropology can be classified according to two criteria. One is the spatial scope of the study—analysis of a single society, analysis of societies in a region, or analysis of a worldwide sample of societies. The other criterion is the temporal scope of the study—historical versus nonhistorical. Combinations of these criteria are shown in Table 9.1.

Ethnography

Around the beginning of the twentieth century, anthropologists started to live among the people they were studying. They observed, and even took part in, the important events of those societies and carefully questioned the people about their native customs. This method is known as **participant-observation**. Participant-observation always involves **fieldwork**, which is firsthand experience with the people being studied, but fieldwork may also involve other methods, such as conducting a census or a survey.[16]

Fieldwork, the cornerstone of modern anthropology, is the means by which most anthropological information is obtained. Regardless of other methods that anthropologists may use, participant-observation is regarded as fundamental. In contrast to the casual descriptions of travelers and adventurers, anthropologists' descriptions record, describe, analyze, and eventually formulate a picture of the culture, or at least part of it.[17] After doing fieldwork, an anthropologist may prepare an *ethnography*, a description and analysis of the society studied.

How an anthropologist goes about doing participant-observation in another culture depends on the person, the culture, and the interaction between the two. Without a doubt, the experience is physically and psychologically demanding. Although it helps enormously to learn the local language before one goes, often it is not possible to do so, and so most anthropologists find themselves struggling to communicate in addition to trying to figure out how to behave properly. Participant-observation involves a

Table 9.1 Types of Research in Cultural Anthropology		
Scope	Nonhistorical	Historical
Single society	Ethnography Within-culture comparison	Ethnohistory Within-culture comparison
Region	Controlled comparison	Controlled comparison
Worldwide sample	Cross-cultural research	Cross-historical research

dilemma. Participation implies living like the people you have come to study, trying to understand subjectively what they think and feel by doing what they do, whereas observation implies a certain amount of objectivity and detachment.[18] Because participant-observation is such a personal experience, anthropologists have begun to realize that *reflecting* on their experiences and their personal interaction with the people they live with is an important part of the enterprise.

An essential part of the participant-observation process is finding some knowledgeable people who are willing to work with you (anthropologists call them *informants*), to help you interpret what you observe and tell you about aspects of the culture that you may not have a chance to see, or may not be entitled to see. For example, it is not likely that you will see many weddings in a village of 200 people in a year of fieldwork. So how can you know who will be a good informant? It is obviously important to find people who are easy to talk to and who understand what information you need. But how do you know who is knowledgeable? You can't just assume that the people you get along with have the most knowledge. (Besides, knowledge is often specialized; one person may know a whole lot more about some subjects than others.) At a minimum, you have to try out a few different people to compare what they tell you about a subject. What if they disagree? How do you know who is more trustworthy or accurate? Fortunately, formal methods have been developed to help select the most knowledgeable informants. One method called the "cultural consensus model" relies on the principle that those things that most informants agree on are probably cultural. After you establish which things appear to be cultural by asking a sample of informants the same questions about a particular cultural domain, it will be easy to discover which informants are very likely to give answers that closely match the cultural consensus. These individuals are your best bets to be the most knowledgeable in that domain.[19] It may seem paradoxical, but the most knowledgeable and helpful individuals are not necessarily "typical" individuals. Many anthropologists have pointed out that key informants are likely to feel somewhat marginal in their culture. After all, why would they want to spend so much time with the visiting anthropologist?[20]

Ethnohistorians need to analyze pieces of information from a variety of sources, such as the accounts of explorers in the Pacific. Pictured here is a painting of the arrival of a French explorer in Maui, Hawaii in the late 1700s.

Participant-observation is valuable for understanding some aspects of culture, particularly the things that are the most public, readily talked about, and most widely agreed upon. But more systematic methods are important too: mapping, house-to-house censuses, behavior observations (e.g., to determine how people spend their time), as well as focused interviews with a sample of informants.

Ethics in Fieldwork   Anthropologists have many ethical obligations—to the people they study, to their anthropological colleagues, to the public and world community. But anthropologists agree that should a conflict arise in ethical obligations, the most important obligation is to protect the interests of the people they study. According to the profession's code of ethics, anthropologists should tell people in the field site about the research and they should respect the right of people to remain anonymous if they so choose.[21] It is for this reason that informants are often given "pseudonyms" or fake names; many anthropologists have extended this principle to using a fake name for the community as well. But the decision to create a fake name for a community is questionable in many circumstances.[22] First, anthropologists "stick out" and it is not hard for anyone interested to figure out where they lived and worked. Governments may have to be asked for research clearance, which means that they know where the anthropologist is going to do the fieldwork. Second, people who are studied are often proud of their place and their customs and they may be insulted if their community is called something else. Third, important geographic information is often vital to understanding the community. You have to reveal if it is located at the confluence of two major rivers, or if it is the trading center of the region. And lastly, it may be difficult for a future anthropologist to conduct a follow-up study if the community is disguised.

Honest, objective reporting is also an obligation to the anthropological profession and to the public at large. But suppose a custom or trait that appears perfectly reasonable to the observed community is considered objectionable by outsiders? Such customs could range from acts that outsiders consider criminal, such as infanticide, to those that are considered repugnant, such as eating dogs. An anthropologist may believe that publication of the information could bring harm to the population. Kim Hill and Magdalena Hurtado faced this situation when they realized that infanticide rates were high in the group they studied in South America. They did not want to play up their findings, nor did they want to dissimulate. After they met with community leaders to discuss the situation, they agreed not to publish their findings in Spanish to minimize the possibility that the local media or neighboring groups might learn of their findings.[23]

Everyday decisions like how to compensate people for their time are not easy either. Nowadays, many if not most informants expect to be paid or receive gifts. But in the early days of anthropology, in places where money was not an important part of the native economy, the decision to pay people was not a clear ethical choice. Payments or nonmonetary gifts can increase inequalities or create jealousies. On the other hand, doing nothing by way of compensation doesn't seem right either. As an alternative some anthropologists try to find some community project that they can help with. This is not to say that the anthropologist is necessarily a burden on the community. People often like to talk about their customs, and they may want others to appreciate their way of life. And anthropologists are often amusing. They may ask "funny" questions, and when they try to say or do customary things they often do them all wrong. Probably every anthropologist has been laughed at sometimes in the field.

Within-Culture Comparisons

Ethnographers could test a theory within one society if they decide to compare individuals, families, households, communities, or districts. The natural variability that exists can be used to make a comparison. Suppose we want to verify Whiting's assumption that in a society with a low-protein diet, longer postpartum taboos enhance the survival of babies. Although almost all couples might practice a long postpartum sex taboo because it is customary, some couples might not adhere to the taboo consistently and some couples might not conceive quickly after the taboo is lifted. So we would expect some variation in spacing between births. If we collected information on the births of each mother and the survival outcome of each birth, we would be able to compare the survival rates of children born a short time after the mother's last pregnancy with those of children born after longer intervals. A significantly higher survival rate for the births after longer intervals would support Whiting's theory. What if some communities within the society had access to more protein than others? If Whiting's theory is correct, those communities with more protein should also have a higher survival rate for babies. If there were variation in the length of the postpartum sex taboo, the communities with more protein should have shorter taboos.

Whether or not we can design intracultural tests of hypotheses depends on whether we have sufficient variability in the variables in our hypotheses. More often than not we do, and we can make use of that variation to test hypotheses within a culture.

Regional Controlled Comparisons

In a regional controlled comparison, the anthropologist compares ethnographic information obtained from societies found in a particular region—societies that presumably have similar histories and occupy similar environments. The anthropologist who conducts a regional comparison is apt to be familiar with the complex of cultural features associated with that region. These features may provide a good understanding of the context of the phenomenon that is to be explained. Because some of the societies being compared will have the characteristic that is to be explained and some will not, the anthropologist can determine whether the conditions hypothesized to be related are in fact related, at least in that region. We must remember, however, that two or more conditions may be related in one region for reasons peculiar to that region. Therefore, an explanation supported in one region may not fit others.

Cross-Cultural Research

The most common use of worldwide comparisons has been to test explanations. An example is Whiting's test of his theory about the adaptive functions of a long postpartum sex taboo. Recall that Whiting hypothesized that if his theory is correct, variation in protein supplies in the adult diet should predict variation in the duration of the postpartum sex taboo. Cross-cultural researchers first identify conditions that should generally be associated if a particular theory is correct. Then they look at a worldwide sample of societies to see if the expected association generally holds true. Most cross-culturalists choose a published sample of societies that was not constructed for any specific hypothesis test. Two of the most widely used samples are the Standard Cross-Cultural (SCCS) sample of 186 societies and the *Human Relations Area Files (HRAF) Collection of Ethnography,* an annually growing collection of original ethnographic books and articles on approximately 400 cultures, past and present, around the world.[24] Since the HRAF collection actually contains full-text ethnographies that are subject-indexed by paragraph, a researcher can quickly find the information to code a variable across a large number of societies. In contrast, the SCCS sample contains pointers to ethnography, not ethnographies themselves. But thousands of variables have now been coded by researchers for this sample, so those researchers who want to use the data coded by others tend to use this sample.

The advantage of cross-cultural research is that the conclusion drawn from it is probably applicable to most societies, if the sample used for testing has been more or less randomly selected and therefore is representative of the world. In other words, in contrast with the results of a regional comparison, which may or may not be applicable to other regions, the results of a cross-cultural study are probably applicable to most societies and most regions.

Historical Research

Ethnohistory consists of studies based on descriptive materials about a single society at more than one point in time. It provides the essential data for historical studies of all types, just as ethnography provides the essential data for all nonhistorical types of research. Ethnohistorical data may consist of sources other than the ethnographic reports prepared by anthropologists—accounts by explorers, missionaries, traders, and government officials. Ethnohistorians, like historians, cannot simply assume that all the documents they find are simply descriptions of fact; they were written by very different kinds of people with very different goals and purposes. So they need to separate carefully what may be fact from what may be speculative interpretation. To reconstruct how a culture changed over hundreds of years, where the natives left few or no written accounts, anthropologists have to seek out travelers' accounts and other historical documents that were written by non-natives.

The goal of theory in cultural anthropology is to explain variation in cultural patterns, that is, to specify what conditions will favor one cultural pattern rather than another. Such specification requires us to assume that the supposed causal, or favoring, conditions antedated the pattern to be explained. Theories or explanations, then, imply a sequence of changes over time, which are the stuff of history. Therefore, if we want to come closer to an understanding of the reasons for the cultural variations we are investigating, we should examine historical sequences. They will help us determine whether the conditions we think caused various phenomena truly antedated those phenomena and thus might more reliably be said to have caused them. In the chapters that follow, we discuss not only what we strongly suspect about the determinants of cultural variation but also what we do not know or only dimly suspect. We devote a lot of our discussion to what we do not know—what has not yet been the subject of research that tests hypotheses and theories—because we want to convey a sense of what cultural anthropology might discover in the future.

Summary

1. Culture may be defined as the learned behaviors and ideas (beliefs, attitudes, values, and ideals) generally shared by the members of a society or other social group.

2. When anthropologists refer to *a* culture, they are usually referring to the cultural patterns of a particular society—that is, a particular territorial population speaking a language not generally understood by neighboring territorial populations.

3. Ethnocentrism, judging other cultures in terms of your own, and its opposite—the glorification of other cultures—impede anthropological inquiry. An important tenet in anthropology is the principle of cultural relativism: the attitude that a society's customs and ideas should be studied objectively and understood in the context of that society's culture.

4. Anthropologists seek to discover the customs and ranges of acceptable behavior that constitute the culture of a society under study. In doing so, they focus on general or shared patterns of behavior rather than on individual variations.

5. One important factor that limits the range of individual variation is the culture itself, which acts directly or indirectly as a constraint on behavior. The existence of cultural constraints, however, is not necessarily incompatible with individuality.

6. Several assumptions are frequently made about culture. First, culture is generally adapted to the particular conditions of its physical and social environment. What may be adaptive in one environment may not be adaptive in another. Second, culture is mostly integrated, in that the elements or traits that make up the culture are mostly adjusted to or consistent with one another. Third, culture is always changing.

7. Cultural anthropologists use several different methods to conduct research. The types of research in cultural anthropology can be classified according to two criteria: the spatial scope of the study (analysis of a single society, analysis of several or more societies in a region, or analysis of a worldwide sample of societies) and the temporal scope of the study (historical versus nonhistorical). The basic research methods, then, are ethnography and ethnohistory, within-culture comparisons, historical and nonhistorical regional controlled comparisons, and historical and nonhistorical cross-cultural research.

Glossary Terms

adaptive customs (p. 224)   maladaptive customs (p. 224)
cultural relativism (p. 219)   norms (p. 221)
culture (p. 213)   participant-observation (p. 227)
ethnocentric (p. 216)   society (p. 213)
ethnocentrism (p. 216)   subculture (p. 214)
fieldwork (p. 227)

Critical Questions

1. Would it be adaptive for a society to have everyone adhere to the cultural norms? Why do you think so?

2. Why does culture change more rapidly in some societies than in others? What external and internal factors might affect the rapidity of culture change?

3. Does the concept of cultural relativism promote international understanding, or does it hinder attempts to have international agreement on acceptable behavior, such as human rights?

CHAPTER 10

LANGUAGE AND COMMUNICATION

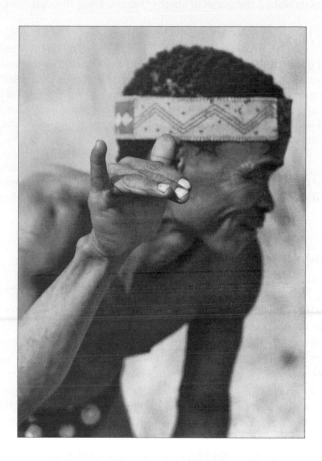

Chapter Outline

- Communication
- Origins of Language
- Descriptive Linguistics
- Historical Linguistics
- Processes of Linguistic Divergence

- Relationships between Language and Culture
- Ethnography of Speaking
- Writing and Literacy

Few of us can remember when we first became aware that words signified something. Yet that moment was a milestone for us, not just in the acquisition of language but in becoming acquainted with all the complex, elaborate behavior that constitutes our culture. Without language, the transmission of complex traditions would be virtually impossible, and each person would be trapped within his or her own world of private sensations.

Helen Keller, left deaf and blind by illness at the age of 19 months, gives a moving account of the afternoon she first established contact with another human being through words:

> [My teacher] brought me my hat, and I knew I was going out into the warm sunshine. This thought, if a wordless sensation may be called a thought, made me hop and skip with pleasure.
>
> We walked down the path to the well house, attracted by the fragrance of the honeysuckle with which it was covered. Someone was drawing water and my teacher placed my hand under the spout. As the cool stream gushed over one hand she spelled into the other the word water, first slowly, then rapidly. Suddenly I felt a misty consciousness as of something forgotten—a thrill of returning thought; and somehow the mystery of language was revealed to me. I knew then that w-a-t-e-r meant the wonderful cool something that was flowing over my hand. That living word awakened my soul, gave it light, hope, joy, set it free! There were barriers still, it is true, barriers that could in time be swept away. I left the well house eager to learn. Everything had a name, and each name gave birth to a new thought. As we returned to the house every object which I touched seemed to quiver with life. That was because I saw everything with the strange, new sight that had come to me.[1]

Communication

Against all odds, Helen Keller had come to understand the essential function that language plays in all societies—namely, that of communication. The word *communicate* comes from the Latin verb *communicare,* "to impart," "to share," "to make *common.*" We communicate by agreeing, consciously or unconsciously, to call an object, a movement, or an abstract concept by a common name. For example, speakers of English have agreed to call the color of grass *green,* even though we have no way of comparing precisely how two persons actually experience this color. What we share is the agreement to call similar sensations *green.* Any system of language consists of publicly accepted symbols by which individuals try to share private experiences. Spoken or vocal language is probably the major transmitter of culture, allowing us to share and pass on our complex configuration of attitudes, beliefs, and patterns of behavior.

Nonverbal Human Communication

As we all know from experience, the spoken word does not communicate all that we know about a social situation. We can usually tell when someone says, "It was good to meet you," whether he or she really means it. We can tell if people are sad from their demeanor, even if they say, "I'm fine," in response to the question "How are you?" Obviously, our communication is not limited to spoken language. We communicate directly through facial expression, body stance, gesture, and tone of voice and indirectly through systems of signs and symbols, such as writing, algebraic equations, musical scores, dancing, painting, code flags, and road signs. As Anthony Wilden put it, "every act, every pause, every movement in living and social systems is also a message; silence is communication; short of death it is impossible for an organism or person not to communicate."[2] How can silence be a communication? Silence may reflect companionship, as when two people work side by side on a project, but silence can also communicate unfriendliness. An anthropologist can learn a great deal from what people in a society do not talk about. For example, in India, sex is not supposed to be talked about. HIV infection is spreading very fast in India, so the unwillingness of people to talk about sex makes it extraordinarily difficult for medical anthropologists and health professionals to do much to reduce the rate of spread.[3]

Some nonverbal communication appears to be universal in humans. For example, humans the world over appear to understand facial expression in the same way; that is, they are able to recognize a happy, sad, surprised, angry, disgusted, or afraid face. But nonverbal communication is also culturally variable. Different cultures have different rules about the emotions that are acceptable to express. One study compared how Japanese and Americans express emotion. Individuals from both groups were videotaped while they were shown films intended to evoke feelings of fear and disgust. When the subjects saw the films by themselves, without other people present, they showed the same kinds of facial expressions of fear and disgust. But culture could affect expression too. When an authority figure was present during the videotaping, the Japanese subjects tried to mask their negative feelings with a half-smile more often than did the Americans.[4]

Nonverbal communication can even involve the voice. Consider how we might know that a person is not fine even though she just said "I'm fine." A depressed person might speak very quietly and use a flat tone of voice. If a person thought about explaining what was really wrong but thought better of it, a significant pause or silence might come before the words "I'm fine." A person's **accent** (differences in pronunciation) can tell a lot about the person's background, such as place of origin and education. There are also nonverbal (nonword) sounds that people make—grunts, laughs, giggles, moans, and sighs.

Nonhuman Communication

Systems of communication are not unique to human beings, nor is communication by sound. Other animal species communicate in a variety of ways. One way is by sound. A bird may communicate by a call that "this is my territory"; a squirrel may utter a cry that leads other squirrels to flee from danger. Another means of animal communication is odor. An ant releases a chemical when it dies, and its fellows then carry it away to the compost heap. Apparently the communication is highly effective; a healthy ant painted with the death chemical will be dragged to the funeral heap again and again. Another means of communication, body movement, is used by bees to convey the location of food sources. Karl von Frisch discovered that the black Austrian honeybee—by choosing a round dance, a wagging dance, or a short, straight run—can communicate not only the precise direction of the source of food but also its distance from the hive.[5]

One of the biggest scholarly debates is the degree to which nonhuman animals, particularly nonhuman primates, differ from humans in their capacity for language. Some scholars see so much discontinuity that they postulate that humans must have acquired (presumably through mutation) a specific genetic capability for language. Others see much more continuity between humans and nonhuman primates and point to research that shows much more cognitive capacity in nonhuman primates than previously thought possible. They point out that the discontinuity theorists are constantly raising the standards for the capacities thought necessary for language.[6] For example, in the past, only human communication was thought to be symbolic. But recent research suggests that some monkey and ape calls in the wild are also symbolic.

When we say that a call, word, or sentence is **symbolic communication**, we mean at least two things. First, the communication has meaning even when its *referent* (whatever is referred to) is not present. Second, the meaning is arbitrary; the receiver of the message could not guess its meaning just from the sound(s) and does not know the meaning instinctively. In other words, symbols have to be learned. There is no compelling or "natural" reason that the word *dog* in English should refer to a smallish four-legged omnivore that is sometimes the bane of letter carriers.

Apes lack the human capacity for speech, so researchers have explored the capacity of chimpanzees and other apes to communicate with hand gestures. A variety of signs from American Sign Language, used by the hearing impaired, are shown on the left. On the right, researcher Joyce Butler teaches Nim, a chimpanzee, a sign for "drink."

Vervet monkeys in Africa are not as closely related to humans as are African apes. Nevertheless, scientists who have observed vervet monkeys in their natural environment consider at least three of their alarm calls to be symbolic because each of them *means* (refers to) a different kind of predator—eagles, pythons, or leopards—and monkeys react differently to each call. For example, they look up when they hear the "eagle" call. Experimentally, in the absence of the referent, investigators have been able to evoke the normal reaction to a call by playing it back electronically. Another indication that the vervet alarm calls are symbolic is that infant vervets appear to need some time to learn the referent for each. When they are very young, infants apply a particular call to more animals than adult vervets apply the call to. So, for example, infant vervets will often make the eagle warning call when they see any flying bird. The infants learn the appropriate referent apparently through adult vervets' repetition of infants' "correct" calls; in any case, the infants gradually learn to restrict the call to eagles.[7]

How is human vocalization different? Since monkeys and apes appear to use symbols at least some of the time, it is not appropriate to emphasize symbolism as the distinctive feature of human language. However, there is a significant quantitative difference between human language and other primates' systems of vocal communication. All human languages employ a much larger set of symbols.

Another often-cited difference between human and nonhuman vocalizations is that the other primates' vocal systems are *closed*—that is, different calls are not combined to produce new, meaningful utterances. In contrast, human languages are *open* systems, governed by complex rules about how sounds and sequences of sounds can be combined to produce an infinite variety of meanings.[8] For example, an English speaker can combine *care* and *full* (*careful*) to mean one thing, then use each of the two elements in other combinations to mean different things. *Care* can be used to make *carefree, careless,* or *caretaker; full* can be used to make *powerful* or *wonderful.* And because language is a system of shared symbols, it can be re-formed into an infinite variety of expressions and be understood by all who share these symbols. In this way, for example, T. S. Eliot could form a sentence never before formed—"In the room the women come and go/talking of Michelangelo"[9]—and the sense of his sentence, though not necessarily his private meaning, could be understood by all speakers of English.

While no primatologist disputes the complexity and infinite variety with which human languages can combine sounds, the closed versus open distinction has been called into question by research on cotton-top tamarins, pygmy marmosets, capuchin monkeys, and rhesus macaques. These nonhuman primates also combine calls in orderly sequences,[10] but not nearly as much as humans do.

Another trait thought to be unique to humans is the ability to communicate about past or future events. But Sue Savage-Rumbaugh has observed wild bonobos leaving what appear to be messages to other bonobos to follow a trail. They break off vegetation where trails fork and point the broken plants in the direction to follow.

Perhaps most suggestive are the successful attempts to teach apes to communicate with humans and with each other using human-created signs. These successes have led many scholars to question the traditional assumption that the gap between human and other animal communication is enormous. Even a parrot, which has a small brain, has been taught to communicate with a human trainer in ways once thought impossible. Alex (the parrot) could correctly answer questions in English about what objects are made of, how many objects of a particular type there are, and even what makes two objects the same or different.[11] When he was not willing to continue a training session, Alex said: "I'm sorry . . . Wanna go back."[12] Chimpanzees Washoe and Nim and the gorilla Koko were taught hand signs based on American Sign Language (ASL, used by the hearing impaired in the United States). Subsequently, many chimpanzees were trained on symbol keyboards connected to computers. For example, Sherman and Austin began to communicate with each other about actions they were intending to do, such as the types of tools they needed to solve a problem. And they were able to classify items into categories, such as "food" and "tools."

Some of the best examples of linguistic ability come from a chimpanzee named Kanzi. In contrast to other apes, Kanzi initially learned symbols just by watching his mother being taught, and he spontaneously began using the computer symbols to communicate with humans, even indicating his intended actions. Kanzi did not need rewards or to have his hands put in the right position. And he understood a great deal of what was spoken to him in English. For example, when he was 5 years old, Kanzi heard someone talk about throwing a ball in the river, and he turned around and did so. Kanzi has come close to having a primitive English grammar when he strings symbols together.[13] If chimpanzees and other primates have the capacity to use nonspoken language and even to understand spoken language, then the difference between humans and nonhumans may not be as great as people used to think.

Are these apes really using language in some minimal way? Many investigators agree about one thing—nonhuman primates have the ability to "symbol," to refer to something (or a class of things) with an arbitrary "label" (gesture or sequence of sounds).[14] The gorilla Koko (with a repertoire of about 375 signs) extended the sign for *drinking straw* to plastic tubing, hoses, cigarettes, and radio antennae. Washoe originally learned the sign *dirty* to refer to feces and other soil and then began to use it insultingly, as in "dirty Roger," when her trainer Roger Fouts refused to give her things she wanted. Even the mistakes made by the apes suggest that they are using signs symbolically, just as words are used in spoken language. For example, the sign *cat* may be used for dog if the animal learned *cat* first (just as our daughter Kathy said "dog" to all pictures of four-footed animals, including elephants, when she was 18 months old).

When we discuss the structure of sounds (phonology) later in this chapter, we will see that every human language has certain ways of combining sounds and ways of not combining those sounds. Apes do not have anything comparable to linguistic rules for allowed and not allowed combinations of sounds. In addition, humans have many kinds of discourse. We make lists and speeches, tell stories, argue, and recite poetry. Apes do none of these things.[15] But apes do have at least some of the capacities for language. Therefore, understanding their capacities may help us better understand the evolution of human language.

Origins of Language

How long humans have had spoken language is not known. Some think that the earliest *Homo sapiens,* perhaps 100,000 years ago, may have had the beginnings of language. Others believe that language developed only in the last 40,000 years or so, with the emergence of modern humans. Because the only unambiguous remains of language are found on written tablets, and the earliest stone tablets date back only about 5,000 years,[16] pinpointing the emergence of earliest languages remains speculative. Theories about when language developed are based on nonlinguistic information such as when cranial capacity expanded dramatically, when complex technology and symbolic artifacts (such as art) started to be made, and when the anatomy of the throat, as inferred from fossil remains, began to resemble what we see in modern humans.

Noam Chomsky and other theoreticians of grammar suggest that there is an innate *language-acquisition device* in the human brain, as innate to humans as call systems are to other animals.[17] If humans are unique in having an innate capacity for language, then some mutation or series of mutations had to be favored in human evolution, not before the human line separated from apes. Whether such a mechanism in fact exists is not clear. But we do know that the actual development of individual language is not completely biologically determined; if it were, all human beings would speak the same brain-generated language. Instead, about 4,000 to 5,000 mutually unintelligible languages have been identified. More than 2,000 of them were still spoken as of recently, most by peoples who did not traditionally have a system of writing.

Can we learn anything about the origins of language by studying the languages of nonliterate (no writing) and technologically simpler societies? The answer is no, because such languages are not simpler or less developed than ours. The sound systems, vocabularies, and grammars of technologically simpler peoples are in no way inferior to those of peoples with more complex technology.[18] Of course, people in other societies, and even some people in our own society, will not be able to name the sophisticated machines used in our society. All languages, however, have the potential for doing so. As we will see later in this chapter, all languages possess the amount of vocabulary their speakers need, and all languages expand in response to cultural changes. A language that lacks terminology for some of our conveniences may have a rich vocabulary for events or natural phenomena that are of particular importance to the people in that society.

If there are no primitive languages, and if the earliest languages have left no traces that would allow us to reconstruct them, does that mean we cannot investigate the origins of language? Some linguists think that understanding the way children acquire language, which we discuss shortly, can help us understand the origins of language. Other linguists have suggested that an understanding of how creole languages develop will also tell us something about the origins of language.

Creole Languages

Some languages developed in various areas where European colonial powers established commercial enterprises that relied on imported labor, generally slaves. The laborers in one place often came from several different societies and in the beginning would speak with their masters and with each other in some kind of *pidgin* (simplified) version of the masters' language. Pidgin languages lack many of the building blocks found in the languages of whole societies, building blocks such as prepositions (*to, on,* and so forth) and auxiliary verbs (designating future and other tenses). Many pidgin languages developed into and were replaced by so-called *creole languages,* which incorporate much of the vocabulary of the masters' language but also have a grammar that differs from it and from the grammars of the laborers' native languages.[19]

Derek Bickerton argues that there are striking grammatical similarities in creole languages throughout the world. This similarity, he thinks, is consistent with the idea that some grammar is inherited by all humans. Creole languages, therefore, may resemble early human languages. All creoles use intonation instead of a change in word order to ask a question. The creole equivalent of the question "Can you fix this?" would be "You can fix this?" The creole version puts a rising inflection at the end; in contrast, the English version reverses the subject and verb without much inflection at the end. All creoles express the future and the past in the same grammatical way, by the use of particles (such as the English *shall*) between subject and verb, and they all employ double negatives, as in the Guyana English creole "Nobody no like me."[20]

It is possible that many other things about language are universal, that all languages are similar in many respects, because of the way humans are "wired" or because people in all societies have similar experiences. For example, names for frogs may usually contain *r* sounds because frogs make them.[21]

Children's Acquisition of Language

Apparently a child is equipped from birth with the capacity to reproduce all the sounds used by the world's languages and to learn any system of grammar. Research on 6-months-old infants finds that they can distinguish sounds of approximately 600 consonants and 200 vowels—all the sounds of all the languages of the world. But by about the time of their first birthdays, babies become better at recognizing the salient sounds and sound clusters of their parents or caretakers and become less adept at distinguishing those of other languages.[22]

Children's acquisition of the structure and meaning of language has been called the most difficult intellectual achievement in life. If that is so, it is pleasing to note that they accomplish it with relative ease and vast enjoyment. Many believe that this "difficult intellectual achievement" may in reality be a natural response to the capacity for language that is one of humans' genetic characteristics. All over the world children begin to learn language at about the same age, and in no culture do children wait until they are 7 or 10 years old. By 12 or 13 months of age, children are able to name a few objects and actions, and by 18 to 20 months they can make one key word stand for a whole sentence: "Out!" for "Take me out for a walk right now"; "Juice!" for "I want some juice now." Evidence suggests that children acquire the concept of a word as a whole, learning sequences of sounds that are stressed or at the ends of words (e.g., "raffe" for giraffe). Even hearing-impaired children learning signs in ASL tend to acquire and use signs in a similar fashion.[23]

A lot of language instruction is by pointing to something and saying what it is called.

Children the world over tend to progress to two-word sentences at about 18 to 24 months of age. In their sentences they express themselves in "telegraph" form—using noun-like words and verb-like words but leaving out the seemingly less important words. So a two-word sentence such as "Shoes off" may stand for "Take my shoes off," or "More milk" may stand for "Give me more milk, please."[24] They do not utter their two words in random order, sometimes saying "off" first, other times saying "shoes" first. If a child says "Shoes off," then he or she will also say "Clothes off" and "Hat off." They seem to select an order that fits the conventions of adult language, so they are likely to say "Daddy eat," not "Eat Daddy." In other words, they tend to put the subject first, as adults do. And they tend to say "Mommy coat" rather than "Coat Mommy" to indicate "Mommy's coat."[25] Adults do not utter sentences such as "Daddy eat," so children seem to know a lot about how to put words together with little or no direct teaching from their caretakers.

If there is a basic grammar imprinted in the human mind, we should not be surprised that children's early and later speech patterns seem to be similar in different languages. We might also expect children's later speech to be similar to the structure of creole languages. And it is, according to Derek Bickerton.[26] The "errors" children make in speaking are consistent with the grammar of creoles. For example, English-speaking children three to four years old tend to ask questions by intonation alone, and they tend to use double negatives, such as "I don't see no dog," even though the adults around them do not speak that way and consider the children's speech "wrong."

But some linguists argue that the evidence for an innate grammar is weak because children the world over do not develop the same grammatical features at similar ages. For example, word order is a more important determinant of meaning in English than in Turkish; the endings of words are more important in Turkish. The word at the beginning of the sentence in English is likely to be the subject. The word with a certain ending in Turkish is the likely subject. Consistent with this difference, English-speaking children learn word order earlier than Turkish children do.[27]

Future research on children's acquisition of language and on the structure of creole languages may bring us closer to an understanding of the origins of human language. But even if much of grammar is universal, we still need to understand how and why the thousands of languages in the world vary, which brings us to the conceptual tools linguists have had to invent in order to study languages.

Descriptive Linguistics

In every society children do not need to be taught "grammar" to learn how to speak. They begin to grasp the essential structure of their language at a very early age, without direct instruction. If you show English-speaking children a picture of one "gork" and then a picture of two of these creatures, they will say there are two "gorks." Somehow they know that adding an *s* to a noun means more than one. But they do not know this consciously, and adults may not either. One of the most surprising features of human language is that meaningful sounds and sound sequences are combined according to rules that often are not consciously known by the speakers.

These rules should not be equated with the "rules of grammar" you were taught in school so that you would speak "correctly." Rather, when linguists talk about rules, they are referring to the patterns of speaking that are discoverable in actual speech. Needless to say, there is some overlap between the actual rules of speaking and the rules taught in school. But there are rules that children never hear about in school, because their teachers are not linguists and are not aware of them. When linguists use the term *grammar,* they are *not* referring to the prescriptive rules that people are supposed to follow in speaking. Rather, *grammar* to the linguist consists of the actual, often unconscious principles that predict how most people talk. As we have noted, young children may speak two-word sentences that conform to a linguistic rule, but their speech is hardly considered "correct."

Discovering the mostly unconscious rules operating in a language is a very difficult task. Linguists have had to invent special concepts and methods of transcription (writing) to permit them to describe: (1) the rules or principles that predict how sounds are made and how they are used (slightly varying sounds are often used interchangeably in words without creating a difference in meaning—this aspect of language is called **phonology**); (2) how sound sequences (and sometimes even individual sounds) convey meaning and how meaningful sound sequences are strung together to form words (this aspect is called **morphology**); and (3) how words are strung together to form phrases and sentences (this aspect is called **syntax**).

Phonology

Most of us have had the experience of trying to learn another language and finding that some sounds are exceedingly difficult to make. Although the human vocal tract theoretically can make a very large number of different sounds—**phones**, to linguists—each language uses only some of them. It is not that we cannot make the sounds that are strange to us; we just have not acquired the habit of making those sounds. And until the sounds become habitual for us, they continue to be difficult to form.

Finding it difficult to make certain sounds is only one of the reasons we have trouble learning a "foreign" language. Another problem is that we may not be used to combining certain sounds or making a certain sound in a particular position in a word. Thus, English speakers find it difficult to combine z and d, as Russian speakers often do (because we never do so in English), or to pronounce a word in Samoan, a South Pacific language, that begins with the sound English speakers write as *ng,* even though we have no trouble putting that sound at the end of words, as in the English *sing* and *hitting.*

In order to study the patterning of sounds, linguists who are interested in *phonology* have to write down speech utterances as sequences of sound. This task would be almost impossible if linguists were restricted to using their own alphabet (say, the one we use to write English), because other languages use sounds that are difficult to represent with the English alphabet or because the alphabet we use in English can represent a particular sound in different ways. (English writing represents the sound *f* by *f* as in *food,* but also as *gh* in *tough* and *ph* in *phone.*) In addition, in English different sounds may be represented by the same letter. English has 26 letters but more than 40 significant sounds (sounds that can change the meaning of a word).[28] To overcome these difficulties in writing sounds with the letters of existing writing systems, linguists have developed systems of transcription with special alphabets in which each symbol represents only one particular sound.

Once linguists have identified the sounds or phones used in a language, they try to identify which sounds affect meaning and which sounds do not. One way is to start with a simple word like *lake* and change the first sound to *r* to make the word *rake.* The linguist will ask if this new combination of sounds means the same thing. An English speaker would say *lake* means something completely different from *rake.* These minimal contrasts enable linguists to identify a **phoneme** in a language—a sound or set of sounds that makes a difference in meaning in that language.[29] So the sound *l* in *lake* is different phonemically from the sound *r* in *rake.* The ways in which sounds are grouped together into phonemes vary from language to language. We are so used to phonemes in our own language that it may be hard to believe that the contrast between *r* and *l* may not make a difference in meaning in some languages. For example, in Samoan, *l* and *r* can be used interchangeably in a word without changing the meaning (therefore, these two sounds belong to the same phoneme in Samoan). So Samoan speakers may say "Leupena" sometimes and "Reupena" at other times when they are referring to someone who in English would be called "Reuben."

English speakers may joke about languages that "confuse" *l* and *r,* but they are not usually aware that we do the same thing with other sets of sounds. For example, in English, the word we spell *and* may be pronounced quite differently by two different English speakers without changing the meaning, and no one would think that a different word was spoken. We can pronounce the *a* in *and* as in the beginning of the word *air,* or we can pronounce it as the *a* in *bat.* If you say those varying *a* sounds and try to think about how you are forming them in your mouth, you will realize that they are two different sounds. English speakers might recognize a slight difference in pronunciation but pay little or no attention to it because the two ways to pronounce the *a* in *and* do not change the meaning. Now think about *l* and *r.* If you form them in your mouth, you will notice that they are only slightly different with respect to how far the tongue is from the ridge behind the upper front teeth. Languages do tend to consider sounds that are close as belonging to the same phoneme, but why they choose some sounds and not others to group together is not yet fully understood.

Why, for example, are two or more consonants strung together in some languages, whereas in other languages vowels are *almost* always put between consonants? The Samoan language now has a word for "Christmas" borrowed from English, but the borrowed word has been changed to fit the rules of Samoan. In the English word, two consonants come first, *k* and *r,* which we spell as *ch* and *r.* The Samoan word is *Kerisimasi* (pronounced as if it were spelled Keh-ree-see-mah-see). It has a vowel after each consonant, or five consonant-vowel syllables.

Why do some languages like Samoan alternate consonants and vowels more or less regularly? Recent cross-cultural research suggests three predictors of this variation. One predictor is a warmer climate. Where people live in warmer climates, the typical syllable is more likely to be a consonant-vowel syllable. Linguists have found that consonant-vowel syllables provide the most contrast in speech. Perhaps when people converse outdoors at a distance, which they are likely to do in a warmer climate, they need more contrast between sounds to be understood. A second predictor of consonant-vowel alternation is literacy. Languages that are written have fewer consonant-vowel syllables. If communication is often in written form, meaning does not have to depend so much on contrast between adjacent sounds. A third (indeed the strongest) predictor of consonant-vowel alternation is the degree to which babies are held by others. Societies with a great deal of baby-holding have a lot of consonant-vowel syllables. A cross-cultural study relates baby-holding to a societal preference for regular rhythm in music. The theory is that when babies are held on a person much of the day, they begin to associate regular rhythm with pleasurable experiences. The baby senses the regular rhythm of the caretaker's heartbeats or the caretaker's rhythmic work, and the reward value of that experience generalizes to a preference for all regular rhythms in adult life, including apparently a regular consonant-vowel alternation in adult speech. Compare the rhythm of the Samoan word *Kerisimasi* with the English word *Christmas.*[30]

Morphology

A phoneme in a language usually does not mean something by itself. Usually phonemes are combined with other phonemes to form a meaningful sequence of sounds. *Morphology* is the study of sequences of sounds that have meaning. Often these meaningful sequences of sounds make up what we call *words,* but a word may be composed of a number of smaller meaningful units. We take our words so much for granted that we do not realize how complicated it is to say what words are. People do not usually pause very much between words when they speak; if we did not know our language, a sentence would seem like a continuous stream of sounds. This is how we first hear a foreign language. It is only when we understand the language and write down what we say that we separate (by spaces) what we call words. But a word is really only an arbitrary sequence of sounds that has a meaning; we would not "hear" words as separate units if we did not understand the language spoken.

Because anthropological linguists traditionally investigated unwritten languages, sometimes without the aid of interpreters, they had to figure out which sequences of sounds conveyed meaning. And because words in many languages can often be broken down into smaller meaningful units, linguists had to invent special words to refer to those units. Linguists call the smallest unit of language that has a meaning a **morph**. Just as a phoneme may have one or more phones, one or more morphs with the same meaning may make up a **morpheme**. For example, the prefix *in-*, as in *indefinite*, and the prefix *un-*, as in *unclear*, are morphs that belong to the morpheme meaning *not*. Although some words are single morphs or morphemes (e.g., *for* and *giraffe* in English), many words are a combination of morphs, generally prefixes, roots, and suffixes. Thus *cow* is one word, but the word *cows* contains two meaningful units—a root (*cow*) and a suffix (pronounced like *z*) meaning more than one. The **lexicon** of a language, which a dictionary approximates, consists of words and morphs and their meanings.

In English, the meaning of an utterance (containing a subject, verb, object, and so forth) usually depends on the order of the words. "The dog bit the child" is different in meaning from "The child bit the dog." But in many other languages, the grammatical meaning of an utterance does not depend much, if at all, on the order of the words. Rather, meaning may be determined by how the morphs in a word are ordered. For example, in Luo, a language of East Africa, the same bound morpheme may mean the subject or object of an action. If the morpheme is the prefix to a verb, it means the subject; if it is the suffix to a verb, it means the object. Another way that grammatical meaning may be conveyed is by altering or adding a bound morpheme to a word to indicate what part of speech it is. For example, in Russian, the word for "mail" when it is the subject of a sentence is pronounced something like "pawchtah." When "mail" is used as the object of a verb, as in "I gave her the mail," the ending of the word changes to "pawchtoo." And if I say, "What was in the mail?" the word becomes "pawchtyeh."

Some languages have so many bound morphemes that they might express as a complex but single word what is considered a sentence in English. For example, the English sentence "He will give it to you" can be expressed in Wishram, a Chinookan dialect that was spoken along the Columbia River in the Pacific Northwest, as *acimluda* (a-c-i-m-l-ud-a, literally "will-he-him-thee-to-give-will"). Note that the pronoun *it* in English is gender-neutral; Wishram requires that *it* be given a gender, in this case, "him."[31]

Syntax

Because language is an open system, we can make up meaningful utterances that we have never heard before. We are constantly creating new phrases and sentences. The rules or syntax that predict how phrases and sentences are generally formed may be partly learned in school, but children know many of them even before they get to school. In adulthood, our understanding of morphology and syntax is so intuitive that we can even understand a nonsense sentence, such as this famous one from Lewis Carroll's *Through the Looking Glass:*

'Twas brillig, and the slithy toves
Did gyre and gimble in the wabe

Simply from the ordering of the words in the sentence, we can surmise which part of speech a word is, as well as its function in the sentence. *Brillig* is an adjective; *slithy* an adjective; *toves* a noun and the subject of the sentence; *gyre* and *gimble* verbs; and *wabe* a noun and the object of a prepositional phrase. Of course, an understanding of morphology helps too. The *-y* ending in *slithy* is an indication that the latter is an adjective, and the *-s* ending in *toves* tells us that we most probably have more than one of these creatures. In addition to producing and understanding an infinite variety of sentences, speakers of a language can tell when a sentence is not "correct" without consulting grammar books. Speakers of a language know these implicit rules of syntax but are not usually consciously aware of them. The linguist's description of the syntax of a language tries to make these rules explicit.

Historical Linguistics

The field of historical linguistics focuses on how languages change over time. Written works provide the best data for establishing such changes. For example, the following short passage from Chaucer's *Canterbury Tales,* written in the English of the fourteenth century, has recognizable elements but is different enough from modern English to require a translation.

> A Frere ther was, a wantowne and a merye,
> A lymytour, a ful solempne man.
> In alle the ordres foure is noon that kan
> So muche of daliaunce and fair language.
> He hadde maad ful many a mariage
> Of yonge wommen at his owene cost.

> A friar there was, wanton and merry,
> A limiter [a friar limited to certain districts], a very important man.
> In all the orders four there is none that knows
> So much of flirting and engaging language.
> He had arranged many a marriage
> Of young women at his own cost.[32]

In this passage we can recognize several changes. Many words are spelled differently today, and in some cases, meaning has changed: *Full,* for example, would be translated today as *very.* What is less evident is that changes in pronunciation have occurred. For example, the *g* in *mariage* (marriage) was pronounced *zh,* as in the French from which it was borrowed, whereas now it is usually pronounced like either *g* in *George.*

Because languages spoken in the past leave no traces unless they were written, and most of the languages known to anthropology were not written by their speakers, you might think that historical linguists can study linguistic change only by studying written languages such as English. But that is not the case. Linguists can reconstruct changes that have occurred by comparing contemporary languages that are similar. Such languages show phonological, morphological, and syntactical similarities because they usually derive from a common ancestral language. For example, Romanian, Italian, French, Spanish, and Portuguese have many similarities. On the basis of these similarities, linguists can reconstruct what the ancestral language was like and how it changed into what we call the Romance languages. Of course, these reconstructions can easily be tested and confirmed because we know from many surviving writings what the ancestral language, Latin, was like; and we know from documents how Latin diversified as the Roman Empire expanded. Thus, common ancestry is frequently the reason why neighboring, and sometimes even separated, languages show patterns of similarity.

But languages can be similar for other reasons too. Contact between speech communities, often with one group dominant over another, may lead one language to borrow from the other. For example, English borrowed a lot of vocabulary from French after England was conquered by the French-speaking Normans in A.D. 1066. Languages may also show similarities even though they do not derive from a common ancestral language and even though there has been no contact or borrowing between them. Such similarities may reflect common or universal features of human cultures or human brains or both. (As we noted

This reproduced page dates from a 1433 book authored by John Lydgate. The language is described by linguists as Middle English, spanning approximately 1100–1500.

earlier in the chapter, the grammatical similarities exhibited by creole languages may reflect how the human brain is "wired.") Finally, even unrelated and separated languages may show some similarities because of the phenomenon of convergence; similarities can develop because some processes of linguistic change may have only a few possible outcomes.

Language Families and Culture History

Latin is the ancestral language of the Romance languages. We know this from documentary (written) records. But if the ancestral language of a set of similar languages is not known from written records, linguists still can reconstruct many features of that language by comparing the derived languages. (Such a reconstructed language is called a **protolanguage**.) That is, by comparing presumably related languages, linguists can become aware of the features that many of them have in common, features that were probably found in the common ancestral language. The languages that derive from the same protolanguage are called a *language family.* The language family that English belongs to is called *Indo-European,* because it includes most of the languages of Europe and some of the languages of India. About 50 percent of the world's more than 6 billion people speak Indo-European languages.[33] Another very large language family, now spoken by more than a billion people, is Sino-Tibetan, which includes the languages of northern and southern China as well as those of Tibet and Burma.

The field of historical linguistics got its start in 1786, when a British scholar living in India, Sir William Jones, noticed similarities between Sanskrit (a language spoken and written in ancient India) and classical Greek, Latin, and more recent European languages.[34] In 1822, Jakob Grimm, one of the brothers

Grimm of fairytale fame, formulated rules to describe the sound shifts that had occurred when the various Indo-European languages diverged from each other. So, for example, in English and the other languages in the Germanic branch of the Indo-European family, *d* regularly shifted to *t* (compare the English *two* and *ten* with the Latin *duo* and *decem*) and *p* regularly shifted to *f* (English *father* and *foot*, Latin *pater* and *pes*). Scholars generally agree that the Indo-European languages derive from a language spoken 5,000 to 6,000 years ago.[35] The ancestral Indo-European language, many of whose features have now been reconstructed, is called *proto-Indo-European*.

The Bantu languages in Africa (spoken by perhaps 100 million people) form a subfamily of the larger Niger-Congo family of languages. Bantu speakers currently live in a wide band across the center of Africa and down the eastern and western sides of southern Africa. All of the Bantu languages presumably derive from people who spoke proto-Bantu. But where was their homeland? Most historical linguists now agree with Joseph Greenberg's suggestion that the origin of Bantu was in what is now the Middle Benue area of eastern Nigeria.[36] The point of origin is presumably where there is the greatest diversity of related languages and *dialects* (varying forms of a language); it is assumed that the place of origin has had the most time for linguistic diversity to develop, compared with an area only recently occupied by a related language. For example, England has more dialect diversity than New Zealand or Australia.

Why were the Bantu able to spread so widely over the last few thousand years? Anthropologists have only begun to guess.[37] Initially, the Bantu probably kept goats and practiced some form of agriculture and thereby were able to spread, displacing hunter-gatherers in the area. As the Bantu speakers expanded, they began to cultivate certain cereal crops and herd sheep and cattle. Around this time, after 1000 B.C., they also began to use and make iron tools, which may have given them significant advantages. In any case, by 1,500 to 2,000 years ago, Bantu speakers had spread throughout central Africa and into the northern reaches of southern Africa. But speakers of non-Bantu languages still live in eastern, southern, and southwestern Africa.

Processes of Linguistic Divergence

The historical or comparative linguist hopes to do more than record and date linguistic divergence. Just as the physical anthropologist may attempt to develop explanations for human variation, so the linguist investigates the possible causes of linguistic variation. Some of the divergence undoubtedly comes about gradually. When groups of people speaking the same language lose communication with one another because they become separated, either physically or socially, they begin to accumulate small changes in phonology, morphology, and syntax (which occur continuously in any language). These variant forms of language are considered **dialects** when the differences in phonology, morphology, and syntax are not great enough to produce unintelligibility. Eventually, if the separation continues, the former dialects of the same language will become separate languages; that is, they will become mutually unintelligible, as German and English now are. Geographic barriers, such as large bodies of water, deserts, and mountains, may separate speakers of what was once the same language, but distance by itself can also produce divergence. For example, if we compare dialects of English in the British Isles, it is clear that the regions farthest away from each other are the most different linguistically (compare the northeast of Scotland and London).[38]

Whereas isolation brings gradual divergence between speech communities, contact results in greater resemblance. This effect is particularly evident when contact between mutually unintelligible languages introduces borrowed words, which usually name some new item borrowed from the other culture— *tomato, canoe, sushi,* and so on. Bilingual groups within a culture may also introduce foreign words, especially when the mainstream language has no real equivalent. Thus, *salsa* has come into English, and *le weekend* into French.

Conquest and colonization often result in extensive and rapid borrowing, if not linguistic replacement. The Norman conquest of England introduced French as the language of the new aristocracy. It was 300 years before the educated classes began to write in English. During this time the English borrowed words from French and Latin, and the two languages—English and French—became more alike than they would otherwise have been. About 50 percent of the English general vocabulary originated in French. Different social classes may react to language contact differentially. For example, English aristocrats eventually called their meat "pork" and "beef" (derived from the French words), but the people who raised the animals and prepared them for eating continued (at least for a while) to refer to the meat as "pig" and "bull," the original Anglo-Saxon words.

In those 300 years of extensive contact, the grammar of English remained relatively stable. English lost most of its inflections or case endings, but it adopted little of the French grammar. In general, the borrowing of words, particularly free morphemes,[39] is much more common than the borrowing of grammar.[40] As we might expect, borrowing by one language from another can make the borrowing language more different from its *sibling languages* (those derived from a common ancestral language) than it would otherwise be. Partly as a result of the French influence, the English vocabulary looks quite different from the languages to which it is actually most similar in terms of phonology and grammar—German, Dutch, and the Scandinavian languages.

Relationships between Language and Culture

Some attempts to explain the diversity of languages have focused on the possible interactions between language and other aspects of culture. On the one hand, if it can be shown that a culture can affect the structure and content of its language, then it would follow that linguistic diversity derives at least in part from cultural diversity. On the other hand, the direction of influence between culture and language might work in reverse: Linguistic features and structures might affect other aspects of the culture.

Cultural Influences on Language

One way a society's language may reflect its corresponding culture is in **lexical content**, or vocabulary. Which experiences, events, or objects are singled out and given words may be a result of cultural characteristics.

Basic Words for Colors, Plants, and Animals   Early in the twentieth century many linguists pointed to the lexical domain (vocabulary) of color words to illustrate the supposed truth that languages vary arbitrarily or without apparent reason. Different languages not only had different numbers of basic color words (from 2 to 12 or so; for example, the words *red, green,* and *blue* in English), but they also, it was thought, had no consistency in the way they classified or divided the colors of the spectrum. But findings from a comparative (cross-linguistic) study contradicted these traditional presumptions about variation in the number and meaning of basic color words. On the basis of their study of at first 20 and later over 100 languages, Brent Berlin and Paul Kay found that languages did not encode color in completely arbitrary ways.[41]

Although different languages do have different numbers of basic color words, most speakers of any language are very likely to point to the same color chips as the best representatives of particular colors. For example, people the world over mean more or less the same color when they are asked to select the best "red." Moreover, there appears to be a nearly universal sequence by which basic color words are added to a language.[42] If a language has just two basic color words, its speakers will always refer to "black" (or dark) hues and "white" (or light) hues. If a language has three basic color words, the third word will nearly always be "red." The next category to appear is either "yellow" or "grue" (green/blue); then different words for green and blue; and so on. To be sure, we usually do not see the process by which basic color words are added to a language. But we can infer the usual sequence because, for example, if a language has a word for "yellow," it will almost always have a word for "red," whereas having a word for "red" does not mean that the language will have a word for "yellow."

What exactly is a *basic* color word? All languages, even the ones with only two basic color terms, have many different ways of expressing how color varies. For example, in English we have words such as turquoise, blue-green, scarlet, crimson, and sky blue. Linguists do not consider these to be basic color words. In English the basic color words are *white, black, red, green, yellow, blue, brown, pink, purple, orange,* and *gray.* One feature of a basic color word is that it consists of a single morph; it cannot include two or more units of meaning. This feature eliminates combinations such as *blue-green* and *sky blue.* A second feature of a basic color word is that the color it represents is not generally included in a higher-order color term. For example, scarlet and crimson are usually considered variants of red, turquoise a variant of blue. A third feature is that basic terms tend to be the first-named words when people are asked for color words. Finally, for a word to be considered a basic color word, many individual speakers of the language have to agree on the central meaning (in the color spectrum) of the word.[43]

Why do different societies (languages) vary in number of basic color terms? Berlin and Kay suggest that the number of basic color terms in a language increases with technological specialization as color is used to decorate and distinguish objects.[44] Cross-linguistic variation in the number of basic color terms does not mean that some languages make more color distinctions than others. Every language could make a particular distinction by combining words (e.g., "fresh leaf" for green); a language need not have a separate basic term for that color.

There may also be many basic color terms because of a biological factor.[45] Peoples with darker (more pigmented) eyes seem to have more trouble distinguishing colors at the dark (blue-green) end of the spectrum than do peoples with lighter eyes. It might be expected, then, that peoples who live nearer the equator (who tend to have darker eyes, presumably for protection against damaging ultraviolet radiation) would tend to have fewer basic color terms. And they do.[46] Moreover, it seems that both cultural and biological factors are required to account for cross-linguistic variation in the number of basic color terms. Societies tend to have six or more such terms (with separate terms for blue and green) only when they are relatively far from the equator and only when their cultures are more technologically specialized.[47] As we will see in later chapters, technological specialization tends to go with larger communities, more centralized governments, occupational specialization, and more social inequality. Societies with such traits are often referred to in a shorthand way as more "complex," which should not be taken to mean "better."

Cecil Brown has found what seem to be developmental sequences in other lexical domains. Two such domains are general, or *life-form,* terms for plants and for animals. Life-form terms are higher-order classifications. All languages have lower-order terms for specific plants and animals. For example, English has words such as *oak* and *pine, sparrow,* and *salmon.* English speakers make finer distinctions too—*pin oak* and *white pine, white-throated sparrow,* and *red salmon.* But why in some languages do people have a larger number of general terms such as *tree, bird,* and *fish?* It seems that these general terms show a universal developmental sequence too. That is, general terms seem to be added in a somewhat consistent order. After "plant" comes a term for "tree"; then one for "grerb" (small, green, leafy, nonwoody plant); then "bush" (for plants between tree and grerb in size); then "grass"; then "vine."[48] The life-form terms for animals also seem to be added in sequence; after "animal" comes a term for "fish," then "bird," then "snake," then "wug" (for small creatures other than fish, birds, and snakes—for example, worms and bugs), then "mammal."[49]

More complex societies tend to have a larger number of general, or life-form, terms for plants and animals than do simpler societies, just as they tend to have a larger number of basic color terms. Do all realms or domains of vocabulary increase in size as social complexity increases? If we look at the total vocabulary of a language (as can be counted in a dictionary), more complex societies do have larger vocabularies.[50] But we have to remember that complex societies have many kinds of specialists, and dictionaries will include the terms used by such specialists. If we look instead at the nonspecialist **core vocabulary** of languages, it seems that all languages have a core vocabulary of about the same size.[51] Indeed, although some domains increase in size with social complexity, some remain the same and still others decrease. An example of a smaller vocabulary domain in complex societies is that of specific names for plants. Urban North Americans may know general terms for plants, but they know relatively few names for specific plants. The typical individual in a small-scale society can commonly name 400 to 800 plant species; a typical person in our own and similar societies may be able to name only 40 to 80.[52] The number of life-form terms is larger in societies in which ordinary people know less about particular plants and animals.[53]

The evidence now available strongly supports the idea that the vocabulary of a language reflects the everyday distinctions that are important in the society. Those aspects of environment or culture that are of special importance will receive greater attention in the language. For example, many languages lack the possessive transitive verb we write as "have," as in "I have." Instead, the language may say something such as "it is to me." A cross-cultural study has suggested that a language may develop the verb "have" after the speakers of that language have developed a system of private property or personal ownership of resources.[54]

Linguistic Influences on Culture: The Sapir–Whorf Hypothesis

There is general agreement that culture influences language. But there is less agreement about the opposite possibility—that language influences other aspects of culture. Edward Sapir and Benjamin Lee Whorf suggested that language is a force in its own right, that it affects how individuals in a society perceive and conceive reality. This suggestion is known as the *Sapir–Whorf hypothesis*.[55] In comparing the

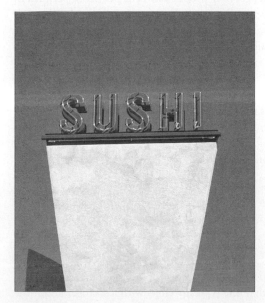

The word *sushi* has been borrowed in North America to identify a Japanese style of food.

English language with Hopi, Whorf pointed out that English-language categories convey discreteness with regard to time and space, but Hopi does not. English has a discrete past, present, and future, and things occur at a definite time. Hopi expresses things more as ongoing processes without time being apportioned into fixed segments. According to Ronald Wardhaugh, Whorf believed that these language differences lead Hopi and English speakers to see the world differently.[56]

As intriguing as that idea is, the relevant evidence is mixed. Linguists today do not generally accept the view that language coerces thought, but some suspect that particular features of language may facilitate certain patterns of thought.[57] The influences may be clearest in poetry and metaphors, where words and phrases are applied to other than their ordinary subjects, as in "all the world's a stage."[58] One of the serious problems in testing the Sapir–Whorf hypothesis is that researchers need to figure out how to separate the effects of other aspects of culture from the effects of language.

One approach that may reveal the direction of influence between language and culture is to study how children in different cultures (speaking different languages) develop concepts as they grow up. If language influences the formation of a particular concept, we might expect that children will acquire that concept earlier in societies where the languages emphasize that concept. For example, some languages make more of gender differences than others. Do children develop gender identity earlier when their language emphasizes gender? (Very young girls and boys seem to believe they can switch genders by dressing in opposite-sex clothes, suggesting that they have not yet developed a stable sense that they are unchangeably girls or boys.) Alexander Guiora and his colleagues have studied children growing up in Hebrew-speaking homes (Israel), English-speaking homes (the United States), and Finnish-speaking homes (Finland). Hebrew has the most gender emphasis of the three languages; all nouns are either masculine or feminine, and even second-person and plural pronouns are differentiated by gender. English emphasizes gender less, differentiating by gender only in the third-person singular (*she* or *her* or *hers*, *he* or *him* or *his*). Finnish emphasizes gender the least; although some words, such as *man* and *woman*, convey gender, differentiation by gender is otherwise lacking in the language. Consistent with the idea that language may influence thought, Hebrew-speaking children acquire the concept of stable gender identity the earliest on the average, Finnish-speaking children the latest.[59]

Another approach is to predict from language differences how people may be expected to perform in experiments. Comparing the Yucatec Mayan language and English, John Lucy predicted that English speakers might recall the *number* of things presented more than Yucatec Mayan speakers. For most classes of nouns, English requires a linguistic way of indicating whether something is singular or plural. You cannot say "I have dog" (no indication of number), but must say "I have a dog," "I have dogs," or "I have one (two, three, several, many) dogs." Yucatec Maya, like English, can indicate a plural, but allows the noun to be neutral with regard to number. In a number of experiments, Yucatec Mayan and American English speakers were equally likely to recall the objects in a picture, but they differed in how often they described the number of a particular object in the picture. Yucatec Mayan speakers did so less often, consistent with their language's lack of insistence on indicating number.[60] So the salience of number in the experiments was probably a consequence of how the languages differ.

Ethnography of Speaking

Many linguists are concerned with the *ethnography of speaking*—that is, with cultural and subcultural patterns of speech variation in different social contexts.[61] The sociolinguist might ask, for example, what kinds of things one talks about in casual conversation with a stranger. A foreigner may know English vocabulary and grammar well but may not know that one typically chats with a stranger about the weather or where one comes from, and not about what one ate that day or how much money one earns.

A foreigner may be familiar with much of the culture of a North American city, but if that person divulges the real state of his or her health and feelings to the first person who says, "How are you?" he or she has much to learn about "small talk" in North American English.

Similarly, North Americans tend to get confused in societies where greetings are quite different from ours. People in some other societies may ask as a greeting, "Where are you going?" or "What are you cooking?" Some Americans may think such questions are rude; others may try to answer in excruciating detail, not realizing that only vague answers are expected, just as we don't really expect a detailed answer when we ask people how they are.

Social Status and Speech

That a foreign speaker of a language may know little about the small talk of that language is but one example of the sociolinguistic principle that what we say and how we say it are not wholly predictable by the rules of our language. Who we are socially and whom we are talking to may greatly affect what we say and how we say it.

In a study interviewing children in a New England town, John Fischer noted that in formal interviews, children were likely to pronounce the ending in words such as *singing* and *fishing*, but in informal conversations they said *"singin'"* and *"fishin'."* Moreover, he noted that the phenomenon also appeared to be related to social class; children from higher-status families were less likely to drop the ending than were children from lower-status families. Subsequent studies in English-speaking areas tend to support Fischer's observations with regard to this speech pattern.[62]

Status can also influence the way people speak to each other. Terms of address are a good example. In English, forms of address are relatively simple. One is called either by a first name or by a title (such as *Doctor, Professor, Ms.,* or *Mister*) followed by a last name. Terms of address in English vary with the nature of the relationship between the speakers.[63] The reciprocal use of first names generally signifies an informal or intimate relationship between two persons. A title and last name used reciprocally usually indicates a more formal or business-like relationship between individuals who are roughly equal in status. Nonreciprocal use of first names and titles in English is reserved for speakers who recognize a marked difference in status between them. This status difference can be a function of age, as when a child refers to her mother's friend as Mrs. Miller and is in turn addressed as Sally, or can be due to occupational hierarchy, as when a person refers to his boss as Ms. Ramirez and is in turn addressed as Joe.

Strangers in North America shake hands when they meet; friends touch each other more warmly. How we speak to others also differs according to the degree of friendship.

Gender Differences in Speech

In many societies the speech of men differs from the speech of women. The variation can be slight, as in our own society, or more extreme, as with the Carib Indians in the Lesser Antilles of the West Indies, among whom women and men use different words for the same concepts.[64] In Japan, males and females use entirely different words for numerous concepts (e.g., the male word for water is *mizu,* the female version is *ohiya*), and females often add the polite prefix *o-* (females tend to say *ohasi* for chopsticks; males tend to say *hasi*).[65] In the United States and other Western societies, there are differences in the speech of females and males, but they are not as dramatic as in the Carib and Japanese cases. For example, earlier we noted the tendency for the *g* to be dropped in words such as *singing* when the situation is informal and when the social class background is lower. Women are more likely than men to keep the *g* sound and less likely than men to drop the *h* in words such as *happy.*[66] Gender differences occur in intonation and in phrasing of sentences as well. Robin Lakoff found that, in English, women tend to answer questions with sentences that have rising inflections at the end instead of a falling intonation associated with a firm answer. Women also tend to add questions to statements, such as "They caught the robber last week, didn't they?"[67]

One explanation for the gender differences, particularly with regard to pronunciation, is that women in many societies may be more concerned than men with being "correct."[68] In societies with social classes, what is considered more correct by the average person may be what is associated with the upper class. In other societies, what is older may be considered more correct. Gender differences in speech may parallel some of the gender differences noted in other social behavior (as we will see in the chapter on sex and gender): Girls are more likely than boys to behave in ways that are acceptable to adults.

There are not enough studies to know just how common it is for women to exhibit more linguistic "correctness." We do know of some instances where it is not the case. For example, in a community in Madagascar where people speak Merina, a dialect of Malagasy, it is considered socially correct to avoid explicit directives. So instead of directly ordering an action, a Merina speaker will try to say it indirectly. Also, it is polite to avoid negative remarks, such as expressing anger toward someone. In this community, however, it is women, not men, who often break the rules; women speak more directly and express anger more often.[69] This difference may be related to the fact that women are more involved in buying and selling in the marketplace.

Men and women typically differ in what they talk about, or do not talk about. Deborah Tannen offers some examples. When women hear about someone else's troubles they are likely to express understanding of the other's feelings; in contrast, men are likely to offer solutions. Men tend not to ask for directions; women do. Women tend to talk a lot in private settings; men talk more in public settings. These and other differences can cause friction and misunderstanding between the genders. When women express their troubles and men offer solutions, women feel that their feelings are not understood; men are frustrated that the women do not take their solutions seriously. Men may prefer to sit at home quietly and feel put-upon to have to engage in conversation; women feel slighted when men avoid extended conversations with them. Why these differences? Tannen suggests that misunderstanding between men and women arises because boys and girls grow up in somewhat different cultures. Girls typically play in small groups, talk frequently, and are intimate with others. Boys more often play in large groups in which jockeying for status and attention are more of a concern. Higher-status individuals give directions and solutions; they do not seek directions or solutions. So asking for directions is like acknowledging lower status. But large play groups resemble public settings, and so later in life men feel more comfortable speaking in public. Women, in contrast, are more comfortable speaking in small, intimate groups.[70]

Multilingualism and Codeswitching

For many people the ability to speak more than one language is a normal part of life. One language may be spoken at home and another in school, the marketplace, or government. Or more than one language may be spoken at home if family members come from different cultures and still other languages are spoken outside. Some countries explicitly promote multilingualism. For example, Singapore has four official languages—English, Mandarin (one of the Chinese languages), Tamil, and Malay. English is stressed for trade, Mandarin as the language of communication with most of China, Malay as the language of the general region, and Tamil as the language of an important ethnic group. Moreover, most of the population speaks Hokkien, another Chinese language. Education is likely to be in English and Mandarin.[71]

What happens when people who know two or more languages communicate with each other? Very often you find them **codeswitching**, using more than one language in the course of conversing.[72] Switching can occur in the middle of a Spanish-English bilingual sentence, as in "No van a bring it up in the meeting" ("They are not going to bring it up in the meeting").[73] Or switching can occur when the topic or situation changes, such as from social talk to schoolwork. Codeswitching involves a great deal of knowledge of two or more languages and an awareness of what is considered appropriate or inappropriate in the community. For example, in the Puerto Rican community in New York City, codeswitching within the same sentence seems to be common in speech among friends, but if a stranger who looks like a Spanish speaker approaches, the language will shift entirely to Spanish.[74]

Codeswitching may need to be understood in terms of the broader political and historical context. For example, German speakers in Transylvania, where Romanian is the national language, hardly ever codeswitch to Romanian. Perhaps the reason is that, before the end of World War II, German speakers were a privileged economic group who looked down upon landless Romanians and their language. Under socialism, the German speakers lost their economic privilege, but they continued to speak German among themselves. In the rare cases that Romanian is used among German speakers, it tends to be associated with low-status speech, such as singing bawdy songs. The opposite situation occurred in a Hungarian region of German-speaking Austria. The people of this agricultural region, annexed to Austria in 1921, were fairly poor peasant farmers. After World War II, business expansion began to attract labor from rural areas, so many Hungarians eagerly moved into jobs in industry. German was seen by the younger generations as a symbol of higher status and upward mobility; not surprisingly, codeswitching between Hungarian and German became part of their conversations. Indeed, in the third generation, German has become the language of choice, except when speaking to the oldest Hungarians. The Hungarian-Austrian situation is fairly common in many parts of the world, where the language of the politically dominant group ends up being "linguistically dominant."[75]

Writing and Literacy

Most of us have come to depend on writing for so many things that it is hard to imagine a world without it. Yet humans spent most of their history on earth without written language and many, if not most, important human achievements predate written language. Parents and other teachers passed on their knowledge by oral instruction and demonstration. Stories, legends, and myths abounded—the stuff we call oral literature—even in the absence of writing. This is not to say that writing is not important. Far more information and far more literature can be preserved for a longer period of time with a writing system. The earliest writing systems are only about 6,000 years old and are associated with early cities and

WHY ARE "MOTHER TONGUES" RETAINED, AND FOR HOW LONG?

The longer an immigrant group lives in another country, the more they incorporate the culture of their new home. At some point the original language is no longer even partially understood. Consider people who originally came from Wales, the region west of England in Great Britain. In that region, until about 100 years ago, most people spoke the Welsh language, which belongs to the Celtic subfamily of Indo-European along with Irish and Scottish Gaelic and Breton. (Celtic is a different subfamily from the one English belongs to, which is Germanic.) In 1729, the Welsh in Philadelphia established the Welsh Society, the oldest ethnic organization in the United States. Many of the members, if not all, spoke Welsh in addition to English at that time, but by the twentieth century hardly any of their descendants did.

If immigrant groups eventually lose their "mother tongues" in many if not most countries, this doesn't mean that the process occurs at the same speed in every group. Why is that? Why do some immigrant groups lose their language faster than others? Is it because they do not live in tightly knit ethnic enclaves? Or because they marry outside their ethnic group? Or because they do not have traditional festivals or celebrations marking their separate identity? A comparative study by Robert Schrauf discovered the most likely reasons. First, Schrauf assessed the degree to which immigrant groups coming to North America retained their native language over time. The greatest retention was defined as when the third generation (the grandchildren of immigrants) continued to use the native language. Examples were Chicanos, Puerto Ricans, Cubans, and Haitians. On the other hand, in some groups the third generation had no comprehension of the native language except for isolated words. Even the second generation (the children of immigrants) mostly spoke and understood only English. Examples were Italians, Armenians, and Basques. Chinese and Koreans were in the middle, with some evidence that the third generation understands a little of the native language. Schrauf then measured seven social factors that might explain longer versus shorter retention of the mother tongue. He looked at whether the group lived in tightly knit communities, retained religious rituals from the old country, had separate schools and special festivals, visited their homeland, did not intermarry, or worked with others of their ethnic group.

Schrauf used data on 11 North American ethnic groups drawn from the HRAF Collection of Ethnography. The major advantage of the HRAF materials is that ethnographies written for more general purposes, or for purposes other than linguistic ones, contain a wealth of information concerning sociocultural features of ethnic groups that may be tested for their possible effects on language retention and loss.

We might suspect that all of the factors measured by Schrauf would lead people to retain their native language (and presumably other native cultural patterns). But not all do, apparently. Only living in tightly knit communities and retaining religious rituals strongly predict retention of the mother tongue in the home into the third generation. Why? Possibly because living in an ethnic community and religious ritual are experienced early in life. Conditions associated with early socialization might have more lasting effects than conditions experienced later in life, such as schooling, visits to the homeland, marriage, and work. Participation in celebrations and festivals is probably important, too, but it does not have quite as strong an effect, perhaps because celebrations and festivals are not everyday experiences.

As always, in the case of research, this study raises questions for future research. Would the same effects be found outside of North America? Would the results be the same if we looked also at other immigrant groups in North America? Do some immigrant groups live in close-knit communities because of discrimination or choice? If choice, are some groups more interested in assimilating than others? And if so, why?

Sources: D. Douglas Caulkins, "Welsh," in David Levinson and Melvin Ember, eds., *American Immigrant Cultures: Builders of a Nation,* 2 vols. (New York: Macmillan Reference, 1997), vol. 2, pp. 935–41; Robert W. Schrauf, "Mother Tongue Maintenance among North American Ethnic Groups," *Cross-Cultural Research,* 33 (1999): 175–92.

Children do not need help learning the language spoken in their homes. However, reading and writing cannot usually be learned without instruction. Nowadays children in most cultures are expected to learn to read and write in school. These Trobriand children from Papua New Guinea are allowed to wear their traditional clothes to school once a week.

states. Early writing is associated with systematic record-keeping—keeping of ledgers for inventorying goods and transactions. In early times probably only the elite could read and write—indeed it is only recently that universal literacy (the ability to read and write) has become the goal of most countries. But in most countries the goal of universal literacy is far from achieved. Even in countries with universal education the quality of education and the length of education varies considerably between subcultures and genders. Just as some ways of speaking are considered superior to others, a high degree of literacy is usually considered superior to illiteracy.[76] But literacy in what language or languages? Recent efforts to preserve languages have encouraged writing of texts in languages that were only spoken previously. Obviously, there will be few texts in those languages; other languages have vast numbers of written texts. As more and more accumulated knowledge is written and stored in books, journals, and databases, attainment of literacy in those written languages will be increasingly critical to success. And texts do not only convey practical knowledge—they may also convey attitudes, beliefs, and values that are characteristic of the culture associated with the language in which the texts are written.

Summary

1. The essential function language plays in all societies is that of communication. Although human communication is not limited to spoken language, such language is of overriding importance because it is the primary vehicle through which culture is shared and transmitted.

2. Systems of communication are not unique to humans. Other animal species communicate in a variety of ways—by sound, odor, body movement, and so forth. The ability of chimpanzees and gorillas to learn and use sign language suggests that symbolic communication is not unique to humans. Still, human language is distinctive as a communication system in that its spoken and symbolic nature permits an infinite number of combinations and recombinations of meaning.

3. Nonverbal human communication includes posture, mannerisms, body movement, facial expressions, and signs and gestures. Nonverbal human communication also includes tone of voice, accent, nonword sounds, and all the optional vocal features that communicate meaning apart from the language itself.

4. Descriptive (or structural) linguists try to discover the rules of phonology (the patterning of sounds), morphology (the patterning of sound sequences and words), and syntax (the patterning of phrases and sentences) that predict how most speakers of a language talk.

5. By comparative analysis of cognates (words similar in sound and meaning) and grammar, historical linguists test the notion that certain languages derive from a common ancestral language, or protolanguage. The goals are to reconstruct the features of the protolanguage, to hypothesize how the offspring languages separated from the protolanguage or from each other, and to establish the approximate dates of such separations.

6. When two groups of people speaking the same language lose communication with each other because they become separated either physically or socially, they begin to accumulate small changes in phonology, morphology, and syntax. If the separation continues, the two former dialects of the same language will eventually become separate languages—that is, they will become mutually unintelligible.

7. Whereas isolation brings about divergence between speech communities, contact results in greater resemblance. This effect is particularly evident when contact between mutually unintelligible languages introduces borrowed words, most of which name some new item borrowed from the other culture.

8. Some attempts to explain the diversity of languages have focused on the possible interaction between language and other aspects of culture. On the one hand, if it can be shown that a culture can affect the structure and content of its language, then it would follow that linguistic diversity derives at least in part from cultural diversity. On the other hand, the direction of influence between culture and language might work in reverse; the linguistic structures might affect other aspects of the culture.

9. In recent years, some linguists have begun to study variations in how people actually use language when speaking. This type of linguistic study, called sociolinguistics, is concerned with the ethnography of speaking—that is, with cultural and subcultural patterns of speaking in different social contexts.

10. In bilingual or multilingual populations, codeswitching (using more than one language in the course of conversing) has become increasingly common.

11. Written language dates back only about 6,000 years, but writing and written records have become increasingly important; literacy is now a major goal of most countries.

Glossary Terms

accent (p. 235)
codeswitching (p. 253)
core vocabulary (p. 249)
dialects (p. 246)
lexical content (p. 247)
lexicon (p. 243)
morph (p. 243)
morpheme (p. 243)

morphology (p. 241)
phones (p. 241)
phoneme (p. 241)
phonology (p. 241)
protolanguage (p. 245)
syntax (p. 241)
symbolic communication (p. 235)

Critical Questions

1. Why might natural selection have favored the development of true language in humans but not in apes?

2. Would the world be better off with many different languages spoken or with just one universal language? Why do you think so?

3. Discuss some new behavior or way of thinking that led people to adopt or invent new vocabulary or some new pattern of speech.

CHAPTER 11

ECONOMICS

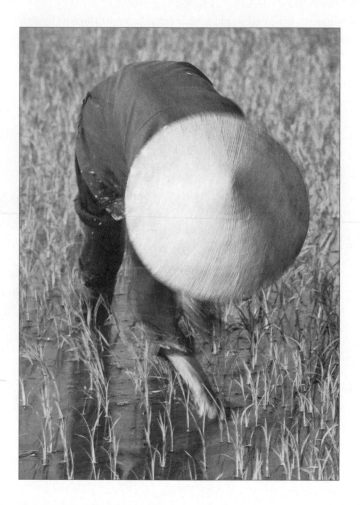

Chapter Outline

- Getting Food
- The Origin, Spread, and Intensification of Food Production
- Allocation of Resources
- Conversion of Resources
- Distribution of Goods and Services

When we think of economics, we think of things and activities involving money. We think of the costs of goods and services, such as food, rent, haircuts, and movie tickets. We may also think of factories, farms, and other enterprises that produce the goods and services we need, or think we need. In industrial societies, workers may stand before a moving belt for eight hours, tightening identical bolts that glide by. For this task they are given bits of paper that may be exchanged for food, shelter, and other goods or services. But many societies—indeed, most that are known to anthropology—did not have money or the equivalent of the factory worker. Still, all societies have economic systems, whether or not they involve money. All societies have customary ways to get food. They also have rules specifying how people gain access to natural resources and ways of transforming or converting those resources, through labor, into necessities and other goods and services. Finally, all societies have customs for distributing goods and services.

As we shall see in this chapter, a great deal of the cross-cultural variation in economic systems is related to how a society gets its food.

Getting Food

For most people in our society, getting food is a trip to the supermarket. Within an hour, we can gather enough food from the shelves to last us a week. Seasons don't daunt us. Week after week, we know food will be there. But we do not think of what would happen if the food were not delivered to the supermarket. We wouldn't be able to eat, and without eating for a while, we would die. Despite the old adage "Man [or woman] does not live by bread alone," without bread or the equivalent we could not live at all. Food-getting activities, then, take precedence over other activities important to survival. Reproduction, social control (the maintenance of peace and order within a group), defense against external threat, and the transmission of knowledge and skills to future generations—none could take place without energy derived from food. But it is not merely energy that is required for survival and long-term reproduction. Food-getting strategies need to provide the appropriate combination of nutrients throughout varying seasons and changing environmental conditions.

In this section we look first at the ways different societies get food and discuss some of the features associated with the different patterns.

Food Collection

Food collection may be generally defined as a food-getting strategy that obtains wild plant and animal resources through gathering, hunting, scavenging, or fishing. Although this was the way humans got their food for most of human history, food collectors in the world today, also referred to as **foragers** or **hunter-gatherers**, are not very numerous and most of them live in what have been called the *marginal areas* of the earth—deserts, the Arctic, and dense tropical forests—habitats that do not allow easy exploitation by modern agricultural technologies. In the last few hundred years only about 5 million people are or were foragers.[1]

Anthropologists are interested in studying the relatively few food-collecting societies still available for observation because these groups may help us understand some aspects of human life in the past, when all people were foragers. But we must be cautious in drawing inferences about the past from our observations of recent and contemporary food collectors, for three reasons. First, early foragers lived in almost all types of environments, including some very bountiful ones. Therefore, what we observe among recent and contemporary food collectors, who generally live in deserts, the Arctic, and tropical forests, may not be comparable to what would have been observable in more favorable environments in the past.[2] Second, contemporary foragers are not relics of the past. Like all contemporary societies, they have evolved and are still evolving. Third, recent and contemporary foragers have been interacting with kinds of societies that did not exist until after 10,000 years ago—agriculturalists, pastoralists, and intrusive, powerful state societies.[3] Many foraging people increasingly depend on agriculture, trade, or commercial activities, so what we see recently may be very different from the past. Let us examine one area of the world where recent food collectors were the only inhabitants until about 200 years ago.

Australian Aborigines   Before Europeans came to the Australian continent, all the people who lived there (who are referred to as *aborigines*) depended on food collection. Although the way of life of Australian aborigines is now considerably altered, we consider the life of the Ngatatjara as described by Richard Gould in the 1960s, when they still lived by gathering wild plants and hunting wild animals in the Gibson Desert of western Australia.[4]

The desert environment of the Ngatatjara averages less than 8 inches of rain per year, and the temperature in summer may rise to 118°F. The few permanent waterholes are separated by hundreds of square miles of sand, scrub, and rock. Even before Europeans arrived in Australia, the area was sparsely populated—fewer than one person per 35 to 40 square miles. Now there are even fewer people, because the aboriginal population was decimated by introduced diseases and mistreatment after the Europeans arrived.

On a typical day, the camp begins to stir just before sunrise, while it is still dark. Children are sent to fetch water, and the people breakfast on water and food left over from the night before. In the cool of the early morning, the adults talk and make plans for the day. The talking goes on for a while. Where should they go for food—to places they have been to recently or to new places? Sometimes there are other considerations. For example, one woman may want to search for plants whose bark she needs to make new sandals. When the women decide which plants they want to collect and where they think those plants are most likely to be found, they take up their digging sticks and set out with large wooden bowls of drinking water on their heads. Their children ride on their hips or walk alongside. Meanwhile, the men may have decided to hunt emus, 6-foot-tall ostrich-like birds that do not fly. The men go to a creekbed where they will wait to ambush any game that may come along. They lie patiently behind a screen of brush they have set up, hoping for a chance to throw a spear at an emu or even a kangaroo. They can throw only once, because if they miss, the game will run away.

By noon, the men and women are usually back at camp, the women with their wooden bowls each filled with up to 15 pounds of fruit or other plant foods, the men more often than not with only some small game, such as lizards and rabbits. The men's food-getting is less certain of success than the women's, so most of the Ngatatjara aborigines' diet is plant food. The daily cooked meal is eaten toward evening, after an afternoon spent resting, gossiping, and making or repairing tools.

The aborigines traditionally were nomadic, moving their campsites fairly frequently. The campsites were isolated and inhabited by only a small number of people, or they were clusters of groups including as many as 80 persons. The aborigines never established a campsite right next to a place with water. If they were too close, their presence would frighten game away and might cause tension with neighboring bands, who also would wait for game to come to the scarce watering spots.

Today many aborigines live in small settled villages. For example, in the 1980s, Victoria Burbank worked in a village she calls "Mangrove" in the Northern Territory of Australia. The once-nomadic aborigines live in a village of about 600, which was founded in the 1950s around a Protestant mission.

Their houses have stoves, refrigerators, toilets, washing machines, and even television sets. Their children attend school full time, and there is a health clinic for their medical needs. They still do some foraging, but most of their food comes from the store. Some earn wages, but many subsist on government welfare checks.[5]

General Features of Food Collectors   Despite the differences in terrain and climate under which they live and the different food-collecting technologies they use, Australian aborigines, Inuit (Eskimo), and most other recent foragers had certain characteristic cultural patterns (see Table 11.1). Most lived in small communities in sparsely populated territories and followed a nomadic lifestyle, forming no permanent settlements. As a rule, they did not recognize individuals' land rights. Their communities generally did not have different classes of people and tended to have no specialized or full-time political officials.[6] Division of labor in food-collecting societies was based largely on age and gender: Men exclusively hunted large marine and land animals and usually did most of the fishing, and women usually gathered wild plant foods.[7]

When we say that food collectors tend to have certain traits, this does not mean that all of them have those traits. There is considerable variability among societies that depend on foraging. Food-collecting societies that depend heavily on fishing (such as on the Pacific Coast of the northwestern United States

Table 11.1   Variation in Food-Getting and Associated Features

	Food Collectors		Food Producers	
	Foragers	**Horticulturalists**	**Pastoralists**	**Intensive Agriculturalists**
Population density	Lowest	Low-moderate	Low	Highest
Maximum community size	Small	Small-moderate	Small	Large (towns and cities)
Nomadism/ permanence of settlements	Generally nomadic or seminomadic	More sedentary: communities may move after several years	Generally nomadic or seminomadic	Permanent communities
Food shortages	Infrequent	Infrequent	Frequent	Frequent
Trade	Minimal	Minimal	Very important	Very important
Full-time craft specialists	None	None or few	Some	Many (high degree of craft specialization)
Individual differences in wealth	Generally none	Generally minimal	Moderate	Considerable
Political leadership	Informal	Some part-time political officials	Part- and full-time political officials	Many full-time political officials

and Canada or on the south coast of New Guinea) are more likely to have bigger and more permanent communities and somewhat more social inequality than do those societies elsewhere who mostly forage for game and plants.[8] The Pacific Coast and New Guinea coastal people also tend to have higher population densities, food storage,[9] occupational specialization, resource ownership, slavery, and competitiveness.[10] For example, two foraging groups that depended heavily on annual salmon runs were the Tlingit of southeastern Alaska and the Nimpkish of British Columbia. Both groups had a three-tiered class system with a high class, commoners, and slaves. The high-status individuals were obliged to stage competitive elaborate feasts with distributions of valuables.[11] This type of inequality and competitiveness was very different from what we find in typical food collectors, who generally show little social differentiation.

Is there a typical pattern of food-getting among food collectors? Many anthropologists have assumed that foragers typically get their food more from gathering than from hunting, and that women contribute more than men to subsistence, because women generally do the gathering.[12] Although gathering is the most important food-getting activity for some food collectors (e.g., the Ngatatjara aborigines and the !Kung of southern Africa), this is not true for most food-collecting societies known to us. A survey of 180 such societies indicates that there is a lot of variation with regard to which food-getting activity is most important to the society. Gathering is the most important activity for 30 percent of the surveyed societies, hunting for 25 percent, and fishing for 38 percent. (Perhaps, then, we should call most recent food collectors fisher-gatherer-hunters.) In any case, because men generally do the fishing as well as the hunting, the men usually contribute more to food-getting than do the women among recent food collectors.[13]

Because food collectors move their camps often and walk great distances, it may seem that the food-collecting way of life is difficult. Although we do not have enough quantitative studies to tell us what is typical of most food collectors, studies of two Australian aborigine groups[14] and of one !Kung group[15] indicate that those food collectors do not spend many hours getting food. For example, !Kung adults spend an average of about 17 hours per week collecting food. Even when you add the time spent making tools (about 6 hours a week) and doing housework (about 19 hours a week), the !Kung seem to have more leisure time than many agriculturalists, as we discuss later.

Food Production

Beginning about 10,000 years ago, certain peoples in widely separated geographic locations made the revolutionary changeover to **food production**. That is, they began to cultivate and then domesticate plants and animals. (Domesticated plants and animals are different from the ancestral wild forms.) With domestication of these food sources, people acquired control over certain natural processes, such as animal breeding and plant seeding. Today, most peoples in the world depend for their food on some combination of domesticated plants and animals.

Anthropologists generally distinguish three major types of food production systems—horticulture, intensive agriculture, and pastoralism.

Horticulture   The word **horticulture** may conjure up visions of people with "green thumbs" growing orchids and other flowers in greenhouses. But to anthropologists, the word means the growing of crops of all kinds with relatively simple tools and methods, in the absence of permanently cultivated fields. The tools are usually hand tools, such as the digging stick or hoe, not plows or other equipment pulled by animals or tractors. And the methods used do not include fertilization, irrigation, or other ways to restore soil fertility after a growing season.

There are two kinds of horticulture. The more common one involves a dependence on **extensive** or **shifting cultivation**. The land is worked for short periods and then left idle for some years. During the years when the land is not cultivated, wild plants and brush grow; when the fields are later cleared by *slash-and-burn techniques,* nutrients are returned to the soil. The other kind of horticulture involves a dependence on long-growing tree crops. The two kinds of horticulture may be practiced in the same society, but in neither case is there permanent cultivation of field crops.

Most horticultural societies do not rely on crops alone for food. Many also hunt or fish; a few are nomadic for part of the year. For example, the Kayapo of the Brazilian Amazon leave their villages for as long as three months at a time to trek through the forest in search of game. The entire village participates in a trek, carrying large quantities of garden produce and moving their camp every day.[16] Other horticulturalists raise domestic animals, but these are usually not large animals, such as cattle and camels.[17] More often than not, the animals raised by horticulturalists are smaller ones, such as pigs, chickens, goats, and sheep.

Let us look now at a recent horticultural society, the Yanomamö of the Brazilian-Venezuelan Amazon.

THE YANOMAMÖ   Dense tropical forest covers most of Yanomamö territory. From the air, the typical village is located in a forest clearing and looks like a single, large, circular lean-to with its inner side open to the central plaza. Each individual family has its own portion of the lean-to under the common roof. Each family's portion of the lean-to has a back wall (part of the closed back wall around the circular village structure), but the portions are open on the sides to each other as well as onto the central plaza of the village. The Yanomamö get most of their calories from garden produce, but according to Raymond Hames, the Yanomamö actually spend most of their time foraging.[18]

Before the people can plant, the forest must be cleared of trees and brush. Like most shifting cultivators, the Yanomamö use a combination of techniques: slashing the undergrowth, felling trees, and using controlled burning to clear a garden spot—in other words, **slash-and-burn** horticulture. Before the 1950s, the Yanomamö had only stone axes, so felling trees was quite difficult. Now they have steel machetes and axes given or traded to them by missionaries.

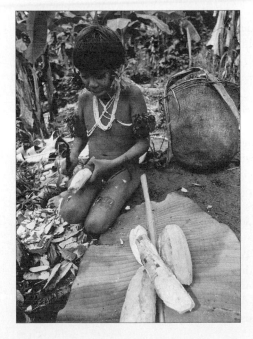

A Yanomamö boy peels cassava.

Because of the work involved in clearing a garden, the Yanomamö prefer to make use of forest patches that have little thorny brush and not too many large trees.[19] After the ground is cleared, the Yanomamö plant plantains, manioc, sweet potatoes, taro, and a variety of plants for medicine, condiments, and craft materials. Men do the heavy clearing work to prepare a garden, and they as well as women plant the crops. Women usually go to the gardens daily to weed and harvest. After two or three years the yields diminish and the forest starts growing back, making continued cultivation less desirable and more difficult, so they abandon the garden and clear a new one. If they can, they clear adjacent forest, but if gardens are far from the village they will move the village to a new location. Villages are moved about every five years because of gardening needs and warfare. There is a great deal of intervillage raiding, so villages are often forced to flee to another location.

Extensive cultivation requires a lot of territory because new gardens are not cleared until the forest grows back. What is often misunderstood is why it is so important to shift gardens. Not only is a burned field easier to plant, but the organic matter that is burned provides necessary nutrients for a good yield. If horticulturalists come back too quickly to a spot with little plant cover, a garden made there will not produce a satisfactory yield.

The Yanomamö crops do not provide much protein, so hunting and fishing are important to their diet. Men hunt birds, peccaries, monkeys, and tapir with bows and arrows. Fishing is enjoyed by women, men, and children. They catch fish by hand, with small bows and arrows, and by stream poisoning. Everybody gathers honey, hearts of palm, Brazil nuts, and cashews, although the men usually climb trees to shake down the nuts. Much of the foraging is done from the village base, but the Yanomamö, like the Kayapo, may go on treks to forage from time to time.

General Features of Horticulturalists   In most horticultural societies, simple farming techniques have tended to yield more food from a given area than is generally available to food collectors. Consequently, horticulture is able to support larger, more densely populated communities. The way of life of horticulturalists is more sedentary than that of food collectors, although communities may move after some years to farm a new series of plots. (Some horticulturalists have permanent villages because they depend mostly on food from trees that keep producing for a long time.) In contrast with most recent food-collecting groups, horticultural societies exhibit the beginnings of social differentiation. For example, some individuals may be part-time craftworkers or part-time political officials, and certain members of a kin group may have more status than other individuals in the society.

Intensive Agriculture   People engaged in **intensive agriculture** use techniques that enable them to cultivate fields permanently. Essential nutrients may be put back in the soil through the use of fertilizers, which may be organic material (most commonly dung from humans or other animals) or inorganic (chemical) fertilizers. But there are other ways to restore nutrients. The Luo of western Kenya plant beans around corn plants. Bacteria growing around the roots of the bean plant replace lost nitrogen, and the corn plant conveniently provides a pole for the bean plant to wind around as it grows. Some intensive agriculturalists use irrigation from streams and rivers to ensure an adequate supply of waterborne nutrients. Crop rotation and plant stubble that has been plowed under also restore nutrients to the soil.

In general, the technology of intensive agriculturalists is more complex than that of horticulturalists. Plows rather than digging sticks are generally employed. But there is enormous variation in the degree to which intensive agriculturalists rely on mechanization rather than hand labor. In some societies the most complex machine is an animal-drawn plow; in the corn and wheat belts of the United States, huge tractors till, seed, and fertilize 12 rows at a time.[20]

Let's look at one group of intensive agriculturalists, those of the Mekong Delta in Vietnam.

RURAL VIETNAM: THE MEKONG DELTA   The village of Khanh Hau, situated along the flat Mekong Delta, comprised about 600 families when it was described by Gerald Hickey in the late 1950s, before the Vietnam War.[21] The delta area has a tropical climate, with a rainy season that lasts from May to November. As a whole, the area has been made habitable only through extensive drainage.

Wet rice cultivation is the principal agricultural activity of Khanh Hau. It is part of a complex, specialized arrangement that involves three interacting components: (1) a complex system of irrigation and water control; (2) a variety of specialized equipment, including plows, waterwheels, threshing sledges, and winnowing machines; and (3) a clearly defined set of socioeconomic roles—from those of landlord, tenant, and laborer to those of rice miller and rice merchant.

In the dry season, the farmer decides what sort of rice crop to plant, whether of long (120 days) or short (90 days) maturation. The choice depends on the capital at his disposal, the current cost of fertilizer, and the anticipated demand for rice. The seedbeds are prepared as soon as the rains have softened the ground in May. The soil is turned over (plowed) and broken up (harrowed) as many as six separate times, with two-day intervals for "airing" between operations. During this time, the rice seeds are soaked in water for at least two days to stimulate sprouting. Before the seedlings are planted, the paddy is plowed once more and harrowed twice in two directions at right angles.

Planting is a delicate, specialized operation that must be done quickly and is performed most often by hired male laborers. But efficient planting is not enough to guarantee a good crop. Proper fertilization and irrigation are equally important. In the irrigating, steps must be taken to ensure that the water level remains at exactly the proper depth over the entire paddy. Water is distributed by means of scoops, wheels, and mechanical pumps. Successive crops of rice ripen from late September to May; all members of the family may be called upon to help with the harvest. After each crop is harvested, it is threshed, winnowed, and dried. Normally, the rice is sorted into three portions: One is set aside for use by the household in the following year; one is for payment of hired labor and other services (such as loans from agricultural banks); and one is for cash sale on the market. Aside from the harvesting, women do little work in the fields, spending most of their time on household chores. In families with little land, however, young daughters help in the fields and older daughters may hire themselves out to other farmers.

The villagers also cultivate vegetables, raise pigs, chickens, and the like, and frequently engage in fishing. The village economy usually supports three or four implement makers and a much larger number of carpenters.

Extensive drainage has made the Mekong Delta region of Vietnam able to support intensive agriculture.

General Features of Intensive Agricultural Societies   Societies with intensive agriculture are more likely than horticulturalists to have towns and cities, a high degree of craft specialization, complex political organization, and large differences in wealth and power. Studies suggest that intensive agriculturalists work longer hours than horticulturalists.[22] For example, men engaged in intensive agriculture average nine hours of work a day, seven days a week; women average almost eleven hours of work per day. Most of the work for women in intensive agricultural societies involves food processing and work in and around the home, but they also spend a lot of time working in the fields. We discuss some of the implications of the work patterns for women in the chapter on sex and gender.

Intensive agricultural societies are more likely than horticultural societies to face famines and food shortages, even though intensive agriculture is generally more productive than horticulture.[23] Why, if more food can be produced per acre, is there more risk of shortage among intensive agriculturalists? Intensive agriculturalists may be more likely to face food shortages because they are often producing crops for a market. Producing for a market pushes farmers to cultivate plants that give them the highest yield rather than cultivating plants that are drought-resistant or that require fewer nutrients. Farmers producing for a market also tend to concentrate on one crop. Crop diversity is often a protection against total crop failure because fluctuations in weather, plant diseases, or insect pests are not likely to affect all the crops. There are also fluctuations in market demand. If the market demand drops and the price falls for a particular crop, farmers may not have enough cash to buy the other food they need.

The Commercialization and Mechanization of Agriculture   Some intensive agriculturalists produce very little for sale; most of what they produce is for their own use. But there is a worldwide trend for intensive agriculturalists to produce more and more for a market. This trend is called **commercialization**, which may occur in any area of life and which involves increasing dependence on buying and selling, usually with money as the medium of exchange.

The increasing commercialization of agriculture is associated with several other trends. One is that farm work is becoming more and more mechanized as hand labor becomes scarce, because of migration to industrial and service jobs in towns and cities, or too expensive. A second trend is the emergence and spread of *agribusiness,* large corporation-owned farms that may be operated by multinational companies and worked by hired, as opposed to family, labor. For example, consider how cotton farming has changed in the southeastern United States. In the 1930s, mules and horses used in plowing were replaced by tractors. This change allowed some landowners to evict their sharecroppers and expand their holdings. After World War II, mechanical cotton pickers replaced most of the harvest laborers. But a farmer had to have a good deal of money or be a corporation to acquire those machines, each of which cost many tens of thousands of dollars.[24] So the mechanization of cotton farming sent many rural farm laborers off to the cities of the North in search of employment, and the agricultural sector increasingly became big business. A third trend associated with the commercialization of agriculture, including animal raising, is a reduction in the proportion of the population engaged in food production. In the United States today, for example, less than 1 percent of the total population work on farms.[25]

Later, in the chapter on culture change and globalization, we more fully discuss some of the apparent consequences of the worldwide changeover to commercial or market economies.

Pastoralism   Most agriculturalists keep and breed some animals (practice animal husbandry), but a small number of societies depend mostly for their living on domesticated herds of animals that feed on natural pasture.[26] We call such a system **pastoralism**. We might assume that pastoralists breed animals to eat their meat, but most do not. Pastoralists more often get their animal protein from live animals in the form of milk, and some pastoralists regularly take blood, which is rich in protein, from their animals to mix with other foods. The herds often indirectly provide food because many pastoralists trade animal products for plant foods and other necessities. In fact, a large proportion of their food may actually come from trade with agricultural groups.[27] For example, some pastoral groups in the Middle East derive much of their livelihood from the sale of what we call oriental rugs, which are made on hand looms from the wool of their sheep. One pastoral society we shall examine are the Lapps or Saami of Scandinavia.

THE LAPPS   The Lapps or Saami practice reindeer herding in northwestern Scandinavia where Finland, Sweden, and Norway share common frontiers. It is a typical Arctic habitat: cold, windswept, with long, dark days for half the year. Considerable change has occurred recently, so we first discuss the food-getting strategy in the 1950s, as described by Ian Whitaker and T. I. Itkonen.[28]

The Lapps herd their reindeer either intensively or, more often, extensively. In the *intensive system,* the herd is constantly under observation within a fenced area for the whole year. Intensively herded reindeer and other animals are accustomed to human contact. Hence, the summer corralling of the females for milking and the breaking in of the ox-reindeer for use as work animals are not difficult tasks. The *extensive system* involves allowing the animals to migrate over a large area. It requires little surveillance and encompasses large herds. Under this system, the reindeer are allowed to move through their seasonal feeding cycles watched by only one or two scouts. The other Lapps stay with the herd only when it has settled in its summer or winter habitat. But milking, breaking in, and corralling are harder in the extensive than in the intensive system because the animals are less accustomed to humans.

Even under the extensive system, which theoretically permits Lapps to engage in subsidiary economic activities such as hunting and fishing, the reindeer herd is the essential, if not the only, source of income. A family might possess as many as 1,000 reindeer, but usually the figure is half that number. Studies show 200 to be the minimum number of reindeer needed to provide for a family of four or five adults. Women may have shared the herding chores in the past under the intensive system, but now, under the extensive system, men do the herding. Women still do the milking. The Lapps eat the meat of the bull reindeer; the female reindeer are kept for breeding purposes. Bulls are slaughtered in the fall, after the mating season. Meat and hides are frequently sold or bartered for other food and necessities.

Reindeer are still herded nowadays, but snowmobiles, all-terrain vehicles, and even helicopters (instead of sleds) are used for herding. Ferries move reindeer to and from different pastures, and the herders

A Saami reindeer herder feeds two of her animals in the snow.

communicate by field telephones. With faster transportation, many Lapps now live in permanent homes and can still get to their herds in hours. Lapp children spend much of their time in school and, consequently, do not learn much of the herding ways. The Norwegian government now regulates pastoralism, licensing pastoralists and trying to limit the number of reindeer they can herd.[29] And many Lapps (they prefer to call themselves Saami) no longer have reindeer.

General Features of Pastoralism   In recent times, pastoralism has been practiced mainly in grassland and other semiarid habitats that are not especially suitable for cultivation without some significant technological input such as irrigation. Most pastoralists are nomadic, moving camp fairly frequently to find water and new pasture for their herds. But other pastoralists have somewhat more sedentary lives. They may move from one settlement to another in different seasons, or they may send some people out to travel with the herds in different seasons. Pastoral communities are usually small, consisting of a group of related families.[30] Individuals or families may own their own animals, but decisions about when and where to move the herds are made by the community. There is a great deal of interdependence between pastoral and agricultural groups. Trade is usually necessary for pastoral groups to survive. Like agriculturalists, pastoralists are more vulnerable than foragers and horticulturalists to famine and food shortages. Pastoralists usually inhabit drought-prone regions, but recent pastoralists have had their access to grazing lands reduced, and political pressures have pushed them to decrease their movement over large areas. Mobility kept the risk of overgrazing to a minimum, but overgrazing in small territories has increased the risk of desertification.[31]

The Origin, Spread, and Intensification of Food Production

We see the first evidence of a changeover to food production—the cultivation and domestication of plants and animals—in the Near East about 8000 B.C. This shift occurred, probably independently, in other areas as well. There is evidence of cultivation some time around 6000 B.C. in China, Southeast Asia (what is now Malaysia, Thailand, Cambodia, and Vietnam), and Africa. In the New World, there appear to have been several places of original cultivation and domestication. The highlands of Mexico (about 7000 B.C.) and the central Andes around Peru (by about 6000 B.C.) were probably the most important in terms of food plants used today.

Wheat is now grown in many areas of the United States where hunting and gathering was practiced.

There are many theories of why food production developed; most have tried to explain the origin of domestication in the Near East. Most of the theories currently considered suggest that people made the changeover because they were pushed into it. The possible reasons include the following:

1. Population growth in regions of bountiful wild resources pushed people to move to marginal areas, where they tried to reproduce their former abundance.
2. Global population growth filled up most of the world's habitable regions and forced people to utilize a broader spectrum of wild resources and to domesticate plants and animals.
3. Climatic change—hotter, drier summers and colder winters—favored settling near seasonal stands of wild grain; population growth in such areas would force people to plant crops and raise animals.

Whatever the reasons for the switch to food production, we still need to explain why food production has supplanted food collection as the primary mode of subsistence. We cannot assume that collectors would automatically adopt production as a superior way of life once they understood the process of domestication. After all, as we have noted, domestication may entail more work and provide less security than the food-collecting way of life.

The spread of agriculture may be linked to the need for territorial expansion. As a sedentary, food-producing population grew, it may have been forced to expand into new territory. Some of this territory may have been vacant, but much of it was probably already occupied by food collectors. Although food production is not necessarily easier than collection, it is generally more productive per unit of land. Greater productivity enables more people to be supported in a given territory. In the competition for land between the faster-expanding food producers and the food collectors, the food producers may have had a significant advantage: They had more people in a given area. Thus, the foraging groups may have been more likely to lose out in the competition for land. Some groups may have adopted cultivation, abandoning the foraging way of life in order to survive. Other groups, continuing as food collectors, may have been forced to retreat into areas not desired by the cultivators. Today, as we have seen, the small number of remaining food collectors inhabit areas not particularly suitable for cultivation—dry lands, dense tropical forests, and polar regions.

Just as prior population growth might account for the origins of domestication, so at later periods further population growth and ensuing pressure on resources might at least partly explain the transformation of horticultural systems into intensive agricultural systems. Ester Boserup suggested that intensification of agriculture, with a consequent increase in yield per acre, is not likely to develop naturally out of horticulture because intensification requires much more work.[32] She argued that people will be willing to intensify their labor only if they have to. Where emigration is not feasible, the prime mover behind intensification may be prior population growth. The need to pay taxes or tribute to a political authority may also stimulate intensification.

However, Boserup's assumption that more work is required with intensive agriculture has recently been questioned. Comparing horticultural (swidden or shifting) rice production with rice produced on permanent fields using irrigation, Robert Hunt found that *less,* not more, labor is required with irrigation.[33] Still, population increase may generally provide the impetus to intensify production in order to increase yields to support the additional people.

Intensive agriculture has not yet spread to every part of the world. Horticulture continues to be practiced in certain tropical regions, and there still are some pastoralists and food collectors. Some environments may make it somewhat more difficult to adopt certain subsistence practices. For example, intensive agriculture cannot supplant horticulture in some tropical environments without tremendous investments

FOOD ON THE MOVE

People in North America get most of their food from stores. Where the food comes from originally—where it was first grown or raised—is unknown to most people. Partly this is because relatively few are directly involved in food-getting (less than 1 percent of the workers in the United States). Even when you count all the activities related to food-getting, such as marketing and transportation, only 14 percent of U.S. workers have anything to do with the production and distribution of food. But nowadays many of the foods we buy in markets—tacos, salsa, bagels, pasta, pizza, sausage, soy sauce, and teriyaki—have become mainstream "North American" food. Where did these foods come from? Originally they were eaten only by ethnic and immigrant minorities who came to the United States and Canada. Some, but not all, of their foods caught on and became widely consumed. They became as "American" as apple pie.

The ingredients in many of these food items resulted from previous movements of people even further back in time. Consider the ingredients in pizza, a favorite food now for many of us. The dough is made from wheat flour, which was first grown in the Middle East, perhaps as much as 10,000 years ago. How do anthropologists know that? Archaeologists have discovered wheat kernels that old in Middle Eastern sites, and they have found flat stones and stone rolling pins from that time that we know were used to grind kernels into flour (we can tell from microscopic analysis of the residue on the stone). What about other ingredients that may be found in pizza? Cheese was first made in the Middle East too, at least 5,000 years ago (we have writings from that time that mention cheese). Tomatoes were first grown in South America, probably several thousand years ago. They got to Italy, the birthplace of the tomato pie (which became transformed into pizza), less than 200 years ago. Just 100 years ago, tomatoes (the key ingredient in pizza for some) were so new in eastern Europe that people were afraid to eat them because their leaves are poisonous to humans and some other animals. Another food we associate with Italian cuisine, spaghetti-type noodles, came to Italy (from China) less than 500 years ago. So the major ingredients of pizza, just like round-noodle *pasta*, are all not native to Italy.

The amazing thing about foods is that they so often travel far and wide, generally carried by the people who like to eat them. And some of our foods, when alive, also travel widely. For example, the bluefin tuna (which can weigh more than a thousand pounds) swims thousands of miles from feeding to breeding grounds in the North Atlantic, Mediterranean, and Caribbean. This largest of all existing fishes is being hunted into extinction because its meat is so prized for what the Japanese call *sushi*, a kind of food that has spread from Japan throughout the world.

Sources: Michelle Diament, "Diversifying Their Crops: Agriculture Schools, Focusing on Job Prospects, Reach Out to Potential Students from Cities and Suburbs," *The Chronicle of Higher Education,* May 6, 2005, pp. A32–34; Andrew C. Revkin, "Tracking the Imperiled Bluefin from Ocean to Sushi Platter," *The New York Times,* May 3, 2005, pp. F1, F4.

in chemical fertilizers and pesticides, not to mention the additional labor required.[34] And enormous amounts of water may be required to make agriculturalists out of foragers and pastoralists who now exploit semiarid environments. However, difficulty is not impossibility. Anna Roosevelt points out that although horticulture was a common food-getting strategy in Amazonia in recent times, archaeological evidence indicates that there were complex societies practicing intensive agriculture on raised, drained fields in the past.[35] The physical environment does not completely control what can be done with it.

Allocation of Resources

Natural Resources: Land

Every society has access to natural resources—land, water, plants, animals, minerals—and every society has cultural rules for determining who has access to particular resources and what can be done with them. In societies like the United States, where land and many other things may be bought and sold, land is divided into precisely measurable units, the borders of which may be visible or invisible. Relatively small plots of land and the resources on them are usually owned by individuals. Large plots of land are generally owned collectively. The owner may be a government agency, such as the National Park Service, which owns land on behalf of the entire population of the United States. Or the owner may be a corporation—a private collective of shareholders. In the United States, property ownership entails a more or less exclusive right to use land or other resources (called *usufruct*) in whatever ways the owner wishes, including the right to withhold or prevent use by others. In the United States and many other societies, property ownership also includes the right to "alienate" property—that is, to sell, give away, bequeath, or destroy the resources owned. This type of property ownership is often referred to as a *private property* system.

Private property in regard to land is uncommon among most food collectors and most horticulturalists. There is no individual ownership of land or ownership by a group of unrelated people. If there is collective ownership, it is always by groups of related people (kinship groups) or by territorial groups (bands or villages). Land is not bought and sold.

Society specifies what is considered property and the rights and duties associated with that property.[36] These specifications are social in nature, for they may be changed over time. For example, France declared all its beaches to be public, thereby stating, in effect, that the ocean shore is not a resource that can be owned by an individual. As a result, all the hotels and individuals that had fenced off portions of the best beaches for their exclusive use had to remove the barriers. Even in countries with private property, such as the United States, people cannot do anything that they want with their property. Federal, state, and local governments have adopted legislation to prevent the pollution of the air and the water supply. Such regulation may be new, but the rights of ownership in the United States have been limited for some time. For example, land may be taken by the government for use in the construction of a highway; compensation is paid, but the individual cannot prevent confiscation. Similarly, people are not allowed to burn their houses or to use them as brothels or munitions arsenals. In short, even with an individualistic system of ownership, property is not entirely private.

How societies differ in their rules for access to land and other natural resources seems to be related in part to how they differ in food-getting. Let us now examine how food collectors, horticulturalists, pastoralists, and intensive agriculturalists structure rights to land in different ways. We look at traditional patterns first. As we shall see later, traditional rights to land have been considerably affected by state societies that have spread to and colonized native societies in the New World, Africa, and Asia.

Food Collectors   As we have noted, members of food-collecting societies generally do not have private ownership of land. The reason is probably that land itself has no intrinsic value for food collectors; what is of value is the presence of game and wild plant life on the land. If game moves away or food resources become less plentiful, the land is less valuable. Therefore, the greater the possibility that the wild food supply in a particular locale will fluctuate, the less desirable it is to parcel out small areas of land to individuals and the more advantageous it is to make land ownership communal. The Hadza of Tanzania, for example, do not believe that they have exclusive rights over the land on which they hunt. Any member of the group can hunt, gather, or draw water wherever he or she likes.[37] This is not to say that private ownership of land does not exist among foragers. Among foragers heavily dependent on fishing in rivers, individual or family ownership is more common,[38] perhaps because the fishing in rivers is more predictable than other kinds of foraging. It is more common in food-collecting societies for a group of individuals, usually kin, to "own" land. To be sure, such ownership is not usually exclusive; typically some degree of access is provided to members of neighboring bands.[39]

Horticulturalists   Like food collectors, most horticulturalists do not have individual or family ownership of land. This may be because rapid depletion of the soil necessitates letting some of the land lie fallow for a period of years or abandoning an area after a few years and moving to a new location. There is no reason for individuals or families to claim permanent access to land that, given available technology, is not usable permanently. But, in contrast to food collectors, horticulturalists are more likely to allocate particular plots of land to individuals or families for their use, although these individuals or families do not commonly own the land in our sense of potentially permanent ownership. For example, among the Mundurucu of Brazil, the village controls the rights to use land. People in the community can hunt and fish where they like, and they have the right to clear a garden plot wherever land belonging to the community is not being used. Gardens can be cultivated for only two years before the soil is exhausted; then the land reverts to the community. The Mundurucu distinguish between the land and the produce on the land, so that a person who cultivates the land owns the produce. Similarly, the person who kills an animal or catches a fish owns it, no matter where it was obtained. But because all food is shared with others, it does not really matter who owns it. Rights to land became more individualized when Mundurucu men began to tap rubber trees for sale. Rights to a particular path in the forest where trees were tapped could not be bought and sold, but the rights could be inherited by a son or son-in-law.[40]

Shown here is a Surui village in the Amazon with cleared land for horticulture in the foreground and the surrounding rainforest in the background.

Pastoralists   The territory of pastoral nomads usually far exceeds that of most horticultural societies. Since their wealth ultimately depends on mobile herds, uncultivated pasture for grazing, and water for drinking, pastoralists often combine the adaptive potential of both food collectors and horticulturalists. Like food collectors, they generally need to know the potential of a large area of land. The Basseri of Iran moved over an area of 15,000 square miles to obtain supplies of grass and water. And, like horticulturalists, pastoralists must move on when a resource is exhausted (in this case, until grass renews itself). Also like horticulturalists, they depend for subsistence on human manipulation of a natural resource—animals—as opposed to the horticulturalists' land.

Because land is only good if there is sufficient pasture and water, there would be considerable risk to individuals or families to own land that did not predictably have grass and water. So, like most foragers and horticulturalists, community members generally have free access to pasture land.[41] Although grazing land tends to be communally held, it is customary among pastoralists for animals to be owned by individuals.[42]

As among hunter-gatherers, pastoralists vary in how much a group actually has ownership rights to the territories through which they move their animals. The Basseri have rights to pass through certain areas, including agricultural areas and even cities, but they do not own the entire territory. The Baluch, another pastoralist group in the border region between Iran, Pakistan, and Afghanistan, claim a "tribal" territory, which they defend by force, if necessary.[43]

Intensive Agriculturalists   Individual ownership of land resources—including the right to use the resources and the right to sell or otherwise dispose of them—is common among intensive agriculturalists. The development of such ownership is partly a result of the possibility of using land season after season, which gives the land more or less permanent value. But the concept of individual ownership is also partly a political and social matter. So, for example, the occupation and cultivation of frontier land in the United States was transformed by law into individual ownership. Under the Homestead Act of 1862, if a person cleared a 160-acre piece of land and farmed it for five years, the federal government would consider that person the owner of the land. This practice is similar to the custom in some societies by which a kin group, a chief, or a community is obligated to assign a parcel of land to anyone who wishes to farm it. The difference is that once the American homesteader had become the owner of the land, the laws of the country gave the homesteader the right to dispose of it at will by selling or giving it away. Once individual ownership of land has become established, property owners may use their economic, and hence political, power to pass laws that favor themselves. In the early years of the United States, only property owners could vote.

Colonialism and Land Rights   Almost universally around the world, colonial conquerors and settlers have taken land away from the natives or aborigines. Even if the natives were given other land in exchange, as in Brazil and the United States, these reservations were often, if not always, poorer in potential than the original land. (If the reservation land hadn't been poorer in quality, the settlers would have taken it for themselves.) In addition, the new centralized governments often tried to change how land was owned by the natives, almost always in the direction of individual or private ownership. If kin groups or larger social entities owned the land, it would be more difficult for the settlers to get the natives to give it up, either by sale or threat. Individual owners could be dispossessed more easily.[44]

This is not to say that native peoples in Africa, Asia, and the New World were never guilty of conquering and exploiting others on their continents or elsewhere. They were. The Aztecs in Mexico and Central America, the native kingdoms in West Africa after about 800 years ago, and the Arabs after the rise of Islam were just some of the expanding state societies of the past, before the rise of the West. Wherever there have been "civilized" (urban) societies, there have been imperialism and colonialism.

Colonial governments have often taken land away from native peoples to establish enterprises such as plantations. Even after independence such lands remain as private enterprises. Here, a Nepali girl harvests tea on a tea plantation.

The taking of land by state authorities does not just happen with colonialism and imperialism. Indigenous revolutionary movements have collectivized land after 1918, as in Russia, or broken up large private landholdings, as in Mexico over the years. Typically, state authorities do not like communal land-use systems. Mobile pastoralists in particular are viewed unfavorably by state authorities, because their mobility makes them difficult to control. Governments usually try to settle pastoralists or break up communally held pasture into small units.[45]

Conversion of Resources

In all societies, resources have to be transformed or converted through labor into food, tools, and other goods. These activities constitute what economists call *production*. In this section, after briefly reviewing different types of production, we examine how societies divide up the work to be done.

Types of Economic Production

At the times they were first described, most of the societies known to anthropology had a *domestic*—family or kinship—mode of production. People labored to get food and to produce shelter and implements for themselves and their kin. Usually families had the right to exploit productive resources and control the products of their labor. Even part-time specialists, such as potters, could still support themselves without that craft if they needed to. At the other extreme are *industrial* societies, where much of the work is based on mechanized production, as in factories but also in mechanized agriculture. Because machines and materials are costly, only some individuals (capitalists), corporations, or governments can afford the expenses of production. Therefore, most people in industrial societies labor for others as wage earners. Although wages can buy food, people out of work lose their ability to support themselves, unless they are protected by welfare payments or unemployment insurance. Then there is the *tributary* type

In postindustrial economies, computers and robots rather than people do much of the work in factories. There are few people in this Bavarian brewery.

of production system, found in nonindustrial societies in which most people still produce their own food but an elite or aristocracy controls a portion of production (including the products of specialized crafts). The feudal societies of medieval western Europe were examples of tributary production, as was czarist Russia under serfdom.[46]

Many people have suggested that our own and other developed economies are now moving from *industrialism* to *postindustrialism*. In many areas of commerce, computers have radically transformed the workplace. Computers "drive" machines and robots, and much of the manual work required in industry is disappearing. Businesses are now more knowledge-and service-oriented. Information is more accessible with telecommunication, so much so that *telecommuting* has entered our vocabulary to describe how people can now work (for wages) at home. This economic transformation has important implications for both home life and the workplace. With inexpensive home computers and speedy data transmission by telephone and other means, more and more people are able to work at home. In addition, when information and knowledge become more important than capital equipment, more and more people can own and have access to the productive resources of society.[47]

Forced and Required Labor

Thus far we have mostly discussed *voluntary labor*—voluntary in the sense that no formal organization within the society compels people to work and punishes them for not working. Social training and social pressure are powerful enough to persuade an individual to perform some useful task. In both food-collecting and horticultural societies, individuals who can stand being the butt of jokes about laziness will still be fed. At most, they will be ignored by the other members of the group. There is no reason to punish them and no way to coerce them to do the work expected of them.

More complex societies have ways of forcing people to work for the authorities, whether those authorities are kings or presidents. An indirect form of forced labor is taxation. The average tax in the United States (local, state, and federal) is about 33 percent of income, which means that the average person works four months out of the year for the various levels of government. If a person decides not to pay the tax, the money will be taken forcibly or the person may be put in prison.

Money is the customary form of tax payment in a commercial society. In a politically complex but non-monetary society, persons may pay their taxes in other ways—by performing a certain number of hours

The Great Wall of China, like many monumental works in ancient societies, was built with forced labor.

of labor or by giving up a certain percentage of what they produce. The **corvée**, a system of required labor, existed in the Inca Empire in the central Andes before the Spanish conquest. Each male commoner was assigned three plots of land to work: a temple plot, a state plot, and his own plot. The enormous stores of food that went into state warehouses were used to supply the nobles, the army, the artisans, and all other state employees. In addition to subsistence work for the state, Inca commoners were subject to military service, to duty as personal servants for the nobility, and to other "public" service.[48]

The draft, or compulsory military service, is also a form of corvée, in that a certain period of service is required, and failure to serve can be punished by a prison term or involuntary exile. Emperors of China had soldiers drafted to defend their territory and to build the Great Wall along the northern borders of the empire. The wall extends over 1,500 miles, and thousands were drafted to work on it. Slavery is the most extreme form of forced work, in that slaves have little control over their labor. Because slaves constitute a category or class of persons in many societies, we discuss slavery more fully in the chapter on social stratification.

Division of Labor

All societies have some division of labor, some customary assignment of different kinds of work to different kinds of people. Universally, males and females and adults and children do not do the same kinds of work. In a sense, then, division of labor by gender and age is a kind of universal specialization of labor. Many societies known to anthropology divide labor only by gender and age; other societies have more complex specialization.

By Gender and Age   All societies make use of gender differences to some extent in their customary assignment of labor. In the chapter on sex and gender, we discuss the division of labor by gender in detail.

Age is also a universal basis for division of labor. Clearly, children cannot do work that requires a great deal of strength. But in many societies girls and boys contribute much more in labor than do children in our own society. For example, they help in animal tending, weeding, and harvesting and do a variety of domestic chores such as child care, fetching water and firewood, and cooking and cleaning. In agricultural communities in the Ivory Coast, children's tasks mirror the tasks of same-sex adults (see Figure 11.1). In some societies, a child who is six years old is considered old enough to be responsible for a younger sibling for a good part of the day.[49] Animal tending is often important work for children. Children in some societies spend more time at this task than adults.[50]

Beyond Gender and Age   In societies with relatively simple technologies, there is little specialization of labor beyond that of gender and age. But as a society's technology becomes more complex and it is able to produce large quantities of food, more of its people are freed from subsistence work to become specialists in some other tasks—canoe builders, weavers, priests, potters, artists, and the like.

In contrast with food collectors, horticultural societies may have some part-time specialists. Some people may devote special effort to perfecting a particular skill or craft—pottery making, weaving, house building, doctoring—and in return for their products or services be given food or other gifts. Among some horticultural groups, the entire village may specialize part time in making a particular product, which can then be traded to neighboring people. With the development of intensive agriculture, full-time specialists—potters, weavers, blacksmiths—begin to appear.

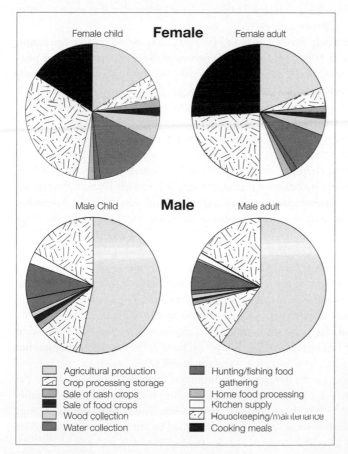

Figure 11.1   A Comparison of the Proportion of Work Tasks Done by Adults and Children

Source: From James A. Levine, Robert Weisell, Simon Chevassus, Claudio D. Martinez, and Barbara Burlingame, "The Distribution of Work Tasks for Male and Female Children and Adults Separated by Gender," in "Looking at Child Labor," *Science, 296* (May 10, 2002): 1025.

Distribution of Goods and Services

Goods and services are distributed in all societies by systems that can be classified under three general types: reciprocity, redistribution, and market or commercial exchange.[51] The three systems often coexist in a society, but one system usually predominates. The predominant system seems to be associated with the society's food-getting technology and, more specifically, its level of economic development.

Reciprocity

Reciprocity consists of giving and taking without the use of money; it mainly takes the form of gift giving or generalized reciprocity. There may also be exchanges of equal value (trade) or balanced reciprocity, without the use of money.[52]

Generalized Reciprocity   When goods or services are given to another, without any apparent expectation of a return gift, we call it **generalized reciprocity**. Generalized reciprocity sustains the family in all societies. Parents give food, clothing, and labor to children because they want to or perhaps feel obliged to, but they do not usually calculate exactly how their children will reciprocate years later. These gifts are one-way transfers. In this sense, all societies have some kind of generalized reciprocity. But some societies depend on it almost entirely to distribute goods and services.

Lorna Marshall recounted how the !Kung divided an eland brought to a site where five bands and several visitors were camping—more than 100 people in all. The owner of the arrow that had first penetrated the eland was, by custom, the owner of the meat. He first distributed the forequarters to the two hunters who had aided him in the kill. After that, the distribution depended on kinship: Each hunter shared with his wives' parents, wives, children, parents, and siblings, and they in turn shared with their kin. Sixty-three gifts of raw meat were recorded, after which further sharing of raw and cooked meat was begun. The !Kung distribution of large game—clearly, generalized reciprocity—is common among foragers.[53]

Parent-child giving may seem easy to understand, but giving beyond the family is more of a problem. Why do some societies rely more on generalized reciprocity than others, particularly beyond the family? Sharing may be most likely when people are not sure they can get the food and water they need. In other words, sharing may be most likely if resources are unpredictable. So a !Kung band may share its water with other bands because they may have water now but not in the future. A related group in the Kalahari, the G//ana,[54] has been observed to share less than other groups. It turns out that the resources available to the G//ana are more predictable, because the G//ana supplement their hunting and gathering with plant cultivation and goat herding. Cultivated melons (which store water) appear to buffer the G//ana against water shortages, and herded goats buffer them against shortages of game. Thus, whereas the !Kung distribute the meat right after a kill, the G//ana dry it and then store it in their houses.[55]

Does food sharing increase the food supply for an individual? Calculations for the Aché of eastern Paraguay, who get most of their food from hunting when they go on food-collecting trips, suggest that the average individual gets more food when food is shared. Even the males who actually do the hunting get more, although the benefits are greater for the females and children on the trip.[56] Mathematically, the risk that an individual food collector will not find enough food on a particular day will be appreciably reduced if at least six to eight adult collectors share the food they collect. Food-collecting bands may often contain only 25 to 30 people, which is about the size that is needed to ensure that there are six to eight adult collectors.[57]

Sharing can occur even in a socially stratified society. Here we see men in a village in Yunnan, China, cutting the meat from a steer into 72 portions for the families of the village.

What happens to a system of generalized reciprocity when resources are very scarce because of a drought or other disaster? Does the ethic of giving break down? Evidence from a few societies suggests that the degree of sharing may actually *increase* during the period of food shortage.[58] For example, in describing the Netsilik Inuit, Asen Balikci said, "Whenever game was abundant, sharing among non-relatives was avoided, since every family was supposedly capable of obtaining the necessary catch. In situations of scarcity, however, caribou meat was more evenly distributed throughout camp."[59] Sharing may increase during mild scarcity because people can minimize their deprivation, but generalized reciprocity may be strained by extreme scarcity. Ethnographic evidence from a few societies suggests that during famine, when individuals are actually dying from hunger, sharing may be limited to the household.[60]

Researchers generally have difficulty explaining sharing because they assume that, other things being equal, individuals would tend to be selfish. Most of the ideas about sharing have postulated that sharing is, in fact, advantageous to individuals in certain circumstances. And it is in those circumstances that societies have found ways to make sharing a moral issue or to otherwise make nonsharers extremely uncomfortable. But experimental evidence suggests that sharing is likely even with people who do not know each other or who have no expectation of any return in the future from that person. Experimenters have set up "games" in which they can control for or eliminate certain responses. For example, in one game a particular player is given a certain amount of money and he or she decides how much of the money to offer to the second player in the game. The second player can accept or reject the offer. If the division is rejected, no one gets any money. If the division is accepted, both players receive the proposed division. If selfishness were normal, one would expect that the proposer of the division would try to give away as little as possible and the second player should always accept whatever is offered because otherwise nothing is gained. Surprisingly, equal divisions are commonly proposed and low offers are commonly rejected because they are viewed as unfair. If a person views the offer as unfair and forfeits any money, he or she seems willing to "punish" the greedy individual. While such experiments were mostly done at first in Western societies, we now have results from over 15 other societies that largely confirm the earlier results.[61] And there is now evidence suggesting that cooperation may even evoke pleasure. Researchers studying brain activity in women, who are playing a game allowing either cooperative or greedy strategies, found to their surprise that cooperation made certain areas of the brain light up. These areas are normally associated with pleasure, such as when eating desserts. So cooperation may be more "natural" than some people think.[62]

Balanced Reciprocity　**Balanced reciprocity** is explicit and short term in its expectations of return. In contrast to generalized reciprocity or a one-way transfer, which has no expectation of a return, balanced reciprocity involves either an immediate exchange of goods or services or an agreed-upon exchange over a limited period of time. In the 1600s, the Iroquois of the North American Northeast traded deerskin to Europeans for brass kettles, iron hinges, steel axes, woven textiles, and guns.[63] The Iroquois acquired trade goods by balanced reciprocity, but such exchanges were not crucial to their economies.

Sometimes the line between generalized and balanced reciprocity is not so clear. Consider our gift giving at Christmas. Although such gift giving may appear to be generalized reciprocity, there may be strong expectations of balance. Two friends or relatives may try to exchange presents of fairly equal value, based on calculations of what last year's gift cost. If a person receives a $5 present when he or she gave a $25 present, that person will be hurt and perhaps angry. On the other hand, a person who receives a $500 present when he or she gave a $25 present may well be dismayed.

Redistribution

Redistribution is the accumulation of goods or labor by a particular person, or in a particular place, for the purpose of subsequent distribution. Although redistribution is found in all societies, it becomes an important mechanism only in societies that have political hierarchies—that is, chiefs or other specialized officials and agencies. In all societies, there is some redistribution, at least within the family. Members of the family pool their labor, products, or income for the common good. But in many societies, there is little or no redistribution beyond the family. It seems that redistribution on a territorial basis emerges when there is a political apparatus to coordinate centralized collection and distribution of goods or to mobilize labor for some public purpose.

Why do redistribution systems develop? Elman Service suggested that they develop in agricultural societies that contain subregions suited to different kinds of crops or natural resources. Food collectors can take advantage of environmental variation by moving to different areas. With agriculture, the task is more difficult; it might be easier to move different products across different regions.[64] If the demand for different resources or products becomes too great, reciprocity between individuals might become awkward. So it might be more efficient to have someone—a chief, perhaps—coordinate the exchanges.

Marvin Harris agreed that redistribution becomes more likely with agriculture, but for a somewhat different reason. He argued that competitive feasting, as in New Guinea, is adaptive because it encourages people to work harder to produce somewhat more than they need. Why would this feature be adaptive? Harris argued that with agriculture, people really have to produce more than they need so that they can protect themselves against crises such as crop failure. The groups that make feasts may be indirectly ensuring themselves against crises by storing up social credit with other villages, who will reciprocate by making feasts for them in the future. On the other hand, inducements to collect more than they need may not be advantageous to food-collecting groups, who might lose in the long run by overcollecting.[65]

Market or Commercial Exchange

When we think of markets we usually think of bustling, colorful places where goods are bought and sold. The exchanges usually involve money. In our own society we have supermarkets and the stock market and other places for buying and selling that we call shops, stores, and malls. In referring to

market or **commercial exchange**, economists and economic anthropologists are referring to exchanges or transactions in which the "prices" are subject to supply and demand, whether or not the transactions actually occur in a marketplace.[66] Market exchange involves not only the exchange (buying and selling) of goods but also transactions of labor, land, rentals, and credit.

Kinds of Money   Although market exchange need not involve money, most commercial transactions, particularly nowadays, do involve what we call money. Some anthropologists define money according to the functions and characteristics of the **general-purpose money** used in our own and other complex societies, for which nearly all goods, resources, and services can be exchanged. According to this definition, money performs the basic functions of serving as an accepted medium of exchange, a standard of value, and a store of wealth. As a medium of exchange, it allows all goods and services to be valued in the same objective way; we say that an object or service is worth so much money. Also, money is nonperishable, and therefore savable or storable, and almost always transportable and divisible, so transactions can involve the buying and selling of goods and services that differ in value. Money has little or no intrinsic value; rather, it is society that determines its value. In the United States today, paper bills, bank checks, and credit and debit cards are fully accepted as money, and money is increasingly transferred electronically.

Degrees of Commercialization   Most societies were not commercialized at all, or only barely so, when first described in the ethnographic record by explorers, missionaries, and anthropologists. That is, most societies as first described did not rely on market or commercial exchange to distribute goods and services. But commercial exchange has become the dominant form of distribution in the modern world. Most societies of the ethnographic past are now incorporated into larger nation-states. Selling today goes far beyond the nation-state. The world is now a multinational market.[67]

But there is considerable variation in the degree to which societies today depend on market or commercial exchange. Many societies still allocate land without purchase and distribute food and other goods primarily by reciprocity and redistribution, participating only peripherally in market exchange. These are societies in transition; their traditional subsistence economies are becoming commercialized. In the chapter on culture change and globalization, we discuss some of the implications and effects of this transition to a more commercialized economy—a transition that is a worldwide phenomenon.

What anthropologists call *peasant economies* are somewhat more commercialized than transitional subsistence economies. Although **peasants** also produce food largely for their own consumption, they regularly sell part of their surplus (food, other goods, or labor) to others, and land is one of the commodities they buy, rent, and sell. But, although their production is somewhat commercialized, peasants still are not like the fully commercialized farmers in industrialized societies, who rely on the market to exchange all or almost all of their crops for all or almost all of the goods and services they need.

In fully commercialized societies such as our own, market or commercial exchange dominates the economy; prices and wages are regulated, or at least significantly affected, by the forces of supply and demand. A modern industrial or postindustrial economy may involve international as well as national markets in which everything has a price, stated in the same money terms—natural resources, labor, goods, services, prestige items, religious and ceremonial items. Reciprocity is reserved for family members and friends or remains behind the scenes in business transactions. Redistribution, however, is an important mechanism. It is practiced in the form of taxation and the use of public revenue for transfer payments and other benefits to low-income families—welfare, Social Security, health care, and so on. But commercial exchange is the major way goods and services are distributed.

Summary

1. All societies have economic systems, whether or not these involve the use of money. All societies have customs specifying who has access to natural resources; customary ways of transforming or converting those resources, through labor, into necessities and other desired goods and services; and customs for distributing and perhaps exchanging goods and services.

2. Food collection or foraging—hunting, gathering, and fishing—depends on wild plants and animals and is the oldest human food-getting technology. Today, only a small number of societies depend largely on food collection and they tend to inhabit marginal environments.

3. Food collectors tend to have low population density, small bands, limited personal possessions, little recognition of individuals' land rights, division of labor along age and gender lines only, and no class differences.

4. Beginning about 10,000 years ago, certain peoples in widely separated geographic locations began to make the revolutionary changeover to food production—the cultivation and raising of plants and animals.

5. Horticulturalists farm with relatively simple tools and methods and do not cultivate fields permanently. They have more densely populated communities than food collectors. Their way of life is sedentary, although communities may move after some years to farm a new series of plots.

6. Intensive agriculture is characterized by techniques such as fertilization and irrigation that allow fields to be cultivated permanently. In contrast with horticultural societies, intensive agriculturalists are more likely to have towns and cities, a high degree of craft specialization, large differences in wealth and power, and more complex political organization. They are also more likely to face food shortages. In the modern world, intensive agriculture is increasingly mechanized and geared to production for a market.

7. Pastoralism is a subsistence technology involving principally the raising of large herds of animals. It is generally found in low-rainfall areas. Pastoralists tend to be nomadic, to have small communities consisting of related families, and to depend significantly on trade because they do not produce items (including certain types of food) they need.

8. We see the first evidence of a changeover to food production in the Near East about 8000 B.C. Most archaeologists think that certain conditions must have pushed people to switch from collecting to producing food. Some possible reasons are: (1) population growth in regions of bountiful wild resources; (2) global population growth; and (3) the emergence of hotter and drier summers and colder winters.

9. Individual or private ownership of land—including the right to use its resources and the right to sell or otherwise dispose of them—is common among intensive agriculturalists and is generally lacking amongst food collectors, horticulturalists, and pastoralists.

10. Division of labor by gender is universal.

11. Goods and services are distributed in all societies by systems that can be classified under three types: reciprocity, redistribution, and market or commercial exchange.

12. Redistribution becomes an important mechanism of distribution only in societies with political hierarchies.

13. Market or commercial exchange usually involves an all-purpose medium of exchange—money. Most societies today are at least partly commercialized; the world is becoming a single market system.

Glossary Terms

balanced reciprocity (p. 280)

commercialization (p. 266)

corvée (p. 276)

extensive or shifting cultivation (p. 262)

food collection (p. 259)

food production (p. 262)

foragers (p. 259)

generalized reciprocity (p. 278)

general-purpose money (p. 281)

horticulture (p. 262)

hunter-gatherers (p. 259)

intensive agriculture (p. 264)

market or commercial exchange (p. 281)

pastoralism (p. 266)

peasants (p. 281)

reciprocity (p. 278)

redistribution (p. 280)

slash-and-burn (p. 263)

Critical Questions

1.   Why might meat be valued more than plant foods in many societies?

2.   Why might foragers be less likely than intensive agriculturalists to suffer from food shortages?

3.   What are the possible effects of a postindustrial economy in which a large proportion of the population has inexpensive access to computers and information?

4.   Do you expect any appreciable change in the future in the degree to which resources are privately owned? State your reasons.

CHAPTER 12

SOCIAL STRATIFICATION:
CLASS, ETHNICITY, AND RACISM

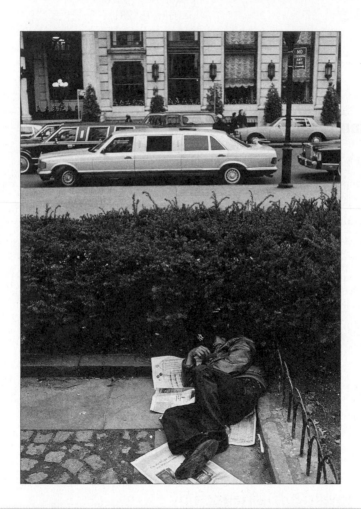

Chapter Outline

A long-enduring value in the United States is the belief that "all men are created equal." These famous words from the American Declaration of Independence do not mean that all people are equal in wealth or status but rather that all (including women nowadays) are supposed to be equal before the law. Equality before the law is the ideal. But the ideal is not always the actuality. Some people have advantages in legal treatment, and they generally also tend to have advantages of other kinds, including economic advantages. Without exception, recent and modern industrial and postindustrial societies such as our own are *socially stratified*—that is, they contain social groups such as families, classes, or ethnic groups that have unequal access to important advantages such as economic resources, power, and prestige.

Hasn't such inequality always existed? Anthropologists, based on firsthand observations of recent societies, would say not. To be sure, even the simplest societies (in the technological sense) have some differences in advantages based on age, ability, or gender—adults have higher status than children, the skilled more than the unskilled, men more than women (we discuss gender stratification in the next chapter). But anthropologists would argue that *egalitarian* societies exist where *social groups* (e.g., families) have more or less the same access to rights or advantages. As we noted in the previous chapter, the economic systems of many food collectors and horticulturalists promote equal access to economic resources for all families in the community. Moreover, such societies also tend to emphasize the sharing of food and other goods, which tends to equalize any small inequalities in resources between families.

Until about 10,000 years ago, all human societies depended on food they hunted, gathered, and/or fished. And so we might expect that egalitarianism characterized most of human history. That is indeed what archaeology suggests. Substantial inequality generally appears only with permanent communities, centralized political systems, and intensive agriculture, which are cultural features that began to appear in the world only in the last 10,000 years. Before that time, then, most societies were probably egalitarian. In the world today, egalitarian societies have all but disappeared because of two processes—the global spread of commercial or market exchange and the voluntary or involuntary incorporation of many diverse people into large, centralized political systems. In modern societies, some groups have more advantages than others. These groups may include *ethnic* groups. That is, ethnic diversity is almost always associated with differential access to advantages. When ethnic diversity is also associated with differences in physical features such as skin color, the social stratification may involve *racism,* the belief that some "racial" groups are inferior.

Systems of social stratification are strongly linked to the customary ways in which economic resources are allocated, distributed, and converted through labor into goods and services. So we would not expect much inequality if all people had relatively equal access to economic resources. But stratification cannot be understood solely in terms of economic resources; there are other benefits such as prestige and power that may be unequally distributed. We first examine how societies vary in their systems of stratification. Then we turn to possible explanations of why they vary.

Variation in Degree of Social Inequality

Societies vary in the extent to which social groups, as well as individuals, have unequal access to advantages. In this chapter we are concerned with differential or unequal access to three types of advantages: (1) wealth or economic resources, (2) power, and (3) prestige. **Economic resources** are things that have value in a culture; they include land, tools and other technology, goods, and money. **Power**, a second but related advantage, is the ability to make others do what they do not want to do; power is influence based on the threat of force. When groups in a society have rules or customs that give them unequal access to wealth or resources, they generally also have unequal access to power. So, for example, when we speak of a "company town" in the United States, we are referring to the fact that the company that employs most of the residents of the town usually has considerable control over them. Finally, there is the advantage of **prestige**. When we speak of prestige, we mean that someone or some group is accorded particular respect or honor. Even if it is true that there is always unequal individual access to prestige (because of differences in age, gender, or ability), there are some societies in the ethnographic record that have no social groups with unequal access to prestige.

Thus, anthropologists conventionally distinguish three types of society in terms of the degree to which different social groups have unequal access to advantages: *egalitarian, rank,* and *class societies* (see Table 12.1). Some societies in the ethnographic record do not fit easily into any of these three types; as with any classification scheme, some cases seem to straddle the line between types.[1] **Egalitarian societies** contain no social groups with greater or lesser access to economic resources, power, or prestige. **Rank societies** do not have very unequal access to economic resources or to power, but they do contain social groups with unequal access to prestige. Rank societies, then, are partly stratified. **Class societies** have unequal access to all three advantages—economic resources, power, and prestige.

Egalitarian Societies

Egalitarian societies can be found not only among foragers such as the !Kung, Mbuti, Australian aborigines, Inuit, and Aché, but also among horticulturalists such as the Yanomamö and pastoralists such as the Lapps or Saami. An important point to keep in mind is that egalitarian does not mean that all people within such societies are the same. There will always be differences among individuals in age and gender and in such abilities or traits as hunting skill, perception, health, creativity, physical prowess, attractiveness, and intelligence. According to Morton Fried, egalitarian means that within a given society "there are as many positions of prestige in any given age/sex grade as there are persons capable of filling them."[2] For instance, if a person can achieve high status by fashioning fine spears, and if many persons in the society fashion such spears, then many acquire high status as spear makers. If high status is also acquired by carving bones into artifacts, and if only three people are considered expert carvers of bones, then only

Table 12.1	Stratification in Three Types of Societies			
	Some Social Groups Have Greater Access to:			
Type of Society	**Economic Resources**	**Power**	**Prestige**	**Examples**
Egalitarian	No	No	No	!Kung, Mbuti, Australian aborigines, Inuit, Aché, Yanomamö
Rank	No	No	Yes	Samoans, Tahiti, Trobriand Islands, Ifaluk
Class/caste	Yes	Yes	Yes	United States, Canada, Greece, India, Inca

In egalitarian societies, such as among the Mbuti hunter-gatherers, houses tend to look the same.

those three achieve high status as carvers. But the next generation might produce 8 spear makers and 20 carvers. In an egalitarian society, the number of prestigious positions is adjusted to fit the number of qualified candidates. We would say, therefore, that such a society is not socially stratified.

There are, of course, differences in position and prestige arising out of differences in ability. Even in an egalitarian society, differential prestige exists. But, although some persons may be better hunters or more skilled artists than others, there is still *equal access* to status positions for people of the same ability. Any prestige gained by achieving high status as a great hunter, for instance, is neither transferable nor inheritable. Because a man is a great hunter, it is not assumed that his sons are also great hunters. There also may be individuals with more influence, but it cannot be inherited, and there are no groups in the society with appreciably more influence over time. An egalitarian society keeps inequality at a minimal level.

Any differences in prestige that do exist are not related to economic differences. Egalitarian groups depend heavily on *sharing*, which ensures equal access to economic resources despite differences in acquired prestige. For instance, in some egalitarian communities, some members achieve higher status through hunting. But even before the hunt begins, how the animal will be divided and distributed among the members of the band has already been decided according to custom. The culture works to separate the status achieved by members—recognition as great hunters—from actual possession of the wealth, which in this case would be the slain animal.

Just as egalitarian societies do not have social groups with unequal access to economic resources, they also do not have social groups with unequal access to power. As we will see later in the chapter on political life, unequal access to power by social groups seems to occur only in state societies, which have full-time political officials and marked differences in wealth. Egalitarian societies use a number of customs to keep leaders from dominating others. Criticism and ridicule can be very effective. The Mbuti of central Africa shout down an overassertive leader. When a Hadza man (in Tanzania) tried to get people to work for him, other Hadza made fun of him. Disobedience is another strategy. If a leader tries to command, people just ignore the command. In extreme cases, a particularly domineering leader may be killed by community agreement; this behavior was reported among the !Kung and the Hadza. Finally, particularly among more nomadic groups, people may just move away from a leader they don't like. The active attempts to put down upstarts in many egalitarian societies prompts Christopher Boehm to suggest that dominance comes naturally to humans. Egalitarian societies work hard to reverse that tendency.[3] The Mbuti provide an example of a society almost totally equal: "Neither in ritual, hunting, kinship nor band relations do they exhibit any discernible inequalities of rank or advantage."[4] Their hunting bands have no leaders, and recognition of the achievement of one person is not accompanied by privilege of any sort. Economic resources such as food are communally shared, and even tools and weapons are frequently passed from person to person. Only within the family are rights and privileges differentiated.

Rank Societies

Most societies with social *ranking* practice agriculture or herding, but not all agricultural or pastoral societies are ranked. Ranking is characterized by social groups with unequal access to prestige or status but *not* significantly unequal access to economic resources or power. Unequal access to prestige is often reflected in the position of chief, a rank to which only some members of a specified group in the society can succeed.

Unusual among rank societies were the nineteenth-century Native Americans who lived along the northwestern coast of the United States and the southwestern coast of Canada. An example were the Nimpkish, a Kwakiutl group.[5] These societies were unusual because their economy was based on food collecting. But huge catches of salmon—which were preserved for year-round consumption—enabled them to support fairly large and permanent villages. These societies were similar to food-producing societies in many ways, not just in their development of social ranking. Still, the principal means of proving one's high status was to give wealth away. The tribal chiefs celebrated solemn rites by grand feasts called *potlatches* at which they gave gifts to every guest.[6]

In rank societies, the position of chief is at least partly hereditary. The criterion of superior rank in some Polynesian societies, for example, was genealogical. Usually the eldest son succeeded to the position of chief, and different kinship groups were differentially ranked according to their genealogical distance from the chiefly line. In rank societies, chiefs are often treated with deference by people of lower rank. For example, among the Trobriand Islanders of Melanesia, people of lower rank must keep their heads lower than a person of higher rank. So, when a chief is standing, commoners must bend low. When commoners have to walk past a chief who happens to be sitting, he may rise and they will bend. If the chief chooses to remain seated, they must crawl.[7]

While there is no question that chiefs in a rank society enjoy special prestige, there is some controversy over whether they really do not also have material advantages. Chiefs may sometimes look as if they are substantially richer than commoners, for they may receive many gifts and have larger storehouses. In some instances, the chief may even be called the "owner" of the land. However, Marshall Sahlins maintains that the chief's storehouses only house temporary accumulations for feasts or other redistributions. And although the chief may be designated the "owner" of the land, others have the right to use the land. Furthermore, Sahlins suggests that the chief in a rank society lacks power because he usually cannot make people give him gifts or force them to work on communal projects. Often the chief can encourage production only by working furiously on his own cultivation.[8]

This picture of economic equality in rank societies is beginning to be questioned. Laura Betzig studied patterns of food sharing and labor on Ifaluk, a small atoll in the Western Carolines.[9] Chiefly status

In societies with rank and class, deference is usually shown to political leaders, as in the case of this Fon chief in the lowlands of Cameroon, Africa.

is inherited geneaologically in the female line, although most chiefs are male. (In the sex and gender chapter, we discuss why political leaders are usually male, even in societies structured around women.) As in other chiefly societies, Ifaluk chiefs are accorded deference. For example, during collective meals prepared by all the island women, chiefs were served first and were bowed to. The Ifaluk chiefs are said to control the fishing areas. Were the catches equitably distributed? Betzig measured the amount of fish each household got. All the commoners received an equal share, but the chiefs got extra fish; their households got twice as much per person as other households. Did the chiefs give away more later?

Theoretically, it is generosity that is supposed to even things out, but Betzig found that the gifts from chiefs to other households did not equal the amount the chiefs received from others. Furthermore, while everyone gave to the chiefs, the chiefs gave mostly to their close relatives. On Ifaluk, the chiefs did not work harder than others; in fact, they worked less. Is this true in other societies conventionally considered to be rank societies? We do not know. However, we need to keep in mind that the chiefs in Ifaluk were not noticeably better off either. If they lived in palaces with servants, had elaborate meals, or were dressed in fine clothes and jewelry, we would not need measures of food received or a special study to see if the chiefs had greater access to economic resources, because their wealth would be obvious. But rank societies may not have had as much economic equality as we used to think.

Class Societies

In class societies, as in rank societies, there is unequal access to prestige. But, unlike rank societies, class societies are characterized by groups of people that have substantially greater or lesser access to economic resources and power. That is, not every social group has the same opportunity to obtain land, animals, money, or other economic benefits or the same opportunity to exercise power that other groups have. Fully stratified or class societies range from somewhat open to virtually closed class, or caste, systems.

Open Class Systems

A **class** is a category of persons who all have about the same opportunity to obtain economic resources, power, and prestige. Different classes have differing opportunities. We call class systems *open* if there is some possibility of moving from one class to another. Although class status is not fully determined at birth in open class societies, there is a high probability that most people will stay close to the class into which they were born and will marry within that class. Classes tend to perpetuate themselves through the inheritance of wealth. John Brittain suggested that, in the United States, the transfer of money through bequests accounts for much of the wealth of the next generation. As we might expect, the importance of inheritance seems to increase at higher levels of wealth. That is, the wealth of richer people comes more from inheritance than does the wealth of not-so-rich people.[10]

Other mechanisms of class perpetuation may be more subtle, but they are still powerful. In the United States there are many institutions that make it possible for an upper-class person to have little contact with other classes. Private day and boarding schools put upper-class children in close contact mostly with others of their class. Attending these schools makes it more likely they will get into universities with higher prestige. Debutante balls and exclusive private parties ensure that young people meet the "right people." Country clubs, exclusive city clubs, and service in particular charities continue the process of limited association. People of the same class also tend to live in the same neighborhoods. Before 1948, explicit restrictions kept certain groups out of particular neighborhoods, but after the U.S. Supreme Court ruled such discrimination unconstitutional, more subtle methods were developed. For instance, zoning restrictions may prohibit multiple-family dwellings in a town or neighborhood and lots below a certain acreage.[11]

Identification with a social class begins early in life. In addition to differences in occupation, wealth, and prestige, social classes vary in many other ways, including religious affiliation, closeness to kin, ideas about child rearing, job satisfaction, leisure-time activities, style of clothes and furniture, and (as noted in the chapter on language and communication) even in styles of speech.[12] People from each class tend to be more comfortable with those from the same class; they talk similarly and are more likely to have similar interests and tastes.

People of the same social class tend to socialize together, where they live or where they vacation. Pictured here is an upscale hotel in Victoria, British Columbia.

Degree of Openness   Some class systems are more open than others; that is, it is easier in some societies to move from one class position to another. Social scientists typically compare the class of a person with the class of his or her parent or parents to measure the degree of mobility. Although most people aspire to move up, mobility also includes moving down. Obtaining more education, particularly a university education, is one of the most effective ways to move upward in contemporary societies. For example, in the United States, college-educated individuals have on average 60 percent more income than those without a college education.[13] In fact, in many countries educational attainment predicts one's social class better than parents' occupation does.[14]

How do the United States and Canada compare with other countries in degree of class mobility? Canada and Sweden have more mobility than the United States, France, and Britain. Japan and Italy have less mobility. If we focus on the ease of moving into the highest class, Italy, France, Spain, Germany, and Japan are more difficult than Britain and the United States.[15]

Class openness also varies over time. In "Paradise," Ontario, Barrett found that the rigid stratification system of the 1950s opened up considerably as new people moved into the community. No one disputed who belonged to the elite in the past. They were of British background, lived in the largest houses, had new cars, and vacationed in Florida. Moreover, they controlled all the leadership positions in the town. By the 1980s, though, the leaders came mostly from the middle and working classes.[16]

Degree of Inequality   Degree of class mobility, however, is not the same as degree of economic inequality. For example, Japan, Italy, and Germany have less mobility than the United States, but less inequality. Degree of inequality can vary considerably over time. In the United States, inequality has fluctuated considerably from the 1900s to the present. The greatest inequality was just before the 1929 stock market crash, when the top 1 percent had 42.6 percent of all the wealth. The least inequality was in the mid-1970s after the stock market declined by 42 percent. Then the top 1 percent controlled 17.6 percent of the wealth.

Change over time in the degree of inequality sometimes appears to have economic causes; for example, the 1929 crash made the wealthy less wealthy. But some of the change over time is due to shifts in public policy. During the New Deal of the 1930s, tax changes and work programs shifted more income to ordinary people; in the 1980s, tax cuts for the wealthy helped the rich get richer. In the 1990s, the rich continued to get richer and the poor got poorer.[17] One way of calculating the disparity between rich and poor is to use the ratio of income held by the top fifth of the households divided by the income held by the bottom fifth. Comparatively speaking, the United States presently has more inequality than any of the countries in western Europe, with a ratio of 9 to 1 (see Figure 12.1 on page 292). That is, the top 20 percent of U.S. households controls nine times the wealth controlled by the bottom 20 percent. Norway, on the other hand, has a ratio of about 3.5 to 1. And Germany has a ratio of about 4.5 to 1. The degree of inequality in the United States exceeds that of India, with a ratio of about 5.5 to 1. South Africa and Brazil are among the most unequal countries, with ratios of 22 to 1 and 24 to 1, respectively.

Recognition of Class

Societies that have open class systems vary in the degree to which members of the society recognize that there are classes, albeit somewhat open classes. The United States is unusual. Despite objective evidence of multiple social classes, many people in the United States deny their existence. The ideology that hard work and strong character can transform anyone into a success appears to be so powerful that it masks the realities of social inequality.[18] A recent poll found that more people in the United States now believe that the chance of moving up has improved in the last few decades when in reality mobility has declined.[19] When we were growing up we were told that "Anyone can be President of the United States." As "proof"

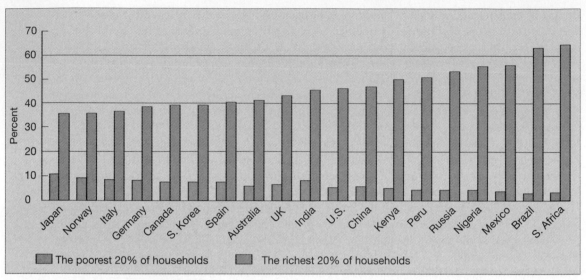

Figure 12.1   Proportion of National Income Earned by the Richest 20 Percent of Households Compared with the Poorest 20 Percent: Selected Country Comparisons

Source: These data are abstracted from *2001 World Development Indicators* (Washington, D.C.: The World Bank, 2001), pp. 70–73.

people pointed to a few individuals who rose from humble beginnings. But consider the odds. How many presidents have come from poor families? How many were not European in background? How many were not Protestant? (And, as we discuss in the next chapter, how many were not male?) So far, all of the presidents of the United States have been European in ancestry, all but one have been Protestant, and all have been male. And only a handful came from humble beginnings. In the Canadian town of "Paradise" the ideology of "classlessness" became more prevalent over time, paralleling the trend in the United States where most people see themselves as "middle class."[20] To move up the social ladder people seem to have to believe that it is possible to do so. However, it is one thing to believe in mobility; it is another thing to deny the existence of classes. Why would people deny that classes exist?

Caste Systems

Some societies have classes that are virtually closed. They are called castes. A **caste** is a ranked group in which membership is determined at birth, and marriage is restricted to members of one's own caste. The only way you can belong is by being born into the group; and since you cannot marry outside the group, your children cannot acquire another caste status either. In India, for example, there are several thousand hereditary castes. Although the precise ranking of these thousands of groups is not clear, there appear to be four main levels of hierarchy. The castes in India are often thought to be associated with different occupations, but that is not quite true. Most Indians live in rural areas and have agricultural occupations, but their castes vary widely.[21]

Castes may exist in conjunction with a more open class system. Indeed, in India today, members of a low caste who can get wage-paying jobs, chiefly those in urban areas, may improve their social standing in the same ways available to people in other class societies. In general, however, they still cannot marry someone in a higher caste, so the caste system is perpetuated.

India has witnessed a marked increase in service and high technology jobs as companies around the world outsource many of their service activities to India. Caste is less important now for jobs.

Questions basic to all stratified societies, and particularly to a caste society, were posed by John Ruskin, a nineteenth-century British essayist: "Which of us . . . is to do the hard and dirty work for the rest—and for what pay? Who is to do the pleasant and clean work, and for what pay?"[22] In India those questions have been answered by the caste system, which mainly dictates how goods and services are exchanged, particularly in rural areas.[23]

Japan also had a caste group within a class society. Now called *burakumin* (instead of the pejorative *Eta*), this group traditionally had occupations that were considered unclean.[24] Comparable to India's Untouchables, they were a hereditary, endogamous (in-marrying) group. Their occupations were traditionally those of farm laborer, leatherworker, and basket weaver; their standard of living was very low. The burakumin are physically indistinguishable from other Japanese.[25] Discrimination against the burakumin was officially abolished by the Japanese government in 1871, but it was not until the twentieth century that the burakumin began organizing to bring about change. These movements appear to be paying off as more active steps have been taken recently by the Japanese government to alleviate discrimination and poverty. As of 1995, 73 percent of burakumin marriages were with non-burakumin. In public opinion polls, two-thirds of burakumin now said that they had not encountered discrimination. However, most burakumin still live in segregated neighborhoods where unemployment, crime, and alcoholism rates are high.[26]

In Rwanda, a country in east-central Africa, a longtime caste system was overthrown, first by an election and then by a revolution in 1959 to 1960. Three castes had existed, each distinguished from the others by physical appearance and occupation.[27] It is believed that the three castes derived from three different language groups that came together through migration and conquest. Later, however, they began to use a common language, although remaining endogamous and segregated by hereditary occupations. The taller and leaner ruling caste, the Tutsi, constituted about 15 percent of the population. They were the landlords and practiced the prestigious occupation of herding. The shorter and stockier agricultural caste, the Hutu, made up about 85 percent of the population. As tenants of the Tutsi, they produced most of the country's food. The much shorter Twa, accounting for less than 1 percent of the population, were foragers who formed the lowest caste.

Colonial rule, first by the Germans and then by the Belgians after World War I, strengthened Tutsi power. When the Hutu united to demand more of the rewards of their labor in 1959, the king and many of the Tutsi ruling caste were driven out of the country. The Hutu then established a republican form of government and declared independence from Belgium in 1962. In this new government, however, the forest-dwelling Twa were generally excluded from full citizenship. In 1990, Tutsi rebels invaded from

Uganda, and attempts were made to negotiate a multiparty government. However, civil war continued, and in 1994 alone over a million people, mostly Tutsi, were killed. Almost 2 million refugees, mostly Hutu, fled to Zaire (now Congo) as the Tutsi-led rebels established a new government.[28]

In the United States, African Americans used to have more of a caste-like status determined partly by the inherited characteristic of skin color. Until recently, some states even had laws prohibiting an African American from marrying a European American. When interethnic marriage did occur, children of the union were often regarded as having lower status than European-American children, even though they may have had blond hair and light skin. In the South, where treatment of African Americans as a caste was most apparent, European Americans refused to eat with African Americans or sit next to them at lunch counters, on buses, and in schools. Separate drinking fountains and toilets reinforced the idea of ritual uncleanness. The economic advantages and gains in prestige enjoyed by European Americans are well documented.[29] In the following sections, on slavery, racism, and inequality, we discuss the social status of African Americans in more detail.

Slavery

Slaves are persons who do not own their own labor, and as such they represent a class. We may associate slavery with a few well-known examples, such as ancient Egypt, Greece, and Rome or the southern United States, but slavery has existed in some form in almost every part of the world at one time or another, in simpler as well as in more complex societies. Slaves are often obtained from other cultures directly: kidnapped, captured in war, or given as tribute. Or they may be obtained indirectly as payment in barter or trade. Slaves sometimes come from the same culture; one became a slave as payment of a debt, as a punishment for a crime, or even as a chosen alternative to poverty. Slave societies vary in the degree to which it is possible to become freed from slavery.[30] Sometimes the slavery system has been a closed class, or caste, system, sometimes a relatively open class system. In different slave-owning societies, slaves have had different, but always some, legal rights.[31]

In ancient Greece, slaves often were conquered enemies. Because city-states were constantly conquering one another or rebelling against former conquerors, slavery was a threat to everyone. After the Trojan War, the transition of Hecuba from queen to slave was marked by her cry, "Count no one happy, however fortunate, before he dies."[32] Nevertheless, Greek slaves were considered human beings, and they could even acquire some higher-class status along with freedom. Andromache, Hecuba's daughter-in-law, was taken as a slave and concubine by one of the Greek heroes. When his legal wife produced no children, Andromache's slave son became heir to his father's throne. Although slaves had no rights under law, once they were freed, either by the will of their master or by purchase, they and their descendants could become assimilated into the dominant group. In other words, slavery in Greece was not seen as the justified position of inferior people. It was regarded, rather, as an act of fate—"the luck of the draw"— that relegated one to the lowest class in society.

Among the Nupe, a society in central Nigeria, slavery was of quite another type.[33] The methods of obtaining slaves—as part of the booty of warfare and, later, by purchase—were similar to those of Europeans, but the position of the slaves was very different. Mistreatment was rare. Male slaves were given the same opportunities to earn money as other dependent males in the household—younger brothers, sons, or other relatives. A slave might be given a garden plot of his own to cultivate, or he might be given a commission if his master was a craftsman or a tradesman. Slaves could acquire property, wealth, and even slaves of their own. But all of a slave's belongings went to the master at the slave's death.

Manumission—the granting of freedom to slaves—was built into the Nupe system. If a male slave could afford the marriage payment for a free woman, the children of the resulting marriage were free; the man himself, however, remained a slave. Marriage and concubinage were the easiest ways out of bondage

When people support themselves by what they collect and produce, as most did until a few thousand years ago, it's difficult to compare the standards of living of different societies because we cannot translate what people have into market or monetary value. It's only when people are at least partly involved in the world market economy that we can measure the standard of living in monetary terms. Today this comparison is possible for most of the world. Many in most societies depend on buying and selling for a living, and the more who depend on international exchange, the more possible it is to compare them in terms of standard economic indicators. We don't have such indicators for all different societies, but we do have them for many countries. Those indicators suggest that the degree of economic inequality in the world is not only very substantial but has generally increased over time.

This conveys just how economically unequal the world is: Surveying households in 91 countries, Branko Milanovic calculated that the richest 1 percent of people in the world have as much total income as 57 percent of the people at the bottom. Over one billion people on earth live on less than one U.S. dollar a day. This level of inequality exceeds the degree of inequality within any individual country. The disparities are not just in terms of income; there are vast inequalities in literacy, access to clean water, and mortality from a wide range of diseases.

Global inequality has increased substantially in the last three decades. To measure the changes, we can compare the ratio between the richest and poorest fifths over time across countries. In 1997, the ratio was 70.4 to 1, which is calculated by dividing the income for the top fifth by the income for the bottom fifth. That ratio has increased since the 1970s, when the ratio was 33.7 to 1. Higher inequality over time does not necessarily mean that the poor are worse off than before; it is possible that the rich can get much richer and the poor remain the same. However, it does seem that the poor have gotten poorer and the rich have gotten richer in the countries of the world. Between 1988 and 1993 Milanovic calculated that the real incomes of the bottom 5 percent dropped by 25 percent, while the incomes of the richest 20 percent grew by about 12 percent.

If the world as a whole is seeing improvements in technology and economic development, why is inequality in the world increasing? As we shall see in the chapter on culture change and globalization, it is often the rich within a society who benefit most from new technology, at least initially. They are not only the most likely to be able to afford it, but also the only ones who can afford to take the risks that it involves. The same may be true for nations. Those that already have capital are more likely than the poorer nations to take advantage of improvements in technology. Also, the poorer countries generally have the highest rates of population growth, so income per capita can fall if population increases faster than the rate of economic development. Economists tell us that a developing country may, at least initially, experience an increase in inequality, but the inequality often decreases over time. Will the inequalities among countries also decrease as the world economy develops further?

The prospect is not entirely bleak. It's true that the disparity between rich and poor countries has increased in recent years, but it's also true that the world economy has improved in some respects. The United Nations has computed a "human development index" for 114 countries, combining measures of life expectancy, literacy, and a measure of per capita purchasing power. According to this index, all countries but Zambia have improved over a period of 30 years, many of them substantially. A child in the world today can expect to live 8 more years than 30 years ago. Literacy has increased from 47 percent in 1970 to 73 percent in 1999. The most progress has occurred in East Asia and the Pacific, the least in sub-Saharan Africa. World leaders at the United Nations Millennium Declaration have committed themselves to a number of goals by the year 2015, including halving the proportion of people living in extreme poverty and halving the proportion of people suffering from hunger. Even if those goals are achieved, much more will remain to be done if we are to achieve a more equal world.

Sources: Human Development Report, UN Development Programme (New York: Oxford University Press, 2001), pp. 9–25; Branko Milanovic, *The Economic Journal,* 112 (2002): 51–92; *State of the World* (New York: Norton, 1994), pp. 1–8; Peter Donaldson, *Worlds Apart* (London: British Broadcasting Corporation, 1971); Philips Foster, *The World Food Problem* (Boulder: Lynne Rienner, 1992), pp. 149–51.

for a slave woman. Once she had produced a child by her master, both she and the child had free status. The woman, however, was only figuratively free; if a concubine, she had to remain in that role. As might be expected, the family trees of the nobility and the wealthy were liberally grafted with branches descended from slave concubines.

The most fortunate slaves among the Nupe were the house slaves. They could rise to positions of power in the household as overseers and bailiffs, charged with law enforcement and judicial duties. (Recall the Old Testament story of Joseph, who was sold into slavery by his brothers. Joseph became a household slave of the pharaoh and rose to the position of second in the kingdom because he devised an ingenious system of taxation.) There was even a titled group of Nupe slaves, the Order of Court Slaves, who were trusted officers of the king and members of an elite. Slave status in general, though, placed one at the bottom of the social ladder. In the Nupe system, few slaves, mainly princes from their own societies, ever achieved membership in the titled group. Nupe slavery was abolished at the beginning of the twentieth century.

In the United States, slavery originated as a means of obtaining cheap labor, but the slaves soon came to be regarded as deserving of their low status because of their alleged inherent inferiority. Because the slaves were from Africa and dark-skinned, some European Americans justified slavery and the belief in "black" people's inferiority by quoting Scripture out of context ("They shall be hewers of wood and drawers of water"). Slaves could not marry or make any other contracts, nor could they own property. In addition, their children were also slaves, and the master had sexual rights over the female slaves. Because the status of slavery was determined by birth in the United States, slaves constituted a caste. During the days of slavery, therefore, the United States had both a caste and a class system. And even after the abolition of slavery, as we have noted, some caste-like elements remained. It is important to note that these caste-like elements were not limited to the American South where slavery had been practiced. For example, although Indiana was established as a "free" state in 1816, in its first constitution "Negros" did not have the right to vote nor could they intermarry with "Whites." In the constitution of 1851 Indiana did not allow "Negros" to come into the state, nor did it allow the existing African-American residents to attend public schools even though they had to pay school taxes.[34] In Muncie, Indiana, in the first half of the twentieth century, there was customary segregation in shows, restaurants, and parks. It was not until the 1950s that the public swimming pool was desegregated.[35]

As to why slavery may have developed in the first place, cross-cultural research is as yet inconclusive. We do know, however, that slavery is not an inevitable stage in economic development, contrary to what some have assumed. In other words, slavery is not found mainly in certain economies, such as those dependent on intensive agriculture. Unlike the United States until the Civil War, many societies with intensive agriculture did not develop any variety of slavery. Also, the hypothesis that slavery develops where available resources are plentiful but labor is scarce is not supported by the cross-cultural evidence. All we can say definitely is that slavery does not occur in developed or industrial economies; either it disappears or it was never present in them.[36]

Racism and Inequality

Racism is the belief that some "races" are inferior to others. In a society composed of people with noticeably different physical features, such as differences in skin color, racism is almost invariably associated with social stratification. Those "races" considered inferior make up a larger proportion of the lower social classes or castes. Even in more open class systems, where individuals from all backgrounds can achieve higher status positions, individuals from "racial" groups deemed inferior may be subject to discrimination in housing or may be more likely to be searched or stopped by the police.

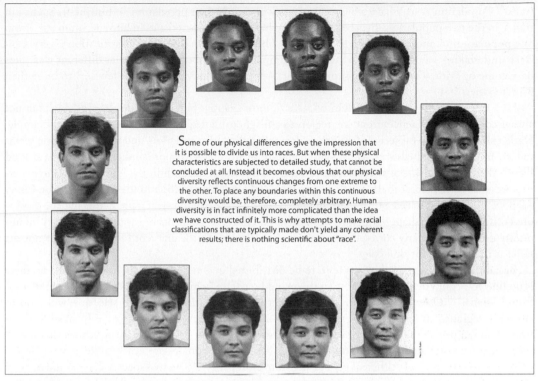

Some of our physical differences give the impression that it is possible to divide us into races. But when these physical characteristics are subjected to detailed study, that cannot be concluded at all. Instead it becomes obvious that our physical diversity reflects continuous changes from one extreme to the other. To place any boundaries within this continuous diversity would be, therefore, completely arbitrary. Human diversity is in fact infinitely more complicated than the idea we have constructed of it. This is why attempts to make racial classifications that are typically made don't yield any coherent results; there is nothing scientific about "race".

It is an illusion that there are races. The diversity of human beings is so great and so complicated that it is impossible to classify the 5.8 billions of individuals into discrete "races."

In some societies, such as the United States, the idea that humans are divided into "races" is taken so much for granted that people are asked for their "race" on the census. Most Americans probably assume that "races" are real, meaningful categories, reflecting important biological variation. But that is not necessarily the case. You may have noticed that we put "races" in quotes. We have done so deliberately because most anthropologists are persuaded that "race" is a meaningless concept as applied to humans. To understand why we say that, we first need to consider what the concept of *race* means in biology.

Race as a Construct in Biology

While all members of a species can potentially interbreed with others, most reproduction takes place within smaller groups or breeding populations. Through time, populations inhabiting different geographic regions may develop some differences in biological traits. Biologists may then classify different geographic populations into different *varieties,* or **races**. If the term *race* is understood to be just a shorthand or classificatory way in which biologists describe variation within a species from one population to the next, the concept of race would probably not be controversial. But, as applied to humans, racial classifications have often been thought to imply that some "races" are innately inferior to others.

The misuse and misunderstanding of the term *race,* and its association with racist thinking, are two of the reasons that anthropologists and others have suggested that the concept of race may hinder the search to explain the development of biological differences in humans. In any case, racial classifications are not scientifically useful in that search because different populations are not clearly classifiable into discrete groups that can be defined in terms of the presence or absence of particular sets of biological traits.[37] Population A may have a higher frequency of trait X than population B, but the frequency of trait Y in the two populations may be the same. So biological characteristics in humans often vary from one population to another in uncorrelated ways. This situation makes racial classification a very arbitrary undertaking when it comes to humans. Compare the number of "races" that different classifiers have come up with. The number of supposed racial categories has varied from as few as 3 to more than 37 categories.[38]

How can groups be clearly divided into "races" if most adaptive biological traits show gradual, but not always correlated, differences from one region to a neighboring region?[39] Skin color is a good example. Darker skin appears to protect the body from damaging ultraviolet radiation, and natural selection seems to have favored individuals with darker skin in environments that have more sunlight. In the area around Egypt, there is a gradient of skin color as you move from north to south in the Nile Valley. Skin generally becomes darker closer to the equator (which is south) and lighter closer to the Mediterranean. Other adaptive traits may not have north-south gradients, because the environmental predictors may be distributed differently. Nose shape varies with humidity, but **clines**, or gradients of varying frequencies, in humidity do not particularly correspond to variation in latitude. So the gradient for nose shape is not the same as the gradient for skin color.

Because individual adaptive traits tend to be distributed in clines that do not always coincide, there is no line you could draw on a world map that would separate "white" from "black" people, or "whites" from "Asians."[40] Only traits that are neutral in terms of adaptation or natural selection will tend to cluster in regions.[41] It should also be noted that the traits we have mentioned are superficial surface features. Human populations do vary biologically in some ways, but it is important to realize that few of these ways are correlated with each other. And under the skin humans are nearly alike genetically. Indeed, humans are not very different genetically from chimpanzees! The two species share as much as 99 percent of their genes.[42]

Race as a Social Category

If race, in the opinion of many biological anthropologists, is not a particularly useful device for classifying humans, why is it so widely used as a category in various societies? Anthropologists suggest the reasons are social. That is, racial classifications are social categories to which individuals are assigned, by themselves and others, to separate "our" group from others. We have seen that people tend to be *ethnocentric,* to view their culture as better than other cultures. Racial classifications may reflect the same tendency to divide "us" from "them," except that the divisions are supposedly based on biological differences.[43] The "them" are almost always viewed as inferior to "us."

We know that racial classifications have often been, and still are, used by certain groups to justify discrimination, exploitation, or even genocide. The "Aryan race" was supposed to be the group of blond-haired, blue-eyed, white-skinned people whom Adolf Hitler wanted to dominate the world, to which end he and others attempted to destroy as many members of the Jewish "race" as they could. (It is estimated that 6 million Jews and others were murdered in what is now called the Holocaust.[44]) But who were the Aryans? Technically, Aryans are any people, including the German-speaking Jews in Hitler's Germany, who speak one of the Indo-European languages. The Indo-European languages include such disparate modern tongues as Greek, Spanish, Hindi, Polish, French, Icelandic, German, Gaelic, and English. And many Aryans speaking these languages have neither blond hair nor blue eyes. Similarly, all kinds of people may be Jews, whether or not they descend from the ancient Near Eastern population that spoke the Hebrew language. There are light-skinned Danish Jews and darker Jewish Arabs. One of the most orthodox Jewish groups in the United States is based in New York City and is composed entirely of African Americans.

The arbitrary and social basis of most racial classifications becomes apparent when you compare how they differ from one place to another. Consider, for example, what used to be thought about the "races" in South Africa. Under apartheid, which was a system of racial segregation and discrimination, someone with mixed "white" and "black" ancestry was considered "colored." However, when important people of African ancestry (from other countries) would visit South Africa, they were often considered "white." Chinese were considered "Asian"; but the Japanese, who were important economically to South Africa, were considered "white."[45] In some parts of the United States, laws against interracial marriage continued in force through the 1960s. You would be considered a "negro" if you had an eighth or more "negro" ancestry (if one or more of your eight grandparents were "negro"). So only a small amount of "negro" ancestry made a person "negro." But a small amount of "white" ancestry did not make a person "white." Biologically speaking, this makes no sense, but socially it was another story.[46]

If people of different "races" are viewed as inferior, they are almost inevitably going to end up on the bottom of the social ladder in a socially stratified society. Discrimination will keep them out of the better-paying or higher-status jobs and in neighborhoods that are poorer.

Ethnicity and Inequality

If "race" is not a scientifically useful category because people cannot be clearly divided into different "racial" categories based on sets of physical traits, then racial classifications such as "black" and "white" in the United States might better be described as *ethnic* classifications. How else can we account for the following facts? Groups in the United States that are now thought of as "white" were earlier thought of as belonging to inferior "races." For example, in the latter half of the nineteenth century, newspapers would often talk about the new immigrants from Ireland as belonging to the Irish "race." Similarly, before World War II, Jews were thought of as a separate "racial" group, and only became "white" afterward.[47] It is hard to escape the idea that changes in "racial" classification occurred as the Irish, Jews, and other immigrant groups became more accepted by the majority in the United States.[48]

It is apparent that *ethnic groups* and *ethnic identities* emerge as part of a social and political process. Defining **ethnicity** usually separates a group of people with common origins and language, shared history, and selected cultural difference such as a difference in religion. Those doing the defining can be outside or inside the ethnic group. Outsiders and insiders often perceive ethnic groups differently. In a country with one large core majority group, often the majority group doesn't think of itself as an ethnic group. Rather, they consider only the minority groups to have ethnic identities. For example, in the United States it is not common for the majority to call themselves European Americans, but other groups may be called African Americans, Asian Americans, or Native Americans. The minority groups, on the other hand, may have different named identities.[49] Asian Americans may identify themselves more specifically as Japanese Americans, Korean Americans, Chinese Americans, or Hmong. The majority population often uses derogatory names to identify people who are different. The majority may also tend to lump people of diverse ethnicities together. Naming a group establishes a social boundary between it and other ethnic groups.[50]

Ethnic identity may be manipulated, by insiders and by outsiders, in different situations. A particularly repressive regime that emphasizes nationalism and loyalty to the state may not only suppress the assertiveness of ethnic claims; it may also act to minimize communication among people who might otherwise embrace the same ethnic identity.[51] More democratic regimes may allow more expression of difference and celebrate ethnic difference. However, manipulation of ethnicity does not come just from the top. It may be to the advantage of minority groups to lobby for more equal treatment as a larger entity, such as Asian American, rather than as Japanese, Chinese, Hmong, Filipino, or Korean American.

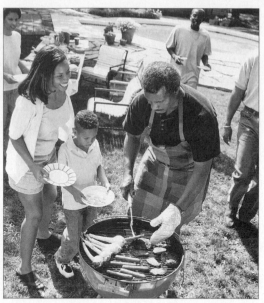

Members of minority ethnic groups are more often at the bottom of the socioeconomic "ladder," but not always, as these pictures from the United States illustrate.

Similarly, even though there are hundreds of American Indian groups, originally speaking different languages, there may be political advantages for all if they are treated as Native Americans.

In many multiethnic societies, ethnicity and diversity are things to be proud of and celebrated. Shared ethnic identity often makes people feel comfortable with similar people and gives them a strong sense of belonging. Still, ethnic differences in multiethnic societies are usually associated with inequities in wealth, power, and prestige. In other words, ethnicity is part of the system of *stratification*.

Although there are some people who believe that inequities are deserved, the origins of ethnic stereotypes, prejudice, and discrimination usually follow from historical and political events that give some groups dominance over others. For example, even though there were many early stories of help given by native peoples to the English settlers in the seventeenth century in the land now known as North America, the English were the invaders, and negative stereotypes about native peoples developed to justify taking their land and their lives. Referring to the negative stereotypes of Native Americans that developed, J. Milton Yinger said: "One would almost think that it had been the Indian who had invaded Europe, driven back the inhabitants, cut their population to one-third of its original size, unilaterally changed treaties, and brought the dubious glories of firewater and firearms."[52]

Similarly, as we noted in the section on slavery, African slaves were initially acquired as cheap labor, but inhumane treatment of slaves was justified by beliefs about their inferiority. Unfortunately, stereotypes can become self-fulfilling prophesies, especially if those discriminated against come to believe the stereotypes. It is easy to see how this can happen. If there is a widespread belief that a group is inferior, and that group is given inferior schools and little chance for improvement or little chance for a good job, the members of that group may acquire few skills and not try hard. The result is often a vicious cycle.[53]

And yet, the picture is not all bleak. Change has occurred. The ethnic identity forged by a minority group can help promote political activism, such as the nonviolent civil rights movement in the United States in the 1960s. That activism, helped by some people in the more advantaged groups, helped break down many of the legal barriers and segregationist practices that reinforced inequality.

The traditional barriers in the United States have mostly been lifted in recent years, but the "color line" has not disappeared. African Americans are found in all social classes, but they remain underrepresented in the wealthiest group and overrepresented at the bottom. Discrimination may be lessened, but it is still not gone. In research done with matched pairs of "whites" and "blacks" applying for jobs or for housing, discrimination is still evident.[54] Thus, African Americans may have to be better than others to get promoted, or it may be assumed that they got ahead just because they were African American and were hired because of affirmative action programs. European Americans often expect African Americans to be "ambassadors," to be called on mainly for knowledge about how to handle situations involving other African Americans. African Americans may work with others, but they usually go home to African American neighborhoods. Or they may live in mixed neighborhoods and experience considerable isolation. Few African Americans can completely avoid the anguish of racism.[55]

The Emergence of Stratification

Anthropologists are not certain why social stratification developed. Nevertheless, they are reasonably sure that higher levels of stratification emerged relatively recently in human history. Archaeological sites dating before about 8,000 years ago do not show extensive evidence of inequality. Houses do not appear to vary much in size or content, and different communities of the same culture are similar in size and otherwise. Signs of inequality appear first in the Near East, about 2,000 years after agriculture emerged in that region. Inequality in burial suggests inequality in life. Particularly telling are unequal child burials. It is unlikely that children could achieve high status by their own achievements. So when archaeologists find statues and ornaments only in some children's tombs, as at the 7,500 year-old site of Tell es-Sawwan in Iraq,[56] the grave goods suggest that those children belonged to a higher-ranking family or a higher class.

Another indication that stratification is a relatively recent development in human history is the fact that certain cultural features associated with stratification also developed relatively recently. For example, most societies that depend primarily on agriculture or herding have social classes.[57] Agriculture and herding developed within the past 10,000 years, so we may assume that most food collectors in the distant past lacked social classes. Other recently developed cultural features associated with class stratification include fixed settlements, political integration beyond the community level, the use of money as a medium of exchange, and the presence of at least some full-time specialization.[58]

In 1966, the comparative sociologist Gerhard Lenski suggested that the trend since 8,000 years ago toward increasing inequality was reversing. He argued that inequalities of power and privilege in industrial societies—measured in terms of the concentration of political power and the distribution of income—are less pronounced than inequalities in complex preindustrial societies. Technology in industrialized societies is so complex, he suggested, that those in power are compelled to delegate some authority to subordinates if the system is to work. In addition, a decline in the birth rate in industrialized societies, coupled with the need for skilled labor, has pushed the average wage of workers far above the subsistence level, resulting in greater equality in the distribution of income. Finally, Lenski also suggested that the spread of the democratic ideology, and particularly its acceptance by elites, has significantly broadened the political power of the lower classes.[59] A few studies have tested and supported Lenski's hypothesis that inequality has decreased with industrialization. In general, nations that are highly industrialized exhibit a lower level of inequality than nations that are only somewhat industrialized.[60] But, as we have seen, even the most industrialized societies may still have an enormous degree of inequality.

Why did social stratification develop in the first place? On the basis of his study of Polynesian societies, Marshall Sahlins suggested that an increase in agricultural productivity results in social stratification.[61] According to Sahlins, the degree of stratification is directly related to the production of a surplus, which is made possible by greater technological efficiency. The higher the level of productivity and the larger the agricultural surplus, the greater the scope and complexity of the distribution system. The status of the chief, who serves as redistributing agent, is enhanced. Sahlins argued that the differentiation between distributor and producer inevitably gives rise to differentiation in other aspects of life:

> First, there would be a tendency for the regulator of distribution to exert some authority over production itself—especially over productive activities which necessitate subsidization, such as communal labor or specialist labor. A degree of control of production implies a degree of control over the utilization of resources, or, in other words, some preeminent property rights. In turn, regulation of these economic processes necessitates the exercise of authority in interpersonal affairs; differences in social power emerge.[62]

Sahlins later rejected the idea that a surplus leads to chiefships, postulating instead that the relationship may be the other way around—that is, leaders encourage the development of a surplus so as to enhance their prestige through feasts, potlatches, and other redistributive events.[63] Of course, both trajectories are possible—surpluses may generate stratification, and stratification may generate surpluses; they are not mutually exclusive.

Lenski's theory of the causes of stratification is similar to Sahlins's original idea. Lenski, too, argued that production of a surplus is the stimulus in the development of stratification, but he focused primarily on the conflict that arises over control of that surplus. Lenski concluded that the distribution of the surplus will be determined on the basis of power. Thus, inequalities in power promote unequal access to economic resources and simultaneously give rise to inequalities in privilege and prestige.[64]

The "surplus" theories of Sahlins and Lenski do not really address the question of why the redistributors or leaders will want, or be able, to acquire greater control over resources. After all, the redistributors or leaders in many rank societies do not have greater wealth than others, and custom seems to keep things that way. One suggestion is that as long as followers have mobility, they can vote with their feet by moving away from leaders they do not like. But when people start to make more permanent "investments" in land or technology (e.g., irrigation systems or weirs for fishing), they are more likely to put up with a leader's aggrandizement in exchange for protection.[65] Another suggestion is that access to economic resources becomes unequal only when there is population pressure on resources in rank or chiefdom societies.[66] Such pressure may be what induces redistributors to try to keep more land and other resources for themselves and their families.

C. K. Meek offered an example of how population pressure in northern Nigeria may have led to economic stratification. At one time, a tribal member could obtain the right to use land by asking permission of the chief and presenting him with a token gift in recognition of his higher status. But by 1921, the reduction in the amount of available land had led to a system under which applicants offered the chief large payments for scarce land. As a result of these payments, farms came to be regarded as private property, and differential access to such property became institutionalized.[67]

Future research by archaeologists, sociologists, historians, and anthropologists should provide more understanding of the emergence of social stratification in human societies and how and why it varies in degree.

Summary

1. Without exception, recent and modern industrial and postindustrial societies such as our own are socially stratified—that is, they contain social groups such as families, classes, or ethnic groups that have unequal access to important advantages, such as economic resources, power, and prestige. Anthropologists, based on firsthand observations, would say that such inequality has not always existed among the societies they have studied. While even the simplest societies (in the technological sense) have some differences in advantages based on age, ability, or gender—adults have higher status than children, the skilled more than the unskilled, men more than women (we discuss gender stratification in the next chapter)—anthropologists would argue that egalitarian societies exist where social groups (e.g., families) have more or less the same access to rights or advantages.

2. The presence or absence of customs or rules that give certain groups unequal access to economic resources, power, and prestige can be used to distinguish three types of societies. In egalitarian societies, social groups do not have unequal access to economic resources, power, or prestige; they are unstratified. In rank societies, social groups do not have very unequal access to economic resources or power, but they do have unequal access to prestige. Rank societies, then, are partially stratified. In class societies, social groups have unequal access to economic resources, power, and prestige. They are more completely stratified than are rank societies.

3. Stratified societies range from somewhat open class systems to caste systems, which are extremely rigid, since caste membership is fixed permanently at birth.

4. Slaves are persons who do not own their own labor; as such, they represent a class and sometimes even a caste. Slavery has existed in various forms in many times and places, regardless of "race" and culture. Sometimes slavery is a rigid and closed, or caste, system; sometimes it is a relatively open class system.

5. Within a society composed of people from widely divergent backgrounds and different physical features, such as skin color, racism is almost invariably associated with social stratification. Those "races" considered inferior make up a larger proportion of the lower social classes or castes. In the opinion of many biological anthropologists, "race" is not a scientifically useful device for classifying humans. "Racial" classifications should be recognized for what they mostly are—social categories to which individuals are assigned, by themselves and others, on the basis of supposedly shared biological traits.

6. In multiethnic societies, ethnic differences are usually associated with inequities in wealth, power, and prestige. In other words, ethnicity is part of the system of stratification.

7. Social stratification appears to have emerged relatively recently in human history, about 8,000 years ago. This conclusion is based on archaeological evidence and on the fact that certain cultural features associated with stratification developed relatively recently.

8. One theory suggests that social stratification developed as productivity increased and surpluses were produced. Another suggestion is that stratification can develop only when people have "investments" in land or technology and therefore cannot move away from leaders they do not like. A third theory suggests that stratification emerges only when there is population pressure on resources in rank societies.

Glossary Terms

caste (p. 292)

class (p. 290)

class societies (p. 286)

clines (p. 298)

economic resources (p. 285)

egalitarian societies (p. 286)

ethnicity (p. 299)

manumission (p. 294)

power (p. 285)

prestige (p. 286)

races (p. 297)

racism (p. 296)

rank societies (p. 286)

slaves (p. 294)

Critical Questions

1. What might be some of the social consequences of large differences in wealth? Explain your reasoning.

2. Is an industrial or a developed economy incompatible with a more egalitarian distribution of re-sources? Why or why not?

3. In a multiethnic society, does ethnic identity help or hinder social equality? Explain your answer.

4. Why do you suppose the degree of inequality has decreased in some countries in recent years?

CHAPTER 13

SEX AND GENDER

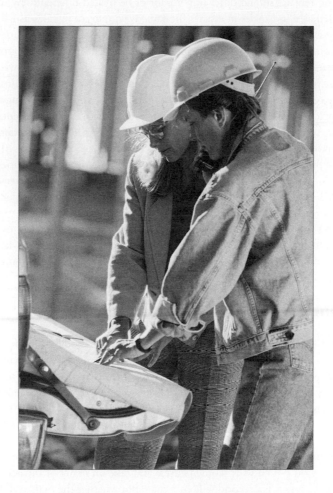

Chapter Outline

- Gender Concepts
- Physique and Physiology
- Gender Roles
- Relative Contributions to Work
- Political Leadership and Warfare
- The Relative Status of Women
- Personality Differences
- Sexuality

We all know that humans come in two major varieties—female and male. The contrast between them is one of the facts of life we share with most animal species. But the fact that males and females always have different organs of reproduction does not explain why males and females may also differ in other physical ways. After all, there are many animal species—such as pigeons, gulls, and laboratory rats—in which the two sexes differ little in appearance.[1] Thus, the fact that we are a species with two sexes does not really explain why human females and males typically look different. Also, the fact that humans reproduce sexually does not explain why human males and females should differ in behavior or be treated differently by society. Yet no society we know of treats females and males in exactly the same way; indeed, females usually have fewer advantages than males. That is why in the previous chapter we were careful to say that egalitarian societies have no *social groups* with unequal access to resources, power, and prestige. But within social groups (e.g., families), even egalitarian societies usually allow males greater access to economic resources, power, and prestige.

Because many of the differences between females and males may reflect cultural expectations and experiences, many researchers now prefer to speak of **gender differences**, reserving the term **sex differences** for purely biological differences.[2] Unfortunately, biological and cultural influences are not always clearly separable, so it is sometimes hard to know which term to use. As long as societies treat males and females differently, we may not be able to separate the effects of biology from the effects of culture, and both kinds of effect may be present. As we focus our discussion on differences and similarities between females and males, keep in mind that not all cultures conceive of gender as including just two categories. Sometimes "maleness" and "femaleness" are thought of as opposite ends of a continuum, or there might be three or more categories of gender, such as "female," "male," and "other."[3]

In this chapter we discuss what we know cross-culturally about how and why females and males may differ physically, in gender roles, and in personality. We also discuss how and why sexual behavior and attitudes about sex vary from culture to culture. First we focus on culturally varying concepts about gender.

Gender Concepts

In the United States and many Western societies your gender is thought of as female or male. There is no other category. In the instances where the baby's genitalia are ambiguous or when an adult desires a sex-change operation, there is a strong value on having the individual fit clearly into one or the other category. Many societies around the world share the male/female dichotomy when it comes to gender concepts. But a strict dichotomy is far from universal.

Some societies, like the Cheyenne Native Americans of the Great Plains, recognized male, female, and a third gender, referred to by the Cheyennes as "two-spirits." "Two-spirit" persons were usually young males. Their status as "two-spirit" persons was often recognized after their preadolescent vision quest. A two-spirit person would then wear women's dress and take on many of the activities of women. A two-spirit might even be taken as a second wife by a man, but whether the man and the two-spirit engaged in sex is not known. Europeans referred to a two-spirit individual as a *berdache*.[4] Accounts of "two-spirit" biological females who take on the role of men are relatively rare, but they do occur in a number of native North American societies, such as the Kaska of Yukon Territory, the Klamath of southern Oregon, and the Mohave of the Colorado River area in the southwestern United States. These biologically female "two-spirits" could marry women and such relationships were known to be lesbian relationships.[5]

In Oman there is a third gender role called *xanith*. Anatomically male, *xaniths* speak of themselves as "women." However, *xaniths* have their own distinctive dress—they wear clothes that are neither male nor female. In fact, their clothes and dress seem in-between. Men wear white clothes, women bright patterns, and *xaniths* wear unpatterned pastels. Men have short hair, women long, and *xaniths* are medium-length. Women are generally secluded in their houses and can only go out with permission from their husbands, but the *xanith* is free to come and go and works as a servant and/or a homosexual prostitute. But the *xanith* gender role is not necessarily forever. A *xanith* may decide to marry, and if he is able to have intercourse with his bride he becomes a "man." An older *xanith* who is no longer attractive may decide to become an "old-man."[6]

Physique and Physiology

As we noted at the outset, biological males and females of many animal species cannot readily be distinguished. Although they differ in chromosome makeup and in their external and internal organs of reproduction, they do not differ otherwise. In contrast, humans are **sexually dimorphic**—that is, the females and males of our species are generally different in size and appearance. Females have proportionately wider pelvises. Males typically are taller and have heavier skeletons. Females have a larger proportion of their body weight in fat; males have a larger proportion of body weight in muscle. Males typically have greater grip strength, proportionately larger hearts and lungs, and greater aerobic capacity (greater intake of oxygen during strenuous activity).

There is a tendency in our society to view "taller" and "more muscled" as better, which may reflect the bias toward males in our culture. Natural selection may have favored these traits in males but different ones in females. For example, because females bear children, selection may have favored earlier cessation of growth, and therefore less ultimate height, in females so that the nutritional needs of a fetus would not compete with a growing mother's needs.[7] (Females achieve their ultimate height shortly after puberty, but boys continue to grow for years after puberty.) Similarly, there is some evidence that females are less affected than males by nutritional shortages, presumably because they tend to be shorter and have proportionately more fat.[8] Natural selection may have favored those traits in females because they resulted in greater reproductive success.

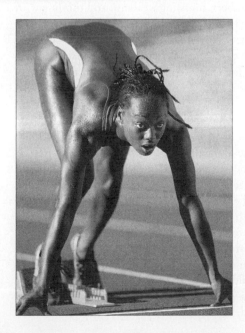

Training can greatly increase muscle strength and aerobic capacity.

Both female and male athletes can build up their muscle strength and increase their aerobic work capacity through training. Given that fact, cultural factors, such as how much a society expects and allows males and females to engage in muscular activity, could influence the degree to which females and males differ muscularly and in aerobic capacity. Similar training may account for the recent trend toward decreasing differences between females and males in certain athletic events, such as marathons and swim meets. Even when it comes to female and male physique and physiology, then, what we see may be the result of both culture and genes.[9]

Gender Roles

Productive and Domestic Activities

In the chapter on economics, we noted that all societies assign or divide labor somewhat differently between females and males. Because role assignments have a clear cultural component, we speak of them as **gender roles**. What is of particular interest here about the gender division of labor is not so much that every society has different work for males and females but rather that so many societies divide up work in similar ways. The question, then, is why there are universal or near-universal patterns in such assignments.

Table 13.1 summarizes the worldwide patterns. We note which activities are performed by which gender in all or almost all societies, which activities are usually performed by one gender, and which activities are commonly assigned to either gender or both. Does the distribution of activities in the table suggest why females and males generally do different things?

One possible explanation may be labeled the **strength theory**. The greater strength of males and their superior capacity to mobilize their strength in quick bursts of energy (because of their greater aerobic work capacity) have commonly been cited as the reasons for the universal or near-universal patterns in the division of labor by gender. Certainly, activities that require lifting heavy objects (hunting large animals, butchering, clearing land, working with stone, metal, or lumber), throwing weapons, and running with great speed (as in hunting) may generally be performed best by males. And none of the activities females usually perform, with the possible exception of collecting firewood, seems to require the same degree of physical strength or quick bursts of energy. But the strength theory is not completely convincing, if only because it cannot readily explain all the observed patterns. For example, it is not clear that the male activities of trapping small animals, collecting wild honey, or making musical instruments require much physical strength.

Another possible explanation of the worldwide patterns in division of labor can be called the **compatibility-with-child-care theory**. The argument here is that women's tasks tend to be those that are compatible with child care. Although males can take care of infants, most traditional societies rely on breast-feeding of infants, which men cannot do. (In most societies, women breast-feed their children for two years on the average.) Women's tasks may be those that do not take them far from home for long periods, that do not place children in potential danger if they are taken along, and that can be stopped and resumed if an infant needs care.[10]

The compatibility theory may explain why *no* activities other than infant care are listed in the right-hand column of Table 13.1. That is, it may be that there are practically no universal or near-universal women-only activities because until recently most women have had to devote much of their time to nursing and caring for infants, as well as caring for other children. The compatibility theory may also explain why men usually perform tasks such as hunting, trapping, fishing, collecting honey, lumbering, and mining. Those tasks are dangerous for infants to be around, and in any case would be difficult to coordinate with infant care.[11]

Table 13.1 Worldwide Patterns in the Division of Labor by Gender

Type of Activity	Males Almost Always	Males Usually	Either Gender or Both	Females Usually	Females Almost Always
Primary subsistence activities	Hunt and trap animals, large and small	Fish Herd large animals Collect wild honey Clear land and prepare soil for planting	Collect shellfish Care for small animals Plant crops Tend crops Harvest crops Milk animals	Gather wild plants	

Secondary subsistence and household activities		Butcher animals	Preserve meat and fish	Care for children
				Cook
				Prepare
				  vegetable
				  foods
				  drinks
				  dairy
				  products
				Launder
				Fetch water
				Collect fuel
					Care for infants

Other	Lumber Mine and quarry Make boats musical instruments bone, horn, and shell objects Engage in combat	Build houses Make nets rope Exercise political leadership	Prepare skins Make leather products baskets mats clothing pottery	Spin yarn	

Sources: Mostly adapted from George P. Murdock and Caterina Provost, "Factors in the Division of Labor by Sex: A Cross-Cultural Analysis," *Ethnology,* 12 (1973): 203–25. The information on political leadership and warfare comes from Martin K. Whyte, "Cross-Cultural Codes Dealing with the Relative Status of Women," *Ethnology,* 17 (1978): 217. The information on child care comes from Thomas S. Weisner and Ronald Gallimore, "My Brother's Keeper: Child and Sibling Caretaker," *Current Anthropology,* 18 (1977): 169–80.

Finally, the compatibility theory may also explain why men seem to take over certain crafts in societies with full-time specialization. Although the distinction is not shown in Table 13.1, crafts such as making baskets, mats, and pottery are women's activities in noncommercial societies but tend to be men's activities in societies with full-time craft specialists.[12] Similarly, weaving tends to be a female activity unless it is produced for trade.[13] Why should commercial activities change the gender division of labor? Full-time specialization and production for trade may increase incompatibility with child care. Cooking is a good example in our own society. Women may be fine cooks, but chefs and bakers tend to be men, even though

In many farming societies, women can do some agriculture and take care of their young children at the same time, as this mother in Zambia demonstrates.

women traditionally do most of the cooking at home. Women might be more likely to work as cooks and chefs if they could leave their babies and young children in safe places to be cared for by other people.

But the compatibility theory does not explain why men usually prepare soil for planting, make objects out of wood, or work bone, horn, and shell. All of those tasks could probably be stopped to tend to a child, and none of them is any more dangerous to children nearby than is cooking. Why, then, do males tend to do them? The **economy-of-effort theory** may help explain patterns that cannot readily be explained by the strength and compatibility theories. For example, it may be advantageous for men to make musical instruments because men generally collect the hard materials involved (e.g., by lumbering).[14] And because they collect those materials, men may be more knowledgeable about the physical properties of the materials and so more likely to know how to work with them. The economy-of-effort interpretation also suggests that it would be advantageous for one gender to perform tasks that are located near each other. Thus, if women have to be near home to take care of young children, it would be economical for them to perform other chores that are located in or near the home.

A fourth explanation of division of labor is the **expendability theory**. This theory suggests that men, rather than women, will tend to do the dangerous work in a society because men are more expendable, because the loss of men is less disadvantageous reproductively than the loss of women. If some men lose their lives in hunting, deep-water fishing, mining, quarrying, lumbering, and the like, reproduction need not suffer as long as most fertile women have sexual access to men—for example, if the society permits two or more women to be married to the same man.[15] When would anybody, male or female, be willing to do dangerous work? Perhaps only when society glorifies those roles and endows them with high prestige and other rewards.

Although the various theories, singly or in combination, seem to explain much of the division of labor by gender, there are some unresolved problems. Critics of the strength theory have pointed out that in some societies women do engage in very heavy labor.[16] If women in some societies can develop the strength to do such work, perhaps strength is more a function of training than traditionally has been believed.

The compatibility theory also has some problems. It suggests that labor is divided to conform to the requirements of child care. But sometimes it seems the other way around. For example, women who spend a good deal of time in agricultural work outside the home often ask others to watch and feed their infants while they are unavailable to nurse.[17] Consider, too, the mountain areas of Nepal, where agricultural work is incompatible with child care; heavy loads must be carried up and down steep slopes, fields are far apart, and labor takes up most of the day. Yet women do this work anyway and leave their infants with others for long stretches of time.[18]

Furthermore, in some societies women hunt—one of the activities most incompatible with child care and generally not done by women. Many Agta women of the Philippines regularly hunt wild pig and deer; women alone or in groups kill almost 30 percent of the large game.[19] The women's hunting does not seem to be incompatible with child care. Women take nursing babies on hunting trips, and the women who hunt do not have lower reproductive rates than the women who choose not to hunt. Agta women may find it possible to hunt because the hunting grounds are only about a half-hour from camp, the dogs that accompany the women assist in the hunting and protect the women and babies, and the women generally hunt in groups, so others can help carry babies as well as carcasses. Hunting by women is also fairly common among the Aka, forest foragers in the Central African Republic. Aka women participate in and sometimes lead in organizing cooperative net-hunting, in which an area is circled and animals are flushed out and caught in nets. Women spend approximately 18 percent of their time net-hunting, which is more than men do.[20]

As the cases just described suggest, we need to know a lot more about labor requirements. More precisely, we need to know exactly how much strength is required in particular tasks, how dangerous those tasks are, and whether a person could stop working at a task to care for a child. So far, we have mostly guesses. When there is more systematically collected evidence on such aspects of particular tasks, we will be in a better position to evaluate the theories we have discussed. In any case, it should be noted that none of the available theories implies that the worldwide patterns of division of labor shown in Table 13.1 on page 309 will persist. As we know from our own and other industrial societies, when machines replace human strength, when women have fewer children, and when women can assign child care to others, a strict gender division of labor begins to disappear.

Relative Contributions to Work

In the United States there has been a tendency to equate "work" with a job that brings in income. Until relatively recently, being a "homemaker" was not counted as an occupation. Anthropologists have not been immune from ignoring household work; indeed, most of the research on division of labor by gender has focused on **primary subsistence activities**—gathering, hunting, fishing, herding, and farming—and relatively less attention has been paid to gender contributions to **secondary subsistence activities** that involve the processing and preparation of food for eating or storing.

Overall Work

If we count all kinds of economic work, whether it be for primary subsistence, secondary subsistence, manufacturing, crafts, or for maintenance of the household, the studies that have been done largely suggest that women typically work more total hours per day than men in both intensive agricultural and horticultural societies.[21] We do not have that many studies yet—so we do not know if this is a cross-cultural universal. We do know though that in many societies, where women earn wages, they are still responsible for the bulk of household work as well as child care at home.

Subsistence Work

Researchers have focused mostly on primary subsistence activities, and they usually measure how much each gender's work in these primary activities contributes to the diet in terms of caloric intake. Alternatively, contribution to primary subsistence activities—generally outside activities, away from the home—can also be measured in terms of time spent doing them. Measures of caloric versus time contribution can yield different results. As we saw in the chapter on economics, more time is spent by the Yanomamö in hunting than in horticulture, but horticulture yields more calories.

In some societies women traditionally have contributed more to the economy than men by any measure. For example, among the Tchambuli of New Guinea in the 1930s, the women did all the fishing—going out early in the morning by canoe to their fish traps and returning when the sun was hot. Some of the catch was traded for sago (a starch) and sugarcane, and it was the women who went on the long canoe trips to do the trading.[22]

In contrast, men did almost all of the primary subsistence work among the Toda of India. As they were described early in the twentieth century, they depended for subsistence almost entirely on the dairy products of their water buffalo, either by using the products directly or by selling them for grain. Women were not allowed to have anything to do with dairy work; only men tended the buffalo and prepared the dairy products. Women's work was largely household work. Women prepared the purchased grain for cooking, cleaned house, and decorated clothing.[23]

A worldwide survey of a wide variety of societies has revealed that both women and men typically contribute to primary food-getting activities, but men usually contribute more in terms of calories.[24] Women are almost always occupied with infant-and child-care responsibilities in most societies, so it is not surprising that men usually do most of the primary food-getting work, which generally has to be done away from the home.

Some of the variation in gender contribution to primary subsistence relates directly to the type of food-getting activities in the society. In societies that depend on hunting, fishing, and herding—generally male activities—for most of their calories, men usually contribute more than women.[25] For example, among the Inuit, who traditionally depended mostly on hunting and fishing, and among the Toda, who depended mostly on herding, men did most of the primary subsistence work. In societies that depend on gathering,

Grinding corn is very time-consuming and is hard work. Women near Lake Titicaca in Peru grind corn between two large stones.

primarily women's work, women tend to do most of the food-getting in terms of calories. The !Kung are an example. But the predominant type of food getting is not always predictive. Among the Tchambuli, who depended mostly on fishing, women did most of the work. Most societies known to anthropology depend primarily on plant cultivation for their calories, not on hunting, gathering, fishing, or herding. And, with the exception of clearing land, preparing the soil, and herding large animals, which are usually men's tasks, the work of planting, crop tending (weeding, irrigating), and harvesting is done by men, women, or both (see Table 13.1 on page 309). So we need some explanation of why women do most of the farming work in some societies but men do it in others. Different patterns predominate in different areas of the world. In Africa south of the Sahara, women generally do most of the farming. But in much of Asia and Europe and the areas around the Mediterranean, men do more.[26]

One explanatory factor is the kind of plant cultivation. With intensive agriculture, particularly plow agriculture, men's caloric contribution to primary subsistence tends to be much higher than women's. In horticultural societies, in contrast, women's contribution is relatively high compared with men's. Women usually contribute the most when horticulture is practiced, either root and tree crop horticulture or shifting/slash-and-burn cultivation. According to Ester Boserup, when population increases and there is pressure to make more intensive use of the land, cultivators begin to use the plow and irrigation, and males start to do more.[27] But it is not clear why.

Why should women not continue to contribute a lot to farming just because plows are used? In trying to answer this question, most researchers shift to considering how much time males and females spend in various farming tasks, rather than estimating the total caloric contribution of females versus males. The reason for this shift is that gender contribution to farming varies substantially over the various phases of the production sequence, as well as from one crop to another. Thus, the total amount of time females versus males work at farming tasks is easier to estimate than how much each gender contributes to the diet in terms of calories. How would caloric contribution be judged, for example, if men do the clearing and plowing, women do the planting and weeding, and both do the harvesting?

One suggestion about why males contribute more to agriculture when the plow is used is that plow agriculture involves a great deal of labor input in the clearing and preparation phases of cultivation and at the same time minimizes subsequent weeding time. Men usually clear land anyway, but clearing is a more time-consuming process if intensive agriculture is practiced. It has been estimated that in one district in Nigeria, 100 days of work are required to clear one acre of virgin land for plowing by tractor; only 20 days are required to prepare the land for shifting cultivation. Weeding is a task that probably can be combined with child care, and perhaps for that reason it may have been performed mostly by women previously.[28] But the fact that men do the plowing, which may take a lot of time, does not explain why women do relatively fewer farming tasks, including weeding, in societies that have the plow.[29]

Another explanation for why women contribute less time than men to intensive agriculture is that household chores increase with intensive agriculture and thus limit the time women can spend in the fields. Intensive agriculturalists typically rely heavily on grain crops, which take much more work to make edible. Cereal grains (corn, rice, wheat, oats, millet) are usually dried before storing and thus take a long time to cook if they are left whole. More cooking requires more time to collect water and firewood (usually women's work) and more time to clean pots and utensils. A variety of techniques can reduce cooking time (such as soaking, grinding, or pounding), but the process that speeds up cooking the most—grinding—is itself time-consuming (unless done by machine).[30] Finally, household work may increase substantially with intensive agriculture because women in such societies have more children than women in horticultural societies.[31] If household work increases in these ways, it is easy to understand why women cannot contribute more time than men, or as much time as men, to intensive agriculture. But women's contribution, although less than men's, is nonetheless substantial; they seem to work outside the home four and a half hours a day, seven days a week, on the average.[32]

We still have not explained why women contribute so much to horticulture in the first place. They may not have as much household work as intensive agricultural women, but neither do the men. Why, then, don't men do relatively more in horticulture also? One possibility is that in horticultural societies men are often drawn away from cultivation into other types of activities. There is evidence that if males are engaged in warfare when primary subsistence work has to be done, the women must do that work.[33] Men may also be withdrawn from primary subsistence work if they have to work in distant towns and cities for wages or if they periodically go on long-distance trading trips.[34]

When women contribute a lot to primary food-getting activities, we might expect their behavior and attitudes concerning children to be affected. Several cross-cultural studies suggest that this expectation is correct. In societies with a high female contribution to primary subsistence (in terms of contributing calories), infants are fed solid foods earlier (so that other persons besides mothers can feed them) than in societies with a low female contribution.[35] Girls are likely to be trained to be industrious (probably to help their mothers), and girl babies are more valued.[36]

Political Leadership and Warfare

In almost every known society, men rather than women are the leaders in the political arena. One cross-cultural survey found that, in about 85 percent of the surveyed societies, only men were leaders. In the societies in which some women occupied leadership positions, the women were either outnumbered by or less powerful than the male leaders.[37] If we look at countries, not cultures, women on the average make up only around 10 percent of the representatives in national parliaments or legislative bodies.[38] Whether or not we consider warfare to be part of the political sphere of life, we find an almost universal dominance of males in that arena. In 87 percent of the world's societies, women never participate actively in war.[39] (See the box "Why Some Societies Let Women Participate in Combat" for a discussion of women in combat in the remaining 13 percent of societies.)

Even in *matrilineal* societies, which seem to be oriented around women (see the chapter on marriage, family, and kinship), men usually occupy political positions. For example, among the Iroquois of what is now New York State, women had control over resources and a great deal of influence, but men, not women, held political office. The highest political body among the League of the Iroquois, which comprised five tribal groups, was a council of 50 male chiefs. Although women could not serve on the council, they could nominate, elect, and impeach their male representatives. Women also could decide between life and death for prisoners of war, forbid the men of their households to go to war, and intervene to bring about peace.[40]

Why have men (at least so far) almost always dominated the political sphere of life? Some scholars have suggested that men's role in warfare gives them the edge in all kinds of political leadership, particularly because they control weapons, an important resource.[41] But evidence suggests that force is rarely used to obtain leadership positions;[42] superior strength is not the deciding factor. Still, warfare may be related to political leadership for another reason. Warfare clearly affects survival, and it occurs regularly in most societies. Therefore, decision making about war may be among the most important kinds of politics in most societies. If so, then the persons who know the most about warfare should be making the decisions about it.

To explain why males and not females usually engage in fighting, let us refer to three of the possible explanations of the worldwide patterns in the gender division of labor. Warfare, like hunting, requires strength (for throwing weapons) and quick bursts of energy (for running). And certainly combat is one of the most dangerous and uninterruptible activities imaginable, hardly compatible with child care. Also, even if they do not at the time have children, women may generally be kept out of combat because their

Women can serve in the U.S. military but are not usually in units directly engaged in combat. Some women feel that such exclusion is unfair and decreases their chances of promotion in the military. Other people, including some women, insist that female participation in combat would be detrimental to military performance or is inappropriate for women. Women in the U.S. military have been attacked in the course of their duties in Iraq and some have died. Some countries currently allow women to engage in combat. And in the eighteenth and nineteenth centuries women made up one wing of the standing army in the West African Kingdom of Dahomey and at one point constituted one-third of the armed forces. Most societies, however, have excluded women from combat and some have excluded women from any involvement in military activities or planning.

Why, then, do some societies allow women to be warriors? Psychologist David Adams compared about 70 societies studied by anthropologists to try to answer that question. Although most societies exclude women from war, Adams found that women are active warriors, at least occasionally, in 13 percent of the sample societies. In native North America, such societies included the Comanche, Crow, Delaware, Fox, Gros Ventre, and Navajo. In the Pacific, there were active warrior women among the Maori of New Zealand, on Majuro Atoll in the Marshall Islands, and among the Orokaiva of New Guinea. In none of these societies were the warriors usually women, but women were allowed to engage in combat if they wanted to.

Societies with women warriors differ from those that exclude women from combat in one of two ways: Either they conduct war only against people in other societies (i.e., "purely external" war) or they marry within their own community. Adams argues that these two conditions, which are not particularly common, preclude the possibility of conflicts of interest between wives and husbands, and therefore women can be permitted to engage in combat because their interests are the same as their husbands'. Because marriages in most cases involve individuals from the same society, husbands and wives will have the same loyalties if the society has purely external war. And even if war occurs between communities and larger groups in the same society (i.e., "internal" war), there will be no conflict of interest between husband and wife if they both grew up in the same community. In contrast, internal war occurs at least occasionally in most societies, and wives usually marry in from other communities that might have been or will be at war with the husband's community. In this situation, there may be a conflict of interest between husband and wife; if women were to engage in combat, they might have to fight against their fathers, paternal uncles, and brothers. And wouldn't the wives try to warn kin in their home communities if the husbands planned to attack them? Indeed, the men's fear of their wives' disloyalty would explain why women in these societies are forbidden to make or handle weapons or go near meetings in which war plans are discussed.

Many countries today engage in purely external war between societies; so other things being equal, we would not expect conflicts of interest to impede women's participation in combat. Therefore, extrapolating from Adams's findings, we might expect that the barriers against female participation in combat will disappear completely. But other conditions may have to be present before women and men participate equally in combat. In Adams's study, not all societies with purely external war or intracommunity marriage had women warriors. So we may also have to consider the degree to which the society seeks to maximize reproduction (and therefore protect women from danger) and the degree to which the society depends on women for subsistence during wartime.

There are other related questions to explore: Does military participation by women increase women's participation in politics? Does the presence of war in a society decrease or increase women's political participation? Does women's participation in politics or in the military change the nature of war?

Sources: From David B. Adams, "Why There Are So Few Women Warriors," in *Behavior Science Research,* 18 (1983): 196–212; Joshua S. Goldstein, "War and Gender," in Carol R. Ember and Melvin Ember, eds., *Encyclopedia of Sex and Gender: Men and Women in the World's Cultures,* vol. 1 (New York: Kluwer Academic/Plenum Publishers, 2004), pp. 10/–16.

Women as well as men serve on political councils in many Coast Salish communities. Here we see a swearing-in ceremony for the Special Chief's Council in Sardis, British Columbia.

potential fertility is more important to a population's reproduction and survival than their potential usefulness as warriors.[43] So the strength theory, the compatibility theory, and the expendability theory might all explain the predominance of men in warfare.

Two other factors may be involved in male predominance in politics. One is the generally greater height of men. Why height should be a factor in leadership is unclear, but studies suggest that taller persons are more likely to be leaders.[44] Finally, there is the possibility that men dominate politics because they get around more in the outside world than do women. Men's activities typically take them farther from home; women tend to work more around the home. If societies choose leaders at least in part because of what they know about the larger world, then men will generally have some advantage. In support of this reasoning, Patricia Draper found that in !Kung bands that had settled down, women no longer engaged in long-distance gathering, and they lost much of their former influence in decision making.[45] Involvement in child care may also detract from such influence. In a study of village leadership among the Kayapo of Brazil, Dennis Werner found that women with heavy child-care burdens were less influential than women not as involved in child care; perhaps they had fewer friends and missed many details of what was going on in the village.[46]

These various explanations suggest why men generally dominate politics, but we still need to explain why women participate in politics more in some societies than in others. Political scientist Marc Ross investigated this question in a cross-cultural survey of 90 societies.[47] In that sample, the degree of female participation in politics varied considerably. For example, among the Mende of Sierra Leone, women regularly held high office, but among the Azande of Zaire, women took no part in public life. One factor that appeared to predict the exclusion of women from politics was the organization of communities around male kin. As we will see later, when they marry, women usually have to leave their communities and move to their husband's place. If women are "strangers" in a community with many related males, then the males will have political advantages because of their knowledge of community members and past events.

The Relative Status of Women

There are probably as many definitions of status as there are researchers interested in the topic. To some, the relative status of the sexes means how much importance society confers on females versus males. To others, it means how much power and authority men and women have relative to each other. And to still others, it means what kinds of rights women and men possess to do what they want to do. In any case, many social scientists are asking why the status of women appears to vary from one society to another. Why do women have few rights and little influence in some societies and more of each in other societies? In other words, why is there variation in degree of **gender stratification**?

In the small Iraqi town of Daghara, women and men live very separate lives.[48] In many respects, women appear to have very little status. Like women in much of the Islamic world, women in Daghara live their lives mostly in seclusion, staying in their houses and interior courtyards. If women must go out, which they can do only with male approval, they must shroud their faces and bodies in long black cloaks. These cloaks must be worn in mixed company, even at home. Women are essentially excluded from political activities. Legally, they are considered to be under the authority of their fathers and husbands. Even the sexuality of women is controlled. There is strict emphasis on virginity before marriage. Because women are not permitted even casual conversations with strange men, the possibilities for extramarital or even premarital relationships are very slight. In contrast, hardly any sexual restrictions are imposed on men.

But some societies such as the Mbuti seem to approach equal status for males and females. Like most food collectors, the Mbuti have no formal political organization to make decisions or to settle disputes. Public disputes occur, and both women and men take part in the uproar that is part of such disputes. Not only do women make their positions known, but their opinions are often heeded. Even in domestic quarrels involving physical violence between husband and wife, others usually intervene to stop them, regardless of who hit whom first.[49] Women control the use of dwellings; they usually have equal say over the disposal of resources they or the men collect, over the upbringing of their children, and about whom their children should marry. One of the few signs of inequality is that women are somewhat more restricted than men with respect to extramarital sex.[50]

There are many theories about why women have relatively high or low status. One of the most common is that women's status will be high when they contribute substantially to primary subsistence activities. According to this theory, then, women should have very little status when food-getting depends

In some cultures, wives defer to their husbands in many contexts.

largely on hunting, herding, or intensive agriculture. A second theory suggests that where warfare is especially important, men will be more valued and esteemed than women. A third theory suggests that where there are centralized political hierarchies, men will have higher status. The reasoning in this theory is essentially the same as the reasoning in the warfare theory: Men usually play the dominant role in political behavior, so men's status should be higher wherever political behavior is more important or frequent. Finally, there is the theory that women will have higher status where kin groups and couples' place of residence after marriage are organized around women.

One of the problems in evaluating these theories is that decisions have to be made about the meaning of *status*. Does it mean value? Rights? Influence? And do all these aspects of status vary together? Cross-cultural research by sociologist Martin Whyte suggests that they do not. For each sample society in his study, Whyte rated 52 items that might be used to define the relative status of the sexes. These items included such things as which sex can inherit property, who has final authority over disciplining unmarried children, and whether the gods in the society are male, female, or both. The results of the study indicate that very few of these items are related. Therefore, Whyte concluded, we cannot talk about status as a single concept. Rather, it seems more appropriate to talk about the relative status of women in different spheres of life.[51]

Even though Whyte found no necessary connection between one aspect of status and another, he decided to ask whether some of the theories correctly predict why some societies have many, as opposed to few, areas in which the status of women is high. Let us turn first to the ideas that are not supported by the available cross-cultural evidence. The idea that generally high status derives from a greater caloric contribution to primary subsistence activities is not supported at all.[52] Women in intensive agricultural societies (who contribute less than men to primary subsistence) do tend to have lower status in many areas of life, just as in the Iraqi case described earlier. But in societies that depend mostly on hunting (where women also do little of the primary subsistence work), women seem to have higher status, which contradicts the theoretical expectation. Similarly, there is no consistent evidence that a high frequency of warfare generally lowers women's status in different spheres of life.[53]

What does predict higher status for women in many areas of life? Although the results are not strong, there is some support in Whyte's study for the theory that where kin groups and marital residence are organized around women, women have somewhat higher status. (We discuss these features of society more fully in the chapter on marriage, family, and kinship.) The Iroquois are a good example. Even though Iroquois women could not hold political office, they had considerable authority within and beyond the household. Related women lived together in longhouses with husbands who belonged to other kin groups. In the longhouse, the women's authority was clear, and they could ask objectionable men to leave. The women controlled the allocation of the food they produced. Allocation could influence the timing of war parties, since men could not undertake a raid without provisions. Women were involved in the selection of religious leaders, half of whom were women. Even in politics, although women could not speak or serve on the council, they largely controlled the selection of councilmen and could institute impeachment proceedings against those to whom they objected.[54]

If we look at nonindustrial or preindustrial societies, a generally lower status for women is more likely in societies with political hierarchies.[55] Lower status for women appears to be associated with other indicators of cultural complexity—social stratification, plow and irrigation agriculture, large settlements, private property, and craft specialization. One type of influence for women increases with cultural complexity—informal influence. But, as Whyte pointed out, informal influence may simply reflect a lack of *real* influence.[56] Why cultural complexity is associated with women having less authority in the home, less control over property, and more restricted sexual lives is not yet understood. However, the relationship between cultural complexity and gender equality appears to change when we include industrial and postindustrial societies. Judging by a comparative study of gender attitudes in 61 countries, it seems that developing countries relying on agriculture such as Nigeria and Peru have the least favorable attitudes toward gender equality, industrial societies such as Russia and Taiwan have moderately favorable attitudes, and postindustrial societies such as Sweden and the United States have the most favorable attitudes toward gender equality.[57]

Western colonialism appears to have been generally detrimental to women's status, perhaps because Westerners were accustomed to dealing with men. There are plenty of examples of Europeans restructuring landownership around men and teaching men modern farming techniques, even in places where women were usually the farmers. In addition, men more often than women could earn cash through wage labor or through sales of goods (such as furs) to Europeans.[58] Although the relative status of men and women may not have been equal before the Europeans arrived, colonial influences seem generally to have undermined the position of women.

Personality Differences

Much of the research on gender differences in personality has taken place in the United States and other Western countries where psychology is a major field of study. While such studies are informative, they do not tell us whether the observed differences hold true in cultures very different from our own. Fortunately, we now have systematic observational studies for various non-Western societies. These studies recorded the minute details of behavior of substantial numbers of males and females. Any conclusions about female-male differences in aggressiveness, for example, are based on actual counts of the number of times a particular individual tried to hurt or injure another person during a given amount of observation time. Almost all of these differences are subtle and a matter of degree, not a matter of a behavior being present or absent in females or males.

Which differences in personality are suggested by these systematic studies? Most of them have observed children in different cultural settings. The most consistent difference is in the area of aggression; boys try to hurt others more frequently than girls do. In an extensive comparative study of children's behavior, the Six Cultures project, this difference showed up as early as three to six years of age.[59] In the Six Cultures project, six different research teams observed children's behavior in Kenya (among the Gusii), Mexico, India, the Philippines, Okinawa, and the United States. A more recent cross-cultural comparison of four other cultures (the Logoli of Kenya, Nepal, Belize, and American Samoa) supports the sex difference in aggression.[60] Studies in the United States are consistent with the cross-cultural findings: In a large number of observation and experimental studies, boys exhibited more aggression than girls.[61]

Other female-male differences have turned up with considerable consistency, but we have to be cautious in accepting them, either because they have not been documented as well or because there are more exceptions. There seems to be a tendency for girls to exhibit more responsible behavior, including nurturance (trying to help others). Girls seem more likely to conform to adult wishes and commands. Boys try more often to exert dominance over others in order to get their own way. In play, boys and girls show a preference for their own gender. Boys seem to play in large groups, girls in small ones. And boys seem to maintain more distance between each other than girls do.[62]

If we assume that these differences are consistent across cultures, how can we explain them? Many writers and researchers believe that because certain female-male differences are so consistent, they are probably rooted in the biological differences between the two sexes. Aggression is one of the traits talked about most often in this connection, particularly because this male-female difference appears so early in life.[63] But an alternative argument is that societies bring up boys and girls differently because they almost

Cross-culturally, girls more often play in small, intimate groups, boys in larger groups.

universally require adult males and females to perform different types of roles. If most societies expect adult males to be warriors or to be prepared to be warriors, shouldn't we expect most societies to encourage or idealize aggression in males? And if females are almost always the caretakers of infants, shouldn't we also expect societies generally to encourage nurturant behaviors in females?

Researchers tend to adopt either the biological or the socialization view, but it is possible that both kinds of causes are important in the development of gender differences. For example, parents might turn a slight genetic difference into a large gender difference by maximizing that difference in the way they socialize boys versus girls.

It is difficult for researchers to distinguish the influence of genes and other biological conditions from the influence of socialization. We have research indicating that as early as birth, parents treat boy and girl infants differently.[64] In spite of the fact that objective observers can see no major "personality" differences between girl and boy infants, parents often claim to.[65] But parents may unconsciously want to see differences and may therefore produce them in socialization. So even early differences could be learned rather than genetic. Remember, too, that researchers cannot do experiments with people; for example, parents' behavior cannot be manipulated to find out what would happen if boys and girls were treated in exactly the same ways.

However, there is considerable experimental research on aggression in nonhuman animals. These experiments suggest that the hormone androgen is partly responsible for higher levels of aggression. For example, in some experiments, females injected with androgen at about the time the sexual organs develop (before or shortly after birth) behave more aggressively when they are older than do females without the hormone. These results may or may not apply to humans of course, but some researchers have investigated human females who were "androgenized" in the womb because of drugs given to their mothers to prevent miscarriage. By and large the results of these studies are similar to the experimental studies—androgenized human females show similar patterns of higher aggression.[66] Some scholars take these results to indicate that biological differences between males and females are responsible for the male-female difference in aggression;[67] others suggest that even these results are not conclusive, because females who get more androgen show generally disturbed metabolic systems, and general metabolic disturbance may itself increase aggressiveness. Furthermore, androgen-injected females may look more like males because they develop male-like genitals; therefore, they may be treated like males.[68]

Is there any evidence that socialization differences may account for differences in aggression? Although a cross-cultural survey of ethnographers' reports on 101 societies does show that more societies encourage aggression in boys than in girls, most societies show no difference in aggression training.[69] The few societies that do show differences in aggression training can hardly account for the widespread sex differences in actual aggressiveness. But the survey does not necessarily mean that there are no consistent differences in aggression training for boys and girls. All it shows is that there are no *obvious* differences. For all we know, the learning of aggression and other "masculine" traits by boys could be produced by subtle types of socialization.

One possible type of subtle socialization that could create gender differences in behavior is the chores children are assigned. It is possible that little boys and girls learn to behave differently because their parents ask them to do different kinds of work. Beatrice and John Whiting reported from the Six Cultures project that in societies where children were asked to do a great deal of work, they generally showed more responsible and nurturant behavior. Because girls are almost always asked to do more work than boys, they may be more responsible and nurturant for this reason alone.[70] If this reasoning is correct, we should find that if boys are asked to do girls' work, they will learn to behave more like girls.

A study of Luo children in Kenya supports this view.[71] Girls were usually asked to babysit, cook, clean house, and fetch water and firewood. Boys were usually asked to do very little because boys' traditional work was herding cattle, and most families in the community studied had few cattle. But more boys than girls had been born during that period, and many mothers without girls at home asked their sons to do girls' chores. Systematic behavior observations showed that much of the behavior of the boys who did girls' work was intermediary between the behavior of other boys and the behavior of girls. The boys who did girls' work were more like girls in that they were less aggressive, less domineering, and more responsible than other boys, even when they weren't working. So it is possible that task assignment has an important influence on how boys and girls learn to behave. These and other subtle forms of socialization need to be investigated more thoroughly.

Misconceptions about Differences in Behavior

Before we leave the subject of behavior differences, we should note some widespread beliefs about them that are not supported by research. Some of these mistaken beliefs are that girls are more dependent than boys, that girls are more sociable, and that girls are more passive. The results obtained by the Six Cultures project cast doubt on all these notions.[72] First, if we think of dependency as seeking help and emotional support from others, girls are generally no more likely to behave this way than boys. To be sure, the results do indicate that boys and girls have somewhat different styles of dependency. Girls more often seek help and contact; boys more often seek attention and approval. As for sociability, which means seeking and offering friendship, the Six Cultures results showed no reliable differences between the sexes. Of course, boys and girls may be sociable in different ways because boys generally play in larger groups than girls. As for the supposed passivity of girls, the evidence is also not particularly convincing. Girls in the Six Cultures project did not consistently withdraw from aggressive attacks or comply with unreasonable demands. The only thing that emerged as a female-male difference was that older girls were less likely than boys to respond to aggression with aggression. But this finding may not reflect passivity as much as the fact that girls are less aggressive than boys, which we already knew.

So some of our common ideas about female-male differences are unfounded. Others, such as those dealing with aggression and responsibility, cannot be readily dismissed and should be investigated further.

As we noted, an observed difference in aggression does not mean that males are aggressive and females are not. Perhaps because males are generally more aggressive, aggression in females has been studied less often. For that reason, Victoria Burbank focused on female aggression in an Australian aborigine community she calls Mangrove. During the 18 months that she was there, Burbank observed some act of aggression almost every other day. Consistent with the cross-cultural evidence, men initiated aggression more often than women, but women were initiators about 43 percent of the time. The women of

Mangrove engaged in almost all the same kinds of aggression as men did, including fighting, except that it tended not to be as lethal as male violence. Lethal weapons were most often used by men; when women fought with weapons, they mostly used sticks, not spears, guns, or knives. Burbank points out that, in contrast to Western cultures, female aggression is not viewed as unnatural or deviant but rather as a natural expression of anger.[73]

Sexuality

In view of the way the human species reproduces, it is not surprising that sexuality is part of our nature. But no society we know of leaves sexuality to nature; all have at least some rules governing "proper" conduct. There is much variation from one society to another in the degree of sexual activity permitted or encouraged before marriage, outside marriage, and even within marriage. And societies vary markedly in their tolerance of nonheterosexual sexuality.

Cultural Regulations of Sexuality: Permissiveness versus Restrictiveness

All societies seek to regulate sexual activity to some degree, and there is a lot of variation cross-culturally. Some societies allow premarital sex; others forbid it. The same is true for extramarital sex. In addition, a society's degree of restrictiveness is not always consistent throughout the life span or for all aspects of sex. For example, a number of societies ease sexual restrictions somewhat for adolescents, and many become more restrictive for adults.[74] Then, too, societies change over time. The United States has traditionally been restrictive, but until recently—before the emergence of the AIDS epidemic—more permissive attitudes were gaining acceptance.

Premarital Sex   The degree to which sex before marriage is approved or disapproved of varies greatly from society to society. The Trobriand Islanders, for example, approved of and encouraged premarital sex, seeing it as an important preparation for later marriage roles. Both girls and boys were given complete instruction in all forms of sexual expression at the onset of puberty and were allowed plenty of opportunity for intimacy. Some societies not only allow premarital sex on a casual basis but specifically encourage trial marriages between adolescents. Among the Ila-speaking peoples of central Africa, at harvest time girls were given houses of their own where they could play at being wife with the boys of their choice.[75]

Some cultures are more relaxed about sexuality than others. Does public sculpture reflect that? A park in Oslo, Norway, is dedicated to sculptures by Gustav Vigeland.

On the other hand, in many societies premarital sex was discouraged. For example, among the Tepoztlan Indians of Mexico, a girl's life became "crabbed, cribbed, confined" from the time of her first menstruation. She was not to speak to or encourage boys in the least way. To do so would be to court disgrace, to show herself to be crazy. The responsibility of guarding the chastity and reputation of one or more daughters of marriageable age was often a burden for the mother. One mother said she wished her 15-year-old daughter would marry soon because it was inconvenient to "spy" on her all the time.[76] In many Muslim societies, a girl's premarital chastity was tested after her marriage. After the wedding night, blood-stained sheets were displayed as proof of the bride's virginity.

Attitudes and practices can change markedly over time, as in the United States. Sex was generally delayed in the past until after marriage; in the 1990s, most Americans accepted or approved of premarital sex.[77]

Sex in Marriage   In most societies some form of face-to-face sexual intercourse or coitus is the usual pattern, most preferring the woman on her back and the man on top. Couples in most cultures prefer privacy. This is easier in societies with single family dwellings or separate rooms, but in societies with unpartitioned dwellings and multiple families living there, privacy is difficult to attain in the house. For example, the Siriono of Bolivia had as many as 50 hammocks 10 feet apart in their houses. Not surprisingly, couples in such societies prefer to have sex outdoors in a secluded location.[78]

Night is often preferred for sex, but some cultures specifically opted for day. For example, the Chenchu of India believed that a child conceived at night might be born blind. In some societies couples engage in sex quickly with little or no foreplay; in others foreplay may take hours.[79] Attitudes toward marital sex and the frequency of it vary widely from culture to culture. In one cross-cultural survey, 70 percent of the surveyed societies believe that frequent marital sex is viewed as a good thing, but in 9 percent frequent sex by married couples is viewed as undesirable, causing weakness, illness, and sometimes death.[80] People in most societies abstain from intercourse during menstruation, during at least part of pregnancy, and for a period after childbirth. Some societies prohibit sexual relations before various activities, such as hunting, fighting, planting, brewing, and iron smelting. Our own society is among the most lenient regarding restrictions on intercourse within marriage, imposing only rather loose restraints during mourning, menstruation, and pregnancy.[81]

Extramarital Sex   Extramarital sex is not uncommon in many societies. In about 69 percent of the world's societies men have extramarital sex more than occasionally, and in about 57 percent so do women. The frequency of such sexual activity is higher than we might expect, given that only a slight majority of societies (54 percent) say they allow extramarital sex for men, and only a small number (11 percent) say they allow it for women.[82]

In quite a few societies, then, there is quite a difference between the restrictive rule and actual practice. The Navajo of the 1940s were said to forbid adultery, but young married men under the age of 30 had 27 percent of their heterosexual contacts with women other than their wives.[83] And although people in the United States in the 1970s almost overwhelmingly rejected extramarital sex, 41 percent of married men and about 18 percent of married women had had extramarital sex. In the 1990s, proportionately more men and women reported that they had been faithful to their spouses.[84] Cross-culturally, most societies have a double standard with regard to men and women, with restrictions considerably greater for women.[85] A substantial number of societies openly accept extramarital relationships. The Chukchee of Siberia, who often traveled long distances, allowed a married man to engage in sex with his host's wife, with the understanding that he would offer the same hospitality when the host visited him.[86]

Although a society may allow extramarital sex, a recent cross-cultural study of individual reactions to extramarital sex finds that men and women try a variety of strategies to curtail such sex. Men are much more likely than women to resort to physical violence against their wives; women are more likely to distance themselves from their husbands. Gossip may be employed to shame the relationship and in more complex societies a higher authority may be asked to intervene. The researchers conclude that married women and men universally consider extramarital sex inappropriate, even in societies that permit it sometimes.[87]

Homosexuality　　When most anthropologists discuss homosexuality they usually refer to sex between males or sex between females. But while the biological male/female dichotomy corresponds to the gender male/female dichotomy in the West, other societies do not have the same gender concepts, so that the meaning of homosexuality may be different in different societies. For example, the Navajo of the American Southwest traditionally recognized four genders. Only relationships between people of the same gender would be considered homosexual and they considered such relationships inappropriate.[88] Biologically speaking, some of the cross-gender relationships would be considered homosexual in the Western view. Most of the research to date has adopted the biological view that homosexuality is between people of the same biological sex.

The range in permissiveness or restrictiveness toward homosexual relations is as great as that for any other kind of sexual activity. Among the Lepcha of the Himalayas, a man was believed to become homosexual if he ate the flesh of an uncastrated pig. But the Lepcha said that homosexual behavior was practically unheard of, and they viewed it with disgust.[89] Perhaps because many societies deny that homosexuality exists, little is known about homosexual practices in the restrictive societies. Among the permissive ones, there is variation in the type and pervasiveness of homosexuality. In some societies homosexuality is accepted but limited to certain times and certain individuals. For example, among the Papago of the southwestern United States there were "nights of saturnalia" in which homosexual tendencies could be expressed. The Papago also had many male transvestites, who wore women's clothing, did women's chores, and, if not married, could be visited by men.[90] A woman did not have the same freedom of expression. She could participate in the saturnalia feasts but only with her husband's permission, and female transvestites were nonexistent.

Homosexuality occurs even more widely in other societies. The Berber-speaking Siwans of North Africa expected all males to engage in homosexual relations. In fact, fathers made arrangements for their unmarried sons to be given to an older man in a homosexual arrangement. Siwan custom limited a man to one boy. Fear of the Egyptian government made this a secret matter, but before 1909 such arrangements were made openly. Almost all men were reported to have engaged in a homosexual relationship as boys; later, when they were between 16 and 20, they married girls.[91] Such prescribed homosexual relationships between persons of different ages are a common form of homosexuality.[92] Among the most extremely prohomosexual societies, the Etoro of New Guinea preferred homosexuality to heterosexuality. Heterosexuality was prohibited as many as 260 days a year and was forbidden in or near the house and gardens. Male homosexuality, on the other hand, was not prohibited at any time and was believed to make crops flourish and boys become strong.[93] Even among the Etoro, however, men were expected to marry women after a certain age.[94]

It is only recently that researchers have paid much attention to erotic relationships between females. Although early studies found relatively few societies with female-female sexual relationships, Evelyn Blackwood located reports of ninety-five societies with such practices, suggesting that it is more common than previously thought.[95] As with male homosexuality, some societies institutionalize same-sex sexual relationships—the Kaguru of Tanzania have female homosexual relationships between older and younger women as part of their initiation ceremonies, reminiscent of the male-male "mentor" relationships in ancient Greece.

Reasons for Restrictiveness

The research to date suggests that societies that are restrictive with regard to one aspect of heterosexual sex tend to be restrictive with regard to other aspects. Thus, societies that frown on sexual expression by young children also punish premarital and extramarital sex.[96] Furthermore, such societies tend to insist on modesty in clothing and are constrained in their talk about sex.[97] But societies that are generally restrictive about heterosexuality are not necessarily restrictive about homosexuality. Societies restrictive about premarital sex are neither more nor less likely to restrict homosexuality. In the case of extramarital sex, the situation is somewhat different. Societies that have a considerable amount of male homosexuality tend to disapprove of males having extramarital heterosexual relationships.[98] If we are going to explain restrictiveness, then, it appears we have to consider heterosexual and homosexual restrictiveness separately.

Let us consider homosexual restrictiveness first. Research so far has not yielded any clear-cut predictions, although several cross-cultural predictors about male homosexuality are intriguing. One such finding is that societies that forbid abortion and infanticide for married women (most societies permit these practices for illegitimate births) are likely to be intolerant of male homosexuality.[99] This and other findings are consistent with the point of view that homosexuality is less tolerated in societies that would like to increase population. Such societies may be intolerant of all kinds of behaviors that minimize population growth. Homosexuality would have this effect, if we assume that a higher frequency of homosexual relations is associated with a lower frequency of heterosexual relations. The less frequently heterosexual relations occur, the lower the number of conceptions there might be. Another indication that intolerance may be related to a desire for population growth is that societies with famines and severe food shortages are more likely to allow homosexuality. Famines and food shortages suggest population pressure on resources; under these conditions, homosexuality and other practices that minimize population growth may be tolerated or even encouraged.[100] Population pressure may also explain why our own society has become somewhat more tolerant of homosexuality recently. Of course, population pressure does not explain why certain individuals become homosexual or why most individuals in some societies engage in such behavior, but it might explain why some societies view such behavior more or less permissively.

Let us now turn to heterosexual behavior. Greater restrictiveness toward premarital sex tends to occur in more complex societies—societies that have hierarchies of political officials, part-time or full-time craft specialists, cities and towns, and class stratification.[101] It may be that as social inequality increases and various groups come to have differential wealth, parents become more concerned with preventing their children from marrying "beneath them." Permissiveness toward premarital sexual relationships might lead a person to become attached to someone not considered a desirable marriage partner. Even worse, from the family's point of view, such "unsuitable" sexual liaisons might result in a pregnancy that could make it impossible for a girl to marry "well." Controlling mating, then, may be a way of trying to control property. Consistent with this view is the finding that virginity is more likely to be emphasized in rank and stratified societies, in which families are likely to exchange goods and money in the course of arranging marriages.[102]

The biological fact that humans depend on sexual reproduction does not by itself help explain why females and males differ in so many ways across cultures, or why societies vary in the way they handle male and female roles. We are only beginning to investigate these questions. When we eventually understand more about how and why females and males are different or the same in roles, personality, and sexuality, we may be better able to decide how much we want the biology of sex to shape our lives.

Summary

1. That humans reproduce sexually does not explain why males and females tend to differ in appearance and behavior, and to be treated differently, in all societies.

2. All or nearly all societies assign certain activities to females and other activities to males. These worldwide gender patterns of division of labor may be explained by male-female differences in strength,

by differences in compatibility of tasks with child care, or by economy-of-effort considerations and/or the expendability of men.

3. Perhaps because women almost always have infant-and child-care responsibilities, men in most societies contribute more to primary subsistence activities, in terms of calories. But women contribute substantially to primary subsistence activities in societies that depend heavily on gathering and horticulture and in which warfare occurs while primary subsistence work has to be done. When primary and secondary subsistence work are counted, women typically work more hours than men. In most societies men are the leaders in the political arena, and warfare is almost exclusively a male activity.

4. The relative status of women compared with that of men seems to vary from one area of life to another. Whether women have relatively high status in one area does not necessarily indicate that they will have high status in another. Less complex societies, however, seem to approach more equal status for males and females in a variety of areas of life.

5. Recent field studies have suggested some consistent female-male differences in personality: Boys tend to be more aggressive than girls, and girls seem to be more responsible and helpful than boys.

6. Societies that are restrictive toward one aspect of heterosexual sex tend to be restrictive with regard to other aspects. And more complex societies tend to be more restrictive toward premarital heterosexual sex than less complex societies.

7. Societal attitudes toward homosexuality are not completely consistent with attitudes toward sexual relationships between the sexes. Societal tolerance of homosexuality is associated with tolerance of abortion and infanticide and with famines and food shortages.

Glossary Terms

compatibility-with child-care theory (p. 308)
economy-of-effort theory (p. 310)
expendability theory (p. 310)
gender differences (p. 306)
gender roles (p. 308)
gender stratification (p. 317)

primary subsistence activities (p. 311)
secondary subsistence activities (p. 311)
sex differences (p. 306)
sexually dimorphic (p. 307)
strength theory (p. 308)

Critical Questions

1. Would you expect female-male differences in personality to disappear in a society with complete gender equality in the workplace?

2. Under what circumstances would you expect male-female differences in athletic performance to disappear?

3. What conditions make the election of a female head of state most likely?

CHAPTER 14

MARRIAGE, FAMILY, AND KINSHIP

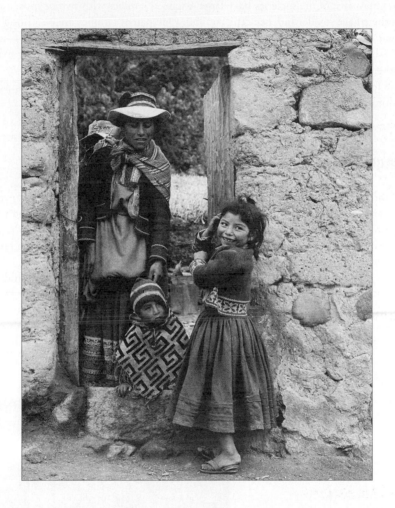

Chapter Outline

- Marriage
- The Family

- Marital Residence and Kinship

Why marriage is customary in nearly every society we know of is a classic and perplexing question, and one we attempt to deal with in this chapter. The universality of marriage does not mean that everyone in every society gets married, nor that marriage and family customs are the same in all societies. On the contrary, there is much variation from society to society in how one marries, whom one marries, and even how many persons a person can be married to simultaneously.

Families also are universal. All societies have parent-child social groups, although the form and size of families may vary. Some societies have large extended families with two or more related parent-child groups; others have smaller independent families. One-parent families are becoming increasingly common in our own and other societies. Marriage has not disappeared in these places—it is still customary to marry—but more individuals are choosing now to have children without being married.

As we will see, kin groups that include several or many families and hundreds or even thousands of people are found in many societies and structure many areas of social life. Kin groups may have important economic, social, political, and religious functions.

Marriage

When anthropologists speak of marriage, they do not mean to imply that couples everywhere must get marriage certificates or have wedding ceremonies, as in our own society. **Marriage** merely means a socially approved sexual and economic union, usually between a woman and a man. It is presumed, by both the couple and others, to be more or less permanent, and it subsumes reciprocal rights and obligations between the two spouses and between spouses and their future children.[1]

It is a socially approved sexual union in that a married couple does not have to hide the sexual nature of their relationship. A woman might say, "I want you to meet my husband," but she could not say, "I want you to meet my lover" without causing some embarrassment in most societies. Although the union may ultimately be dissolved by divorce, couples in all societies begin marriage with some idea of permanence in mind. Implicit too in marriage are reciprocal rights and obligations. These may be more or less

Weddings in some societies are very elaborate. Here a Minangkabau bride dressed in elaborate clothes sits in the windowsill of a home in Padang, West Sumatra, Indonesia.

specific and formalized regarding matters of property, finances, and child rearing. Marriage entails both a sexual and an economic relationship, as George Peter Murdock noted: "Sexual relations can occur without economic cooperation, and there can be a division of labor between men and women without sex. But marriage unites the economic and the sexual."[2]

Why Is Marriage Universal?

Because virtually all societies practice female-male marriage as we have defined it, we can assume that the custom is adaptive. Several interpretations have traditionally been offered to explain why all human societies have the custom of marriage. Each suggests that marriage solves problems found in all societies—how to share the products of a gender division of labor; how to care for infants, who are dependent for a long time; and how to minimize sexual competition. To evaluate the plausibility of these interpretations, we must ask whether marriage provides the best or the only reasonable solution to each problem. After all, we are trying to explain a custom that is presumably a universal solution. The comparative study of other animals, some of which have something like marriage, may help us to evaluate these explanations.

Gender Division of Labor   We noted in the chapter on sex and gender that males and females in every society perform different economic activities. This gender division of labor has often been cited as a reason for marriage because society has to have some mechanism by which women and men share the products of their labor.[3] But it seems unlikely that marriage is the only possible solution. All the products brought in by both women and men could be shared in the group. Or a small group of men and women, such as brothers and sisters, might be pledged to cooperate economically. Thus, although marriage may solve the problem of sharing the fruits of a division of labor, it clearly is not the only possible solution.

Prolonged Infant Dependency   Humans exhibit the longest period of infant dependency of any primate. The child's prolonged dependence places the greatest burden on the mother, who is the main child caregiver in most societies. Prolonged child care may limit the kinds of work mothers can do. Also, they may need the help of a man to do certain types of work, such as hunting, that are incompatible with child care. Because of this prolonged dependency, it has been suggested, marriage is necessary.[4] But here the argument becomes essentially the same as the division-of-labor argument, and it has the same logical weakness. It is not clear why a group of women and men, such as a hunter-gatherer band, could not cooperate in providing for dependent children without marriage.

Sexual Competition   Unlike most other female primates, the human female may engage in intercourse at any time throughout the year. Some scholars have suggested that more or less continuous female sexuality created a serious problem—considerable sexual competition between males for females. It is argued that society had to prevent such competition in order to survive, that it had to develop marriage to minimize the rivalry among males for females in order to reduce the chance of lethal and destructive conflict.[5]

There are several problems with this argument. First, why should continuous female sexuality make for more sexual competition in the first place? One might argue the other way around. There might be more if females were less frequently interested in sex. Second, males of many animal species, even some that have relatively frequent female sexuality (as do many of our close primate relatives), do not show much aggression over females. Third, why couldn't sexual competition, even if it existed, be regulated by cultural rules other than marriage? For instance, society might have adopted a rule whereby men and women circulated among all the opposite-sex members of the group, each person staying a specified length of time with each partner. Such a system presumably would solve the problem of sexual competition. On the other hand, such a system might not work particularly well if individuals came to prefer certain other individuals. Jealousies attending those attachments might give rise to even more competition.

Other Mammals and Birds: Postpartum Requirements   None of the theories we have discussed explains convincingly why marriage is the only or the best solution to a particular problem. Also, we now have some comparative evidence on mammals and birds that casts doubt on those theories.[6] How can evidence from other animals help us evaluate theories about human marriage? If we look at the animals that, like humans, have some sort of stable female-male mating, as compared with those that are completely promiscuous, we can perhaps see what sorts of factors may predict male-female bonding in the warm-blooded animal species. Most species of birds, and some mammals such as wolves and beavers, have "marriage." In a random sample of 40 mammal and bird species, none of the 3 factors previously discussed —division of labor, prolonged infant dependency, and greater female sexuality—predicts or is correlated strongly with male-female bonding. With respect to division of labor by sex, most other animals have nothing comparable to a human-like division of labor, but many have stable female-male matings anyway. The two other supposed factors—prolonged infant dependency and female sexuality—predict just the opposite of what we might expect. Mammal and bird species that have longer dependency periods or more female sexuality are less likely to have stable matings.

Does anything predict male-female bonding? One factor does among mammals and birds, and it may also help explain human marriage. Animal species in which females can simultaneously feed themselves and their babies after birth (*postpartum*) tend not to have stable matings; species in which postpartum mothers cannot feed themselves and their babies at the same time tend to have stable matings. Among the typical bird species, a mother would have difficulty feeding herself and her babies simultaneously. Because the young cannot fly for a while and must be protected in a nest, the mother risks losing them to other animals if she goes off to obtain food. But if she has a male bonded to her (as most bird species do), he can bring back food or take a turn watching the nest. Among animal species that have no postpartum feeding problem, babies almost immediately after birth are able to travel with the mother as she moves about to eat (as do grazers such as horses), or the mother can transport the babies as she moves about to eat (as do baboons and kangaroos). We think the human female has a postpartum feeding problem. When humans lost most of their body hair, babies could not readily travel with the mother by clinging to her fur. And when humans began to depend on certain kinds of food-getting that could be dangerous (such as hunting), mothers could not engage in such work with their infants along.[7]

"I do love you. But, to be perfectly honest, I would have loved
any other lovebird who happened to turn up."
(Rothco Cartoons)

Recent research on the Hadza foragers of Tanzania appears to support this view. Frank Marlowe found that the caloric contribution of mothers and fathers depends on whether or not they have a nursing infant. Women may generally contribute more calories than men to the diet, but married women who are nursing contribute substantially less than other married women. The lower contribution of nursing mothers appears to be made up by the father. Fathers with nursing children contribute significantly more food to the household than fathers with older children.[8]

Even if we assume that human mothers have a postpartum feeding problem, we still have to ask if marriage is the most likely solution to the problem. We think so, because other conceivable solutions probably would not work as well. For example, if a mother took turns babysitting with another mother, neither might be able to collect enough food for both mothers and the two sets of children dependent on them. But a mother and father share the same set of children, and therefore it would be easier for them to feed themselves and their children adequately. Another possible solution is no pair bonding at all, just a promiscuous group of males and females. But in that kind of arrangement, we think, a particular mother probably would not always be able to count on some male to watch her baby when she had to go out for food or to bring her food when she had to watch her baby. Thus, it seems to us that the problem of postpartum feeding by itself helps to explain why some animals, including humans, have relatively stable male-female bonds.[9] Of course, there is still the question of whether research on other animals can be applied to human beings. We think it can, but not everybody will agree.

How Does One Marry?

When we say that marriage is a socially approved sexual and economic union, we mean that all societies have some way of marking the onset of a marriage, but the ways of doing so vary considerably. For reasons that we don't fully understand, some cultures mark marriages by elaborate rites and celebrations, others mark marriages in much more informal ways. And most societies have economic transactions before, during, or even after the onset of the marriages.

Economic Aspects of Marriage   "It's not man that marries maid, but field marries field, vineyard marries vineyard, cattle marry cattle." In its down-to-earth way, this German peasant saying indicates that in many societies marriage involves economic considerations. In about 75 percent of the societies known to anthropology,[10] one or more explicit economic transactions take place before or after the marriage.

BRIDE PRICE   **Bride price or bride wealth** is a gift of money or goods from the groom or his kin to the bride's kin. The gift usually grants the groom the right to marry the bride and the right to her children. Bride price is the most common form of economic transaction. In one cross-cultural sample, 44 percent of the societies with economic transactions at marriage practiced bride price; in almost all of those societies the bride price was substantial.[11] Bride price occurs all over the world but is especially common in Africa and Oceania. Payment can be made in different currencies; livestock and food are two of the more common. With the increased importance of commercial exchange, money has increasingly become part of the bride price payments.

What kinds of societies are likely to have the custom of bride price? Cross-culturally, societies with bride price are likely to practice horticulture and lack social stratification. Bride price is also likely where women contribute a great deal to primary subsistence activities[12] and where they contribute more than men to all kinds of economic activities.[13] Although these findings might suggest that women are highly valued in such societies, recall that the status of women relative to men is not higher in societies in which women contribute a lot to primary subsistence activities. Indeed, bride price is likely to occur in societies in which men make most of the decisions in the household,[14] and decision making by men is one indicator of lower status for women.

BRIDE SERVICE   **Bride service**, which is the next most common type of economic transaction at marriage—occurring in about 19 percent of the societies with economic transactions—requires the groom to work for the bride's family, sometimes before the marriage begins, sometimes after. Bride service varies in duration. In some societies it lasts for only a few months; in others, as long as several years. Native North and South American societies were likely to practice bride service, particularly if they were egalitarian food collectors.[15]

EXCHANGE OF FEMALES   Of the societies that have economic transactions at marriage, 6 percent have the custom whereby a sister or female relative of the groom is exchanged for the bride. These societies tend to be horticultural, egalitarian, and to have a relatively high contribution of women to primary subsistence.[16]

GIFT EXCHANGE   Gift exchange, which involves the exchange of gifts of about equal value by the two kin groups about to be linked by marriage, occurs somewhat more often than the exchange of females (about 11 percent of those with economic transactions).[17] For example, among the Andaman Islanders, as soon as a boy and girl indicate their intention to marry, their respective sets of parents cease all communication and begin sending gifts of food and other objects to each other through a third party. This arrangement continues until the marriage is completed and the two kin groups are united.[18]

DOWRY   A **dowry** is usually a substantial transfer of goods or money from the bride's family to the bride, the groom, or the couple.[19] Unlike the types of transactions we have discussed so far, the dowry, which occurs in about 8 percent of the societies with economic transactions, is usually not a transaction between the kin of the bride and the kin of the groom. A family has to have wealth to give a dowry, but because the goods go to the new household, no wealth comes back to the family that gave the

Quilts that are part of a dowry in the Kyrgyz Republic.

dowry. Payment of dowries was common in medieval and Renaissance Europe, where the size of the dowry often determined the desirability of the daughter. The custom is still practiced in parts of eastern Europe and in sections of southern Italy and France, where land is often the major item provided by the bride's family. Parts of India also practice the dowry. In contrast to societies with bride price, societies with dowry tend to be those in which women contribute relatively little to primary subsistence activities, there is a high degree of social stratification, and a man is not allowed to be married to more than one woman simultaneously.[20]

INDIRECT DOWRY   The dowry is provided by the bride's family to the bride, the groom, or the couple. But sometimes the payments to the bride originate from the groom's family. Because the goods are sometimes first given to the bride's father, who passes most if not all of them to her, this kind of transaction is called **indirect dowry**.[21] Indirect dowry occurs in about 12 percent of the societies in which marriage involves an economic transaction.

Restrictions on Marriage: The Universal Incest Taboo

Hollywood and its press agents notwithstanding, marriage is not always based solely on mutual love, independently discovered and expressed by the two life-partners-to-be. Nor is it based on sex or wealth alone. Even when love, sex, and economics are contributing factors, regulations specify whom one may or may not marry. Perhaps the most rigid regulation, found in *all* cultures, is the **incest taboo**, which prohibits sexual intercourse or marriage between some categories of kin.

The most universal aspect of the incest taboo is the prohibition of sexual intercourse or marriage between mother and son, father and daughter, and brother and sister. No society in recent times has permitted either sexual intercourse or marriage between those pairs. A few societies in the past, however, did permit incest, mostly within the royal and aristocratic families, though generally it was forbidden to the rest of the population. For example, the Incan and Hawaiian royal families allowed marriage within the family. Probably the best-known example of allowed incest involved Cleopatra of Egypt. Cleopatra was married to two of her younger brothers at different times.[22] The reasons seem to have been partly religious—a member of the family of the pharaoh, who was considered a god, could not marry any "ordinary" human—and partly economic, for marriage within the family kept the royal property undivided. In Egypt, between 30 B.C. and A.D. 324, incest was allowed not just in the royal family; an estimated 8 percent of commoner marriages were brother-sister marriages.[23] But, despite these exceptions, the fact remains that no culture we know of today permits or accepts incest within the nuclear family.

Whom Should One Marry?

Probably every child in our society knows the story of Cinderella—the poor, downtrodden, but lovely girl who accidentally meets, falls in love with, and eventually marries a prince. It is a charming tale, but as a guide to mate choice in our society it is misleading. In addition to the incest taboo, societies often have rules restricting marriage with other persons, as well as preferences about which other persons are the most desirable mates. Even in a modern, urbanized society such as ours, where theoretically mate choice is free, people tend to marry within their own class and geographic area.

Arranged Marriages   In an appreciable number of societies, marriages are arranged; negotiations are handled by the immediate families or by go-betweens. Sometimes betrothals are completed while the future partners are still children. This was formerly the custom in much of Hindu India, China, Japan,

A priest in India prays for young women to get good husbands and to have many sons. Marriages are often still arranged.

and eastern and southern Europe. Implicit in the arranged marriage is the conviction that the joining together of two kin groups to form new social and economic ties is too important to be left to free choice.

In many places arranged marriages are beginning to disappear, and couples are beginning to have more say about their marriage partners. As recently as 1960, marriages were still arranged on the Pacific island of Rotuma, and sometimes the bride and groom did not meet until the wedding day. Today weddings are much the same, but couples are allowed to "go out" and have a say about whom they wish to marry.[24]

Exogamy and Endogamy   Marriage partners often must be chosen from outside one's own kin group or community; this is known as a rule of **exogamy**. Exogamy may mean marrying outside a particular group of kin or outside a particular village or group of villages. When there are rules of exogamy, violations are often believed to cause harm. On the islands of Yap in Micronesia, people who are related through women are referred to as "people of one belly." The elders say that if two people from the same kinship group married, they would not have any female children and the group would die out.[25]

A study of foragers and horticulturalists found a clear relationship between population density and the distance between the communities of the husband and wife—the lower the density, the greater the marriage distance. Because foragers generally have lower densities than horticulturalists, they generally have further to go to find mates. Among the !Kung, for instance, the average husband and wife had lived 65 kilometers (40 miles) from each other before they were married.[26]

A rule of **endogamy** obliges a person to marry within some group. The caste groups of India traditionally have been endogamous. The higher castes believed that marriage with lower castes would "pollute" them, and such unions were forbidden. Caste endogamy is also found in some parts of Africa.

Cousin Marriages   Kinship terminology for most people in the United States does not differentiate between types of cousins. In some other societies such distinctions may be important, particularly with regard to first cousins; the terms for the different kinds of first cousins may indicate which cousins are suitable marriage partners (sometimes even preferred mates) and which are not. Although most societies prohibit marriage with all types of first cousins,[27] some societies allow and even prefer particular kinds of cousin marriage.

Cross-cousins are children of **siblings** of the opposite sex; that is, a person's cross-cousins are father's sisters' children and mother's brothers' children. **Parallel cousins** are children of siblings of the same sex; a person's parallel cousins, then, are father's brothers' children and mother's sisters' children. The Chippewa Indians used to practice cross-cousin marriage, as well as cross-cousin joking. With his female cross-cousins, a Chippewa man was expected to exchange broad, risqué jokes, but he would not do so with his parallel cousins, with whom severe propriety was the rule. In general, in any society in which cross-cousin marriage is allowed but parallel-cousin is not, there is a joking relationship between a man and his female cross-cousins. This attitude contrasts with the formal and very respectful relationship the man maintains with female parallel cousins. Apparently, the joking relationship signifies the possibility of marriage, whereas the respectful relationship signifies the extension of the incest taboo to parallel cousins.

Parallel-cousin marriage is fairly rare, but Muslim societies usually prefer such marriages, allowing other cousin marriages as well. The Kurds, who are mostly Sunni Muslims, prefer a young man to marry his father's brother's daughter (for the young woman this would be her father's brother's son). The father and his brother usually live near each other, so the woman will stay close to home in such a marriage. The bride and groom are also in the same kin group, so marriage in this case also entails kin group endogamy.[28]

There is evidence from cross-cultural research that cousin marriages are most apt to be permitted in relatively large and densely populated societies. Perhaps this is because the likelihood of such marriages, and therefore the risks of harmful inbreeding effects, are minimal in those societies.[29]

How Many Does One Marry?

We are accustomed to thinking of marriage as involving just one man and one woman at a time—**monogamy**—but most societies known to anthropology have allowed a man to be married to more than one woman at the same time—**polygyny**. At any given time, however, the majority of men in societies permitting polygyny are married monogamously; few or no societies have enough women to permit most men to have at least two wives. Polygyny's mirror image—one woman being married to more than one man at the same time, called **polyandry**—is practiced in very few societies. Polygyny and polyandry are the two types of **polygamy**, or plural spouse marriage. **Group marriage**, in which more than one man is married to more than one woman at the same time, sometimes occurs but is not customary in any known society.

Polygyny   The Old Testament has many references to men with more than one wife simultaneously: King David and King Solomon are just two examples of men polygynously married. Polygyny in many societies is a mark of a man's great wealth or high status. In such societies only the very wealthy can, and are expected to, support more than one wife. But a man does not always have to be wealthy to be polygynous; indeed, in some societies in which women are important contributors to the economy, it seems that men try to have more than one wife in order to become wealthier. For example, among the Siwai, a society in the South Pacific, status is achieved through feast giving. Pork is the main dish at these feasts, so the Siwai associate pig raising with prestige. This interest in pigs sparks an interest in wives, because in Siwai society women raise the food needed to raise pigs. Thus, although having many wives does not in itself confer status among the Siwai, the increase in pig herds that may result from polygyny is a source of prestige for the owner.[30]

Polygynously married Siwai men do seem to have greater prestige, but they complain that a household with multiple wives is difficult. Sinu, a Siwai, described his plight:

There is never peace for a long time in a polygynous family. If the husband sleeps in the house of one wife, the other one sulks all the next day. If the man is so stupid as to sleep two consecutive nights in the house of one wife, the other one will refuse to cook for him, saying, "So-and-so is your wife; go to her for food. Since I am not good enough for you to sleep with, then my food is not good enough for you to eat."[31]

Why might there be little or no jealousy between co-wives in a society? One possible reason is that a man is married to two or more sisters—**sororal polygyny**; it seems that sisters, having grown up together, are more likely to get along and cooperate as co-wives than are co-wives who are not also sisters—**nonsororal polygyny**. Other customs may also lessen jealousy between co-wives:

1. Co-wives who are not sisters tend to have separate living quarters; sororal co-wives almost always live together.
2. Co-wives have clearly defined equal rights in matters of sex, economics, and personal possessions.
3. Senior wives often have special prestige, which may compensate the first wife for her loss of physical attractiveness.[32]

We must remember that, although jealousy is commonly mentioned in polygynous marriages, people who practice polygyny think it has considerable advantages. In a study conducted by Philip and Janet Kilbride in Kenya, female as well as male married people agreed that polygyny had economic and political advantages. Because they tend to be large, polygynous families provide plenty of farm labor and extra food that can be marketed. They also tend to be influential in their communities and are likely to produce individuals who become government officials.[33] And in South Africa, Connie Anderson found that women choose to be married to a man with other wives because the other wives could help with child care and household work, provide companionship, and allow more freedom to come and go. Some women said they chose polygynous marriages because there was a shortage of marriageable males.[34]

How can we account for the fact that polygyny is allowed and often preferred in most of the societies known to anthropology? One theory is that polygyny will be permitted in societies that have a long **postpartum sex taboo**.[35] Recall that John Whiting suggested that couples, particularly in societies where

Polygyny is practiced by some in this country, even though it is prohibited by law.

staple foods have little protein, abstain from sexual intercourse for a long time after their child is born to protect their child from *kwashiorkor*. If a child gets protein from mother's milk during its first few years, the likelihood of contracting kwashiorkor may be greatly reduced. Societies with long postpartum sex taboos also tend to be polygynous. Perhaps, Whiting suggests, a man's having more than one wife is a cultural adjustment to the taboo since men may seek other sexual relationships during the period of a long postpartum sex taboo. However, it is not clear why polygyny is the only possible solution to the problem. After all, it is conceivable that all of a man's wives might be subject to the postpartum sex taboo at the same time. Furthermore, there may be sexual outlets outside marriage.

Another explanation of polygyny is that it is a response to an excess of women over men due largely to the prevalence of warfare in a society. Because men and not women are generally the warriors, warfare almost always takes a greater toll of men's lives. Given that almost all adults in noncommercial societies are married, polygyny may be a way of providing spouses for surplus women. Indeed, there is evidence that societies with imbalanced sex ratios in favor of women tend to have both polygyny and high male mortality in warfare. Conversely, societies with balanced sex ratios tend to have both monogamy and low male mortality in warfare.[36]

A third explanation is that a society will allow polygyny when men marry at an older age than women. The argument is similar to the sex ratio interpretation. Delaying the age of marriage for men would produce an artificial, though not an actual, excess of marriageable women. Why marriage for men is delayed is not clear, but the delay does predict polygyny.[37]

Is one of these explanations better than the others, or are all three factors—long postpartum sex taboo, an imbalanced sex ratio in favor of women, and delayed age of marriage for men—important in explaining polygyny? One way of trying to decide among alternative explanations is to do what is called a *statistical-control analysis,* which allows us to see if a particular factor still predicts when the effects of other possible factors are removed. In this case, when the possible effect of sex ratio is removed, a long postpartum sex taboo no longer predicts polygyny and hence is probably not a cause of polygyny.[38] But both an actual excess of women and a late age of marriage for men seem to be strong predictors of polygyny. Added together, these two factors predict even more strongly.[39]

Behavioral ecologists have also suggested ecological reasons why both men and women might prefer polygynous marriages. If there are enough resources, men might prefer polygyny because they can have more children if they have more than one wife. If resources are highly variable and men control resources, women might find it advantageous to marry a man with many resources even if she is a second wife. A recent study of foragers suggests that foraging societies in which men control more hunting or fishing territory are more likely to be polygynous.[40] The main problem with the theory of variable resources and their marital consequences is that many societies, particularly in the "modern" world, have great variability in wealth, but little polygyny. So behavioral ecologists have had to argue that polygyny is lacking because of socially imposed constraints. Degree of disease in the environment may also be a factor. Bobbi Low has suggested that a high incidence of disease may reduce the prevalence of "healthy" men. In such cases it may be to a woman's advantage to marry a "healthy" man even if he is already married, and it may be to a man's advantage to marry several unrelated women to maximize genetic variation (and disease resistance) among his children. Indeed, societies with many pathogens are more likely to have polygyny.[41] Further research is needed to compare the degree of disease explanation of polygyny with the imbalanced sex-ratio explanation.

Polyandry   George Peter Murdock's "World Ethnographic Sample" included only four societies (less than 1 percent of the total) in which polyandry, or the marriage of several men to one woman, was practiced.[42] When the husbands are brothers we call it *fraternal polyandry*; if they are not brothers, it is *nonfraternal polyandry*. Some Tibetans, the Toda of India, and the Sinhalese of Sri Lanka have practiced fraternal polyandry. Among the Tibetans who practice fraternal polyandry, biological paternity seems to be of no particular concern; there is no attempt to link children biologically to a particular brother, and all children are treated the same.[43]

One possible explanation for the practice of polyandry is a shortage of women. The Toda practiced female infanticide;[44] the Sinhalese had a shortage of women but denied the practice of female infanticide.[45] A correlation between shortage of women and polyandry would account for why polyandry is so rare in the ethnographic record; an excess of men is rare cross-culturally.

Another possible explanation is that polyandry is an adaptive response to severely limited resources. Melvyn Goldstein studied Tibetans who live in the northwestern corner of Nepal, above 12,000 feet in elevation. Cultivable land is extremely scarce there, with most families having less than an acre. The people say they practice fraternal polyandry in order to prevent the division of a family's farm and animals. Instead of dividing up their land among them and each taking a wife, brothers preserve the family farm by sharing a wife. Although not recognized by the Tibetans, their practice of polyandry minimizes population growth. There are as many women as men of marriageable age. But about 30 percent of the women do not marry, and, although these women do have some children, they have far fewer than married women. Thus, the practice of polyandry minimizes the number of mouths to feed and therefore maximizes the standard of living of the polyandrous family.[46]

The Family

All societies have families. A **family** is a social and economic unit consisting minimally of one or more parents and their children. Members of a family always have certain reciprocal rights and obligations, particularly economic ones. Family members usually live in one household, but common residence is not a defining feature of families. In simpler societies, the family and the household tend to be indistinguishable; it is only in more complex societies, and in societies becoming dependent on commercial exchange, that some members of a family may live elsewhere.[47]

Variation in Family Form

Most societies have families that are larger than the single-parent family (the parent in such families is usually the mother, in which case the unit is called the **matrifocal family**), the monogamous (single-couple) family (called the **nuclear family**), or the polygamous family. The **extended family** is the prevailing form of family in more than half the societies known to anthropology.[48] It may consist of two or more single-parent, monogamous, polygynous, or polyandrous families linked by a blood tie. Most commonly, the extended family consists of a married couple and one or more of the married children, all living in the same house or household. An extended family, however, is sometimes composed solely of families linked through a sibling tie. Such a family might consist of two married brothers, their wives, and their children. Extended families may be very large, containing many relatives and including three or four generations.

Extended-Family Households

In a society composed of extended-family households, marriage does not bring as pronounced a change in lifestyle as it does in our culture, where the couple typically moves to a new residence and forms a new, and basically independent, family unit. In extended families, the newlyweds are assimilated into an existing family unit. Margaret Mead described such a situation in Samoa:

. . . the young couple live in the main household, simply receiving a bamboo pillow, a mosquito net and a pile of mats for their bed. . . . The wife works with all the women of the household and waits on all the men. The husband shares the enterprises of the other men and boys. Neither in personal service given or received are the two marked off as a unit.[49]

A young couple in Samoa, as in other societies with extended families, generally has little decision-making power over the governing of the household. Often the responsibility of running the household rests with the senior male. Nor can the new family accumulate its own property and become independent; it is a part of the larger corporate structure. Eventually the young people will have authority when the parents die.

Possible Reasons for Extended-Family Households

Why do most societies known to anthropology commonly have extended-family households? Extended-family households are found most frequently in societies with sedentary agricultural economies. M. F. Nimkoff and Russell Middleton suggested that the extended family may be a social mechanism that prevents the economically ruinous division of family property in societies in which property such as cultivated land is important.[50]

But agriculture is only a weak predictor of extended-family households. Many agriculturalists lack them, and many nonagricultural societies have them. A different theory is that extended-family households come to prevail in societies that have incompatible activity requirements—that is, requirements that cannot be met by a mother or a father in a one-family household. In other words, extended-family households are generally favored when the work a mother has to do outside the home (cultivating fields or gathering foods far away) makes it difficult for her to also care for her children and do other household tasks. Similarly, extended families may be favored when the required outside activities of a father (warfare, trading trips, or wage labor far away) make it difficult for him to do the subsistence work required of males. There is cross-cultural evidence that societies with such incompatible activity requirements are more

Kazaks usually live in extended families and collectively herd their livestock. The youngest son will inherit the father's house, and the older sons will build their own houses nearby when they get married.

ONE-PARENT FAMILIES: WHY THE RECENT INCREASE?

Not only is the custom of marriage almost universal, but in most societies known to anthropology most people marry. And they usually remarry if they divorce. This means that, except for the death of a spouse or temporarily during times of divorce or separation, one-parent families are relatively uncommon in most societies.

In many Western countries, however, there has been a dramatic increase recently in the percentage of one-parent families, most of which (about 90 percent) are female-headed families. For example, in the 1960s about 9 percent of families in the United States were one-parent families, but by 2003 the figure jumped to about 30 percent. Whereas Sweden once led the Western countries in percentage of one-parent families—about 13 percent in the 1970s—the United States now has the higher percentage.

Before we examine the reasons for the increase, we need to consider that there are a variety of ways to become a one-parent family. First, many one-parent families result from the divorce or separation of two-parent families. Second, many one-parent families result from births out of wedlock. In addition, some result from the death of a spouse and others from the decision by a single person to have a child.

Many researchers suggest that the ease of divorce is largely responsible for the increase in one-parent families. On the face of it, this explanation seems plausible. But it is flawed. In many countries during the late 1960s and early 1970s, changes in the law made getting a divorce much easier, and the percentage of one-parent families did rise after that. But why did so many countries ease divorce restrictions at the same time? A high divorce rate by itself will make for a higher percentage of one-parent households only if individuals do not remarry quickly. In the United States, for example, remarriage rates did decline sharply in the mid-1960s, particularly among younger, better educated women, and so the percentage of one-parent households may have risen for that reason. In many other countries, divorce rates stabilized in the 1980s, but the percentage of one-parent families still increased. Thus, easier divorce does not fully explain the increase in number of one-parent families.

Although some parents are clearly choosing to stay single, many might prefer to marry if they could find an appropriate spouse. In some countries, and among some ethnic groups within some countries, there are many fewer males than females, and sometimes a high proportion of the males have poor economic prospects. In the former Soviet Union, there are many more women than men because males are more likely to have died from war, alcoholism, and accidents. The United States does not have such a skewed sex ratio, but in some neighborhoods, particularly poor neighborhoods, there are very high mortality rates for young males. And many males in such neighborhoods do not have work. One study by Daniel Lichter and his colleagues estimated that for every 100 African-American women between the ages of 21 and 28, there were fewer than 80 available African-American men. If we count only men who are employed full or part time, the number of available men per 100 women drops below 50. And a comparison of 85 countries finds that single parenthood is much more likely when there is higher male unemployment as well as when there are fewer men than women of a comparable age. So there may be considerable merit to the argument that one-parent families (usually headed by women) will be likely when a spouse (particularly an employed one) is hard to find.

Another popular explanation for the rise in number of one-parent families is that, in contrast to the past, women can manage without husbands because of support from the state. This scenario seems to fit Sweden, where unmarried and divorced mothers receive many social supports and allowances for maternity and educational leave. But Iceland has few social supports from the government and yet has the highest rate of out-of-wedlock births of all the Scandinavian countries. In the United States, the welfare argument fails to predict changes over time. The program called Aid to Families with Dependent Children provided aid largely to single mothers. If the theory about government help was correct, increases in such aid would generally predict increases in the percentage of mother-headed households. But, in fact, during the 1970s the percentage of families receiving aid and the value of aid decreased, while the percentage of mother-headed households increased. In the 1980s it was more difficult to go "on welfare," but the percentage of mother-headed households increased anyway.

Women might be more able to manage alone if they have high-paying employment, and therefore we might expect more one-parent families by choice, as more women enter the job market. But, although this may explain the choices of some women, recent research finds that employed women generally are *more* rather than less likely to marry.

In any case, there seems to be a general association between commercial economies and the possibility of one-parent families. Is there something about subsistence economies that promotes marriage and something about commercial economies that detracts from it? Although marriage is not universally based on love or companionship, it entails a great deal of economic and other kinds of interdependence, particularly in not-so-commercial economies. Market economies allow other possibilities; goods and services can be bought and sold, and governments may take over functions normally handled by kin and family. So the one-parent family is likely to remain an option—either a choice or a necessity—for some people.

Sources: Alisa Burns and Cath Scott, *Mother-Headed Families and Why They Have Increased* (Hillsdale, NJ: Lawrence Erlbaum Associates, 1994); David Popenoe, *Disturbing the Nest: Family Change and Decline in Modern Societies* (New York: Aldine, 1988); Daniel T. Lichter, Diane K. McLaughlin, George Kephart, and David J. Landry, "Race and the Retreat from Marriage: A Shortage of Marriageable Men?" *American Sociological Review,* 57 (1992): 781–99; Nigel Barber, "Paternal Investment Prospects and Cross-National Differences in Single Parenthood," *Cross-Cultural Research,* 37 (2003): 163–77; Jason Fields, *America's Families and Living Arrangements: 2003* (Washington, D.C.: Current Population Reports, P20 553, U.S. Census Bureau, 2003).

likely to have extended-family households than societies with compatible activity requirements, regardless of whether or not the society is agricultural. Even in commercial societies, a family may be able to obtain the necessary help by "buying" the required services so the need for extended families may be lessened.[51] Of course, even in societies with money economies, not everyone can buy required services. Those who are poor may need to live in extended families, and extended-family living may become more common even in the middle class when the economy is depressed.

In many societies there are kin groups even larger than extended families. The rest of this chapter discusses the varieties of such groupings.

Marital Residence and Kinship

In the United States and Canada, as well as in many other industrial societies, a young man and woman usually establish a place of residence apart from their parents or other relatives when they marry, if they have not already moved away before that. Our society is so oriented toward this pattern of marital residence—*neolocal (new-place) residence*—that it seems to be the obvious and natural one to follow. Young adults of all income levels learn to live away from home most of the year if they join the army or attend an out-of-town college. In any case, when a young person marries, he or she generally lives apart from family.

So familiar is neolocal residence to us that we tend to assume that all societies must practice the same pattern. On the contrary, of the 565 societies in George Peter Murdock's "World Ethnographic Sample," only about 5 percent followed this practice.[52] About 95 percent of the world's societies have had some other pattern of residence whereby a new couple settles within, or very close to, the household of the parents or some other close relative of either the groom or the bride. As we shall see, marital residence largely predicts the types of kin groups found in a society.

Patterns of Marital Residence

In societies in which newly married couples customarily live with or close to their kin, the pattern of residence varies. Children in all societies are required to marry outside the nuclear family, because of the incest taboo, and, with few exceptions, couples in almost all societies live together after they are married. Therefore some children have to leave home when they marry. But which married children remain at home and which reside elsewhere? Societies vary in the way they deal with this question, but there are not many different patterns. The prevailing one could be one of the following (the percentages of each in the ethnographic record do not sum to 100 because of rounding):

1. **Patrilocal residence.**   The son stays and the daughter leaves, so that the married couple lives with or near the husband's parents (67 percent of all societies in the ethnographic record).
2. **Matrilocal residence.**   The daughter stays and the son leaves, so that the married couple lives with or near the wife's parents (15 percent of all societies).
3. **Bilocal residence.**   Either the son or the daughter leaves, so that the married couple lives with or near either the wife's or the husband's parents (7 percent of all societies).

In many societies known to anthropology, the bride goes to live with or near the husband's family. In the town of Itako, Japan, a bride is transported to the bridegroom's place.

4. **Avunculocal residence.**   Both son and daughter normally leave, but the son and his wife settle with or near his mother's brother (4 percent of all societies).[53]

In these definitions, we use the phrase "the married couple lives *with or near*" a particular set of in-laws. When couples live with or near the kin of a spouse, the couple may live in the same household with those kin, creating an *extended-family* household, or they may live separately in an *independent-family* household, but nearby. (Because matrilocal, patrilocal, and avunculocal residence specify just one pattern, they are often called nonoptional or **unilocal residence** patterns.) A fifth pattern of residence is neolocal, in which the newly married couple does not live with or near kin.

5. **Neolocal residence.**   Both son and daughter leave; married couples live apart from the relatives of both spouses (5 percent of all societies). This is in the ethnographic record; in the modern world neolocal residence is customary more often.

How does place of residence affect the social life of the couple? Because the pattern of residence governs with whom or near whom individuals live, it largely determines which people those individuals interact with and have to depend on. If a married couple is surrounded by the kin of the husband, for example, chances are that those relatives will figure importantly in the couple's future. Whether the couple lives with or near the husband's or the wife's kin can also have important consequences for the status of the husband or wife. If married couples live patrilocally, as occurs in most societies, the wife may be far from her own kin. In any case, she will be an outsider among a group of male relatives who have grown up together. The feeling of being an outsider is particularly strong when the wife has moved into a patrilocal extended-family household.

Among the Tiv of central Nigeria,[54] the patrilocal extended family consists of the "great father," who is the head of the household, and his younger brothers, his sons, and his younger brothers' sons. Also included are the in-marrying wives and all unmarried children. (The sisters and daughters of the household head who have married would have gone to live where their husbands lived.) Authority is strongly vested in the male line, particularly the oldest of the household, who has authority over bride price, disputes, punishment, and plans for new buildings.

A somewhat different situation exists if the husband comes to live with or near his wife's parents. In this case, the wife and her kin take on somewhat greater importance, and the husband is the outsider. As we shall see, however, the matrilocal situation is not quite the mirror image of the patrilocal, because in matrilocal societies the husband's kin often are not far away. Moreover, even though residence is matrilocal, women often do not have as much to say in decision making as their brothers do.

If the married couple does not live with or near the parents or close kin of either spouse, the situation is again quite different. It should not be surprising that relatives and kinship connections do not figure very largely in everyday life in neolocal residence situations. Toward the end of this chapter we consider the factors that may explain residential variation; these same factors may also help explain the types of kinship groups that develop.

The Structure of Kinship

In noncommercial societies, kinship connections structure many areas of social life—from the kind of access an individual has to productive resources to the kind of political alliances formed between communities and larger territorial groups. In some societies, in fact, kinship connections have an important bearing on matters of life and death.

If kinship is important, which set of kin does a person affiliate with and depend on? After all, if every single relative were counted as equally important, there would be an unmanageably large number of people in each person's kinship network. Consequently, in most societies in which kinship connections are important, rules allocate each person to a particular and definable set of kin.

Types of Affiliation with Kin   We distinguish three main types of affiliation with kin: *unilineal descent*, *ambilineal descent*, and *bilateral kinship*. The first two types (unilineal descent and ambilineal descent) are based on **rules of descent**, rules that connect individuals with particular sets of kin because of known or presumed common ancestry.

Unilineal descent refers to the fact that a person is affiliated with a group of kin through descent links of one sex only—either males only or females only. Thus unilineal descent can be either patrilineal or matrilineal.

1. **Patrilineal descent** affiliates an individual with kin of both sexes related to him or her *through men only*. As Figure 14.1 indicates, in patrilineal systems the children in each generation belong to the kin group of their father; their father, in turn, belongs to the group of his father; and so on. Although a man's sons and daughters are all members of the same descent group, affiliation with that group is transmitted only by the sons to their children. Just as patrilocal residence is much more common than matrilocal residence, patrilineal descent is more common than matrilineal descent.

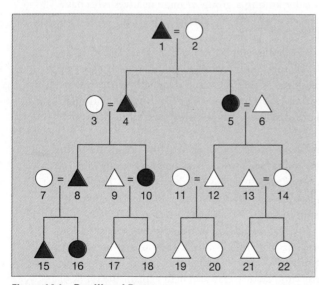

Note: A triangle represents a male; a circle represents a female; an equal sign (=) represents a marriage; vertical lines show descent; horizontal lines indicate siblings.

Figure 14.1   Patrilineal Descent

Individuals 4 and 5, who are the children of 1 and 2, affiliate with their father's patrilineal kin group, represented by the color blue. In the next generation, the children of 3 and 4 also belong to the blue kin group, since they take their descent from their father, who is a member of that group. However, the children of 5 and 6 do not belong to this patrilineal group, since they take their descent from their father, who is a member of a different group. That is, although the mother of 12 and 14 belongs to the blue patrilineal group, she cannot pass on her descent affiliation to her children, and since her husband (6) does not belong to her patrilineage, her children (12 and 14) belong to their father's group. In the fourth generation, only 15 and 16 belong to the blue patrilineal group, since their father is the only male member of the preceding generation who belongs to the blue patrilineal group. In this diagram, then, 1, 4, 5, 8, 10, 15, and 16 are affiliated by the patrilineal descent; all the other individuals belong to other patrilineal groups.

2. **Matrilineal descent** affiliates an individual with kin of both sexes related to him or her *through women only.* In each generation, then, children belong to the kin group of their mother (see Figure 14.2). Although a woman's sons and daughters are all members of the same descent group, only her daughters can pass on their descent affiliation to their children.

Unilineal rules of descent affiliate an individual with a line of kin extending back in time and into the future. By virtue of this line of descent, whether it extends through males or females, some very close relatives are excluded. For example, in a patrilineal system, your mother and your mother's parents do not belong to your patrilineal group, but your father and his father (and their sisters) do. In your own generation in a matrilineal or patrilineal system, some cousins are excluded, and in your children's generation, some of your nieces and nephews are excluded.

Unilineal rules of descent can form clear-cut, nonoverlapping and hence unambiguous, groups of kin, which can act as separate units even after the death of individual members. Referring again to Figures 14.1 and 14.2, we can see that the individuals in the highlight color belong to the same patrilineal or matrilineal descent group without ambiguity; individuals in the fourth generation belong to the group just as much as those in the first generation. In contrast to unilineal descent, **ambilineal descent** affiliates an individual with kin related to him or her through men *or* women. In other words, some people in the society affiliate with a group of kin through their fathers; others, through their mothers. Consequently, the descent groups show both female and male genealogical links and they often if not usually overlap in membership

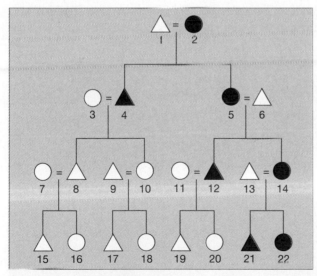

Figure 14.2 Matrilineal Descent

Individuals 4 and 5, who are the children of 1 and 2, affiliate with their mother's kin group, represented by the color blue. In the next generation, the children of 5 and 6 also belong to the blue kin group, since they take their descent from their mother, who is a member of that group. However, the children of 3 and 4 do not belong to this matrilineal group, since they take their descent from their mother, who is a member of a different group; their father, although a member of the blue matrilineal group, cannot pass his affiliation on to them under the rule of matrilineal descent. In the fourth generation, only 21 and 22 belong to the blue matrilineal group, since their mother is the only female member of the preceding generation who belongs. Thus, individuals 2, 4, 5, 12, 14, 21, and 22 belong to the same matrilineal group.

These three rules of descent (patrilineal, matrilineal, and ambilineal) are usually, but not always, mutually exclusive. Most societies can be characterized as having only one rule of descent, but sometimes two principles are used to affiliate individuals with different sets of kin for different purposes. Some societies have, then, what is called **double descent or double unilineal descent**, whereby an individual affiliates for some purposes with a group of matrilineal kin and for other purposes with a group of patrilineal kin.

Many societies, including our own, do not have lineal (matrilineal, patrilineal, or ambilineal) descent groups—sets of kin who believe they descend from a common ancestor. These are societies with **bilateral kinship**. *Bilateral* means "two-sided," and in this case it refers to the fact that one's relatives on both the mother's and father's sides are equal in importance or, more usually, in unimportance. Kinship reckoning in bilateral societies does not refer to common descent but rather is horizontal, moving outward from close to more distant relatives rather than upward to common ancestors (see Figure 14.3).

The term **kindred** describes a person's bilateral set of relatives who may be called upon for some purpose. Most bilateral societies have kindreds that overlap in membership. In North America, we think of the kindred as including the people we might invite to weddings, funerals, or some other ceremonial occasion; a kindred, however, is not usually a definite group. As anyone who has been involved in creating a wedding invitation list knows, a great deal of time may be spent deciding which relatives ought to be invited and which ones can legitimately be excluded. Societies with bilateral kinship differ in precisely how distant relatives have to be before they are lost track of or before they are not included in ceremonial activities.

The distinctive feature of bilateral kinship is that, aside from brothers and sisters, no two persons belong to exactly the same kin group. Your kindred contains close relatives spreading out on both your mother's and father's sides, but the members of your kindred are affiliated only by way of their connection to you (**ego**, or the focus). Thus, the kindred is an *ego-centered* group of kin. Because different people (except for brothers and sisters) have different mothers and fathers, your first cousins will have different kindreds, and even your own children will have a different kindred from yours. It is the ego-centered nature

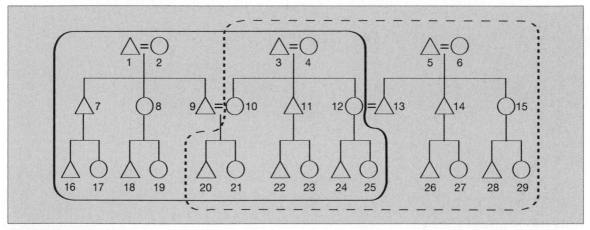

Figure 14.3 Bilateral Kinship

In a bilateral system the kindred is ego-centered; hence, it varies with different points of reference (except for brothers and sisters). In any bilateral society, the kindred minimally includes parents, grandparents, aunts, uncles, and first cousins. So, if we look at the close kindred of the brother and sister 20 and 21 (enclosed by the solid line), it would include their parents (9 and 10), their aunts and uncles (7, 8, 11, 12), their grandparents (1, 2, 3, 4), and their first cousins (16–19, 22–25). But the kindred of the brother and sister 24 and 25 (shown by the dashed line) includes only some of the same people (3, 4, 10–12, 20–23); in addition, the kindred of 24 and 25 includes people not in the kindred of 20 and 21 (5, 6, 13–15, 26–29).

of the kindred that makes it difficult for it to serve as a permanent or persistent group. The only thing the people in a kindred have in common is the ego who brings them together. A kindred usually has no name, no common purpose, and only temporary meetings centered around the ego.[55] Because everyone belongs to several different and overlapping kindreds, the society is not divided into clear-cut groups.

Groups in Unilineal Descent Systems

In a society with unilineal descent, people usually refer to themselves as belonging to a particular unilineal group or set of groups because they believe they share common descent in either the male (patrilineal) or female (matrilineal) line. Several types of unilineal descent groups are distinguished by anthropologists: lineages, clans, phratries, and moieties.

Lineages A **lineage** is a set of kin whose members trace descent from a common ancestor through known links. There may be *patrilineages* or *matrilineages*, depending on whether the links are traced through males only or through females only. Lineages are often designated by the name of the common male or female ancestor. In some societies, people belong to a hierarchy of lineages. That is, they first trace their descent back to the ancestor of a minor lineage, then to the ancestor of a larger and more inclusive major lineage, and so on.

Clans A **clan** (also sometimes called a **sib**) is a set of kin whose members believe themselves to be descended from a common ancestor, but the links back to that ancestor are not specified. In fact, the common ancestor may not even be known. Clans with patrilineal descent are called *patriclans;* clans with matrilineal descent are called *matriclans.* Clans often are designated by an animal name (Bear, Wolf), called a **totem**, which may have some special significance for the group and, at the very least, is a means of group identification. The word *totem* comes from the Ojibwa Indian word *ototeman,* "a relative of mine."

Totem poles often symbolize the history of a descent group. A totem pole in Ketchikan, Alaska.

Phratries   A **phratry** is a unilineal descent group composed of supposedly related clans or sibs. As with clans, the descent links in phratries are unspecified.

Moieties   When a whole society is divided into two unilineal descent groups, we call each group a **moiety**. (The word *moiety* comes from a French word meaning "half.") The people in each moiety believe themselves to be descended from a common ancestor, although they cannot specify how. Societies with moiety systems usually have relatively small populations (fewer than 9,000 people). Societies with phratries and clans tend to be larger.[56]

Combinations   Many societies have two or more types in various combinations. For example, some societies have lineages and clans; others may have clans and phratries but no lineages; and still others may have clans and moieties but neither phratries nor lineages. Even if societies have more than one type of unilineal kin group—for example, lineages and clans—there is no ambiguity about membership. Small groups are simply subsets of larger units; the larger units include people who say they are unilineally related further back in time.

Patrilineal Organization   Patrilineal organization is the most frequent type of descent system. The Kapauku Papuans, a people living in the central highlands of western New Guinea, are an example of a patrilineal society with various types of descent groups.[57] The male members of a patrilineage—all the living males who can trace their actual relationship through males to a common ancestor—constitute the male population of a single village or, more likely, a series of adjoining villages. The male members of the lineage live together by virtue of a patrilocal rule of residence and a fairly stable settlement pattern. A son stays near his parents and brings his wife to live in or near his father's house; the daughters leave home and go to live with their husbands. If the group lives in one place over a long period, the male descendants of one man will live in the same territory.

   The members of the same patrilineage address each other affectionately, and within this group law and order are maintained by a headman. Killing within the lineage is considered a serious offense, and any fighting that takes place is done with sticks rather than lethal weapons such as spears.

   The Kapauku also belong to larger and more inclusive patrilineal descent groups—clans and phratries. If a member of the patriclan eats the clan's plant or animal totem, it is believed that the person will become deaf. A Kapauku is also forbidden to marry anyone from his or her clan. In other words, the clan is exogamous. Unlike the members of the patrilineage, the male members of the patriclan do not all live together. The lineage is also the largest group of kinsmen that acts together politically. Among clan members there is no mechanism for resolving disputes, and members of the same patriclan (who belong to different lineages) may even go to war with one another.

   The most inclusive patrilineal descent group among the Kapauku is the phratry, each of which is composed of two or more clans. The members of a phratry observe all the totemic taboos of the clans that belong to that phratry. Intermarriage of members of the same clan is forbidden, but members of the same phratry, if they belong to different clans, may marry.

Matrilineal Organization   Although societies with matrilineal descent seem in many respects like mirror images of their patrilineal counterparts, they differ in one important way. That difference has to do with who exercises authority. In patrilineal systems, descent affiliation is transmitted through males, and it is also the males who exercise authority. Consequently, in the patrilineal system, lines of descent and of authority converge. In a matrilineal system, however, although the line of descent passes through females, females rarely exercise authority in their kin groups. Usually males do. Thus, the lines of authority and descent do not converge.[58] Since males exercise authority in the kin group, an individual's mother's brother becomes an important authority figure, because he is the individual's closest male matrilineal relative in the parental generation. The individual's father does not belong to the individual's matrilineal kin group and thus has no say in that kin group.

The divergence of authority and descent in a matrilineal system has some effect on community organization and marriage. Most matrilineal societies practice matrilocal residence. Daughters stay at home after marriage and bring their husbands to live with them; sons leave home to join their wives. But the sons who are required to leave will be the ones who eventually exercise authority in their kin groups. This situation presents a problem. The solution that seems to have been arrived at in most matrilineal societies is that, although the males move away to live with their wives, they usually do not move too far away; indeed, they often marry women who live in the same village. Thus, matrilineal societies tend not to be locally exogamous—that is, members often marry people from inside the village—whereas patrilineal societies are often locally exogamous.[59]

The matrilineal organization on Chuuk, a group of small islands in the Pacific, illustrates the general pattern of authority in matrilineal systems.[60] The Chuukese have both matrilineages and matriclans. The matrilineage is a property-owning group whose members trace descent from a known common ancestor in the female line. The female lineage members and their husbands occupy a cluster of houses on the matrilineage's land. The property of the lineage group is administered by the oldest brother of the group, who allocates the productive property of his matrilineage and directs the work of the members. He also represents the group in dealings with the district chief and all outsiders, and he must be consulted on any matter that affects the group. There is also a senior woman of the lineage who exercises some authority, but only insofar as the activities of the women are concerned. She may supervise the women's cooperative work (they usually work separately from the men) and manage the household.

Within the nuclear family, the father and mother have the primary responsibility for raising and disciplining their children. When a child reaches puberty, however, the father's right to discipline or exercise authority over the child ceases. The mother continues to exercise her right of discipline, but her brother may interfere, especially after puberty. On Chuuk, men rarely move far from their birthplace. As Ward Goodenough pointed out, "Since matrilocal residence takes the men away from their home lineages, most of them marry women whose lineage houses are within a few minutes' walk of their own."[61]

Functions of Unilineal Descent Groups

Unilineal descent groups exist in societies at all levels of cultural complexity.[62] Apparently, however, they are most common in noncommercial food-producing, as opposed to food-collecting, societies.[63] Unilineal descent groups often have important functions in the social, economic, political, and religious realms of life:

1. **Regulating marriage.** In unilineal societies, individuals are not usually permitted to marry within their own unilineal descent groups. In general, the incest taboo in unilineal societies is extended to some, if not all, presumed unilineal relatives.

2. **Economic functions.** Members of a person's lineage or clan are often required to side with that person in any quarrel or lawsuit, to help him or her get established economically, to contribute to a bride price or fine, and to support the person in life crises. Mutual aid often extends to economic cooperation on a regular basis. The unilineal descent group may act as a corporate unit in landownership.

3. **Political functions.** Headmen or elders may also have the right to settle disputes between two members within a lineage, although they generally lack power to force a settlement. And they may act as intermediaries in disputes between a member of their own clan and a member of an

opposing kin group. One of the most important political functions of unilineal descent groups is their role in warfare—the attempt to resolve disputes within and without the society by violent action. In societies without towns or cities, the organization of such fighting is often in the hands of descent groups.

4. **Religious Functions.**   A clan or lineage may have its own religious beliefs and practices, worshiping its own gods or goddesses and ancestral spirits.

Ambilineal Systems

Societies with ambilineal descent groups are far less numerous than unilineal or even bilateral societies. Ambilineal societies, however, resemble unilineal ones in many ways. For instance, the members of an ambilineal descent group believe that they are descended from a common ancestor, although frequently they cannot specify all the genealogical links. The descent group is commonly named and may have an identifying emblem or even a totem; land and other productive resources may be owned by the descent group; and myths and religious practices are often associated with the group. Marriage is often regulated by group membership, just as in unilineal systems, although kin group exogamy is not nearly as common as in unilineal systems. Moreover, ambilineal societies resemble unilineal ones in having various levels or types of descent groups. They may have lineages and higher orders of descent groups, distinguished (as in unilineal systems) by whether or not all the genealogical links to the supposed common ancestors are specified.[64]

Explaining Variation in Residence

If in most societies married couples live with or near kin, then why in some societies, such as our own, do couples typically live apart from kin? And, among the societies in which couples live with or near kin, why do most choose the husband's side (patrilocal residence), but some the wife's side (matrilocal residence)? Why do some non-neolocal societies allow a married couple to go to either the wife's or the husband's kin (bilocal residence), whereas most others do not allow a choice?

Neolocal Residence   Many anthropologists have suggested that neolocal residence is related to the presence of a money or commercial economy. They argue that when people can sell their labor or their products for money, they can buy what they need to live, without having to depend on kin. Indeed, neolocal residence tends to occur in societies with monetary or commercial exchange, whereas societies without money tend to have patterns of residence that locate a couple near or with kin.[65] The presence of money, then, partially accounts for neolocal residence: Money seems to allow couples to live on their own. Still, this fact does not quite explain why they choose to do so. One reason may be that in commercial societies, couples do better on their own because the jobs available require physical or social mobility. Or perhaps couples prefer to live apart from kin because they want to avoid some of the interpersonal tensions and demands that may be generated by living with or near kin.

Matrilocal versus Patrilocal Residence   It was traditionally assumed that in societies in which married children live near or with kin, the pattern of residence will tend to be patrilocal if males contribute more to the economy and matrilocal if women contribute more. However plausible that assumption may seem, the cross-cultural evidence does not support it. Where men do most of the primary subsistence work, residence is patrilocal no more often than would be expected by chance. Conversely, where women do an equal amount or more of the subsistence work, residence is no more likely to be matrilocal than patrilocal.[66] And if we counted all work inside and outside the home, most societies should be matrilocal because women usually do more. But that is not true either; most societies are not matrilocal.

We can predict whether residence will be matrilocal or patrilocal from the type of warfare practiced in the society. In most societies known to anthropology, neighboring communities or districts are enemies. The type of warfare that breaks out periodically between such groups is called *internal,* because the fighting occurs between groups that speak the same language. In other societies, the warfare is never within the same society but only with other language groups. This pattern of warfare is referred to as purely *external.* Cross-cultural evidence suggests that in societies where warfare is at least sometimes internal, residence is almost always patrilocal rather than matrilocal. In contrast, residence is usually matrilocal when warfare is purely external.[67]

How can we explain this relationship between type of warfare and matrilocal versus patrilocal residence? One theory is that patrilocal residence tends to occur with internal warfare because there may be concern over keeping sons close to home to help with defense. Because women do not usually constitute the fighting force in any society, having sons reside at home after marriage might be favored as a means of maintaining a loyal and quickly mobilized fighting force in case of surprise attack from nearby. If warfare is purely external, however, people may not be so concerned about keeping their sons at home because families need not fear attack from neighboring communities or districts.

With purely external warfare, then, the pattern of residence may be determined by other considerations, especially economic ones. If in societies with purely external warfare the women do most of the primary subsistence work, families might want their daughters to remain at home after marriage, so the pattern of residence might become matrilocal. If warfare is purely external but men still do more of the primary subsistence work, residence should still be patrilocal. Thus, the need to keep sons at home after marriage when there is internal warfare may take precedence over any considerations based on division of labor. It is perhaps only when internal warfare is nonexistent that a female-dominant division of labor may give rise to matrilocal residence.[68]

The frequent absence of men because of long-distance trade or wage labor in distant places may also provide an impetus for matrilocal residence even after warfare ceases. For example, among the Miskito of eastern Central America, matrilocality allowed domestic and village life to continue without interruption when men were away from home for long periods of time, working as lumberers, miners, and river transporters. Even though some men would always be away from home, the Miskito continued to get food in their traditional ways, from farming (done mostly by the women) and from hunting and fishing (which was mostly men's work).[69]

Bilocal Residence   In societies that practice bilocal residence, a married couple goes to live with or near either the husband's or the wife's parents. Although this pattern seems to involve a choice for the married couple, theory and research suggest that bilocal residence may occur out of necessity instead. Elman Service suggested that bilocal residence is likely to occur in societies that have recently suffered a severe and drastic loss of population because of the introduction of new infectious diseases.[70] Over the past 500 years, contact with Europeans in many parts of the world has resulted in severe population losses among non-European societies that lacked resistance to the Europeans' diseases. If couples need to live with some set of kin in order to make a living in noncommercial societies, it seems likely that couples in depopulated, noncommercial societies might have to live with whichever spouse's parents and other relatives are still alive. This interpretation is supported by the cross-cultural evidence. Recently depopulated societies tend to have bilocal residence or frequent departures from unilocality, whereas societies that are not recently depopulated tend to have one pattern or another of unilocal residence.[71]

In hunter-gatherer societies, a few other circumstances may also favor bilocal residence. Bilocality tends to be found among those hunter-gatherers who have very small bands or unpredictable and low rainfall. Residential "choice" in these cases may be a question of adjusting marital residence to where the couple will have the best chance to survive or to find close relatives with whom to live and work.[72]

Avunculocal Residence   Now that we have learned about matrilineal systems, the avunculocal pattern of residence, whereby married couples live with or near the husband's mother's brother, may become clearer. Although avunculocal residence is relatively rare, just about all avunculocal societies are matrilineal. As we have seen, the mother's brother plays an important role in decision making in most matrilineal societies. Aside from his brothers, who is a boy's closest male matrilineal relative? His mother's brother. Going to live with the mother's brother, then, provides a way of localizing male *matrilineal* relatives. But why should some matrilineal societies practice that form of residence? The answer may involve a recent change in the prevailing type of warfare.

Avunculocal societies, in contrast with matrilocal societies, fight internally. Just as patrilocality may be a response to keep patrilineally related men home after marriage, so avunculocality may be a way of keeping related—in this case, matrilineally related—men together after marriage to provide for quick mobilization in case of surprise attack from nearby. Societies that already have strong, functioning matrilineal descent groups may choose initially, when faced with the emergence of fighting close to home, to switch to avunculocality rather than patrilocality. Avunculocal residence would keep a higher number of related men together after marriage, compared with patrilocality, because there would be more possible links through women than through men if many men were dying relatively young in the warfare.[73]

The Emergence of Unilineal Systems

Unilineal kin groups play very important roles in the organization of many societies. But not all societies have such groups. In societies that have complex systems of political organization, officials and agencies take over many of the functions that might be performed by kin groups, such as the organization of work and warfare and the allocation of land. But not all societies that lack complex political organization have unilineal descent systems. Why, then, do some societies have unilineal descent systems, but others do not?

Trobriand Islanders have avunculocal residence and matrilineal descent groups.

It is generally assumed that unilocal residence, patrilocal or matrilocal, is necessary for the development of unilineal descent. Patrilocal residence, if practiced for some time in a society, will generate a set of patrilineally related males who live in the same territory. Matrilocal residence over time will similarly generate a localized set of matrilineally related females. It is no wonder, then, that matrilocal and patrilocal residence are cross-culturally associated with matrilineal and patrilineal descent, respectively.[74]

But, although unilocal residence might be necessary for the formation of unilineal descent groups, it is apparently not the only condition required. For one thing, many societies with unilocal residence lack unilineal descent groups. For another, merely because related males or related females live together by virtue of a patrilocal or matrilocal rule of residence, it does not necessarily follow that the related people will actually view themselves as a descent group and function as such. Thus, it appears that other conditions are needed to supply the impetus for the formation of unilineal descent groups.

There is evidence that unilocal societies that engage in warfare are more apt to have unilineal descent groups than unilocal societies without warfare.[75] It may be, then, that the presence of fighting in societies lacking complex systems of political organization provides an impetus to the formation of unilineal descent groups. Unilineal descent groups provide individuals with unambiguous groups of persons who can fight or form alliances as discrete units.[76] There is no ambiguity about an individual's membership. It is perfectly clear whether someone belongs to a particular clan, phratry, or moiety. It is this feature of unilineal descent groups that enables them to act as separate and distinct units—mostly, perhaps, in warfare.

Summary

1. All societies known today have the custom of marriage. Marriage is a socially approved sexual and economic union usually between a man and a woman that is presumed to be more or less permanent and that subsumes reciprocal rights and obligations between the two spouses and between the spouses and their children.

2. Marriage arrangements often include an economic element including bride-price (the most common form of economic transaction), bride-service, female exchange, dowry, and indirect dowry.

3. Every society tells people whom they cannot marry, whom they can marry, and sometimes even whom they should marry. No society in recent times has allowed sex or marriage between brothers and sisters, mothers and sons, or fathers and daughters.

4. Most societies allow a man to be married to more than one woman at a time (polygyny). Monogamy is less common and polyandry, the marriage of one woman to several husbands, is rare.

5. The prevailing form of family in most societies is the extended family. It consists of two or more single-parent, monogamous (nuclear), polygynous, or polyandrous families linked by blood ties.

6. In our society, and in many other industrial societies, a newly married couple usually establishes a place of residence apart from parents or relatives (neolocal residence). But about 95 percent of the world's societies have some pattern of residence whereby the new couple settles within or very close to the household of the parents or some other close relative of the groom or bride. The four major patterns in which married couples live with or near kinsmen are these: patrilocal residence (the most common), matrilocal residence, bilocal residence, and avunculocal residence.

7. In most societies where kinship is important, rules of affiliation allocate each person to a particular and definable set of kin. The three main types of affiliation with kin are unilineal descent, ambilineal descent, and bilateral kinship.

8. With unilineal descent people usually refer to themselves as belonging to a particular unilineal group or set of groups because they believe they share common descent in either the male or the female line. These people form what is called a unilineal descent group. There are several types, and a society may have more than one type: lineages, clans, phratries, and moieties.

Glossary Terms

ambilineal descent (p. 345)

avunculocal residence (p. 343)

bilateral kinship (p. 346)

bilocal residence (p. 342)

bride price or bride wealth (p. 331)

bride service (p. 332)

clan or sib (p. 347)

cross-cousins (p. 335)

double descent or double unilineal
    descent (p. 346)

dowry (p. 332)

ego (p. 346)

endogamy (p. 334)

exogamy (p. 334)

extended family (p. 338)

family (p. 338)

group marriage (p. 335)

incest taboo (p. 333)

indirect dowry (p. 333)

kindred (p. 346)

lineage (p. 347)

marriage (p. 328)

matrifocal family (p. 338)

matrilineal descent (p. 345)

matrilocal residence (p. 342)

moiety (p. 348)

monogamy (p. 335)

neolocal residence (p. 343)

nonsororal polygyny (p. 336)

nuclear family (p. 338)

parallel cousins (p. 335)

patrilineal descent (p. 344)

patrilocal residence (p. 342)

phratry (p. 348)

polyandry (p. 335)

polygamy (p. 335)

polygyny (p. 335)

postpartum sex taboo (p. 336)

rules of descent (p. 344)

siblings (p. 335)

sororal polygyny (p. 336)

totem (p. 347)

unilineal descent (p. 344)

unilocal residence (p. 343)

Critical Questions

1. Do you think extended-family households will become more common in our society? Explain your answer.

2. Why is polyandry so much less common than polygyny?

3. Why might it be important for unilineal descent groups to be nonoverlapping in membership?

CHAPTER 15

POLITICAL LIFE

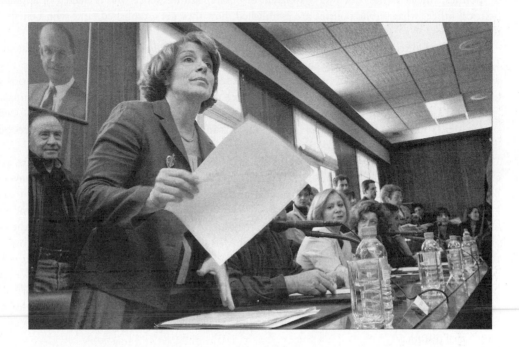

Chapter Outline

- Types of Political Organization
- The Spread of State Societies
- Variation in Political Process
- Resolution of Conflict

For people in the United States, the phrase *political life* has many connotations. It may call to mind the various branches of government: the executive branch, from the president on the national level to governors on the state level to mayors on the local level; legislative institutions, from Congress to state legislatures to city councils; and administrative bureaus, from federal government departments to local agencies.

Political life may also evoke thoughts of political parties, interest groups, lobbying, campaigning, and voting. In other words, when people living in the United States think of political life, they may think first of "politics," the activities (not always apparent or public) that influence who is elected or appointed to political office, what public policies are established, how they get established, and who benefits from those policies.

But in the United States and in many other countries, *political life* involves even more than government and politics. Political life also involves ways of preventing or resolving troubles and disputes both within and outside the society. Internally, a complex society such as ours may employ mediation or arbitration to resolve industrial disputes, a police force to prevent crimes or track down criminals, and courts and a penal system to deal with lawbreakers as well as with social conflict in general. Externally, such a society may establish embassies in other nations and develop and utilize its armed forces both to maintain security and to support domestic and foreign interests.

Formal governments have become more widespread around the world over the last 100 years, as powerful colonizing countries have imposed political systems upon others or as people less formally organized realized that they needed governmental mechanisms to deal with the larger world. But many societies known to anthropology did not have political officials or political parties or courts or armies. Indeed, the band or village was the largest autonomous political unit in 50 percent of the societies in the ethnographic record, as of the times they were first described. And those units were only informally organized; that is, they did not have individuals or agencies formally authorized to make and implement policy or resolve disputes. Does this mean they did not have political life? If we mean political life as we know it in our own society, then the answer has to be that they did not. But if we look beyond our formal institutions and mechanisms—if we ask what functions these institutions and mechanisms perform—we find that all societies have had political activities and beliefs to create and maintain social order and cope with social disorder.

Many kinds of groups including descent groups have political functions. But when anthropologists talk about *political organization* or *political life,* they are particularly focusing on activities and beliefs pertaining to *territorial groups.* Territorial groups, in whose behalf political activities may be organized, range from small communities, such as bands and villages, to large communities, such as towns and cities, to multilocal groups, such as districts or regions, entire nations, or even groups of nations.

As we shall see, the different types of political organization, as well as how people participate in politics and how they cope with conflict, are often strongly linked to variation in food-getting, economy, and social stratification.

Types of Political Organization

Societies in the ethnographic record vary in *level of political integration*—that is, the largest territorial group on whose behalf political activities are organized—and in the degree to which political authority is centralized or concentrated in the integrated group. When we describe the political integration of particular societies, we focus on their traditional political systems.

Elman Service suggested that most societies can be classified into four principal types of political organization: bands, tribes, chiefdoms, and states.[1] Although Service's classification does not fit all societies, it is a useful way to show how societies vary in trying to create and maintain social order. We often use the present tense in our discussion, because that is the convention in ethnographic writing, but the reader should remember that most societies that used to be organized at the band, tribe, or chiefdom level are now incorporated into larger political entities. With a handful of exceptions, there are no politically autonomous bands or tribes or chiefdoms in the world anymore.

Band Organization

Some societies were composed of fairly small and usually nomadic groups of people. Each of these groups is conventionally called a **band** and is politically autonomous. That is, in **band organization** the local group or community is the largest group that acts as a political unit. Because most recent food collectors had band organization, some anthropologists contend that this type of political organization characterized nearly all societies before the development of agriculture, or until about 10,000 years ago. But we have to remember that almost all of the described food-collecting societies are or were located in marginal environments; and almost all were affected by more dominant societies nearby.[2] So it is possible that what we call "band organization" may not have been typical of food collectors in the distant or prehistoric past.

Bands are typically small, with less than 100 people usually, often considerably less. Each small band occupies a large territory, so population density is low. Band size often varies by season, with the band breaking up or recombining according to the food resources available at a given time and place. Inuit bands, for example, are smaller in the winter, when food is hard to find, and larger in the summer, when there is sufficient food to feed a larger group.

Political decision making within the band is generally informal. The "modest informal authority"[3] that does exist can be seen in the way decisions affecting the group are made. Because the formal, permanent office of leader typically does not exist, decisions such as when camp has to be moved or how a hunt is to be arranged are either agreed upon by the community as a whole or made by the best-qualified member. Leadership, when it is exercised by an individual, is not the consequence of bossing or throwing one's weight about. Each band may have its informal **headman**, or its most proficient hunter, or a person most accomplished in rituals. There may be one person with all these qualities, or several persons, but such a person or persons will have gained status through the community's recognition of skill, good sense, and humility. Leadership, in other words, stems not from power but from influence, not from office but from admired personal qualities. For example, among the Iglulik Inuit:

> Within each settlement . . . there is as a rule an older man who enjoys the respect of the others and who decides when a move is to be made to another hunting center, when a hunt is to be started, how the spoils are to be divided, when the dogs are to be fed . . . . He is called *isumaitoq*, "he who thinks." It is not always the oldest man, but as a rule an elderly man who is a clever hunter or, as head of a large family, exercises great authority. He cannot be called a chief; there is no obligation to follow his counsel; but they do so in most cases, partly because they rely on his experience, partly because it pays to be on good terms with this man.[4]

A summary of the general features of band organization can be found in Table 15.1 on page 358. Note, however, that there are exceptions to these generalizations. For example, not all known food collectors are organized at the band level or have all the features of a band type of society. Classic exceptions are the Native American societies of the Northwest Pacific coast, who had enormous resources of salmon and other fish, relatively large and permanent villages, and political organization beyond the level of the typical band societies in the ethnographic record.

				Community		
Type of Organization	**Highest Level of Political Integration**	**Specialization of Political Officials**	**Predominant Mode of Subsistence**	**Size and Population Density**	**Social Differentiation**	**Major Form of Distribution**
Band	Local group or band	Little or none: informal leadership	Food collecting	Very small communities, very low density	Egalitarian	Mostly reciprocity
Tribe	Sometimes multilocal group	Little or none: informal leadership	Extensive (shifting) agriculture and/or herding	Small communities, low density	Egalitarian	Mostly reciprocity
Chiefdom	Multilocal group	Some	Extensive or intensive agriculture and/or herding	Large communities, medium density	Rank	Reciprocity and redistribution
State	Multilocal group, often entire language group	Much	Intensive agriculture and herding	Cities and towns, high density	Class and caste	Mostly market exchange

Table 15.1   Suggested Trends in Political Organization and Other Social Characteristics

Tribal Organization

When local communities mostly act autonomously but there are kinship groups (such as clans or lineages) or associations (such as age-sets—see page 359) that can potentially integrate several local groups into a larger unit (**tribe**), we say that the society has **tribal organization**. The term *tribe* is sometimes used to refer to an entire society; that is, an entire language group may be called a tribe. But a tribal type of political system does not usually permit the entire society to act as a unit; all the communities in a tribal society may be linked only occasionally for some political (usually military) purpose. Thus, what distinguishes tribal from band political organization is the presence in the former of some multilocal, but not usually society-wide, integration. The multilocal integration, however, is *not permanent,* and it is *informal* in the sense that it is not headed by political officials. Frequently, the integration is called into play only when an outside threat arises; when the threat disappears, the local groups revert to self-sufficiency.[5] Tribal organization may seem fragile—and, of course, it usually is—but the fact that there are social ways to integrate local groups into larger political entities means that societies with tribal organization are militarily a good deal more formidable than societies with band organization.

Societies with tribal political organization are similar to band societies in their tendency to be egalitarian (see Table 15.1). At the local level, informal leadership is also characteristic. In those tribal societies where kinship provides the basic framework of social organization, the elders of the local kin groups tend to have considerable influence; where age-sets are important, a particular age-set is looked to for leadership. But, in contrast to band societies, societies with tribal organization generally are food producers.

And because cultivation and animal husbandry are generally more productive than hunting and gathering, the population density of tribal societies is generally higher, local groups are larger, and the way of life is more sedentary than in hunter-gatherer bands.

Kinship Bonds Frequently communities are linked to each other by virtue of belonging to the same kin group, usually a unilineal group such as a lineage or clan. A **segmentary lineage system** is one type of tribal integration based on kinship. A society with such a system is composed of segments, or parts, each similar to the others in structure and function. Every local segment belongs to a hierarchy of lineages stretching farther and farther back genealogically. The hierarchy of lineages, then, unites the segments into larger and larger genealogical groups. The closer two groups are genealogically, the greater their general closeness. In the event of a dispute between members of different segments, people related more closely to one contestant than to another take the side of their nearest kinsman.

The Tiv of northern Nigeria offer a classic example of a segmentary lineage system, one that happens to link all the Tiv into a single genealogical structure or tribe. The Tiv are a large society, numbering more than 800,000. There are four levels of lineages. Each of the smallest lineages is in turn embedded in more inclusive lineages. Territorial organization follows lineage hierarchy. The most closely related lineages have territories near each other. All of Tivland is said to descend from one ancestor.[6]

Tiv lineage organization is the foundation of Tiv political organization. A dispute between the smallest neighboring lineages (and territories) remains minor, since no more than "brother" segments are involved. But a dispute between two small lineages from different larger lineages involves those larger lineages as well, with the requirement that smaller lineages within the larger support each other. This process of mutual support, called **complementary opposition**, means that segments will unite only in a confrontation with some other group. Groups that will fight with each other in a minor dispute might coalesce at some later time against a larger group.

The segmentary lineage system was presumably very effective in allowing the Tiv to intrude into new territory and take land from other tribal societies with smaller descent groups. Individual Tiv lineage segments could call on support from related lineages when faced with border troubles. Conflicts within the society—that is, between segments—especially in border areas, were often turned outward, "releasing internal pressure in an explosive blast against other peoples."[7]

A segmentary lineage system may generate a formidable military force, but the combinations of manpower it produces are temporary, forming and dissolving as the occasion demands.[8] Tribal political organization does not make for a political system that more or less permanently integrates a number of communities.

Age-Set Systems Age-sets (groups of males of a certain age-range) can function as the basis of a tribal type of political organization, as among the Karimojong of northeastern Uganda.[9] As herders, Karimojong adults are often separated from their usual settlements. Herders will meet, mingle for a while, then go their separate ways, but each may call upon other members of his age-set wherever he goes. The age-set system is important among the Karimojong because it immediately allocates a place to each individual in the system and thereby establishes for him an appropriate pattern of response. A quarrel in camp will be settled by the representatives of the senior age-set who are present, regardless of which section of the tribe they may belong to.

Among the Karimojong, political leaders are not elected from among the elders of a particular age-set, nor are they appointed; they acquire their positions informally. Usually a man's background, and the ability he has demonstrated in public debates over a period of time, will result in his being considered by the men of his neighborhood to be their spokesman. His function is to announce what course of action seems required in a particular situation, to initiate that action, and then to coordinate it after it has begun.

Chiefdom Organization

Whereas a tribe has some informal mechanism that can integrate more than one community, a **chiefdom** has some *formal* structure that integrates more than one community into a political unit. The formal structure could consist of a council with or without a chief, but most commonly there is a person—the **chief**—who has higher rank or authority than others. Most societies at the chiefdom level of organization contain more than one multicommunity political unit or chiefdom, each headed by a district chief or a council. There may also be more than one level of chief beyond the community, such as district chiefs and higher-level chiefs. Compared with tribal societies, societies with chiefdoms are more densely populated and their communities more permanent, partly as a consequence of their generally greater economic productivity (see Table 15.1 on page 358).

The position of chief, which is sometimes hereditary and generally permanent, bestows high status on its holder. Most chiefdoms have social ranking and accord the chief and his family greater access to prestige. The chief may redistribute goods, plan and direct the use of public labor, supervise religious ceremonies, and direct military activities on behalf of the chiefdom. In South Pacific chiefdoms, the chiefs carried out most of these duties. In Fijian chiefdoms, for example, the chief was responsible for the redistribution of goods and the coordination of labor:

> [The chief] could summon the community's labor on his own behalf, or on behalf of someone else who requested it, or for general purposes . . . . Besides his right to summon labor he accumulated the greater proportion of the first fruits of the yam crop . . . and he benefited from other forms of food presentation, or by the acquisition of special shares in ordinary village distribution . . . . Thus, the paramount [chief] would collect a significant part of the surplus production of the community and redistribute it in the general welfare.[10]

In contrast to leaders in tribal societies, who generally have to earn their privileges by their personal qualities, hereditary chiefs are said to have those qualities in their "blood." A high-ranking chief in Polynesia, a huge triangular area of islands in the South Pacific, inherited special religious power called *mana*. Mana sanctified his rule and protected him.[11] Chiefs in Polynesia had so much religious power that missionaries could convert people to Christianity only after their chiefs had been converted.[12]

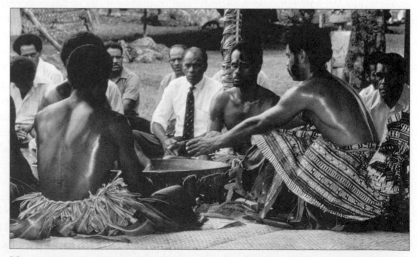

Men present *kava*, a special drink, to a chief in Fiji. The chief wears a tie.

In most chiefdoms, the chiefs did not have the power to compel people to obey them; people would act in accordance with the chief's wishes because the chief was respected and often had religious authority. But in the most complex paramount chiefdoms, such as those of Hawaii and Tahiti, the chiefs seemed to have more compelling sanctions than the "power" of respect or mana. Substantial amounts of goods and services collected by the chiefs were used to support subordinates, including specialists such as high priests, political envoys, and warriors who could be sent to quell rebellious factions.[13] When redistributions do not go to everybody—when chiefs are allowed to keep items for their own purposes—and when a chief begins to use armed force, the political system is on the way to becoming what we call a state.

State Organization

A **state**, according to one more or less standard definition, is "an autonomous political unit, encompassing many communities within its territory and having a centralized government with the power to collect taxes, draft men for work or war, and decree and enforce laws."[14] States, then, have a complex, centralized political structure that includes a wide range of permanent institutions with legislative, executive, and judicial functions and a large bureaucracy. Central to this definition is the concept of legitimate force used to implement policies both internally and externally. In states, the government tries to maintain a monopoly on the use of physical force.[15] This monopoly can be seen in the development of formal and specialized instruments of social control: a police force, a militia, or a standing army.

Just as a particular society may contain more than one band, tribe, or chiefdom, so may it contain more than one state. The contiguously distributed population speaking a single language may or may not be politically unified in a single state. Ancient Greece was composed of many city-states; so, too, was Italy until the 1870s. German speakers are also not politically unified; Austria and Germany are separate states, and Germany itself was not politically unified until the 1870s. We say that a society has **state organization** when it is composed of one or more political units that are states.

A state may include more than one society. Multisociety states often are the result of conquest or colonial control when the dominant political authority, itself a state, imposes a centralized government over a territory with many different societies and cultures, as the British did in Nigeria and Kenya. Colonialism is a common feature of state societies.

Nearly all of the multisociety states that emerged after World War II were the results of successful independence movements against colonial powers.[16] Most have retained their political unity despite the fact that they still contain many different societies. Multisociety or multiethnic states may also form voluntarily, in reaction to external threat. Switzerland comprises cantons, each of which speaks mainly French, German, Italian, or Romansch; the various cantons confederated originally to shake off control by the Holy Roman Empire. But some states have lost their unity recently, including the former Union of Soviet Socialist Republics (USSR) and much of Yugoslavia.

In addition to their strictly political features, state-organized societies are generally supported by intensive agriculture. The high productivity of the agriculture allows for the emergence of cities, a high degree of economic and other kinds of specialization, and market or commercial exchange. In addition, state societies usually have class stratification (see Table 15.1 on page 358). Cities have grown tremendously in the past 100 years, largely as a result of migration and immigration.

When states come into existence, people's access to scarce resources is radically altered. So, too, is their ability not to listen to leaders: You cannot refuse to pay taxes and go unpunished. Of course, the rulers of a state do not maintain the social order by force alone. The people must believe, at least to some extent, that those in power have a legitimate right to govern. If the people think otherwise, history suggests that those in power may eventually lose their ability to control. Witness the recent downfall of Communist parties throughout most of eastern Europe and the former Soviet Union.

Humans are a social bunch. They generally live in groups or communities. These groups range in size from bands to villages to town and cities. Each may function as a political entity; activities are organized in their behalf by headmen, mayors, councils, and other political "officials" and groups. Nearly half of the world's human population now live in cities, which are usually defined as communities in which few are directly involved in food getting. An even larger proportion of humanity will be urban dwellers 30 years from now.

The growth of cities over the past century or so is not due to more births than deaths in the cities. Rather, cities have grown mostly because of migration from rural areas within and outside of the country. Recall the exodus of the Irish to Britain and the United States because of the "potato famine," the massive migrations from the villages of Germany, Italy, and Greece in the nineteenth and twentieth centuries, and the huge migrations, particularly in the past 50 years, from rural Mexico and China. It is probably safe to say that millions of people in many parts of the world would move to the United States, Canada, and Western Europe tomorrow, if they could. Poverty is one "push" factor. Fleeing from persecution is another. Many parts of the world are not safe, particularly for poor people. Or other places look more promising. Think of the state of California in the United States. The vast majority of its inhabitants were born elsewhere. True, in the modern world it is possible for some people to go "home" for a visit, even halfway around the world. But for many migrants, now and in the recent past, the move was one way. Because you may have run away from poverty, persecution, and war, you couldn't (or wouldn't) go home again.

An increasing number of anthropologists call themselves "urban anthropologists." They study why people move, and how they adjust to new places. They do so because so many people are moving now. There are villages in rural Spain and France that are mostly empty during the week. The owners live and work in Barcelona or Paris, and they hardly ever go "home." Indeed, their village houses may not even be available to them much, because they are usually rented to tourists! From across the Atlantic, no less.

Cities everywhere have problems, even in the most developed countries. It is difficult and expensive to provide water, power, sanitation, and other services to perhaps millions of city-dwellers. Yet in every country people are leaving rural areas and going to cities for a variety of reasons. Some are political refugees, like the Hmong from Laos. Then there are the people from Congo, Sudan, Kosovo, and Northern Ireland who have fled civil wars. There are other reasons to leave, too. Technological improvements may have reduced the need for rural labor, as happened in the U.S. South after the 1930s. Or the rural opportunities cannot support the increased number of mouths to be fed. Then people go to cities where there are jobs available. In the more urbanized countries the cities have acquired "suburbs," where many of the people in a metropolitan area may actually live, but hardly anyone is left on the farm—just a few percent of the population in the more developed countries.

With the building of suburbs in many countries in the last half of the twentieth century, cities lost population as people moved to the suburbs to have more living space or "better" schools for their children, or to escape the threat of violence. But recently the flow has started to reverse in North America and elsewhere. People are coming back to the cities, perhaps because they are tired of commuting long distances to jobs and recreation. This is particularly so with wealthier people whose children have grown up and moved away; with more people living longer, many want to move closer to the places where they mostly spend their time. Despite the social inequality and violence, cities have always been the places to go for jobs and other activities. Theaters, restaurants, museums, hospitals, and professional sports stadiums have always been located in or near cities.

The "push" out of the rural areas, the "pull" of the cities, is hard to resist, despite the enormous political problems of urban living. As the old song laments, "How ya gonna keep 'em down on the farm after they've seen Paree?"

Source: Melvin Ember and Carol R. Ember, eds., *Encyclopedia of Urban Cultures: Cities and Cultures around the World,* 4 vols. (Danbury, CT: Grolier/Scholastic, 2002).

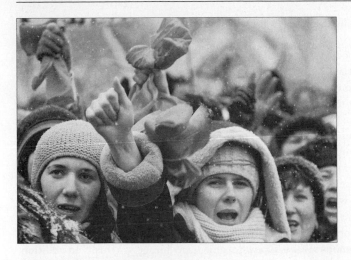

Popular will can change governments. Massive protest in Ukraine led a newly elected president to resign.

A state society can retain its legitimacy, or at least its power, for a long time. For example, the Roman Empire was a complex state society that dominated the Mediterranean and Near East for hundreds of years. It began as a city-state that waged war to acquire additional territory. At its height, the Roman Empire embraced more than 55 million people;[17] the capital city of Rome had a population of well over a million.[18] The empire included parts of what are now Great Britain, France, Spain, Portugal, Germany, Rumania, Turkey, Greece, Armenia, Egypt, Israel, and Syria.

Factors Associated with Variation in Political Organization

The kinds of political organization we call band, tribal, chiefdom, and state are points on a continuum of levels of political integration or unification, from small-scale local autonomy to large-scale regional unification. There also is variation in political authority, from a few temporary and informal political leaders to large numbers of permanent, specialized political officials, from the absence of coercive political power to the monopoly of public force by a central authority. These aspects of variation in political organization are generally associated with shifts from food collection to more intensive food production, from small to large communities, from low to high population densities, from an emphasis on reciprocity to redistribution to market exchange, and from egalitarian to rank to fully stratified class societies.

The associations just outlined, which seem to be confirmed by the available cross-cultural evidence, are summarized in Table 15.1 on page 358. With regard to the relationship between level of subsistence technology and political complexity, it was found that the greater the importance of agriculture in a society, the larger the population that is politically unified and the greater the number and types of political officials.[19] Another cross-cultural survey reported a similar trend: The more intensive the agriculture, the greater the likelihood of state organization; conversely, societies with no more than local political institutions are likely to depend on hunting, gathering, and fishing.[20]

With regard to community size, the first of these studies also suggested that the larger the leading community, the wider the range of political officials in the society.[21] Robert Textor presented a similar finding: Societies with state organization tend to have cities and towns, whereas those with only local political organization are more likely to have communities with an average population of fewer than 200 persons.[22] Cross-cultural research also tends to confirm that societies with higher levels of political integration are more likely to exhibit social differentiation, especially in the form of class distinctions.[23]

Does this evidence provide us with an explanation for why political organization varies? Clearly, the data indicate that several factors are associated with political development, but exactly why changes in organization occur is not yet understood. Although economic development may be a necessary condition for political development,[24] that relation does not fully explain why political organization should become more complex just because the economy can support it. Some theorists have suggested that competition between groups may be a more important reason for political consolidation. For example, Elman Service suggested competition as a reason why a society might change from a band level of political organization to a tribal level. Band societies are generally hunter-gatherers. With a changeover to agriculture, population density and competition between groups may increase. Service believed that such competition would foster the development of some informal organization beyond the community—namely, tribal organization—for offense and defense.[25] Indeed, both unilineal kinship groups and age-set systems seem to be associated with warfare.

Among agriculturalists, defensive needs might also be the main reason for switching from informal multivillage political organization to more formal chiefdom organization. Formally organized districts are probably more likely to defeat autonomous villages or even segmentary lineage systems.[26] In addition, there may be economic reasons for political development. With regard to chiefdoms, Service suggested that chiefdoms will emerge when redistribution between communities becomes important or when large-scale coordinated work groups are required. The more important these activities are, the more important—and hence more "chiefly"—the organizer and his family presumably become.[27] But redistribution is far from a universal activity of chiefs.[28]

Theory and research on the anthropology of political development have focused mostly on the high end of the scale of political complexity, and particularly on the origins of the first state societies. Those earliest states apparently rose independently of one another, after about 3500 B.C., in what are now southern Iraq, Egypt, northwestern India, northern China, and central Mexico. Several theories have been proposed to explain the rise of the earliest states, but no one theory seems to fit all the known archaeological sequences culminating in early state formation. The reason may be that different conditions in different places favored the emergence of centralized government. The state, by definition, implies the power to organize large populations for collective purposes. In some areas, the impetus may have been the need to organize necessary local or long-distance trade or both. In other areas, the state may have emerged as a way to control defeated populations that could not flee. In still other instances, other factors or a combination of factors may have fostered the development of states. It is still not clear what the specific conditions were that led to the emergence of the state in each of the early centers.[29]

The Spread of State Societies

The state level of political development has come to dominate the world. Societies with states have larger communities and higher population densities than do band, tribal, and chiefdom societies. They also have armies that are ready to fight at almost any time. State systems that have waged war against chiefdoms and tribes have almost always won, and the result has usually been the political incorporation of the losers. For example, the British and, later, the U.S. colonization of much of North America led to the defeat and incorporation of many Native American societies.

The defeat and incorporation of the Native Americans was at least partly due to the catastrophic depopulations they suffered because of epidemic diseases, such as smallpox and measles, that European colonists introduced. Catastrophic depopulation was commonly the outcome of the first contacts between European Americans and the natives of North and South America, as well as the natives of the far islands in the Pacific. People in the New World and the Pacific had not been exposed, and therefore were not

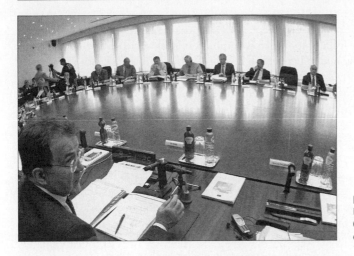

In the governance structure of the European Union (EU), the executive branch (the European Commission) consists of one representative from each EU country.

resistant, to the diseases the European Americans carried with them when they began to colonize the world. Before the expansion of Europeans, the people of the New World and the Pacific had been separated for a long time from the people and diseases on the geographically continuous landmass we separate into Europe, Africa, and Asia. Smallpox, measles, and the other former scourges of Europe had largely become childhood diseases that most individuals of European ancestry survived.[30]

Whether by depopulation, conquest, or intimidation, the number of independent political units in the world has decreased strikingly in the last 3,000 years, and especially in the last 200 years. Robert Carneiro estimated that in 1000 B.C., there may have been between 100,000 and 1 million separate political units in the world; today there are fewer than 200.[31] In the ethnographic record, about 50 percent of the 2,000 or so societies described within the last 150 years had only local political integration. That is, the highest level of political integration in one out of two recent societies was the local community.[32] Thus, most of the decrease in the number of independent political units has occurred fairly recently.

But the recent secessions from the former Soviet Union and Yugoslavia and other separatist movements around the world suggest that ethnic rivalries may make for departures from the trend toward larger and larger political units. Ethnic groups that have been dominated by others in multinational states may opt for political autonomy, at least for a while. On the other hand, the separate nations of Western Europe are becoming more unified every day, both politically and economically. So the trend toward larger and larger political units may be continuing, even if there are departures from it now and then.

Extrapolating from past history, a number of investigators have suggested that the entire world will eventually come to be politically integrated, perhaps as soon as the twenty-third century and no later than A.D. 4850.[33] Only the future will tell if this prediction will come true. And only the future will tell if further political integration in the world will occur peacefully—with all parties agreeing—or by force or the threat of force, as has happened so often in the past.

Variation in Political Process

Anthropologists are increasingly interested in the politics, or political processes, of the societies they study: who acquires influence or power, how they acquire it, and how political decisions are made. But even though we have descriptive accounts of politics in many societies, there is still relatively little comparative or cross-cultural research on what may explain variation in politics.

Getting to Be a Leader

In those societies that have hereditary leadership, which is common in rank societies and in state societies with monarchies, rules of succession usually establish how leadership is inherited. But for societies whose leaders are *chosen,* either as informal leaders or as elected political officials, we need a lot more research to understand why some kinds of people are chosen over others.

A few studies have investigated the personal qualities of leaders in tribal societies. One study, conducted among the Mekranoti-Kayapo of central Brazil, found that leaders, in contrast to followers, tend to be rated by their peers as higher in intelligence, generosity, knowledgeability, ambitiousness, and aggressiveness. Leaders also tend to be older and taller. And despite the egalitarian nature of Mekranoti society (at least with respect to sharing resources), sons of leaders are more likely than others to become leaders.[34]

Research in another Brazilian society, the Kagwahiv of the Amazon region, suggests another personal quality of leaders: They seem to have positive feelings about their fathers and mothers.[35] In many respects, studies of leaders in the United States show them to be not that different from their counterparts in Brazil. But there is one major difference: Mekranoti and Kagwahiv leaders are not wealthier than others; in fact, they give their wealth away. U.S. leaders are generally wealthier than others.[36]

"Big Men"   In some egalitarian tribal societies, the quest for leadership seems quite competitive. In parts of New Guinea and South America, "big men" compete with other ambitious men to attract followers. Men who want to compete must show that they have magical powers, success in gardening, and bravery in war. But, most important, they have to collect enough goods to throw big parties at which the goods are given away. Big men have to work very hard to attract and keep their followings, for dissatisfied followers can always join other aspiring men.[37] The wives of big men are often leaders too. Among the Kagwahiv, for example, a headman's wife is usually the leader of the women in the community; she is responsible for much of the planning for feasts and often distributes the meat at them.[38]

How does a man get to be a big man? Among the Kumdi-Engamoi, a central Highlands group, a man who wants to be considered a *wua nium* (literally, a "great-important-wealthy man") needs to have many wives and daughters, because the amount of land controlled by a man and how much can be produced on that land depend on the number of women in his family. The more wives he has, the more land he is given to cultivate. He must also be a good speaker. Everyone has the right to speak and give speeches, but to get to be known as a big man requires speaking well and forcefully and knowing when to sum up a consensus. It usually takes a man until his thirties or forties to acquire more than one wife and to make his name through exchanges. When a man wants to inaugurate an exchange, he needs to get shells and pigs from his family and relatives. Once he has achieved a reputation as a *wua nium,* he can keep it only if he continues to perform well—that is, if he continues to distribute fairly, make wise decisions, speak well, and conduct exchanges.[39]

"Big Women"   In contrast to most of mainland New Guinea, the islands off the southeastern coast are characterized by matrilineal descent. But, like mainland New Guinea, the islands also have a shifting system of leadership in which people compete for "big" status. Here, though, the people competing are women as well as men, and so there are "big women" as well as "big men." On the island of Vanatinai, for example, women and men compete with each other to exchange valuables. Women lead canoe expeditions to distant islands to visit male as well as female exchange partners, women mobilize relatives and exchange partners to mount large feasts, and the women get to keep the ceremonial valuables exchanged, at least for a while.[40]

The prominence of women on Vanatinai may be linked to the disappearance of warfare—the colonial powers imposed peace; we call this "pacification." Inter-island exchanges became frequent when war

In many egalitarian societies, leadership shifts informally from one person to another. In much of New Guinea, there is more competition for achieving "big" status. On Vanatinai, the women compete as well as the men, so there are "big women" as well as "big men." Here a "big woman" paints the face of her cousin's widow for a feast honoring the dead man.

became less common in the early twentieth century, giving women and men more freedom to travel. For men, but not women, war provided a path to leadership; champion warriors would acquire great renown and influence. It is not that women did not participate in war; they did, which is unusual cross-culturally, but a woman could not become a war leader. Now, in the absence of war, women have an opportunity through exchanges to become leaders, or "big women."

Political Participation

Political scientist Marc Ross conducted cross-cultural research on variation in degree of political participation. Ross phrased the research question: "Why is it that in some polities there are relatively large numbers of persons involved in political life, while in others political action is the province of very few?"[41]

Political participation in preindustrial societies ranges from widespread to low or nonexistent. In 16 percent of the societies examined, there is widespread participation; decision-making forums are open to all adults. The forums may be formal (councils and other governing bodies) or informal. Next in degree of political participation are societies (37 percent) that have widespread participation by some but not all adults (men but not women, certain classes but not others). Next are societies (29 percent) that have some but not much input by the community. Finally, 18 percent of the societies have low or nonexistent participation, which means that leaders make most decisions, and involvement of the average person is very limited.

Degree of political participation seems to be high in small-scale societies, as well as in modern democratic nation-states, but not in between (feudal states and preindustrial empires). Why? In small-scale societies leaders do not have the power to force people to act; thus a high degree of political participation may be the only way to get people to go along with decisions. In modern democracies, which have many powerful groups outside the government—corporations, unions, and other interest groups are examples—the central authorities may only theoretically have the power to force people to go along; in reality, they rely mostly on voluntary compliance. For example, the U.S. government failed when it tried with force (Prohibition, 1920–1933) to stop the manufacture, transport, and sale of alcoholic beverages.

A high degree of political participation seems to have an important consequence. In the modern world, democratically governed states rarely go to war with each other.[42] So, for example, the United States invaded three countries—Grenada, Panama, and Iraq—between 1980 and 1993 but no democracies. Similarly, it appears that more participatory, that is, more "democratic," political units in the ethnographic record fight with each other significantly less often than do less participatory political units, just as seems to be the case among modern nation-states.[43] Does this mean that democracies are more peaceful in general? Here there is more controversy. Judging by the frequency of war, modern democratic states do not look very different from autocratic states in their tendency to go to war. However, if you look at the severity of war as measured by casualty rates, democratic societies do look less war-like.[44] Exactly why more participation or more democracy is likely to lead to peace remains to be established. But there are policy implications of the relationship, which we explore in the chapter on global issues.

Resolution of Conflict

As we noted in the beginning of this chapter, political life involves more than the making of policy, its administration, and its enforcement. Political life also involves the resolution of conflict, which may be accomplished peacefully by avoidance, community action, mediation or the negotiation of compromises, apology, appeal to supernatural forces, or adjudication by a third party. As we shall see, the procedures used usually vary with degree of social complexity; decisions by third parties are more likely in hierarchical societies.[45] But peaceful solutions are not always possible, and disputes may erupt into violent conflict. When violence occurs within a political unit in which disputes are usually settled peacefully, we call such violence crime, particularly when committed by an individual. When the violence occurs between groups of people from separate political units—groups between which there is no procedure for settling disputes—we call such violence *warfare*. When violence occurs between subunits of a population that had been politically unified, we call it *civil war*.

Peaceful Resolution of Conflict

Most modern industrialized states have formal institutions and offices, such as police, district attorneys, courts, and penal systems, to deal with minor disputes and more serious conflicts that may arise in society. All these institutions generally operate according to **codified laws**—that is, a set of explicit, usually written rules stipulating what is permissible and what is not. Transgression of the law by individuals gives the state the right to take action against them. The state has a monopoly on the legitimate use of force in the society, for it alone has the right to coerce subjects into agreement with regulations, customs, political edicts, and procedures.

Many societies lack such specialized offices and institutions for dealing with conflict. Yet, because all societies have peaceful, regularized ways of handling at least certain disputes, some anthropologists speak of the *universality of law*. E. Adamson Hoebel, for example, stated the principle as follows:

> Each people has its system of social control. And all but a few of the poorest of them have as a part of the control system a complex of behavior patterns and institutional mechanisms that we may properly treat as law. For, "anthropologically considered, law is merely one aspect of our culture—the aspect which employs the force of organized society to regulate individual and group conduct and to prevent redress or punish deviations from prescribed social norms."[46]

Law, then, whether informal as in simpler societies, or formal as in more complex societies, provides a means of dealing peacefully with whatever conflicts develop. That does not mean that conflicts are always resolved peacefully. But that also does not mean that people cannot learn to resolve their conflicts peacefully. The fact that there are societies with little or no violent conflict means that it may be possible to learn from them; it may be possible to discover how to avoid violent outcomes of conflicts. How come South Africa could move relatively peacefully from a society dominated by people from Europe to one with government and civil rights shared by all groups? On the other hand, Bosnia had very violent conflict between ethnic groups and needed intervention by outside parties to keep the warring sides apart.[47]

Avoidance   Violence can often be avoided if the parties to a dispute voluntarily avoid each other or are separated until emotions cool down. Anthropologists have frequently remarked that foragers are particularly likely to make use of this technique. People may move to other bands or move their dwellings to opposite ends of camp. Shifting horticulturalists may also split up when conflicts get too intense. Avoidance is obviously easier in societies such as band societies that are nomadic or seminomadic and in which people have temporary dwellings. And avoidance is more feasible when people live independently and self-sufficiently (e.g., in cities and suburbs).[48]

Community Action   Societies have found various ways of resolving disputes peacefully. One such way involves action by a group or the community as a whole; collective action is common in simpler societies that lack powerful authoritarian leaders.[49] Many Inuit societies, for example, frequently resolve disputes through community action. An individual's failure to heed a taboo or to follow the suggestions of a shaman leads to expulsion from the group, because the community cannot accept a risk to its livelihood. A person who fails to share goods voluntarily will find them confiscated and distributed to the community, and he or she may be executed in the process. A single case of murder, as an act of vengeance (usually because of the abduction of a wife or as part of a blood feud), does not concern the community, but repeated murders do. Franz Boas gave a typical example:

> There was a native of Padli by the name Padlu. He had induced the wife of a native of Cumberland Sound to desert her husband and follow him. The deserted husband, meditating revenge . . . visited his friends in Padli, but before he could accomplish his intention of killing Padlu, the latter shot him . . . . A brother of the murdered man went to Padli to avenge the death . . . but he also was killed by Padlu. A third native of Cumberland Sound, who wished to avenge the death of his relatives, was also murdered by him.
>
> On account of these outrages the natives wanted to get rid of Padlu, but yet they did not dare to attack him. When the *pimain* (headman) of the Akudmurmuit learned of these events he started southward and *asked every man in Padli whether Padlu should be killed. All agreed;* so he went with the latter deer hunting . . . and . . . shot Padlu in the back.[50]

The killing of an individual is the most extreme action a community can take—we call it *capital punishment.* The community as a whole or a political official or a court may decide to administer such punishment, but capital punishment seems to exist in nearly all societies, from the simplest to the most complex.[51] It is often assumed that capital punishment deters crime. If it did, we would expect the abolition of capital punishment to be followed by an increase in homicide rates. But that does not seem to happen. A cross-national study indicates that the abolition of capital punishment tends to be followed by a decrease in homicide rates.[52]

Negotiation and Mediation   In many conflicts, the parties to a dispute may come to a settlement themselves by **negotiation**. There aren't necessarily any rules for how they will do so, but any solution is "good" if it restores peace.[53] Sometimes an outside or third party is used to help bring about a settlement between the disputants. We call it **mediation** when the outside party tries to help bring about a settlement, but that third party does not have the formal authority to force a settlement. Both negotiation and mediation are likely when the society is relatively egalitarian and it is important for people to get along.[54]

Among the Nuer of East Africa, a pastoral and horticultural people, disputes within the community can be settled with the help of an informal mediator called the "leopard-skin chief." This man is not a political chief but a mediator. His position is hereditary, has religious overtones, and makes its holder responsible for the social well-being of the district. Matters such as cattle stealing rarely come to the attention of the leopard-skin chief; the parties involved usually prefer to settle in their own private way. But if, for example, a murder has been committed, the culprit will go at once to the house of the leopard-skin chief. Immediately the chief cuts the culprit's arm so that blood flows; until the cut has been made the murderer may not eat or drink. If the murderer is afraid of vengeance by the slain man's family, he will remain at the house of the leopard-skin chief, which is considered sanctuary. Then, within the next few months, the chief attempts to mediate between the parties to the crime.

The chief elicits from the slayer's kin that they are prepared to pay compensation to avoid a feud, and he persuades the dead man's kin that they ought to accept compensation, usually in the form of cattle. During this period neither party may eat or drink from the same vessels as the other, and they may not, therefore, eat in the house of the same third person. The chief then collects the cattle—some 40 to 50 beasts—and takes them to the dead man's home, where he performs various sacrifices of cleansing and atonement.[55]

Throughout the process, the chief acts as a go-between. He has no authority to force either party to negotiate, and he has no power to enforce a solution once it has been arrived at. However, he is able to take advantage of the fact that because both disputants belong to the same community and are anxious to avoid a blood feud, they usually are willing to come to terms.

Ritual Reconciliation—Apology   The desire to restore a harmonious relationship may also explain ceremonial apologies. An apology is based on deference—the guilty party shows obeisance and asks for forgiveness. Such ceremonies tend to occur in recent chiefdoms.[56] Among the Fijians of the South Pacific, there is a strong ethic of harmony and mutual assistance, particularly within a village. When a person offends someone of higher status, the offended person and other villagers begin to avoid, and gossip about, the offender. If offenders are sensitive to village opinion, they will perform a ceremony of apology called *i soro*. One of the meanings of *soro* is "surrender." In the ceremony the offender bows the head and remains silent while an intermediary speaks, presents a token gift, and asks the offended person for forgiveness. The apology is rarely rejected.[57]

Oaths and Ordeals   Still another way of peacefully resolving disputes is through oaths and ordeals, both of which involve appeals to supernatural power. An **oath** is the act of calling upon a deity to bear witness to the truth of what one says. An **ordeal** is a means used to determine guilt or innocence by submitting the accused to dangerous or painful tests believed to be under supernatural control.[58]

A common kind of ordeal, found in almost every part of the world, is scalding. Among the Tanala of Madagascar, the accused person, having first had his hand carefully examined for protective covering, has to reach his hand into a cauldron of boiling water and grasp, from underneath, a rock suspended there. He then plunges his hand into cold water, has it bandaged, and is led off to spend the night under guard. In the morning his hand is unbandaged and examined. If there are blisters, he is guilty.

Oaths and ordeals have also been practiced in Western societies. Both were common in medieval Europe. Even today, in our own society, vestiges of oaths can be found. Children can be heard to say, "Cross my heart and hope to die," and witnesses in courts of law are obliged to swear to tell the truth.

Why do some societies use oaths and ordeals? John Roberts suggested that their use tends to be found in fairly complex societies in which political officials lack sufficient power to make and enforce judicial decisions or would make themselves unnecessarily vulnerable were they to attempt to do so. So the officials may use oaths and ordeals to let the gods decide guilt or innocence. When political officials gain more power, oaths and ordeals seem to decline or disappear.[59] In contrast, smaller and less complex societies probably have no need for elaborate mechanisms such as courts and oaths and ordeals to ascertain guilt. In such societies, everyone is aware of what crimes have been committed and who the guilty parties probably are.

Adjudication, Courts, and Codified Law We call it **adjudication** when a third party acting as judge makes a decision that the disputing parties have to accept. Judgment may be rendered by one person (a judge), a panel of judges, a jury, or a political agent or agency (a chief, a royal personage, a council). Courts are often open to an audience, but they need not be. Judges and courts may rely on codified law and stipulated punishments, but codified law is not necessary for decisions to be made. Our own society relies heavily on codified law and courts to resolve disputes peacefully, but courts often, if not usually, rely on precedent—that is, the outcomes of previous, similar cases. Codified laws and courts are not limited to Western societies. From the late seventeenth to the early twentieth centuries, for example, the Ashanti of West Africa had a complex political system with legal codes.[60] Ashanti punishments could be severe. Physical mutilation, such as slicing off the nose or an ear—even castration in sexual offenses—was often employed. Fines were more frequent, however, and death sentences could often be commuted to banishment and confiscation of goods.

Why do some societies have codified systems and others do not? One explanation, advanced by E. Adamson Hoebel, A. R. Radcliffe-Brown, and others, is that in small, closely knit communities there is little need for formal legal guidelines because competing interests are minimal. Hence, simple societies need little codified law. There are relatively few matters to quarrel about, and the general will of the group is sufficiently well known and demonstrated frequently enough to deter transgressors.

Many societies have adopted courts to resolve disputes, as here in Papua New Guinea.

This point of view is echoed in Richard Schwartz's study of two Israeli settlements. In one communal kibbutz, a young man aroused a good deal of community resentment because he had accepted an electric teakettle as a gift. It was the general opinion that he had overstepped the code about not having personal possessions, and he was so informed. Accordingly, he gave the kettle to the communal infirmary. Schwartz observed that "no organized enforcement of the decision was threatened, but had he disregarded the expressed will of the community, his life . . . would have been made intolerable by the antagonism of public opinion."[61]

In this community, where people worked and ate together, not only did everyone know about transgressions, but a wrongdoer could not escape public censure. Thus, public opinion was an effective sanction. In another Israeli community, however, where individuals lived in widely separated houses and worked and ate separately, public opinion did not work as well. Not only were community members less aware of problems, but they had no quick way of making their feelings known. As a result, they established a judicial body to handle trouble cases.

Larger, more heterogeneous and stratified societies are likely to have more frequent disputes, which at the same time are less visible to the public. Individuals in stratified societies are generally not so dependent on community members for their well-being and hence are less likely to know of, or care about, others' opinions. It is in such societies that codified laws and formal authorities for resolving disputes develop—in order, perhaps, that disputes may be settled impersonally enough so that the parties can accept the decision and social order can be restored.

A good example of how more formal systems of law develop is the experience of towns in the American West during the gold-rush period. These communities were literally swamped by total strangers. The townsfolk, having no control (authority) over these intruders because the strangers had no local ties, looked for ways to deal with the trouble cases that were continually flaring up. A first attempt at a solution was to hire gunslingers, who were also strangers, to act as peace officers or sheriffs, but this strategy usually failed. Eventually, towns succeeded in having federal authorities send in marshals backed by federal power.

Is there some evidence to support the theory that codified law is necessary only in larger, more complex societies? Data from a large, worldwide sample of societies suggest that codified law is associated with political integration beyond the local level. Murder cases, for example, are dealt with informally in societies that have only local political organization. In societies with multilocal political units, murder cases tend to be judged or adjudicated by specialized political authorities.[62] There is also some cross-cultural evidence that violence within a society tends to be less frequent when there are formal authorities (chiefs, courts) who have the power to punish murderers.[63] In general, adjudication or enforced decisions by outside authorities tend to occur in hierarchical societies with social classes and centralized power.[64]

Violent Resolution of Conflict

People are likely to resort to violence when regular, effective alternative means of resolving a conflict are not available. Some societies consider violence between individuals to be appropriate under certain circumstances; when it is not, we call it **crime**. When violence occurs between political entities such as communities, districts, or nations, we call it **warfare**. The type of warfare, of course, varies in scope and complexity from society to society. Sometimes a distinction is made among feuding, raiding, and large-scale confrontations.

Some scholars talk about a cultural pattern of violence. But are some cultures more violent than others? The answer seems to be yes. More often than not, societies with one type of violence have others. Societies with more war tend to have war-like sports, malevolent magic, severe punishment for crimes, high murder rates, feuding, and family violence. What might explain this tendency? One suggestion is that if war is frequent, the society may have to encourage boys to be aggressive, so that they can grow up to be effective warriors. But this socializing for aggression can spill over into other areas of life; high rates of crime and other violence may be inadvertent or unintended consequences of the encouragement of aggressiveness.[65]

Individual Violence   Although at first it may seem paradoxical, violent behavior itself is often used to try to control behavior. In some societies it is considered necessary for parents to beat children who misbehave. They don't consider this criminal behavior or child abuse; they consider it punishment (see the discussion of family violence in the chapter on global issues). Similar views may attach to interpersonal behavior between adults. If a person trespasses on your property or hurts someone in your family, some societies consider it appropriate or justified to kill or maim the trespasser. Is this social control, or is it just lack of control? Most societies have norms about when such "punishment" is or is not appropriate, so the behavior of anyone who contemplates doing something wrong, as well as the behavior of the person wronged, is likely to be influenced by the "laws" of their society. For example, systems of individual self-help are characteristic of egalitarian societies.[66] How is this different from "community action," which earlier we classified under peaceful resolution of conflict? Because community action is explicitly based on obtaining a consensus, it is likely to lead to the ending of a particular dispute. Individual action, or self-help, particularly if it involves violence, is not.

Feuding   Feuding is an example of how individual self-help may not lead to a peaceful resolution of conflict. **Feuding** is a state of recurring hostilities between families or groups of kin, usually motivated by a desire to avenge an offense—whether insult, injury, deprivation, or death—against a member of the group. The most common characteristic of the feud is that responsibility to avenge is carried by all members of the kin group. The killing of any member of the offender's group is considered appropriate revenge, because the kin group as a whole is regarded as responsible. Feuds are by no means limited to small-scale societies; they occur as frequently in societies with high levels of political organization.[67]

Raiding   Raiding is a short-term use of force, planned and organized, to realize a limited objective. This objective is usually the acquisition of goods, animals, or other forms of wealth belonging to another, often neighboring community.

Raiding is especially prevalent in pastoral societies, in which cattle, horses, camels, or other animals are prized and an individual's own herd can be augmented by theft. Raids are often organized by temporary leaders or coordinators whose authority may not last beyond the planning and execution of the venture. Raiding may also be organized for the purpose of capturing people. Sometimes people are taken to marry—the capture of women to be wives or concubines is fairly common[68]—or to be slaves. Slavery has been practiced in about 33 percent of the world's known societies, and war has been one way of obtaining slaves either to keep or to trade for other goods.[69] Raiding, like feuding, is often self-perpetuating: the victim of a raid today becomes the raider tomorrow.[70]

Large-Scale Confrontations   Individual episodes of feuds and raids usually involve relatively small numbers of persons and almost always an element of surprise. Because they are generally attacked without warning, the victims are often unable to muster an immediate defense. Large-scale confrontations, in contrast, involve a large number of persons and planning by both sides of strategies of attack and defense. Large-scale warfare is usually practiced among societies with intensive agriculture or industrialization. Only these societies possess a technology sufficiently advanced to support specialized armies, military leaders, strategists, and so on. But large-scale confrontations are not limited to state societies; they occur, for example, among the horticultural Dugum Dani of central New Guinea.

The military history of the Dani, with its shifting alliances and confederations, is reminiscent of that of Europe, although Dani battles involve far fewer fighters and less sophisticated weaponry. Among the Dani, long periods of ritual warfare are characterized by formal battles announced through a challenge sent by one side to the opposing side. If the challenge is accepted, the protagonists meet at the agreed-upon battle site to set up their lines. Fighting with spears, sticks, and bows and arrows begins at midmorning and continues either until nightfall or until rain intervenes. There may also be a rest period during the midday heat during which the two sides shout insults at each other or talk and rest among themselves.

The front line of battle is composed of about a dozen active warriors and a few leaders. Behind them is a second line, still within arrow range, composed of those who have just left the forward line or are preparing to join it. The third line, outside arrow range, is composed of noncombatants—males too old or too young to participate and those recovering from wounds. This third line merely watches the battle taking place on the grassy plain. On the hillsides far back from the front line, some of the old men help to direct ancestral ghosts to the battle by gouging a line in the ground that points in the direction of the battlefield.[71]

Yet, as total as large-scale confrontations may be, even warfare has cultural rules. Among the Dani, for instance, no fighting occurs at night, and weapons are limited to simple spears and bows and arrows. Similarly, in state societies, governments will sign "self-denying" pacts restricting the use of poison gas, germ warfare, and so forth. Unofficially, private arrangements are common. One has only to glance through the memoirs of national leaders of the two world wars to become aware of locally arranged truces, visits to one another's front positions, exchanges of prisoners of war, and so on.

Explaining Warfare

Most societies anthropology knows about have had warfare between communities or larger territorial groups. The vast majority of the societies in a recent cross-cultural study had at least occasional wars when they were first described, unless they had been pacified or incorporated by more dominant societies.[72] Yet relatively little research has been done on the possible causes of war and why it varies in type and frequency. For instance, why have some people fought a great deal, and others only infrequently? Why in some societies does warfare occur internally, within the society or language group?

We have answers, based on cross-cultural studies, to some of those questions. There is evidence that people in preindustrial societies go to war mostly out of fear, particularly a fear of expectable but unpredictable natural disasters (e.g., droughts, floods, locust infestations) that will destroy food resources. People may think they can protect themselves against such disasters ahead of time by taking things from defeated enemies. In any case, preindustrial societies with higher frequencies of war are very likely to have had a history of expectable but unpredictable disasters. The fact that chronic (annually recurring and therefore predictable) food shortages do not predict higher frequencies of war suggests that people go to war in an attempt to cushion the impact of the disasters they expect to occur in the future but cannot predict. Consistent with this tentative conclusion is the fact that the victors in war almost always take land or other resources from the defeated. And this is true for simpler as well as more complex preindustrial societies.[73] Might similar motives affect decisions about war and peace in the modern world?

We know that complex or politically centralized societies are likely to have professional armies, hierarchies of military authority, and sophisticated weapons.[74] But surprisingly, the frequency of warfare seems to be not much greater in complex societies than in simple band or tribal societies.[75] We have some evidence that warfare is unlikely to occur internally (within a society) if it is small in population (21,000 or fewer people) or territory; in a larger society there is a high likelihood of warfare within the society, between communities or larger territorial divisions.[76] In fact, complex societies, even if they are politically unified, are not less likely than simpler societies to have internal warfare.[77]

What about the idea that men in band and tribal societies may mostly go to war over women?[78] If this were true, those band and tribal societies with the most frequent wars should have shortages of women, and those with little or no war—less often than once in 10 years—should have more equal numbers of women and men. But the cross-cultural evidence clearly contradicts this theory. Band and tribal societies with more wars do not have fewer women.[79]

What, if anything, do we know about recent warfare between nation-states? Although many people think that military alliances lessen the chance of war, it turns out that nations formally allied with other nations do not necessarily go to war less often than nations lacking formal alliances. Countries that are allies are, of course, less likely to go to war with each other; however, alliances can drag dependent allies into wars they don't want. Countries that are economically interdependent, that trade with each other for necessities, are less likely to go to war with each other.[80] Finally, military equality between nations, particularly when preceded by a rapid military buildup, seems to increase rather than lessen the chance of war between those nations.[81]

Clearly, these findings contradict some traditional beliefs about how to prevent war. Military buildups do not make war less likely, but trade does. What else may? We have already noted that participatory ("democratic") political systems are less likely to go to war with each other than are authoritarian political systems. Later, in the chapter on global issues, we discuss how the results of cross-cultural and cross-national studies may translate into policies that could minimize the risk of war in the world.

Summary

1. All societies have customs or procedures that, organized on behalf of territorial groups, result in decision making and the resolution of disputes. These ways of creating and maintaining social order and coping with social disorder vary from society to society.

2. Societies with a band type of political organization are composed of fairly small, usually nomadic groups. Each of these bands is politically autonomous, the band being the largest group that acts as a political unit. Authority within the band is usually informal. Societies with band organization generally are egalitarian hunter-gatherers. But band organization may not have been typical of food collectors in the distant past.

3. Societies with tribal organization are generally egalitarian. But in contrast with band societies, they generally are food producers, have a higher population density, and are more sedentary. Tribal organization is defined by the presence of groupings, such as clans and age-sets, that can integrate more than one local group into a larger whole.

4. The personal qualities of leaders in tribal societies seem to be similar to the qualities of leaders in the United States, with one major difference: U.S. leaders are generally wealthier than others in their society.

5. Chiefdom organization differs from tribal organization in having formal authority structures that integrate multicommunity political units. Compared with societies with tribal organization, societies with chiefdoms are more densely populated, their communities are more permanent, and there is some form of social ranking. Chiefs generally hold their positions permanently.

6. A state has been defined as a political unit composed of many communities and having a centralized government with the authority to make and enforce laws, collect taxes, and draft men for military service. In state societies, the government tries to maintain a monopoly on the use of physical force. In addition, states are generally characterized by class stratification, intensive agriculture, commercial exchange, a high degree of economic and other specialization, and extensive foreign trade.

7. Degree of political participation seems to be high in small-scale societies, as well as in modern democratic nation-states, but not in those in between, such as feudal states and preindustrial empires.

8. Many societies lack specialized offices and institutions for dealing with conflict. Yet all societies have peaceful, regularized ways of handling at least certain disputes. Avoidance, community action, and negotiation and mediation are more common in simpler societies. Ritual apology occurs frequently in chiefdoms. Oaths and ordeals tend to occur in complex societies in which political officials lack power to enforce judicial decisions. Adjudication is more likely in stratified, more complex societies. Capital punishment seems to exist in nearly all societies, from the simplest to the most complex.

9. People are likely to resort to violence when regular, effective alternative means of resolving a conflict are not available. Violence that occurs between political entities such as communities, districts, or nations is generally referred to as warfare. Preindustrial societies with higher warfare frequencies are likely to have had a history of unpredictable disasters that destroyed food supplies. More often than not, societies with one type of violence have others.

Glossary Terms

adjudication (p. 371)   negotiation (p. 370)
band (p. 357)   oath (p. 370)
band organization (p. 357)   ordeal (p. 370)
chief (p. 360)   raiding (p. 373)
chiefdom (p. 360)   segmentary lineage system (p. 359)
codified laws (p. 368)   state (p. 361)
complementary opposition (p. 359)   state organization (p. 361)
crime (p. 372)   tribal organization (p. 358)
feuding (p. 373)   tribe (p. 358)
headman (p. 357)   warfare (p. 372)
mediation (p. 370)

Critical Questions

1. When, if ever, do you think the world will be politically unified? Why do you think so?

2. Why don't informal methods of social control work well in societies like our own? Why don't formal methods work better than they do?

3. What does research on war and violence suggest about how to minimize them?

CHAPTER 16

RELIGION AND MAGIC

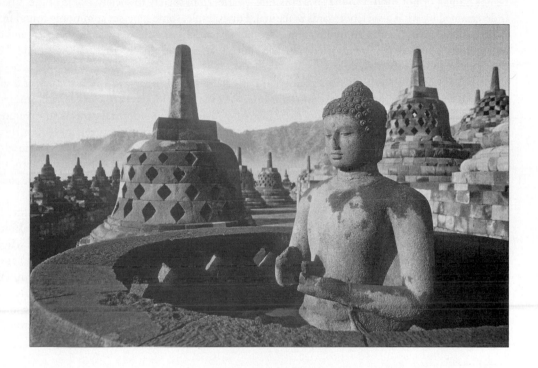

Chapter Outline

- Variation in Religious Beliefs
- Variation in Religious Practices
- Religion and Adaptation

As far as we know, all societies have possessed beliefs that can be grouped under the term *religion*. These beliefs vary from culture to culture and from time to time. Yet, despite their variety, we shall define **religion** as any set of attitudes, beliefs, and practices pertaining to *supernatural power*, whether that power be forces, gods, spirits, ghosts, or demons.

In our society, we divide phenomena into the natural and the supernatural, but not all languages or cultures make such a neat distinction. Moreover, what is considered **supernatural**—powers believed to be not human or not subject to the laws of nature—varies from society to society. Some of the variation is determined by what a society regards as natural. For example, some illnesses commonly found in our society are believed to result from the natural action of bacteria and viruses. In other societies, and even among some people in our own society, illness is thought to result from supernatural forces, and thus it forms a part of religious belief.

Beliefs about what is, or is not, a supernatural occurrence also vary within a society at a given time or over time. In Judeo-Christian traditions, for example, floods, earthquakes, volcanic eruptions, comets, and epidemics were once considered evidence of supernatural powers intervening in human affairs. It is now generally agreed that they are simply natural occurrences—even though many still believe that supernatural forces may be involved. Thus, the line between the natural and the supernatural varies in a society according to what people believe about the causes of things and events in the observable world. Similarly, what is considered sacred in one society may not be so considered in another.

In many cultures, what we would consider religious is embedded in other aspects of everyday life. That is, it is often difficult to separate the religious, economic, or political from other aspects of the culture. Such cultures have little or no specialization of any kind; there are no full-time priests, no purely religious activities. So the various aspects of culture we distinguish (e.g., in the chapter titles of this book) are not separate and easily recognized in many societies, as they are in complex societies such as our own. However, it is sometimes difficult for us to agree whether or not a particular custom of ours is religious. After all, the categorizing of beliefs as religious, political, or social is a relatively new custom. The ancient Greeks, for instance, did not have a word for religion, but they did have many concepts concerning the behavior of their gods and their own expected duties to the gods.

Variation in Religious Beliefs

There is no general agreement among scholars as to why people need religion, or how spirits, gods, and other supernatural beings and forces come into existence. Yet there is general recognition of the enormous variation in the details of religious beliefs and practices. Societies differ in the kinds of supernatural beings or forces they believe in and the character of those beings. They also differ in the structure or hierarchy of those beings, in what the beings actually do, and in what happens to people after death. Variation exists also in the ways in which the supernatural is believed to interact with humans.

Types of Supernatural Forces and Beings

Supernatural Forces   Some supernatural forces have no person-like character. For example, a supernatural, impersonal force called **mana**, after its Malayo-Polynesian name, is thought to inhabit some objects but not others, some people but not others. A farmer in Polynesia places stones around a field; the crops are bountiful; the stones have mana. During a subsequent year the stones may lose their mana and the

THE USEFULNESS OF RELIGION: TABOOS AMONG NEW ENGLAND FISHERMEN

People who engage in risky activities may try to ensure their safety by carrying or wearing lucky charms. They believe the charms protect them by invoking the help of supernatural beings or forces. We might also believe we can protect ourselves by not doing some things. For example, baseball players on a hitting streak may choose not to change their socks or sweatshirt for the next game (to continue their luck). Or we obey a prohibition because we think that by doing so we can avoid supernatural punishment. For example, we may fast or give up certain foods for a period of time. Why? God knows!

Whether or not religious beliefs and practices can affect our success or reduce our risk, we may consider them useful or adaptive if they reduce our anxieties. And reducing anxiety might indirectly maximize our success. Doesn't an actor try to reduce his or her "stage fright" before a performance? Prohibitions (taboos) are perhaps particularly likely to be adaptive in this way. Consider some research on New England fishermen that suggests how their taboos, or "rituals of avoidance," may reduce anxiety.

John Poggie and Richard Pollnac interviewed a random sample of 108 commercial fishermen from three New England ports. They were trying to explain the number of taboos among the fishermen, as measured by asking them to describe all the superstitions related to fishing they could remember. The fishermen were often embarrassed when they talked about their ritual beliefs and practices. They would say they did not really believe in their taboos, but they admitted that they would not break them while fishing. The taboos prohibited saying or doing a certain thing, or something bad would happen. Most frequently mentioned were "Don't turn a hatch cover upside down," "Don't whistle on a boat," and "Don't mention the word *pig* on board." When the fishermen were asked what these taboos meant, they talked about personal safety and preventing bad luck.

The results of the study suggest that anxiety about personal danger while fishing is the main stimulus for the taboo behavior observed among the fishermen. For example, there are more taboos reported when the duration of exposure to danger is longer. Fishermen who go out just for the day report significantly fewer taboos than fishermen who go out for longer periods of time. And longer trips are clearly more dangerous because they are farther from shore. If there is a storm, the farther out you are, the more risk of disaster because you are exposed longer to rough seas. And it is more difficult to deal with illness, injury, breakdowns, and damage to the boat far from shore. Also consistent with the conclusion that the fishermen's taboos reduce anxiety is the fact that inshore fishermen (those who are after shellfish close to shore) report a significantly smaller number of taboos than offshore fishermen (who go out farther in trawlers).

On shore, the fishermen express some disbelief in the effectiveness of their taboos. (They are called "superstitions," you know!) But at sea it seems that the omnipresence of danger raises anxiety levels and discourages the fishermen from testing their disbelief. It won't hurt to practice the taboo at sea, they say, but it might hurt not to!

Sources: John J. Poggie, Jr., and Richard B. Pollnac, "Danger and Rituals of Avoidance among New England Fishermen," *MAST: Maritime Anthropological Studies,* 1 (1988): 66–78; John J. Poggie, Jr., Richard B. Pollnac, and Carl Gersuny, "Risk as a Basis for Taboos among Fishermen in Southern New England," *Journal for the Scientific Study of Religion,* 15 (1976): 257–62.

crops will be poor. People may also possess mana, as, for example, the chiefs in Polynesia were said to do. However, such power is not necessarily possessed permanently; chiefs who were unsuccessful in war or other activities were said to have lost their mana.

There's room in the world for all religions—those who believe in rocks, those who believe in trees, those who believe in clouds . . . .
(© 1984 by Sidney Harris)

The word *mana* may be Malayo-Polynesian, but a similar concept is also found in our own society. We can compare mana to the power that golfers may attribute to some but, unhappily not all, of their clubs. A ballplayer might think a certain sweatshirt or pair of pants has supernatural power or force, and that more runs or points will be scored when they are worn. A four-leaf clover has mana; a three-leaf clover does not.

Objects, persons, or places can be considered **taboo**. Anthony Wallace distinguished mana from taboo by pointing out that things containing mana are to be touched, whereas taboo things are not to be touched, for their power can cause harm.[1] Thus, those who touch them may themselves become taboo. Taboos surround food not to be eaten, places not to be entered, animals not to be killed, people not to be touched sexually, people not to be touched at all, and so on. An Australian aborigine could not normally kill and eat the animal that was his totem; Hebrew tribesmen were forbidden to touch a woman during menstruation or for seven days afterward.

Supernatural Beings   Supernatural beings fall within two broad categories: those of nonhuman origin, such as gods and spirits, and those of human origin, such as ghosts and ancestral spirits. Chief among the beings of nonhuman origin, **gods** are named personalities. They are often *anthropomorphic*—that is, conceived in the image of a person—although they are sometimes given the shapes of other animals or of celestial bodies, such as the sun or moon. Essentially, the gods are believed to have created themselves, but some of them then created, or gave birth to, other gods. Although some are seen as creator gods, not all peoples include the creation of the world as one of the acts of gods.

After their efforts at creation, many creator gods retire. Having set the world in motion, they are not interested in its day-to-day operation. Other creator gods remain interested in the ordinary affairs of human beings, especially the affairs of one small, chosen segment of humanity. Whether or not a society has a creator god, the job of running the creation is often left to lesser gods. The Maori of New Zealand, for example, recognize three important gods: a god of the sea, a god of the forest, and a god of agriculture. They call upon each in turn for help and try to get all three to share their knowledge of how the universe runs. The gods of the ancient Romans, on the other hand, specialized to a high degree. There were three gods of the plow, one god to help with the sowing, one for weeding, one for reaping, one for storing grain, one for manuring, and so on.[2]

Beneath the gods in prestige, and often closer to people, are multitudes of unnamed **spirits**. Some may be guardian spirits for people. Some, who become known for particularly efficacious work, may be promoted to the rank of named gods. Some spirits who are known to the people but are never invoked by them are of the hobgoblin type. Hobgoblins delight in mischief and can be blamed for any number of small mishaps; still other spirits take pleasure in deliberately working evil on behalf of people.

Many Native American groups believed in guardian spirits that had to be sought out, usually in childhood. For example, among the Sanpoil of northeastern Washington, boys and sometimes girls would be sent out on overnight vigils to acquire their guardians. Most commonly the spirits were animals, but they could also be uniquely shaped rocks, lakes, mountains, whirlwinds, or clouds. The vigil was not always successful. When it was, the guardian spirit appeared in a vision or dream, and always at first in human form. Conversation with the spirit would reveal its true identity.[3]

Ghosts are supernatural beings who were once human and **ancestor spirits** are ghosts of dead relatives. The belief that ghosts or their actions can be perceived by the living is almost universal.[4] The near-universality of the belief in ghosts may not be difficult to explain. There are many cues in everyday experience that are associated with a loved one, and even after the death those cues might arouse the feeling that the dead person is still somehow present. The opening of a door or the smell of tobacco or cologne in a room may evoke the idea that the person is still present, if only for a moment. Then, too, loved ones live on in dreams. Small wonder, then, that most societies believe in ghosts. If the idea of ghosts is generated by these familiar associations, we might expect that ghosts in most societies would be close relatives and friends, not strangers—and they are.[5]

Although the belief in ghosts is nearly universal, the spirits of the dead do not play an active role in the life of the living in all societies. In his cross-cultural study of 50 societies, Swanson found that people are likely to believe in active ancestral spirits where descent groups are important decision-making units. The descent group is an entity that exists over time, back into the past as well as forward into the future,

A Guatemalan Maya family visits a cemetery on the Day of the Dead. It is believed that the spirits of the dead return for a visit on that day.

despite the deaths of individual members.[6] The dead feel concern for the fortunes, the prestige, and the continuity of their descent group as strongly as the living. As a Lugbara elder (in northern Uganda in Africa) put it, "Are our ancestors not people of our lineage? They are our fathers and we are their children whom they have begotten. Those that have died stay near us in our homes and we feed and respect them. Does not a man help his father when he is old?"[7]

The Character of Supernatural Beings

Whatever type they may be, the gods or spirits venerated in a given culture tend to have certain personality or character traits. They may be unpredictable or predictable, aloof from or interested in human affairs, helpful or punishing. Why do the gods and spirits in a particular culture exhibit certain character traits rather than others?

We have some evidence from cross-cultural studies that the character of supernatural beings may be related to the nature of child training. Melford Spiro and Roy D'Andrade suggested that the god-human relationship is a projection of the parent-child relationship, in which case child-training practices might well be relived in dealings with the supernatural.[8] For example, if a child was nurtured immediately by her parents when she cried or waved her arms about or kicked, she might grow up expecting to be nurtured by the gods when she attracted their attention by performing a ritual. On the other hand, if her parents often punished her, she would grow up expecting the gods to punish her if she disobeyed them. William Lambert, Leigh Minturn Triandis, and Margery Wolf, in another cross-cultural study, found that societies with hurtful or punitive child-training practices are likely to believe that their gods are aggressive and malevolent; societies with less punitive child training are more likely to believe that the gods are benevolent.[9] These results are consistent with the Freudian notion that the supernatural world should parallel the natural. It is worth noting in this context that some peoples refer to the god as their father and to themselves as his children.

Structure or Hierarchy of Supernatural Beings

The range of social structures in human societies from egalitarian to highly stratified has its counterpart in the supernatural world. Some societies have gods or spirits that are not ranked; one god has about as much power as another. Other societies have gods or spirits that are ranked in prestige and power. For example, on the Pacific islands of Palau, which was a rank society, gods were ranked as people were. Each clan worshiped a god and a goddess that had names or titles similar to clan titles. Although a clan god was generally important only to the members of that clan, the gods of the various clans in a village were believed to be ranked in the same order that the clans were. Thus, the god of the highest-ranking clan was respected by all the clans of the village. Its shrine was given the place of honor in the center of the village and was larger and more elaborately decorated than other shrines.[10]

Although the Palauans did not believe in a high god or supreme being who outranked all the other gods, some societies do. Consider Judaism, Christianity, and Islam, which we call **monotheistic** religions. Although *monotheism* means "one god," most monotheistic religions actually include more than one supernatural being (e.g., demons, angels, the Devil). But the supreme being or high god, as the creator of the universe or the director of events (or both), is believed to be ultimately responsible for all events.[11] A **polytheistic** religion recognizes many important gods, no one of which is supreme.

Why do some societies have a belief in a high god and others do not? Recall Swanson's suggestion that people invent gods who personify the important decision-making groups in their society. He therefore hypothesized that societies with hierarchical political systems should be more likely to believe in a high god. In his cross-cultural study of 50 societies (none of which practiced any of the major world religions), he found that belief in a high god is strongly associated with three or more levels of "sovereign" (decision-making) groups. Of the 20 sample societies that had a hierarchy of 3 or more sovereign groups—for instance, family, clan, and chiefdom—17 possessed the idea of a high god. Of the 19 societies that had fewer than 3 levels of decision-making groups, only 2 had a high god.[12] Consistent with Swanson's findings, societies dependent on food production are more likely to have a belief in a high god than are food-collecting societies.[13] These results strongly suggest, then, that the realm of the gods parallels and may reflect the everyday social and political worlds. In the past, many state societies had state religions in which the political officials were also the officials of the temples (e.g., the pharaohs in Egypt). In recent times most state societies have separated church and state, as in the United States and Canada.

Intervention of the Gods in Human Affairs

According to Clifford Geertz, it is when faced with ignorance, pain, and the unjustness of life that a person explains events by the intervention of the gods.[14] Thus, in Greek religion the direct intervention of Poseidon as ruler of the seas prevented Odysseus from getting home for ten years. In the Old Testament, the direct intervention of Yahweh caused the great flood that killed most of the people in the time of Noah. In other societies, people may search their memories for a violated taboo that has brought punishment through supernatural intervention.

In addition to unasked-for divine interference, there are numerous examples of requests for divine intervention, either for good for oneself and friends or for evil for others. Gods are asked to intervene in the weather and make the crops grow, to send fish to the fisherman and game to the hunter, to find lost things, and to accompany travelers and prevent accidents. They are asked to stop the flow of lava down the side of a volcano, to stop a war, or to cure an illness.

The gods do not intervene in all societies. In some, they intervene in human affairs; in others, they are not the slightest bit interested; and in still others, they interfere only occasionally. We have little research on why gods are believed to interfere in some societies and not in others. We do, however, have some evidence suggesting when the gods will take an interest in the morality or immorality of human behavior. Swanson's study suggests that the gods are likely to punish people for immoral behavior when there are considerable differences in wealth in the society.[15] His interpretation is that supernatural support of moral behavior is particularly useful where inequalities tax the ability of the political system to maintain social order and minimize social disorder. Envy of others' privileges may motivate some people to behave immorally; the belief that the gods will punish such behavior might deter it.

Variation in Religious Practices

Beliefs are not the only elements of religion that vary from society to society. There is also variation in how people interact with the supernatural. The manner of approach to the supernatural varies from supplication—requests, prayers, and so on—to manipulation. And societies vary in the kinds of religious practitioners they have.

Ways to Interact with the Supernatural

How to get in touch with the supernatural is a universal problem. Wallace identified a number of ways used by people the world over, though not necessarily all together, including, but not limited to, prayer (asking for supernatural help), physiological experience (doing things to the body and mind), simulation

A worshipper makes offerings at the feet of a statue in an Indian temple.

(manipulating imitations of things), feasts, and sacrifices.[16] Prayer can be spontaneous or memorized, private or public, silent or spoken. The Lugbara do not say the words of a prayer aloud, for doing so would be too powerful; they simply think about the things that are bothering them. The gods know all languages.[17]

Doing things to the body or mind may involve drugs (hallucinogenics such as peyote or opiates) or alcohol; social isolation or sensory deprivation; dancing or running until exhausted; being deprived of food, water, and sleep; and listening to repetitive sounds such as drumming. Such behaviors may induce trances or altered states of consciousness.[18] Erika Bourguignon found that achieving these altered states, which she generally referred to as *trances,* is part of religious practice in 90 percent of the world's societies.[19] In some societies, trances are thought to involve the presence of a spirit or power inside a person that changes or displaces that person's personality or soul. These types are referred to as possession trances. Other types of trances may involve the journey of a person's soul, experiencing visions, or transmitting messages from spirits. Possession trances are especially likely in societies that depend on agriculture and have social stratification, slavery, and more complex political hierarchies. Nonpossession trances are most likely to occur in food-collecting societies. Societies with moderate levels of social complexity have both possession and nonpossession trances.[20]

One puzzle is why there is a preponderance of women thought to be possessed. Alice Kehoe and Dody Giletti suggested that women are more likely than men to suffer from nutritional deficiencies because of pregnancy, lactation, and men's priority in gaining access to food. Calcium deficiency in particular can cause muscular spasms, convulsive seizures, and disorientation, all of which may foster the belief that an individual is possessed.[21] Douglas Raybeck and his colleagues suggest that women's physiology makes them more susceptible to calcium deficiency even with an equivalent diet. In addition, women are subject to more stress because they are usually less able to control their lives. Higher levels of stress, they suggest, lowers the body's reserves of calcium.[22] Erika Bourguignon suggests a more psychological explanation of women's preponderance in possession trances. In many societies, women are brought up to be submissive. But when possessed, women are taken over by spirits and they are not responsible for what they do or say—therefore they can unconsciously do what they are not able to do consciously.[23]

Voodoo employs simulation, or the imitation of things. Dolls are made in the likeness of an enemy and then are maltreated in hopes that the original enemy will experience pain and even death.

Divination seeks practical answers from the supernatural about anything that is troublesome: decisions to be made, interpersonal problems, or illness. Diviners use a variety of methods, including altered states of consciousness and simulation through the use of objects such as Ouija boards or tarot cards.[24]

Omar Moore suggested that among the Naskapi hunters of Labrador, divination is an adaptive strategy for successful hunting. The Naskapi consult the diviner every three or four days when they have no luck in hunting. The diviner holds a caribou bone over the fire, as if the bone were a map, and the burns and cracks that appear in it indicate where the group should hunt. Moore, unlike the Naskapi, did not believe that the diviner really can find out where the animals will be; the cracks in the bones merely provide a way of randomly choosing where to hunt. Because humans are likely to develop customary patterns of action, they might be likely to look for game according to some plan. But game might learn to avoid hunters who operate according to a plan. Thus, any method of ensuring against patterning or predictable plans—any random strategy—may be advantageous. Divination by "reading" the bones would seem to be a random strategy. It also relieves any individual of the responsibility of deciding where to hunt, a decision that might arouse anger if the hunt failed.[25]

The eating of a sacred meal is found in many religions. For instance, Holy Communion is a simulation of the Last Supper. Australian aborigines, normally forbidden to eat their totem animal, have one totem feast a year at which they eat the totem. Feasts are often part of marriage and funeral ceremonies, as well as a fringe benefit of the sacrifice of food to the gods.

Some societies make sacrifices to a god in order to influence the god's action, either to divert anger or to attract goodwill. Characteristic of all sacrifices is that something of value is given up to the gods, whether it be food, drink, sex, household goods, or the life of an animal or person. Some societies feel that the god is obligated to act on their behalf if they make the appropriate sacrifice. Others use the sacrifice in an attempt to persuade the god, realizing there is no guarantee that the attempt will be successful.

Of all types of sacrifice, we probably think that the taking of human life is the ultimate. Nevertheless, human sacrifice is not rare in the ethnographic and historical records. Why have some societies practiced it? One cross-cultural study found that among preindustrial societies, those with full-time craft specialists, slavery, and the corvée are most likely to practice human sacrifice. The suggested explanation is that the sacrifice mirrors what is socially important: Societies that depend mainly on human labor for energy (rather than animals or machines) may think of a human life as an appropriate offering to the gods when people want something very important.[26]

Magic

All these modes of interacting with the supernatural can be categorized in various ways. One dimension of variation is how much people in society rely on pleading or asking or trying to persuade the supernatural to act on their behalf, as opposed to whether they believe they can compel the supernatural to help by performing certain acts. For example, prayer is asking; performing voodoo is presumably compelling. When people believe their action can compel the supernatural to act in some particular and intended way, anthropologists often refer to the belief and related practice as **magic**.

Magic may involve manipulation of the supernatural for good or for evil. Many societies have magical rituals designed to ensure good crops, the replenishment of game, the fertility of domestic animals, and the avoidance and cure of illness in humans. We tend to associate the belief in magic with societies simpler than our own. But as many as 80,000 people in the United States take magic seriously.[27] Many claim to be witches. An understanding of why magic appeals to some individuals but not others in our own society may help us explain why magic is an important part of religious behavior in many societies.

As we will see, the witch doctor and the shaman often employ magic to effect a cure. But the use of magic to bring about harm has evoked perhaps the most interest.

Sorcery and Witchcraft   Sorcery and witchcraft are attempts to invoke the spirits to work harm against people. Although the words *sorcery* and *witchcraft* are often used interchangeably, they are also often distinguished. **Sorcery** may include the use of materials, objects, and medicines to invoke supernatural malevolence. **Witchcraft** may be said to accomplish the same ills by means of thought and emotion alone. Evidence of witchcraft can never be found. This lack of visible evidence makes an accusation of witchcraft both harder to prove and harder to disprove.

To the Azande of Zaire, in central Africa, witchcraft was part of everyday living. It was not used to explain events for which the cause was known, such as carelessness or violation of a taboo, but to explain the otherwise unexplainable. A man is gored by an elephant. He must have been bewitched, because he had not been gored on other elephant hunts. A man goes to his beer hut at night, lights some straw, and holds it aloft to look at his beer. The thatch catches fire and the hut burns down. The man has been bewitched, for huts did not catch fire on hundreds of other nights when he and others did the same thing. Some of the pots of a skilled potter break; some of the bowls of a skilled carver crack. Witchcraft. Other pots, other bowls treated exactly the same have not broken.[28]

The witch craze in Europe during the sixteenth and seventeenth centuries and the witch trials in 1692 in Salem, Massachusetts, remind us that the fear of others, which the belief in witchcraft presumably represents, can increase and decrease in a society within a relatively short period of time. Many scholars have tried to explain these witch hunts. One factor often suggested is political turmoil, which may give rise to widespread distrust and a search for scapegoats. In the case of Europe during the sixteenth and seventeenth centuries, small regional political units were being incorporated into national states, and political allegiances were in flux. In addition, as Swanson noted, the commercial revolution and related changes were producing a new social class, the middle class, and "were promoting the growth of Protestantism and other heresies from Roman Catholicism."[29] In the case of Salem, the government of Massachusetts colony was unstable and there was much internal dissension. In 1692, the year of the witchcraft hysteria, Massachusetts was left without an English governor, and judicial practices broke down. These extraordinary conditions saw the accusation of a single person for witchcraft become the accusation of hundreds and the execution of 20 people. Swanson suggested that the undermining of legitimate political procedures may have generated the widespread fear of witches.[30]

It is also possible that epidemics of witchcraft accusation, as in Salem as well as other New England and European communities, may be the result of real epidemics—epidemics of disease. The disease implicated in Salem and elsewhere is the fungus disease called ergot, which can grow on rye plants. (The rye flour that went into the bread that the Salem people ate may have been contaminated by ergot.) It is now known that people who eat grain products contaminated by ergot suffer from convulsions, hallucinations, and other symptoms, such as crawling sensations in the skin. We also now know that ergot contains LSD, the drug that produces hallucinations and other delusions that resemble those occurring in severe mental disorders.

The presumed victims of bewitchment in Salem and other places had symptoms similar to victims of ergot poisoning today. They suffered from convulsions and the sensations of being pricked, pinched, or bitten. They had visions and felt as if they were flying through the air. We cannot know for sure that ergot poisoning occurred during those times when witchcraft accusations flourished. There is no direct evidence, of course, since the "bewitched" were not medically tested. But we do have some evidence that seems to be consistent with the ergot theory. Ergot is known to flourish on rye plants under certain climatic conditions, particularly a very cold winter followed by a cool, moist spring and summer. Tree-ring growth indicates that the early 1690s were particularly cold in eastern New England; and the outbreaks of witchcraft accusation in Europe seem to have peaked with colder winter temperatures.[31] Interestingly, too, when witchcraft hysteria was greatest in Europe, Europeans were using an ointment containing a skin-penetrating substance that we now know produces hallucinations and a vivid sensation of flying.[32] It may not be cause for wonder, then, that our popular image of witches is of people flying through the air on broomsticks.

But whether or not epidemics of witchcraft hysteria are due to epidemics of ergot poisoning or episodes of political turmoil or both, we still have to understand why so many societies in the ethnographic record believe in witchcraft and sorcery in the first place. Why do so many societies believe that there are ways to invoke the spirits to work harm against people? One possible explanation, suggested by Beatrice Whiting, is that sorcery or witchcraft will be found in societies that lack procedures or judicial authorities to deal with crime and other offenses. Her theory is that all societies need some form of social control—some way of deterring most would-be offenders and of dealing with actual offenders. In the absence of judicial officials who, if present, might deter and deal with antisocial behavior, sorcery may be a very effective social-control mechanism. If you misbehave, the person you mistreated might cause you to become ill or even die. The cross-cultural evidence seems to support this theory. Sorcery is more important in societies that lack judicial authorities than in those that have them.[33]

Types of Practitioners

Individuals may believe that they can directly contact the supernatural, but almost all societies also have part-time or full-time religious or magical practitioners. Research suggests there are four major types of practitioners: shamans, sorcerers or witches, mediums, and priests. As we shall see, the number of types of practitioners in a society seems to vary with degree of cultural complexity.[34]

The Shaman   The word *shaman* may come from a language that was spoken in eastern Siberia. The **shaman** is usually a part-time male specialist who has fairly high status in his community and is often involved in healing.[35] We discuss the role of the shaman as healer in the chapter on applied and practicing anthropology, where we discuss medical anthropology. More generally the shaman deals with the spirit world to try to get their help or to keep them from causing harm.[36] Here we focus on the methods used by shamans to help others.

The shaman enters into a trance, or some other altered state of consciousness, and then journeys to other worlds in order to get help from guardians or other spirits. Dreams may be used to provide insight or as a way for shamans to commune with spirits. People may seek help for practical matters, such as where to get food resources or whether to relocate, but solving a health problem is most often the goal of the shaman.[37] Shamans may also bring news from spirits, such as a warning about an impending disaster.[38]

Shamans are usually male, but here we see female shamans in Korea perform a healing ritual.

Someone may receive a "call" to the role of shaman in recovering from an illness, through a vision quest, or in a dream. Shamans-in-training may enhance the vividness of their imagery by using hallucinogens, sleep or food deprivation, or engaging in extensive physical activity such as dancing. An important part of the process of being a shaman is learning to control the imagery and the spirit powers. Shamanistic training can take several years under the guidance of a master shaman.[39]

Westerners often call shamans "witch doctors" because they don't believe that shamans can effectively cure people. Do shamans effectively cure people? Actually, Westerners are not the only skeptics. A Native American named Quesalid from the Kwakiutl of the Pacific Northwest didn't believe that shamanism was effective either. So he began to associate with the shamans in order to spy on them and was taken into their group. In his first lessons, he learned

> a curious mixture of pantomime, prestidigitation, and empirical knowledge, including the art of simulating fainting and nervous fits, . . . sacred song, the technique for inducing vomiting, rather precise notions of auscultation or listening to sounds within the body to detect disorders and obstetrics, and the use of "dreamers," that is, spies who listen to private conversations and secretly convey to the shaman bits of information concerning the origins and symptoms of the ills suffered by different people. Above all, he learned the *ars magna*. . . . The shaman hides a little tuft of down in the corner of his mouth, and he throws it up, covered with blood at the proper moment—after having bitten his tongue or made his gums bleed—and solemnly presents it to his patient and the onlookers as the pathological foreign body extracted as a result of his sucking and manipulations.[40]

His suspicions were confirmed, but his first curing was a success. The patient had heard that Quesalid had joined the shamans and believed that only he could heal him. Quesalid remained with the shamans for the four-year apprenticeship, during which he could take no fee, and he became increasingly aware that his methods worked. He visited other villages, competed with other shamans in curing hopeless cases and won, and finally seemed convinced that his curing system was more valid than those of other shamans. Instead of denouncing the trickery of shamans, he continued to practice as a renowned shaman.[41]

Sorcerers and Witches   In contrast with shamans, who have fairly high status, sorcerers and witches of both sexes tend to have very low social and economic status in their societies.[42] Suspected sorcerers and witches are usually feared because they are thought to know how to invoke the supernatural to cause illness, injury, and death. Because sorcerers use materials for their magic, evidence of sorcery can be found, and suspected sorcerers are often killed for their malevolent activities. Because witchcraft supposedly is accomplished by thought and emotion alone, it may be harder to prove that someone is a witch, but the difficulty of proving witchcraft has not prevented people from accusing and killing others for being witches.

Mediums   Mediums tend to be females. These part-time practitioners are asked to heal and divine while in possession trances—that is, when they are thought to be possessed by spirits. Mediums are described as having tremors, convulsions, seizures, and temporary amnesia.

Priests   Priests are generally full-time male specialists who officiate at public events. They have very high status and are thought to be able to relate to superior or high gods who are beyond the ordinary person's control. In most societies with priests, the people who get to be priests obtain their offices through inheritance or political appointment.[43] Priests are sometimes distinguished from other people by special clothing or a different hairstyle. The training of a priest can be vigorous and long, including fasting, praying, and physical labor, as well as learning the dogma and the ritual of his religion. Priests in the United States complete four years of theological school and sometimes serve first as apprentices under established priests. The priest does not receive a fee for his services but is supported by donations from parishioners or followers. Priests often have some political power as a result of their office—the chief priest is sometimes also the head of state or is a close adviser to the chief of state—and their material well-being is a direct reflection of their position in the priestly hierarchy.

It is the dependence on memorized ritual that both marks and protects the priest. If a shaman repeatedly fails to effect a cure, he will probably lose his following, for he has obviously lost the support of the spirits. But if a priest performs his ritual perfectly and the gods choose not to respond, the priest will usually retain his position and the ritual will preserve its assumed effectiveness. The nonresponse of the gods will be explained in terms of the people's unworthiness of supernatural favor.

Practitioners and Social Complexity   More complex societies tend to have more types of religious or magical practitioners. If a society has only one type of practitioner, it is almost always a shaman; such societies tend to be nomadic or seminomadic food collectors. Societies with two types of practitioners (usually shaman-healers and priests) have agriculture. Those with three types of practitioners are agriculturalists or pastoralists with political integration beyond the community (the additional practitioner type tends to be either a sorcerer-witch or a medium). Finally, societies with all four types of practitioners have agriculture, political integration beyond the community, and social classes.[44]

Religion and Adaptation

Many anthropologists take the view that religions are adaptive because they reduce the anxieties and uncertainties that afflict all peoples. We do not really know that religion is the only means of reducing anxiety and uncertainty, or even that individuals or societies *have* to reduce their anxiety and uncertainty. Still, it seems likely that certain religious beliefs and practices have directly adaptive consequences. For example, the Hindu belief in the sacred cow has seemed to many to be the very opposite of a useful or adaptive custom. Their religion does not permit Hindus to slaughter cows. Why do the Hindus retain such a belief? Why do they allow all those cows to wander around freely, defecating all over the place, and not slaughter any of them? The contrast with our own use of cows could hardly be greater.

Marvin Harris suggested that the Hindu use of cows may have beneficial consequences that some other use of cows would not have. Harris pointed out that there may be a sound economic reason for not slaughtering cattle in India. The cows, and the males they produce, provide resources that could not easily be gotten otherwise. At the same time, their wandering around to forage is no strain on the food-producing economy.

The resources provided by the cows are varied. First, a team of oxen and a plow are essential for the many small farms in India. The Indians could produce oxen with fewer cows, but to do so they would have to devote some of their food production to the feeding of those cows. In the traditional system, they do not feed the cows, and even though poor nutrition makes the cows relatively infertile, males, which are castrated to make oxen, are still produced at no cost to the economy. Second, cow dung is essential as a cooking fuel and fertilizer. The National Council of Applied Economic Research estimated that an amount of dung equivalent to 45 million tons of coal is burned annually. Moreover, it is delivered practically to the door each day at no cost. Alternative sources of fuel, such as wood, are scarce or costly. In addition, about 340 million tons of dung are used as manure—essential in a country obliged to derive three harvests a year from its intensively cultivated land. Third, although Hindus do not eat beef, cattle that die naturally or are butchered by non-Hindus are eaten by the lower castes, who, without the upper-caste taboo against eating beef, might not get this needed protein. Fourth, the hides and horns of the cattle that die are used in India's enormous leather industry. Therefore, because the cows do not themselves consume resources needed by people and it would be impossible to provide traction, fuel, and fertilizer as cheaply by other means, the taboo against slaughtering cattle may be very adaptive.[45]

Religious Change

The long history of religion includes periods of strong resistance to change as well as periods of radical change. Anthropologists have been especially interested in the founding of new religions or sects. The appearance of new religions is one of the things that may happen when cultures are disrupted by contact with dominant societies. Various terms have been suggested for these religious movements—cargo cults, nativistic movements, messianic movements, millenarian cults. Wallace suggested that they are all examples of **revitalization movements**, efforts to save a culture by infusing it with a new purpose and new life.[46] Change may come about more directly by the presence of missionaries who try to convert people to their religion.

Revitalization Movements: The Seneca and the Religion of Handsome Lake   The Seneca reservation of the Iroquois on the Allegheny River in New York State was a place of "poverty and humiliation" by 1799.[47] Demoralized by whiskey and dispossessed from their traditional lands, unable to compete with the new technology because of illiteracy and lack of training, the Seneca were at an impasse. In this setting, Handsome Lake, the 50-year-old brother of a chief, had the first of a number of visions. In them, he met with emissaries of the Creator who showed him heaven and hell and commissioned him to revitalize Seneca religion and society. This he set out to do for the next decade and a half. He used as his principal text the *Gaiwiio,* or "Good Word," a gospel that contains statements about the nature of religion and eternity and a code of conduct for the righteous. The *Gaiwiio* is interesting both for the influence of Quaker Christianity it clearly reveals[48] and for the way the new material was merged with traditional Iroquois religious concepts.

Handsome Lake's teaching seems to have led to a renaissance among the Seneca. Temperance was widely accepted, as were schooling and new farming methods. By 1801, corn yields had been increased tenfold, new crops (oats, potatoes, flax) had been introduced, and public health and hygiene had improved considerably. Handsome Lake himself acquired great power among his people. He spent the remainder of his life fulfilling administrative duties, acting as a representative of the Iroquois in Washington, and preaching his gospel to neighboring tribes. By the time of Handsome Lake's death in 1815, the Seneca clearly had undergone a dramatic rebirth, attributable at least in part to the new religion. Later in the century, some of Handsome Lake's disciples founded a church in his name that, despite occasional setbacks and political disputes, survives to this day.

Although many scholars believe cultural stress gives rise to these new religious movements, it is still important to understand exactly what the stresses are and how strong they have to become before a new movement emerges. Do different kinds of stresses produce different kinds of movements? And does the nature of the movement depend on the cultural elements already present?

Religious Conversion

Religious change usually does not occur in a vacuum, but is often associated with economic and political changes. Missionaries are some of the earliest settlers in interior regions and out-of-the-way places. Of course, the presence of missionaries does not always mean that people convert to the new religion.

A revitalization movement that became known as the Ghost Dance spread eastward from the Northwest from the 1870s to the 1890s. It was generally believed that if people did the dance correctly, ghosts would come to life with sufficient resources to allow the people to return to their old ways, and, as a result of some cataclysm, the whites would disappear.

Source: Ogallala Sioux performing the Ghost Dance at the Pine Ridge Indian Agency, South Dakota. Illustration by Frederic Remington, 1890. The Granger Collection.

Missionaries have not met with equal success in all parts of the world. In some places, large portions of the native population have converted to the new religion with great zeal. In others, missionaries have been ignored, forced to flee, or even killed. We do not fully understand why missionaries have been successful in some societies and not in others. Yet, in many parts of the world, Western missionary activity has been a potent force for all kinds of cultural change. One possible reason is that missionaries offer resources that enable natives to minimize economic and other risks in the new, Western-dominated social environment.[49]

Christianity on Tikopia   Tikopia was one of the few Polynesian societies to retain its traditional religious system into the first decades of the twentieth century. An Anglican mission was first established on the island in 1911. With it came a deacon and the founding of 2 schools for about 200 pupils. By 1929, approximately half the population had converted, and in the early 1960s almost all Tikopia gave at least nominal allegiance to Christianity.[50]

Traditional Tikopian belief embraced a great number of gods and spirits of various ranks who inhabited the sky, the water, and the land. One god in particular—the original creator and shaper of the culture—was given a place of special importance, but he was in no way comparable to the all-powerful God of Christianity. Unlike Christianity, Tikopian religion made no claim to universality. The Tikopian gods did not rule over all creation, only over Tikopia. It was thought that if one left Tikopia, one left the gods behind.

The people of Tikopia interacted with their gods and spirits primarily through religious leaders who were also the heads of descent groups. Clan chiefs presided over rituals associated with the everyday aspects of island life, such as house construction, fishing, planting, and harvesting. The chief was expected to intercede with the gods on the people's behalf, to persuade them to bring happiness and prosperity to the group. Indeed, when conditions were good it was assumed that the chief was doing his job well. When disaster struck, the prestige of the chief often fell in proportion. Why did the Tikopia convert to Christianity? Firth suggested several contributing factors.

First, the mission offered the people the prospect of acquiring new tools and consumer goods. Although conversion alone did not provide such benefits, attachment to the mission made them more attainable. Later, it became apparent that education, particularly in reading and writing English, was helpful in getting ahead in the outside world. Mission schooling became valued and provided a further incentive for adopting Christianity.

Second, conversion may have been facilitated by the ability of chiefs, as religious and political leaders, to bring over entire descent groups to Christianity. Should a chief decide to transfer his allegiance to Christianity, the members of his kin group usually followed him. In 1923, when Tafua, chief of the Faea district of Tikopia, converted to the new religion, he brought with him his entire group—nearly half the population of the island. The ability of the chiefs to influence their kin groups, however, was both an asset and a hindrance to missionary efforts, since some chiefs steadfastly resisted conversion.

A final blow to traditional Tikopian religion came in 1955, when a severe epidemic killed at least 200 people in a population of about 1,700. According to Firth, "the epidemic was largely interpreted as a sign of divine discrimination," because three of the outstanding non-Christian religious leaders died.[51] Subsequently, the remaining non-Christian chiefs voluntarily converted to Christianity, and so did their followers. By 1966, all Tikopia, with the exception of one old woman, had converted to the new faith.

Although many Tikopians feel their conversion to Christianity has been a unifying, revitalizing force, the changeover from one religion to another has not been without problems. Christian missionaries on Tikopia have succeeded in eliminating the traditional Tikopian population-control devices of abortion, infanticide, and male celibacy. It is very possible that the absence of these controls will continue to intensify population pressure. The island, with its limited capacity to support life, can ill afford this outcome. Firth summed up the situation Tikopian society faced:

> In the history of Tikopia complete conversion of the people to Christianity was formerly regarded as a solution to their problems; it is now coming to be realized that the adoption and practice of Christianity itself represents another set of problems. As the Tikopia themselves are beginning to see, to be Christian Polynesians in the modern technologically and industrially dominated world, even in the Solomon Islands, poses as many questions as it supplies answers.[52]

Fundamentalism

For some scholars one of the main attributes of fundamentalism is the literal interpretation of a sacred scripture. But recent scholars have suggested that fundamentalist movements need to be understood more broadly as religious/political movements that appear in response to the rapidly changing environment of the modern world. In this broader view, fundamentalism occurs in many religions, including Christian, Jewish, Islam, Sikh, Buddhist, and Hindu. Although each movement is different in content, Richard Antoun suggests that fundamentalist movements have the following elements in common: the selective use of scripture to inspire and assert proof of particular certainties; the quest for purity and traditional values in what is viewed as an impure world; active opposition to what is viewed as a permissive secular society and a nation-state that separates religion from the state; and an incorporation of selected modern elements such as television to promote the movements' aims.[53]

Fundamentalist religious movements do appear to be linked to the anxieties and uncertainties associated with culture change in general and globalization in particular. Many people in many countries are repelled by new behaviors and attitudes, and react in a way that celebrates the old. As Judith Nagata puts it, fundamentalism is a "quest for certainty in an uncertain world."[54] Protestant fundamentalism flourished at the end of the nineteenth century in the United States as immigrant groups came into the country in great numbers and the country became industrialized and increasingly urbanized. The fundamentalists denounced foreign influences, the decline of the Bible as a guide to moral behavior, and the teaching of evolution; and they succeeded in getting the country to prohibit the sale of alcoholic beverages. Recent Islamic fundamentalist movements seem to be responses to a different kind of challenge to the social order—increasing Westernization. Westernization may have first arrived in conjunction with colonial rule. Later it may have been promoted by Western-educated native elites.[55] Antoun suggests that fundamentalist movements deliberately push certain practices because the leaders know they will outrage the secular opposition. Examples in recent Islamic fundamentalist movements are the extreme punishment of cutting off a hand for theft and requiring women to be covered by veils or head-to-toe covering in public.[56] Unfortunately, in present-day discourse, fundamentalism tends to be equated by Westerners with Islam itself. But, in historical perspective, all major religions have had fundamentalist movements in times of rapid culture change.

The Appeal of Religion

There are many religions in the United States today, and new sects, often derisively called cults, emerge regularly. Few of us realize that nearly all of the major churches or religions in the world began as minority sects or cults. Indeed, some of the most established and prestigious Protestant churches were considered radical social movements at first. For example, what we now know as the United Church of Christ, which includes the Congregational Church, was founded by radicals in England who wanted church governance to be in the hands of the local congregation. Many of these radicals became the people we call Pilgrims, who had to flee to the New World. But they were very fundamentalist in their beliefs; for example, as late as the 1820s, Congregationalist-dominated towns in Connecticut prohibited celebrations of Christmas outside of church because such celebrations were not mentioned in the Bible. Nowadays, Congregationalists are among the most liberal Protestants.

We should not be surprised to learn that most of the various Protestant churches today, including some considered very conservative, began as militant sects that set out to achieve a better world. After all, that's why we call them "Protestant." At first, the rebellion was against Rome and the Catholic Church. Later, sects developed in opposition to church and government hierarchies. And remember that Christianity itself began as a radical group in the hinterland of the Roman Empire. So new sects or cults were probably always political and social, as well as religious, movements. Recall that the word *millennium,* as used in discussions of religious movements, refers to a wished-for or expected future time when human life and society will be perfect and free of troubles; the world will then be prosperous, happy, and peaceful.[57] Nowadays, the wish for a better world may or may not be religiously inspired. Some people who seek a more perfect world believe that humans alone must achieve it.

How should we categorize this wish for a better world? Should we call it "conservative" because the imagined world may have existed in the past? If the imagined world does not yet exist, is it "radical" to believe it can be achieved? Maybe the wish for a more perfect world is neither conservative nor radical. Maybe it is just that people who are not satisfied with the world as it is think that something can be done to improve things, with or without divine assistance. However it will come, the "millennium" will be different from now, and better.

Ideas about the millennium, and the origins of new cults and religions, might best be viewed then as human hopes: Which ones do people have? Do they vary from culture to culture, and why? Are some hopes universal? And how might they be achieved?

Summary

1. Religion is any set of attitudes, beliefs, and practices pertaining to supernatural power. Such beliefs may vary within a culture as well as among societies, and they may change over time.

2. There are wide variations in religious beliefs. Societies vary in the number and kinds of supernatural entities in which they believe. There may be impersonal supernatural forces (e.g., mana and taboo), supernatural beings of nonhuman origin (gods and spirits), and supernatural beings of human origin (ghosts and ancestor spirits). The religious belief system of a society may include any or all such entities.

3. Gods and spirits may be unpredictable or predictable, aloof from or interested in human affairs, helpful or punishing. In some societies, all gods are equal in rank; in others, there is a hierarchy of prestige and power among gods and spirits, just as among the humans in those societies.

4. A monotheistic religion is one in which there is one high god, as the creator of the universe or the director of events (or both); all other supernatural beings are either subordinate to, or function as alternative manifestations of, this god. A high god is generally found in societies with a high level of political development.

5. Faced with ignorance, pain, and injustice, people frequently explain events by claiming intervention by the gods. Such intervention has also been sought by people who hope it will help them achieve their own ends. The gods are likely to punish the immoral behavior of people in societies that have considerable differences in wealth.

6. Various methods have been used to attempt communication with the supernatural. Among them are prayer, taking drugs or otherwise affecting the body and mind, simulation, feasts, and sacrifices.

7. When people believe that their actions can compel the supernatural to act in a particular and intended way, anthropologists refer to the belief and related practice as magic. Sorcery and witchcraft are attempts to make the spirits work harm against people.

8. Almost all societies have part-time or full-time religious or magical practitioners. Recent cross-cultural research suggests that there are four major types of practitioners: shamans, sorcerers or witches, mediums, and priests. The number of types of practitioners seems to vary with degree of cultural complexity: the more complex the society, the more types of practitioners.

9. The history of religion includes periods of strong resistance to change and periods of radical change. One explanation for this cycle is that religious practices always originate during periods of stress. Religious movements have been called revitalization movements—efforts to save a culture by infusing it with a new purpose and new life. Religious change is often promoted by the efforts of missionaries, but it is not clearly understood why some societies are more likely to convert than others. Finally, fundamentalist movements appear in response to the rapidly changing environment of the modern world.

10. One appeal of religion may be the wish for a better world.

Glossary Terms

ancestor spirits (p. 381)

divination (p. 384)

ghosts (p. 381)

gods (p. 380)

magic (p. 385)

mana (p. 378)

mediums (p. 388)

monotheistic (p. 382)

polytheistic (p. 382)

priests (p. 388)

religion (p. 378)

revitalization movements (p. 390)

shaman (p. 387)

sorcery (p. 386)

spirits (p. 381)

supernatural (p. 378)

taboo (p. 380)

witchcraft (p. 386)

Critical Questions

1. How does your conception of God compare with beliefs about supernatural beings in other religious systems?

2. What do you think is the future of religion? Explain your answer.

3. Could any of the religious practices you know about be classified as magic? Are they associated with anxiety-arousing situations?

CULTURE CHANGE AND GLOBALIZATION

Chapter Outline

- How and Why Cultures Change
- Culture Change and Adaptation
- Types of Culture Change in the Modern World

- Ethnogenesis: The Emergence of New Cultures
- Globalization: Problems and Opportunities
- Cultural Diversity in the Future

Most of us are aware that "times have changed," especially when we compare our lives with those of our parents. Witness the recent changes in attitudes about sex and marriage, as well as the changes in women's roles. But such culture change is not unusual. Throughout history humans have replaced or altered customary behaviors and attitudes as their needs have changed. Just as no individual is immortal, no particular cultural pattern is impervious to change. Anthropologists, therefore, want to understand how and why culture change occurs.

Three general questions can be asked about culture change: What is the source of a new trait? Why are people motivated, unconsciously as well as consciously, to adopt it? And is the new trait adaptive? The source of the change may be inside or outside the society. That is, a new idea or behavior may originate within the society, or it may come from another society. With regard to motivation, people may adopt the new idea or behavior voluntarily, even if unconsciously, or they may be forced to adopt it. Finally, the outcome of culture change may or may not be beneficial. In this chapter, we first discuss the various processes of culture change in terms of the three dimensions of source, motivation, and outcome. Then we discuss some of the major types of culture change in the modern world. As we will see, these changes are associated largely with the expansion of Western societies over the last 500 years. New cultures and new identities may arise, in a process called *ethnogenesis*. Finally, we discuss *globalization*—the ongoing spread of cultural features around the world—and what it portends for the future of cultural diversity.

How and Why Cultures Change

Discoveries and inventions, which may originate inside or outside a society, are ultimately the sources of all culture change. But they do not necessarily lead to change. If an invention or discovery is ignored, no change in culture results. It is only when society accepts an invention or discovery and uses it regularly that we can begin to speak of culture change.

Discovery and Invention

The new thing discovered or invented, the innovation, may be an object—the wheel, the plow, the computer—or it may involve behavior and ideas—buying and selling, democracy, monogamy. According to Ralph Linton, a discovery is any addition to knowledge and an invention is a new application of knowledge.[1] Thus, a person might discover that children can be persuaded to eat nourishing food if the food is associated with an imaginary character that appeals to them. And then someone might exploit that discovery by inventing a character named Popeye who appears in a series of animated cartoons, acquiring miraculous strength by devouring cans of spinach.

Unconscious Invention In discussing the process of invention, we should differentiate between various types of inventions. One type is the consequence of a society's setting itself a specific goal, such as eliminating tuberculosis or placing a person on the moon. Another type emerges less intentionally. This second process of invention is often referred to as *accidental juxtaposition* or *unconscious invention*. Linton suggested that some inventions, especially those of prehistoric days, were probably the consequences of literally dozens of tiny initiatives by "unconscious" inventors. These inventors made their small contributions, perhaps over many hundreds of years, without being aware of the part they were playing in bringing one invention, such as the wheel or a better form of hand ax, to completion.[2] In reconstructing the process of invention in prehistoric times, however, we should be careful not to look back on our ancestors with a smugness generated by our more highly developed technology. We have become accustomed to turning to the science sections of our magazines and newspapers and finding, almost daily, reports of miraculous new discoveries and inventions. From our point of view, it is difficult to imagine such a simple invention as the wheel taking so many centuries to come into being. We are tempted to surmise that early humans were less intelligent than we are. But the capacity of the human brain has been the same for perhaps 100,000 years; there is no evidence that the inventors of the wheel were any less intelligent than we are.

Intentional Innovation   Some discoveries and inventions arise out of deliberate attempts to produce a new idea or object. It may seem that such innovations are obvious responses to perceived needs. For example, during the Industrial Revolution there was a great demand for inventions that would increase productivity. James Hargreaves, in eighteenth-century England, is an example of an inventor who responded to an existing demand. Textile manufacturers were clamoring for such large quantities of spun yarn that cottage laborers, working with foot-operated spinning wheels, could not meet the demand. Hargreaves, realizing that prestige and financial rewards would come to the person who invented a method of spinning large quantities of yarn in a short time, set about the task and developed the spinning jenny.

A study of innovation among Ashanti artist-carvers in Ghana suggests that creativity is more likely in some socioeconomic groups than in others.[3] Some carvers produced only traditional designs; others departed from tradition and produced "new" styles of carving. Two groups were found to innovate the most—the wealthiest and the poorest carvers. These two groups of carvers may tolerate risk more than the middle socioeconomic group. Innovative carving entails some risk because it may take more time and it may not sell. Wealthy carvers can afford the risk, and they may gain some prestige as well as income if their innovation is appreciated. The poor are not doing well anyway, and they have little to lose by trying something new.

Some societies encourage innovativeness more than others and this can vary substantially over time. Patricia Greenfield and her colleagues describe the changes in weaving in a Mayan community in the Zinacantán region of Chiapas, Mexico.[4] In 1969 and 1970, innovation was not valued. Rather, tradition was; there was the old "true way" to do everything, including how one dressed. There were only four simple weaving patterns, and virtually all males wore ponchos with the same pattern. By 1991, virtually no poncho was the same and the villagers had developed elaborate brocaded and embroidered designs. In a period of 20 years, innovation had increased dramatically.

Who Adopts Innovations?   Once someone discovers or invents something, there is still the question of whether the innovation will be adopted by others. Many researchers have studied the characteristics of "early adopters." Such individuals tend to be educated, high in social status, upwardly mobile, and, if they are property owners, to have large farms and businesses. The individuals who most need technological improvements—those who are less well off—are generally the last to adopt innovations. The theory is that only the wealthy can afford to take the substantial risks associated with new ways of doing things. In periods of rapid technological change, therefore, the gap between rich and poor is likely to widen because the rich adopt innovations sooner, and benefit more from them, than the poor.[5]

Costs and Benefits   An innovation that is technologically superior is not necessarily going to be adopted. There are costs as well as benefits for both individuals and large-scale industries. Take the computer keyboard. The keyboard used most often on computers today is called the QWERTY keyboard (named after the letters on the left side of the line of keys below the row of number keys). This keyboard was actually invented to slow typing speed down! Early typewriters had mechanical keys that jammed if the typist went too fast.[6] Computer keyboards don't have that problem, so an arrangement of keys that allowed faster typing would probably be better. Different keyboard configurations have been invented, but they haven't caught on. Most people probably would find it too hard or too time-consuming to learn a new style of typing, so the original style of keyboard persists.

Diffusion

The source of new cultural elements in a society may also be another society. The process by which cultural elements are borrowed from another society and incorporated into the culture of the recipient group is called **diffusion**. Borrowing sometimes enables a group to bypass stages or mistakes in the development of a process or institution. For example, Germany was able to accelerate its program of industrialization in the nineteenth century because it was able to avoid some of the errors made by its English and Belgian competitors by taking advantage of technological borrowing. Japan did the same somewhat later. Indeed, in recent years some of the earliest industrialized countries have fallen behind their imitators in certain areas of production, such as automobiles, televisions, cameras, and computers.

In a known well passage, Linton conveyed the far reaching effects of diffusion by considering the first few hours in the day of an American man in the 1930s. This man

> . . . awakens in a bed built on a pattern which originated in the Near East but which was modified in northern Europe before it was transmitted to America. He throws back covers made from cotton, domesticated in India, or linen, domesticated in the Near East, or silk, the use of which was discovered in China. All of these materials have been spun and woven by processes invented in the Near East . . . . He takes off his pajamas, a garment invented in India, and washes with soap invented by the ancient Gauls. He then shaves, a masochistic rite which seems to have derived from either Sumer or ancient Egypt.

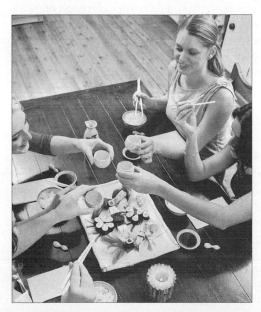

Americans have not adopted most features of Japanese culture, but the interest in sushi is spreading.

Before going out for breakfast he glances through the window, made of glass invented in Egypt, and if it is raining puts on overshoes made of rubber discovered by the Central American Indians and takes an umbrella, invented in southeastern Asia . . . .

On his way to breakfast he stops to buy a paper paying for it with coins, an ancient Lydian invention . . . . His plate is made of a form of pottery invented in China. His knife is of steel, an alloy first made in southern India, his fork a medieval Italian invention, and his spoon a derivative of a Roman original . . . . After his fruit (African watermelon) and first coffee (an Abyssinian plant) . . . he may have the egg of a species of bird domesticated in Indo-China, or thin strips of the flesh of an animal domesticated in Eastern Asia which have been salted and smoked by a process developed in northern Europe . . . .

While smoking (an American Indian habit) he reads the news of the day, imprinted in characters invented by the ancient Semites upon a material invented in China by a process invented in Germany. As he absorbs the accounts of foreign troubles he will, if he is a good conservative citizen, thank a Hebrew deity in an Indo-European language that he is 100 percent American.[7]

The Selective Nature of Diffusion   Although there is a temptation to view the dynamics of diffusion as similar to a stone sending concentric ripples over still water, this would be an oversimplification of the way diffusion actually occurs. Not all cultural traits are borrowed as readily as the ones we have mentioned, nor do they usually expand in neat, ever-widening circles. Rather, diffusion is a selective process. The Japanese, for instance, accepted much from Chinese culture, but they also rejected many traits. Rhymed tonal poetry, civil service examinations, and foot binding, which were favored by the Chinese, were never adopted in Japan. The poetry form was unsuited to the structure of the Japanese language; the examinations were unnecessary in view of the entrenched power of the Japanese aristocracy; and foot binding was repugnant to a people who abhorred body mutilation of any sort.

Not only would we expect societies to reject items from other societies that are repugnant, we would also expect them to reject ideas and technology that do not satisfy some psychological, social, or cultural need. After all, people are not sponges; they don't automatically soak up the things around them. If they did, the amount of cultural variation in the world would be extremely small, which is clearly not the case.

Finally, diffusion is selective because the overt form of a particular trait, rather than its function or meaning, frequently seems to determine how the trait will be received. For example, the enthusiasm in women for bobbed hair (short haircuts) that swept through much of North America in the 1920s never caught on among the Native Americans of northwestern California. To many women of European ancestry, short hair was a symbolic statement of their freedom. To Native American women, who traditionally cut their hair short when in mourning, it was a reminder of death.[8]

Acculturation

On the surface, the process of change called **acculturation** seems to include much of what we have discussed under the label of diffusion, since acculturation refers to the changes that occur when different cultural groups come into intensive contact. As in diffusion, the source of new cultural items is the other society. But more often than not, the term *acculturation* is used by anthropologists to describe a situation in which one of the societies in contact is much more powerful than the other. Thus, acculturation can be seen as a process of extensive cultural borrowing in the context of superordinate-subordinate relations between societies.[9] The borrowing may sometimes be a two-way process, but generally it is the subordinate or less powerful society that borrows the most. The concept of diffusion can then be reserved for the voluntary borrowing of cultural elements, in contrast with borrowing under external pressure, which characterizes acculturation.

A subordinate society may acculturate to a dominant society even in the absence of direct or indirect force. The dominated people may elect to adopt cultural elements from the dominant society in order to survive in their changed world. Or, perceiving that members of the dominant society enjoy more secure living conditions, the dominated people may identify with the dominant culture in the hope that by doing so they will be able to share some of its benefits. For example, in Arctic areas many Inuit and Lapp groups seemed eager to replace dog sleds with snowmobiles without any coercion.[10]

But many millions of people never had a chance to acculturate after contact with Europeans. They simply died, sometimes directly at the hands of the conquerors, but probably more often as a result of the new diseases the Europeans inadvertently brought with them. Depopulation because of measles, smallpox, and tuberculosis was particularly common in North and South America and on the islands of the Pacific. Those areas had previously been isolated from contact with Europeans and from the diseases of that continuous landmass we call the Old World—Europe, Asia, and Africa.[11]

Nowadays, many powerful nations—and not just Western ones—may seem to be acting in more humanitarian ways to improve the life of previously subjugated as well as other "developing" peoples. For better or worse, these programs, however, are still forms of external pressure. The tactic used may be persuasion rather than force, but most of the programs are nonetheless designed to bring about acculturation in the direction of the dominant societies' cultures. For example, the introduction of formal schooling cannot help but instill new values that may contradict traditional cultural patterns. And even healthcare programs may alter traditional ways of life by undermining the authority of shamans and other leaders and by increasing population beyond the number that can be supported in traditional ways. Confinement to "reservations" or other kinds of direct force are not the only ways a dominant society can bring about acculturation.

The process of acculturation also applies to immigrants, most of whom, at least nowadays, choose to leave one country for another. Immigrants are almost always a minority in the new country and therefore are in a subordinate position. If the immigrant's culture changes, it is almost always in the direction of the dominant culture. Immigrant groups vary considerably in the degree and speed with which they

Students and teachers stand outside of the Lincoln Institution, an Indian girls' school in Delaware County, Pennsylvania. This picture was taken in October 1884.

adopt the new culture and the social roles of the new society in which they live. An important area of research is explaining the variation in acculturation and assimilation. (*Assimilation* is a concept very similar to acculturation, but assimilation is a term more often used by sociologists to describe the process by which individuals acquire the social roles and culture of the dominant group.) Why do some immigrant groups acculturate or assimilate faster than others? Recall the comparative study by Robert Schrauf that assessed the degree to which immigrant groups coming to North America retained their native language over time. He looked at whether they lived in tightly knit communities, retained religious rituals, had separate schools and special festivals, visited their homeland, did not intermarry, or worked with others of their ethnic group. All of these factors might be expected to lead to retention of the native language (and presumably other cultural patterns), but only living in tightly knit communities and retaining religious rituals strongly predicted retaining the native language over a long period of time.[12]

Revolution

Certainly the most drastic and rapid way a culture can change is as a result of **revolution**—replacement, usually violent, of a country's rulers. Historical records, as well as our daily newspapers, indicate that people frequently rebel against established authority. Rebellions, if they occur, almost always occur in state societies, where there is a distinct ruling elite. They take the form of struggles between rulers and ruled, between conquerors and conquered, or between representatives of an external colonial power and segments of the native society. Rebels do not always succeed in overthrowing their rulers, so rebellions do not always result in revolutions. And even successful rebellions do not always result in culture change; the individual rulers may change, but customs or institutions may not. The sources of revolution may be mostly internal, as in the French Revolution, or partly external, as in the Russian-supported 1948 revolution in Czechoslovakia and the U.S.-supported 1973 revolution against President Allende in Chile.

The American War of Independence toward the end of the eighteenth century is a good example of a colonial rebellion, the success of which was at least partly a result of foreign intervention. The American rebellion was a war of neighboring colonies against the greatest imperial power of the time, Great Britain. In the nineteenth century and continuing into the middle and later years of the twentieth century, there would be many other wars of independence, in Latin America, Europe, Asia, and Africa. We don't always remember that the American rebellion was the first of these anti-imperialist wars in modern times, and the model for many that followed. And just like many of the most recent liberation movements, the American rebellion was also part of a larger worldwide war, involving people from many rival nations. Thirty thousand German-speaking soldiers fought, for pay, on the British side; an army and navy from France fought on the American side. There were volunteers from other European countries, including Denmark, Holland, Poland, and Russia.

One of these volunteers was a man named Kosciusko from Poland, which at the time was being divided between Prussia and Russia. Kosciusko helped win a major victory for the Americans, and subsequently directed the fortification of what later became the American training school for army officers, West Point. After the war he returned to Poland and led a rebellion against the Russians, which was only briefly successful. In 1808 he published the *Manual on the Maneuvers of Horse Artillery*, which was used for many years by the American army. When he died he left money to buy freedom and education for American slaves. The executor of Kosciusko's will was Thomas Jefferson.

As in many revolutions, those who were urging revolution were considered "radicals." At a now famous debate in Virginia in 1775, delegates from each colony met at a Continental Congress. Patrick Henry put forward a resolution to prepare for defense against the British armed forces. The motion barely passed, by a vote of 65 to 60. Henry's speech is now a part of American folklore. He rose to declare

Revolutionary leaders are often from high-status backgrounds. Here we see a depiction of Patrick Henry giving his famous speech to the aristocratic landowners in the Virginia Assembly on March 23, 1775. Urging the Virginians to fight the British, Henry said that the choice was "liberty or death."

Source: Currier & Ives, "Give Me Liberty or Give Me Death!" 1775. Lithograph, 1876. © The Granger Collection, New York.

that it was insane not to oppose the British and that he was not afraid to test the strength of the colonies against Great Britain. Others might hesitate, he said, but he would have "liberty or death." The "radicals" who supported Henry's resolution included many aristocratic landowners, two of whom, George Washington and Thomas Jefferson, became the first and third occupants of the highest political office in what became the United States of America.[13]

Not all peoples who are suppressed, conquered, or colonialized eventually rebel against established authority. Why this is so, and why rebellions and revolts are not always successful in bringing about culture change, are still open questions. The classic revolutions of the past occurred in countries that were industrialized only incipiently at best. For the most part, the same is true of the rebellions and revolutions in recent years; they have occurred mostly in countries we call "developing." The evidence from a worldwide survey of developing countries suggests that rebellions have tended to occur where the ruling classes depended mostly on the produce or income from land, and therefore were resistant to demands for reform from the rural classes that worked the land. In such agricultural economies, the rulers are not likely to yield political power or give greater economic returns to the workers, because to do so would eliminate the basis (landownership) of the rulers' wealth and power.[14]

The idea of revolution has been one of the central myths and inspirations of many groups both in the past and in the present. The colonial empire building of countries such as England and France created a worldwide situation in which rebellion became nearly inevitable. In numerous technologically underdeveloped lands, which have been exploited by more powerful countries for their natural resources and cheap labor, a deep resentment has often developed against the foreign ruling classes or their local clients. Where the ruling classes, native or foreign, refuse to be responsive to those feelings, rebellion becomes the only alternative. In many areas, it has become a way of life.

Culture Change and Adaptation

The chapter on the study of culture discussed the general assumption that most of the customary behaviors of a culture are probably adaptive, or at least not maladaptive, in that environment. A custom is adaptive if it increases the likelihood that the people practicing it will survive and reproduce. Even though customs are learned and not genetically inherited, cultural adaptation may be like biological adaptation or evolution in another respect. The frequency of certain genetic alternatives is likely to increase over time if those genetic traits increase their carriers' chances of survival and reproduction. Similarly, the frequency of a new learned behavior will increase over time and become customary in a population if the people with that behavior are most likely to survive and reproduce. Thus, if a culture is adapted to its environment, culture change should also be adaptive—not always, to be sure, but commonly.

One of the most important differences between cultural evolution and genetic evolution is that individuals can often decide whether or not to accept and follow the way their parents behave or think, whereas they cannot decide whether or not to inherit certain genes. When enough individuals change their behavior and beliefs, we say that the culture has changed. Therefore, it is possible for culture change to occur much more rapidly than genetic change.

Robert Boyd and Peter Richerson have shown mathematically that when the environment is relatively stable and individual mistakes are costly, staying with customary modes of behavior (usually transmitted by parents) is probably more adaptive than changing.[15] But what happens when the environment, particularly the social environment, is changing? There are plenty of examples in the modern world: People have to migrate to new places for work; medical care leads to increased population so that land is scarcer; people have had land taken away from them and are forced to make do with less land; and so on.

It is particularly when circumstances change that individuals are likely to try ideas or behaviors that are different from those of their parents. Most people would want to adopt behaviors that are more suited to their present circumstances, but how do they know which behaviors are better? There are various ways to find out. One way is by experimenting, trying out various new behaviors. Another way is to evaluate the experiments of others. If a person who tries a new technique seems successful, we would expect that person to be imitated, just as we would expect people to stick with new behaviors they have personally tried and found successful. Finally, one might choose to do what most people in the new situation decide to do.[16]

We can expect, then, that the choices individuals make may often be adaptive ones. But it is important to note that adopting an innovation from someone in one's own society or borrowing an innovation from another society is not always or necessarily beneficial, either in the short or the long run. First, people may make mistakes in judgment, especially when some new behavior seems to satisfy a physical need. Why, for example, have smoking and drug use diffused so widely even though they are likely to reduce a person's chances of survival? Second, even if people are correct in their short-term judgment of benefit, they may be wrong in their judgment about long-run benefit. A new crop may yield more than the old crop for five consecutive years, but the new crop may fail miserably in the sixth year because of lower than normal rainfall or because the new crop depleted soil nutrients. Third, people may be forced by the more powerful to change, with few if any benefits for themselves.

Whatever the motives for humans to change their behavior, the theory of natural selection suggests that new behavior is not likely to become cultural or remain cultural over generations if it has harmful reproductive consequences, just as a genetic mutation with harmful consequences is not likely to become frequent in a population.[17] Still, we know of many examples of culture change that seem maladaptive—the switch to bottle-feeding rather than nursing infants, which may spread infection because contaminated water is used, or the adoption of alcoholic beverages, which may lead to alcoholism and early death. In the last few hundred years, the major stimulus to culture change, adaptive and maladaptive, has been the new social environment produced by the arrival of people from Western societies and the growth of a global economy.

Types of Culture Change in the Modern World

Many of the cultural changes in the world from A.D. 1500 to the present have been caused, directly or indirectly, by the dominance and expansion of Western societies.[18] Thus, much of the culture change in the modern world has been externally induced, if not forced. This is not to say that cultures are changing now only because of external pressures; but externally induced changes have been the changes most frequently studied by anthropologists and other social scientists. Most of the external pressures have come from Western societies, but not all. Far Eastern societies, such as Japan and China, have also stimulated culture change. And the expansion of Islamic societies after the eighth century A.D. made for an enormous amount of culture change in the Near East, Africa, Europe, and Asia.

Commercialization

One of the most important changes resulting from the expansion of Western societies is the increasingly worldwide dependence on commercial exchange. The borrowed customs of buying and selling may at first be supplementary to traditional means of distributing goods in a society. But as the new commercial customs take hold, the economic base of the receiving society alters. Inevitably, this alteration is accompanied by other changes, which have broad social, political, and even biological and psychological ramifications.

In examining contemporary patterns of change, however, we should bear in mind that commercialization has occurred in many parts of the world in the ancient past. The Chinese, Persians, Greeks, Romans, Arabs, Phoenicians, and Hindus were some of the early state societies that pushed commercial enterprises in other areas. We may cast some light on how and why some earlier cultures changed when we consider several questions: How, and why, does a contemporary society change from a subsistence to a commercial economic base? What are the resultant cultural changes? Why do they occur?

In general, the evidence available suggests that a previously noncommercial people may begin to sell and buy things simply in order to live, not just because they may be attracted by goods they can obtain only by commercial exchange. If the resources available to a group have been significantly reduced per person—because the group has been forced to resettle on a small "reservation" or because population has increased—the group may be likely to take advantage of any commercial opportunities that become available, even if such opportunities require considerably more work, time, and effort.[19]

Migratory Labor   One way commercialization can occur is for some members of a community to move to a place that offers the possibility of working for wages. This happened in Tikopia, an island near the Solomon Islands in the South Pacific. In 1929, when Raymond Firth first studied the island, its economy was still essentially noncommercial—simple, self-sufficient, and largely self-contained.[20] Some Western goods were available but, with the exception of iron and steel in limited quantities, not sought after. Their possession and use were associated solely with Europeans. This situation changed dramatically with World War II. During the war, military forces occupied neighboring islands, and people from Tikopia migrated to those islands to find employment. In the period following the war, several large commercial interests extended their activities in the Solomons, thus creating a continued demand for labor. As a result, when Firth revisited Tikopia in 1952, he found the economic situation significantly altered.

Here we see girls plucking tea leaves in Sabah, Borneo, Malaysia.

More than 100 Tikopians had left the island to work for varying periods. The migrants wanted to earn money because they aspired to standards of living previously regarded as appropriate only to Europeans. Already, living conditions on Tikopia were changing. Western cooking and water-carrying utensils, mosquito nets, kerosene storm lamps, and so forth had come to be regarded as normal items in a Tikopia household.

The introduction of money into the economy of Tikopia not only altered the economic system but also affected other areas of life. Compared with the situation in 1929, land was under more intensive cultivation in 1952, with introduced manioc and sweet potatoes supplementing the old principal crop, taro. Pressures on the food supply resulting from improved living standards and an increased population seem to have weakened the ties of extended kinship. For example, the nuclear families constituting the extended family (the landholding and land-using unit in 1929) were not cooperating as much in 1952. In many cases, in fact, the land had actually been split up among the constituent nuclear families; land rights had become more individualized. People were no longer as willing to share with members of their extended family, particularly with respect to the money and goods acquired by working in the Solomons.

Nonagricultural Commercial Production   Commercialization can also occur when a self-sufficient hunting or agricultural society comes to depend more and more on trading for its livelihood. Such a change is exemplified by the Mundurucú of the Amazon Basin, who largely abandoned general horticulture for commercial rubber production. A similar change may also be seen in the Montagnais of northeastern Canada, who came to depend increasingly on commercial fur trapping, rather than hunting, for subsistence. Robert Murphy and Julian Steward found that when modern goods from industrialized areas became available through trade, both the Mundurucú and the Montagnais devoted their energies to producing specialized cash crops or other trade items. They did this to obtain other industrially made objects.[21] The primary socioeconomic change that occurred among the Mundurucú and the Montagnais was a shift from cooperative labor and community autonomy to individualized economic activity and a dependence on an external market.

Among the Mundurucú, for example, before close trading links were established, the native population and the Europeans had been in contact for some 80 years without the Mundurucú way of life being noticeably altered. The men did give up their independent military activities in order to perform as mercenaries for the Brazilians, but they continued to maintain their horticultural economy. Some trading took place with Brazilians, with the chief acting as agent for the village. Barter was the method of exchange. Traders first distributed their wares, ranging from cheap cottons to iron hatchets, trinkets, and so on; they returned about three months later to collect manioc, India rubber, and beans from the Mundurucú. At this time (1860), however, rubber was only a secondary item of commerce.

The rapidly growing demand for rubber from the 1860s onward increased the importance of Mundurucú-trader relationships. Traders now openly began to appoint agents, called *capitoes,* whose job it was to encourage greater rubber production. *Capitoes* were given economic privileges and hence power, both of which began to undercut the position of the traditional chief. In addition, the process of rubber collection itself began to alter Mundurucú social patterns by moving people away from their jungle-based communities.

Wild rubber trees are found only along rivers, which are often a considerable distance from the jungle habitat of the Mundurucú and can be exploited only during the dry season (late May to December). So the Mundurucú man who elected to gather rubber had to separate himself from his family for about half the year. Furthermore, rubber collecting is a solitary activity. Each tapper must work his territory, consisting of about 150 trees, daily, and he must live close to his trees because the work lasts all day. Therefore, the tapper usually lives alone or in a small group except during the rainy season, when he returns to his village.

At this stage in the commercialization process, the Mundurucú became increasingly dependent on goods supplied by the trader. Firearms were useless without regular quantities of gun powder and lead or shot; clothing required needles and thread for repairs. But these items could be earned only through increased rubber production, which in turn led to greater dependency on the outside world. Inevitably, the ability to work with traditional materials and the desire to maintain traditional crafts disappeared. Metal pots took the place of clay ones, and manufactured hammocks replaced homemade ones. Gradually the village agricultural cycle ceased to be followed by all in the community so that rubber production would not suffer. The authority of the traditional chiefs was weakened as that of the *capitoes* was enhanced.

The point of no return was reached when significant numbers of Mundurucú abandoned the villages for permanent settlements near their individual territories of trees. These new settlements lacked the unity, the sense of community, of former village life. Property was held by nuclear families and carefully maintained in the interest of productivity.

With the discovery of gold, many Mundurucú young men have turned to panning for gold in rivers. The required equipment is simple, and gold is easier to transport and trade than rubber. Because gold can be sold for cash, which is then used for purchases, trading relationships are no longer so important. Cash is now used to buy transistor radios, tape recorders, watches, bicycles, and new kinds of clothing, in addition to firearms, metal pots, and tools. With money as a medium of exchange, the traditional emphasis on reciprocity has declined. Even food may now be sold to fellow Mundurucú, a practice that would have been unthinkable in the 1950s.[22]

Supplementary Cash Crops   A third way commercialization occurs is when people cultivating the soil produce a surplus above their subsistence requirements, which is then sold for cash. In many cases, this cash income must be used to pay rent or taxes. Under these circumstances, commercialization may be said to be associated with the formation of a peasantry. Peasants are rural people who produce food for their own subsistence, but they must also contribute or sell their surpluses to others, in towns and cities, who do not produce their own food.

Peasants first appeared with the emergence of state and urban civilizations about 5,000 to 6,000 years ago, and they have been associated with civilization ever since.[23] To say that peasants are associated with urban societies perhaps needs some qualification. The contemporary, highly industrialized urban socie-ty has little need of peasants. Their scale of production is small and their use of land "uneconomic." A highly industrialized society with a large population of nonfood producers requires mechanized agricul-ture. As a result, the peasant has passed, or is passing, out of all but the most peripheral existence in in-dustrial countries. It is the preindustrial city, and the social organization it represents, that generates and maintains peasants. They cultivate land; they furnish the required quantity of food, rent, and profit on which the remainder of society, particularly the people in the cities, depends.

What changes does the development of a peasantry entail? In some respects there is little disturbance of the cultivator's (now peasant's) former way of life. The peasant still has to produce enough food to meet family needs, to replace what has been consumed, to cover a few ceremonial obligations (e.g., the marriage of a child, village festivals, and funerals). But in other respects the peasant's situation is rad-ically altered. For in addition to the traditional obligations—indeed, often in conflict with them—the peasant now has to produce extra crops to meet the requirements of a group of outsiders—landlords or officials of the state. These outsiders expect to be paid rent or taxes in produce or currency, and they are able to enforce their expectations because they control the military and the police.

Introduction of Commercial and Industrial Agriculture   Commercialization can come about through the introduction of commercial agriculture, cultivation for sale rather than personal consumption. The system of agriculture may come to be industrialized. In other words, some of the production processes, such as plowing, weeding, irrigation, and harvesting, can be done by machine. Commercial agriculture is, in fact, often as mechanized as any manufacturing industry. Land is worked for the maximum return it will yield, and labor is hired and fired just as impersonally as in other industries.

The introduction of commercial agriculture brings several important social consequences. Gradu-ally, a class polarization develops. Farmers and landlords become increasingly separated from laborers and tenants, just as in the town the employer becomes socially separated from the employees. Gradu-ally, too, manufactured items of all sorts are introduced into rural areas. Laborers migrate to urban cen-ters in search of employment, often meeting even less sympathetic conditions there than exist in the country.

The changeover to commercial agriculture may result in an improved standard of living in the short and long run. But sometimes the switch is followed by a decline in the standard of living if the market price for the commercial crop declines. For example, the changeover of the farmer-herders of the arid *sertão* region of northeastern Brazil after 1940 to the production of sisal (a plant whose fibers can be made into twine and rope) seemed to be a move that could provide a more secure living in their arid environment. But when the world price for sisal dropped (because of the availability of nylon and Dacron rope) and the wages of sisal workers declined, many workers were forced to curtail the caloric intake of their chil-dren. The poorer people were obliged to save their now more limited food supplies for the money earn-ers, at the expense of the children.[24]

Commercialization can start in various ways: People can begin to sell and buy because they begin to work near home or away for wages, or because they begin to sell nonagricultural products, surplus food, or cash crops (crops grown deliberately for sale). One type of commercialization does not exclude anoth-er; all types can occur in any society. However commercialization begins, it seems to have predictable ef-fects on traditional economics. The ethic of generalized reciprocity declines, particularly with respect to giving money away. (Perhaps because it is nonperishable and hideable, money seems more likely than other goods to be kept for one's immediate family rather than shared with others.) Property rights become in-dividualized rather than collective when people begin to buy and sell. And even in societies that were pre-viously egalitarian, commercialization usually results in more unequal access to resources and hence a greater degree of social stratification.

Contact with the West first brought medical devastation to many populations previously unexposed to European illnesses. However, with the acceptance of modern medical care throughout much of the developing world, infant mortality has declined and life expectancies have gone up. These achievements have largely come about because of the control of major epidemic diseases, such as smallpox (now eradicated), cholera, yellow fever, syphilis, and tuberculosis, as well as the inoculation of children against childhood diseases. Improvements in medical health are by no means uniform. The AIDS epidemic, which we discuss in the chapter on applied and practicing anthropology, is spreading throughout much of the world. Overall deaths from infectious diseases may have declined, but other health problems have increased. As more people survive into older ages, problems of hypertension, heart disease, cancer, and diabetes increase. Some of the increase in these chronic diseases is due to the aging of populations, but much of it appears to be due to changes in lifestyle that accompany modernization.

A lot of research has focused on the Samoans of the South Pacific. The Samoans traditionally depended on root and tree crop horticulture. As did many other people in the modern world, Samoans increasingly moved to urban areas, worked for wages, and started buying most of their food. Researchers reported substantial increases, within a relatively short time, in rates of hypertension, diabetes, and obesity across a wide range of age groups. For example, in 1990 about two-thirds of American Samoans were severely overweight, up substantially from the situation in the 1970s. And Samoans from more rural areas show less hypertension and physiological signs of stress. Among the lifestyle changes thought to be responsible are less physical activity and changes in diet to low-fiber, high-calorie foods. Stress may also increase as more individuals buy material things and status goods without having the economic resources to support them.

When food is not plentiful, the "thrifty gene" helps people survive on less. But when the food supply becomes plentiful and reliable, people may become overweight, as in the Marquesas.

What about genetic factors? Could some genetic predisposition be interacting with modernization to create obesity in the Samoan population? One possibility is referred to as the "thrifty" gene. The geneticist James Neel suggested that individuals who have very efficient metabolisms and can store calories in fatty tissue are most apt to survive and reproduce in environments with frequent famines or chronic food shortages. In time, populations in such environments would have a high prevalence of individuals with "thrifty" genes. What happens, though, when such individuals no longer need to exercise much, or have access to high-calorie foods? Neel suggested that adult-onset diabetes might result, a scenario that is consistent with the increase in diabetes in Samoa and other parts of Polynesia. It is also consistent with the increase in obesity and hypertension.

The "thrifty" gene theory does not just pertain to Samoans and other Polynesian populations. Probably most human populations have had to cope with food uncertainty. If the food supply increases with modernization, accompanied by a reduction in physical activity and a switch to high-calorie diets, then increases in obesity, diabetes, and hypertension may often accompany modernization. Understanding both biological and cultural factors is essential in helping populations adapt to conditions of urban life.

Sources: John S. Allen and Susan M. Cheer, "The Non-Thrifty Genotype," *Current Anthropology*, 37 (1996): 831–42; James R. Bindon and Douglas E. Crews, "Changes in Some Health Status Characteristics of American Samoan Men," *American Journal of Human Biology*, 5 (1993): 31–37; James R. Bindon, Amy Knight, William W. Dressler, and Douglas E. Crews, "Social Context and Psychosocial Influences on Blood Pressure among American Samoans," *American Journal of Physical Anthropology*, 103 (1997): 7–18; Stephen T. McGarvey, "The Thrifty Gene Concept and Adiposity Studies in Biological Anthropology," *Journal of the Polynesian Society*, 103 (1994): 29–42; J. D. Pearson, Gary D. James, and Daniel E. Brown, "Stress and Changing Lifestyles in the Pacific," *American Journal of Human Biology*, 5 (1993): 49–60; World Bank, *World Development Report 1995: Workers in an Integrating World* (Oxford: Oxford University Press, 1995).

Political and Social Change

In addition to commercialization and religious change brought about by the expansion of Western and other countries, political changes have often occurred when a foreign system of government has been imposed. But, as recent events in the former Soviet Union and South Africa indicate, dramatic changes in a political system can also occur more or less voluntarily. Perhaps the most striking type of political change in recent years is the spread of participatory forms of government—"democracy."

To political scientists, democracy is usually defined in terms of voting by a substantial proportion of the citizenry, governments brought to power by periodic contested elections, a chief executive either popularly elected or responsible to an elected legislature, and often also civil liberties such as free speech. Depending on which criteria are used, only 12 to 15 countries qualified as democracies as of the beginning of the twentieth century. The number decreased after World War I, as emerging democratic institutions were replaced by dictatorships in Russia, Italy, Germany, central Europe, Japan, and elsewhere. After World War II, despite all the rhetoric associated with the founding of the United Nations, the picture was not much different. Some members of the new North Atlantic Treaty Organization (NATO) were not democracies, and neither were many members of the wider Western alliance system, in Latin America, the Middle East, and Asia.

It was not until the 1970s and 1980s that people, not just political scientists, started noticing that democracy was becoming more common in the world. By the early 1990s, President George H. W. Bush and then-candidate Bill Clinton were talking about the spread of the "democratic peace." As of 1992, about half of the countries in the world had more or less democratic governments, and others were in transition to democracy.[25] Social scientists do not yet understand why this change is happening. But it is possible that the global communication of ideas has a lot to do with it. Authoritarian governments can censor their own newspapers and prevent group meetings, but they really cannot stop the movement of ideas via telephone lines and the Internet. The movement of ideas, of course, does not explain the acceptance of those ideas. Why democracy has recently diffused to more countries than ever before still requires explanation.

Another frequent type of culture change in the modern world is increasing social stratification. Because of economic change, some groups become more privileged and powerful than others. For example, it has been suggested that the introduction of new technology may generally make for an increase in degree of social stratification.[26] When the snowmobile began to be used for herding by the Lapps or Saami, those who for various reasons could participate in the "snowmobile revolution" gained economic, social, and political advantages. But those who could not acquire the new machines tended to become an economically and generally deprived class—without machines *or* reindeer.[27]

Ethnogenesis: The Emergence of New Cultures

Many of the processes that we have discussed—the expansion and domination by the West and other powerful nations, the deprivation of the ability of peoples to earn their livelihoods by traditional means, the imposition of schools or other methods to force acculturation, the attempts to convert people to other religions, and globalization—have led to profound changes in culture. But if culture change in the modern world has made cultures more alike in some ways, it has not eliminated cultural differences. Indeed, people are still quite variable culturally from one place to the next. New differences have also emerged. Often, in the aftermath of violent events such as depopulation, relocation, enslavement, and genocide by dominant powers, deprived peoples have created new cultures in a process called **ethnogenesis**.[28]

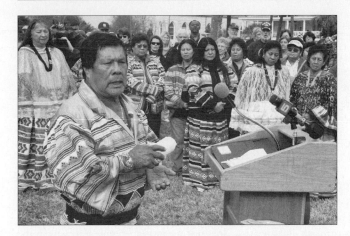

Bobby Henry, a Seminole medicine man, sings a song in 2003 during ceremonies honoring a Seminole chief who died 165 years before.

The emergence of the Seminole in Florida is an example of ethnogenesis. The early settlers who moved to what is now Florida and later became known as Seminole largely derived from the Lower Creek Kawita chiefdom. The Kawita chiefdom, like other southeastern Muskogean chiefdoms, was a large, complex, multiethnic paramount chiefdom. Its ruler, Kawita, relied on allegiance and tribute from outlying districts; ritual and linguistic hegemony was imposed by the ruler.[29]

A combination of internal divisions among the Lower Creek, vacant land in northern Florida, and weak Spanish control over northern Florida apparently prompted dissidents to move away and settle in three different areas in Florida. Three new chiefdoms were established, essentially similar to those the settlers left and still under the supposed control of Kawita.[30] But the three chiefdoms began to act together under the leadership of Tonapi, the Talahassi chief. After 1780, over a period of 40 or so years, the three Seminole chiefdoms formally broke with Kawita. Not only was geographic separation a factor, but the political and economic interests of the Creek Confederacy and of the Seminole had diverged. For example, the Creek supported neutrality in the American Revolution, but the Seminole took the side of the British. It was during this time that the British encouraged slaves to escape by promising freedom in Florida. These Maroon communities allied themselves with the emerging Seminole. The composition of the Seminole population again changed dramatically after the War of 1812 and the Creek War of 1814.[31] First, a large number of Creek refugees, mostly Upper Creek Talapusa (who spoke a different Muskogean language), became Seminole. Second, the Seminole ranks were also expanded by a large number of escaped slaves and Maroons who fled when the Americans destroyed a British fort in 1816. Larger-scale political events continued to influence Seminole history. When the Americans conquered Florida, they insisted on dealing with one unified Seminole council, they removed the Seminole to a reserve in Florida, and later, after the second Seminole war, removed most of them to Oklahoma.[32]

Globalization: Problems and Opportunities

Investment capital, people, and ideas are moving around the world at an ever faster rate.[33] Transportation now allows people and goods to circle the globe in days; telecommunications and the Internet make it possible to send a message around the world in seconds and minutes. Economic exchange is enormously more global and transnational. The word **globalization** is often used nowadays to refer to "the massive flow of goods, people, information, and capital across huge areas of the earth's surface."[34] The process of globalization has resulted in the worldwide spread of cultural features, particularly in the domain of economics and international trade. We buy from the same companies (that have factories all over the world), we sell our products and services for prices that are set by world market forces. We can eat pizza, hamburgers, curry, or sushi in most urban centers. In some ways, cultures are changing in similar directions. They have become more commercial, more urban, and more international. The job has become more important, and kinship less important, as people travel to and work in other countries, and return only periodically to their original homes. Ideas about democracy, the rights of the individual, alternative medical practices and religions, have become more widespread; people in many countries of the world watch the same TV shows, wear similar fashions, listen to the same or similar music. In short, people are increasingly sharing behaviors and beliefs with people in other cultures, and the cultures of the world are less and less things "with edges," as Paul Durrenberger says.[35]

But diffusion of a culture trait does not mean that it is incorporated in exactly the same way, and the spread of certain products and activities through globalization does not mean that change happens in the same way everywhere. For example, the spread of multinational fast-food restaurants like McDonald's or Kentucky Fried Chicken has come to symbolize globalization. But the behavior of the Japanese in such restaurants is quite different from behavior in the United States. Perhaps the most surprising difference is that the Japanese in McDonald's actually have more familial intimacy and sharing than in more traditional restaurants. We imagine that establishments like McDonald's promote fast eating. But Japan has long had fast food—noodle shops at train stations, street vendors, and boxed lunches. Sushi, which is usually ordered in the United States at a sit-down restaurant, is usually served in Japan at a bar with a conveyor belt—individuals only need to pluck off the wanted dish as it goes by. Observations at McDonald's in Japan suggest that mothers typically order food for the family while the father spends time with the children at a table, a rare event since fathers often work long hours and cannot get home for dinner often. Food, such as French fries, is typically shared by the family. Even burgers and drinks are passed around with many people taking a bite or a sip. Such patterns typify long-standing family practices.

Democracy—contested elections with widespread voting—is spreading around the world. In this rural area of South Africa, people line up to vote.

Japan has historically borrowed food, such as the Chinese noodle soup, now called ramen. Indeed, in a survey, ramen was listed as the most representative Japanese food. The burger was the second most-often listed. McDonald's has become Japanese—the younger generation does not even know that McDonald's is a foreign company—they think it is Japanese.[36]

Globalization is not new. The world has been global and interdependent since the sixteenth century.[37] What we currently call "globalization" is a more widespread version of what we used to call by various other names—diffusion, acculturation, colonialism, imperialism, or commercialization. But globalization is now on a much grander scale; enormous amounts of international investment fuel world trade. Shifts in the world marketplace may drastically affect a country's well-being more than ever before. For example, 60 percent of Pakistan's industrial employment is in textile and apparel manufacturing, but serious unemployment resulted when that manufacturing was crippled by restrictive American import policies and fears about war between India and Afghanistan.[38]

As we have seen in this chapter, there are many negative effects of colonialism, imperialism, and globalization. Many native peoples in many places lost their land and have been forced to work for inadequate wages in mines and plantations and factories that are owned by foreign capitalists. Frequently, there is undernutrition if not starvation. But are there any positive consequences? As we discussed in the social stratification chapter, the "human development indicators" collected by the United Nations suggest an improvement in many respects, including increases in most countries in life expectancy and literacy. Much of the improvement in life expectancy is undoubtedly due to the spread of medicines developed in the advanced economies of the West. There is generally less warfare as colonial powers enforced pacification within the colonies that later became independent states. Most important, perhaps, has been the growth of middle classes all over the world, whose livelihoods depend on globalizing commerce. The middle classes in many countries have become strong and numerous enough to pressure governments for democratic reforms and the reduction of injustice.

World trade is the primary engine of economic development. Per capita income is increasing. Forty years ago, the countries of Asia were among the poorest countries in the world in terms of per capita income. Since then, because of their involvement in world trade, their incomes have risen enormously. In 1960, South Korea was as poor as India. Now its per capita income is 20 times higher than India's. Singapore is an even more dramatic example. In the late 1960s, its economy was a disaster. Today its per capita income is higher than Britain's.[39] Mexico used to be a place where North Americans built factories to produce garments for the North American market. Now its labor is no longer so cheap. But because it has easy access to the North American market and because its plentiful labor is acquiring the necessary skills, Mexico is now seeing the development of high-tech manufacturing with decent salaries.[40]

There is world trade also in people. Many countries of the world now export people to other countries. Mexico has done so for a long time. Virtually every family in a Bangladesh village depends on someone who works overseas and sends money home. Without those remittances, many would face starvation. The government encourages people to go abroad to work. Millions of people from Bangladesh are now overseas on government-sponsored work contracts.[41]

But does a higher per capita income mean that life has improved generally in a country? Not necessarily. As we saw in the chapter on social stratification, inequality within countries can increase with technological improvements because the rich often benefit the most. In addition, economic wealth is increasingly concentrated in a relatively small number of countries. Obviously, then, not everyone is better off even if on average most countries are doing better. Poverty has become more common as countries have become more unequal.

While many of the changes associated with globalization seem to be driven by the economic and political power of the richer countries, the movement of ideas, art, music, and food is more of a two-way process. A large part of that process involves the migration of people who bring their culture with them. As we have seen in the boxes on migrants and immigrants in previous chapters, movements of people have played a large role in the entry of food such as tortilla chips and salsa, sushi, and curries into the United States, music like reggae and many types of dance music from Latin America, and African carvings and jewelry such as beaded necklaces. Recently there has even been increased interest in acquiring indigenous knowledge of plants, the knowledge of indigenous healers, and learning about shamanistic trances. As indigenous knowledge comes to be viewed as potentially valuable, shamans have been able to speak out on national and international issues. In Brazil, shamans have organized to speak out against "biopiracy"— what is perceived as the unethical appropriation of biological knowledge for commercial purposes. In a more globalized world, shamans and other indigenous activists can be heard by more people than ever before. Despite the fact that indigenous people constitute less than one percent of the Brazilian population, some activist groups have been able to keep in touch with international environmentalists, using tape recorders and video cameras to convey information about their local situation.[42]

It is probably not possible to go back to a time when societies were not so dependent on each other, not so interconnected through world trade, not so dependent on commercial exchange. Even those who are most upset with globalization find it difficult to imagine that it is possible to return to a less connected world. For better or worse, the world is interconnected and will remain so. The question now is whether the average economic improvements in countries will eventually translate into economic improvements for most individuals.

Cultural Diversity in the Future

Measured in terms of travel time, the world today is much smaller than it has ever been. It is possible now to fly halfway around the globe in the time it took people less than a century ago to travel to the next state. In the realm of communication, the world is even smaller. We can talk to someone on the other side of the globe in a matter of minutes, we can send that person a message (by fax or Internet) in seconds, and through television we can see live coverage of events in that person's country. More and more people are drawn into the world market economy, buying and selling similar things and, as a consequence, altering the patterns of their lives in sometimes similar ways. Still, although modern transportation and communication facilitate the rapid spread of some cultural characteristics to all parts of the globe, it is highly unlikely that all parts of the world will end up the same culturally. Cultures are bound to retain some of their original characteristics or develop distinctive new adaptations. Even though television has diffused around the world, local people continue to prefer local programs when they are available. And even when people all over the world watch the same program, they may interpret it in very different ways. People are not just absorbing the messages they get; they often resist or revise them.[43]

Until recently, researchers studying culture change generally assumed that the differences between people of different cultures would become minimal. But in the last 30 years or so, it has become increasingly apparent that, although many differences disappear, many people are affirming ethnic identities in a process that often involves deliberately introducing cultural difference.[44] Eugeen Roosens describes the situation of the Huron of Quebec, who in the late 1960s seemed to have disappeared as a distinct culture. The Huron language had disappeared and the lives of the Huron were not obviously distinguishable from those of the French Canadians around them. The Huron then developed a new identity as they actively worked to promote the rights of indigenous peoples like themselves. That their new defining cultural symbols bore no resemblance to the past Huron culture is beside the point.

One fascinating possibility is that ethnic diversity and ethnogenesis may be a result of broader processes. Elizabeth Cashdan found that ethnic diversity appears to be related to environmental unpredictability, which is associated with greater distance from the equator.[45] There appear to be many more cultural groups nearer to the equator than in very northern and southern latitudes. Perhaps, Cashdan suggests, environmental unpredictability in the north and south necessitates wider ties between social groups to allow cooperation in case local resources fail. This may minimize the likelihood of cultural divergence, that is, ethnogenesis. Hence there will be fewer cultures farther from the equator.

Future research on culture change should increase our understanding of how and why various types of change are occurring. If we can increase our understanding of culture change in the present, we should be better able to understand similar processes in the past. We may be guided in our efforts to understand culture change by the large number of cross-cultural correlations that have been discovered between a particular cultural variation and its presumed causes.[46] All cultures have changed over time; variation is the product of differential change. Thus, the variations we see are the products of change processes, and the discovered predictors of those variations may suggest how and why the changes occurred.

Summary

1. Culture is always changing. Because culture consists of learned patterns of behavior and belief, cultural traits can be unlearned and learned anew as human needs change.

2. Discoveries and inventions, though ultimately the sources of all culture change, do not necessarily lead to change. Only when society accepts an invention or discovery and uses it regularly can culture change be said to have occurred.

3. The process by which cultural elements are borrowed from another society and incorporated into the culture of the recipient group is called diffusion. Cultural traits do not necessarily diffuse; that is, diffusion is a selective, not automatic, process. A society accepting a foreign cultural trait is likely to adapt it in a way that effectively harmonizes it with the society's own traditions.

4. When a group or society is in contact with a more powerful society, the weaker group is often obliged to acquire cultural elements from the dominant group. This process of extensive borrowing in the context of superordinate-subordinate relations between societies is called acculturation. In contrast with diffusion, acculturation comes about as a result of some sort of external pressure.

5. Perhaps the most drastic and rapid way a culture can change is by revolution—a usually violent replacement of the society's rulers. Rebellions occur primarily in state societies, where there is a distinct ruling elite. However, not all peoples who are suppressed, conquered, or colonized eventually rebel or successfully revolt against established authority.

6. Even though customs are not genetically inherited, cultural adaptation may be somewhat similar to biological adaptation. Traits (cultural or genetic) that are more likely to be reproduced (learned or inherited) are likely to become more frequent in a population over time. And if culture is generally adapted to its environment, then culture change should also be generally adaptive.

7. Many of the cultural changes observed in the modern world have been generated, directly or indirectly, by the dominance and expansion of Western societies. One of the principal changes resulting from the expansion of Western culture is the increasing dependence of much of the world on commercial exchange. The borrowed custom of buying and selling may at first be supplementary to

traditional means of distributing goods, but as the new commercial customs take hold, the economic base of the receiving society alters.

8. One way commercialization can occur is for members of a community to become migratory workers, traveling to a place nearby that offers the possibility of working for wages. Commercialization can also occur when a simple, self-sufficient hunting or agricultural society comes to depend more and more on trading for its livelihood. A third way commercialization occurs is when those cultivating the soil produce more than they require for subsistence. The surplus is then sold for cash. In many instances, this cash income must be used to pay rent or taxes; under such circumstances, commercialization may be said to be associated with the formation of a peasantry. A fourth way in which commercialization can come about is through the introduction of commercial agriculture, in which all the cultivated commodities are produced for sale rather than for personal consumption. Along with this change, the system of agriculture may be industrialized, with some of the production processes being done by machine.

9. One of the most striking types of culture change in the modern world is the spread of democracies. Participatory political institutions are now found in a majority of the world's countries.

10. Ethnogenesis is the process by which new cultures are created.

11. Globalization—the spread of cultural features around the world—is minimizing cultural diversity, but it is not eliminating it.

Glossary Terms

acculturation (p. 400)
diffusion (p. 399)
ethnogenesis (p. 410)

globalization (p. 411)
revolution (p. 402)

Critical Questions

1. What kinds of cultural items might most easily be borrowed by another culture? Why do you think so?

2. The expansion of the West has had terrible consequences for many peoples. Have there been any beneficial consequences?

3. Why might an increasing understanding of cultural variation also provide an increasing understanding of culture change?

CHAPTER 18

GLOBAL ISSUES

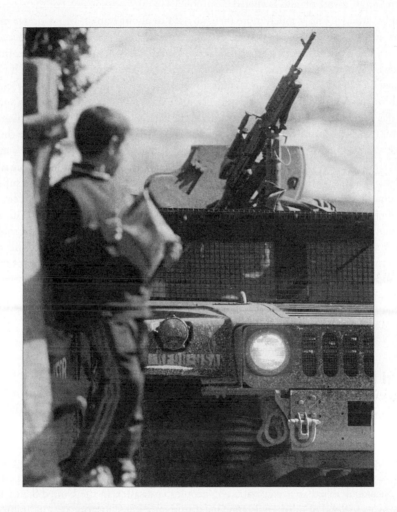

Chapter Outline

- Natural Disasters and Famine
- Inadequate Housing and Homelessness
- Family Violence and Abuse
- Crime
- War
- Terrorism
- Making the World Better

The news on television and in the newspapers makes us aware every day that terrible social problems threaten people around the world. War, crime, family violence, natural disasters, poverty, famine—all these and more are the lot of millions of people in many places. And now there is an increasing threat of terrorism. Can anthropological and other research help us solve these global social problems? Many anthropologists and other social scientists think so.

High-tech communications have increased our awareness of problems all over the world, and we seem to be increasingly aware of, and bothered by, problems in our own society. For these two reasons, and perhaps also because we know much more than we used to about human behavior, we may be more motivated now to try to solve those problems. We call them "social problems" not just because a lot of people worry about them but also because they have social causes and consequences, and treating or solving them requires changes in social behavior. Even AIDS, which we discuss in the next chapter, is partly a social problem. It may be caused by a virus, but it is mostly transmitted by social (sexual) contact with another person. And the main ways to avoid it—abstinence and "safe" sex—require changes in social behavior.

The idea that we can solve social problems, even the enormous ones such as war and family violence, is based on two assumptions. First, we have to assume that it is possible to discover the causes of a problem. And two, we have to assume that we may be able to do something about the causes, once they are discovered, and thereby eliminate or reduce the problem. Not everyone would agree with these assumptions. Some would say that our understanding of a social problem cannot ever be sufficient to suggest a solution guaranteed to work. To be sure, no understanding in science is perfect or certain; there is always some probability that even a well-supported explanation is wrong or incomplete. But the uncertainty of knowledge does not rule out the possibility of application. With regard to social problems, the possible payoff from even incomplete understanding could be a better and safer world. This possibility is what motivates many researchers who investigate social problems. After all, the history of the various sciences strongly supports the belief that scientific understanding can often allow humans to control nature, not just predict and explain it. Why should human behavior be any different?

So what do we know about some of the global social problems, and what policies or solutions are suggested by what we know?

Natural Disasters and Famine

Natural events such as floods, droughts, earthquakes, and insect infestations are usually but not always beyond human control, but their effects are not.[1] We call such events accidents or emergencies when only a few people are affected, but we call them disasters when large numbers of people or large areas are affected. The harm caused is not just a function of the magnitude of the natural event. Between 1960 and 1980, 43 natural disasters in Japan killed an average of 63 people per disaster. During the same period, 17 natural disasters in Nicaragua killed an average of 6,235 people per disaster. In the United States, between 1960 and 1976, the average flood or other environmental disturbance killed just one person, injured a dozen, and destroyed fewer than five buildings. These comparative figures demonstrate that climatic and other events in the physical environment become disasters because of events or conditions in the social environment.

If people live in houses that are designed to withstand earthquakes—if governing bodies require such construction and the economy is developed enough so that people can afford such construction—the effects of an earthquake will be minimized. If poor people are forced to live in deforested floodplains in order to be able to find land to farm (as in coastal Bangladesh), if the poor are forced to live in shanties built on precarious hillsides (like those of Rio de Janeiro), the floods and landslides that follow severe hurricanes and rainstorms can kill thousands and even hundreds of thousands.

Thus, natural disasters can have greater or lesser effects on human life, depending on social conditions. And therefore disasters are also social problems, problems that have social causes and possible social solutions. Legislating safe construction of a house is a social solution. The 1976 earthquake in Tangsham, China, killed 250,000 people, mostly because they lived in top-heavy adobe houses that could not withstand severe shaking, whereas the 1989 Loma Prieta earthquake in California, which was of comparable intensity, killed 65 people.

One might think that floods, of all disasters, are the least influenced by social factors. After all, without a huge runoff from heavy rains or snow melt, there cannot be a flood. But consider why so many people have died from Hwang River floods in China. (One such flood, in 1931, killed nearly 4 million people, making it the deadliest single disaster in history.) The floods in the Hwang River basin have occurred mostly because the clearing of nearby forests for fuel and farmland has allowed enormous quantities of silt to wash into the river, raising the riverbed and increasing the risk of floods that burst the dams that normally would contain them. The risk of disastrous flooding would be greatly reduced if different social conditions prevailed—if people were not so dependent on firewood for fuel, or if they did not have to farm close to the river, or if the dams were higher and more numerous.

Famines, episodes of severe starvation and death, often appear to be triggered by physical events such as a severe drought or a hurricane that kills or knocks down food trees and plants. But famines do not inevitably follow such an event. Social conditions can prevent a famine or increase the likelihood of one. Consider what is likely to happen in Samoa after a hurricane.[2] Whole villages that have lost their coconut and breadfruit trees, as well as their taro patches, pick up and move for a period of time to other villages where there are relatives and friends. The visitors stay and are fed until some of their cultivated trees and plants start to bear food again, at which point they return home. This kind of intervillage reciprocity probably could occur only in a society that has relatively little inequality in wealth. Nowadays, the central government or international agencies may also help out by providing food and other supplies.

The average flood in the United States does not kill that many people, but the storm surges from Hurricane Katrina and inadequate levees caused major flooding, massive homelessness, and hundreds of deaths in New Orleans (pictured here) and surrounding areas of the Gulf Coast in 2005.

Researchers point out that famine rarely results from just one bad food production season. During one bad season, people can usually cope by getting help from relatives, friends, and neighbors or by switching to less desirable foods. The famine in the African Sahel in 1974 occurred after eight years of bad weather; a combination of drought, floods, and a civil war in 1983 to 1984 contributed to the subsequent famine in the Sahel, Ethiopia, and Sudan.[3] Famine almost always has some social causes. Who has rights to the available food, and do those who have more food distribute it to those who have less? Cross-cultural research suggests that societies with individual property rights rather than shared rights are more likely to suffer famine.[4] Nonetheless, government assistance can lessen the risk of famine in societies with individual property.

Relief provided by government may not always get to those who need it the most. In India, for example, the central government provides help in time of drought to minimize the risk of famine. But the food and other supplies provided to a village may end up being unequally distributed, following the rules of social and gender stratification. Members of the local elite arrange to function as distributors and find ways to manipulate the relief efforts to their advantage. Lower-class and lower-caste families still suffer the most. Within the family, biases against females, particularly young girls and elderly women, translate into their getting less food. It is no wonder, then, that in times of food shortage and famine, the poor and other socially disadvantaged persons are especially likely to die.[5]

Thus, the people of a society may not all be equally at risk in case of disaster. In socially stratified societies, the poor particularly suffer. It is they who are likely to be forced to overcultivate, overgraze, and deforest their land, making it more susceptible to degradation. A society most helps those it values the most.

People in the past, and even recently in some places, viewed disasters as divine retribution for human immorality. For example, the great Flood described in the Old Testament was understood to be God's doing. But scientific research increasingly allows us to understand the natural causes of disasters, and particularly the social conditions that magnify or minimize their effects. To reduce the impact of disasters, then, we need to reduce the social conditions that magnify the effects of disasters. If humans are responsible for those social conditions, humans can change them. If earthquakes destroy houses that are too flimsy, we can build stronger houses. If floods caused by overcultivation and overgrazing kill people directly (or indirectly by stripping their soils), we can grow new forest cover and provide new job opportunities to floodplain farmers. If prolonged natural disasters or wars threaten famine, social distribution systems can lessen the risk. In short, we may not be able to do much about the weather or other physical causes of disasters, but we can do a lot—if we want to—about the social factors that make disasters disastrous.

Inadequate Housing and Homelessness

In most nations, the poor typically live in inadequate housing, in areas we call *slums*. In many of the developing nations, where cities are growing very rapidly, squatter settlements emerge as people build dwellings (often makeshift) that are typically declared illegal, either because the land is illegally occupied or because the dwellings violate building codes. Squatter settlements are often located in degraded environments that are subject to flooding and mudslides or have inadequate or polluted water. The magnitude of the problem is made clear in some statistics. As of the 1980s, 40 percent of the population in Nairobi, Kenya, lived in unauthorized housing, and 67 percent of the people in five of El Salvador's major cities lived in illegal dwellings.[6]

But contrary to what some people have assumed, not all dwellers in illegal settlements are poor; all but the upper-income elite may be found in such settlements.[7] Moreover, although squatter settlements have problems, they are not chaotic and unorganized places that are full of crime. Most of the dwellers

Shown here is a homeless boy in Calcutta, India with his belongings.

are employed, aspire to get ahead, live in intact nuclear families, and help each other.[8] People live in such settlements because they cannot find affordable housing and they house themselves as best they can. Many researchers think that such self-help tendencies should be assisted to improve housing, because governments in developing countries can seldom afford costly public housing projects. But they could invest somewhat in infrastructure—sewers, water supplies, roads—and provide construction materials to those who are willing to do the work required to improve their dwellings.[9]

Housing in slum areas or shantytowns does provide shelter, minimal though it may be. But many people in many areas of the world have no homes at all. Even in countries such as the United States, which are affluent by world standards, large numbers of people are homeless. They sleep in parks, over steam vents, in doorways, subways, and cardboard boxes. In 1987 it was estimated that there were more than 1 million homeless people in the United States.[10] Now there are about three quarters of a million homeless.[11]

Who are the homeless, and how did they get to be homeless? We have relatively little research on these questions, but what we do have suggests differences in the causes of homelessness in different parts of the world. In the United States, unemployment and the shortage of decent low-cost housing appear to be at least partly responsible for the large number of homeless persons.[12] But there is also another factor: the deliberate policy to reduce the number of people hospitalized for mental illness and other disabilities. For example, from the mid-1960s to the mid-1990s, New York State released thousands of patients from mental hospitals. Many of these ex-patients had to live in cheap hotels or poorly monitored facilities with virtually no support network. With very little income, they found it especially hard to cope with their circumstances. Ellen Baxter and Kim Hopper, who studied the homeless in New York City, suggest that one event is rarely sufficient to render a person homeless. Rather, poverty and disability (mental or physical) seem to lead to one calamity after another and, finally, homelessness.[13]

Many people cannot understand why homeless individuals do not want to go to municipal shelters. But observations and interviews with the homeless suggest that violence pervades the municipal shelters, particularly the men's shelters. Many feel safer on the streets. Some private charities provide safe shelters and a caring environment. These shelters are filled, but the number of homeless they can accommodate is small.[14] Even single-room-occupancy hotels are hardly better. Many of them are infested with vermin, the common bathrooms are filthy, and they, like the shelters, are often dangerous.[15]

Scientists are increasingly sure that the world is heating up. And they are worried about the consequences. The more the temperature rises, the more the Greenland and Arctic ice will melt. The resulting higher sea level will flood many low-lying coastal areas, including many world cities. The weather in many places will also probably change, and not always for the better. For example, areas that now get enough rainfall to grow crops may turn into deserts.

The world is warming probably for several reasons. One of them is our increasing use of fossil fuels, particularly oil. We burn those fuels to make electricity, to power our cars (with the gasoline made from oil), to heat our homes, and to cook food. The emissions from all that burning may contribute to a "greenhouse effect": The atmosphere reflects the warmth produced on earth, and temperatures rise. And the air gets dirtier, resulting in other harmful consequences such as a higher incidence of breathing disorders.

Can people do anything about global warming and air pollution? Surely the answer is yes. If at least some of the problem is of human making, we could change our behavior and at least partly solve the problem. One way would be to reduce our use of oil as fuel. But how could we do that?

In the year 2000 the first hybrid cars were sold in the United States. These cars are powered by an electric motor and a small gasoline engine. The combination reduces the amount of fuel needed, because the electric motor moves the car much of the time. The battery that powers the electric motor is recharged by braking and by the gasoline engine when it is on, which is not much of the time. (For example, at a stop light, the gasoline engine turns off.) So a hybrid car allows a gallon of gasoline to go a lot farther. If most cars were hybrid cars, we would need much less oil to make the gasoline needed.

It is estimated that hybrid cars could cut greenhouse emissions by up to half, which would help alleviate or even reverse global warming and air pollution. So, given this rosy scenario, what is discouraging the world from switching to hybrid cars?

The answer is probably economics and politics. There is money to be made from the dependence on oil, particularly when supplies are short. The shorter the supplies, the more the oil producers abroad and the refiners at home can charge their customers. And the more the oil comes from abroad, the more the United States and other governments may feel that they have to keep the foreign producers happy. But this obligation runs counter to a foreign policy that would encourage democracy in the world; many of the countries that produce our oil are dictatorships. So the oil companies are dependent on those regimes to keep their refineries going, and they lobby governments (ours included) to maintain friendly relations with many of those regimes. Can we expect the oil companies to want to escape their dependence on foreign suppliers, if they are making a lot of money from that dependence? Hardly.

Our market economy does offer a way out of this dilemma. If hybrid cars and other ways to reduce the need for fossil fuels become more economical, the marketplace will turn the tide. Ironically, it will be the capitalist laws of supply and demand that may reduce the influence of oil companies on politics and help us solve the problems of global warming and air pollution. Even if the automobile manufacturers wanted to continue doing business as usual, they will not be able to resist making more fuel-efficient cars. Consumers will want to buy them to reduce their gasoline expenses. No car company will be able to ignore that kind of pressure from the marketplace. There seems to be more interest now in making and buying hybrid vehicles, and there is the possibility of transforming organic garbage into oil.

Sources: J. Oerlemans, "Extracting a Climate Signal from 169 Glacial Records," *Science* (April 28, 2005): 675–77; Matthew L. Wald, "Hybrid Cars Show Up in M.I.T.'s Crystal Ball," *The New York Times,* November 3, 2000, p. F1; and the special advertisement produced by energy companies, "Energy: Investing for a New Century," *The New York Times,* October 30, 2000, pp. EN1–8; Daniel Duane, "Turning Garbage into Oil," *New York Times Magazine,* December 14, 2003, p. 100.

Some poor individuals may be socially isolated, with few or no friends and relatives and little or no social contact. But a society with many such individuals does not necessarily have much homelessness. Socially isolated individuals, even mentally ill individuals, could still have housing, or so the experience of Melbourne, Australia, suggests. Universal health insurance there pays for health care as well as medical practitioners' visits to isolated and ill individuals, wherever they live. Disabled individuals receive a pension or sickness benefits sufficient to allow them to live in a room or apartment. And there is still a considerable supply of cheap housing in Melbourne. Research in Melbourne suggests that a severe mental disorder often precedes living in marginal accommodations—city shelters, commercial shelters, and cheap single rooms. About 50 percent of the people living in such places were diagnosed as previously having some form of mental illness; this percentage is similar to what seems to be the case for homeless people and people living in marginal accommodations in the United States.

The contrast between the United States and Australia makes it clear that homelessness is caused by social and political policies. Individuals with similar characteristics live in both Australia and the United States, but in the United States a larger percentage of them are homeless.[16]

Because homelessness cannot occur if everybody can afford housing, some people would say that homelessness can happen only in a society with great extremes in income. Statistics on income distribution in the United States clearly show that since the 1970s the rich have gotten much richer and the poor have gotten much poorer. The United States now has more income inequality than most other industrialized countries, such as Japan and Italy. In fact, the profile of inequality in the United States more closely resembles that of developing countries, such as China.[17]

In the United States, and many other countries, most homeless persons are adults. Whereas adults are "allowed" to be homeless, public sensibilities in the United States appear to be outraged by the sight of children living in the streets; when authorities discover homeless children, they try to find shelters or foster homes for them. But many countries have "street children." It has been estimated that 80 million of the world's children live in the streets. Forty million of them live in Latin America, 20 million in Asia, 10 million in Africa and the Middle East, and 10 million elsewhere.[18]

Lewis Aptekar, who studied street children in Cali, Colombia, reported some surprises.[19] Whereas many of the homeless in the United States and Australia are mentally disabled, the street children in Cali, ranging in age from 7 to 16, are mostly free of mental problems; by and large they also test normally on intelligence tests. In addition, even though many street children come from abusive homes or never had homes, they usually seem happy and enjoy the support and friendship of other street children. They cleverly and creatively look for ways to get money, frequently through entertaining passersby.

Although the observer might think that the street children must have been abandoned by their families, in actuality most of them have at least one parent they keep in touch with. Street life begins slowly, not abruptly; children usually do not stay on the streets full time until they are about 13 years old. Though street children in Cali seem to be in better physical and mental shape than their siblings who stay at home, they often are viewed as a "plague." The street children come from poor families and cope with their lives as best they can, so why are they not viewed with pity and compassion? Aptekar suggests that well-off families see the street children as a threat because a life independent of family may appeal to children, even those from well-off families, who wish to be free of parental constraint and authority.

Whether people become homeless, whether there are shantytowns, seems to depend on a society's willingness to share wealth and help those in need. The street children of Cali may remind us that children as well as adults need companionship and care. Addressing physical needs without responding to emotional needs may get people off the streets, but it won't get them a "home."

Family Violence and Abuse

In U.S. society we hear regularly about the abuse of spouses and children, which makes us think that such abuse is increasing—but is it? This seems to be a simple question, but it is not so simple to answer. We have to decide what we mean by *abuse.*

Is physical punishment of a child who does something wrong child abuse? Not so long ago, teachers in public schools in the United States were allowed to discipline children by hitting them with rulers or paddles, and many parents used switches or belts. Many would consider these practices to be child abuse, but were they abusive when they were generally accepted? Some would argue that abuse is going beyond what a culture considers appropriate behavior. Others would disagree and would focus on the violence and severity of parents' or teachers' behavior, not the cultural judgment of appropriateness. And abuse need not involve physical violence. It could be argued that verbal aggression and neglect may be just as harmful as physical aggression. Neglect presents its own problems of definition. People from other cultures might argue that we act abusively when we put an infant or child alone in a room to sleep.[20] Few would disagree about severe injuries that kill a child or spouse or require medical treatment, but other disciplinary behaviors are more difficult to judge.

To avoid having to decide what is or is not abuse, many researchers focus their studies on variation in the frequencies of specific behaviors. For example, one can ask which societies have physical punishment of children without calling physical punishment abusive.

According to three national interview surveys of married or cohabiting couples in the United States conducted in 1975, 1985, and 1992, physical violence against children appears to have decreased in frequency over time, as did serious assaults by husbands against wives. But serious assaults by wives on husbands did not decrease.[21] The decreasing rates of abuse may be mostly due to reporting differences: Wife and child beating is less acceptable now. For example, men report dramatically fewer assaults on their wives, but wives report only slight declines.[22] However, the United States remains a society with a lot of physical violence in families. In 1992 alone, one out of ten couples had a violent assault episode and one out of ten children was severely assaulted by a parent.[23] A survey conducted in the mid-1990s found that about 75 percent of the violence against women comes from a male intimate partner, such as a husband. In contrast, most of the violence men experience comes from strangers and acquaintances. Just as women face more risk from those close to them, so do children. When a child is the target of violence, it usually comes from the birth mother.[24]

Cross-culturally, if one form of family violence occurs, others are also likely. So, for example, wife beating, husband beating, child punishment, and fighting among siblings are all significantly associated with each other. But the relationships between these types of family violence are not that strong, which means that they cannot be considered as different facets of the same phenomenon. Indeed, somewhat different factors seem to explain different forms of family violence.[25] We focus here on two forms of violence that are most prevalent cross-culturally: violence against children and violence against wives.

Violence against Children

Cross-culturally, many societies practice and allow infanticide. Frequent reasons for infanticide include illegitimacy, deformity of the infant, twins, too many children, or that the infant is unwanted. Infanticide is usually performed by the mother, but this does not mean that she is uncaring; it may mean that she cannot adequately feed or care for the infant or that it has a poor chance of surviving. The reasons for infanticide are similar to those given for abortion. Therefore, it seems that infanticide may be performed when abortion does not work or when unexpected qualities of the infant (e.g., deformity) force the mother to reevaluate her ability to raise the child.[26]

Physical punishment of children occurs at least sometimes in over 70 percent of the world's societies.[27] And physical punishment is frequent or typical in 40 percent of the world's societies. Why? A recent cross-cultural study suggests that the major reason parents physically punish children is to prepare them for a life of power inequality, which will require them to fear those more powerful. Societies with class stratification and political hierarchy, either native or introduced (colonialism), are very likely to practice corporal punishment of children.[28] Research in the United States is consistent with the cross-cultural finding: Those at the bottom of the socioeconomic hierarchy are more likely than those at the top to practice corporal punishment of children.[29]

Violence against Wives

Cross-culturally, wife beating is the most common form of family violence; it occurs at least occasionally in about 85 percent of the world's societies. In about half the societies, wife beating is sometimes serious enough to cause permanent injury or death.[30] It is often assumed that wife beating is common in societies in which males control economic and political resources. In a cross-cultural test of this assumption, David Levinson found that not all indicators of male dominance predict wife beating, but many do. Specifically, wife beating is most common when men control the products of family labor, when men have the final say in decision making in the home, when divorce is difficult for women, when remarriage for a widow is controlled by the husband's kin, and when women do not have any female work groups.[31] Similarly, in the United States, the more one spouse in the family makes the decisions and has the power, the more physical violence occurs in the family. Wife beating is even more likely when the husband controls the household and is out of work.[32]

Wife beating appears to be related to broader patterns of violence. Societies that have violent methods of conflict resolution within communities, physical punishment of criminals, high frequency of warfare, and cruelty toward enemies generally have more wife beating.[33] Corporal punishment of children may be related to wife beating. In the United States, many parents think that corporal punishment is necessary to teach children right and wrong. Corporal punishment of children may also teach that it is appropriate to hit people if you think they are misbehaving. As of 1995, one out of four parents hit children with objects.[34] Research in the United States supports the idea that individuals (males and females) who were punished corporally as adolescents are more likely to approve of marital violence and are more likely to commit it.[35]

Reducing the Risk

What can be done to minimize family violence? First, we have to recognize that probably nothing can be done as long as people in a society do not acknowledge that there is a problem. If severe child punishment and wife beating are perfectly acceptable by almost everyone in a society, they are unlikely to be considered social problems that need solutions. In our own society many programs are designed to take abused children or wives out of the family situation or to punish the abuser. (Of course, in these situations the violence has already occurred and was serious enough to have been noticed.) Cross-culturally, at least with respect to wife beating, intervention by others seems to be successful only if the intervention occurs before violence gets serious. As one would expect, however, those societies most prone to a high rate of wife beating are the least likely to practice immediate intervention. More helpful perhaps, but admittedly harder to arrange, is the promotion of conditions of life that are associated with low family violence. Research so far suggests that promoting the equality of men and women and the sharing of child rearing responsibilities may go a long way toward lessening incidents of family violence.[36] And reducing the risk of corporal punishment of children may reduce the risk of violence when they have families.

Crime

What is a crime in one society is not necessarily a crime in another. Just as it is difficult to decide what constitutes abuse, it is difficult to define *crime*. In one society, it may be a crime to walk over someone's land without permission; in another, there might not be any concept of personal ownership, and therefore no concept of trespassing. In seeking to understand variation in crime, it is not surprising that many researchers have preferred to compare those behaviors that are more or less universally considered crimes and that are reliably reported. For example, in a large-scale comparison of crime in 110 nations over a span of 70 years, Dane Archer and Rosemary Gartner concentrated on homicide rates. They argued that homicide is harder for the public to hide and for officials to ignore than are other crimes. A comparison of interviews about crime with police records suggests that homicide is the most reliably reported crime in official records.[37]

One of the clearest findings to emerge from comparative studies of crime is that war is associated with higher rates of homicide. Archer and Gartner compared changes in homicide rates of nations before and after major wars. Whether a nation is defeated or victorious, homicide rates tend to increase after a war. This result is consistent with the idea that a society or nation legitimizes violence during wartime. That is, during wartime, societies approve of killing the enemy; afterward, homicide rates may go up because inhibitions against killing have been relaxed.[38] Ted Gurr suggested that the long-term downtrend in crime in Western societies seems to be consistent with an increasing emphasis on humanistic values and nonviolent achievement of goals. But such goals may be temporarily suspended during wartime. In the United States, for example, surges in violent crime rates occurred during the 1860s and 1870s (during and after the Civil War), after World War I, after World War II, and during the Vietnam War.[39]

In the types of societies that anthropologists have typically studied, homicide statistics were not usually available; so cross-cultural studies of homicide usually measure homicide rates by comparing and rank-ordering ethnographers' statements about the frequency of homicide. For example, the statement that murder is "practically unheard of" is taken to mean that the murder rate is lower than where it is reported that "homicide is not uncommon." Despite the fact that the data on cultural homicide rates are not quantitative, the cross-cultural results are consistent with the cross-national results; more war is usually associated with more homicide and assault, as well as with socially approved aggressive behaviors (as in aggressive games) and severe physical punishment for wrongdoing.[40] A cross-cultural study suggests that the more war a society has, the more socialization or training of aggression in boys it will have, and such socialization strongly predicts higher rates of homicide and assault.[41]

Capital punishment—execution of criminals—is severe physical punishment for wrongdoing. It is commonly thought that would-be murderers are deterred by the prospect of capital punishment. Yet cross-national research suggests otherwise. More countries show murder rates going down rather than up after capital punishment was abolished.[42] Capital punishment may legitimize violence rather than deter it.

Research conducted in the United States suggests that juvenile delinquents (usually boys) are likely to come from broken homes, with the father absent for much of the time the boy is growing up. The conclusion often drawn is that father absence somehow increases the likelihood of delinquency and adult forms of physical violence. But other conditions that may cause delinquency are also associated with broken homes, conditions such as the stigma of not having a "regular" family and the generally low standard of living of such families. It is therefore important to conduct research in other societies, in which father absence does not occur in concert with these other factors, to see if father absence by itself is related to physical violence.

For example, in many polygynous societies, children grow up in a mother-child household; the father lives separately and is seldom around the child. Does the father-absence explanation of delinquency and violence fit such societies? The answer is apparently yes: Societies in which children are reared in mother-child households or the father spends little time caring for the child tend to have more physical violence by males than do societies in which fathers spend time with children.[43] The rate of violent crime is also more frequent in nations that have more women than men, which is consistent with the theory that father absence increases violence.[44]

More research is needed to discover exactly what accounts for these relationships. It is possible, as some suggest, that boys growing up without fathers are apt to act "supermasculine," to show how "male" they are. But it is also possible that mothers who rear children alone have more frustration and more anger, and therefore are likely to provide an aggressive role model for the child. In addition, high male mortality in war predicts polygyny, as we saw in the chapter on marriage, family, and kinship; therefore, boys in polygynous societies are likely to be exposed to a warrior tradition.[45]

Trying to act supermasculine, however, may be likely to involve violence only if aggression is an important component of the male gender role in society. If men were expected by society to be sensitive, caring, and nonviolent, boys who grew up without fathers might try to be supersensitive and supercaring. So society's expectations for males probably shape how growing up in a mother-child household affects behavior in adolescence and later.[46] The expectations for males may also be influenced by the media. Numerous studies in the United States show that even controlling for other factors like parental neglect, family income, and mental illness, more television watching in childhood and adolescence predicts more overt aggression later. Estimates show that an hour of prime-time television depicts 3 to 5 violent acts, and an hour of children's television depicts 20 to 25 violent acts.[47]

One widely held idea is that poor economic conditions increase the likelihood of crime, but the relationship does not appear to be strong. Also, the findings are somewhat different for different types of crime. For example, hundreds of studies in this and other countries do not show a clear relationship between changes in economic well-being as measured by unemployment rates and changes in violent crime as measured by homicide. The rate of homicide does not appear to increase in bad times. Property crimes, however, do increase with increases in unemployment. Violent crime does appear to be associated with one economic characteristic: Homicide is usually highest in nations with high income inequality. Why income inequality predicts homicide but downturns in the economy do not is something of a puzzle.[48]

Evidence indicates that violence on television encourages violence in real life.

The fact that property crime is linked to unemployment is consistent with the cross-cultural finding that theft (but not violent crime) tends to occur less often in egalitarian societies than in stratified ones. Societies with equal access to resources usually have distribution mechanisms that offset any differences in wealth. Hence theft should be less of a temptation and therefore less likely in an egalitarian society. Theft rates are higher in socially stratified societies despite the fact that they are more likely than egalitarian societies to have police and courts to punish crime. Societies may try to deter property and other crimes when the rates of such are high, but we do not know that these efforts actually reduce the rates.

So what does the available research suggest about how we might be able to reduce crime? The results so far indicate that homicide rates are highest in societies that socialize their boys for aggression. Such socialization is linked to war and other forms of socially approved violence—capital punishment, television and movie violence by heroes, violence in sports. The statistical evidence suggests that war encourages socialization for aggression, which in turn results unintentionally in high rates of violence. The policy implication of these results is that if we can reduce socialization for aggression, by reducing the risk of war and therefore the necessity to produce effective warriors, and if we can reduce other forms of socially approved violence, we may thereby reduce the rates of violent crime. The reduction of inequalities in wealth may also help to reduce crime, particularly theft. And although it is not yet clear why, it appears that raising boys with a male role model around may reduce the likelihood of male violence in adulthood.

War

War is an unfortunate fact of life in most societies known to anthropology, judging by the cross-cultural research we referred to in the chapter on political life. Almost every society had at least occasional wars when it was first described, unless it had been pacified (usually by Western colonial powers).[49] Since the Civil War, the United States has not had any wars on its territory, but it is unusual in that respect. Before pacification, most societies had frequent armed combat between communities or larger units that spoke the same language. That is, most warfare was internal to the society or language group. Even some wars in modern times involved speakers of the same language; recall the wars between Italian states before the unification of Italy and many of the "civil" wars of the past two centuries. Although people in some societies might

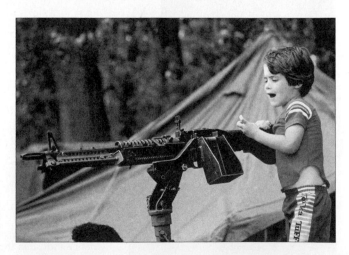

A society might encourage boys to play soldier, perhaps to prepare them to be courageous in combat later on. Cross-culturally, socialization for aggression strongly predicts homicide and assault.

fight against people in other societies, such "external" wars were usually not organized on behalf of the entire society or even a major section of it.[50] That is, warfare in the ethnographic record did not usually involve politically unified societies. Finally, the absolute numbers of people killed may have been small, but this does not mean that warfare in nonindustrial societies was a trivial matter. Indeed, it appears that nonindustrial warfare may have been even more lethal *proportionately* than modern warfare, judging by the fact that wars killed 25 to 30 percent of the males in some nonindustrial societies.[51]

In the chapter on political life, we discussed the possibility that people in nonindustrial societies go to war mostly out of fear, particularly a fear of expectable but unpredictable natural disasters (droughts, floods, hurricanes, among others) that destroy food supplies.[52] People with more history of such disasters have more war. It seems as if people go to war to protect themselves ahead of time from disasters, inasmuch as the victors in war almost always take resources (land, animals, other things) from the defeated, even when the victors have no current resource problems. Another factor apparently making for more war is teaching children to mistrust others. People who grow up to be mistrustful of others may be more likely to go to war than to negotiate or seek conciliation with "enemies." Mistrust or fear of others seems to be partly caused by threat or fear of disasters.[53]

Is warfare in and between modern state societies explainable in much the same way that nonindustrial warfare seems to be explainable? If the answer to that question turns out to be yes, it will certainly be a modified yes, because the realities of industrialized societies require an expanded conception of disasters. In the modern world, with its complex economic and political dependencies among nations, we may not be worried only about weather or pest disasters that could curtail food supplies. Possible curtailments of other resources, particularly oil, may also scare us into going to war. According to some commentators, the decision to go to war against Iraq after it invaded Kuwait in 1991 fits this theory of war.

But even if the "threat-to-resources" theory is true, we may be coming to realize (since the end of the Cold War) that war is not the only way to ensure access to resources. There may be a better way in the modern world, a way that is more cost-effective as well as more preserving of human life. If it is true that war is most likely when people fear unpredictable disasters of any kind, the risk of war should lessen when people realize that the harmful effects of disasters could be reduced or prevented by international cooperation. Just as we have the assurance of disaster relief within our country, we could have the assurance of disaster relief worldwide. That is, the fear of unpredictable disasters and the fear of others, and the consequent risk of war, could be reduced by the assurance ahead of time that the world would help those in need in case of disaster. Instead of going to war out of fear, we could go to peace by agreeing to share. The certainty of international cooperation could compensate for the uncertainty of resources.

Consider how Germany and Japan have fared in the years since their "unconditional surrender" in World War II. They were forbidden to participate in the international arms race and could rely on others, particularly the United States, to protect them. Without a huge burden of armaments, Germany and Japan thrived. But countries that competed militarily, particularly the United States and the Soviet Union at the height of the Cold War, experienced economic difficulties. Doesn't that scenario at least suggest the wisdom of international cooperation, particularly the need for international agreements to ensure worldwide disaster relief? Compared with going to war and its enormous costs, going to peace would be a bargain!

Recent research in political science and anthropology suggests an additional way to reduce the risk of war. Among the societies known to anthropology, studies indicate that people in more participatory—that is, more "democratic"—political systems rarely go to war with each other.[54] Thus, if authoritarian governments were to disappear from the world, because the powerful nations of the world stopped supporting them militarily and otherwise, the world could be more peaceful for this reason too.

Although democratically governed states rarely go to war with each other, it used to be thought that they are not necessarily more peaceful in general, that they are as likely to go to war as are other kinds of

ETHNIC CONFLICTS: ANCIENT HATREDS OR NOT?

Ethnic conflicts appear to be on the rise. In recent years, violent conflicts have erupted between ethnic groups in the former Yugoslavia, Russia, and Spain (in Europe), in Rwanda and Sierra Leone (in Africa), and in Sri Lanka and Indonesia (in Asia)—to name just a few of the many instances. Such conflicts are often thought to be intractable and inevitable because they are supposedly based on ancient hatreds. But is that true?

Social scientists are a long way from understanding the conditions that predict ethnic conflicts, but they do know that ethnic conflicts are not necessarily ancient or inevitable. For example, anthropologists who did field-work in the former Yugoslavia in the 1980s described villages where different ethnic groups had lived side by side for a long time without apparent difficulty. The differences between them were hardly emphasized. Mary Kay Gilliland worked in a midsize town (Slavonski Brod) in the Slavonian region of Croatia, which was part of Yugoslavia. The people in the town identified themselves as from Slavonia, rather than as Croats, Serbs, Hungarians, Czechs, Muslims (from Bosnia or from Albania), or Roma (Gypsies). Mixed marriages were not uncommon and people discussed differences in background without anger. But in 1991, when Gilliland returned to Croatia, people complained about Serb domination of the Yugoslav government and there was talk of Croatia seceding. Symbols of Croat nationalism had appeared—new place names, a new flag—and Croats were now said to speak Croatian, rather than the language they shared with the Serbs (Serbo-Croatian or Croato-Serbian). Later in 1991, violence broke out between Serbs and Croats, and atrocities were committed on both sides. Ethnicity became a matter of life or death and Croatia seceded from Yugoslavia. At the same time, Tone Bringa, a Norwegian anthropologist who worked in Bosnia (which was then still a region of Yugoslavia), reported that the people there also paid little attention to ethnicity. A few years later, however, ethnic violence erupted among Bosnian Serbs, Muslims, and Croats, and only the intervention of the United Nations established a precarious peace.

Ethnic conflict is often associated with secessionist movements; secession often occurs after the eruption of ethnic conflict. In the American Revolution, the region that became the United States seceded from Great Britain and declared independence. The ethnic differences between the Americans and the British were not great—not many years had passed since the first British colonizers had come to America—but there still was a secessionist movement, and there was violence. Ethnic differences do not always lead to violence. Sometimes, probably even most of the time, people of different ethnic backgrounds live in peace with one another. So why do some places with ethnic differences erupt in violence, but not all? Why do different ethnic groups get along in some places?

We need research to answer this question. With all of the forced and voluntary immigration in the world, many countries are becoming more multiethnic or multicultural. The possibility of ethnic violence has become a global social problem. Gilliland suggests, among other things, that discontent over economic and political power (inequitable access to resources and opportunities) drove the Croatians to violence and secession. Other scholars have suggested other possible answers to the question of why ethnic relations do not always become ethnic conflict and violence. Violence may erupt in the absence of strong unifying interests (cross-cutting ties) between the parties. Another suggested factor is the absence of constitutional ways to resolve conflict. What we need now are cross-cultural, cross-national, and cross-historical studies to measure each of the possible explaining factors, so that we can compare how well (or poorly) they predict ethnic conflict throughout the world, controlling for the effects of the other factors. If we knew which factors generally give rise to ethnic violence, we might be able to think of ways to reduce or eliminate the causal conditions.

Sources: Mary Kay Gilliland, "Nationalism and Ethnogenesis in the Former Yugoslavia," in Lola Romanucci-Ross and George A. De Vos, eds., *Ethnic Identity,* 3rd ed. (Walnut Creek, CA: AltaMira Press, 1995), pp. 197–221; Tone Bringa, *Being Muslim the Bosnian Way* (Princeton, NJ: Princeton University Press, 1995), as examined in eHRAF World Cultures on the Web; Marc Howard Ross, "Ethnocentrism and Ethnic Conflict," in *Research Frontiers,* in Carol R. Ember, Melvin Ember, and Peter N. Peregrine, eds., *New Directions in Anthropology* (Upper Saddle River, NJ: Prentice Hall, CD-ROM, 2004).

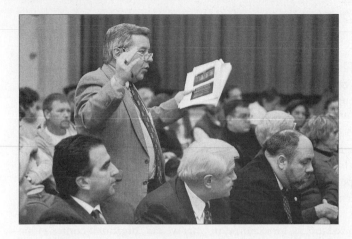

At a public planning meeting in Salina, New York, a town resident raises questions. Societies with participatory democracies are less likely to fight with other democracies.

political systems, but not so much with each other. For example, the United States has gone to war with Grenada, Panama, and Iraq—all authoritarian states—but not with democratic Canada, with which the United States has also had disputes. But now a consensus is emerging among political scientists that democracies are not only unlikely to go to war with each other, they are also less war-like in general.[55] The theory suggested by the cross-national and cross-cultural results is that democratic conflict resolution within a political system generalizes to democratic conflict resolution between political systems, particularly if the systems are both democratic. If our participatory institutions and perceptions allow us to resolve our disputes peacefully, internally and externally, we may think that similarly governed people would also be disposed to settle things peacefully. Therefore, disputes between participatory political systems should be unlikely to result in war.

The understanding that participatory systems rarely fight each other, and knowing why they do not, would have important consequences for policy in the contemporary world. The kinds of military preparations believed necessary and the costs people would be willing to pay for them might be affected. On the one hand, understanding the relationship between democracy and peace might encourage war making against authoritarian regimes to overturn them—with enormous costs in human life and otherwise. On the other hand, understanding the consequences of democracy might encourage us to assist the emergence and consolidation of more participatory systems of government in the countries of eastern Europe, the former Soviet Union, and elsewhere. In any case, the relationship between democracy and peace strongly suggests that it is counterproductive to support any undemocratic regimes, even if they happen to be enemies of our enemies, if we want to minimize the risk of war in the world. The latest cross-national evidence suggests that extending democracy around the world would minimize the risk of war. Encouraging nations to be more interdependent economically, and encouraging the spread of international nongovernmental organizations (like professional societies and trade associations) to provide informal ways to resolve conflicts, would also minimize the risk of war, judging by results of recent research by political scientists.[56]

Terrorism

Ever since September 11, 2001, when terrorists crashed airliners into the World Trade Center towers in New York City and into the Pentagon in Arlington, Virginia, people all over the world realize that terrorism has become a social problem globally. It is now painfully clear that organized groups of terrorists can train their people to kill themselves and thousands of others half a world away, not only by hijacking airliners and flying them into skyscrapers, but also by using easily transported explosives and biological weapons. Social scientists are now actively trying to understand terrorism, in the hope that research may lead to ways to minimize the likelihood of future attacks. But there are lots of questions to answer. What is terrorism and how shall it be defined? How long has terrorist activity been around? What are the causes of terrorism? What kind of people are likely to become terrorists? And what are the consequences of terrorism?

Answering these questions is not so simple. Most people can point to instances that hardly anyone would have trouble calling terrorism—spraying nerve gas in a Japanese subway, Palestinian suicide bombers targeting Israeli civilians, Ku Klux Klan members lynching African Americans.[57] It is harder to identify the boundaries between terrorism, crime, political repression, and warfare.[58] Most researchers agree that terrorism involves the threat or use of violence against civilians. Terrorism is usually also politically or socially organized, in contrast to most crimes, which are usually perpetrated by individuals acting on their own. (To be sure, crime can be socially organized too, as, for example, in what we call "organized crime.") One marker of the difference between most crime and terrorism is that criminals rarely take public credit for their activities, because they want to avoid being caught. In terrorism, the perpetrators usually proclaim their responsibility. In terrorism also, the violence is directed mostly at unarmed people, including women and children. It is intended to frighten the "enemy," to *terrorize* them, to scare them into doing something that the terrorists want to see happen. Generally, then, **terrorism** may be defined as the use or threat of violence to create terror in others, usually for political purposes.[59] Some define terrorism as perpetrated by groups that are not formal political entities. However, this criterion presents some difficulty. What are we to call it when governments support death squads and genocide against their own civilians? Some scholars call this "state terror."[60] And what are we to call the activities of some governments that support secret operations against other countries (often referred to as "state-sponsored terrorism")? Finally, while some nations conducting war explicitly try to avoid civilian casualties and focus primarily on combatants (armed soldiers), their weapons, and resources or "assets" such as factories, air strips, and fuel depots, many attacks in wartime throughout history have purposefully targeted civilians (e.g., the United States dropped atomic bombs on Hiroshima and Nagasaki to persuade the Japanese to end World War II).

One thing is certain about terrorism: It is not a new development. Some of the words we use for terrorists (e.g., "zealots" and "assassins") derive from terrorist movements in the past. The Zealots, Jewish nationalists who revolted against the Romans occupying Judea in the first century, would hide in crowds

People light candles in memory of those killed by terrorist attacks on trains in Madrid, Spain in 2004.

and stab officials and priests as well as soldiers. In the eleventh and twelfth centuries in southwest Asia, the Fedayeen (a group of Muslim Isma'ili Shi'ites) undertook to assassinate Sunni rulers despite the near certainty of their own capture or death. The rulers said that the Fedayeen were under the influence of hashish and called them "Hashshashin," which is the root of the later term "assassin."[61] In the late eighteenth and early nineteenth centuries, the "reign of terror" occurred during and after the French Revolution. In the early and middle twentieth century, the dictator Joseph Stalin ordered the execution of many millions of people who were considered enemies of the Soviet state. Six million Jews and millions of other innocents were exterminated by the German Third Reich in the 1930s and 1940s.[62] And many Latin American regimes, such as that in Argentina, terrorized and killed dissidents in the 1970s and 1980s.[63] Now there is a heightened fear of terrorists who may have access to weapons of mass destruction. In a world made smaller by global transportation, cell phones, and the Internet, terrorism is a greater threat than ever before.

We still lack systematic research that explains why terrorism occurs and why people are motivated to become terrorists. But there is a good deal of research about state terrorism. Political scientist R. J. Rummel estimates that nearly 170 million people have been killed by governments in the twentieth century (he calls this kind of terrorism "democide"). State terrorism has been responsible for four times more deaths than all the wars, civil and international, that occurred in the twentieth century. Regimes in the Soviet Union (1917–1987), China (1923–1987), and Germany (1933–1945) were responsible for killing more than a total of 100 million civilians. Proportionately the Khmer Rouge regime in Cambodia topped them all, killing over 30 percent of its population from 1975 to 1978.[64] What predicts state terrorism against one's own people? Rummel finds one clear predictor—totalitarian governments. By far they have the highest frequencies of domestic state terrorism, controlling for factors such as economic wealth, type of religion, and population size. As Rummel puts it, "power kills; absolute power kills absolutely."[65] Democratic countries are less likely to practice state terrorism, but when they do it occurs during or after a rebellion or a war.[66]

We know relatively little so far about what predicts who will become a terrorist. We do know that terrorists often come from higher social statuses and generally have more education than the average person.[67] If state terrorism is more likely to occur in totalitarian regimes, terrorists and terrorist groups may be more likely to occur in such societies. If so, the spread of democracy may be our best hope of minimizing the risk of terrorism in the world, just as the spread of democracy seems to minimize the likelihood of war between countries.

Making the World Better

Many social problems afflict our world, not just the ones discussed in this chapter.[68] We don't have the space to discuss the international trade in drugs and how it plays out in violence, death, and corruption. We haven't talked about the negative effects of environmental degradations such as water pollution, ozone depletion, and destruction of forests and wetlands. We haven't said much about overpopulation, refugees, the energy crisis, global warming, and a host of other problems that we should care about and do something about if we hope to make this a safer world. But we have tried in this chapter to encourage positive thinking about global issues; we have suggested how the results of past and future scientific research could be applied to solving some of those problems.

We may know enough now that we can do something about some of our problems, and we will discover more through future research. Social problems are mostly of human making and are therefore susceptible to human unmaking.

Summary

1. We may be more motivated now to try to solve social problems because worldwide communication has increased our awareness of them elsewhere, because we seem to be increasingly bothered by problems in our own society, and because we know more than we used to about various social problems that afflict our world.

2. The idea that we can solve global social problems is based on two assumptions. We have to assume that it is possible to discover the causes of a problem, and we have to assume that we will be able to do something about the causes once they are discovered and thereby eliminate or reduce the problem.

3. Disasters such as earthquakes, floods, and droughts can have greater or lesser effects on human life, depending on social conditions. Therefore disasters are partly social problems, with partly social causes and solutions.

4. Whether people become homeless, and whether there are shantytowns, seems to depend on a society's willingness to share wealth and to help those in need.

5. Promoting the equality of men and women and the sharing of child-rearing responsibilities may reduce family violence.

6. We may be able to reduce rates of violent crime if we can reduce socialization and training for aggression. To do that we would have to reduce the likelihood of war, the high likelihood of which predicts more socialization for aggression and other forms of socially approved aggression. The reduction of inequalities in wealth may also help to reduce crime, particularly theft. And raising boys with a male role model around may reduce the likelihood of male violence in adulthood.

7. People seem to be most likely to go to war when they fear unpredictable disasters that destroy food supplies or curtail the supplies of other necessities. Disputes between more participatory (more "democratic") political systems are unlikely to result in war. Therefore, the more democracy spreads in the world, and the more people all over the world are assured of internationally organized disaster relief, the more they might go to peace rather than to war to solve their problems.

8. Terrorism has occurred throughout history. State terrorism has killed more than all wars in the twentieth century and seems to be predicted mostly by totalitarianism.

Glossary Term

terrorism (p. 432)

Critical Questions

1. What particular advantages do anthropologists have in trying to solve practical problems?

2. Select one of the social problems discussed in this chapter and suggest what you think could be done to reduce or eliminate it.

3. Do global problems require solutions by global agencies? If so, which?

CHAPTER 19

APPLIED AND PRACTICING ANTHROPOLOGY

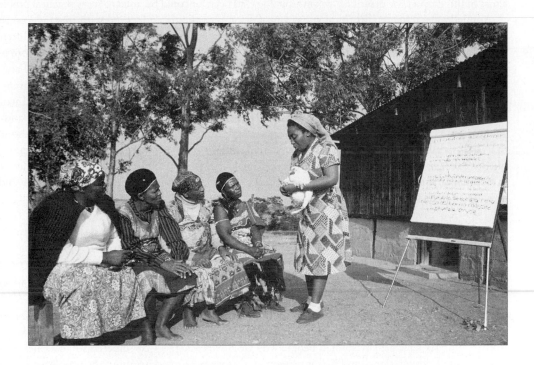

Chapter Outline

- Motives for Applying and Practicing Anthropology
- Ethics of Applied Anthropology
- Evaluating the Effects of Planned Change
- Difficulties in Instituting Planned Change
- Cultural Resource Management
- Forensic Anthropology
- Medical Anthropology

Anthropology is no longer a merely academic subject. One out of two anthropologists in the United States is employed outside of colleges and universities. This situation reflects an increasing realization that anthropology, what it has discovered and can discover about humans, is useful. Anthropologists who call themselves applied or practicing anthropologists are usually employed in nonacademic settings, working for government agencies, international development agencies, private consulting firms, public health organizations, medical schools, public interest law firms, community development agencies, charitable foundations, and even profit-seeking corporations. Why are so many anthropologists hired to help solve practical problems? In this chapter, we describe how anthropology has been, or could be, used to solve practical problems.

Applied or practicing anthropology as a profession is explicitly concerned with making anthropological knowledge useful. Many applied anthropologists participate in or evaluate programs intended to improve people's lives. Applied or practicing anthropologists may be involved in one or more phases of a program: assembling relevant knowledge, developing plans, assessing the likely social and environmental impact of particular plans, implementing the program, and monitoring the program and its effects.[1] And there are still other ways to use anthropology. One frequent type of applied work is **cultural resource management**, the "social impact" studies required by many government and private programs. For example, archaeologists are hired to study, record, and preserve "cultural resources" that will be disturbed or destroyed by construction projects. Another frequent and popular type of applied work is **forensic anthropology**—the use of anthropology to help solve crimes. And then there is **medical anthropology**, the application of anthropological knowledge to the study of health and illness. We devote the second half of this chapter to this fast-growing specialty.

Motives for Applying and Practicing Anthropology

Anthropologists have always cared and worried about the people they study, just as they care and worry about family and friends back home. It is upsetting if most of the families in your place of fieldwork have lost many of their babies to diseases that could be eliminated by medical care. It is upsetting when outside political and economic interests threaten to deprive your fieldwork friends of their resources and pride. Anthropologists have usually studied people who are disadvantaged—by imperialism, colonialism, and other forms of exploitation—and so it is no wonder that we feel protective about the people we have lived and shared with in the field.

A member of the Argentine Forensic Anthropology Team exhumes remains of one of the many "disappeared" Argentine civilians.

But caring is not enough to improve others' lives. We may need basic research that allows us to understand how a condition might be successfully treated. A particular proposed "improvement" might actually not be an improvement; well-meaning efforts have sometimes produced harmful consequences. And even if we know that a change would be an improvement, there is still the problem of how to make that change happen. The people to be affected may not want to change. Is it ethical to try to persuade them? And, conversely, is it ethical *not* to try? Applied anthropologists must take all of these matters into consideration in determining whether and how to act in response to a perceived need.

Applied anthropology in the United States developed out of anthropologists' personal experiences with disadvantaged people in other cultures.[2] Today anthropologists are also interested in studying and solving problems in our own society. Indeed, as noted earlier, there are as many anthropologists now working in nonacademic settings as in academic settings.[3] These practicing anthropologists often work on specific projects that aim to improve people's lives, usually by trying to change behavior or the environment; or the anthropologists monitor or evaluate efforts by others to bring about change.[4] Usually the problems and projects are defined by the employers or clients (the client is sometimes the "target" population), not by the anthropologists.[5] But anthropologists are increasingly called upon to participate in deciding exactly what improvements might be possible, as well as how to achieve them.

Ethics of Applied Anthropology

An anthropologist's first responsibility is to those who are being studied; everything should be done to ensure that their welfare and dignity will be protected. Anthropologists also have a responsibility to those who will read about their research; research findings should be reported openly and truthfully.[6] But because applied anthropology often deals with planning and implementing changes in some target population, ethical responsibilities can become complicated. Perhaps the most important ethical question is: Will the change truly benefit the target population?

In May 1946, the Society for Applied Anthropology established a committee to draw up a specific code of ethics for professional applied anthropologists. After many meetings and revisions, a statement on ethical responsibilities was finally adopted in 1948, and in 1983 the statement was revised.[7] According to the code, the target community should be included as much as possible in the formulation of policy, so that people in the community may know in advance how the program will affect them. Perhaps the most important aspect of the code is the pledge not to recommend or take any action that is harmful to the interests of the community. The National Association of Practicing Anthropologists goes further: If the work the employer expects of the employee violates the ethical principles of the profession, the practicing anthropologist has the obligation to try to change those practices or, if change cannot be brought about, to withdraw from the work.[8]

Thayer Scudder described the situation of Gwembe Tonga villagers who were relocated after a large dam was built in the Zambezi Valley of central Africa. Economic conditions improved during the 1960s and early 1970s, as the people increasingly produced goods and services for sale. But then conditions deteriorated. By 1980, the villagers were in a miserable state; rates of mortality, alcoholism, theft, assault, and murder were up. Why? One reason was that they had cut back on producing their own food in favor of producing for the world market. Such a strategy works well when world market prices are high; however, when prices fall, so does the standard of living.[9] The situation described by Scudder illustrates the ethical dilemma for many applied anthropologists. As he said: "So how is it that I can still justify working for the agencies that fund such projects?" He points out that large-scale projects are almost impossible to stop. The anthropologist can choose to stand on the sidelines and complain or try to influence the project to benefit the target population as much as possible.[10]

The problem described by Scudder comes about in part because the anthropologist is not often involved until after a decision is made to go ahead with a change program. This situation has begun to change as applied anthropologists are increasingly asked to participate in earlier stages of the planning process. Anthropologists are also increasingly asked to help in projects initiated by the affected party. Such requests may range from help in solving problems in corporate organizations to helping Native Americans with land claims. If the project is consistent with the wishes of the affected population, the results are not likely to put the anthropologist into an ethical dilemma.

Evaluating the Effects of Planned Change

The decision as to whether a proposed change would benefit the target population is not always easy to make. In certain cases, as when improved medical care is involved, the benefits offered to the target group would seem to be unquestionable—we all feel sure that health is better than illness. However, this may not always be true. Consider a public health innovation such as inoculation against disease. Although it would undoubtedly have a beneficial effect on the survival rate of a population, a reduction in the mortality rate might have unforeseen consequences that would in turn produce new problems. Once the inoculation program was begun, the number of children surviving would probably increase. But it might not be possible to increase the rate of food production, given the level of technology, capital, and land resources possessed by the target population. Thus, the death rate, because of starvation, might rise to its previous level and perhaps even exceed it. The inoculation program would not affect the death rate; it might merely change the causes of death. This example shows that even if a program of planned change has beneficial consequences in the short run, a great deal of thought and investigation have to be given to its long-term effects.

Debra Picchi raised questions about the long-term effects on the Bakairí Indians of a program by the National Brazilian Indian Foundation (FUNAI) to produce rice with machine technology.[11] The Bakairí of the Mato Grosso region largely practice slash-and-burn horticulture in gallery forests along rivers, with supplementary cattle raising, fishing, and hunting. In the early part of the twentieth century their population had declined to 150 people and they were given a relatively small reserve. Some of it was gallery forest, but a larger part was parched and infertile (*cerrado*). When the Bakairí population began to increase, FUNAI introduced a scheme to plant rice on formerly unused *cerrado* land, using machinery, insecticides, and fertilizer. FUNAI paid the costs for the first year and expected that by the third year the scheme would be self-supporting. The project did not go so well because FUNAI did not deliver all the equipment needed and did not provide adequate advice. So only half the expected rice was produced. Still, it was more food than the Bakairí had previously, so the program should have been beneficial to them.

But there were unanticipated negative side effects. Nutritionally, to be sure, the Bakairí are growing an additional starchy food. But use of the *cerrado* for agriculture reduces the area on which cattle can be grazed; cattle are an important source of high-quality protein. So the now-mechanized agriculture has reduced the availability of animal protein. The mechanization also makes the Bakairí more dependent on cash for fuel, insecticides, fertilizer, and repairs. But cash is hard to come by. Only some individuals can be hired—usually men with outside experience who have the required knowledge of machinery. So the cash earned in the now-mechanized agriculture goes mainly to a relatively small number of people. It is debatable whether the new inequalities of income provide long-term effects that are beneficial to most Bakairí.

These failures were not the fault of anthropologists—indeed, most instances of planned change by governments and other agencies usually have begun without the input of anthropologists at all. Applied anthropologists have played an important role in pointing out the problems with programs like these that fail to evaluate long-term consequences. Such evaluations are an important part of convincing governments and other agencies to ask for anthropological help in the first place.

Difficulties in Instituting Planned Change

Whether a program of planned change can be successfully implemented depends largely on whether the targeted population wants the proposed change and likes the proposed program. Before an attempt can be made at cultural innovation, the innovators must determine whether the target population is aware of the benefits of the proposed change. Lack of awareness can be a barrier to solving the problem at hand. For example, health workers have often had difficulty convincing people that they were becoming ill because something was wrong with their water supply. Many people do not believe that disease can be transmitted by water. At other times, the target population is perfectly aware of the problem. A case in point involved Taiwanese women who were introduced to family-planning methods beginning in the 1960s. The women knew they were having more children than they wanted or could easily afford, and they wanted to control their birth rate. They offered no resistance—they merely had to be given the proper devices and instructions, and the birth rate quickly fell to a more desirable, and more manageable, level.[12]

Resistance by the Target Population

Not all proposed change programs are beneficial to the target population. Sometimes resistance is rational. Applied anthropologists have pointed to cases where the judgment of the affected population has been better than that of the agents of change. One such example occurred during a Venezuelan government-sponsored program to give infants powdered milk. The mothers rejected the milk, even though it was free, on the grounds that it implied that the mothers' milk was no good.[13] But who is to say that the resistance was not in fact intuitively smart, reflecting an awareness that such a milk program would not benefit the children? Medical research now indicates quite clearly that mothers' milk is far superior to powdered milk or formula. First, human milk best supplies the nutrients needed for human development. Second, it is now known that the mother, through her milk, is able to transmit antibodies (disease resistances) to the baby. And third, nursing delays ovulation and usually increases the spacing between births.[14]

The switchover to powdered milk and formula in many underdeveloped areas has been nothing short of a disaster, resulting in increased malnutrition and misery. For one thing, powdered milk must be mixed with water, but if the water and the bottles are not sterilized, more sickness is introduced. Then, too, if powdered milk has to be purchased, mothers without cash are forced to dilute the milk to stretch it. And if a mother feeds her baby formula or powder for even a short time, the process is tragically irreversible, for her own milk dries up and she cannot return to breast-feeding even if she wants to.

As the Venezuelan example suggests, individuals may be able to resist proposed medical or health projects because acceptance is ultimately a personal matter. Large development projects planned by powerful governments or agencies rarely are stoppable, but even they can be resisted successfully. The Kayapo of the Xingu River region of Brazil were able to cancel a plan by the Brazilian government to build dams along the river for hydroelectric power. The Kayapo gained international attention when some of their leaders appeared on North American and European television and then successfully organized a protest in 1989 by members of several tribal groups. Their success seemed to come in part from their ability to present themselves to the international community as guardians of the rain forest—an image that resonated with international environmental organizations that supported their cause. Although to outsiders it might seem that the Kayapo want their way of life to remain as it was, the Kayapo are not opposed to all change. In fact, they want greater access to medical care, other government services, and manufactured goods from outside.[15]

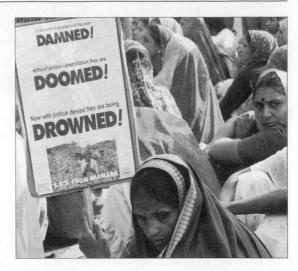

Indians protest construction of a dam in their area.

But even if a project is beneficial to a population, it may still meet with resistance. Factors that may hinder acceptance can be divided roughly into three, sometimes overlapping, categories: *cultural, social,* and *psychological* barriers.

Cultural barriers are shared behaviors, attitudes, and beliefs that tend to impede the acceptance of an innovation. For example, members of different societies may view gift giving in different ways. Particularly in commercialized societies, things received for nothing are often believed to be worthless. When the government of Colombia instituted a program of giving seedling orchard trees to farmers in order to increase fruit production, the farmers showed virtually no interest in the seedlings, many of which proceeded to die of neglect. When the government realized that the experiment had apparently failed, it began to charge each farmer a nominal fee for the seedlings. Soon the seedlings became immensely popular and fruit production increased.[16] The farmers' demand for the seedlings may have increased because they were charged a fee and therefore came to value the trees. The market demand for fruit may also have increased.

It is very important for agents of change to understand what the shared beliefs and attitudes are. First, indigenous cultural concepts or knowledge can sometimes be used effectively to enhance educational programs. For instance, in a program in Haiti to prevent child mortality from diarrhea, change agents used the terminology for traditional native herbal tea remedies (*rafrechi,* or cool refreshment) to identify the new oral rehydration therapy, which is a very successful medical treatment. In native belief, diarrhea is a "hot" illness and appropriate remedies have to have cooling properties.[17] Second, even if indigenous beliefs are not helpful to the campaign, not paying attention to contrary beliefs can undermine the campaign. But uncovering contrary beliefs is not easy, particularly when they do not emerge in ordinary conversation. (Later in this chapter, concerning medical anthropology, we discuss cultural theories about illness more extensively.) The acceptance of planned change may also depend on social factors. Research suggests that acceptance is more likely if the change agent and the target or potential adopter are similar socially. But change agents may have higher social status and more education than the people they are trying to influence. So change agents may work more with higher-status individuals because they are more likely to accept new ideas. If lower-status individuals also have to be reached, change agents of lower status may have to be employed.[18]

Finally, acceptance may depend on psychological factors—that is, how the individuals perceive both the innovation and the agents of change. In the course of trying to encourage women in the southeastern

United States to breast-feed rather than bottle-feed their infants, researchers discovered a number of reasons why women were reluctant to breast-feed their infants, even though they heard it was healthier. Many women did not have confidence that they would produce enough milk for their babies; they were embarrassed about breast-feeding in public; and their family and friends had negative attitudes.[19] In designing an educational program, change agents may have to address such psychological concerns directly.

Discovering and Utilizing Local Channels of Influence

In planning a project involving cultural change, the administrator of the project should find out what the normal channels of influence are in the population. In most communities, there are preestablished networks for communication, as well as persons of high prestige or influence who are looked to for guidance and direction. An understanding of such channels of influence is extremely valuable when deciding how to introduce a program of change. In addition, it is useful to know at what times, and in what sorts of situations, one channel is likely to be more effective in spreading information and approval than another.

An example of the effective use of local channels of influence occurred when an epidemic of smallpox broke out in the Kalahandi district of the state of Orissa in India. The efforts of health workers to vaccinate villagers against the disease were consistently resisted. The villagers, naturally suspicious and fearful of these strange men with their equally strange medical equipment, were unwilling to offer themselves, and particularly their babies, to the peculiar experiments the strangers wished to perform. Afraid of the epidemic, the villagers appealed for help to their local priest, whose opinions on such matters they trusted. The priest went into a trance, explaining that the illness was the result of the goddess Thalerani's anger with the people. She could be appeased, he continued, only by massive feasts, offerings, and other demonstrations of the villagers' worship of her. Realizing that the priest was the village's major opinion leader, at least in medical matters, the frustrated health workers tried to get the priest to convince his people to undergo vaccination. At first, the priest refused to cooperate with the strange men, but when his favorite nephew fell ill, he decided to try any means available to cure the boy. He thereupon went into another trance, telling the villagers that the goddess wished all her worshippers to be vaccinated. Fortunately, the people agreed, and the epidemic was largely controlled.[20]

If channels of influence are not stable, using influential persons in a campaign can sometimes backfire. In the educational campaign in Haiti to promote the use of oral rehydration therapy to treat diarrhea in children, Mme. Duvalier, the first lady of Haiti at the time, lent her name to the project. Because there were no serious social or cultural barriers to the treatment and mothers reported that children took to the solutions well, success was expected. But in the middle of the campaign, Haiti became embroiled in political turmoil and the first lady's husband was overthrown. Some of the public thought that the oral rehydration project was a plot by the Duvaliers to sterilize children, and this suspicion fueled resistance.[21] Even after the Duvalier regime was toppled, people in Haiti were suspicious of any government-sponsored program.

Cultural Resource Management

Large-scale programs of planned change have an impact not only on living people. They can also have an impact on the archaeological record left by the ancestors of living people. Recovering and preserving the archaeological record before programs of planned change disturb or destroy it is called *cultural resource management (CRM)*. CRM work is carried out by archaeologists who are often called "contract archaeologists" because they typically work under contract to a government agency, a private developer, or a native group.

Commuters look at fourth century ruins uncovered as part of a large-scale CRM project associated with construction of the Athens metro system.

What kinds of impact can programs of planned change have on the archaeological record? In the 1960s a large number of hydroelectric dam projects were initiated to provide flood control and to bring a stable source of electrical power to developing nations. In Egypt a dam was built on the Nile River at a site called Aswan. Archaeologists realized that once the dam was in place a huge lake would form behind it, submerging thousands of archaeological sites, including the massive temple of Rameses II. Something needed to be done; the archaeological record had to be salvaged or protected. In the language of CRM, there needed to be a *mitigation plan* put into action. And there was. As the Aswan dam was being built, archaeologists went to work excavating sites that would be flooded. Archaeologists and engineers designed a way to take apart the temple of Rameses II and rebuild it, piece by piece, on higher ground where it would not be flooded. By the time the dam was completed in 1965, hundreds of sites had been investigated and two entire temple complexes moved.

Large-scale development projects are not the only projects that involve CRM archaeologists. In many nations, including the United States and Canada, historic preservation laws require any project receiving federal funds to ensure that archaeological resources are protected or their damage mitigated. Highway construction projects in the United States are common places to find CRM archaeologists at work. Virtually all highway projects rely on federal funding, and before a highway can be built a complete archaeological survey of the proposed right-of-way has to be made. If archaeological sites are found, potential damage to them must be mitigated. A CRM archaeologist will work with the construction company, the state archaeologist, and perhaps a federal archaeologist to decide on the best course of action. In some cases the archaeological site will be excavated. In others, the right-of-way may be moved. In still others, the decision is to allow the archaeological site to be destroyed, because it would be too costly to excavate or the site may not be significant enough to warrant excavation. Regardless of the decision, the CRM archaeologist plays a crucial role in assessing and protecting the archaeological record.

CRM archaeologists do not work only for state or federal agencies. In many nations today CRM archaeologists are also working with native peoples to protect, preserve, and manage archaeological materials for them. Indeed, archaeologist John Ravesloot recently stated that "the future of American archaeology is with Indian communities functioning as active, not passive, participants in the interpretation, management, and preservation of their rich cultural heritage."[22] One example of such a working relationship is the Zuni Heritage and Historic Preservation Office. During the 1970s the Pueblo of Zuni decided it needed to train tribal members in archaeology in order to ensure that Zuni cultural resources and properties were managed properly. It hired three professional archaeologists and, with additional assistance from the National Park Service and the Arizona State Museum, initiated a program to train and employ tribal members in cultural resource management. Working with these non-Zuni archaeologists, the Pueblo of Zuni was able to establish its own historic preservation office that today manages and coordinates all historic preservation on the Zuni reservation, a task that was managed by the federal government until 1992. The Pueblo also established the Zuni Cultural Resource Enterprise, a Zuni-owned CRM business that employs both Zuni and non-Zuni archaeologists and carries out contract archaeology projects both on and off the Zuni reservation.[23]

Cultural resource management is a growing field. Indeed, a 1994 survey conducted by the Society for American Archaeology showed that more than 25 percent of archaeologists in the United States were employed in private CRM firms working on federally funded contracts, and another 25 percent worked directly for state and federal agencies. Thus 50 percent of all employed archaeologists in the United States had jobs directly related to CRM.[24] As development and construction projects continue to affect the archaeological record, the need for well-trained CRM archaeologists is not likely to decline.

Forensic Anthropology

Many of us are fascinated by detective stories. We are interested in crimes and why they occur, and we like to read about them, fictional or not. Forensic anthropology is the specialty in anthropology that is devoted to solving crimes. It is attracting increasing attention by the public, and an increasing number of practitioners. One forensic anthropologist says she is called "the bone lady" by law enforcement personnel.[25] Like others in her line of work, she is asked to dig up or examine human bones to help solve crimes. Often the task is simple: Are these the bones of a man or woman? How old was the person? Forensic anthropologists can answer such questions fairly easily, particularly if the remains include most bones of the skeleton. Other times the question may be more difficult to answer. For example, can the forensic anthropologist say that a skull is probably from an Asian male? (The police suspect that the skeletal remains they found are from an Asian man who disappeared under mysterious circumstances five years before.) But it is difficult enough to assign an unambiguous "racial" classification to living persons. Bones alone are even more ambiguous because different features in the skeleton do not all vary in correlated ways, as we noted in our earlier discussion of "race" in the chapter on social stratification. Still, the forensic anthropologist can suggest whether the skeletal remains show a constellation of features typically associated with a particular region of the world. Sometimes the forensic anthropologist can suggest the cause of death when the law enforcement people are stumped.

Some cultural anthropologists have also done forensic work, often in connection with legal cases involving Native Americans. For example, Barbara Joans was asked in 1978 to advise the defense in a trial of six older Bannock-Shoshoni women from the Fort Hall reservation who were accused of fraud. They had received "supplemental security income (SSI)," which the social service agency claimed they had no right to receive because they had not reported receiving rent money on land that they owned. Joans presented evidence that the women, although they spoke some English, did not have enough proficiency to understand the nuances of what the SSI people told them. The judge agreed with the defense and ruled that in the future the SSI would have to use a Bannock-Shoshoni interpreter when they went to the reservation to describe the requirements of the program.[26]

In recent years, Clyde Snow and other forensic anthropologists have been called on to confirm horrendous abuses of human rights. Governments have been responsible for the systematic killing of their citizens, and forensic anthropologists have helped to bring the perpetrators to justice. For example, Snow

444   Chapter 19

and other forensic anthropologists helped to confirm that the military dictatorship in Argentina in the 1980s was responsible for the deaths of many Argentine civilians who had "disappeared." The forensic anthropologists were also able to determine the location of mass graves and the identity of victims of state-organized brutality in Guatemala. In addition to bringing the perpetrators to justice, confirming the massacres and identifying the victims help the families of the "disappeared" put their anguish behind them.

Medical Anthropology

Illness and death are significant events for people everywhere. No one is spared. So it should not be surprising that how people understand the causes of illness and death, how they behave, and what resources they marshal to cope with these events are extremely important. Some argue that we will never completely understand how to treat illness effectively until we understand the cultural behaviors, attitudes, values, and the larger social and political milieux in which people live. Others argue that society and culture have little to do with the outcome of illness—the reason that people die needlessly is that they do not get the appropriate medical treatment.

But anthropologists, particularly medical anthropologists, who are actively engaged in studying health and illness, are increasingly realizing that biological *and* social factors need to be considered if we are to reduce human suffering. For instance, some populations have an appalling incidence of infant deaths due to diarrhea. The origin of this situation is mostly biological, in the sense that the deaths are caused by bacterial infection. But why are so many infants exposed to those bacteria? Usually, the main reason is social. The affected infants are likely to be poor. Because they are poor, they are likely to live with infected drinking water. Similarly, malnutrition may be the biological result of a diet poor in protein, but such a diet is usually also a cultural phenomenon, reflecting a society with classes of people with very unequal access to the necessities of life. In many ways, therefore, medical anthropology, and anthropology in general, are developing in the direction of a "biocultural synthesis."[27]

Cultural Understandings of Health and Illness

Medical researchers and medical practitioners in the United States and other Western societies do not exist in a social vacuum. Many of their ideas and practices are influenced by the culture in which they live. We may think of medicine as purely based on "fact," but on reflection it is clear that many ideas stem from the culture in which the researchers reside. Consider the recent shift in attitudes toward birth. It was not so long ago in the United States that fathers were excluded from the birth, hospitals whisked the baby away from the mother and only brought the baby to her infrequently, and visitors (but not attending nurses and doctors) had to wear masks when holding the baby. Rationalizations were given for those practices, but looking back at them, they do not appear to be based on scientific evidence. Many medical anthropologists now argue that the *biomedical paradigm* (the system in which physicians are trained) itself needs to be understood as part of the culture.

Discovering the health-related beliefs, knowledge, and practices of a cultural group—its **ethnomedicine**—is one of the goals of medical anthropology. How do cultures view health and illness? What are their theories about the causes of illness? Do those theories impact on how illnesses are treated? What is the therapeutic process? Are there specialized medical practitioners, and how do they heal? Are there special medicines, and how are they administered? These are just some of the questions asked by the anthropological study of ethnomedicine.

Concepts of Balance or Equilibrium   In many cultures it is thought that the body should be kept in equilibrium or balance. The balance may be between hot and cold, or wet and dry, as in many cultures of Latin America and the Caribbean.[28] The notion of balance is not limited to opposites. For example, the ancient Greek system of medicine, stemming from Hippocrates, assumed that there were four "humors"— blood, phlegm, yellow bile, and black bile—that must be kept in balance. These humors have hot and cold and wet and dry properties. The Greek medical system was widely diffused in Europe and spread to parts of the Islamic world. In Europe, the humoral medical system was dominant until it was replaced by the germ theory in the 1900s.[29] In the Ayurvedic system, whose practice dates back 4,000 years in North India, Pakistan, Bangladesh, Sri Lanka, and in the Arab world, there are three humors (phlegm, bile, and flatulence), and a balance between hot and cold is also important.[30] The Chinese medical system, which dates back about 3,500 years, initially stressed the balance between the contrasting forces of *yin* and *yang* and later added the concept of humors, which were six in number in Chinese medicine.[31]

The concepts of hot and cold and *yin* and *yang* are illustrated in Emily Ahern's ethnographic description of the medical system of the Taiwanese Hokkien.[32] Both hot and cold substances are required by the body; when the body is out of balance, a lack of one substance can be restored by eating or drinking the missing substance. So, for example, when Ahern was faint with heat, she was told to drink some bamboo-shoot soup because it was "cold." In the winter, you need more hot substances; in the summer, you want fewer. Some people can tolerate more imbalance than others; the old, for instance, can tolerate less imbalance than the young. A loss of blood means a loss of heat. So, for a month after childbirth, women eat mostly a soup made of chicken, wine, and sesame oil—all "hot" ingredients. Hot things to eat are generally oily, sticky, or come from animals; cold things tend to be soupy, watery, or made from plants.

Supernatural Forces   The Taiwanese Hokkien believe that most illnesses have natural or physiological causes, but around the world it is more common to believe that illnesses are caused by supernatural forces. In fact, in a cross-cultural study of 139 societies, George P. Murdock found that only two societies did not have the belief that gods or spirits could cause illness, making such a belief a near-universal. And 56 percent of those sample societies thought that gods or spirits were the major causes of illness.[33] As we discussed in the chapter on religion and magic, sorcery and witchcraft are common in the world's societies. Although both sorcery and witchcraft are practiced by humans and may be used for good or evil, making people ill is one of their major uses. Illness can also be thought of as caused by the loss of one's soul,

In China and elsewhere, tai chi exercises are believed to bring harmony and balance.

fate, retribution for violation of a taboo, or contact with a polluting or tabooed substance or object. Sorcery is believed to be a cause of illness by most societies on all continents; retribution because of violation of a taboo is also very frequent in all but one region of the world. The belief that soul loss can cause illness is absent in the area around the Mediterranean, uncommon in Africa, infrequent in the New World and the Pacific, and has its highest frequency in Eurasia.[34]

On Chuuk (Truk), an atoll in the central Pacific, serious illnesses and death are mainly believed to be the work of spirits. Occasionally, the spirits of relatives are to blame, although they usually do not cause serious damage. More often, illness is caused by the spirit of a particular locality or a ghost on a path at night.[35] Nowadays, one of two therapeutic options or their combination is often chosen—hospital medicine or Chuuk medicine. Chuuk medical treatment requires a careful evaluation of symptoms by the patient and his or her relatives, because different spirits inflict different symptoms. If the symptom match is clear, the patient may choose an appropriate Chuuk medical formula to cure the illness. The patient may also ask whether he or she has done something wrong, and if so, what might point to the appropriate spirit and countervailing formula. For example, there is a taboo on having sexual relations before going to sea. If a person who violated this prohibition becomes ill, the reef spirits will be suspected. The Chuuk medical formula is supposed to cure illness quickly and dramatically. It is for this reason that Chuuk patients ask for a discharge from a hospital if their condition does not improve quickly. If treatment fails, the Chuukese believe that they need to reevaluate the diagnosis, sometimes with the aid of a diviner.[36] In contrasting their theories of illness to the American germ theory, the people of Chuuk point out that while they have seen ghosts, they have never seen the germs that Americans talk about. Using both methods, some people recover and some do not, so the ultimate cause is a matter of faith.[37]

The Biomedical Paradigm   In most societies, people simply think that their ideas about health and illness are true. Often it is not until they confront another medical system that people develop any awareness that there may be another way of viewing things. Western medical practice has spread widely. People with other medical systems have had to recognize that their ideas about health and illness may be considered deficient by Western practitioners, so it is often necessary to decide which course (Western or non-Western) to follow in dealing with illness. Change, however, is not entirely one-way. For example, for a long time the Chinese practice of acupuncture was disparaged by the Western medical profession, but now more medical practitioners are recognizing that acupuncture may provide effective treatment of certain conditions.

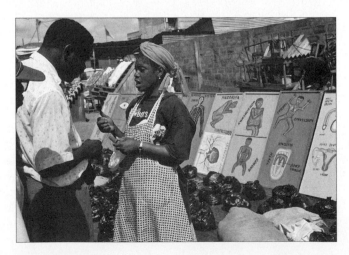

People treat themselves with herbal medicines
bought from an herbalist in Ghana.

Most medical anthropologists use the term **biomedicine** to refer to the dominant medical paradigm in Western cultures today, with the *bio* part of the word emphasizing the biological emphasis of this medical system. As Robert Hahn points out, biomedicine appears to focus on specific diseases and cures for those diseases. Health is not the focus, as it is thought to be the *absence* of disease. Diseases are considered to be purely natural, and there is relatively little interest in the person or the larger social and cultural systems. Doctors generally do not treat the whole body but tend to specialize, with the human body partitioned into zones that belong to different specialties. Death is seen as a failure, and biomedical practitioners do everything they can to prolong life, regardless of the circumstances under which the patient would live his or her life.[38]

Treatment of Illness

Anthropologists who study diseases in this and other cultures can be roughly classified into two camps. First, there are those (the more relativistic) who think that the culture so influences disease symptoms, incidence, and treatment that there are few if any cultural universals about any illness. If each culture is unique, we should expect its conception and treatment of an illness to be unique too, not like beliefs and practices in other cultures. Second, there are those (the more universalistic) who see cross-cultural similarities in the conception and treatment of illness, despite the unique qualities (particularly in the belief system) of each culture. For example, native remedies may contain chemicals that are the same as, or similar in effect to, chemicals used in remedies by Western biomedicine.[39] The reader should note that our classification here of medical anthropologists is a crude one; many medical anthropologists do not fall unambiguously into one or the other group. And the reality might be that a given culture is very much like other cultures in some respects but unique in other respects.

In their extensive research on Maya ethnomedicine, Elois Ann Berlin and Brent Berlin make a strong case that although studies of the Maya have emphasized beliefs about illness that are based on supernatural causes, a good deal of Maya ethnomedicine is about natural conditions, their signs and symptoms, and the remedies used to deal with those conditions. In regard to gastrointestinal diseases, the Berlins found that the Maya have a wide-ranging and accurate understanding of anatomy, physiology, and symptoms. Furthermore, the remedies they use, including recommendations for food, drink, and herbal medicines, have properties that are not that different from those of the biomedical profession.[40]

Carole Browner also suggests that the emphasis on "hot-cold" theories of illness in Latin America has been overemphasized, to the neglect of other factors that influence choices about reproductive health and female health problems. In a study of the medical system in a highland Oaxacan community, Browner finds that certain plants are used to expel substances from the uterus—to facilitate labor at full term, to produce an abortion, or to induce menstrual flow. Other plants are used to retain things in the uterus— to prevent excess blood loss during menstruation, to help healing after delivery, and to prevent miscarriage. Most of these plant remedies appear to work.[41]

The biomedical establishment has become increasingly aware of the value of studying the "traditional" medicinal remedies discovered or invented by people around the world. In studying the indigenous medicines of the Hausa of Nigeria, Nina Etkin and Paul Ross asked individuals to describe the physical attributes of more than 600 plants and their possible medicinal uses, more than 800 diseases and symptoms, and more than 5,000 prepared medicines. While many medicines were used for treating sorcery, spirit aggression, or witchcraft, most medicines were used for illnesses regarded by the Hausa as having natural causes. Malaria is a serious endemic medical problem in the Hausa region, as in many areas of Africa. The Hausa use approximately 72 plant remedies for conditions connected with malaria—among them anemia, intermittent fever, and jaundice. Experimental treatment of malaria in laboratory animals supports the efficacy of many of the Hausa remedies.

But perhaps the most important part of the Etkin and Ross findings is the role of diet. While most medical research does not consider the possible medical efficacy of the *foods* that people eat in combating illness, food is, of course, consumed in much larger quantities and more often than medicine. It is noteworthy, therefore, that the Hausa eat many plants with antimalarial properties; in fact, dietary consumption of these plants appears to be greatest during the time of year when the risk of malarial infection is at its highest. Recent research has also discovered that foods and spices like garlic, onions, cinnamon, ginger, and pepper have antiviral or antibacterial properties.[42]

Medical Practitioners   In our society we may be so used to consulting a full-time medical specialist (if we do not feel better quickly) that we tend to assume that biomedical treatment is the only effective medical treatment. If we are given a medicine, we expect it to have the appropriate medical effect and make us feel better. So many in the biomedical system, practitioners and patients alike, are perplexed by the seeming effectiveness of other medical systems that involve symbolic or ritual healing.

Illness may be viewed as being due to something being out of order in one's social life. The cause could be retribution for one's own bad behavior or thoughts, or the work of an angry individual practicing sorcery or witchcraft. Or a bad social situation or a bad relationship may be thought of as provoking physical symptoms because of anxiety or stress. In societies with occupational specialization, priests, who are formally trained full-time religious practitioners, may be asked to convey messages or requests for healing to higher powers.[43] Societies with beliefs in sorcery and witchcraft as causes of illness typically have practitioners who are believed to be able to use magic in reverse—that is, to undo the harm invoked by sorcerers and witches. Sometimes sorcerers or witches themselves may be asked to reverse illnesses caused by others. However, they may not be sought out because they are often feared and have relatively low status.[44] Shamans are perhaps the most important medical practitioners in societies lacking full-time occupational specialization.

After working with shamans in Africa, E. Fuller Torrey, a psychiatrist and anthropologist, concluded that they use the same mechanisms and techniques to cure patients as psychiatrists and achieve about the same results. He isolated four categories used by healers the world over:

1. **The naming process.**   If a disease has a name—"neurasthenia" or "phobia" or "possession by an ancestral spirit" will do—then it is curable; the patient realizes that the doctor understands his case.
2. **The personality of the doctor.**   Those who demonstrate some empathy, nonpossessive warmth, and genuine interest in the patient get results.
3. **The patient's expectations.**   One way of raising the patient's expectations of being cured is the trip to the doctor; the longer the trip, the easier the cure. An impressive setting (the medical center) and impressive paraphernalia (the stethoscope, the couch, attendants in uniform, the rattle, the whistle, the drum, the mask) also raise the patient's expectations. The healer's training is important: High fees also help to raise a patient's expectations. (The Paiute doctors always collect their fees before starting a cure; if they don't, it is believed that they will fall ill.)
4. **Curing techniques.**   Drugs, shock treatment, conditioning techniques, and so on have long been used in many different parts of the world.[45]

Biomedical research is not unaware of the effect of the mind on healing. In fact, considerable evidence has accumulated that psychological factors can be very important in illness. Patients who believe that medicine will help them often recover quickly even if the medicine is only a sugar pill or a medicine not particularly relevant to their condition. Such effects are called *placebo* effects.[46] Placebos do not just have psychological effects. Although the mechanisms are not well understood, they may also alter body chemistry and bolster the immune system.[47]

Shamans may coexist with medical doctors. Don Antonio, a respected Otomi Indian shaman in central Mexico, has many patients, perhaps not as many as before modern medicine, but still plenty. In his view, when he was born God gave him his powers to cure, but his powers are reserved for removing "evil" illnesses (those caused by sorcerers). "Good" illnesses can be cured by herbs and medicine, and he refers patients with those illnesses to medical doctors; he believes that doctors are more effective than he could be in those cases. The doctors, however, do not seem to refer any patients to Don Antonio or other shamans![48]

The most important full-time medical practitioner in the biomedical system is the physician, and the patient-physician relationship is central. In the ideal scheme of things, the physician is viewed as having the ability, with some limits, of being able to treat illness, alleviate suffering, and prolong the life of the patient, as well as offering promises of patient confidentiality and privacy. The patient relies on the physician's knowledge, skill, and ethics. Consistent with the biomedical paradigm, doctors tend to treat patients as having "conditions" rather than as complete persons. Physicians presumably rely on science for authoritative knowledge, but they place a good deal of importance on the value of their own clinical experience. Often physicians consider their own observations of the patient to be more valuable than the reports by the patient. Since patients commonly go to physicians to solve a particular condition or sickness, physicians tend to try to do something about it even in the face of uncertainty. Physicians tend to rely on technology for diagnoses and treatment and place relatively low value on talking with patients. In fact, physicians tend to give patients relatively little information, and they may not listen very well.[49]

Despite the importance of physicians in biomedicine, patients do not always seek physician care. In fact, one-third of the population of the United States regularly consults with alternative practitioners, such as acupuncturists or chiropractors, often unbeknown to the physician. Somewhat surprisingly, individuals with more education are more likely to seek alternative care.[50]

A Navajo medicine man performs a healing ceremony involving a snake painted on the ground.

Political and Economic Influences on Health

People with more social, economic, and political power in a society are generally healthier.[51] Inequality in health in socially stratified societies is not surprising. The poor usually have more exposure to disease because they live in more crowded conditions. And the poor are more likely to lack the resources to get quality care. For many diseases, health problems, and death rates, incidence or relative frequency varies directly with social class. In the United Kingdom, for example, people in the higher social classes are less likely to have headaches, bronchitis, pneumonia, heart disease, arthritis, injuries, and mental disorders, to name just a few of the differences.[52] Ethnic differences also predict health inequities. In South Africa under apartheid, the 14 percent minority population, referred to as "white," controlled most of the income of the country and most of the high-quality land. "Blacks" were restricted to areas with shortages of housing, inadequate housing, and little employment. To get a job, families often had to be disrupted; usually the husband would have to migrate to find work. "Blacks" lived, on average, about nine years less than "whites" in 1985 and "black" infants died at about seven times the rate of "white" infants. In the United States recently, the differences between African Americans and European Americans in health are not as stark as in South Africa, but those favoring European Americans are still substantial. As of 2004, the difference in life expectancy was approximately five years, and African-American infant mortality was about twice the rate for European American infants. Robert Hahn has estimated that poverty accounts for about 19 percent of the overall mortality in the United States.[53]

Inequities, because of class and ethnicity, are not limited to within-society differences. Power and economic differentials *between* societies also have profound health consequences. Over the course of European exploration and expansion, indigenous peoples died in enormous numbers from introduced diseases, wars, and conquests; they had their lands expropriated and diminished in size and quality. When incorporated into colonial territories or into countries, indigenous people usually become minorities and they are almost always very poor. These conditions of life not only affect the incidence of disease, they also tend to lead to greater substance abuse, violence, depression, and other mental pathologies.[54] Medical anthropologists have studied an enormous variety of health conditions and diseases. We focus here on AIDS and undernutrition.

AIDS

We may think that epidemics are a thing of the past. But the sudden emergence of the disease we call **AIDS (acquired immune deficiency syndrome)** reminds us that new diseases, or new varieties of old diseases, can appear at any time. Like all other organisms, disease-causing organisms also evolve. The human immunodeficiency virus (HIV) that causes AIDS emerged only a couple of decades ago. Viruses and bacteria are always mutating, and new strains emerge that are initially a plague on our genetic resistance and on medical efforts to contain them.

AIDS is a leading cause of death of people between the ages of 25 and 44 in the United States and Western Europe. It is the leading cause of adult death in many countries as well.[55] AIDS is a frightening epidemic not only because of its death toll. It is also frightening because it takes a long time (on average, four years) after exposure for symptoms to appear. This means that many people who have been infected by HIV but do not know they are infected may continue, unknowingly, to transmit the virus to others.[56]

Transmission occurs mostly via sexual encounters, through semen and blood. Drug users may also transmit HIV by way of contaminated needles. Transmission by blood transfusion has been virtually eliminated in this and other societies by medical screening of blood supplies. In many countries, however, there is still no routine screening of blood prior to transfusions. HIV may be passed from a pregnant woman to her offspring through the placenta and after birth through her breast milk. The rate of transmission between a mother and her baby is 20 to 40 percent. Children are also at great risk because they are likely to be orphaned by a parent's death from AIDS. At the turn of the twenty-first century approximately 14 million children were parentless because of AIDS.[57]

Many people think of AIDS as only a medical problem that requires only a medical solution, without realizing that there are behavioral, cultural, and political issues that need to be addressed as well. It is true that developing a vaccine or a drug to prevent people from getting AIDS and finding a permanent cure for those who have it will finally solve the problem. But, for a variety of reasons, we can expect that the medical solution alone will not be sufficient, at least not for a while. First, to be effective worldwide, or even within a country, a vaccine has to be inexpensive and relatively easy to produce in large quantities; the same is true of any medical treatment. Second, governments around the world have to be willing and able to spend the money and hire the personnel necessary to manage an effective program.[58] Third, future vaccination and treatment will require the people at risk to be willing to get vaccinated and treated, which is not always the case. Witness the fact that the incidence of measles is on the rise in the United States because many people are not having their children vaccinated.

There are now expensive drug treatments that significantly reduce the degree of HIV infection, but we do not know if an effective and inexpensive vaccine or treatment will be developed soon. In the meantime, the risk of HIV infection can be reduced only by changes in social, particularly sexual, behavior. But to persuade people to change their sexual behavior, it is necessary to find out exactly what they do sexually, and why they do what they do.

Research so far suggests that different sexual patterns are responsible for HIV transmission in different parts of the world. In the United States, England, northern Europe, Australia, and Latin America, the recipients of anal intercourse, particularly men, are the most likely individuals to acquire HIV infection; vaginal intercourse can also transmit the infection, usually from the man to the woman. Needle sharing can transmit the infection, too. In Africa, the most common mode of transmission is vaginal intercourse, and so women get infected more commonly in Africa than elsewhere.[59] In fact, in Africa there are slightly more cases of HIV in women as compared with men.[60]

A neighborhood self-help group in Tamil Nadu, India, collects rice for people with HIV and AIDS. Each member of the group puts aside one handful of rice every time she cooks a meal. The group members also contribute money to pay for drugs to treat neighbors with HIV and AIDs.

·As of now, there are only two known ways to reduce the likelihood of sexual HIV transmission. One way is to abstain from sexual intercourse; the other is to use condoms. Educational programs that teach how AIDS spreads and what one can do about it may reduce the spread somewhat, but such programs may fail where people have incompatible beliefs and attitudes about sexuality. For example, people in some central African societies believe that deposits of semen after conception are necessary for a successful pregnancy and generally enhance a woman's health and ability to reproduce. It might be expected then that people who have these beliefs about semen would choose not to use condoms; after all, condoms in their view are a threat to public health.[61] Educational programs may also emphasize the wrong message. Promiscuity may increase the risk of HIV transmission, so hardly anyone would question the wisdom of advertising to reduce the number of sexual partners. And, at least in the homosexual community in the United States, individuals report fewer sexual partners than in the past. What was not anticipated, however, was that individuals in monogamous relationships, who may feel safe, are less likely to use condoms or to avoid the riskiest sexual practices. Needless to say, sex with a regular partner who is infected is not safe![62] In what may seem like something of a paradox, the United Nations observed that for most women in the world today, the major risk factor for being infected with HIV is being married.[63] It is not marriage, *per se,* that causes the risk of HIV infection; rather, the proximate cause may be the lower likelihood of condom use or abstinence between a husband and wife.

Undernutrition

What people eat is intrinsically connected to their survival and the ability of a population to reproduce itself, so we would expect that the ways people obtain, distribute, and consume food have been generally adaptive.[64] For example, the human body cannot synthesize eight amino acids. Meat can provide all of these amino acids, and combinations of particular plants can also provide them for a complete complement of protein. The combination of maize and beans in many traditional Native American diets, or *tortillas* and *frijoles* in Mexico, can provide all the needed amino acids. In places where wheat (often made into bread) is the staple, dairy products combined with wheat also provide complete protein.[65] Even the way that people have prepared for scarcity, such as breaking up into mobile bands, cultivating crops that can better withstand drought, and preserving food in case of famine, are probably adaptive practices in unpredictable environments. As we saw in the feature box on obesity, hypertension, and diabetes in the chapter on culture change and globalization, geneticists have proposed that populations in famine-prone areas may have had genetic selection for "thrifty genes"— genes that allow individuals to need a minimum of food and store the extra in fatty tissue to get them past serious scarcity.

Often the switch to commercial or cash crops has harmful effects on nutrition. As we noted in the chapter on culture change and globalization, when the farmer-herders of the arid region in northeastern Brazil started growing sisal, a drought-resistant plant used for making twine and rope, many of them abandoned subsistence agriculture. The small landholders used most of their land for sisal growing and when the price of sisal fell they had to work as laborers for others to try to make ends meet. Food then had to be mostly bought, but if a laborer or sisal grower didn't earn enough, there was not enough food for the whole family.

Analysis of allocation of food in some households by Daniel Gross and Barbara Underwood suggests that the laborer and his wife received adequate nutrition, but the children often received much less than required. Lack of adequate nutrition usually results in retarded weight and height in children. As is commonly the case when there is substantial social inequality, the children from lower-income

Cultures differ in what is considered beautiful. In many cultures, fat people are deemed more beautiful than thin people. Melvin Ember did fieldwork years ago on the islands of American Samoa. When he returned to the main island after three months on a distant island, he met with a Samoan chief. The chief said: "You look good. You gained weight." In reality, Ember had lost 30 pounds. The chief did not remember how heavy Ember had been, but clearly he thought that fat was better than thin. As another example, the Azawagh Arabs of Niger ensure that young girls become fat by sometimes forcing them to drink large quantities of milk-based porridge.

Worldwide, fatness is generally deemed more desirable than thinness, particularly for women. Fatness is valued in many cultures because it is seen as a marker of health, fertility, and higher status in societies with social stratification. This view is in strong contrast to the ideal in the United States and other Western societies, where fatness is thought to be unattractive and to reflect laziness, a lack of self-control, and poor health. Thinness, particularly in the upper classes, is considered beautiful. How can we explain these differences in what is considered beautiful?

People who have efficient metabolisms and can store calories in fatty tissue may be most apt to survive and reproduce in environments with famines or food shortages, so natural selection may favor "thrifty genes" in such environments. Would such societies also be likely to value fatness? Recent cross-cultural research suggests something more complicated. It appears that societies with unpredictable resources actually value thinness, particularly when they have no way of storing food. Shouldn't someone who stores calories on the body be better off than someone who is thin when facing starvation, particularly if there is no food storage? Perhaps, but ten thin people will generally consume less than ten heavier people, so there is a group advantage to being thin. Indeed, many societies with famine encourage fasting or eating light meals, as among the Gurage of Ethiopia. The strongest cross-cultural predictor of valuing fatness in women is "machismo" or "protest masculinity." Societies with a strong emphasis on male aggression, strength, and sexuality are the most likely to value fatness in women; those with little machismo value thinness. Why machismo is associated with valuing fatness in women is not clear. One suggestion is that machismo reflects male insecurity and fear of women. Macho men may not look for intimacy with their wives, but they may want to show how potent they are by having many children. If fatness suggests fertility, men may look for wives who are fatter. Along these lines, the ideal of thinness in women became common in North America with the rise of women's movements in the 1920s and late 1960s. Thin became more popular when women began to question early marriage and having many children.

Cultural beliefs about what is a beautiful body can impose pressures on females to achieve the ideal body type, whether it be fat or thin. In the United States and other Western countries, the effort to be thin can be carried to an extreme, resulting in the eating disorders anorexia and bulimia. Those who have these often fatal illnesses regularly eat little and regularly force themselves to throw up, thus depriving their bodies of nutrients in their quest to be thinner. The irony of "thinness" being idealized in the United States and other Western countries is that obesity is becoming more common in those societies. In 2001 the incidence of obesity increased in the United States to 31 percent and medical researchers worried about the increase in heart disease and diabetes. Whether or not obesity is a result of eating disorders is debatable. Researchers are finding biological causes of obesity, such as resistance to the hormone leptin, which regulates appetite, suggesting that much of the obesity "epidemic" has biological causes. Still, fast food, increasing sedentariness, and large portion sizes are probably contributing factors.

Sources: Peter J. Brown, "Culture and the Evolution of Obesity," in Aaron Podolefsky and Peter J. Brown, eds., *Applying Cultural Anthropology*, 4th ed. (Mountain View, CA: Mayfield, 1999), p. 100; Martha O. Loustaunau and Elisa J. Sobo, *The Cultural Context of Health, Illness, and Medicine* (Westport, CT: Bergin and Garvey, 1997), p. 85; Naomi Wolf, *The Beauty Myth* (New York: Morrow, 1991); Rebecca Popenoe, *Feeding Desire* (London: Routledge, 2004); Carol R. Ember, Melvin Ember, Andrey Korotayev, and Victor de Munck, "Valuing Thinness or Fatness in Women," *Evolution and Human Behavior*, 26 (2005): 257–70; J. L. Anderson, C. B. Crawford, J. Nadeau, and T. Lindberg, "Was the Duchess of Windsor Right?" *Ethology and Sociobiology*, 13 (1992): 197–227; Jeffrey M. Friedman, "A War on Obesity, Not the Obese," *Science* (February 7, 2003), pp. 856–58.

Shown here is a sisal plant in Bahia, Brazil. The switch to sisal production led to undernutrition in children.

groups weigh substantially less than those from higher-income groups. But even though there were some economic differences before sisal production, the effects on nutrition appeared negligible before, judging from the fact that there was little or no difference in weight among adults from higher and lower socioeconomic positions who grew up prior to sisal production. But more recently, 45 percent of the children from lower economic groups were undernourished as compared with 23 percent of those children from the higher economic groups.[66]

This is not to say that commercialization is always deleterious to adequate nutrition. For example, in the Highlands of New Guinea there is evidence that the nutrition of children improved when families started growing coffee for sale. However, in this case the families still had land to grow some crops for consumption. The extra money earned from coffee enabled them to buy canned fish and rice, which provided children with higher amounts of protein than the usual staple of sweet potatoes.[67]

Nutritional imbalances for females have a far-reaching impact on reproduction and the health of the infants they bear. In some cultures, the lower status of women has a direct bearing on their access to food. While the custom of feeding males first is well known, it is less often realized that females end up with less nutrient-dense food such as meat. Deprivation of food sometimes starts in infancy where girl babies, as in India, are weaned earlier than boy babies.[68] Parents may be unaware that their differential weaning practice has the effect of reducing the amount of high-quality protein that girl infants receive. Indeed, in Ecuador, Lauris McKee found that parents thought that earlier weaning of girls was helpful to them. They believed that mothers' milk transmitted sexuality and aggression, both ideal male traits, to their infants and so it was important that girl babies be weaned early. Mothers weaned their girls at about 11 months and their boys about 20 months, a 9-month difference. McKee found that girl infants had a significantly higher mortality than boy infants in their second year of life, suggesting that the earlier weaning time for girls and their probable undernutrition may have been responsible.[69]

Applied and practicing anthropologists are not the only ones interested in solving problems. Many researchers in anthropology and the other social sciences do *basic research* on social problems. Such research may involve fieldwork to get a broad understanding of cultural ideas and practices about health, illness, or violence. Or basic research may involve testing theories about the possible causes of specific problems. The results of such tests could suggest solutions to the problems if the causes, once discovered, can be reduced or eliminated. It is often the case that basic research has unintended payoffs. Even if a study is not directed to a practical problem, it may end up suggesting a solution.

Summary

1. Applied, or practicing, anthropologists may be involved in one or more phases of programs that are designed to change peoples' lives: assembling relevant knowledge, constructing alternative plans, assessing the likely social and environmental impact of particular plans, implementing the programs, and monitoring the programs and their effects. Today many anthropologists are finding employment outside of anthropology departments—in medical schools, health centers, development agencies, urban-planning agencies, and other public and private organizations.

2. The code of ethics for those who work professionally as applied anthropologists specifies that the target population should be included as much as possible in the formulation of policy. The most important aspect of the code is the pledge not to be involved in any plan whose effect will not be beneficial. It is often difficult to evaluate the effects of planned changes. Long-term consequences may be detrimental even if the changes are beneficial in the short run.

3. Even if a planned change will prove beneficial to its target population, the people may not accept it. Target populations may reject or resist a proposed innovation for various reasons: because they are unaware of the need for the change; because they misinterpret the symbols used to explain the change or fail to understand its real purpose; because their customs and institutions conflict with the change; because they are afraid of it; or because they unconsciously or consciously know it is not good for them. To be effective, change agents may have to discover and use the traditional channels of influence in introducing their projects to the target population.

4. Cultural resource management (CRM) usually takes the form of "contract archaeology" to record and/or conserve the archaeology of a building site.

5. Forensic anthropology is the use of anthropology to help solve crimes.

6. Medical anthropologists suggest that biological and social factors need to be considered if we are to understand how to treat illness effectively and reduce the suffering in human life.

7. Researchers are finding evidence that many of the plant remedies used by indigenous peoples contain chemicals that are the same as, or similar in effect to, chemicals used in remedies by Western biomedicine.

8. People with more social, economic, and political power in a society are generally healthier.

9. Many people think of AIDS as only a medical problem that requires only a medical solution, without realizing that there are behavioral, cultural, and political issues that need to be addressed as well. It is true that developing a vaccine or a drug to prevent people from getting AIDS and finding a permanent cure for those who have it will finally solve the problem.

10. The ways that people obtain, distribute, and consume food have been generally adaptive. Geneticists have proposed that populations in famine-prone areas may have had genetic selection for "thrifty genes." Many of the serious nutritional problems of today are due to rapid culture change, particularly those making for an increasing degree of social inequality.

Glossary Terms

AIDS (acquired immune deficiency
    syndrome) (p. 450)
biomedicine (p. 447)
cultural resource management (CRM) (p. 436)

ethnomedicine (p. 444)
forensic anthropology (p. 436)
medical anthropology (p. 436)

Critical Questions

1. What particular advantages do anthropologists have in trying to solve practical problems?

2. Is it ethical to try to influence people's lives when they have not asked for help? Explain your answer.

3. If you were interested in solving a practical problem, would you do basic or applied research on the problem? Why?

4. Do people get sick just because they are exposed to germs?

5. Why do native remedies often contain chemicals that are the same as, or similar in effect to, chemicals used in remedies by Western biomedicine?

GLOSSARY

Absolute dating A method of dating fossils in which the actual age of a deposit or specimen is measured. Also known as *chronometric dating*.

Accent Differences in pronunciation characteristic of a group.

Acclimatization Impermanent physiological changes that people make when they encounter a new environment.

Acculturation The process of extensive borrowing of aspects of culture in the context of superordinate-subordinate relations between societies; usually occurs as the result of external pressure.

Acheulian A stone toolmaking tradition dating from 1.5 million years ago. Compared with the Oldowan tradition, Acheulian assemblages have more large tools created according to standardized designs or shapes. One of the most characteristic and prevalent tools in the Acheulian tool kit is the so-called hand axe, which is a teardrop-shaped bifacially flaked tool with a thinned sharp tip. Other large tools might have been cleavers and picks.

Adapid A type of prosimian with many lemur-like features; appeared in the early Eocene.

Adaptation Refers to genetic changes that allow an organism to survive and reproduce in a specific environment.

Adaptive customs Customs that enhance survival and reproductive success in a particular environment. Usually applied to biological evolution, the term is also often used by cultural anthropologists to refer to cultural traits that enhance reproductive success.

Adjudication The process by which a third party acting as judge makes a decision that the parties to a dispute have to accept.

Aegyptopithecus An Oligocene anthropoid and probably the best-known propliopithecid.

Agriculture The practice of raising domesticated crops.

AIDS (Acquired Immune Deficiency Syndrome) A disease caused by the HIV virus.

Allele One member of a pair of genes.

Allen's rule The rule that protruding body parts (particularly arms and legs) are relatively shorter in the cooler areas of a species' range than in the warmer areas.

Ambilineal descent The rule of descent that affiliates an individual with groups of kin related to him or her through men or women.

Ancestor spirits Supernatural beings who are the ghosts of dead relatives.

Anthropoids One of the two suborders of primates; includes monkeys, apes, and humans.

Anthropological linguistics The anthropological study of languages.

Anthropology A discipline that studies humans, focusing on the study of differences and similarities, both biological and cultural, in human populations. Anthropology is concerned with typical biological and cultural characteristics of human populations in all periods and in all parts of the world.

Applied (practicing) anthropology The branch of anthropology that concerns itself with applying anthropological knowledge to achieve practical goals, usually in the service of an agency outside the traditional academic setting.

^{40}Ar–^{39}Ar dating Used in conjunction with potassium-argon dating, this method gets around the problem of needing different rock samples to estimate potassium and argon. A nuclear reactor is used to convert the ^{39}Ar to ^{39}K, on the basis of which the amount of ^{40}K can be estimated. In this way, both argon and potassium can be estimated from the same rock sample.

Arboreal Adapted to living in trees.

Archaeology The branch of anthropology that seeks to reconstruct the daily life and customs of peoples who lived in the past and to trace and explain cultural changes. Often lacking written records for study, archaeologists must try to reconstruct history from the material remains of human cultures. See also **Historical archaeology**.

Archaic Time period in the New World during which food production first developed.

Ardipithecus ramidus Perhaps the first hominid, dating to about 4.5 million years ago. Its dentition combines ape-like and australopithecine-like features, and its skeleton suggests it was bipedal.

Artifact Any object made by a human.

Atlatl Aztec word for "spear-thrower."

Australopithecus   Genus of Pliocene and Pleistocene hominids.

Australopithecus aethiopicus   An early robust australopithecine.

Australopithecus afarensis   A species of *Australopithecus* that lived 4 million to 3 million years ago in East Africa and was definitely bipedal.

Australopithecus africanus   A species of *Australopithecus* that lived between about 3 million and 2 million years ago.

Australopithecus anamensis   A species of *Australopithecus* that lived perhaps 4.2 million years ago.

Australopithecus bahrelghazali   An early gracile australopithecine, dating to about 3 million years ago, and currently represented by only a single jaw. It is an interesting species because it is found in western Chad, distant from the East African Rift Valley where all other early australopithecines have been found.

Australopithecus boisei   An East African robust australopithecine species dating from 2.2 million to 1.3 million years ago with somewhat larger cranial capacity than *A. africanus*. No longer thought to be larger than other australopithecines, it is robust primarily in the skull and jaw, most strikingly in the teeth. Compared with *A. robustus*, *A. boisei* has even more features that reflect a huge chewing apparatus.

Australopithecus garhi   A gracile australopithecine, dating to about 2.5 million years ago.

Australopithecus robustus   A robust australopithecine species found in South African caves dating from about 1.8 million to 1 million years ago. Not as large in the teeth and jaws as *A. boisei*.

Avunculocal residence   A pattern of residence in which a married couple settles with or near the husband's mother's brother.

Balanced reciprocity   Giving with the expectation of a straightforward immediate or limited-time trade.

Balancing selection   A type of selection that occurs when a heterozygous combination of alleles is positively favored even though a homozygous combination is disfavored.

Band   A fairly small, usually nomadic local group that is politically autonomous.

Band organization   The kind of political organization where the local group or band is the largest territorial group in the society that acts as a unit.

Behavioral ecology   The study of how all kinds of behavior may be related to the environment. The theoretical orientation involves the application of biological evolutionary principles to the behavior (including social behavior) of animals, including humans. Also called sociobiology, particularly when applied to social organization and social behavior.

Bergmann's rule   The rule that smaller-sized subpopulations of a species inhabit the warmer parts of its geographic range and larger-sized subpopulations the cooler areas.

Bifacial tool   A tool worked or flaked on two sides.

Bilateral kinship   The type of kinship system in which individuals affiliate more or less equally with their mother's and father's relatives.

Bilocal residence   A pattern of residence in which a married couple lives with or near either the husband's parents or the wife's parents.

Bilophodont   Having four cusps on the molars that form two parallel ridges. This is the common molar pattern of Old World monkeys.

Biological (physical) anthropology   The study of humans as biological organisms, dealing with the emergence and evolution of humans and with contemporary biological variations among human populations.

Biomedicine   The dominant medical paradigm in Western societies today.

Bipedalism   Locomotion in which an animal walks on its two hind legs.

Blade   A thin flake whose length is usually more than twice its width. In the blade technique of toolmaking, a core is prepared by shaping a piece of flint with hammerstones into a pyramidal or cylindrical form. Blades are then struck off until the core is used up.

Brachiators   Animals that move through the trees by swinging hand over hand from branch to branch. They usually have long arms and fingers.

Bride price (or Bride wealth)   A substantial gift of goods or money given to the bride's kin by the groom or his kin at or before the marriage.

Bride service   Work performed by the groom for his bride's family for a variable length of time either before or after the marriage.

Burin   A chisel-like stone tool used for carving and for making such artifacts as bone and antler needles, awls, and projectile points.

Canines   The cone-shaped teeth immediately behind the incisors; used by most primates to seize food and in fighting and display.

Carpolestes   A mouse-sized arboreal creature living about 56 million years ago; a strong candidate for the common primate ancestor.

Caste   A ranked group, often associated with a certain occupation, in which membership is determined at birth and marriage is restricted to members of one's own caste.

Catarrhines   The group of anthropoids with narrow noses and nostrils that face downward. Catarrhines include monkeys of the Old World (Africa, Asia, and Europe), as well as apes and humans.

Ceramics   Objects shaped from clay and baked at high temperature (fired) to make them hard. Containers such as pots and jars are typical ceramics, though they can take on many forms and uses.

Cercopithecoids   Old World monkeys.

Cerebral cortex   The "gray matter" of the brain; the center of speech and other higher mental activities.

Chief   A person who exercises authority, usually on behalf of a multicommunity political unit. This role is generally found in rank societies and is usually permanent and often hereditary.

Chiefdom   A political unit, with a chief at its head, integrating more than one community but not necessarily the whole society or language group.

Chromosomes   Paired rod-shaped structures within a cell nucleus containing the genes that transmit traits from one generation to the next.

Chronometric dating   See **Absolute dating**.

Civilization   Urban society, from the Latin word for "city-state."

Clan   A set of kin whose members believe themselves to be descended from a common ancestor or ancestress but cannot specify the links back to that founder; often designated by a totem. Also called a *sib*.

Class   A category of persons who have about the same opportunity to obtain economic resources, power, and prestige.

Class society   A society containing social groups that have unequal access to economic resources, power, and prestige.

Cline   The gradually increasing (or decreasing) frequency of a gene from one end of a region to another.

Codeswitching   Using more than one language in the course of conversing.

Codified laws   Formal principles for resolving disputes in heterogeneous and stratified societies.

Commercialization   The increasing dependence on buying and selling, with money usually as the medium of exchange.

Compatibility-with-child-care theory   An explanation for the gender division of labor that suggests that women's work will typically involve tasks that do not take women far from home for long periods, do not place children in potential danger if they are taken along, and can be stopped and resumed if an infant needs care.

Complementary opposition   The occasional uniting of various segments of a segmentary lineage system in opposition to similar segments.

Conservation   Techniques used on archaeological materials to stop or reverse the process of decay.

Context   The relationships between and among artifacts, ecofacts, fossils, and features.

Continental drift   The movement of the continents over the past 135 million years. In the early Cretaceous (ca. 135 million years ago) there were two "supercontinents": *Laurasia*, which included North America and Eurasia; and *Gondwanaland*, which included Africa, South America, India, Australia, and Antarctica. By the beginning of the Paleocene (ca. 65 million years ago), Gondwanaland had broken apart, with South America drifting west away from Africa, India drifting east, and Australia and Antarctica drifting south.

Core vocabulary   Nonspecialist vocabulary.

Corvée   A system of required labor.

Cretaceous   Geological epoch 135 million to 65 million years ago, during which dinosaurs and other reptiles ceased to be the dominant land vertebrates, and mammals and birds began to become important.

Crime   Violence not considered legitimate that occurs within a political unit.

Cro-magnons   Humans who lived in western Europe about 35,000 years ago. Once thought to be the earliest specimens of modern-looking humans, or *Homo sapiens sapiens*. But it is now known that modern-looking humans appeared earlier outside of Europe; the earliest so far found lived in Africa.

Cross-cousins   Children of siblings of the opposite sex. One's cross-cousins are father's sisters' children and mother's brothers' children.

Cross-cultural researcher   An ethnologist who uses ethnographic data about many societies to test possible explanations of cultural variation to discover general patterns about cultural traits—what is universal, what is variable, why traits vary, and what the consequences of the variability might be.

Crossing-over   Exchanges of sections of chromosomes from one chromosome to another.

Cultural anthropology   The study of cultural variation and universals in the past and present.

Cultural relativism   The attitude that a society's customs and ideas should be viewed within the context of that society's problems and opportunities.

Cultural resource management (CRM)   The branch of applied anthropology that seeks to recover and preserve the archaeological record before programs of planned change disturb or destroy it.

Culture   The set of learned behaviors, beliefs, attitudes, values, and ideals that are characteristic of a particular society or other social group.

Culture history   A history of the cultures that lived in a given area over time. Until the 1950s, building such culture histories was a primary goal of archaeological research.

Cuneiform   Wedge-shaped writing invented by the Sumerians around 3000 B.C.

Descriptive or structural linguistics   The study of how languages are constructed.

Dialect   A variety of a language spoken in a particular area or by a particular social group.

Diastema   A gap between the canine and first premolar found in apes.

Diffusion   The borrowing by one society of a cultural trait belonging to another society as the result of contact between the two societies.

Directional selection   A type of natural selection that increases the frequency of a trait (the trait is said to be positively favored, or adaptive).

Diurnal   Active during the day.

Divination   Getting the supernatural to provide guidance.

DNA   Deoxyribonucleic acid; a long, two-stranded molecule in the genes that directs the makeup of an organism according to the instructions in its genetic code.

Domestication   Modification or adaptation of plants and animals for use by humans. When people plant crops, we refer to the process as cultivation. It is only when the crops cultivated and the animals raised have been modified—are different from wild varieties—that we speak of plant and animal domestication.

Dominant   The allele of a gene pair that is always phenotypically expressed in the heterozygous form.

Double descent or double unilineal descent   A system that affiliates an individual with a group of matrilineal kin for some purposes and with a group of patrilineal kin for other purposes.

Dowry   A substantial transfer of goods or money from the bride's family to the bride.

Dryopithecus   Genus of ape from the later Miocene found primarily in Europe. It had thin tooth enamel and pointed molar-cusps very similar to those of the fruit-eating chimpanzees of today.

Ecofacts   Natural items that have been used by humans. Things such as the remains of animals eaten by humans or plant pollens found on archaeological sites are examples of ecofacts.

Economic resources   Things that have value in a culture, including land, tools and other technology, goods, and money.

Economy-of-effort theory   An explanation for the gender division of labor that suggests that it may be advantageous for a gender to do tasks that follow in a production sequence (e.g., those who cut lumber make wooden objects; those who quarry stone make stone objects); it may also be advantageous for one gender to perform tasks that are located near each other (e.g., child care and other chores done in or near the home).

Egalitarian society   A society in which all persons of a given age-sex category have equal access to economic resources, power, and prestige.

Ego   In the reckoning of kinship, the reference point or focal person.

Electron spin resonance dating   Like thermoluminescence dating, this technique measures trapped electrons from surrounding radioactive material. The material to be dated is exposed to varying magnetic fields in order to obtain a spectrum of the microwaves absorbed by the tested material. Because heat is not required for this technique, electron spin resonance is especially useful for dating organic materials, such as bone and shell, that decompose if heated.

Endogamy   The rule specifying marriage to a person within one's own group (kin, caste, community).

Eocene   A geological epoch 55 million to 34 million years ago during which the first definite primates appeared.

Epipaleolithic   Time period during which food production first developed in the Near East.

Ethnicity   The process of defining ethnicity usually involves a group of people emphasizing common origins and language, shared history, and selected aspects of cultural difference such as a difference in religion. Since different groups are doing the perceiving, ethnic identities often vary with whether one is inside or outside the group.

Ethnocentric   Refers to judgment of other cultures solely in terms of one's own culture.

Ethnocentrism   The attitude that other societies' customs and ideas can be judged in the context of one's own culture.

Ethnogenesis   Creation of a new culture.

Ethnographer   A person who spends some time living with, interviewing, and observing a group of people to describe their customs.

Ethnographic analogy   Method of comparative cultural study that extrapolates to the past from recent or current societies.

Ethnography   A description of a society's customary behaviors, and ideas.

Ethnohistorian   An ethnologist who uses historical documents to study how a particular culture has changed over time.

Ethnology   The study of how and why recent cultures differ and are similar.

Ethnomedicine   The health-related beliefs, knowledge, and practices of a cultural group.

Evolutionary psychology   The study of how evolution may have produced lasting variation in the way humans behave, interact, and perceive the world.

Exogamy   The rule specifying marriage to a person from outside one's own group (kin or community).

Expendability theory   An explanation for the gender division of labor that suggests that men, rather than women, will tend to do the dangerous work in a society because the loss of men is less disadvantageous reproductively than the loss of women.

Explanation   An answer to a *why* question. In science, there are two kinds of explanation that researchers try to achieve: associations and theories.

Extended family   A family consisting of two or more single-parent monogamous, polygynous, or polyandrous families linked by a blood tie.

Extensive or shifting cultivation   A type of horticulture in which the land is worked for short periods and then left to regenerate for some years before being used again.

Family   A social and economic unit consisting minimally of a parent and a child.

Fayum   A site southwest of Cairo, Egypt, where the world's best record of Oligocene primate fossils has been found.

Features   Artifacts of human manufacture that cannot be removed from an archaeological site. Hearths, storage pits, and buildings are examples of features.

Feuding   A state of recurring hostility between families or groups of kin, usually motivated by a desire to avenge an offense against a member of the group.

Fieldwork   Firsthand experience with the people being studied and the usual means by which anthropological information is obtained. Regardless of other methods (e.g., censuses, surveys) that anthropologists may use, fieldwork usually involves participant-observation for an extended period of time, often a year or more. See **Participant-observation**.

Fission-track dating   A chronometric dating method used to date crystal, glass, and many uranium-rich materials contemporary with fossils or deposits that are from 20 billion to 5 billion years old. This dating method entails counting the tracks or paths of decaying uranium-isotope atoms in the sample and then comparing the number of tracks with the uranium content of the sample.

Food collection   All forms of subsistence technology in which food-getting is dependent on naturally occurring resources—wild plants and animals.

Food production   The form of subsistence technology in which food-getting is dependent on the cultivation and domestication of plants and animals.

Foragers   People who subsist on the collection of naturally occurring plants and animals. Also referred to as *hunter-gatherers* or *food collectors*.

Foramen magnum   Opening in the base of the skull through which the spinal cord passes en route to the brain.

Forensic anthropology   The use of anthropology to help solve crimes.

Fossils   The hardened remains or impressions of plants and animals that lived in the past.

Gender differences   Differences between females and males that reflect cultural expectations and experiences.

Gender roles   Roles that are culturally assigned to genders.

Gender stratification   The degree of unequal access by the different genders to prestige, authority, power, rights, and economic resources.

Gene   Chemical unit of heredity.

Gene flow   The process by which genes pass from the gene pool of one population to that of another through mating and reproduction.

Generalized reciprocity   Gift giving without any immediate or planned return.

General-purpose money   A universally accepted medium of exchange.

Genetic drift   The various random processes that affect gene frequencies in small, relatively isolated populations.

Genotype   The total complement of inherited traits or genes of an organism.

Genus   A group of related species; pl., genera.

Ghosts   Supernatural beings who were once human; the souls of dead people.

Globalization   The ongoing spread of goods, people, information, and capital around the world.

Gloger's rule   The rule that populations of birds and mammals living in warm, humid climates have more melanin (and therefore darker skin, fur, or feathers) than populations of the same species living in cooler, drier areas.

Gods   Supernatural beings of nonhuman origin who are named personalities; often anthropomorphic.

Gracile australopithecines   The earliest group of australopithecines, usually differentiated from the robust australopithecines by their lighter dentition and smaller faces.

Group marriage   Marriage in which more than one man is married to more than one woman at the same time; not customary in any known human society.

Half-life   The time it takes for half of the atoms of a radioactive substance to decay into atoms of a different substance.

Hand axe   A teardrop-shaped stone tool characteristic of Acheulian assemblages.

Hard hammer   A technique of stone tool manufacture where one stone is used to knock flakes from another stone. Flakes produced through hard hammer percussion are usually large and crude.

Headman   A person who holds a powerless but symbolically unifying position in a community within an egalitarian society; may exercise influence but has no power to impose sanctions.

Heterozygous   Possessing differing genes or alleles in corresponding locations on a pair of chromosomes.

Hieroglyphics   "Picture writing," as in ancient Egypt and in Mayan sites in Mesoamerica (Mexico and Central America).

Historical archaeology   A specialty within archaeology that studies the material remains of recent peoples who left written records.

Historical linguistics   The study of how languages change over time.

Holistic   Refers to an approach that studies many aspects of a multifaceted system.

Hominids   The group of hominoids consisting of humans and their direct ancestors. It contains at least two genera: *Homo* and *Australopithecus*.

Hominoids   The group of catarrhines that includes both apes and humans.

Homo erectus   The first hominid species to be widely distributed in the Old World. The earliest finds are possibly 1.8 million years old. The brain (averaging 895–1,040 cc) was larger than that found in any of the australopithecines or *H. habilis* but smaller than the average brain of a modern human.

Homo floresiensis   A small-bodied species related to *Homo erectus*, found only on the Indonesian island of Flores.

Homo habilis   Early species belonging to our genus, *Homo*, with cranial capacities averaging about 630–640 cc, about 50 percent of the brain capacity of modern humans. Dating from about 2 million years ago.

Homo heidelbergensis   A transitional species between *Homo erectus* and *Homo sapiens*.

Homo neandertalensis   The technical name for the Neandertals, a group of robust and otherwise anatomically distinct hominids that are close relatives of modern humans—so close that some believe they should be classified as *Homo sapiens neandertalensis*.

Homo rudolfensis   Early species belonging to our genus, *Homo*. Similar enough to *Homo habilis* that some paleoanthropologists make no distinction between the two.

Homo sapiens   All living people belong to one biological species, *Homo sapiens*, which means that all human populations on earth can successfully interbreed. The first *Homo sapiens* may have emerged by 200,000 years ago.

Homo sapiens sapiens   Modern-looking humans, undisputed examples of which appeared about 50,000 years ago; may have appeared earlier.

Homozygous   Possessing two identical genes or alleles in corresponding locations on a pair of chromosomes.

Horticulture   Plant cultivation carried out with relatively simple tools and methods; nature is allowed to replace nutrients in the soil, in the absence of permanently cultivated fields.

Human paleontology   The study of the emergence of humans and their later physical evolution. Also called *paleoanthropology*.

Human variation   The study of how and why contemporary human populations vary biologically.

Hunter-gatherers   People who collect food from naturally occurring resources, that is, wild plants, animals, and fish. The phrase *hunter-gatherers* minimizes sometimes heavy dependence on fishing. Also referred to as *foragers* or *food collectors*.

Hybridization   The creation of a viable offspring from the mating of two different species.

Hylobates   The family of hominoids that includes gibbons and siamangs; often referred to as the lesser apes (as compared with the great apes such as gorillas and chimpanzees).

Hypotheses Predictions, which may be derived from theories, about how variables are related.

Hypoxia A condition of oxygen deficiency that often occurs at high altitudes. The percentage of oxygen in the air is the same as at lower altitudes, but because the barometric pressure is lower, less oxygen is taken in with each breath. Often, breathing becomes more rapid, the heart beats faster, and activity is more difficult.

Incest taboo Prohibition of sexual intercourse or marriage between mother and son, father and daughter, and brother and sister.

Incisors The front teeth; used for holding or seizing food and preparing it for chewing by the other teeth.

Indirect dowry Goods given by the groom's kin to the bride (or her father, who passes most of them to her) at or before her marriage.

Indicator artifacts and ecofacts Items that changed relatively rapidly and which, thus, can be used to indicate the relative age of associated items.

Indirect percussion A toolmaking technique common in the Upper Paleolithic. After shaping a core into a pyramidal or cylindrical form, the toolmaker can put a punch of antler or wood or another hard material into position and strike it with a hammer. Using a hammer-struck punch enabled the toolmaker to strike off consistently shaped blades.

Insectivore The order or major grouping of mammals, including modern shrews and moles, that is adapted to feeding on insects.

Intensive agriculture Food production characterized by the permanent cultivation of fields and made possible by the use of the plow, draft animals or machines, fertilizers, irrigation, water-storage techniques, and other complex agricultural techniques.

Kenyanthropus platyops A nearly complete 3.5 million year old skull found in western Kenya. It is thought by some scholars to be a species of gracile australopithecine (and hence should not be regarded as a separate genus).

Kenyapithecus An ape-like primate from the Middle Miocene found in East Africa. It had very thickly enameled teeth and robust jaws, suggesting a diet of hard, tough foods. Probably somewhat terrestrial.

Kindred A bilateral set of close relatives.

Knuckle walking A locomotor pattern of primates such as the chimpanzee and gorilla in which the weight of the upper part of the body is supported on the thickly padded knuckles of the hands.

Laws (scientific) Associations or relationships that are accepted by almost all scientists.

Levalloisian method A method that allowed flake tools of a predetermined size to be produced from a shaped core. The toolmaker first shaped the core and prepared a "striking platform" at one end. Flakes of predetermined and standard sizes could then be knocked off. Although some Levallois flakes date from as far back as 400,000 years ago, they are found more frequently in Mousterian tool kits.

Lexical content Vocabulary or lexicon.

Lexicon The words and morphs, and their meanings, of a language; approximated by a dictionary.

Lineage A set of kin whose members trace descent from a common ancestor through known links.

Lithics The technical name for tools made from stone.

Lower Paleolithic The period of the Oldowan and Acheulian stone tool traditions.

Magic The performance of certain rituals that are believed to compel the supernatural powers to act in particular ways.

Maladaptive customs Customs that diminish the chances of survival and reproduction in a particular environment. Usually applied to biological evolution, the term is often used by cultural anthropologists to refer to behavioral or cultural traits that are likely to disappear because they diminish reproductive success.

Mana A supernatural, impersonal force that inhabits certain objects or people and is believed to confer success and/or strength.

Manumission The granting of freedom to a slave.

Market or commercial exchange Transactions in which the "prices" are subject to supply and demand, whether or not the transactions occur in a marketplace.

Marriage A socially approved sexual and economic union, usually between a man and a woman, that is presumed, both by the couple and by others, to be more or less permanent, and that subsumes reciprocal rights and obligations between the two spouses and their future children.

Matrifocal family A family consisting of a mother and her children.

Matrilineal descent The rule of descent that affiliates an individual with kin of both sexes related to him or her through women only.

Matrilocal residence A pattern of residence in which a married couple lives with or near the wife's parents.

Measure To describe how something compares with other things on some scale of variation.

Mediation The process by which a third party tries to bring about a settlement in the absence of formal authority to force a settlement.

Medical anthropology The application of anthropological knowledge to the study of health and illness.

Medium Part-time religious practitioner who is asked to heal and divine while in a trance.

Meiosis The process by which reproductive cells are formed. In this process of division, the number of chromosomes in the newly formed cells is reduced by half, so that when fertilization occurs the resulting organism has the normal number of chromosomes appropriate to its species, rather than double that number.

Mesolithic The archaeological period in the Old World beginning about 12,000 B.C. Humans were starting to settle down in semipermanent camps and villages, as people began to depend less on big game (which they used to have to follow over long distances) and more on relatively stationary food resources such as fish, shellfish, small game, and wild plants rich in carbohydrates, proteins, and oils.

Messenger RNA (mRNA) A type of ribonucleic acid that is used in the cell to copy the DNA code for use in protein synthesis.

Microlith A small, razor-like blade fragment that was probably attached in a series to a wooden or bone handle to form a cutting edge.

Middle Paleolithic The time period of the Mousterian stone tool tradition.

Miocene The geological epoch from 24 million to 5.2 million years ago.

Mitosis Cellular reproduction or growth involving the duplication of chromosome pairs.

Moiety A unilineal descent group in a society that is divided into two such maximal groups; there may be smaller unilineal descent groups as well.

Molars The large teeth behind the premolars at the back of the jaw; used for chewing and grinding food.

Monogamy Marriage to only one spouse at a time, usually one man and one woman.

Monotheistic Believing that there is only one high god and that all other supernatural beings are subordinate to, or are alternative manifestations of, this supreme being.

Morph The smallest unit of a language that has a meaning.

Morpheme One or more morphs with the same meaning.

Morphology The study of how sound sequences convey meaning.

Mousterian tool assemblage Named after the tool assemblage found in a rock shelter at Le Moustier in the Dordogne region of southwestern France. Compared with an Acheulian assemblage, the Middle Paleolithic (40,000–300,000 years ago) Mousterian has a smaller proportion of large core tools such as hand axes and cleavers and a bigger proportion of small flake tools such as scrapers. Flakes were often altered or "retouched" by striking small flakes or chips from one or more edges.

Mutation A change in the DNA sequence, producing an altered gene.

Natural selection The outcome of processes that affect the frequencies of traits in a particular environment. Traits that enhance survival and reproductive success increase in frequency over time.

Neandertal The common name for the species *Homo neandertalensis*.

Negotiation The process by which the parties to a dispute try to resolve it themselves.

Neolithic Originally meaning "the new stone age," now meaning the presence of domesticated plants and animals. The earliest evidence of domestication comes from the Near East about 8000 B.C.

Neolocal residence A pattern of residence whereby a married couple lives separately, and usually at some distance, from the kin of both spouses.

Nocturnal Active during the night.

Nonsororal polygyny Marriage of a man to two or more women who are not sisters.

Normalizing selection The type of natural selection that removes harmful genes that arose by mutation.

Norms Standards or rules about acceptable behavior in a society. The importance of a norm usually can be judged by how members of a society respond when the norm is violated.

Nuclear family A family consisting of a married couple and their young children.

Oath The act of calling upon a deity to bear witness to the truth of what one says.

Obsidian A volcanic glass that can be used to make mirrors or sharp-edged tools.

Occipital torus A ridge of bone running horizontally across the back of the skull in apes and some hominids.

Oldowan The earliest stone toolmaking tradition, named after the tools found in Bed I at Olduvai Gorge, Tanzania; from about 2.5 million years ago. The stone artifacts include core tools and sharp-edged flakes made by striking one stone against another. Flake tools predominate. Among the core tools, so-called choppers are common.

Oligocene The geological epoch 34 million to 24 million years ago during which definite anthropoids emerged.

Omnivorous Eating both meat and vegetation.

Omomyid A type of prosimian with many tarsier-like features that appeared in the early Eocene.

Operational definition A description of the procedure that is followed in measuring a variable.

Opposable thumb A thumb that can touch the tips of all the other fingers.

Ordeal A means of determining guilt or innocence by submitting the accused to dangerous or painful tests believed to be under supernatural control.

Orrorin tugenensis An apparently bipedal primate dating to between 5.8 and 6 million years, making it possibly the earliest known hominid.

Paleoanthropologists Anthropologists who work in the field of paleoanthropology or human paleontology.

Paleoanthropology See **Human paleontology**.

Paleocene The geological epoch 65 million to 55 million years ago.

Paleomagnetic dating A method of dating archaeological and fossil deposits based on reversals and changes in the earth's magnetic field over time. By comparing the magnetic characteristics of a deposit to those known from the earth's past, a date when the deposit was formed can be determined.

Parallel cousins Children of siblings of the same sex. One's parallel cousins are father's brothers' children and mother's sisters' children.

Parapithecids Small monkey-like Oligocene primates found in the Fayum area of Egypt.

Participant-observation Living among the people being studied—observing, questioning, and (when possible) taking part in the important events of the group. Writing or otherwise recording notes on observations, questions asked and answered, and things to check out later are parts of participant-observation.

Pastoralism A form of subsistence technology in which food-getting is based directly or indirectly on the maintenance of domesticated animals.

Patrilineal descent   The rule of descent that affiliates an individual with kin of both sexes related to him or her through men only.

Patrilocal residence   A pattern of residence in which a married couple lives with or near the husband's parents.

Peasants   Rural people who produce food for their own subsistence but who must also contribute or sell their surpluses to others (in towns and cities) who do not produce their own food.

Percussion flaking   A toolmaking technique in which one stone is struck with another to remove a flake.

Pierolapithecus   A middle Miocene ape that has wrists and vertebrae that would have made it capable of brachiation, but also has relatively short fingers like modern monkeys.

Phenotype   The observable physical appearance of an organism, which may or may not reflect its genotype or total genetic constitution.

Phone   A speech sound in a language.

Phoneme   A sound or set of sounds that makes a difference in meaning to the speakers of the language.

Phonology   The study of the sounds in a language and how they are used.

Phratry   A unilineal descent group composed of a number of supposedly related clans (sibs).

Platyrrhines   The group of anthropoids that have broad, flat-bridged noses, with nostrils facing outward; these monkeys are currently found only in the New World (Central and South America).

Plesiadipis   The most well known of the plesiadipiforms, possibly an archaic primate.

Pliocene   The geological epoch 5.2 million to 1.6 million years ago during which the earliest definite hominids appeared.

Polyandry   The marriage of one woman to more than one man at a time.

Polygamy   Plural marriage; marriage to more than one spouse simultaneously.

Polygyny   The marriage of one man to more than one woman at a time.

Polytheistic   Recognizing many gods, none of whom is believed to be superordinate.

Pongids   Hominoids whose members include both the living and extinct apes.

Potassium-argon (K-Ar) dating   A chronometric dating method that uses the rate of decay of a radioactive form of potassium (^{40}K) into argon (^{40}Ar) to date samples from 5,000 to 3 billion years old. The K-Ar method dates the minerals and rocks in a deposit, not the fossils themselves.

Postpartum sex taboo   Prohibition of sexual intercourse between a couple for a period of time after the birth of their child.

Power   The ability to make others do what they do not want to do or influence based on the threat of force.

Prehensile   Adapted for grasping objects.

Prehistory   The time before written records.

Premolars   The teeth immediately behind the canines; used in chewing, grinding, and shearing food.

Pressure flaking   Toolmaking technique whereby small flakes are struck off by pressing against the core with a bone, antler, or wooden tool.

Prestige   Being accorded particular respect or honor.

Priest   Generally a full-time specialist, with very high status, who is thought to be able to relate to superior or high gods beyond the ordinary person's access or control.

Primary subsistence activities   The food-getting activities: gathering, hunting, fishing, herding, and agriculture.

Primate   A member of the mammalian order Primates, including prosimians, monkeys, apes, and humans.

Primatologists   People who study primates.

Proconsul   The best-known genus of proto-apes from the Early Miocene.

Prognathic   A physical feature that is sticking out or pushed forward, such as the faces in apes and some hominid species.

Propliopithecids   Ape-like anthropoids dating from the early Oligocene, found in the Fayum area of Egypt.

Prosimians   Literally "premonkeys," one of the two suborders of primates; includes lemurs, lorises, and tarsiers.

Protolanguage   A hypothesized ancestral language from which two or more languages seem to have derived.

Quadrupeds   Animals that walk on all fours.

Race   In biology, race refers to a subpopulation or variety of a species that differs somewhat in gene frequencies from other varieties of the species. All members of a species can interbreed and produce viable offspring. Many anthropologists do not think that the concept of race is usefully applied to humans because humans do not fall into geographic populations that can be easily distinguished in terms of different sets of biological or physical traits. Thus, race in humans is largely a culturally assigned category.

Rachis   The seed-bearing part of a plant. In the wild variety of grain, the rachis shatters easily, releasing the seeds. Domesticated grains have a tough rachis, which does not shatter easily.

Racism   The belief, without scientific basis, that one "race" is superior to others.

Radiocarbon (or carbon-14, ^{14}C) dating   A dating method that uses the decay of carbon-14 to date organic remains. It is reliable for dating once-living matter up to 50,000 years old.

Raiding   A short-term use of force, generally planned and organized, to realize a limited objective.

Rank society   A society that does not have any unequal access to economic resources or power, but with social groups that have unequal access to status positions and prestige.

Recessive   An allele phenotypically suppressed in the heterozygous form and expressed only in the homozygous form.

Reciprocity   Giving and taking (not politically arranged) without the use of money.

Redistribution   The accumulation of goods (or labor) by a particular person or in a particular place and their subsequent distribution.

Relative dating   A method of dating fossils that determines the age of a specimen or deposit relative to a known specimen or deposit.

Religion Any set of attitudes, beliefs, and practices pertaining to supernatural power, whether that power rests in forces, gods, spirits, ghosts, or demons.

Revitalization movement A new religious movement intended to save a culture by infusing it with a new purpose and life.

Revolution A usually violent replacement of a society's rulers.

Ribosome A structure in the cell used in making proteins.

Robust australopithecines A later group of australopithecines usually differentiated from the gracile australopithecines by their heavier dentition and larger faces.

Rules of descent Rules that connect individuals with particular sets of kin because of known or presumed common ancestry.

Sagittal crest A ridge of bone running along the top of the skull in apes and early hominids.

Sagittal keel An inverted V-shaped ridge running along the top of the skull in *Homo erectus*.

Sahelanthropus tchadensis A hominoid found in Chad dating to around 7 million years ago.

Savanna Tropical grassland.

Secondary subsistence activities Activities that involve the preparation and processing of food either to make it edible or to store it.

Sedentarism Settled life.

Segmentary lineage system A hierarchy of more and more inclusive lineages; usually functions only in conflict situations.

Segregation The random sorting of chromosomes in meiosis.

Sex differences The typical differences between females and males that are most likely due to biological differences.

Sexual dimorphism A marked difference in size and appearance between males and females of a species.

Shaman A religious intermediary, usually part time, whose primary function is to cure people through sacred songs, pantomime, and other means; sometimes called witch doctor by Westerners.

Siblings A person's brothers and sisters.

Sickle-cell anemia (sicklemia) A condition in which red blood cells assume a crescent (sickle) shape when deprived of oxygen, instead of the normal (disk) shape. The sickle-shaped red blood cells do not move through the body as readily as normal cells, and thus cause damage to the heart, lungs, brain, and other vital organs.

Sites Locations where the material remains of human activity have been preserved in a way that archaeologists or paleoanthropologists can recover them.

Sivapithecus A genus of ape from the later Miocene known for its thickly enameled teeth, suggesting a diet of hard, tough, or gritty items. Found primarily in western and southern Asia and now thought to be ancestral to orangutans.

Slash-and-burn A form of shifting cultivation in which the natural vegetation is cut down and burned off. The cleared ground is used for a short time and then left to regenerate.

Slaves A class of persons who do not own their own labor or the products thereof.

Society A group of people who occupy a particular territory and speak a common language not generally understood by neighboring peoples. By this definition, societies do not necessarily correspond to nations.

Sociobiology See **Behavioral ecology**.

Sociolinguistics The study of cultural and subcultural patterns of speaking in different social contexts.

Soft hammer A technique of stone tool manufacture in which a bone or wood hammer is used to strike flakes from a stone.

Sorcery The use of certain materials to invoke supernatural powers to harm people.

Sororal polygyny The marriage of a man to two or more sisters at the same time.

Speciation The development of a new species.

Species A population that consists of organisms able to interbreed and produce viable and fertile offspring.

Spirits Unnamed supernatural beings of nonhuman origin who are beneath the gods in prestige and often closer to the people; may be helpful, mischievous, or evil.

State A form of political organization that includes class stratification, three or more levels of hierarchy, and leaders with the power to govern by force.

State organization A society is described as having state organization when it includes one or more states.

Statistical association A relationship or correlation between two or more variables that is unlikely to be due to chance.

Stratified An archaeological deposit that contains successive layers or strata.

Stratigraphy The study of how different rock formations and fossils are laid down in successive layers or strata. Older layers are generally deeper or lower than more recent layers.

Strength theory An explanation for the gender division of labor suggesting that men's work typically involves tasks (like hunting and lumbering) requiring greater strength and greater aerobic work capacity.

Subculture The shared customs of a subgroup within a society.

Supernatural Believed to be not human or not subject to the laws of nature.

Symbolic communication An arbitrary (not obviously meaningful) gesture, call, word or sentence that has meaning even when its *referent* is not present.

Syntax The ways in which words are arranged to form phrases and sentences.

Taboo A prohibition that, if violated, is believed to bring supernatural punishment.

Taphonomy The study of how natural processes form and disturb archaeological sites.

Taurodontism Having teeth with an enlarged pulp cavity.

Terrestrial Adapted to living on the ground.

Terrorism The use or threat of violence to create terror in others, usually for political purposes.

Theoretical construct Something that cannot be observed or verified directly.

Theories Explanations of associations or laws.

Thermoluminescence dating A dating technique that is well suited to samples of ancient pottery, brick, tile, or terra cotta, which (when they were made) were heated to a high temperature that released trapped electrons. Such an object continues over time to trap electrons from radioactive elements around it, and the electrons trapped after manufacture emit light when heated. Thus the age of the object can be estimated by measuring how much light is emitted when the object is heated.

Totem A plant or animal associated with a clan (sib) as a means of group identification; may have other special significance for the group.

Tribal organization The kind of political organization in which local communities mostly act autonomously but there are kin groups (such as clans) or associations (such as age-sets) that can temporarily integrate a number of local groups into a larger unit.

Tribe A territorial population in which there are kin or non-kin groups with representatives in a number of local groups.

Typology A way of organizing artifacts in categories based on their particular characteristics.

Unifacial tool A tool worked or flaked on one side only.

Unilineal descent Affiliation with a group of kin through descent links of one sex only.

Unilocal residence A pattern of residence (patrilocal, matrilocal, or avunculocal) that specifies just one set of relatives that the married couple lives with or near.

Upper Paleolithic The time period associated with the emergence of modern humans and their spread around the world.

Uranium-series dating A technique for dating fossil sites that uses the decay of two kinds of uranium (^{235}U and ^{238}U) into other isotopes (such as ^{230}Th, thorium). Particularly useful in cave sites. Different types of uranium-series dating use different isotope ratios.

Variable A thing or quantity that varies.

Vertical clinging and leaping A locomotor pattern characteristic of several primates, including tarsiers and galagos. The animal normally rests by clinging to a branch in a vertical position and uses its hind limbs alone to push off from one vertical position to another.

Warfare Violence between political entities such as communities, districts, or nations.

Witchcraft The practice of attempting to harm people by supernatural means, but through emotions and thought alone, not through the use of tangible objects.

NOTES

CHAPTER 1

1. Harrison 1975; Durham 1991: 228–37.
2. Chen and Li 2001.
3. Chambers 1989, as referred to in Kushner 1991.
4. Miracle 2004; Kushner 1991.
5. Hempel 1965: 139.
6. J. Whiting 1964.
7. Nagel 1961: 88–89.
8. Ibid., pp. 83–90.
9. Ibid., p. 85. See also McCain and Segal 1988: 75–79.
10. McCain and Segal 1988: 62–64.
11. Caws 1969: 1378.
12. McCain and Segal: 56–57, 131–32.
13. J. Whiting 1964: 519–20.
14. McCain and Segal 1988: 67–69.
15. Blalock 1972: 15–20 and Thomas 1986: 18–28. See also M. Ember 1970: 701–703.
16. Ogburn 1922: 200–80.

CHAPTER 2

1. R. Martin 1990: 42.
2. R. Etienne 1992.
3. Dibble, Chase, McPherron, and Tuffreau 1997.
4. Schiffer 1987.
5. Isaac 1997.
6. B. Fowler 2000.
7. A. Underhill 2002.
8. Michel, McGovern, and Badler 1993.
9. Sinopoli 2002.
10. Wynn 1979.
11. Keeley 1977.
12. Kay 2000a.
13. B. Wood 1994.
14. Conroy 1990.
15. Peregrine 1992.
16. Leakey 1965: 73–78.
17. F. H. Brown 1992.
18. Aitken 1985: 191–202.
19. Aitken 1985: 4, 211–13.
20. Kappelman 1993.
21. Gentner and Lippolt 1963.
22. F. H. Brown 2000: 225.
23. Schwarcz 1993.
24. Fleischer and Hart 1972: 474.
25. Fleischer, Price, Walker, and Leakey 1965: 72–74.
26. Trigger 1989.
27. Waldbaum 2005.

CHAPTER 3

1. Sagan 1975.
2. A. Lovejoy 1964: 58–63
3. A. Lovejoy 1964: 63.
4. Eiseley 1958: 17–26; Mayr 1982: 171–75, 340–41.
5. Mayr 1982: 339–60.
6. Wallace 1970 (1858).
7. Mayr 1982: 423.
8. Darwin had a still longer title. It continued, *Or the Preservation of the Favoured Races in the Struggle for Life*. Darwin's notion of "struggle for life" is often misinterpreted to refer to a war of all against all. Although animals may fight with each other at times over access to resources, Darwin was referring mainly to their metaphorical "struggle" with the environment, particularly to obtain food.
9. Darwin 1970 (1859).
10. Futuyma 1982 provides an overview of this long controversy.
11. Huxley 1970.
12. Brandon 1990: 6–7.
13. G. Williams 1992: 7.
14. J. M. Smith 1989: 42–45.
15. Hooper 2002.
16. Grant 2002.
17. Devillers and Chaline 1993: 22–23.
18. Beadle and Beadle 1966: 216.
19. Golden, Lemonick, and Thompson 2000; Hayden 2000; Marshall 2000; Pennisi 2000; Travis 2000.
20. Daiger 2005.
21. Olsen 2002.
22. Dobzhansky 1962: 138–40.
23. Relethford 1990: 94.
24. G. A. Harrison et al. 1988: 198–200.
25. Brace 1996.
26. Grant and Grant 2002.
27. Rennie 2002: 83.
28. Chatterjee 1997.
29. Paley 1810.
30. Center for Renewal of Science and Culture, "The Wedge Strategy," cited in Forrest 2001: 16.
31. McMullin 2001: 174.
32. Rennie 2002.
33. Barash 1977.
34. Krebs and Davies 1984, 1987.
35. Badcock 2000.
36. Schaller 1972.
37. Hare, Brown, Williamson, and Tomasello 2002.
38. Wilson 1975.
39. B. Low 2004.
40. D. Campbell 1965.
41. Nissen 1958.
42. Boyd and Richerson 1985.
43. Durham 1991.

467

CHAPTER 4

1. See Durham 1991: 154–225 for an extensive discussion of the relationship between genes and culture.
2. Steward, T.D. 1950.
3. *Genesis* 17: 9–15.
4. Hanna, Little, and Austin 1989: 133–36; G. A. Harrison et al. 1988: 504–507.
5. Roberts 1953. Cited in Garn 1971: 73. See also Roberts 1978.
6. Roberts 1953.
7. Harrison et al. 1988: 505.
8. Riesenfeld 1973: 427–59.
9. Riesenfeld 1973: 452–53.
10. Weiner 1954: 615–18; Steegman 1975. See also Larsen 2002.
11. Harrison et al. 1988: 308–10.
12. Polednak 1974: 49–57. See also Branda and Eaton 1978.
13. Loomis 1967.
14. Post, Daniels, and Binford 1975: 65–80.
15. Holden 2000; Jablonski and Chaplin 2000.
16. Stini 1975: 53.
17. Mazess 1975.
18. Greksa and Beall 1989: 223.
19. Greksa and Beall 1989: 226.
20. Frisancho and Greksa 1989: 204.
21. Eveleth and Tanner 1990: 176–79.
22. Eveleth and Tanner 1990: 205–206.
23. Bogin 1988: 105–106.
24. Harrison et al. 1988: 300.
25. Harrison et al. 1988: 198.
26. Huss-Ashmore and Johnston 1985: 482–83.
27. Harrison et al. 1988: 385–86.
28. Martorell 1980: 81–106.
29. Martorell et al. 1991.
30. Landauer and Whiting 1964, 1981; Gunders and Whiting 1968; Gray and Wolfe 1980.
31. Landauer and Whiting, 1964, 1981; Gunders and Whiting 1968.
32. Gray and Wolfe 2002.
33. Landauer and Whiting 1981.
34. Eveleth and Tanner 1990: 205.
35. Landauer 1973.
36. Motulsky 1971: 223.
37. Motulsky 1971: 226.
38. Motulsky 1971: 229.
39. Motulsky 1971: 230.
40. Motulsky 1971: 233.
41. Motulsky 1971: 233.
42. Black 1992.
43. An examination of the epidemic diseases spread by Europeans can be found in chapter 11 of J. Diamond 1997a.
44. Neel et al. 1970; Patrick Tierney in his *Darkness in El Dorado* (New York: Norton, 2000) accused the Neel research team of fueling a measles outbreak among the Yanomamö by administering a harmful measles vaccine. But the scientific evidence indicates that Tierney is wrong. The vaccine used by Neel and associates was widely pretested and there was no way that the vaccine could have caused the epidemic. Measles was already spreading in the Amazon, which was why the vaccination program was initiated. See Gregor and Gross 2004.
45. Relethford 1990: 425–27.
46. Merbs 1992.
47. Durham 1991: 105–107.
48. Durham 1991: 105–107.
49. Durham 1991: 107.
50. Harrison et al. 1988: 231.
51. For a review of the early research, see Durham 1991: 123–27. The particular form of malaria that is discussed is caused by the species *Plasmodium falciparum*.
52. See Madigral 1989 for a report of her own research and a review of earlier studies.
53. Pennisi 2001a.
54. Durham 1991: 124–45.
55. Motulsky 1971: 238.
56. Diamond 1993.
57. Molnar 1998: 158; Pennisi 2001b.
58. Durham 1991: 230.
59. Brodey 1971.
60. Durham 1991: 233–35.
61. Relethford 1990: 127.
62. McCracken 1971; see also references to the work of F. J. Simoons as referred to in Durham 1991: 240–41.
63. McCracken 1971; Huang 2002.
64. Durham 1991: 263–69.
65. Marks 1994; Shanklin 1993: 15–17.
66. Molnar 1998: 19.
67. Brace et al. 1993.
68. Brooks et al. 1993.
69. Brace et al. 1993.
70. Brooks et al. 1993.
71. King and Motulsky 2002.
72. Goodrich 1959: 7–15.
73. Coe 1966: 74–76.
74. Thompson 1966: 89.
75. McNeill 1976.
76. Motulsky 1971: 232.
77. Motulsky 1971: 232.
78. MacArthur and Wilson 1967.
79. Johansen and Edey 1981.
80. Peregrine, C. R. Ember, and M. Ember 2000, 2003.
81. Lieberman 1999.
82. Klineberg 1935, 1944.
83. Jensen 1969.
84. M. W. Smith 1974.
85. Dobzhansky 1973: 11.
86. Dobzhansky 1973: 14–15.
87. Research by Sandra Scarr and others reported in Boyd and Richerson 1985: 56.
88. Dobzhansky 1962: 243.
89. Haldane 1963.
90. Simpson 1971: 297–308.

CHAPTER 5

1. The classic description of common primate traits is Napier and Napier 1967. For primate social organization see Smuts, Cheney, Seyfarth, Wrangham, and Struhsaker 1987.
2. Bearder 1987: 14.
3. Richard 1985: 22ff.
4. Doyle and Martin 1979; Tattersall 1982.
5. Richard 1987: 32.
6. Bearder 1987: 13.
7. MacKinnon and MacKinnon 1980.
8. Cartmill 1992a: 28; Fleagle 1999: 118–22.
9. Napier and Napier 1967: 32–33.
10. Richard 1985: 164–65.
11. Cartmill 1992a: 29; Goldizen 1987: 34; also Eisenberg 1977; Sussman and Kinzey 1984; Fleagle 1999: 168–74.
12. Eisenberg 1977: 15–17.
13. Robinson, Wright, and Kinzey 1987; Crockett and Eisenberg 1987; Robinson and Janson 1987.
14. Hrdy 1977: 18.
15. Napier 1970: 80–82.
16. Fedigan 1982: 11.
17. Fleagle 1999: 302.
18. Clark, LeGros 1964: 184.
19. Preuschoft, Chivers, Brockelman, and Creel 1984.
20. Carpenter 1940; Chivers 1974, 1980.
21. Rijksen 1978: 22.
22. Fossey 1983: xvi.
23. Tuttle 1986: 99–114.
24. Schaller 1963; Schaller 1964.

25. Fossey 1983: 47.
26. Harcourt 1979: 187–92.
27. Susman 1984; White 1996.
28. Goodall 1963; van Lawick-Goodall 1971.
29. Teleki 1973.
30. Stanford 2002.
31. Stanford 2002: 35–41.
32. Tuttle 1986: 266–69.
33. Whiten et al. 1999.
34. M. Goodman 1992.
35. Falk 1987.
36. Female bonobos, or pygmy chimpanzees, engage in sexual intercourse near-ly as often as human females—see Thompson-Handler, Malenky, and Badri-an 1984.
37. By male-female bonding, we mean that at least one of the sexes is "faithful," that is, typically has intercourse with just one opposite-sex partner through-out at least one estrus or menstrual cycle or breeding season. Note that the bonding may not be monogamous; an individual may be bonded to more than one individual of the opposite sex. See M. Ember and C. R. Ember 1979.
38. C.R. Ember and M. Ember 1984: 207.
39. C.R. Ember and M. Ember 1984: 208–209.
40. de Waal and Lanting 1997.
41. Rumbaugh 1970: 52–58.
42. Boesche et al. 1994.
43. Observation by others cited by A. Jolly 1985 (53).
44. Hannah and McGrew 1987.
45. "The First Dentist," *Newsweek,* March 5, 1973, 73.
46. Seyfarth, Cheney, and Marler 1980.
47. Gardner and Gardner 1969.
48. Gardner and Gardner 1980.
49. Greenfield and Savage-Rumbaugh 1990.
50. Gingerich 1986; Szalay 1972; Szalay, Tattersall, and Decker 1975.
51. Fleagle 1994; Ciochon and Etler 1994: 41; Cartmill 2002.
52. Block and Boyer 2002.
53. Conroy 1990: 49–53.
54. Conroy 1990: 53.
55. Habicht 1979.
56. Sussman 1991.
57. Richard 1985: 31; Cartmill 1974.
58. Szalay 1968.
59. Cartmill 1974; for more recent statements see Cartmill 1992b; Cartmill 2002.
60. Sussman and Raven 1978.
61. Fleagle 1994: 22–23.
62. Conroy 1990: 119.
63. Radinsky 1967.
64. Conroy 1990: 105; Fleagle 1994: 21.
65. Alexander 1992; Conroy 1990: 111.
66. Kay, Ross, and Williams 1997.
67. Martin 1990: 46; Conroy 1990: 46.
68. Kay, Ross, and Williams 1997; Fleagle and Kay 1985: 25.
69. Jaeger et al. 1999.
70. Simons 1995; Simons, and Rassmussen 1996.
71. Kay 2000b: 441.
72. Kay 2000b: 441–42; Conroy 1990: 156.
73. Fleagle 1999: 404–409.
74. Rosenberger 1979.
75. Fleagle and Kay 1987.
76. Aiello 1993; Hartwig 1994.
77. Andrews 2000a: 486.
78. Fleagle and Kay 1985: 25, 30; Conroy 1990: 160–61.
79. Fleagle 1999: 413–15; Fleagle and Kay 1983: 205.
80. Conroy 1990: 248–49.
81. Conroy 1990: 56.
82. R. Martin 1990: 56.
83. Begun 2002.
84. Conroy 1990: 206–11.
85. Begun 2002.
86. Andrews 2000b: 485.
87. Begun 2002.
88. Zimmer 1999; Ward, Brown, Hill, Kelley, and Downs 1999.

89. Begun 2002; Kelley 1992: 225.
90. Moyà-Solà et al. 2004.
91. T. Harrison 1986; T. Harrison and Rook 1997.
92. Ward 1997.
93. Begun 2002.
94. Begun 2002.
95. Fleagle 1999: 480–83.
96. Bilsborough 1992: 65.
97. Simons 1992: 207.
98. Sarich and Wilson 1966; Sarich 1968; Lewin 1983a.
99. Jones, Martin, and Pilbeam 1992: 293; R. Martin 1990: 693–709.
100. Clark et al. 2003.
101. The material referred to in this paragraph is drawn from Jones, Martin, and Pilbeam 1992: 8, 293–321.

CHAPTER 6

1. Rose 1984.
2. Bilsborough 1992: 64–65.
3. Oakley 1964.
4. Kingston, Marino, and Hill 1994.
5. Hewes 1961.
6. Shipman 1986; Trinkaus 1987a.
7. Lovejoy 1981.
8. C. Jolly 1970.
9. Washburn 1960.
10. Pilbeam 1972: 153.
11. Wolpoff 1971.
12. Savage-Rumbaugh 1994
13. Wolpoff 1983.
14. Zimmer 2004.
15. Zihlman 1992.
16. Wheeler 1984, 1991.
17. Falk 1988.
18. Zihlman 1992: 414.
19. Lovejoy 1988.
20. Aiello and Dean 1990: 268–74.
21. Aiello and Dean 1990: 507–508.
22. Gibbons 2002.
23. Brunet et al. 2002; Wong 2003.
24. Aiello and Collard 2001; Pickford, Senut, Gommercy and Treil 2002; Wong 2003.
25. White, Suwa, and Asfaw 1995.
26. White, Suwa, and Asfaw 1994.
27. Hailie-Selassie 2001.
28. Susman, Stern, and Jungers 1985; Rose 1984.
29. Conroy 1990: 274; Culotta 1995; Wilford 1995.
30. Culotta 1995.
31. Leakey et al. 1995.
32. Tattersall and Schwartz 2000: 93.
33. Simpson 2002; White, Johanson, and Kimbel 1981; Johanson and White 1979.
34. Johanson and Edey 1981: 17–18.
35. Johanson and White 1979.
36. Lewin 1983b.
37. Conroy 1990: 291–92; Simpson 2002.
38. Fleagle 1999: 515–18.
39. Fleagle 1999: 515, 520.
40. Grine 1988a.
41. Kimbel, White, and Johansen 1984.
42. Jungers 1988a; Clarke and Tobias 1995.
43. Lovejoy 1988.
44. Tattersall and Schwartz 2000: 88–89; Clarke and Tobias 1995.
45. Dart 1925.
46. Bromage and Dean 1985; B. H. Smith 1986.
47. Eldredge and Tattersall 1982: 80–90.
48. Pilbeam 1972: 107.
49. Holloway 1974.
50. Szalay and Delson 1979: 504.

51. Conroy 1990: 280–82.
52. Asfaw et al. 1999.
53. Brunet et al. 1995.
54. Brunet et al. 1995.
55. Leakey et al. 2001.
56. Conroy 1990: 294–303.
57. McHenry 2002.
58. Szalay and Delson 1979: 504; Wood 1992.
59. McHenry 1988; Jungers 1988b.
60. Fleagle 1999: 522.
61. Grine 1993; Walker and Leakey 1988.
62. Broom 1950.
63. Fleagle 1999: 522.
64. McHenry 2002.
65. McHenry 2002.
66. Grine 1988b.
67. Stringer 1985.
68. McHenry 2002.
69. Fleagle 1999: 529.
70. Fleagle 1999: 511–15.
71. Wood 1992.
72. Susman 1994.
73. Susman 1994.
74. Holden 1997.
75. Leakey 1960.
76. Clark 1970: 68; Schick and Toth 1993: 97–99.
77. Schick and Toth 1993: 153–70.
78. Schick and Toth 1993: 129.
79. Schick and Toth 1993: 157–59.
80. Isaac 1984.
81. Whittaker 1994: 283–85.
82. Schick and Toth 1993: 175–76.
83. Speth 2002.
84. Shipman 1986. For the idea that scavenging may have been an important food-getting strategy even for protohominids, see Szalay 1975.
85. Speth and Davis 1976; Blumenschine et al. 2003.
86. Isaac 1971.
87. Leakey 1971.
88. Potts 1988: 253–58.
89. Potts 1984.
90. Potts 1988: 278–81.
91. Boyd and Silk 2000: 249–50.
92. Dobzhansky 1962: 196.
93. Bromage and Dean 1985; B. H. Smith 1986.
94. McHenry 1982.
95. McHenry 1982.
96. Pilbeam and Gould 1974.
97. Leonard 2002.
98. Stedman et al. 2004.
99. McHenry 2002; Tobias 1994.
100. Simpson 2002.
101. Rightmire 2000.
102. Swisher et al. 1994.
103. Balter and Gibbons 2000; Gabunia et al. 2000.
104. Vekua et al. 2002; Gore 2002.
105. Wolpoff and Nkini 1985. See also Rightmire 2000; Balter 2001.
106. Rightmire 1990: 12–14.
107. Swisher et al. 1994.
108. Fleagle 1999: 534–35; Day 1986: 409–12; Kramer 2002.
109. Rightmire 2000; Tobias 1994.
110. Franciscus and Trinkaus 1988.
111. Feibel and Brown 1993.
112. Ruff and Walker 1993.
113. Morwood et al. 2004; Brown et al. 2004.
114. Falk et al. 2005
115. Diamond 2004
116. Wong 2005
117. Fleagle 1999: 306.
118. M. Ember and C. R. Ember 1979; cf. Lovejoy 1981.
119. Clayman 1989: 857–58.

120. Bordes 1968: 51–97.
121. Phillipson 1993: 57.
122. Schick and Toth 1993: 227, 233.
123. Schick and Toth 1993: 231–33; Whittaker 1994: 27.
124. Bordes 1968: 24–25; Whittaker 1994: 27.
125. Schick and Toth 1993: 258–60; Whittaker 1994: 27.
126. Lawrence Keeley's analysis reported in Schick and Toth 1993: 260; see that page for their analysis of tool use.
127. Calvin 1983.
128. Yamei et al. 2000.
129. Ciochon, Olsen, and James 1990: 178–83: Pope 1989.
130. Howell 1966
131. Klein 1987; Binford 1987.
132. L. G. Freeman 1994.
133. A good example of this problem is the ongoing debate about fire use at Zhoukoudian cave, as reported by Weiner et al. 1998.
134. Isaac 1984: 35–36. Other evidence for deliberate use of fire comes from the Swartkans cave in South Africa and is dated 1 million to 1.5 million years ago; see Brain and Sillen 1988.
135. Goren-Inbar et al. 2004.
136. Binford and Ho 1985.
137. Leonard 2002.
138. Clark 1970: 94–95.
139. Clark 1970: 96–97.
140. de Lumley 1969.

CHAPTER 7

1. Stringer 1985.
2. Stringer 1985.
3. Rightmire 1997.
4. Rightmire 1997; Fleagle 1999: 535–37.
5. Spencer 1984.
6. Trinkaus 1985.
7. Stringer 2000.
8. Trinkaus and Shipman 1993a, 1993b.
9. Krings et al. 1997.
10. Cann 1988.
11. Cann 1988.
12. Vigilant et al. 1991.
13. Krings et al. 1997.
14. Ovchinnikov et al. 2000.
15. Tattersall 1999: 115–16; Gibbons 2001.
16. Mellars 1996: 405–19.
17. Mellars 1998.
18. Strauss 1989.
19. Schick and Toth 1993: 288–92.
20. Klein 1989: 291–96.
21. Schick and Toth 1993: 288–92; Whittaker 1994: 30–31.
22. Klein 1989: 421–22.
23. Binford and Binford 1969.
24. Fish 1981: 377.
25. Butzer 1982: 42.
26. Phillipson 1993: 63.
27. For the controversy about whether the inhabitants of the Dordogne Valley lived in their homesites year-round, see Binford 1973.
28. Schick and Toth 1993: 292.
29. Klein 1977.
30. Klein 1974.
31. Bordes 1961.
32. T. Patterson 1981.
33. Phillipson 1993: 64.
34. Klein 1983: 38–39.
35. Binford 1984: 195–97. To explain the lack of complete skeletons of large animals, Klein (1983) suggests that the hunters may have butchered the large animals elsewhere because they could carry home only small cuts.
36. Wilford 1997.
37. Chase and Dibble 1987.
38. Stringer, Hublin, and Vandermeersch 1984: 107.

39. Singer and Wymer 1982: 149.
40. Gibbons 2003.
41. Bräuer 1984: 387–89, 394; Rightmire 1984: 320.
42. Valladas et al. 1988.
43. Stringer, Hublin, and Vandermeersch 1984: 121.
44. For arguments supporting the single-origin theory, see the chapters by Günter Bräuer, F. Clark Howell, and C. B. Stringer et al., in F. Smith and Spencer 1984. For arguments supporting the multiregional theory, see the chapters by C. L. Brace et al., David W. Frayer, Fred H. Smith, and Milford H. Wolpoff et al. in the same volume.
45. Cann, Stoneking, and Wilson 1987.
46. Vigilant et al. 1991.
47. Stoneking 1997.
48. Hammer and Zegura 1996.
49. Hammer and Zegura 2002.
50. Cavalli-Sforza and Feldman 2003.
51. Wolpoff 1999: 501–504, 727–31; Frayer et al. 1993.
52. Wolpoff 1999: 735–43; Frayer et al. 1993.
53. D. Lieberman 1995.
54. Templeton 1993.
55. Trinkaus 1986.
56. Eswaran 2002.
57. Templeton 1996. See also Ayala 1995, 1996.
58. Reed et al. 2004
59. Duarte et al. 1999.
60. Bahn 1998.
61. Tattersall 1999: 198–203.
62. Trinkaus 1986; see also Trinkaus and Howells 1979.
63. Culotta 2005.
64. Klein 2003.
65. R. White 1982.
66. Strauss 1982.
67. Dawson 1992: 24–71.
68. COHMAP 1988.
69. Martin and Wright 1967.
70. Mellars 1994.
71. T. Patterson 1981.
72. Klima 1962.
73. Whittaker 1994: 33; Schick and Toth 1993: 293–99.
74. Whittaker 1994: 31.
75. Bordaz 1970: 68.
76. Whittaker 1994: 33.
77. Phillipson 1993: 60.
78. Bordaz 1970: 68.
79. We thank Robert L. Kelly (personal communication) for bringing this possibility to our attention. See also J. D. Clark 1977: 136.
80. Ascher 1961.
81. Semenov 1970: 103. For a more recent discussion of research following this strategy, see Keeley 1980.
82. Klein 1994: 508.
83. Soffer 1993: 38–40.
84. Phillipson 1993: 74.
85. Morell 1995.
86. Henshilwood et al. 2002.
87. Ucko and Rosenfeld 1967.
88. Rice and Paterson 1985, 1986.
89. Rice and Paterson 1985: 98.
90. Hawkins and Kleindienst 2001.
91. Jayaswal 2002.
92. Peregrine and Bellwood 2001.
93. McDonald 1998.
94. Hoffecker, Powers, and Goebel 1993.
95. Gibbons 1995; Roosevelt et al. 1996.
96. Dillehay 2000.
97. Parry 2002.
98. Greenberg and Ruhlen 1992: 94–99.
99. Turner 1989.
100. Szathmary 1993.
101. McDonald 1998.
102. Wheat 1967.

103. Fagan 1991: 79.
104. Hoffecker, Powers, and Goebel 1993.
105. Jennings 1968: 72–88.
106. Judge and Dawson 1972.
107. Wheat 1967.
108. Fagan 1989: 221.
109. Wheat 1967.
110. Wheat 1967.
111. Fagan 1989: 227.
112. Fagan 1991: 192.
113. Fagan 1989: 227.
114. Collins 1976: 88–125.
115. Chard 1969: 171.
116. G. Clark 1975: 101–61.
117. Petersen 1973: 94–96.
118. Daniel 2001.
119. Sassaman 1996: 58–83.
120. Sassaman 1996: 58–83.
121. J. Brown 1983: 5–10.

CHAPTER 8

1. Miller 1992.
2. Crawford 1992; Phillipson 1993: 118; MacNeish 1991: 256, 268.
3. Flannery 1986: 6–8; Pearsall 1992; B. Smith 1992a.
4. Binford 1971.
5. Flannery 1973a.
6. Simcha et al. 2000.
7. Harlan 1967.
8. Flannery 1971.
9. Mellaart 1961.
10. Henry 1989: 214–15.
11. Brown and Price 1985.
12. Henry 1989: 38–39, 209–10; 1991. See Olszewski 1991 for some questions about the degree of social complexity in Natufian sites.
13. Martin and Wright 1967.
14. A recent analysis of these changes is Kuehn 1998; see also J. Brown 1985.
15. Marcus and Flannery 1996: 49–50.
16. Marcus and Flannery 1996: 50–53.
17. Gorman 1970.
18. Chang 1970; Gorman 1970.
19. J. Clark 1970: 171–72.
20. Phillipson 1993: 111–12.
21. Alroy 2001.
22. Martin 1973.
23. Grayson 1977, 1984. See also L. G. Marshall 1984; Guthrie 1984; Barnosky et al. 2004.
24. Cohen 1977b: 12, 85.
25. Cohen 1977b: 85; Hassan 1981: 207. For the view that hunter-gatherers were very unlikely to have lived in tropical forests before agriculture developed, see Bailey et al. 1989.
26. Cohen 1989: 112–13.
27. Cohen 1989: 113–15.
28. Flannery 1973b.
29. Patterson 1971.
30. G. Johnson 1977; D. Harris 1977.
31. Sussman 1972; Lee 1972.
32. For some examples of societies that have practiced infanticide, D. Harris 1977.
33. Howell 1979; Lee 1979.
34. Frisch 1980; Howell 1979.
35. Zohary 1969.
36. Flannery 1965.
37. Hole 1992; MacNeish 1991: 127–28.
38. Clutton-Brock 1992.
39. Hole, Flannery, and Neely 1969.
40. Marcus and Flannery 1996: 64–66.
41. Flannery 1986: 6–8.
42. Fedoroff 2003.

43. Flannery 1986: 8–9; Marcus and Flannery 1996: 66–67.
44. Marcus and Flannery 1996: 66–68.
45. Piperno and Stothert 2003.
46. MacNeish 1991: 37, 47; Hole 1992.
47. B. Smith 1992b: 163, 287.
48. Asch and Asch 1978.
49. Clutton-Brock 1992.
50. Müller-Haye 1984.
51. Wenke 1984: 350, 397–98.
52. Chang 1981; MacNeish 1991: 159–63.
53. MacNeish 1991: 267–68.
54. Neumann 2003; Denham et al. 2003.
55. Hole 1992.
56. Phillipson 1993: 118.
57. MacNeish 1991: 314.
58. Hanotte et al. 2002; Clutton-Brock 1992.
59. Cited in MacNeish 1991: 6.
60. Braidwood 1960.
61. Wright 1971.
62. Flannery 1986: 10–11.
63. Cohen 1977a, 1977b: 279.
64. Byrne 1987, referred to in Blumler and Byrne 1991; see also Henry 1989: 30–38; McCorriston and Hole 1991.
65. Henry 1989: 41.
66. McCorriston and Hole 1991.
67. Henry 1989: 54.
68. Speth and Spielmann 1983.
69. B. White 1973; see also Kasarda 1971.
70. C. R. Ember 1983.
71. Konner and Worthman 1980.
72. Roosevelt 1984; see also M. N. Cohen and Armelagos 1984b: 585–602; Cohen 1987, 2002. For evidence suggesting that the transition to food production was not generally associated with declining health, see Wood et al. 1992.
73. Roosevelt 1984.
74. Renfrew 1969.
75. Wenke 1990; Connah 1987; Service 1975.
76. Flannery 1972.
77. Flannery 1972; Redman 1978: 215–16.
78. Wright and Johnson 1975.
79. The discussion in the remainder of this section draws from Wright and Johnson 1975; see also G. Johnson 1987.
80. Wright and Johnson 1975.
81. Flannery 1972.
82. Service 1975: 207.
83. Service 1975; Flannery 1972.
84. This description of Sumerian civilization is based on Kramer 1963.
85. Diamond 1989.
86. Helms 1975: 34–36, 54–55; Sanders, Parsons, and Santley 1979.
87. Millon 1967.
88. Millon 1976.
89. Millon 1967.
90. Helms 1975: 61–63; Weaver 1993.
91. Wenke 1984: 289.
92. Connah 1987: 67.
93. Fagan 1989: 428–30.
94. Connah 1987: 216–17.
95. Vogel 2002.
96. Wenke 1984: 305–20.
97. Chang 1981.
98. Chang 1968: 235–55.
99. Solis, Haas, and Creamer 2001; Haas, Creamer, and Ruiz 2004.
100. For an overview, see Lumbreras 1974.
101. M. Fowler 1975.
102. For a more complete review of the available theories, see various chapters in Cohen and Service 1978; see also chapter 1 in Zeder 1991.
103. Wittfogel 1957.
104. R. Adams 1960; H. T. Wright 1986.
105. Wheatley 1971: 291.
106. R. Adams 1960.

107. R. Adams 1981: 244.
108. R. Adams 1981: 243; Service 1975: 274–75.
109. Carneiro 1970; Sanders and Price 1968: 230–32.
110. M. Harris 1979: 101–102.
111. T. C. Young 1972.
112. Sanders and Price 1968: 141.
113. Blanton et al. 1981: 224. For the apparent absence of population pressure in the Teotihuacán Valley, see Brumfiel 1976. For the Oaxaca Valley, see Feinman et al. 1985.
114. Wright and Johnson 1975. Carneiro 1988, however, argued the opposite: that the population grew just before the states emerged in southwestern Iran. Whether or not population declined, Frank Hole 1994 has suggested that climate change around that time may have forced local populations to relocate, some to centers that became cities.
115. Polanyi, Arensberg, and Pearson 1957: 257–62; Sanders 1968.
116. Wright and Johnson 1975.
117. Rathje 1971.
118. Chang 1986: 234–94.
119. For a discussion of how political dynamics may play an important role in state formation, see Brumfiel 1983.
120. Johnson and Earle 1987: 324–26.
121. Childe 1950.
122. Service 1975: 12–15, 89–90.
123. J. Diamond 1997a: 205–207.
124. Dirks 1993.
125. Johnson and Earle 1987: 243–48; 304–306.
126. C. R. Ember and M. Ember 1992.
127. Ferguson and Whitehead 1992.
128. Weiss et al. 1993.
129. Kerr 1998; Grossman 2002.
130. Haug et al. 2003.
131. deMenocal 2001; Haug et al. 2003; Hodell et al. 2001.
132. Holden 1996.

CHAPTER 9

1. Linton 1945: 30.
2. See, for example, Holland and Quinn 1987: 4.
3. Sapir 1938, cited by Pelto and Pelto 1975: 1.
4. Pelto and Pelto 1975: 14–15.
5. de Waal 2001: 269.
6. Hewlett 2004.
7. Miner 1956: 504–505, reproduced by permission of the American Anthropological Association. Although Miner is not a foreign visitor, he wrote this description in a way that shows how these behaviors might be viewed from an outside perspective.
8. Lee 1972.
9. Hatch 1997.
10. Durkheim 1938 [originally published 1895]: 3.
11. Asch 1956.
12. Hall 1966: 159–60.
13. Ibid., p. 120.
14. Wagley 1974.
15. R. Brown 1965: 549–609.
16. Bernard 2001: 323.
17. Peacock 1986: 54.
18. Lawless et al. 1983: xi–xxi; Peacock 1986: 54–65.
19. Romney et al. 1986.
20. Bernard 2001: 190.
21. American Anthropological Association 1991.
22. Szklut and Reed 1991.
23. K. Hill and Hurtado 2004.
24. See Murdock and White 1969 for a description of the SCCS sample; sets of the HRAF Collection of Ethnography in paper and microfiche are found in hundreds of academic libraries in the United States and elsewhere. Many of the cultures in paper and microfiche (along with some additional cultures) can be found in eHRAF World Cultures, available at over 300 libraries. The HRAF Collections, which together now include indexed full-text on approximately 400 cultures past and present,

are described at http://www.yale.edu/hraf; for a description of the available cross-cultural samples see C. R. Ember and M. Ember 2001: 76–88.

CHAPTER 10

1. Keller 1974 [originally published 1902]: 34.
2. Wilden 1987: 124, referred to in Christensen, Hockey, and James 2001.
3. Lambert 2001.
4. Ekman and Keltner 1997: 32.
5. von Frisch 1962.
6. King 1999a; Gibson and Jessee 1999: 189–90.
7. Seyfarth and Cheney 1982: 242, 246.
8. Hockett and Ascher 1964.
9. T. S. Eliot 1963.
10. Snowdon 1999: 81.
11. Pepperberg 1999.
12. Mukerjee 1996: 28.
13. Savage-Rumbaugh 1992: 138–41.
14. J. H. Hill 1978: 94; J. H. Hill 2004.
15. Ibid.
16. Senner 1989b.
17. Chomsky 1975.
18. Southworth and Daswani 1974: 312. See also Boas 1964: 121–23.
19. Bickerton 1983.
20. Ibid., p. 122.
21. B. Berlin 1992; Hays 1994.
22. G. Miller 2004.
23. Gleitman and Wanner 1982; Blount 1981.
24. R. Brown 1980: 93–94.
25. de Villiers and de Villiers 1979: 48; see also Wanner and Gleitman 1982.
26. Bickerton 1983: 122.
27. E. Bates and Marchman 1988 as referred to by Snowdon 1999: 88–91.
28. Crystal 1971: 168.
29. Ibid., pp. 100–101.
30. R. L. Munroe, R. H. Munroe, and Winters 1996; M. Ember and C. R. Ember 1999. The theory about the effect of baby-holding on consonant-vowel alternation is an extension of the theory that regular baby-holding encourages a preference for regular rhythm in music; see Ayres 1973.
31. Sapir and Swadesh 1964: 103.
32. Geoffrey Chaucer 1926: 8. Our modern English translation is based on the glossary in that book.
33. Akmajian, Demers, and Harnish 1984: 356.
34. Baldi 1983: 3.
35. Ibid., p. 12.
36. Greenberg 1972; see also Phillipson 1976: 71.
37. Phillipson 1976: 79.
38. Trudgill 1983: 34.
39. Weinreich 1968: 31.
40. But see Thomason and Kaufman 1988 for a discussion of how grammatical changes due to contact may be more important than was previously assumed.
41. Berlin and Kay 1969.
42. Ibid.
43. Ibid., pp. 5–6.
44. Ibid., p. 104; Witkowski and Brown 1978.
45. Bornstein 1973: 41–101.
46. M. Ember 1978: 364–67.
47. Ibid.
48. C. H. Brown 1977.
49. C. H. Brown 1979.
50. Witkowski and Burris 1981.
51. Ibid.
52. C. H. Brown and Witkowski 1980: 379.
53. C. H. Brown 1984: 106.
54. Webb 1977: 42–49; see also Rudmin 1988.
55. Sapir 1931: 578; see also J. B. Carroll 1956.
56. Wardhaugh 2002: 222.
57. Denny 1979: 97.
58. Friedrich 1986.
59. Guiora et al. 1982.
60. Ibid., pp. 85–148.
61. Hymes 1974: 83–117.
62. Fischer 1958; Wardhaugh 2002: 160–88.
63. R. Brown and Ford 1961.
64. Wardhaugh 2002: 315.
65. Shibamoto 1987: 28.
66. Holmes 2001: 153.
67. Robin Lakoff 1973; Robin Lakoff 1990b.
68. Wardhaugh 2002: 328; Holmes 2001: 158–59; Trudgill 1983: 87–88.
69. Keenan 1989.
70. Tannen 1990: 49–83.
71. Wardhaugh 2002: 100.
72. Heller 1988: 1.
73. Pfaff 1979.
74. Wardhaugh 2002: 108.
75. Gal 1988: 249–55.
76. Collins and Blot 2003: 1–3.

CHAPTER 11

1. Hitchcock and Beisele 2000: 5.
2. C. R. Ember 1978b.
3. Schrire 1984a; Myers 1988.
4. The discussion of the Australian aborigines is based on R. A. Gould 1969.
5. Burbank 1994: 23; Burbank 2004b.
6. Data from Textor 1967 and Service 1979.
7. Murdock and Provost 1973: 207.
8. Palsson 1988; Roscoe 2002.
9. Kelly 1991.
10. R. L. Kelly 1995: 293–315.
11. Mitchell 2004; Tollefson 2004.
12. R. B. Lee 1968; DeVore and Konner 1974.
13. C. R. Ember 1978b.
14. McCarthy and McArthur 1960.
15. R. B. Lee 1979: 256–58, 278–80.
16. D. Werner 1978.
17. Textor 1967.
18. This section is largely based on Hames 2004.
19. Chagnon 1987: 60.
20. S. S. King 1979.
21. Hickey 1964: 135–65.
22. C. R. Ember 1983: 289.
23. Textor 1967; Dirks 2004; Messer 1996: 244.
24. Barlett 1989: 253–91.
25. The farm population is now so small that the Bureau of the Census has stopped counting it.
26. Salzman 1996.
27. Lees and Bates 1974; A. L. Johnson 2002.
28. Whitaker 1955; Itkonen 1951.
29. Paine 1994.
30. Textor 1967.
31. Dirks 2004.
32. Boserup 1993 [1965].
33. R. C. Hunt 2000.
34. Janzen 1973.
35. Roosevelt 1992.
36. Hoebel 1968: 46–63.
37. Woodburn 1968.
38. Pryor 2005: 36.
39. Leacock and Lee 1982a: 8.
40. R. Murphy 1960: 69, 142–43.
41. Salzman 1996.
42. Not all pastoralists have individual ownership. For example, the Tungus of northern Siberia have kin group ownership of reindeer. See Dowling 1975: 422.
43. Salzman 2002.
44. Bodley 1990: 77–93; Wilmsen 1989: 1–14.
45. Salzman 1996: 904–905.
46. Plattner 1989b: 379–96.

47. Hage and Powers 1992.
48. Steward and Faron 1959: 122–25.
49. B. B. Whiting and Edwards 1988: 164.
50. Nag, White, and Peet 1978: 295–96.
51. Polanyi 1957.
52. Sahlins 1972: 188–96.
53. L. Marshall 1961: 239–41.
54. The // sign in the name for the G//ana people symbolizes a click sound not unlike the sound we make when we want a horse to move faster.
55. Cashdan 1980: 116–20.
56. H. Kaplan, Hill, and Hurtado 1990.
57. Winterhalder 1990.
58. Mooney 1978.
59. Balikci 1970 quoted in Mooney 1978: 392.
60. Mooney 1978: 392.
61. Fehr and Fischbacher 2003; Ensminger 2002; Henrich et al. n.d., as cited by Ensminger 2002.
62. Angier 2002: F1, F8.
63. Abler 2004.
64. Service 1962: 145–46.
65. M. Harris 1974: 118–21.
66. Plattner 1985: viii.
67. Plattner 1985: xii.

CHAPTER 12

1. In an analysis of many native societies in the New World, Feinman and Neitzel (1984: 57) argue that egalitarian and rank societies ("tribes" and "chiefdoms," respectively) are not systematically distinguishable.
2. Fried 1967: 33.
3. Boehm 1993: 230–31; Boehm 1999.
4. M. G. Smith 1966: 152.
5. D. Mitchell 2004.
6. Drucker 1965: 56–64.
7. Service 1978: 249.
8. Sahlins 1958: 80–81.
9. Betzig 1988.
10. Brittain 1978.
11. Higley 1995: 1–47.
12. Argyle 1994.
13. Stille 2001: A17, A19.
14. Treiman and Ganzeboom 1990: 117; Featherman and Hauser 1978: 4, 481.
15. Argyle 1994: 36–37, 178.
16. S. R. Barrett 1994: 17, 41.
17. K. Phillips 1990; *New York Times International* 1997: A26; Johnston 1999: 16.
18. Durrenberger 2001b, who refers to Goldschmidt 1999 and Newman 1988, 1993.
19. Scott and Leonhardt 2005.
20. S. R. Barrett 1994: 17, 41.
21. Klass 2004.
22. Ruskin 1963: 296–314.
23. O. Lewis 1958.
24. Kristof 1995: A18.
25. For more information about caste in Japan, see Berreman 1973 and 1972: 403–14.
26. Kristof 1995; Kristof 1997.
27. For more information about caste in Rwanda, see Berreman 1973 and 1972.
28. "Book of the Year (1995): World Affairs: RWANDA," and "Book of the Year (1995): Race and Ethnic Relations: Rwanda's Complex Ethnic History," *Britannica Online,* December 1997.
29. Berreman 1960: 120–27.
30. O. Patterson 1982: vii–xiii, 105.
31. Pryor 1977: 219.
32. Euripides 1937: 52.
33. Nadel 1942.
34. Lassiter et al. 2004: 49–50.
35. Ibid., pp. 59–67.
36. Pryor 1977: 217–47.

37. Marks 1994: 33; Shanklin 1991: 15–17.
38. Molnar 1998: 19.
39. Brace et al. 1993: 17–19.
40. Brooks, Jackson, and Grinker 1993: 11.
41. Brace et al. 1993: 19.
42. J. Cohen 2007.
43. M. D. Williams 2004.
44. S. S. Friedman 1980: 206.
45. M. H. Ross 2004a.
46. Marks 1994: 32.
47. Armelagos and Goodman 1998: 365.
48. O. Patterson 2000.
49. M. Nash 1989: 2.
50. Ibid., p. 10.
51. Barth 1994: 27.
52. Yinger 1994: 169.
53. Ibid., pp. 169–71.
54. Ibid., pp. 216–17.
55. Benjamin 1991; see also M. D. Williams 2004.
56. Flannery 1972.
57. Data from Textor 1967.
58. Ibid.
59. Lenski 1984: 308–18.
60. Treiman and Ganzeboom 1990: 117; Cutright 1967: 564.
61. Sahlins 1958.
62. Ibid., p. 4.
63. Sahlins 1972.
64. Lenski 1984.
65. Gilman 1990.
66. Fried 1967: 201ff; and Harner 1975.
67. Meek 1940: 149–50.

CHAPTER 13

1. Leibowitz 1978: 43–44.
2. Schlegel 1989: 266; Epstein 1988: 5–6; Chafetz 1990: 28.
3. Jacobs and Roberts 1989.
4. Segal 2004; Segal also cites the work of W. Williams 1992.
5. Lang 1999: 93–94; Blackwood 1984b.
6. Wikan 1982: 168–86.
7. Stini 1971.
8. Frayer and Wolpoff 1985: 431–32.
9. For reviews of theories and research on sexual dimorphism and possible genetic and cultural determinants of variation in degree of dimorphism over time and place, see Frayer and Wolpoff 1985 and Gray 1985: 201–209, 217–25.
10. J. K. Brown 1970b: 1074.
11. Among the Aché hunter-gatherers of Paraguay, women collect the type of honey produced by stingless bees (men collect other honey); this division of labor is consistent with the compatibility theory. See Hurtado et al. 1985: 23.
12. Murdock and Provost 1973: 213; Byrne 1994.
13. R. O'Brian 1999.
14. D. R. White, Burton, and Brudner 1977: 1–24.
15. Mukhopadhyay and Higgins 1988: 473.
16. J. K. Brown 1970b: 1073–78; and D. R. White, Burton, and Brudner 1977.
17. Nerlove 1974.
18. N. E. Levine 1988.
19. M. J. Goodman et al. 1985.
20. Noss and Hewlett 2001.
21. C. R. Ember 1983: 288–89.
22. Mead 1950 [originally published 1935]: 180–84.
23. Rivers 1967 [originally published 1906]: 567.
24. M. Ember and C. R. Ember 1971: 573, table 1.
25. Schlegel and Barry 1986.
26. Boserup 1970: 22–25; see also Schlegel and Barry 1986: 144–45.
27. Boserup 1970: 22–25.
28. Ibid., pp. 31–34.
29. C. R. Ember 1983: 286–87; data from Murdock and Provost 1973: 212; Bradley 1995.

30. C. R. Ember 1983.
31. Ibid.
32. Ibid., pp. 287–93.
33. M. Ember and C. R. Ember 1971: 579–80.
34. Ibid., p. 581; see also Sanday 1973: 1684.
35. Nerlove 1974.
36. Schlegel and Barry 1986.
37. Whyte 1978a: 217.
38. Nussbaum 1995: 2, based on data from Human Development Report 1993.
39. Whyte 1978a; D. B. Adams 1983.
40. J. K. Brown 1970a.
41. Sanday 1974; and Divale and Harris 1976.
42. Quinn 1977: 189–90.
43. Graham 1979.
44. D. Werner 1982; and Stogdill 1974, cited in ibid.; see also Handwerker and Crosbie 1982.
45. Draper 1975: 103.
46. D. Werner 1984.
47. M. H. Ross 1986.
48. This description is based on the fieldwork of Elizabeth and Robert Fearnea (1956–1958), as reported in M. K. Martin and Voorhies 1975: 304–31.
49. Begler 1978.
50. Ibid. See also Whyte 1978a: 229–32.
51. Whyte 1978b: 95–120; see also Quinn 1977.
52. Whyte 1978b: 124–29, 145; see also Sanday 1973.
53. Whyte 1978b: 129–30.
54. J. K. Brown 1970.
55. Whyte 1978b: 135–36.
56. Ibid., p. 135.
57. Doyle 2005.
58. Quinn 1977: 85; see also Etienne and Leacock 1980: 19–20.
59. B. B. Whiting and Edwards 1973.
60. R. L. Munroe et al. 2000: 8–9.
61. Maccoby and Jacklin 1974.
62. For a more extensive discussion of behavior differences and possible explanations of them, see C. R. Ember 1981.
63. B. B. Whiting and Edwards 1973.
64. For references to this research, see C. R. Ember 1981: 559.
65. Rubin, Provenzano, and Haskett 1974.
66. For a discussion of this evidence, see Ellis 1986: 525–27; C. R. Ember 1981.
67. For example, Ellis 1986 considers the evidence for the biological view of aggression "beyond reasonable dispute."
68. For a discussion of other possibilities, see C. R. Ember 1981.
69. Rohner 1976.
70. B. B. Whiting and Whiting 1975; see also B. B. Whiting and Edwards 1988: 273.
71. C. R. Ember 1973: 424–39.
72. B. B. Whiting and Edwards 1973: 175–79; see also Maccoby and Jacklin 1974.
73. Burbank 1994.
74. Heise 1967.
75. C. S. Ford and Beach 1951: 191.
76. O. Lewis 1951: 397.
77. Farley 1996: 60.
78. C. S. Ford and Beach 1951: 23–25, 68–71.
79. Ibid., pp. 40–41, 73.
80. Broude 2004b.
81. C. S. Ford and Beach 1951: 82–83.
82. Broude and Greene 1976.
83. Kluckhohn 1948: 101.
84. M. Hunt 1974: 254–57; Lewin 1994.
85. Broude 1980: 184.
86. C. S. Ford and Beach 1951: 114.
87. Jankowiak, Nell, and Buckmaster 2002.
88. Lang 1999: 97, citing Thomas 1993.
89. J. Morris 1938: 191.
90. Underhill 1938: 117, 186.
91. 'Abd Allah 1917: 7, 20.
92. Cardoso and Werner 2004.
93. R. C. Kelly 1974.
94. Cardoso and Werner 2004.
95. Blackwood and Wieringa 1999: 49; Blackwood 1984a.
96. Data from Textor 1967.
97. W. N. Stephens 1972: 1–28.
98. Broude 1976: 243.
99. D. Werner 1979; D. Werner 1975.
100. D. Werner 1979: 345–62; see also D. Werner 1975: 36.
101. Data from Textor 1967.
102. Schlegel 1991.

CHAPTER 14

1. W. N. Stephens 1963: 5.
2. Murdock 1949: 8.
3. Murdock 1949: 7–8.
4. Ibid., pp. 9–10.
5. See, for example, Linton 1936: 135–36.
6. M. Ember and C. R. Ember 1979.
7. Ibid.
8. Marlowe 2003: 221–23.
9. M. Ember and C. R. Ember 1979.
10. Schlegel and Eloul 1987: 119.
11. Schlegel and Eloul 1988: 295, table 1. We used the data to calculate the frequency of various types of economic transaction in a worldwide sample of 186 societies.
12. Schlegel and Eloul 1988: 298–99.
13. Pryor 1977: 363–64.
14. Ibid.
15. Schlegel and Eloul 1988: 296–97.
16. Ibid.
17. Ibid.
18. Radcliffe-Brown 1922: 73.
19. Murdock 1967; Goody 1973: 17–21.
20. Pryor 1977: 363–65; Schlegel and Eloul 1988: 296–99.
21. Schlegel and Eloul 1988, following Goody 1973: 20.
22. Middleton 1962: 606.
23. Durham 1991: 293–94, citing research by Hopkins 1980.
24. A. Howard and Rensel 2004.
25. Lingenfelter 2004.
26. MacDonald and Hewlett 1999: 504–506.
27. M. Ember 1975: 262, table 3.
28. Busby 2004.
29. M. Ember 1975: 260–69; see also Durham 1991: 341–57.
30. Oliver 1955: 352–53.
31. Ibid., pp. 223–24, quoted in W. Stephens 1963: 58.
32. The discussion of these customs is based on W. Stephens 1963: 63–67.
33. Kilbride and Kilbride 1990: 202–206.
34. C. Anderson 2000: 102–103.
35. J. W. M. Whiting 1964.
36. M. Ember 1974b.
37. M. Ember 1984–1985. The statistical relationship between late age of marriage for men and polygyny was first reported by Witkowski 1975.
38. M. Ember 1974: 202–205.
39. M. Ember 1984–1985. For other predictors of polygyny, see D. R. White and Burton 1988.
40. Sellen and Hruschka 2004.
41. Low 1990b.
42. Coult and Habenstein 1965; Murdock 1957.
43. M. C. Goldstein 1987: 39.
44. Stephens 1963: 45.
45. Hiatt 1980.
46. M. C. Goldstein 1987. Formerly, in feudal Tibet, a class of serfs who owned small parcels of land also practiced polyandry. Goldstein suggests that a shortage of land would explain their polyandry too. See M. C. Goldstein 1971.
47. Pasternak 1976: 96.
48. Coult and Habenstein 1965.
49. Mead 1928, quoted in Stephens 1963: 134–35.
50. Nimkoff and Middleton 1960.
51. Pasternak, C. R. Ember, and M. Ember 1976: 109–23.

52. Coult and Habenstein 1965; Murdock 1957.
53. Percentages calculated from Coult and Habenstein 1965.
54. L. Bohannan and P. Bohannan 1953.
55. J. D. Freeman 1961.
56. C. R. Ember, M. Ember, and Pasternak 1974: 84–89.
57. Pospisil 1963.
58. Schneider 1961a.
59. M. Ember and C. R. Ember 1971: 581.
60. Schneider 1961b.
61. Goodenough 1951: 145.
62. Coult and Habenstein 1965.
63. Data from Textor 1967.
64. Davenport 1959.
65. M. Ember 1967.
66. M. Ember and C. R. Ember. 1971. See also Divale 1974.
67. M. Ember and C. R. Ember 1971: 583–85; and Divale 1974.
68. M. Ember and C. R. Ember 1971. For a different theory—that matrilocal residence precedes, rather than follows, the development of purely external warfare—see Divale 1974.
69. Helms 2004; see also M. Ember and C. R. Ember 1971.
70. Service 1962: 137.
71. C. R. Ember and M. Ember 1972.
72. C. R. Ember 1975.
73. M. Ember 1974a.
74. Data from Textor 1967.
75. C. R. Ember, M. Ember, and Pasternak 1974.
76. The importance of warfare and competition as factors in the formation of unilineal descent groups is also suggested by Service 1962 and Sahlins 1961: 332–45.

CHAPTER 15

1. Service 1962.
2. Schrire 1984b; see also Leacock and Lee 1982: 8.
3. Service 1962: 109.
4. Mathiassen 1928: 213.
5. Service 1962: 114–15.
6. Bohannan 1954: 3.
7. Sahlins 1961: 342.
8. Sahlins 1961: 345.
9. N. Dyson-Hudson 1966: chapters 5 and 6.
10. Sahlins 1962: 293–94.
11. Sahlins 1963: 295.
12. Sahlins 1983: 519.
13. Sahlins 1963: 297.
14. Carneiro 1970: 733.
15. Weber 1947: 154.
16. Wiberg 1983.
17. Finley 1983.
18. Carcopino 1940: 18–20.
19. M. Ember 1963.
20. Textor 1967.
21. M. Ember 1963.
22. Textor 1967.
23. Naroll 1961. See also Ross 1981.
24. M. Ember 1963: 244–46.
25. Service 1962; see also Braun and Plog 1982; Haas 1990a.
26. A. Johnson and Earle 1987: 158; Carneiro 1990.
27. Service 1962: 112, 145.
28. Feinman and Nietzel 1984.
29. For a more detailed description and evaluation of the available theories, see chapter 11 in C. R. Ember, M. Ember, and Peregrine 2007. See also Cohen and Service 1978.
30. McNeill 1976.
31. Carneiro 1978: 215.
32. Textor 1967.
33. Carneiro 1978; Hart 1948; Naroll 1967; Marano 1973: 35–40. See also Peregrine, M. Ember, and C. R. Ember 2004 and other articles in Graber 2004.
34. D. Werner 1982.
35. Kracke 1979: 232.
36. D. Werner 1982.
37. Sahlins 1963.
38. Kracke 1979: 41.
39. Brandewie 1991.
40. Lepowsky 1990.
41. Ross 1988: 73. The discussion in this section draws mostly from ibid., pp. 73–89, and from Ross 2004b.
42. For studies of international relations that support these conclusions, see the citations in footnotes 2 and 3 in C. R. Ember, M. Ember, and Russett 1992; see also chapter 3 in Russett and Oneal 2001.
43. C. R. Ember, M. Ember, and Russett 1992.
44. Rummel 2002b.
45. Scaglion 2004b.
46. Hoebel 1968: 4, quoting S. P. Simpson and Field 1946: 858.
47. Fry and Björkqvist 1997.
48. D. Black 1993: 79–83.
49. Ross 1988.
50. Boas 1888: 668.
51. Otterbein 1986: 107.
52. Archer and Gartner 1984: 118–39.
53. Scaglion 2004b; D. Black 1993: 83–86.
54. Ibid.
55. Evans-Pritchard 1940: 291. The discussion of the Nuer follows this source.
56. Hickson 1986.
57. Ibid.; and Koch et al. 1977: 279.
58. J. M. Roberts 1967: 169.
59. Roberts 1967: 192.
60. Hoebel 1968: chapter 9.
61. Schwartz 1954: 475.
62. Textor 1967.
63. Masumura 1977: 388–99.
64. Scaglion 2004b; Black 1993; Newman 1983: 131.
65. C. R. Ember and M. Ember 1994.
66. Newman 1983: 131.
67. Otterbein and Otterbein 1965: 1476.
68. D. R. White 1988.
69. Patterson 1982: 345–52.
70. Gat 1999: 373, as referred to in Wadley 2003.
71. Heider 1970: 105–11; Heider 1979: 88–99.
72. M. Ember and C. R. Ember 1992: 188–89.
73. C. R. Ember and M. Ember 1992; M. Ember 1982. For a discussion of how Dani warfare seems to be motivated mainly by economic considerations, see Shankman 1991. B. W. Kang 2000: 878–79 finds a strong correlation between environmental stress and warfare frequency in Korean history.
74. Otterbein 1970.
75. C. R. Ember and M. Ember 1992; see also Otterbein 1970 and Loftin 1971.
76. C. R. Ember 1974.
77. Otterbein 1968: 283; Ross 1985.
78. Divale and Harris 1976: 521–38; see also Gibbons 1993.
79. C. R. Ember and M. Ember 1992: 251–52.
80. Russett and Oneal 2001: 89.
81. Ibid., pp. 145–48.

CHAPTER 16

1. A. Wallace 1966: 60–61.
2. Malefijt 1968: 153.
3. Ray 1954: 172–89.
4. Rosenblatt, Walsh, and Jackson 1976: 51.
5. Ibid., p. 55.
6. Swanson 1969: 97–108; see also Sheils 1975.
7. Middleton 1971: 488.
8. Spiro and D'Andrade 1958.
9. Lambert, Triandis, and Wolf 1959; Rohner 1975: 108.
10. H. G. Barnett 1960: 79–85.
11. Swanson 1969: 56.

12. Ibid., pp. 55–81; see also W. D. Davis 1971. Peregrine (1996: 84–112) replicated Swanson's finding in North American societies.
13. Textor 1967; R. Underhill 1975.
14. Geertz 1966.
15. Swanson 1969: 153–74.
16. A. Wallace 1966: 52–67.
17. J. Middleton 1971
18. Winkelman 1986: 178–83.
19. Bourguignon 1973a.
20. Bourguignon and Evascu 1977; Winkelman 1986: 196–98.
21. Kehoe and Giletti 1981.
22. Raybeck 1998, referring to Raybeck, Shoobe, and Grauberger 1989.
23. Bourguignon 2004: 572.
24. Winkleman and Peck 2004.
25. O. K. Moore 1957.
26. Sheils 1980.
27. M. Adler 1989: 4–5.
28. Evans-Pritchard 1979: 362–66.
29. Swanson 1969: 150; see also H. R. Trevor-Roper 1971: 444–49.
30. Swanson 1969: 150–51.
31. Caporael 1976; Matossian 1982; and Matossian 1989: 70–80. For possible reasons to dismiss the ergot theory, see Spanos 1983.
32. Harner 1972b.
33. B. B. Whiting 1950: 36–37; see also Swanson 1969: pp. 137–52, 240–41.
34. Winkelman 1986a.
35. Ibid., pp. 28–29.
36. Knecht 2003: 11.
37. Harner and Doore 1987: 3, 8–9; Noll 1987: 49; Krippner 1987: 128.
38. de Laguna 1972. 701C.
39. See Krippner 1987: 126–27; Noll 1987: 49–50.
40. Boas 1930 as reported in Lévi-Strauss 1963a: 169.
41. Boas 1930: 1–41, reported in Lévi-Strauss 1963b: 169–73.
42. Winkelman 1986: 27–28.
43. Ibid., p. 27.
44. Ibid., pp. 35 37.
45. M. Harris 1966.
46. A. Wallace 1966: 30.
47. A. Wallace 1970: 239.
48. The Quakers, long-time neighbors and trusted advisers of the Seneca, took pains not to interfere with Seneca religion, principles, and attitudes.
49. D. O. Larson, Johnson, and Michaelsen 1994.
50. Discussion is based on Firth 1970.
51. Ibid., p. 387.
52. Ibid., p. 418.
53. Antoun 2001.
54. Nagata 2001
55. Antoun 2001: 17–18.
56. Ibid., p. 45.
57. Stark 1985; Trompf 1990.

CHAPTER 17

1. Linton 1936: 306.
2. Ibid., pp. 310–11.
3. Silver 1981.
4. Greenfield, Maynard, and Childs 2000.
5. Rogers 1983: 263–69.
6. Valente 1995: 21.
7. Linton 1936: 326–27.
8. G. M. Foster 1962: 26.
9. Bodley 1990: 7.
10. Pelto and Müller-Wille 1987: 207–43.
11. Bodley 1990: 38–41.
12. Schrauf 1999.
13. The historical information we refer to comes from a book by Nevins 1927. For how radical the American Revolution was, see Wood 1992.
14. Paige 1975.
15. Boyd and Richerson 1996: 106.
16. Ibid., p. 135.

17. D. T. Campbell 1965. See also Boyd and Richerson 1996 and Durham 1991.
18. McNeill 1967: 283–87.
19. See, e.g., Gross et al. 1979.
20. The description of Tikopia is based on Firth 1959: chapters 5, 6, 7, and 9, passim.
21. Most of this discussion is based on R. F. Murphy and Steward 1956.
22. Burkhalter and Murphy 1989.
23. E. Wolf 1966: 3–4.
24. Gross and Underwood 1971.
25. Russett 1993: 10–11, 14, 138.
26. Bernard and Pelto 1987a: 367.
27. Pelto and Müller-Wille 1987: 237.
28. J. D. Hill 1996: 1.
29. Sattler 1996: 42.
30. Ibid., pp. 50–51.
31. Ibid., p. 54.
32. Ibid., pp. 58–59.
33. Bestor 2001: 76.
34. Trouillot 2001: 128.
35. Durrenberger 2001a; see also Hannerz 1996.
36. Traphagan and Brown 2002.
37. Trouillot 2001: 128.
38. Bradsher 2002: 3.
39. Yergin 2002: A29.
40. G. Thompson 2002: A3.
41. Sengupta 2002: A3.
42. Conklin 2002.
43. Kottak 1996: 136, 153.
44. Roosens 1989: 9.
45. Cashdan 2001.
46. C. R. Ember and Levinson 1991.

CHAPTER 18

1. The discussion in this section draws extensively from Aptekar 1994.
2. Information collected during M. Ember's fieldwork in American Samoa, 1955–1956.
3. Mellor and Gavian 1987.
4. Dirks 1993.
5. Torry 1986.
6. Hardoy and Satterthwaite 1987.
7. Rodwin and Sanyal 1987.
8. Mangin 1967.
9. Rodwin and Sanyal 1987; for a critique of self-help programs, see Ward 1982a.
10. A. Cohen and Paul Koegel 2004.
11. U.S. Department of Housing and Urban Development 2007.
12. A. Cohen and Koegel 2004.
13. Baxter and Hopper 1981: 30–33, 50–74.
14. Ibid.
15. A. Cohen and Koegel 2004.
16. Herrman 1990.
17. Barak 1991: 63–65.
18. Aptekar 1991: 326.
19. Ibid., pp. 326–49; Aptekar 1988.
20. Korbin 1981b: 4.
21. Straus 2001: 195–96.
22. Straus and Kantor 1994.
23. Straus 1995: 30–33; Straus and Kantor 1995.
24. "Children as Victims," 2000; "Violent Crime," 1994; "Prevalence, Incidence, and Consequences of Violence against Women," 1998; Straus 1991.
25. Levinson 1989: 11–12, 44.
26. Minturn and Stashak 1982. Using a sociobiological orientation, a study by Daly and Wilson (1988: 43–59) also suggests that infanticide is largely due to the difficulty of raising the infant successfully.
27. Levinson 1989: 26–28.
28. C. R. Ember and M. Ember 2005; see also Petersen, Lee, and Ellis 1982, as cited in Levinson 1989: 63.
29. Lareau 2003: 230.

30. Levinson 1989: 31.
31. Ibid., p. 71.
32. Gelles and Straus 1988: 78–88.
33. Erchak 2004; Levinson 1989: 44–45.
34. Straus 2001: 187.
35. Straus and Yodanis 1996.
36. Levinson 1989: 104–107.
37. Archer and Gartner 1984: 35.
38. Archer and Gartner 1984: 63–97.
39. Gurr 1989a: 47–48.
40. Russell 1972; Eckhardt 1975; Sipes 1973.
41. C. R. Ember and M. Ember 1994.
42. Archer and Gartner 1984: 118–39.
43. Bacon, Child, and Barry 1963; B. B. Whiting 1965.
44. Barber 2000.
45. C. R. Ember and M. Ember 1994: 625.
46. C. R. Ember and M. Ember 1993: 227.
47. C. A. Anderson and Bushman 2002: 2377; J. G. Johnson et al. 2002.
48. Loftin, McDowall, and Boudouris 1989; Krahn, Hartnagel, and Gartrell 1986, as referred to in Daly and Wilson 1988: 287–88; Gartner 2004.
49. C. R. Ember and M. Ember 1997.
50. Most of the discussion in this section comes from M. Ember and C. R. Ember 1992: 204–206.
51. Meggitt 1977: 201; Gat 1999: 563–83.
52. Data from Korea is consistent with this explanation of war: More environmental stress strongly predicts higher frequencies of warfare in Korea between the first century B.C. and the eighth century A.D. B. W. Kang 2000: 878.
53. For the cross-cultural results suggesting the theory of war described here, see C. R. Ember and M. Ember 1992.
54. For the results on political participation and peace in the ethnographic record, see C. R. Ember, M. Ember, and Russett 1992. For the results on political participation and peace in the modern world, see the references in that essay.
55. Russett and Oneal 2001: 49.
56. Ibid., pp. 125ff.
57. Some of these examples are from Henderson 2001.
58. See the discussions in ibid., pp. 3–9, and S. K. Anderson and Sloan 2002: 1–5.
59. S. K. Anderson and Sloan 2002: 465.
60. This definition is adapted from Chomsky, who is quoted in Henderson 2001: 5.
61. S. K. Anderson and Sloan 2002: 6–7.
62. Ibid., pp. 6–8.
63. Suárez-Orozco 1992.
64. Rummel 2002a.
65. R. J. Rummel 2002c.
66. R. J. Rummel 2002d.
67. S. K. Anderson and Sloan 2002: 422.
68. "Crossroads for Planet Earth" 2005.

CHAPTER 19

1. Kushner 1991.
2. Mead 1978: 426–29.
3. Frankel and Trend 1991: 177.
4. Hackenberg 1988: 172.
5. Kushner 1991.
6. "Appendix C: Statements on Ethics . . .," 2002; "Appendix I: Revised Principles . . .," 2002.
7. "Appendix A: Report of the Committee on Ethics . . .," 2002; "Appendix F: Professional and Ethical Responsibilities . . .," 2002.
8. "Appendix H: National Association of Practicing Anthropologists' Ethical Guidelines . . .," 2002.
9. Scudder 1978.
10. Ibid., pp. 204ff.
11. Picchi 1991: 26–38; for a general description of the Bakairi, see Picchi 2004.
12. Niehoff 1966: 255–67.
13. G. M. Foster 1969: 8–9.
14. Jelliffe and Jelliffe 1975.
15. W. H. Fisher 1994.
16. G. M. Foster 1969: 122–23.
17. Coreil 1989: 149–50.
18. Rogers 1983: 321–31.
19. Bryant and Bailey 1990.
20. Niehoff 1966: 219–24.
21. Coreil 1989: 155.
22. Ravesloot 1997: 174.
23. Anyon and Ferguson 1995.
24. Zeder 1997.
25. Manhein 1999.
26. Joans 1997.
27. A. H. Goodman and Leatherman 1998; Kleinman, Das, and Lock 1997.
28. Rubel and Hass 1996: 120; Loustaunau and Sobo 1997: 80–81.
29. Loustaunau and Sobo 1997: 82–83, referring to Magner 1992: 93.
30. Loustaunau and Sobo 1997, referring to Gesler 1991: 16.
31. Loustaunau and Sobo 1997, referring to C. Leslie 1976: 4; and G. Foster 1994: 11.
32. Ahern 1975: 92–97, as appearing in the eHRAF World Cultures on the Web.
33. Murdock 1980: 20.
34. C. C. Moore 1988.
35. T. Gladwin and Sarason 1953: 64–66.
36. Mahony 1971: 34–38, as seen in the eHRAF World Cultures on the Web.
37. Gladwin and Sarason 1953: 65.
38. Hahn 1995: 133–39.
39. For an exhaustively documented presentation of the more universalistic approach, see E. A. Berlin and Berlin 1996; see also Browner 1985; and Rubel, O'Nell, and Collado-Ardón 1984.
40. E. A. Berlin 1996.
41. Browner 1985; Ortiz de Montellano and Browner 1985.
42. Etkin and Ross 1997.
43. Loustaunau and Sobo 1997: 98–101.
44. Winkelman 1986a.
45. Torrey n.d.
46. Loustaunau and Sobo 1997: 101–102; and Moerman 1997.
47. Loustaunau and Sobo 1997: 102.
48. Dow 1986: 6–9, 125.
49. Hahn 1995: 131–72.
50. Ibid., p. 165.
51. For a discussion of some of the relevant research, see ibid., pp. 80–82.
52. Mascie-Taylor 1990: 118–21.
53. See references in Hahn 1995: 82–87.
54. A. Cohen 1999.
55. Herdt 1997: 3–22.
56. Bolton 1989.
57. Reported in Carey et al. 2004: 462.
58. Bolton 1989.
59. Carrier and Bolton 1991; Schoepf 1988: 625, cited in Carrier and Bolton 1991.
60. Simmons, Farmer, and Schoepf 1996: 64.
61. Schoepf 1988: 637–38.
62. Bolton 1992.
63. Farmer 1997: 414. Married men in Thailand are gradually turning away from commercial sex and having affairs with married women who are believed to be safe; see Lyttleton 2000: 299.
64. Quandt 1996.
65. McElroy and Townsend 2002.
66. Gross and Underwood 1971.
67. McElroy and Townsend 2002: 187, referring to Harvey and Heywood 1983: 27–35.
68. Quandt 1996: 277.
69. McKee 1984: 96.

REFERENCES

'Abd Allah, Mahmud M. 1917. "Siwan Customs." *Harvard African Studies,* 1: 1–28.

Abler, Thomas S. 2004. "Iroquois: The Tree of Peace and the War Kettle." In *Portraits of Culture,* in C. R. Ember, M. Ember, and P. N. Peregrine, *New Directions in Anthropology.* Upper Saddle River, NJ: Prentice Hall, CD-ROM.

Adams, David B. 1983. "Why There Are So Few Women Warriors." *Behavior Science Research,* 18: 196–212.

Adams, Robert McC. 1960. "The Origin of Cities." *Scientific American* (September): 153–68.

Adams, Robert McC. 1981. *Heartland of Cities: Surveys of Ancient Settlement and Land Use on the Central Floodplain of the Euphrates.* Chicago: University of Chicago Press.

Adler, Mortimer. 1986. *Drawing Down the Moon.* Boston: Beacon.

Ahern, Emily M. 1975. "Sacred and Secular Medicine in a Taiwan Village: A Study of Cosmological Disorders." In A. Kleinman et al., eds., *Medicine in Chinese Cultures: Comparative Studies of Health Care in Chinese and Other Societies.* Washington, D.C.: U.S. Department of Health, Education, and Welfare, National Institutes of Health, as seen in eHRAF World Cultures on the Web.

Aiello, Leslie C. 1992. "Body Size and Energy Requirements." In S. Jones, R. Martin, and D. Pilbeam, eds., *The Cambridge Encyclopedia of Human Evolution.* New York: Cambridge University Press.

Aiello, Leslie C., and Mark Collard. 2001. "Our Newest Oldest Ancestor?" *Nature,* 410 (November 29): 526–27.

Aiello, Leslie C., and Christopher Dean. 1990. *An Introduction to Human Evolutionary Anatomy.* London: Academic Press, pp. 268–74.

Aitken, M. J. 1985. *Thermoluminescence Dating.* London: Academic Press.

Akmajian, Adrian, Richard A. Demers, and Robert M. Harnish. 1984. *Linguistics: An Introduction to Language and Communication,* 2nd ed. Cambridge, MA: MIT Press.

Alexander, John P. 1992. "Alas, Poor *Notharctus.*" *Natural History* (August): 55–59.

Alroy, John. 2001. "A Multispecies Overkill Simulation of the End-Pleistocene Megafaunal Mass Extinction." *Science* 292 (June 8): 1893–96.

American Anthropological Association. 1991. "Revised Principles of Professional Responsibility, 1990." In C. Fluehr-Lobban, ed., *Ethics and the Profession of Anthropology: Dialogue for a New Era.* Philadelphia: University of Pennsylvania Press, pp. 274–79.

Anderson, Connie M. 2000. "The Persistence of Polygyny as an Adaptive Response to Poverty and Oppression in Apartheid South Africa." *Cross-Cultural Research* 34: 99–112.

Anderson, J. L., C. B. Crawford, J. Nadeau, and T. Lindberg. 1992. "Was the Dutchess of Windsor Right? A Cross-Cultural Review of the Socioecology of Ideal Female Body Shape. *Ethnology and Sociobiology,* 13: 197–227.

Anderson, Sean K., and Stephen Sloan. 2002. *Historical Dictionary of Terrorism,* 2nd ed. Lanham, MD: Scarecrow Press.

Andrews, Peter. 2000. "*Propliopithecidae.*" In I. Tattersall, E. Delson, and J. van Couvering, eds., *Encyclopedia of Human Evolution and Prehistory.* New York, Garland.

Andrews, Peter. 2001. "Proconsul." In I. Tattersall, E. Delson, and J. van Couvering, eds., *Encyclopedia of Human Evolution and Prehistory.* New York: Garland.

Angier, Natalie. 2002. "Why We're So Nice: We're Wired to Cooperate." Science Times in *The New York Times,* July 23, pp. F1, F8.

Antoun, Richard T. 2001. *Understanding Fundamentalism: Christian, Islamic, and Jewish Movements.* Walnut Creek, CA: AltaMira Press.

Anyon, Roger, and T. J. Ferguson. 1995. "Cultural Resources Management at the Pueblo of Zuni, New Mexico, USA." *Antiquity,* 69: 913–30.

"Appendix A: Report of the Committee on Ethics, Society for Applied Anthropology." 2002. In C. Fluehr-Lobban, ed., *Ethics and the Profession of Anthropology.* Philadelphia: University of Pennsylvania Press.

"Appendix C: Statements on Ethics: Principles of Professional Responsibility, Adopted by the Council of the American Anthropological Association, May 1971." 1991. In C. Fluehr-Lobban, ed., *Ethics and the Profession of Anthropology.* Philadelphia: University of Pennsylvania Press.

"Appendix F: Professional and Ethical Responsibilities, SfAA." 2002. In C. Fluehr-Lobban, ed., *Ethics and the Profession of Anthropology.* Philadelphia: University of Pennsylvania Press.

"Appendix H: National Association of Practicing Anthropologists' Ethical Guidelines for Practitioners, 1988." 1991. In C. Fluehr-Lobban, ed., *Ethics and the Profession of Anthropology.* Philadelphia: University of Pennsylvania Press.

Aptekar, Lewis. 1988. *Street Children of Cali.* Durham, NC: Duke University Press.

Aptekar, Lewis. 1991. "Are Colombian Street Children Neglected? The Contributions of Ethnographic and Ethnohistorical Approaches to the Study of Children." *Anthropology and Education Quarterly,* 22: 326–49.

Aptekar, Lewis. 1994. *Environmental Disasters in Global Perspective.* New York: G. K. Hall/Macmillan.

Archer, Dane, and Rosemary Gartner. 1984. *Violence and Crime in Cross-National Perspective.* New Haven, CT: Yale University Press.

Argyle, Michael. 1994. *The Psychology of Social Class.* New York: Routledge.

Armelagos, George J., and Alan H. Goodman. 1998. "Race, Racism, and Anthropology." In A. H. Goodman and T. L. Leatherman, eds., *Building a New Biocultural Synthesis: Political-Economic Perspectives on Human Biology.* Ann Arbor: University of Michigan Press.

Asch, Nancy B., and David L. Asch. 1978. "The Economic Potential of *Iva annua* and Its Prehistoric Importance in the Lower Illinois Valley." In R. Ford, ed., *The Nature and Status of Ethnobotany.* Anthropological Papers No 67, Museum of Anthropology. Ann Arbor: University of Michigan.

Asch, Solomon. 1956. "Studies of Independence and Conformity: A Minority of One against a Unanimous Majority." *Psychological Monographs,* 70: 1–70.

Ascher, Robert. 1961. "Analogy in Archaeological Interpretation." *Southwestern Journal of Anthropology,* 17: 317–25.

Asfaw, Berhane, Tim White, Owen Lovejoy, Bruce Latimer, Scott Simpson, and Glen Suwa. 1999. "*Australopithecus garhi:* A New Species of Early Hominid from Ethiopia." *Science,* 284 (April 23): 629–36.

Ayala, Francisco J. 1995. "The Myth of Eve: Molecular Biology and Human Origins." *Science,* 270 (December 22): 1930–36.

Ayala, Francisco J. 1996. "Communication" in *Science,* 274 (November 29): 1354.

Bacon, Margaret, Irvin L. Child, and Herbert Barry III. 1963. "A Cross-Cultural Study of Correlates of Crime." *Journal of Abnormal and Social Psychology,* 66: 291–300.

Badcock, C. R. 2000. *Evolutionary Psychology: A Critical Introduction.* Cambridge: Blackwell.

Bahn, Paul. 1998. "Neanderthals Emancipated." *Nature,* 394 (August 20): 719–20.

Bailey, Robert C., Genevieve Head, Mark Jenike, Bruce Owen, Robert Rectman, and Elzbieta Zechenter. 1989. "Hunting and Gathering in Tropical Rain Forest: Is It Possible?" *American Anthropologist,* 91: 59–82.

Baldi, Philip. 1983. *An Introduction to the Indo-European Languages.* Carbondale: Southern Illinois University Press.

Balikci, Asen. 1970. *The Netsilik Eskimo.* Garden City, NY: Natural History Press.

Balter, Michael. 2001. "In Search of the First Europeans," *Science,* 291 (March 2): 1722–25.

Balter, Michael, and Ann Gibbons. 2000. "A Glimpse of Humans' First Journey Out of Africa." *Science,* 288 (May 12): 948–50.

Barak, Gregg. 1991. *Gimme Shelter: A Social History of Homelessness in Contemporary America.* New York: Praeger.

Barash, David P. 1977. *Sociobiology and Behavior.* New York: Elsevier.

Barber, Nigel. 2000. "The Sex Ratio as a Predictor of Cross-National Variation in Violent Crime," *Cross-Cultural Research,* 34: 264–82.

Barber, Nigel. 2003. "Paternal Investment Prospects and Cross-National Differences in Single Parenthood." *Cross-Cultural Research,* 37: 163–77.

Barlett, Peggy F. 1989. "Industrial Agriculture." In S. Plattner, ed., *Economic Anthropology.* Stanford, CA: Stanford University Press.

Barnett, H. G. 1960. *Being a Palauan.* New York: Holt, Rinehart & Winston.

Barnosky, Anthony, Paul Koch, Robert Feranec, Scott Wing, and Alan Shabel. 2004. "Assessing the Causes of Late Pleistocene Extinctions on the Continents." *Science,* 306 (October 1): 70–75.

Barrett, Stanley R. 1994. *Paradise: Class, Commuters, and Ethnicity in Rural Ontario.* Toronto: University of Toronto Press.

Barth, Fredrik. 1994. "Enduring and Emerging Issues in the Analysis of Ethnicity." In H. Vermeulen and C. Govers, eds., *The Anthropology of Ethnicity.* Amsterdam: Het Spinhuis.

Bates, E., and V. A. Marchman. 1988. "What Is and Is Not Universal in Language Acquisition." In F. Plum, ed., *Language, Communication, and the Brain.* New York: Raven Press, pp. 19–38.

Baxter, Ellen, and Kim Hopper. 1981. *Private Lives/Public Spaces: Homeless Adults on the Streets of New York City.* New York: Community Service Society of New York.

Beadle, George, and Muriel Beadle. 1966. *The Language of Life.* Garden City, NY: Doubleday.

Bearder, Simon K. 1987. "Lorises, Bushbabies, and Tarsiers: Diverse Societies in Solitary Foragers." In B. Smuts et al., eds., *Primate Societies.* Chicago: University of Chicago Press.

Begler, Elsie B. 1978. "Sex, Status, and Authority in Egalitarian Society." *American Anthropologist,* 80: 571–88.

Begun, David. 2002. "Miocene Apes." In P. N. Peregrine, C. R. Ember, and M. Ember, eds., *Physical Anthropology: Original Readings in Method and Practice.* Upper Saddle River, NJ: Prentice Hall.

Benjamin, Lois. 1991. *The Black Elite: Facing the Color Line in the Twilight of the Twentieth Century.* Chicago: Nelson-Hall.

Berggren, William A., Dennis V. Kent, John D. Obradovich, and Carl C. Swisher III. 1992. "Toward a Revised Paleogene Geochronology." In D. R. Prothero and W. A. Berggren, eds., *Eocene-Oliocene Climatic and Biotic Evolution.* Princeton, NJ: Princeton University Press.

Berlin, Brent. 1992. *Ethnobiological Classification: Principles of Categorization of Plants and Animals in Traditional Societies.* Princeton, NJ: Princeton University Press.

Berlin, Brent, and Paul Kay. 1969. *Basic Color Terms: Their Universality and Evolution.* Berkeley: University of California Press.

Berlin, E. A. 1996. "General Overview of Maya Ethnomedicine." In E. A. Berlin and B. Berlin, *Medical Ethnobiology of the Highland Maya of Chiapas, Mexico.* Princeton, NJ: Princeton University Press, pp. 52–53.

Berlin, Elois Ann, and Brent Berlin. 1996. *Medical Ethnobiology of the Highland Maya of Chiapas, Mexico: The Gastrointestinal Diseases.* Princeton, NJ: Princeton University Press.

Bernard, H. Russell. 2001. *Research Methods in Cultural Anthropology: Qualitative and Quantitative Approaches,* 3rd ed. Walnut Creek, CA: AltaMira Press.

Bernard, H. Russell, and Pertti J. Pelto. 1987. "Technology and Anthropological Theory: Conclusions." In H. R. Bernard and P. J. Pelto, eds., *Technology and Social Change,* 2nd ed. Prospect Heights, IL: Waveland.

Berreman, Gerald D. 1960. "Caste in India and the United States." *American Journal of Sociology,* 66: 120–27.

Berreman, Gerald D. 1972. "Race, Caste and Other Invidious Distinctions in Social Stratification." *Race,* 13: 403–14.

Berreman, Gerald D. 1973. *Caste in the Modern World.* Morristown, NJ: General Learning Press.

Bestor, Theodore C. 2001. "Supply-Side Sushi: Commodity, Market, and the Global City." *American Anthropologist,* 103: 76–95.

Betzig, Laura. 1988. "Redistribution: Equity or Exploitation?" In L. Betzig, M. Borgerhoff Mulder, and P. Turke, eds., *Human Reproductive Behavior.* Cambridge: Cambridge University Press, pp. 49–63.

Bickerton, Derek. 1983. "Creole Languages." *Scientific American* (July): 116–22.

Bilsborough, Alan. 1992. *Human Evolution.* New York: Blackie Academic & Professional.

Bindon, James R., and Douglas E. Crews. 1993. "Changes in Some Health Status Characteristics of American Samoan Men: Preliminary Observations from a 12-Year Follow-Up Study." *American Journal of Human Biology,* 5: 31–37.

Bindon, James R., Amy Knight, William W. Dressler, and Douglas E. Crews. 1997. "Social Context and Psychosocial Influences on Blood Pressure among American Samoans." *American Journal of Physical Anthropology,* 103: 7–18.

Binford, Lewis R. 1971. "Post-Pleistocene Adaptations." In S. Struever, ed., *Prehistoric Agriculture.* Garden City, NY: Natural History Press.

Binford, Lewis R. 1973. "Interassemblage Variability: The Mousterian and the 'Functional' Argument." In C. Renfrew, ed., *The Explanation of Culture Change.* Pittsburgh: University of Pittsburgh Press.

Binford, Lewis R. 1984. *Faunal Remains from Klasies River Mouth.* Orlando, FL: Academic Press.

Binford, Lewis R. 1987. "Were There Elephant Hunters at Torralba?" In M. Nitecki and D. Nitecki, eds., *The Evolution of Human Hunting.* New York: Plenum.

Binford, Lewis R., and Chuan Kun Ho. 1985. "Taphonomy at a Distance: Zhoukoudian, 'The Cave Home of Beijing Man'?" *Current Anthropology,* 26: 413–42.

Binford, Sally R., and Lewis R. Binford. 1969. "Stone Tools and Human Behavior." *Scientific American* (April): 70–84.

Black, Donald. 1993. *The Social Structure of Right and Wrong.* San Diego: Academic Press.

Black, Francis L. 1992. "Why Did They Die?" *Science,* 258 (December 11): 1739–40.

Blackwood, Evelyn. 1984a. Cross-Cultural Dimensions of Lesbian Relations. Master's Thesis. San Francisco State University. As referred to in Blackwood and Wieringa 1999.

Blackwood, Evelyn. 1984b. "Sexuality and Gender in Certain Native American Tribes: The Case of Cross-Gender Females." *Signs,* 10: 27–42.

Blackwood, Evelyn, and Saskia E. Wieringa. 1999. "Sapphic Shadows: Challenging the Silence in the Study of Sexuality." In E. Blackwood and S. E. Weiringa, eds., *Female Desires: Same-Sex Relations and Transgender Practices Across Cultures.* New York: Columbia University Press, pp. 39–63.

Blalock, Hubert M. 1972. *Social Statistics,* 2nd ed. New York: McGraw-Hill.

Blanton, Richard E., Stephen A. Kowalewski, Gary Feinman, and Jill Appel. 1981. *Ancient Mesoamerica: A Comparison of Change in Three Regions.* New York: Cambridge University Press.

Block, Jonathan I. and Doug M. Boyer. 2002. "Grasping Primate Origins," *Science,* 298 (November 22): 1606–10.

Blount, Ben G. 1981. "The Development of Language in Children." In R. H. Munroe, R. L. Munroe, and B. B. Whiting, eds., *Handbook of Cross-Cultural Human Development.* New York: Garland.

Blumenschine, Robert J., et al. 2003. "Late Pliocene *Homo* and Hominid Land Use from Western Olduvai Gorge, Tanzania." *Science,* 299 (February 21): 1217–21.

Blumler, Mark A., and Roger Byrne. 1991. "The Ecological Genetics of Domestication and the Origins of Agriculture." *Current Anthropology,* 32: 23–35.

Boas, Franz. 1888. *Central Eskimos.* Washington, D.C.: Bureau of American Ethnology Annual Report No. 6.

Boas, Franz. 1930. "The Religion of the Kwakiutl." *Columbia University Contributions to Anthropology,* vol. 10, pt. 2. New York: Columbia University.

Boas, Franz. 1964 [1911]. "On Grammatical Categories." In D. Hymes, ed., *Language in Culture and Society.* New York: Harper & Row.

Boaz, Noel T., and Alan J. Almquist. 1999. *Essentials of Biological Anthropology.* Upper Saddle River, NJ: Prentice Hall.

Boaz, Noel T., and Alan J. Almquist. 2001. *Biological Anthropology: A Synthetic Approach to Human Evolution,* 2nd ed. Upper Saddle River, NJ: Prentice Hall.

Bodley, John H. 1990. *Victims of Progress,* 3rd ed. Mountain View, CA: Mayfield.

Boehm, Christopher. 1993. "Egalitarian Behavior and Reverse Dominance Hierarchy." *Current Anthropology,* 34: 230–31.

Boehm, Christopher. 1999. *Hierarchy in the Forest: The Evolution of Egalitarian Behavior.* Cambridge, MA: Harvard University Press.

Boesche, C., et al. 1994. "Is Nut Cracking in Wild Chimpanzees a Cultural Behavior?" *Journal of Human Evolution,* 26: 325–38.

Bogin, Barry. 1988. *Patterns of Human Growth.* Cambridge: Cambridge University Press.

Bohannan, Laura, and Paul Bohannan. 1953. *The Tiv of Central Nigeria.* London: International African Institute.

Bohannan, Paul. 1954. "The Migration and Expansion of the Tiv." *Africa,* 24: 2–16.

Bolton, Ralph. 1989. "Introduction: The AIDS Pandemic, a Global Emergency." *Medical Anthropology,* 10: 93–104.

Bolton, Ralph. 1992. "AIDS and Promiscuity: Muddles in the Models of HIV Prevention." *Medical Anthropology,* 14: 145–223.

"Book of the Year: World Affairs: Rwanda," and "Book of the Year: Race and Ethnic Relations: Rwanda's Complex Ethnic History." 1995. *Britannica Online,* December.

Bordaz, Jacques. 1970. *Tools of the Old and New Stone Age.* Garden City, NY: Natural History Press.

Bordes, François. 1961. "Mousterian Cultures in France." *Science,* 134 (September 22): 803–10.

Bordes, François. 1968. *The Old Stone Age.* New York: McGraw-Hill, pp. 51–97.

Bornstein, Marc H. 1973. "The Psychophysiological Component of Cultural Difference in Color Naming and Illusion Susceptibility." *Behavior Science Notes,* 8: 41–101.

Boserup, Ester. 1970. *Woman's Role in Economic Development.* New York: St. Martin's Press.

Boserup, Ester. 1993 [1965]. *The Conditions of Agricultural Growth: The Economics of Agrarian Change under Population Pressure.* Toronto: Earthscan Publishers.

Bourguignon, Erika. 1973. "Introduction: A Framework for the Comparative Study of Altered States of Consciousness." In E. Bourguignon, ed., *Religion, Altered States of Consciousness, and Social Change.* Columbus: Ohio State University Press.

Bourguignon, Erika. 2004. "Suffering and Healing, Subordination and Power: Women and Possession Trance." *Ethos,* 32: 557–74.

Bourguignon, Erika, and Thomas L. Evascu. 1977. "Altered States of Consciousness within a General Evolutionary Perspective: A Holocultural Analysis." *Behavior Science Research,* 12: 197–216.

Boyd, Robert, and Peter J. Richerson. 1996 [1985]. *Culture and the Evolutionary Process.* Chicago: University of Chicago Press.

Boyd, Robert, and Joan Silk. 2000. *How Humans Evolved,* 2nd ed. New York: Norton.

Brace, C. Loring. 1996. "A Four-Letter Word Called Race." In L. T. Reynolds and L. Leiberman, eds., *Race and Other Misadventures: Essays in Honor of Ashley Montague in His Ninetieth Year.* New York: General Hall.

Brace, C. Loring, David P. Tracer, Lucia Allen Yaroch, John Robb, Kari Brandt, and A. Russell Nelson. 1993. "Clines and Clusters versus 'Race': A Test in Ancient Egypt and the Case of a Death on the Nile." *Yearbook of Physical Anthropology,* 36: 1–31.

Bradley, Candice. 1995. "Keeping the Soil in Good Heart: Weeding, Women, and Ecofeminism." In K. Warren, ed., *Ecofeminism.* Bloomington: Indiana University Press.

Bradsher, Keith. 2002. "Pakistanis Fume as Clothing Sales to U.S. Tumble." *The New York Times,* June 23, p. 3.

Braidwood, Robert J. 1960. "The Agricultural Revolution." *Scientific American,* (September): 130–48.

Brain, C. K., and A. Sillen. 1988. "Evidence from the Swartkrans Cave for the Earliest Use of Fire." *Nature,* 336 December 1: 464–66.

Branda, Richard F., and John W. Eaton. 1978. "Skin Color and Nutrient Photolysis: An Evolutionary Hypothesis." *Science,* 201 (August 18): 625–26.

Brandewie, Ernest. 1991. "The Place of the Big Man in Traditional Hagen Society in the Central Highlands of New Guinea." In F. McGlynn and A. Tuden, eds., *Anthropological Approaches to Political Behavior.* Pittsburgh, PA: University of Pittsburg Press.

Brandon, Robert N. 1990. *Adaptation and Environment.* Princeton, NJ: Princeton University Press.

Bräuer, Günter. 1984. "A Craniological Approach to the Origin of Anatomically Modern *Homo sapiens* in Africa and Implications for the Appearance of Modern Europeans." In F. Smith and F. Spencer, eds., *The Origins of Modern Humans.* New York: Alan R. Liss.

Braun, David P., and Stephen Plog. 1982. "Evolution of 'Tribal' Social Networks: Theory and Prehistoric North American Evidence." *American Antiquity,* 47: 504–25.

Bringa, Tone. 1995. *Being Muslim the Bosnian Way: Identity and Community in a Central Bosnian Village.* Princeton, NJ: Princeton University Press, as examined in eHRAF World Cultures on the Web.

Brittain, John A. 1978. *Inheritance and the Inequality of Material Wealth.* Washington, D.C.: Brookings Institution.

Brodey, Jane E. 1971. "Effects of Milk on Blacks Noted." *The New York Times,* October 15, p. 15.

Bromage, Timothy G., and M. Christopher Dean. 1985. "Reevaluation of the Age at Death of Immature Fossil Hominids." *Nature,* 317 (October 10): 525–27.

Brooks, Alison S., Fatimah Linda Collier Jackson, and R. Richard Grinker. 1993. "Race and Ethnicity in America." *Anthro Notes* (National Museum of Natural History Bulletin for Teachers), 15, no. 3 (fall): 1–3, 11–15.

Broom, Robert. 1950. *Finding the Missing Link.* London: Watts.

Brothwell, Don, and Eric Higgs, eds. 1963. *Science in Archaeology.* New York: Basic Books.

Broude, Gwen J. 1976. "Cross-Cultural Patterning of Some Sexual Attitudes and Practices." *Behavior Science Research,* 11: 227–62.

Broude, Gwen J. 1980. "Extramarital Sex Norms in Cross-Cultural Perspective." *Behavior Science Research,* 15: 181–218.

Broude, Gwen J. 2004. "Variations in Sexual Attitudes, Norms, and Practices." In *Cross-Cultural Research for Social Science,* in C. R. Ember, M. Ember, and P. N. Peregrine, eds., *New Directions in Anthropology.* Upper Saddle River, NJ: Prentice Hall, CD-ROM.

Broude, Gwen J., and Sarah J. Greene. 1976. "Cross-Cultural Codes on Twenty Sexual Attitudes and Practices." *Ethnology,* 15: 409–29.

Brown, Cecil H. 1977. "Folk Botanical Life-Forms: Their Universality and Growth." *American Anthropologist,* 79: 317–42.

Brown, Cecil H. 1979. "Folk Zoological Life-Forms: Their Universality and Growth." *American Anthropologist,* 81: 791–817.

Brown, Cecil H. 1984. "World View and Lexical Uniformities." *Reviews in Anthropology,* 11: 99–112.

Brown, Cecil H., and Stanley R. Witkowski. 1980. "Language Universals." Appendix B in D. Levinson and M. J. Malone, eds., *Toward Explaining Human Culture.* New Haven, CT: HRAF Press.

Brown, Frank H. 1992. "Methods of Dating." In S. Jones, R. Martin, and D. Pilbeam, eds., *The Cambridge Encyclopedia of Human Evolution.* New York: Cambridge University Press.

Brown, Frank H. 2000. "Geochronometry." In I. Tattersall, G. Delson, and J. van Couvering, eds., *Encyclopedia of Human Evolution and Prehistory.* New York: Garland.

Brown, James A. 1983. "Summary." In J. L. Phillips and J. A. Brown, eds., *Archaic Hunters and Gatherers in the American Midwest.* New York: Academic Press, pp. 5–10.

Brown, James A. 1985. "Long-Term Trends to Sedentism and the Emergence of Complexity in the American Midwest." In T. Price and J. Brown, eds., *Prehistoric Hunter-Gatherers.* Orlando, FL: Academic Press, pp. 201–31.

Brown, James A., and T. Douglas Price. 1985. "Complex Hunter-Gatherers: Retrospect and Prospect." In T. Price and J. Brown, eds., *Prehistoric Hunter-Gatherers.* Orlando, FL: Academic Press

Brown, Judith K. 1970a. "Economic Organization and the Position of Women among the Iroquois." *Ethnohistory,* 17: 151–67.

Brown, Judith K. 1970b. "A Note on the Division of Labor by Sex." *American Anthropologist,* 72: 1073–78.

Brown, Peter J. 1999. "Culture and the Evolution of Obesity." In A. Podolefsky and P. J. Brown, eds., *Applying Cultural Anthropology: An Introductory Reader.* Mountain View, CA: Mayfield.

Brown, Peter J., T. Sutikna, M. J. Morwood, R. P. Soejono, Wayhu Saptomo Jatmiko, and Rokus Awe Due. 2004. "A New Small-Bodied Hominin from the Late Pleistocene of Flores, Indonesia." *Nature,* 431 (October 27).

Brown, Roger. 1965. *Social Psychology.* New York: Free Press.

Brown, Roger. 1980. "The First Sentence of Child and Chimpanzee." In T. A. Sebeok and J. Umiker-Sebeok, eds., *Speaking of Apes.* New York: Plenum Press.

Brown, Roger, and Marguerite Ford. 1961. "Address in American English." *Journal of Abnormal and Social Psychology,* 62: 375–85.

Browner, C. H. 1985. "Criteria for Selecting Herbal Remedies." *Ethnology,* 24: 13–32.

Brumfiel, Elizabeth M. 1976. "Regional Growth in the Eastern Valley of Mexico: A Test of the 'Population Pressure' Hypothesis." In K. Flannery, ed., *The Early Mesoamerican Village.* New York: Academic Press.

Brumfiel, Elizabeth M. 1983. "Aztec State Making: Ecology, Structure, and the Origin of the State." *American Anthropologist,* 85: 261–84.

Brunet, Michel, Alain Beauvilain, Yves Coppens, Emile Heintz, Aladji H. E. Moutaye, and David Pilbeam. 1995. "The First Australopithecine 2,500 Kilometres West of the Rift Valley." *Nature,* 378: 273–74.

Brunet, Michel, et al. 2002. "A New Hominid from the Upper Miocene of Chad, Central Africa," *Nature,* 418 (July 11): 145–51.

Bryant, Carol A., and Doraine F. C. Bailey. 1990. "The Use of Focus Group Research in Program Development." In J. van Willigen and T. L. Finan, eds., *Soundings.* NAPA Bulletin No. 10. Washington, D.C.: American Anthropological Association.

Buettner-Janusch, John. 1973. *Physical Anthropology: A Perspective.* New York: Wiley.

Burbank, Victoria K. 1994. *Fighting Women: Anger and Aggression in Aboriginal Australia.* Berkeley: University of California Press.

Burbank, Victoria K. 2004. "Australian Aborigines: An Adolescent Mother and Her Family." In *Portraits of Culture,* in C. R. Ember, M. Ember, and P. N. Peregrine, eds., *New Directions in Anthropology.* Upper Saddle River, NJ: Prentice Hall, CD-ROM.

Burkhalter, S. Brian, and Robert F. Murphy. 1989. "Tappers and Sappers: Rubber, Gold and Money among the Mundurucú." *American Ethnologist,* 16: 100–16.

Burns, Alisa, and Cath Scott. 1994. *Mother-Headed Families and Why They Have Increased.* Hillsdale, NJ: Lawrence Erlbaum Associates.

Busby, Annette. 2004. "Kurds: A Culture Straddling National Borders." In *Portraits of Culture,* in C. R. Ember, M. Ember, and P. N. Peregrine, eds., *New Directions in Anthropology.* Upper Saddle River, NJ: Prentice Hall, CD-ROM.

Butzer, Karl W. 1982. "Geomorphology and Sediment Stratigraphy." In R. Singer and J. Wymer, *The Middle Stone Age at Klasies River Mouth in South Africa.* Chicago: University of Chicago Press.

Byrne, Bryan. 1994. "Access to Subsistence Resources and the Sexual Division of Labor among Potters." *Cross-Cultural Research,* 28: 225–50.

Calvin, William H. 1983. *The Throwing Madonna: Essays on the Brain.* New York: McGraw-Hill.

Campbell, Donald T. 1965. "Variation and Selective Retention in Socio-Cultural Evolution." In H. Barringer, G. Blankstein, and R. Mack, eds., *Social Change in Developing Areas.* Cambridge, MA: Schenkman.

Cann, Rebecca. 1988. "DNA and Human Origins." *Annual Review of Anthropology,* 17: 127–43.

Cann, Rebecca, M. Stoneking, and A. C. Wilson. 1987. "Mitochondrial DNA and Human Evolution." *Nature,* 325 (January 1): 31–36.

Caporael, Linda R. 1976. "Ergotism: The Satan Loosed in Salem?" *Science* (April 2): 21–26.

Cardoso, Fernando Luis, and Dennis Werner. 2004. "Homosexuality." In C. R. Ember and M. Ember, eds., *Encyclopedia of Sex and Gender: Men and Women in the World's Cultures,* vol 1. New York: Kluwer Academic/Plenum Publishers, pp. 204–15.

Carey, James W., Erin Picone-DeCaro, Mary Spink Neumann, Devorah Schwartz, Delia Easton, and Daphne Cobb St. John. 2004. "HIV/AIDS Research and Prevention." In C. R. Ember and M. Ember, eds., *Encyclopedia of Medical Anthropology: Health and Illness in the World's Cultures,* vol. 1. New York: Kluwer Academic/Plenum, pp. 462–79.

Carcopino, Jerome. 1940. *Daily Life in Ancient Rome: The People and the City at the Height of the Empire.* Edited with bibliography and notes by Henry T. Rowell. Translated from the French by E. O. Lorimer. New Haven, CT: Yale University Press.

Carneiro, Robert L. 1970. "A Theory of the Origin of the State." *Science,* 169 (August 21): 733–38.

Carneiro, Robert L. 1978. "Political Expansion as an Expression of the Principle of Competitive Exclusion." In R. Cohen and E. R. Service, eds., *Origins of the State.* Philadelphia: Institute for the Study of Human Issues.

Carneiro, Robert L. 1988. "The Circumscription Theory: Challenge and Response." *American Behavioral Scientist,* 31: 497–511.

Carneiro, Robert L. 1990. "Chiefdom-Level Warfare as Exemplified in Fiji and the Cauca Valley." In J. Haas, ed., *The Anthropology of War.* New York: Cambridge University Press.

Carpenter, C. R. 1940. "A Field Study in Siam of the Behavior and Social Relations of the Gibbon (*Hylobates lar*)." *Comparative Psychology Monographs,* 16, no. 5: 1–212.

Carrier, Joseph, and Ralph Bolton. 1991. "Anthropological Perspectives on Sexuality and HIV Prevention." *Annual Review of Sex Research,* 2: 49–75.

Carroll, John B., ed. 1956. *Language, Thought, and Reality: Selected Writings of Benjamin Lee Whorf.* New York: Wiley.

Cartmill, Matt. 1974. "Rethinking Primate Origins," *Science,* (April 26): 436–37.

Cartmill, Matt. 1992a. "New Views on Primate Origins." *Evolutionary Anthropology,* 1: 105–11.

Cartmill, Matt. 1992b. "Non-Human Primates." In S. Jones, R. Martin, and D. Pilbeam, eds., *The Cambridge Encyclopedia of Human Evolution.* New York: Cambridge University Press.

Cartmill, Matt. 2002. "Explaining Primate Origins." In P. N. Peregrine, C. R. Ember, and M. Ember, eds., *Physical Anthropology: Original Readings in Method and Practice.* Upper Saddle River, NJ: Prentice Hall.

Cashdan, Elizabeth A. 1980. "Egalitarianism among Hunters and Gatherers." *American Anthropologist,* 82: 116–20.

Cashdan, Elizabeth. 2001. "Ethnic Diversity and Its Environmental Determinants: Effects of Climate, Pathogens, and Habitat Diversity." *American Anthropologist,* 103: 968–91.

Caulkins, D. Douglas. 1997. "Welsh." In D. Levinson and M. Ember, eds., *American Immigrant Cultures: Builders of a Nation,* vol. 2. New York: Macmillan Reference, pp. 935–41.

Cavalli-Sforza, L. Luca, and Marcus W. Feldman. 2003. "The Application of Molecular Genetic Approaches to the Study of Human Evolution." *Nature Genetics Supplement* 33: 266–75.

Caws, Peter. 1969. "The Structure of Discovery." *Science,* 166 (December 12): 1375–80.

Center for Renewal of Science and Culture. 2001. "The Wedge Strategy." Cited in Barbara Forrest, "The Wedge at Work," in Robert Pennock, ed., *Intelligent Design Creationism and Its Critics.* Boston: IT Press.

Chafetz, Janet Saltzman. 1990. *Gender Equity: An Integrated Theory of Stability and Change.* Sage Library of Social Research No. 176. Newbury Park, CA: Sage.

Chagnon, Napoleon. 1987. *Yanomamö: The Fierce People,* 3rd ed. New York: Holt, Rinehardt, and Winston.

Chambers, Erve. 1989. *Applied Anthropology: A Practical Guide,* rev. ed. Prospect Heights, IL: Waveland.

Chapman, Jefferson. 1985. *Tellico Archaeology.* Knoxville: Tennessee Valley Authority, figure 1.15.

Chang, Kwang-Chih. 1968. *The Archaeology of Ancient China.* New Haven, CT: Yale University Press.

Chang, Kwang-Chih. 1970. "The Beginnings of Agriculture in the Far East." *Antiquity,* 44: 175–85.

Chang, Kwang-Chih. 1981. "In Search of China's Beginnings: New Light on an Old Civilization." *American Scientist,* 69: 148–60.

Chang, Kwang-Chih. 1986. *Archaeology of Ancient China,* 4th ed. New Haven, CT: Yale University Press.

Chard, Chester S. 1969. *Man in Prehistory.* New York: McGraw-Hill.

Chase, Philip and Harold Dibble. 1987. "Middle Paleolithic Symbolism: A Review of Current Evidence and Interpretations." *Journal of Anthropological Archaeology,* 6: 263–69.

Chatterjee, Sankar. 1997. *The Rise of Birds: 225 Million Years of Evolution.* Baltimore: Johns Hopkins.

Chaucer, Geoffrey. 1926. *The Prologue to the Canterbury Tales, the Knights Tale, the Nonnes Prestes Tale.* Ed. Mark H. Liddell. New York: Macmillan.

Chen, F. C., and W. H. LI. 2001. "Genomic Divergences between Humans and Other Hominoids and the Effective Population Size of the Common Ancestor of Humans and Chimpanzees." *American Journal of Human Genetics,* 68: 445–56.

Childe, V. Gordon. 1950. "The Urban Revolution." *Town Planning Review,* 21: 3–17.

"Children as Victims." 2000. *Juvenile Justice Bulletin 1999.* National Report Series. Washington, D.C.: U.S. Department of Justice.

Chivers, David J. 1974. *The Siamang in Malaya.* Basel, Switzerland: Karger.

Chivers, David J., ed. 1980. *Malayan Forest Primates: Ten Years' Study in Tropical Rain Forest.* New York: Plenum.

Chomsky, Noam. 1975. *Reflections on Language.* New York: Pantheon.

Christensen, Pia, Jenny Hockey, and Allison James. 2001. "Talk, Silence, and the Material World: Patterns of Indirect Communication among Agricultural Farmers in Northern England." In J. Hendry and C. W. Watson, eds., *An Anthropology of Indirect Communication.* London: Routledge, pp. 68–82.

Ciochon, Russell L., and Robert S. Corruccini, eds. 1983. *New Interpretations of Ape and Human Ancestry.* New York: Plenum.

Ciochon, Russell L., and Dennis A. Etler. 1994. "Reinterpreting Past Primate Diversity." In R. Corruccini and R. Ciochon, eds., *Integrative Paths to the Past.* Upper Saddle River, NJ: Prentice Hall.

Ciochon, Russell, John Olsen, and Jamie James. 1990. *Other Origins: The Search for the Giant Ape in Human Prehistory.* New York: Bantam.

Claassen, Cheryl. 1991. "Gender, Shellfishing, and the Shell Mound Archaic." In J. Gero and M. Conkey, eds., *Engendering Archaeology.* Oxford: Blackwell.

Claassen, Cheryl. 2002. "Gender and Archaeology." In P. N. Peregrine, C. R. Ember, and M. Ember, eds., *Archaeology: Original Readings in Method and Practice.* Upper Saddle River, NJ: Prentice Hall.

Clark, Andrew, et al. 2003. "Inferring Nonneutral Evolution from Human-Chimp-Mouse Orthologous Gene Trios." *Science,* 302 (December 12): 1960–63.

Clark, Grahame. 1975. *The Earlier Stone Age Settlement of Scandinavia.* Cambridge: Cambridge University Press.

Clark, J. Desmond. 1970. *The Prehistory of Africa.* New York: Praeger.

Clark, J. Desmond. 1977. "Interpretations of Prehistoric Technology from Ancient Egyptian and Other Sources. Pt. II: Prehistoric Arrow Forms in Africa as Shown by Surviving Examples of the Traditional Arrows of the San Bushmen." *Paleorient,* 3: 127–50.

Clark, W. E. Le Gros. 1964. *The Fossil Evidence for Human Evolution.* Chicago: University of Chicago Press.

Clarke, Ronald J., and P. V. Tobias. 1995. "Sterkfontein Member 2 Foot Bones of the Oldest South African Hominid." *Science,* 269 (July 28): 521–24.

Clayman, Charles B., ed. 1989. *American Medical Association Encyclopedia of Medicine.* New York: Random House.

Clutton-Brock, Juliet. 1992. "Domestication of Animals." In S. Jones, R. Martin, and D. Pilbeam, eds., *The Cambridge Encyclopedia of Human Evolution.* New York: Cambridge University Press.

Coale, Ansley J. 1974. "The History of the Human Population." *Scientific American* (September): 41–51.

Coe, Michael D. 1966. *The Maya.* New York: Praeger.

Cohen, Alex. 1999. *The Mental Health of Indigenous Peoples: An International Overview.* Geneva: Department of Mental Health, World Health Organization.

Cohen, Alex, and Paul Koegel. 2004. "Homelessness." In *Research Frontiers,* in C. R. Ember, M. Ember, and P. N. Peregrine, eds. *New Directions in Anthropology.* Upper Saddle River, NJ: Prentice Hall, CD-ROM.

Cohen, Jon. 2007. "Relative Differences: The Myth of 1%." *Science* (June 29): 1836.

Cohen, Mark Nathan. 1977a. *The Food Crisis in Prehistory: Overpopulation and the Origins of Agriculture.* New Haven, CT: Yale University Press.

Cohen, Mark Nathan. 1977b. "Population Pressure and the Origins of Agriculture." In C. A. Reed, ed., *Origins of Agriculture.* The Hague: Monton.

Cohen, Mark Nathan. 1987. "The Significance of Long Term Changes in Human Diet and Food Economy." In M. Harris and E. Ross, eds., *Food and Evolution.* Philadelphia: Temple University Press.

Cohen, Mark Nathan. 1989. *Health and the Rise of Civilization.* New Haven, CT: Yale University Press.

Cohen, Mark Nathan. 1998. *Culture of Intolerance: Chauvinism, Class, and Racism in the United States.* New Haven, CT: Yale University Press.

Cohen, Mark Nathan. 2002. "Were Early Agriculturalists Less Healthy Than Food Collectors?" In P. N. Peregrine, C. R. Ember, and M. Ember, eds., *Archaeology: Original Readings in Method and Practice.* Upper Saddle River, NJ: Prentice Hall.

Cohen, Mark Nathan, and George J. Armelagos. 1984. "Paleopathology at the Origins of Agriculture: Editors' Summation." In M. N. Cohen and G. J. Armelagos, eds., *Paleopathology at the Origins of Agriculture.* Orlando, FL: Academic Press.

Cohen, Ronald, and Elman R. Service, eds. 1978. *Origins of the State: The Anthropology of Political Evolution.* Philadelphia: Institute for the Study of Human Issues.

COHMAP Personnel. 1988. "Climatic Changes of the Last 18,000 Years." *Science,* 241 (August 26): 1043–52.

Collins, Desmond. 1976. "Later Hunters in Europe." In D. Collins, ed., *The Origins of Europe.* New York: Thomas Y. Crowell.

Collins, James and Richard Blot. 2003. *Literacy and Literacies.* Cambridge: Cambridge University Press.

Conklin, Beth A. 2002. "Shamans versus Pirates in the Amazonian Treasure Chest." *American Anthropologist,* 104: 1050–61.

Connah, Graham. 1987. *African Civilizations: Precolonial Cities and States in Tropical Africa.* Cambridge: Cambridge University Press.

Conroy, Glenn C. 1990. *Primate Evolution.* New York: Norton.

Coreil, Jeannine. 1989. "Lessons from a Community Study of Oral Rehydration Therapy in Haiti." In J. van Willigen, B. Rylko-Bauer, and A. McElroy, eds., *Making Our Research Useful.* Boulder, CO: Westview.

Coult, Allan D., and Robert W. Habenstein. 1965. *Cross Tabulations of Murdock's World Ethnographic Sample.* Columbia: University of Missouri Press.

Crawford, Gary W. 1992. "Prehistoric Plant Domestication in East Asia." In C. Cowan and P. Watson, eds., *The Origins of Agriculture.* Washington, D.C.: Smithsonian Institution Press.

Crockett, Carolyn, and John F. Eisenberg. 1987. "Howlers: Variations in Group Size and Demography." In B. Smuts et al., eds., *Primate Societies.* Chicago: University of Chicago Press.

"Crossroads for Planet Earth." 2005. *Scientific American.* Special Issue, September.

Crystal, David. 1971. *Linguistics.* Middlesex, UK: Penguin.

Culotta, Elizabeth. 1995. "New Hominid Crowds the Field." *Science,* 269 (August 18): 918.

Culotta, Elizabeth. 2005. "Calorie Count Reveals Neandertals Out-Ate Hardiest Modern Humans." *Science,* 307 (February 11): 840.

Cutright, Phillips. 1967. "Inequality: A Cross-National Analysis." *American Sociological Review,* 32: 562–78.

Daiger, Stephen. 2005. "Was the Human Genome Project Worth the Effort?" *Science,* 308 (April 15): 362–64.

Daly, Martin, and Margo Wilson. 1988. *Homicide.* New York: Aldine.

Daniel, I. Randolph. 2001. "Early Eastern Archaic." In P. N. Peregrine and M. Ember, eds., *Encyclopedia of Prehistory, Volume 6: North America.* Kluwer: Academic/Plenum.

Dart, Raymond. 1925. "*Australopithecus africanus:* The Man-Ape of South Africa." *Nature,* 115: 195.

Darwin, Charles. [1859]. "The Origin of Species." In L. B. Young, ed., *Evolution of Man.* New York: Oxford University Press.

Davenport, William. 1959. "Nonunilinear Descent and Descent Groups." *American Anthropologist,* 61: 557–72.

Davis, William D. 1971. "Societal Complexity and the Nature of Primitive Man's Conception of the Supernatural." Ph.D. dissertation; University of North Carolina, Chapel Hill.

Dawson, Alistair. 1992. *Ice Age Earth.* London: Routledge: 24–71.

Day, Michael. 1986. *Guide to Fossil Man,* 4th ed. Chicago: University of Chicago Press.

De Laguna, Frederica. 1972. *Under Mount Saint Elias: The History and Culture of the Yakutat Tlingit.* Washington, D.C.: Smithsonian Institution Press, as seen in eHRAF World Cultures on the Web.

De Lumley, Henry. 1969. "A Paleolithic Camp at Nice." *Scientific American* (May): 42–50.

DeMenocal, Peter. 2001. "Cultural Responses to Climate Change During the Late Holocene." *Science,* 292 (April 27): 667–73.

Devillers, Charles, and Jean Chaline. 1993. *Evolution: An Evolving Theory.* New York: Springer-Verlag.

De Villiers, Peter A., and Jill G. De Villiers. 1979. *Early Language*. Cambridge, MA: Harvard University Press.

De Waal, Frans. 2001. *The Ape and the Sushi Master: Cultural Reflections of a Primatologist*. New York: Basic Books.

De Waal, Frans, and Frans Lanting. 1997. *Bonobo: The Forgotten Ape*. Berkeley: University of California Press.

Deacon, Terrence. 1992. "Primate Brains and Senses." In S. Jones, R. Martin, and D. Pilbeam, eds., *The Cambridge Encyclopedia of Human Evolution*. New York: Cambridge University Press.

Denham, T. P., S. G. Haberle, C. Lentfer, R. Fullagar, J. Field, M. Therin, N. Porch, and B. Winsborough. 2003. "Origins of Agriculture at Kuk Swamp in the Highlands of New Guinea." *Science*, 301 (July 11): 189–93.

Denny, J. Peter. 1979. "The 'Extendedness' Variable in Classifier Semantics: Universal Features and Cultural Variation." In M. Mathiot, ed., *Ethnolinguistics*. The Hague: Mouton.

Devillers, Charles, and Jean Chaline. 1993. *Evolution: An Evolving Theory*. New York: Springer Verlag.

DeVore, Irven, and Melvin J. Konner. 1974. "Infancy in Hunter-Gatherer Life: An Ethological Perspective." In N. F. White, ed., *Ethology and Psychiatry*. Toronto: Ontario Mental Health Foundation and University of Toronto Press.

Diament, Michelle. 2005. "Diversifying Their Crops: Agriculture Schools, Focusing on Job Prospects, Reach out to Potential Students from Cities and Suburbs," *The Chronicle of Higher Education*, pp. A32–34.

Diamond, Jared. 1989. "The Accidental Conqueror." *Discover* (December): 71–76.

Diamond, Jared. 1993. "Who Are the Jews?" *Natural History* (November): 12–19.

Diamond, Jared. 1997. *Guns, Germs, and Steel*. New York: Norton: 205–207.

Diamond, Jared. 2004. "The Astonishing Micropygmies." *Science*, 306 (December 17): 2047–48.

Dibble, Harold P., Chase, S. McPherron, and A. Tuffreau. 1997. "Testing the Reality of a 'Living Floor' with Archaeological Data." *American Antiquity*, 62: 629–51.

Dillehay, Thomas. 2000. *The Settlement of the Americas*. New York: Basic Books.

Dirks, Robert. 1993. "Starvation and Famine." *Cross-Cultural Research*, 27: 28–69.

Dirks, Robert. 2004. "Hunger and Famine." In *Research Frontiers*, in C. R. Ember, M. Ember, and P. N. Peregrine, eds., *New Directions in Anthropology*. Upper Saddle River, NJ: Prentice Hall, CD-ROM.

Divale, William T. 1974. "Migration, External Warfare, and Matrilocal Residence." *Behavior Science Research*, 9: 75–133.

Divale, William T., and Marvin Harris. 1976. "Population, Warfare, and the Male Supremacist Complex." *American Anthropologist*, 78: 521–38.

Dobzhansky, Theodosius. 1962. *Mankind Evolving: The Evolution of the Human Species*. New Haven, CT: Yale University Press.

Dobzhansky, Theodosius. 1973. *Genetic Diversity and Human Equality*. New York: Basic Books.

Donaldson, Peter. 1971. *Worlds Apart: The Economic Gulf between Nations*. London: British Broadcasting Corporation.

Dow, James. 1986. *The Shaman's Touch: Otomi Indian Symbolic Healing*. Salt Lake City: University of Utah Press.

Dowling, John H. 1975. "Property Relations and Productive Strategies in Pastoral Societies." *American Ethnologist*, 2: 419–26.

Doyle, G. A., and R. D. Martin, eds. 1979. *The Study of Prosimian Behavior*. New York: Academic Press.

Doyle, Rodger. 2005. "Leveling the Playing Field: Economic Development Helps Women Pull Even with Men." *Scientific American* (June): 32.

Draper, Patricia. 1975. "!Kung Women: Contrasts in Sexual Egalitarianism in Foraging and Sedentary Contexts." In R. R. Reiter, ed., *Toward an Anthropology of Women*. New York: Monthly Review Press.

Drucker, Philip. 1965. *Cultures of the North Pacific Coast*. San Francisco: Chandler.

Duarte, Cidalia, J. Mauricio, P. B. Pettitt, P. Souto, E. Trinkaus, H. van der Plicht, and J. Zilhao. 1999. "The Early Upper Paleolithic Human Skeleton from the Abrigo do Lagar Velho (Portugal) and Modern Human Emergence in Iberia." *Proceedings of the National Academy of Sciences of the United States*, 96: 7604–609.

Durham, William H. 1991. *Coevolution: Genes, Culture and Human Diversity*. Stanford, CA: Stanford University Press.

Durkheim, Émile. 1938 [1895]. *The Rules of Sociological Method*, 8th ed. Ed. George E. Catlin. Trans. Sarah A. Soloway and John H. Mueller. New York: Free Press.

Durrenberger, E. Paul. 2001a. "Anthropology and Globalization." *American Anthropologist*, 103: 531–35.

Durrenberger, E. Paul. 2001b. "Explorations of Class and Consciousness in the U.S." *Journal of Anthropological Research*, 57: 41–60.

Dyson-Hudson, Neville. 1966. *Karimojong Politics*. Oxford: Clarendon Press.

Eckhardt, William. 1975. "Primitive Militarism." *Journal of Peace Research*, 12: 55–62.

Eiseley, Loren C. 1958. "The Dawn of Evolutionary Theory." In Loren C. Eiseley, *Darwin's Century: Evolution and the Men Who Discovered It*. Garden City, NY: Doubleday.

Eisenberg, John F. 1977. "Comparative Ecology and Reproduction of New World Monkeys." In Devra Kleinman, ed., *The Biology and Conservation of the Callitrichidae*. Washington, D.C.: Smithsonian Institution.

Ekman, Paul, and Dachner Keltner. 1997. "Universal Facial Expressions of Emotion: An Old Controversy and New Findings." In U. Segerstrale and P. Molnar, eds., *Nonverbal Communication: Where Nature Meets Culture*. Mahwah, NJ: Lawrence Erlbaum.

Eldredge, Niles, and Ian Tattersall. 1982. *The Myths of Human Evolution*. New York: Columbia University Press.

Eliot, T. S. 1963. "The Love Song of J. Alfred Prufrock." In *Collected Poems, 1909–1962*. New York: Harcourt, Brace & World.

Ellis, Lee. 1986. "Evidence of Neuroandrogenic Etiology of Sex Roles from a Combined Analysis of Human, Nonhuman Primate and Nonprimate Mammalian Studies." *Personality and Individual Differences*, 7: 519–52.

Ember, Carol R. 1973. "Feminine Task Assignment and the Social Behavior of Boys." *Ethos*, 1: 424–39.

Ember, Carol R. 1974. "An Evaluation of Alternative Theories of Matrilocal versus Patrilocal Residence." *Behavior Science Research*, 9: 135–49.

Ember, Carol R. 1975. "Residential Variation among Hunter-Gatherers." *Behavior Science Research*, 9: 135–49.

Ember, Carol R. 1978. "Myths about Hunter-Gatherers." *Ethnology*, 17: 439–48.

Ember, Carol R. 1981. "A Cross-Cultural Perspective on Sex Differences." In R. H. Munroe, R. L. Munroe, and B. B. Whiting, eds., *Handbook of Cross-Cultural Human Development*. New York, Garland.

Ember, Carol R. 1983. "The Relative Decline in Women's Contribution to Agriculture with Intensification." *American Anthropologist*, 85: 285–304.

Ember, Carol R., and Melvin Ember. 1972. "The Conditions Favoring Multilocal Residence." *Southwestern Journal of Anthropology*, 28: 382–400.

Ember, Carol R., and Melvin Ember. 1984. "The Evolution of Human Female Sexuality: A Cross-Species Perspective." *Journal of Anthropological Research*, 40: 202–10.

Ember, Carol R., and Melvin Ember. 1992. "Resource Unpredictability, Mistrust, and War: A Cross-Cultural Study." *Journal of Conflict Resolution*, 36: 242–62.

Ember, Carol R., and Melvin Ember. 1993. "Issues in Cross-Cultural Studies of Interpersonal Violence." *Violence and Victims*, 8: 217–33.

Ember, Carol R., and Melvin Ember. 1994. "War, Socialization, and Interpersonal Violence: A Cross-Cultural Study." *Journal of Conflict Resolution*, 38: 620–46.

Ember, Carol R., and Melvin Ember. 1997. "Violence in the Ethnographic Record: Results of Cross-Cultural Research on War and Aggression." In D. Martin and D. Frayer, eds., *Troubled Times*. Langhorn, PA: Gordon and Breach.

Ember, Carol R., and Melvin Ember. 2001. *Cross-Cultural Research Methods*. Walnut Creek, CA: AltaMira Press.

Ember, Carol R. and Melvin Ember. 2005. "Explaining Corporal Punishment of Children: A Cross-Cultural Study." *American Anthropologist*, 107: 609–19.

Ember, Carol R., Melvin Ember, and Peter N. Peregrine. 2007. *Anthropology*, 12th ed. Upper Saddle River, NJ: Prentice Hall.

Ember, Carol R., Melvin Ember, Andrey Korotayev, and Victor de Munck. 2005. "Valuing Thinness or Fatness in Women: Reevaluating the Effect of Resource Scarcity." *Evolution and Human Behavior*, 26: 257–70.

Ember, Carol R., Melvin Ember, and Burton Pasternak. 1974. "On the Development of Unilineal Descent." *Journal of Anthropological Research*, 30: 69–94.

Ember, Carol R., Melvin Ember, and Bruce Russett. 1992. "Peace between Participatory Polities: A Cross-Cultural Test of the 'Democracies Rarely Fight Each Other' Hypothesis." *World Politics,* 44: 573–99.

Ember, Carol R., and David Levinson. 1991. "The Substantive Contributions of Worldwide Cross-Cultural Studies Using Secondary Data." *Behavior Science Research* (special issue, "Cross-Cultural and Comparative Research: Theory and Method"), 25: 79–140.

Ember, Melvin. 1963. "The Relationship between Economic and Political Development in Nonindustrialized Societies." *Ethnology,* 2: 228–48.

Ember, Melvin. 1967. "The Emergence of Neolocal Residence." *Transactions of the New York Academy of Sciences,* 30: 291–302.

Ember, Melvin. 1970. "Taxonomy in Comparative Studies." In R. Naroll and R. Cohen, eds., *A Handbook of Method in Cultural Anthropology.* Garden City, NY: Natural History Press.

Ember, Melvin. 1974a. "The Conditions That May Favor Avunculocal Residence." *Behavior Science Research,* 9: 203–209.

Ember, Melvin. 1974b. "Warfare, Sex Ratio, and Polygyny." *Ethnology,* 13: 197–206.

Ember, Melvin. 1975. "On the Origin and Extension of the Incest Taboo." *Behavior Science Research,* 10: 249–81.

Ember, Melvin. 1978. "Size of Color Lexicon: Interaction of Cultural and Biological Factors." *American Anthropologist,* 80: 364–67.

Ember, Melvin. 1985. "Alternative Predictors of Polygyny." *Behavior Science Research,* 19: 1–23.

Ember, Melvin, and Carol R. Ember. 1971. "The Conditions Favoring Matrilocal versus Patrilocal Residence." *American Anthropologist,* 73: 571–94.

Ember, Melvin, and Carol R. Ember. 1979. "Male-Female Bonding: A Cross-Species Study of Mammals and Birds." *Behavior Science Research,* 14: 37–56.

Ember, Melvin, and Carol R. Ember. 1992. "Cross-Cultural Studies of War and Peace: Recent Achievements and Future Possibilities." In S. P. Reyna and R. E. Downs, eds., *Studying War.* New York: Gordon and Breach.

Ember, Melvin, and Carol R. Ember. 1999. "Cross-Language Predictors of Consonant-Vowel Syllables." *American Anthropologist,* 101: 730–42.

Ember, Melvin, and Carol R. Ember, eds. 2002. *Encyclopedia of Urban Cultures: Cities and Cultures around the World,* 4 vols. Danbury, CT: Grolier/Scholastic.

Ember, Melvin, Carol R. Ember, and Ian Skoggard, eds. 2004. *Encyclopedia of Diasporas: Immigrant and Refugee Cultures around the World,* 2 vols. New York: Kluwer Academic/Plenum.

Ensminger, Jean. 2002. "Experimental Economics: A Powerful New Method for Theory Testing in Anthropology." In J. Ensminger, ed., *Theory in Economic Anthropology.* Walnut Creek, CA: AltaMira Press, pp. 59–78.

Epstein, Cynthia Fuchs. 1988. *Deceptive Distinctions: Sex, Gender, and the Social Order.* New York: Russell Sage Foundation.

Erchak, Gerald M. 2004. "Family Violence." In *Research Frontiers,* in C. R. Ember, M. Ember, and P. N. Peregrine, eds., *New Directions in Anthropology.* Upper Saddle River, NJ: Prentice Hall, CD-ROM.

Eswaran, Vinayak. 2002. "A Diffusion Wave Out of Africa." *Current Anthropology,* 43: 749–74.

Etienne, Mona, and Eleanor Leacock, eds. 1980. *Women and Colonization: Anthropological Perspectives.* New York: Praeger.

Etienne, Robert. 1992. *Pompeii: The Day a City Died.* New York: Abrams.

Etkin, Nina L., and Paul J. Ross. 1997. "Malaria, Medicine, and Meals: A Biobehavioral Perspective." In L. Romanucci-Ross, D. E. Moerman, and L. R. Tancredi, eds., *The Anthropology of Medicine.* Westport, CT: Bergin & Garvey, pp. 169–209.

Euripides. 1937. "The Trojan Women." In E. Hamilton, trans., *Three Greek Plays.* New York: Norton.

Evans-Pritchard, E. E. 1940. "The Nuer of the Southern Sudan." In M. Fortes and E. E. Evans-Pritchard, eds., *African Political Systems.* New York: Oxford University Press.

Evans-Pritchard, E. E. 1979. "Witchcraft Explains Unfortunate Events." In W. A. Lessa and E. Z. Vogt, eds., *Reader in Comparative Religion,* 3rd ed. New York: Harper & Row.

Eveleth, Phyllis B., and James M. Tanner. 1990. *Worldwide Variation in Human Growth,* 2nd ed. Cambridge: Cambridge University Press.

Fagan, Brian M. 1989. *People of the Earth: An Introduction to World Prehistory,* 6th ed. Glenview, IL: Scott, Foresman.

Fagan, Brian M. 1991. *Ancient North America: The Archaeology of a Continent.* London: Thames and Hudson.

Falk, Dean. 1987. "Hominid Paleoneurology." *Annual Review of Anthropology,* 16: 13–30.

Falk, Dean. 1988. "Enlarged Occipital/Marginal Sinuses and Emissary Foramina: Their Significance in Hominid Evolution." In F. E. Grine, ed., *Evolutionary History of the "Robust" Australopithecines.* New York: Aldine.

Falk, Dean, C. Hildebolt, K. Smith, M. J. Morwood, T. Sutikna, P. Brown, Jatmiko, E. W. Saptomo, B. Brunsden, F. Prior. 2005. "The Brain of LB1, *Homo floresiensis.*" *Science,* 308 (April 8): 242–45.

Farley, Reynolds. 1996. *The New American Reality: Who We Are, How We Got Here, Where We Are Going.* New York: Russell Sage Foundation.

Farmer, Paul. 1997. "Ethnography, Social Analysis, and the Prevention of Sexually Transmitted HIV Infection among Poor Women in Haiti." In M. C. Inhorn and P. J. Brown, eds., *The Anthropology of Infectious Disease.* Amsterdam: Gordon and Breach, pp. 413–38.

Featherman, David L., and Robert M. Hauser. 1978. *Opportunity and Change.* New York: Academic Press.

Fedigan, Linda Marie. 1982. *Primate Paradigms: Sex Roles and Social Bonds.* Montreal: Eden Press.

Fedoroff, Nina. 2003. "Prehistoric GM Corn." *Science,* 302 (November 14): 1158–59.

Fehr, Ernst, and Urs Fischbacher. 2003. "The Nature of Human Altruism." *Nature* (October 23): 785–91.

Feibel, Craig S., and Francis H. Brown. 1993. "Microstratigraphy and Paleoenvironments." In A. Walker and R. Leakey, eds., *The Nariokotome Homo erectus Skeleton.* Cambridge, MA: Harvard University Press.

Feinman, Gary, and Jill Neitzel. 1984. "Too Many Types: An Overview of Sedentary Prestate Societies in the Americas." In M. B. Schiffer, ed., *Advances in Archaeological Methods and Theory,* vol. 7. Orlando, FL: Academic Press.

Feinman, Gary M., Stephen A. Kowalewski, Laura Finsten, Richard E. Blanton, and Linda Nicholas. 1985. "Long-Term Demographic Change: A Perspective from the Valley of Oaxaca, Mexico." *Journal of Field Archaeology,* 12: 333–62.

Ferguson, R. Brian, and Neil L. Whitehead. 1992. "Violent Edge of Empire." In R. B. Ferguson and N. Whitehead, eds., *War in the Tribal Zone.* Santa Fe, NM: School of American Research Press, pp. 1–30.

Fernea, Elizabeth, and Robert Fernea, as reported in M. Kay Martin and Barbara Voorhies. 1975. *Female of the Species.* New York: Columbia University Press.

Fields, Jason. 2003. *America's Families and Living Arrangements, 2003.* Current Population Reports, P20–553. Washington, D.C.: U.S. Census Bureau.

Finley, M. I. 1983. *Politics in the Ancient World.* Cambridge: Cambridge University Press.

Firth, Raymond. 1959. *Social Change in Tikopia.* New York: Macmillan.

Firth, Raymond. 1970. *Rank and Religion in Tikopia.* Boston: Beacon Press.

Fischer, John L. 1958. "Social Influences on the Choice of a Linguistic Variant." *Word,* 14: 47–56.

Fish, Paul R. 1981. "Beyond Tools: Middle Paleolithic Debitage Analysis and Cultural Inference." *Journal of Anthropological Research,* 37: 374–86.

Fisher, William H. 1994. "Megadevelopment, Environmentalism, and Resistance: The Institutional Context of Kayapo Indigenous Politics in Central Brazil." *Human Organization,* 53: 220–32.

Flannery, Kent V. 1965. "The Ecology of Early Food Production in Mesopotamia." *Science,* 147 (March 12): 1247–56.

Flannery, Kent V. 1971. "The Origins and Ecological Effects of Early Domestication in Iran and the Near East." In S. Struever, ed., *Prehistoric Agriculture.* Garden City, NY: Natural History Press.

Flannery, Kent V. 1972. "The Cultural Evolution of Civilizations." *Annual Review of Ecology and Systematics,* 3: 399–426.

Flannery, Kent V. 1973a. "The Origins of Agriculture." *Annual Review of Anthropology,* 2: 271–310.

Flannery, Kent V. 1973b. "The Origins of the Village as a Settlement Type in Mesoamerica and the Near East: A Comparative Study." In R. Tringham, ed., *Territoriality and Proxemics.* Andover, MA: Warner.

Flannery, Kent V., ed. 1986. *Guila Naquitz: Archaic Foraging and Early Agriculture in Oaxaca, Mexico.* Orlando, FL: Academic Press.

Fleagle, John G. 1994. "Anthropoid Origins." In R. Corruccini and R. Ciochon, eds., *Integrative Paths to the Past.* Upper Saddle River, NJ: Prentice Hall.

Fleagle, John G. 1999. *Primate Adaptation and Evolution,* 2nd ed. San Diego: Academic Press.

Fleagle, John G., and Richard F. Kay. 1983. "New Interpretations of the Phyletic Position of Oligocene Hominoids." In R. Ciochon and R. Corruccini, eds., *New Interpretations of Ape and Human Ancestry.* New York: Plenum

Fleagle, John G., and Richard F. Kay. 1985. "The Paleobiology of Catarrhines." In E. Delson, ed., *Ancestors.* New York: Alan R. Liss.

Fleagle, John G., and Richard F. Kay. 1987. "The Phyletic Position of the *Parapithecidae.*" *Journal of Human Evolution,* 16: 483–531.

Fleischer, Robert L., and Howard R. Hart, Jr. 1972. "Fission-Track Dating: Techniques and Problems." In W. Bishop and J. Miller, eds., *Calibration of Hominid Evolution.* Toronto: University of Toronto Press.

Fleischer, Robert L., P. B. Price, R. M. Walker, and L. S. B. Leakey. 1965. "Fission-Track Dating of Bed I, Olduvai Gorge." *Science,* 148 (April 2): 72–74.

Ford, Clellan S., and Frank A. Beach. 1951. *Patterns of Sexual Behavior.* New York: Harper.

Fossey, Dian. 1983. *Gorillas in the Mist.* Boston: Houghton Mifflin.

Foster, George M. 1962. *Traditional Cultures and the Impact of Technological Change.* New York: Harper & Row.

Foster, George M. 1969. *Applied Anthropology.* Boston: Little, Brown.

Foster, George M. 1994. *Hippocrates' Latin American Legacy: Humoral Medicine in the New World.* Amsterdam: Gordon and Breach.

Foster, Philips. 1992. *The World Food Problem: Tackling the Causes of Undernutrition in the Third World.* Boulder, CO: Lynne Rienner.

Fowler, Brenda. 2000. *Iceman: Uncovering the Life and Times of a Prehistoric Man Found in an Alpine Glacier.* New York: Random House.

Fowler, Melvin L. 1975. "A Pre-Columbian Urban Center on the Mississippi." *Scientific American* (August): 92–101.

Franciscus, Robert G., and Erik Trinkaus. 1988. "Nasal Morphology and the Emergence of *Homo erectus.*" *American Journal of Physical Anthropology,* 75: 517–27.

Frankel, Barbara, and M. G. Trend. 1991. "Principles, Pressures, and Paychecks: The Anthropologist as Employee." In C. Fluehr-Lobban, ed., *Ethics and the Profession of Anthropology.* Philadelphia: University of Pennsylvania Press.

Frayer, David W., and Milford H. Wolpoff. 1985. "Sexual Dimorphism." *Annual Review of Anthropology,* 14: 429–73.

Frayer, David W., M. Wolpoff, A. Thorne, F. Smith, and G. Pope. 1993. "Theories of Modern Human Origins: The Paleontological Test." *American Anthropologist,* 95: 24–27.

Freeman, J. D. 1961. "On the Concept of the Kindred." *Journal of the Royal Anthropological Institute,* 91: 192–220.

Freeman, Leslie G. 1994. "Torralba and Ambrona: A Review of Discoveries." In R. Corruccini and R. Ciochon, eds., *Integrative Paths to the Past.* Upper Saddle River, NJ: Prentice Hall.

Freyman, R. 1987. "The First Technology." *Scientific American* (April): 112.

Fried, Morton H. 1967. *The Evolution of Political Society: An Essay in Political Anthropology.* New York: Random House.

Friedman, Jeffrey M. 2003. "A War on Obesity, Not the Obese." *Science,* 299 (February 7): 856–58.

Friedman, Saul S. 1980. "Holocaust." In *Academic American* [now Grolier] *Encyclopedia,* vol. 10. Princeton, NJ: Areté.

Friedrich, Paul. 1986. *The Language Parallax.* Austin: University of Texas Press.

Frisancho, A. Roberto, and Lawrence P. Greksa. 1989. "Developmental Responses in the Acquisition of Functional Adaptation to High Altitude." In M. Little and J. Haas, eds., *Human Population Biology.* New York: Oxford University Press.

Frisch, Rose. E. 1980. "Fatness, Puberty, and Fertility." *Natural History* (October): 16–27.

Fry, Douglas P., and Kaj Björkqvist, eds. 1997. *Cultural Variation in Conflict Resolution: Alternatives to Violence.* Mahwah, NJ: Lawrence Erlbaum Associates.

Futuyma, Douglas. 1982. *Science on Trial.* New York: Pantheon.

Gabunia, Leo, et al. 2000. "Earliest Pleistocene Hominid Cranial Remains from Dmanisi, Republic of Georgia: Taxonomy, Geological Setting, and Age." *Science,* 288 (May 12): 1019–25.

Gal, Susan. 1988. "The Political Economy of Code Choice." In M. Heller, ed., *Codeswitching.* Berlin: Mouton de Gruyter, pp. 245–64.

Gardner, Beatrice T., and R. Allen Gardner. 1980. "Two Comparative Psychologists Look at Language Acquisition." In K. Nelson, ed., *Children's Language,* vol. 2. New York: Halsted Press.

Gardner, R. Allen, and Beatrice T. Gardner. 1969. "Teaching Sign Language to a Chimpanzee." *Science,* 165 (August 15): 664–72.

Garn, Stanley M. 1971. *Human Races,* 3rd ed. Springfield, IL: Charles C. Thomas.

Gartner, Rosemary. 2004. "Crime Variations across Cultures and Nations." In *Cross-Cultural Research for Social Science,* in C. R. Ember, M. Ember, and P. N. Peregrine, eds., *New Directions in Anthropology.* Upper Saddle River, NJ: Prentice Hall, CD-ROM.

Gat, Azar. 1999. "The Pattern of Fighting in Simple, Small-Scale, Prestate Societies." *Journal of Anthropological Research,* 55: 563–83.

Geertz, Clifford. 1966. "Religion as a Cultural System." In M. Banton, ed., *Anthropological Approaches to the Study of Religion.* New York: Praeger.

Gelles, Richard J., and Murray A. Straus. 1988. *Intimate Violence.* New York: Simon & Schuster.

Gentner, W., and H. J. Lippolt. 1963. "The Potassium-Argon Dating of Upper Tertiary and Pleistocene Deposits." In D. Brothwell and E. Higgs, eds., *Science in Archaeology.* New York: Basic Books.

Gesler, W. 1991. *The Cultural Geography of Health Care.* Pittsburgh, PA: University of Pittsburgh Press.

Gibbons, Ann. 1993. "Warring over Women." *Science,* 261 (August 20): 987–88.

Gibbons, Ann. 1995. "First Americans: Not Mammoth Hunters, but Forest Dwellers?" *Science,* 268 (April 19): 346–47.

Gibbons, Ann. 2001. "The Riddle of Co-Existence." *Science,* 291 (March 2): 1725–29.

Gibbons, Ann. 2002. "One Scientist's Quest for the Origin of Our Species." *Science,* 298 (November 29): 1708–11.

Gibbons, Ann. 2003. "Oldest Members of *Homo sapiens* Discovered in Africa." *Science,* 300 (June 13): 1641.

Gibson, Kathleen R., and Stephen Jessee. 1999. "Language Evolution and Expansions of Multiple Neurological Processing Areas." In B. J. King, ed., *The Origins of Language.* Santa Fe, NM: School of American Research Press, pp. 189–227.

Gilliland, Mary Kay. 1995. "Nationalism and Ethnogenesis in the Former Yugoslavia." In L. Romanucci-Ross and G. A. De Vos, eds., *Ethnic Identity: Creation, Conflict, and Accommodation,* 3rd ed. Walnut Creek, CA: AltaMira Press, pp. 197–221.

Gilman, Antonio. 1990. "The Development of Social Stratification in Bronze Age Europe." *Current Anthropology,* 22: 1–23.

Gingerich, P. D. 1986. "*Pleisiadipis* and the Delineation of the Order Primates." In B. Wood, L. Martin, and P. Andrews, eds., *Major Topics in Primate Evolution.* Cambridge: Cambridge University Press, pp. 32–46.

Gladwin, Thomas, and Seymour B. Sarason. 1953. *Truk: Man in Paradise.* New York: Wenner-Gren Foundation for Anthropological Research.

Gleitman, Lila R., and Eric Wanner. 1982. "Language Acquisition: The State of the State of the Art." In E. Wanner and L. R. Gleitman, eds., *Language Acquisition.* Cambridge: Cambridge University Press.

Golden, Frederic, Michael Lemonick, and Dick Thompson. 2000. "The Race Is Over." *Time* (July 3): 18–23.

Goldizen, Anne Wilson. 1987. "Tamarins and Marmosets: Communal Care of Offspring." In B. Smuts et al., eds., *Primate Societies.* Chicago: University of Chicago Press.

Goldschmidt, Walter. 1999. "Dynamics and Status in America." *Anthropology Newsletter,* 40: 62, 64.

Goldstein, Joshua S. 2004. "War and Gender." In C. R. Ember and M. Ember, eds., *Encyclopedia of Sex and Gender: Men and Women in the World's Cultures,* vol. 1. New York: Kluwer Academic/Plenum Publishers, pp. 107–16.

Goldstein, Melvyn C. 1971. "Stratification, Polyandry, and Family Structure in Central Tibet." *Southwestern Journal of Anthropology,* 27: 65–74.

Goldstein, Melvyn C. 1987. "When Brothers Share a Wife." *Natural History* (March): 39–48.

Goodall, Jane. 1963. "My Life among Wild Chimpanzees." *National Geographic* (August): 272–308.

Goodenough, Ward H. 1951. *Property, Kin, and Community on Truk.* New Haven, CT: Yale University Press.

Goodman, Alan H., and Thomas L. Leatherman, eds. 1998. *Building a New Biocultural Synthesis: Political-Economic Perspectives on Human Biology.* Ann Arbor: University of Michigan Press.

Goodman, Madeleine J., P. Bion Griffin, Agnes A. Estioko-Griffin, and John S. Grove. 1985. "The Compatibility of Hunting and Mothering among the Agta Hunter-Gatherers of the Philippines." *Sex Roles,* 12: 1199–209.

Goodman, Morris. 1992. "Reconstructing Human Evolution from Proteins." In S. Jones, R. Martin, and D. Pilbeam, eds., *The Cambridge Encyclopedia of Human Evolution.* New York: Cambridge University Press.

Goodrich, L. Carrington. 1959. *A Short History of the Chinese People*, 3rd ed. New York: Harper & Row.

Goody, Jack. 1973. "Bridewealth and Dowry in Africa and Eurasia." In J. Goody and S. H. Tambiah, eds., *Bridewealth and Dowry*. Cambridge: Cambridge University Press.

Gore, Rick. 2002. "The First Pioneer?" *National Geographic* (August), Departments.

Goren-Inbar, Naama, N. Alperson, M. Kislev, O. Simchoni, Y. Melamed, A. Ben-Nun, and E. Werker. "Evidence of Hominin Control of Fire at Gesher Benot Ya'aqov, Israel." *Science*, 304 (April 30): 725–27.

Gorman, Chester. 1970. "The Hoabinhian and After: Subsistence Patterns in Southeast Asia during the Late Pleistocene and Early Recent Periods." *World Archaeology*, 2: 315–19.

Gould, Richard A. 1969. *Yiwara: Foragers of the Australian Desert*. New York: Scribner's.

Graber, Robert Bates, ed. 2004. "The Future State of the World: An Anthropological Symposium." *Cross-Cultural Research* (special issue), 38: 95–207.

Graham, Susan Brandt. 1979. "Biology and Human Social Behavior: A Response to van den Berghe and Barash." *American Anthropologist*, 81: 357–60.

Grant, Bruce S. 2002. "Sour Grapes of Wrath." *Science*, 297 (August 9): 940–41.

Grant, Peter R. 1991. "Natural Selection and Darwin's Finches." *Scientific American* (October): 82–87.

Grant, Peter R., and Rosemary Grant. 2002. "Unpredictable Evolution in a 30-Year Study of Darwin's Finches," *Science*, 296 (April 26): 707–11.

Gray, J. Patrick. 1985. *Primate Sociobiology*. New Haven, CT: HRAF Press.

Gray, J. Patrick, and Linda D. Wolfe. 1980. "Height and Sexual Dimorphism of Stature among Human Societies." *American Journal of Physical Anthropology*, 53: 446–52.

Gray, J. Patrick, and Linda Wolfe. 2002. "What Accounts for Population Variation in Height?" In P. N. Peregrine, C. R. Ember, and M. Ember, eds., *Physical Anthropology: Original Readings in Method and Practice*. Upper Saddle River, NJ: Prentice Hall.

Grayson, Donald K. 1977. "Pleistocene Avifaunas and the Overkill Hypothesis." *Science*, 195 (February 18): 691–92.

Grayson, Donald K. 1984. "Explaining Pleistocene Extinctions: Thoughts on the Structure of a Debate." In P. S. Martin and R. Klein, eds., *Quaternary Extinctions*. Tucson: University of Arizona Press.

Greenberg, Joseph H. 1972. "Linguistic Evidence Regarding Bantu Origins." *Journal of African History*, 13: 189–216.

Greenberg, Joseph H., and Merritt Ruhlen. 1992. "Linguistic Origins of Native Americans." *Scientific American* (November): 94–99.

Greenfield, Patricia M., Ashley E. Maynard, and Carla P. Childs. 2000. "History, Culture, Learning, and Development." *Cross-Cultural Research*, 34. 351–74.

Greenfield, Patricia M., and E. Sue Savage-Rumbaugh. 1990. "Grammatical Combination in *Pan paniscus*: Processes of Learning and Invention in the Evolution and Development of Language." In S. Parker and K. Gibson, eds., *"Language" and Intelligence in Monkeys and Apes*. New York: Cambridge University Press.

Gregor, Thomas A., and Daniel R. Gross. 2004. "Guilt by Association: The Culture of Accusation and the American Anthropological Association's Investigation of Darkness in El Dorado." *American Anthropologist*, 106: 687–98.

Greksa, Lawrence P., and Cynthia M. Beall. 1989. "Development of Chest Size and Lung Function at High Altitude." In M. Little and J. Haas, eds., *Human Population Biology*. New York: Oxford University Press.

Grine, Frederick E. 1988a. "Evolutionary History of the 'Robust' Australopithecines: A Summary and Historical Perspective." In F. E. Grine, ed., *Evolutionary History of the "Robust" Australopithecines*. New York: Aldine.

Grine, Frederick E., ed. 1988b. *Evolutionary History of the "Robust" Australopithecines*. New York: Aldine.

Grine, Frederick E. 1993. "Australopithecine Taxonomy and Phylogeny: Historical Background and Recent Interpretation." In R. Ciochon and J. Fleagle, eds., *The Human Evolution Source Book*. Upper Saddle River, NJ: Prentice Hall.

Gross, Daniel R., and Barbara A. Underwood. 1971. "Technological Change and Caloric Costs: Sisal Agriculture in Northeastern Brazil." *American Anthropologist*, 73: 725–40.

Gross, Daniel R., George Eiten, Nancy M. Flowers, Francisca M. Leói, Madeline Latiman Ritter, and Dennis W. Werner. 1979. "Ecology and Acculturation among Native Peoples of Central Brazil." *Science*, 206 (November 30): 1043–50.

Grossman, Daniel. 2002. "Parched Turf Battle." *Scientific American* (December): 32–33.

Grubb, Henry J. 1987. "Intelligence at the Low End of the Curve: Where Are the Racial Differences?" *Journal of Black Psychology*, 14: 25–34.

Grubb, Henry J., and Andrea G. Barthwell. 1996. "Superior Intelligence and Racial Equivalence: A Look at Mensa." Paper presented at the 1996 annual meeting of the Society for Cross Cultural Research.

Guiora, Alexander Z., Benjamin Beit-Hallahmi, Risto Fried, and Cecelia Yoder. 1982. "Language Environment and Gender Identity Attainment." *Language Learning*, 32: 289–304.

Gunders, S., and J. W. M. Whiting. 1968. "Mother-Infant Separation and Physical Growth." *Ethnology*, 7: 196–206.

Gurr, Ted Robert. 1989a. "Historical Trends in Violent Crime: Europe and the United States." In T. R. Gurr, ed., *Violence in America, Volume 1: The History of Crime*. Newbury Park, CA: Sage.

Gurr, Ted Robert. 1989b. "The History of Violent Crime in America: An Overview." In T. R. Gurr, ed., *Violence in America, Volume 1: The History of Crime*. Newbury Park, CA: Sage.

Guthrie, Dale R. 1984. "Mosaics, Allelochemics, and Nutrients: An Ecological Theory of Late Pleistocene Megafaunal Extinctions." In P. S. Martin and R. Klein, eds., *Quaternary Extinctions*. Tucson: University of Arizona Press.

Haas, Jonathan. 1990. "Warfare and the Evolution of Tribal Polities in the Prehistoric Southwest." In J. Haas, ed., *The Anthropology of War*. New York: Cambridge University Press.

Haas, Jonathan, Winifred Creamer, and Alvaro Ruiz. 2004. "Dating the Late Archaic Occupation of the Norte Chico Region in Peru." *Nature*, 432 (December 23): 1020–23.

Habicht, J. K. A. 1979. *Paleoclimate, Paleomagnetism, and Continental Drift*. Tulsa, OK: American Association of Petroleum Geologists.

Hackenberg, Robert A. 1988. "Scientists or Survivors? The Future of Applied Anthropology under Maximum Uncertainty." In R. T. Trotter II, ed., *Anthropology for Tomorrow*. Washington, D.C.: American Anthropological Association.

Hage, Jerald, and Charles H. Powers. 1992. *Post-Industrial Lives: Roles and Relationships in the 21st Century*. Newbury Park, CA: Sage.

Hahn, Robert A. 1995. *Sickness and Healing: An Anthropological Perspective*. New Haven, CT: Yale University Press.

Hailie-Selassie, Yohannes. 2001. "Late Miocene Hominids from the Middle Awash, Ethiopia." *Nature*, 412 (July 12): 178–81.

Haldane, J. B. S. 1963. "Human Evolution: Past and Future." In G. Jepsen, E. Mayr, and G. Simpson, eds., *Genetics, Paleontology, and Evolution*. New York: Atheneum.

Hall, Edward T. 1966. *The Hidden Dimension*. Garden City, NY: Doubleday.

Hames, Raymond. 2004. "Yanomamö: Varying Adaptations of Foraging Horticulturalists." In *Portraits of Culture*, in C. R. Ember, M. Ember, and P. N. Peregrine, eds., *New Directions in Anthropology*. Upper Saddle River, NJ: Prentice Hall, CD-ROM.

Hammer, Michael F., and Stephen L. Zegura. 1996. "The Role of the Y Chromosome in Human Evolutionary Studies." *Evolutionary Anthropology*, 5: 116–34.

Hammer, Michael F., and Stephen L. Zegura. 2002. "The Human Y Chromosome Haplogroup Tree," *Annual Review of Anthropology*, 31: 303–21.

Handwerker, W. Penn, and Paul V. Crosbie. 1982. "Sex and Dominance." *American Anthropologist*, 84: 97–104.

Hanna, Joel M., Michael A. Little, and Donald M. Austin. 1989. "Climatic Physiology." In M. Little and J. Haas, eds., *Human Population Biology*. New York: Oxford University Press.

Hannah, Alison C., and W. C. McGrew. 1987. "Chimpanzees Using Stones to Crack Open Oil Palm Nuts in Liberia." *Primates*, 28: 31–46.

Hannerz, Ulf. 1996. *Transnational Connections: Culture, People, Places*. London: Routledge.

Hanotte, Olivier, et al. 2002. "African Pastoralism: Genetic Imprints of Origins and Migrations." *Science*, 296 (April 12): 336–43.

Harcourt, A. H. 1979. "The Social Relations and Group Structure of Wild Mountain Gorillas." In D. Hamburg and E. McCown, eds., *The Great Apes*. Menlo Park, CA: Benjamin/Cummings.

Hardoy, Jorge, and David Satterthwaite. 1987. "The Legal and the Illegal City." In L. Rodwin, ed., *Shelter, Settlement, and Development*. Boston: Allen & Unwin.

Hare, Brian, Michelle Brown, Christina Williamson, and Michael Tomasello. 2002. "The Domestication of Social Cognition in Dogs." *Science*, 298 (November 22): 1634–36.

Harlan, Jack R. 1967. "A Wild Wheat Harvest in Turkey." *Archaeology,* 20: 197–201.

Harner, Michael. 1972. "The Role of Hallucinogenic Plants in European Witchcraft." In M. Harner, ed., *Hallucinogens and Shamanism.* New York: Oxford University Press.

Harner, Michael J. 1975. "Scarcity, the Factors of Production, and Social Evolution." In S. Polgar, ed., *Population, Ecology, and Social Evolution.* The Hague: Mouton.

Harner, Michael, and Gary Doore. 1987. "The Ancient Wisdom in Shamanic Cultures." In S. Nicholson, comp., *Shamanism.* Wheaton, IL: Theosophical Publishing House.

Harris, David R. 1977. "Settling Down: An Evolutionary Model for the Transformation of Mobile Bands into Sedentary Communities." In J. Friedman and M. Rowlands, eds., *The Evolution of Social Systems.* London: Duckworth.

Harris, Marvin. 1966. "The Cultural Ecology of India's Sacred Cattle." *Current Anthropology,* 7: 51–63.

Harris, Marvin. 1975. *Cows, Pigs, Wars and Witches: The Riddles of Culture.* New York: Random House, Vintage.

Harris, Marvin. 1979. *Cultural Materialism: The Struggle for a Science of Culture.* New York: Random House.

Harrison, G. A., James M. Tanner, David R. Pilbeam, and P. T. Baker. 1988. *Human Biology: An Introduction to Human Evolution, Variation, Growth, and Adaptability,* 3rd ed. Oxford: Oxford University Press.

Harrison, Gail G. 1975. "Primary Adult Lactase Deficiency: A Problem in Anthropological Genetics." *American Anthropologist,* 77: 812–35.

Harrison, T. 1986. "A Reassessment of the Phylogenetic Relationships of *Oreopithecus bamboli.*" *Journal of Human Evolution,* 15: 541–84.

Harrison, T., and L. Rook. 1997. "Enigmatic Anthropoid or Misunderstood Ape? The Phylogenetic Status of *Oreopithecus bamboli* Reconsidered." In D. R. Begun, C. V. Ward, and M. D. Rose, eds., *Function, Phylogeny, and Fossils: Miocene Hominoid Evolution and Adaptation.* New York: Plenum, pp. 327–62.

Hart, Hornell. 1948. "The Logistic Growth of Political Areas." *Social Forces,* 26: 396–408.

Hartwig, W. C. 1994. "Pattern, Puzzles, and Perspectives on Platyrrhine Origins." In R. Corruccini and R. Ciochon, eds., *Integrative Paths to the Past.* Upper Saddle River, NJ: Prentice Hall, pp. 69–93.

Harvey, Philip W., and Peter F. Heywood. 1983. "Twenty-Five Years of Dietary Change in Simbu Province, Papua New Guinea." *Ecology of Food and Nutrition,* 13: 27–35.

Hassan, Fekri A. 1981. *Demographic Archaeology.* New York: Academic Press.

Hatch, Elvin. 1997. "The Good Side of Relativism." *Journal of Anthropological Research,* 53: 371–81.

Haug, Gerald, et al. 2003. "Climate and the Collapse of Maya Civilization." *Science,* 299 (March 14): 1731–35.

Hawkins, Alicia, and M. Kleindienst. 2001. "Aterian." In P. N. Peregrine and M. Ember, eds., *Encyclopedia of Prehistory, Volume 1: Africa.* New York: Kluwer Academic/Plenum, pp. 23–45.

Hayden, Thomas. 2000. "A Genome Milestone." *Newsweek* (July 3): 51–52.

Haynes, Vance. 1973. "The Calico Site: Artifacts or Geofacts?" *Science,* 181 (July 27): 305–10.

Hays, Terence E. 1994. "Sound Symbolism, Onomatopoeia, and New Guinea Frog Names." *Journal of Linguistic Anthropology,* 4: 153–74.

Heider, Karl. 1970. *The Dugum Dani.* Chicago: Aldine.

Heider, Karl. 1979. *Grand Valley Dani: Peaceful Warriors.* New York: Holt, Rinehart & Winston.

Heise, David R. 1967. "Cultural Patterning of Sexual Socialization." *American Sociological Review,* 32: 726–39.

Heller, Monica, ed. 1988. *Codeswitching: Anthropological and Sociolinguistic Perspectives.* Berlin: Mouton de Gruyter.

Helms, Mary W. 1975. *Middle America.* Upper Saddle River, NJ: Prentice Hall.

Helms, Mary W. 2004. "Miskito: Adaptations to Colonial Empires, Past and Present." In *Portraits of Culture,* in C. R. Ember, M. Ember, and P. N. Peregrine, eds., *New Directions in Anthropology.* Upper Saddle River, NJ: Prentice Hall, CD-ROM.

Hempel, Carl G. 1965. *Aspects of Scientific Explanation.* New York: Free Press.

Henderson, Harry. 2001. *Global Terrorism: The Complete Reference Guide.* New York: Checkmark Books.

Henry, Donald O. 1989. *From Foraging to Agriculture: The Levant at the End of the Ice Age.* Philadelphia: University of Pennsylvania Press.

Henry, Donald O. 1991. "Foraging, Sedentism, and Adaptive Vigor in the Natufian: Rethinking the Linkages." In G. A. Clark, ed., *Perspectives on the Past.* Philadelphia: University of Pennsylvania Press.

Henshilwood, Christopher, et al. 2002. "Emergence of Modern Human Behavior: Middle Stone Age Engravings from South Africa." *Science,* 295 (February 15): 1278–80.

Herdt, Gilbert. 1997. "Sexual Cultures and Population Movement: Implications for AIDS/STDs." In G. Herdt, ed., *Sexual Cultures and Migration in the Era of AIDS: Anthropological and Demographic Perspectives.* Oxford: Oxford University Press, pp. 3–22.

Herrman, Helen. 1990. "A Survey of Homeless Mentally Ill People in Melbourne, Australia." *Hospital and Community Psychiatry,* 41: 1291–92.

Herrnstein, Richard J., and Charles Murray. 1994. *The Bell Curve: Intelligence and Class Structure in American Life.* New York: Free Press.

Hewes, Gordon W. 1961. "Food Transport and the Origin of Hominid Bipedalism." *American Anthropologist,* 63: 687–710.

Hewlett, Barry. 2004. "Diverse Contexts of Human Infancy." In *Cross-Cultural Research for Social Science,* in C. R. Ember, M. Ember, and P. N. Peregrine, eds., *New Directions in Anthropology.* Upper Saddle River, NJ: Prentice Hall, CD-ROM.

Hiatt, L. R. 1980. "Polyandry in Sri Lanka: A Test Case for Parental Investment Theory." *Man,* 15: 583–98.

Hickey, Gerald Cannon. 1964. *Village in Vietnam.* New Haven, CT: Yale University Press.

Hickson, Letitia. 1986. "The Social Contexts of Apology in Dispute Settlement: A Cross-Cultural Study." *Ethnology,* 25: 283–94.

Higley, Stephen Richard. 1995. *Privilege, Power, and Place: The Geography of the American Upper Class.* Lanham, MD: Rowman & Littlefield.

Hill, Jane H. 1978. "Apes and Language." *Annual Review of Anthropology,* 7: 89–112.

Hill, Jane H. 2004. "Do Apes Have Language?" In *Research Frontiers,* in C. R. Ember, M. Ember, and P. N. Peregrine, eds., *New Directions in Anthropology.* Upper Saddle River, NJ: Prentice Hall, CD-ROM.

Hill, Jonathan D. 1996. "Introduction: Ethnogenesis in the Americas, 1492–1992." In J. D. Hill, ed., *Ethnogenesis in the Americas.* Iowa City: University of Iowa Press, pp. 1–19.

Hill, Kim, and A. Magdalena Hurtado. 2004. "The Ethics of Anthropological Research with Remote Tribal Populations." In F. M. Salzano and A. M. Hurtado, eds., *Lost Paradises and the Ethics of Research and Publication.* Oxford: Oxford University Press, pp. 193–210.

Hitchcock, Robert K., and Megan Biesele. 2000. "Introduction." In P. P. Schweitzer, M. Biesele, and R. K. Hitchcock, eds., *Hunters and Gatherers in the Modern World: Conflict, Resistance, and Self-Determinations.* New York: Berghahn Books, pp. 1–27.

Hockett, C. F., and R. Ascher. 1964. "The Human Revolution." *Current Anthropology,* 5: 135–68.

Hodell, David, M. Brenner, J. Curtis, and T. Guilderson. 2001. "Solar Forcing of Drought Frequency in the Maya Lowlands." *Science,* 292 (May 18): 1367–70.

Hoebel, E. Adamson. 1968 [1954]. *The Law of Primitive Man.* New York: Atheneum.

Hoffecker, John F., W. Roger Powers, and Ted Goebel. 1993. "The Colonization of Beringia and the Peopling of the New World." *Science,* 259 (January 1): 46–53.

Holden, Constance. 1996. "Last of the Cahokians." *Science,* 272 (April 19): 351–54.

Holden, Constance. 1997. "The First Tool Kit." *Science,* 275 (January 31): 623.

Holden, Constance. 2000. "Selective Power of UV." *Science,* 289 (September 1): 1461.

Hole, Frank. 1992. "Origins of Agriculture." In S. Jones, R. Martin, and D. Pilbeam, eds., *The Cambridge Encyclopedia of Human Evolution.* New York: Cambridge University Press.

Hole, Frank. 1994. "Environmental Shock and Urban Origins." In G. Stein and M. Rothman, eds., *Chiefdoms and Early States in the Near East.* Madison, WI: Prehistory Press.

Hole, Frank, Kent V. Flannery, and James A. Neely. 1969. *Prehistory and Human Ecology of the Deh Luran Plain.* Memoirs of the Museum of Anthropology, No. 1. Ann Arbor: University of Michigan.

Holland, Dorothy, and Naomi Quinn, eds. 1987. *Cultural Models in Language and Thought.* Cambridge: Cambridge University Press.

Holloway, Ralph L. 1974. "The Casts of Fossil Hominid Brains." *Scientific American* (July): 106–15.

Holmes, Janet. 2001. *An Introduction to Sociolinguistics,* 2nd ed. London: Longman.

Hooper, Judith. 2002. *Of Moths and Men: The Untold Story of Science and the Peppered Moth.* New York: W. W. Norton.

Hopkins, K. 1980. "Brother-Sister Marriage in Roman Egypt." *Comparative Studies in Society and History,* 22: 303–54.

Howard, Alan, and Jan Rensel. 2004. "Rotuma: Interpreting a Wedding." In *Portraits of Culture,* in C. R. Ember, M. Ember, and P. N. Peregrine, eds., *New Directions in Anthropology.* Upper Saddle River, NJ: Prentice Hall, CD-ROM.

Howell, F. Clark. 1966. "Observations on the Earlier Phases of the European Lower Paleolithic." *Recent Studies in Paleoanthropology. American Anthropologist* (special publication, April): 88–200.

Howell, Nancy. 1979. *Demography of the Dobe !Kung.* New York: Academic Press.

Hrdy, Sarah Blaffer. 1977. *The Langurs of Abu: Female and Male Strategies of Reproduction.* Cambridge, MA: Harvard University Press.

Huang, H. T. 2002. "Hypolactasia and the Chinese Diet." *Current Anthropology,* 43: 809–19.

Human Development Report 2001, published for the United Nations Development Programme. New York: Oxford University Press.

Hunt, Morton. 1974. *Sexual Behavior in the 1970s.* Chicago: Playboy Press.

Hunt, Robert C. 2000. "Labor Productivity and Agricultural Development: Boserup Revisited." *Human Ecology,* 28: 251–77.

Hurtado, Ana M., Kristen Hawkes, Kim Hill, and Hillard Kaplan. 1985. "Female Subsistence Strategies among the Aché Hunter-Gatherers of Eastern Paraguay." *Human Ecology,* 13: 1–28.

Huss-Ashmore, Rebecca, and Francis E. Johnston. 1985. "Bioanthropological Research in Developing Countries." *Annual Review of Anthropology,* 14: 475–527.

Huxley, Thomas H. 1970. "Man's Place in Nature." In L. B. Young, ed., *Evolution of Man.* New York: Oxford University Press.

Hymes, Dell. 1974. *Foundations in Sociolinguistics: An Ethnographic Approach.* Philadelphia: University of Pennsylvania Press.

Isaac, Glynn. 1971. "The Diet of Early Man: Aspects of Archaeological Evidence from Lower and Middle Pleistocene Sites in Africa." *World Archaeology,* 2: 277–99.

Isaac, Glynn. 1984. "The Archaeology of Human Origins: Studies of the Lower Pleistocene in East Africa, 1971–1981." In F. Wendorf and A. Close, eds., *Advances in World Archaeology.* Orlando, FL: Academic Press.

Isaac, Glynn, ed., assisted by Barbara Isaac. 1997. *Plio-Pleistocene Archaeology.* Oxford: Clarendon Press.

Itkonen, T. I. 1951. "The Lapps of Finland." *Southwestern Journal of Anthropology,* 7: 32–68.

Jablonski, Nina G., and George Chaplin. 2000. "The Evolution of Human Skin Color." *Journal of Human Evolution,* 39: 57–106.

Jacobs, Sue-Ellen, and Christine Roberts. 1989. "Sex, Sexuality, Gender and Gender Variance." In S. Morgen, ed., *Gender and Anthropology.* Washington, D.C.: American Anthropological Association.

Jaeger, J., T. Thein, M. Benammi, Y. Chaimanee, A. N. Soe, T. Lwin, T. Tun, S. Wai, and S. Ducrocq. 1999. "A New Primate from the Middle Eocene of Myanmar and the Asian Early Origins of Anthropoids." *Science,* 286 (October 15): 528–30.

Jankowiak, William, M. Diane Nell, and Ann Buckmaster. 2002. "Managing Infidelity: A Cross-Cultural Perspective." *Ethnology,* 41: 85–101.

Janzen, Daniel H. 1973. "Tropical Agroecosystems." *Science,* 182 (December 21): 1212–19.

Jayaswal, Vidula. 2002. "South Asian Upper Paleolithic." In P. N. Peregrine and M. Ember, eds., *Encyclopedia of Prehistory, Volume 8: South and Southwest Asia.* New York: Kluwer Academic/Plenum.

Jelliffe, Derrick B., and E. F. Patrice Jelliffe. 1975. "Human Milk, Nutrition, and the World Resource Crisis." *Science,* 188 (May 9): 557–61.

Jennings, J. D. 1968. *Prehistory of North America.* New York: McGraw-Hill.

Jensen, Arthur. 1969. "How Much Can We Boost IQ and Scholastic Achievement?" *Harvard Educational Review,* 29: 1–123.

Joans, Barbara. 1997. "Problems in Pocatello: A Study in Linguistic Misunderstanding." In A. Podolefsky and P. J. Brown, eds., *Applying Cultural Anthropology: An Introductory Reader,* 3rd ed. Mountain View, CA: Mayfield, pp. 51–54.

Johanson, Donald C., and Maitland Edey. 1981. *Lucy: The Beginnings of Humankind.* New York: Simon & Schuster.

Johanson, Donald C., and Tim D. White. 1979. "A Systematic Assessment of Early African Hominids." *Science,* 203 (January 26): 321–30.

Johnson, Allen, and Timothy Earle. 1987. *The Evolution of Human Societies: From Foraging Group to Agrarian State.* Stanford, CA: Stanford University Press.

Johnson, Amber Lynn. 2002. "Cross-Cultural Analysis of Pastoral Adaptations and Organizational States: A Preliminary Study." *Cross-Cultural Research,* 36: 151–80.

Johnson, Gregory A. 1977. "Aspects of Regional Analysis in Archaeology." *Annual Review of Anthropology,* 6: 479–508.

Johnson, Gregory A. 1987. "The Changing Organization of Uruk Administration on the Susiana Plain." In F. Hole, ed., *Archaeology of Western Iran.* Washington, D.C.: Smithsonian Institution Press.

Johnson, Jeffrey G., Patricia Cohen, Elizabeth M. Smailies, Stephanie Kasen, and Judith S. Brook. 2002. "Television Viewing and Aggressive Behavior during Adolescence and Adulthood." *Science,* 295 (March 29): 2468–70.

Johnston, David Cay. 1999. "Gap Between Rich and Poor Found Substantially Wider." *New York Times National,* September 5, p. 16.

Jolly, Alison. 1985. *The Evolution of Primate Behavior,* 2nd ed. New York: Macmillan.

Jolly, Clifford. 1970. "The Seed-Eaters: A New Model of Hominid Differentiation Based on a Baboon Analogy." *Man,* 5: 5–28.

Jones, Steve, Robert Martin, and David Pilbeam, eds. 1992. *The Cambridge Encyclopedia of Human Evolution.* New York: Cambridge University Press.

Judge, W. James, and Jerry Dawson. 1972. "Paleo Indian Settlement Technology in New Mexico." *Science,* 176 (June 16): 1210–16.

Jungers, William L. 1988a. "Relative Joint Size and Hominoid Locomotor Adaptations with Implications for the Evolution of Hominid Bipedalism." *Journal of Human Evolution,* 17: 247–65.

Jungers, William L. 1988b. "New Estimates of Body Size in Australopithecines." In F. Grine, ed., *Evolutionary History of the "Robust" Australopithecines.* New York: Aldine.

Kamin, Leon J. 1995. "Behind the Curve." *Scientific American* (February): 99–103.

Kang, Bong W. 2000. "A Reconsideration of Population Pressure and Warfare: A Protohistoric Korean Case." *Current Anthropology,* 41: 873–81.

Kaplan, Hillard, Kim Hill, and A. Magdalena Hurtado. 1990. "Risk, Foraging and Food Sharing among the Aché." In E. Cashdan, ed., *Risk and Uncertainty in Tribal and Peasant Economies.* Boulder, CO: Westview.

Kappelman, John. 1993. "The Attraction of Paleomagnetism." *Evolutionary Anthropology,* 2: 89–99.

Kasarda, John D. 1971. "Economic Structure and Fertility: A Comparative Analysis." *Demography,* 8, no. 3 (August): 307–18.

Kay, Richard F. 2000a. "*Parapithecidae.*" In I. Tattersall, E. Delson, and J. van Couvering, eds., *Encyclopedia of Human Evolution and Prehistory.* New York: Garland.

Kay, Richard F. 2000b. "Teeth." In I. Tattersall, E. Delson, and J. van Couvering, eds., *Encyclopedia of Human Evolution and Prehistory.* New York: Garland.

Kay, Richard F., C. Ross, and B. A. Williams. 1997. "Anthropoid Origins." *Science,* 275 (February 7): 797–804.

Keeley, Lawrence H. 1977. "The Functions of Paleolithic Flint Tools." *Scientific American* (November): 108–26.

Keeley, Lawrence H. 1980. *Experimental Determination of Stone Tool Uses: A Microwear Analysis.* Chicago: University of Chicago Press.

Keeley, Lawrence H. 1991. "Ethnographic Models for Late Glacial Hunter-Gatherers." In N. Barton, A. J. Roberts, and D. A. Roe, eds., *The Late Glacial in North-West Europe: Human Adaptation and Environmental Change at the End of the Pleistocene.* London: Council for British Archaeology, CBA Research Report, pp. 179–90.

Keenan, Elinor. 1989. "Norm-Makers, Norm-Breakers: Uses of Speech by Men and Women in a Malagasy Community." In R. Bauman and J. Sherzer, eds., *Explorations in the Ethnography of Speaking,* 2nd ed. New York: Cambridge University Press.

Kehoe, Alice B., and Dody H. Giletti. 1981. "Women's Preponderance in Possession Cults: The Calcium-Deficiency Hypothesis Extended." *American Anthropologist,* 83: 549–61.

Keller, Helen. 1974 [1902]. *The Story of My Life.* New York: Dell.

Kelley, Jay. 1992. "The Evolution of Apes." In S. Jones, R. Martin, and D. Pilbeam, eds., *The Cambridge Encyclopedia of Human Evolution.* New York: Cambridge University Press.

Kelly, Raymond C. 1974. "Witchcraft and Sexual Relations: An Exploration in the Social and Semantic Implications of the Structure of Belief." Paper presented at the annual meeting of the American Anthropological Association, Mexico City.

Kelly, Robert L. 1995. *The Foraging Spectrum: Diversity in Hunter-Gatherer Lifeways.* Washington, D.C.: Smithsonian Institution Press.

Kerr, Richard A. 1998. "Sea-Floor Dust Shows Drought Felled Akkadian Empire." *Science,* 299 (January 16): 325–26.

Kilbride, Philip L., and Janet C. Kilbride. 1990. "Polygyny: A Modern Contradiction?" In P. L. Kilbride and J. C. Kilbride, *Changing Family Life in East Africa.* University Park: Pennsylvania State University Press.

Kimbel, William H., T. D. White, and D. C. Johansen. 1984. "Cranial Morphology of *Australopithecus afarensis:* A Comparative Study Based on Composite Reconstruction of the Adult Skull." *American Journal of Physical Anthropology,* 64: 337–88.

King, Barbara J. 1999. "Introduction." In B. J. King, ed., *The Origins of Language.* Santa Fe, NM: School of American Research Press, pp. 3–19.

King, Marie-Claire, and Arno Motulsky. 2002. "Mapping Human History," *Science,* 298 (December 20): 2342–43.

King, Seth S. 1979. "Some Farm Machinery Seems Less Than Human." *The New York Times,* April 8, p. E9.

Kingston, John D., Bruno D. Marino, and Andrew Hill. 1994. "Isotopic Evidence for Neogene Hominid Paleoenvironments in the Kenya Rift Valley." *Science,* 264 (May 13): 955–59.

Klass, Morton. 2004. "Is There 'Caste' Outside of India?" In *Cross-Cultural Research for Social Science,* in C. R. Ember, M. Ember, and P. N. Peregrine, eds., *New Directions in Anthropology.* Upper Saddle River, NJ: Prentice Hall, CD-ROM.

Klein, Richard G. 1974. "Ice-Age Hunters of the Ukraine." *Scientific American* (June): 96–105.

Klein, Richard G. 1977. "The Ecology of Early Man in Southern Africa." *Science,* 197 (July 8): 115–26.

Klein, Richard G. 1983. "The Stone Age Prehistory of Southern Africa." *Annual Review of Anthropology,* 12: 25–48.

Klein, Richard G. 1987. "Reconstructing How Early People Exploited Animals: Problems and Prospects." In M. Nitecki and D. Nitecki, eds., *The Evolution of Human Hunting.* New York: Plenum.

Klein, Richard G. 1989. *The Human Career: Human Biological and Cultural Origins.* Chicago: University of Chicago Press.

Klein, Richard G. 1994. "Southern Africa before the Ice Age." In R. Corruccini and R. Ciochon, eds., *Integrative Paths to the Past.* Upper Saddle River, NJ: Prentice Hall.

Klein, Richard G. 2003. "Whither the Neanderthals" *Science,* 299 (March 7): 1525–28.

Kleinman, Arthur, Veena Das, and Margaret Lock, eds. 1997. *Social Suffering.* Berkeley: University of California Press.

Klima, Bohuslav. 1962. "The First Ground-Plan of an Upper Paleolithic Loess Settlement in Middle Europe and Its Meaning." In R. Braidwood and G. Willey, eds., *Courses toward Urban Life.* Chicago: Aldine.

Klineberg, Otto. 1935. *Negro Intelligence and Selective Migration.* New York: Columbia University Press.

Klineberg, Otto, ed. 1944. *Characteristics of the American Negro.* New York: Harper & Brothers.

Kluckhohn, Clyde. 1948. "As an Anthropologist Views It." In A. Deutsch, ed., *Sex Habits of American Men.* Upper Saddle River, NJ: Prentice Hall.

Knecht, Peter. 2003. "Aspects of Shamanism: An Introduction." In C. Chilson and P. Knecht, eds., *Shamans in Asia.* London: RoutledgeCurzon, pp. 1–30.

Koch, Klaus-Friedrich, Soraya Altorki, Andrew Arno, and Letitia Hickson. 1977. "Ritual Reconciliation and the Obviation of Grievances: A Comparative Study in the Ethnography of Law." *Ethnology,* 16: 269–84.

Konner, Melvin, and Carol Worthman. 1980. "Nursing Frequency, Gonadal Function, and Birth Spacing among !Kung Hunter-Gatherers." *Science,* 267 (February 15): 788–91.

Korbin, Jill E. 1981. "Introduction." In J. E. Korbin, ed., *Child Abuse and Neglect.* Berkeley: University of California Press.

Kottak, Conrad P. 1999. "The New Ecological Anthropology." *Current Anthropology,* 101: 23–35.

Kracke, Waud H. 1979. *Force and Persuasion: Leadership in an Amazonian Society.* Chicago: University of Chicago Press.

Krahn, H., T. F. Hartnagel, and J. W. Gartrell. 1986. "Income Inequality and Homicide Rates: Cross-National Data and Criminological Theories." *Criminology,* 24: 269–95.

Kramer, Andrew. 2002. "The Natural History and Evolutionary Fate of *Homo erectus.*" In P. N. Peregrine, C. R. Ember, and M. Ember, eds., *Physical Anthropology: Original Readings in Method and Practice.* Upper Saddle River, NJ: Prentice Hall.

Kramer, Samuel Noel. 1963. *The Sumerians: Their History, Culture, and Character.* Chicago: University of Chicago Press.

Krebs, J. R., and N. B. Davies, eds. 1984. *Behavioural Ecology: An Evolutionary Approach,* 2nd ed. Sunderland, MA: Sinauer.

Krebs, J. R., and N. B. Davies. 1987. *An Introduction to Behavioural Ecology,* 2nd ed. Sunderland, MA: Sinauer.

Krings, Matthias, A. Stone, R. W. Schmitz, H. Krainitzki, M. Stoneking, and S. Paabo. 1997. "Neandertal DNA Sequences and the Origin of Modern Humans." *Cell,* 90: 19–30.

Krippner, Stanley. 1987. "Dreams and Shamanism." In S. Nicholson, comp., *Shamanism.* Wheaton, IL: Theosophical Publishing House, pp. 125–32.

Kristof, Nicholas D. 1995. "Japan's Invisible Minority: Better Off Than in Past, but Still Outcasts." *New York Times International,* November 30, p. A18.

Kristof, Nicholas D. 1997. "Japan's Invisible Minority: Burakumin," *Britannica Online.* December.

Kuehn, Steven. 1998. "New Evidence for Late Paleoindian–Early Archaic Subsistence Behavior in the Western Great Lakes." *American Antiquity,* 63: 457–76.

Kushner, Gilbert. 1991. "Applied Anthropology." In W. G. Emener and M. Darrow, eds., *Career Explorations in Human Services.* Springfield, IL: Charles C. Thomas.

Lakoff, Robin. 1973. "Language and Woman's Place." *Language in Society,* 2: 45–80.

Lakoff, Robin. 1990. "Why Can't a Woman Be Less Like a Man?" In R. Lakoff, *Talking Power.* New York: Basic Books.

Lambert, Helen. 2001. "Not Talking about Sex in India: Indirection and the Communication of Bodily Intention." In J. Hendry and C. W. Watson, eds., *An Anthropology of Indirect Communication.* London: Routledge, pp. 51–67.

Lambert, William W., Leigh Minturn Triandis, and Margery Wolf. 1959. "Some Correlates of Beliefs in the Malevolence and Benevolence of Supernatural Beings: A Cross-Societal Study." *Journal of Abnormal and Social Psychology,* 58: 162–69.

Landauer, Thomas K. 1973. "Infantile Vaccination and the Secular Trend in Stature." *Ethos,* 1: 499–503.

Landauer, Thomas K., and John W. M. Whiting. 1964. "Infantile Stimulation and Adult Stature of Human Males." *American Anthropologist,* 66: 1007–28.

Landauer, Thomas K., and John W. M. Whiting. 1981. "Correlates and Consequences of Stress in Infancy." In R. H. Munroe, R. Munroe, and B. B. Whiting, eds., *Handbook of Cross-Cultural Human Development.* New York: Garland.

Lang, Sabine. 1999. "Lesbians, Men-Women, and Two-Spirits: Homosexuality and Gender in Native American Cultures." In E. Blackwood and S. E. Weiringa, eds., *Female Desires: Same-Sex Relations and Transgender Practices across Cultures.* New York: Columbia University Press, pp. 91–116.

Lareau, Annette. 2003. *Unequal Childhoods: Class, Race, and Family Life.* Berkeley, CA: University of California Press.

Larsen, Clark Spenser. 2002. "Bare Bones Anthropology: The Bioarchaeology of Human Remains." In P. N. Peregrine, C. R. Ember, and M. Ember, eds., *Archaeology: Original Readings in Method and Practice.* Upper Saddle River, NJ: Prentice Hall.

Larson, Daniel O., John R. Johnson, and Joel C. Michaelsen. 1994. "Missionization among the Coastal Chumash of Central California: A Study of Risk Minimization Strategies." *American Anthropologist,* 96: 263–99.

Lassiter, Luke Eric, Hurley Goodall, Elizabeth Campbell, and Michelle Natasya Johnson, eds. 2004. *The Other Side of Middletown: Exploring Muncie's African-American Community.* Walnut Creek, CA: AltaMira Press.

Lawless, Robert, Vinson H. Sutlive, Jr., and Mario D. Zamora, eds. 1983. *Fieldwork: The Human Experience.* New York: Gordon and Breach.

Leacock, Eleanor, and Richard Lee. 1982. "Introduction." In E. Leacock and R. Lee, eds., *Politics and History in Band Societies.* Cambridge: Cambridge University Press.

Leakey, Louis S. B. 1960. "Finding the World's Earliest Man." *National Geographic* (September): 420–35.

Leakey, Louis S. B. 1965. *Olduvai Gorge, 1951–1961, Volume I: A Preliminary Report on the Geology and Fauna.* Cambridge: Cambridge University Press.

Leakey, Maeve, C. S. Feibel, I. McDougall, and A. Walker. 1995. "New Four-Million-Year-Old Hominid Species from Kanapoi and Allia Bay, Kenya." *Nature,* 376 (August 17): 565–71.

Leakey, Maeve, Fred Spoor, Frank Brown, Patrick Gathogo, Christopher Kiarie, Louise Leakey, Ian McDougall. 2001. "New Hominin Genus from Eastern Africa Shows Diverse Middle Pliocene Lineages." *Nature,* 410 (March 22): 433–51.

Leakey, Mary. 1971. *Olduvai Gorge: Excavations in Beds I and II.* Cambridge: Cambridge University Press.

Lee, Richard B. 1968. "What Hunters Do for a Living, or, How to Make Out on Scarce Resources." In R. B. Lee and I. DeVore, eds., *Man the Hunter.* Chicago: Aldine.

Lee, Richard B. 1972. "Population Growth and the Beginnings of Sedentary Life among the !Kung Bushmen." In B. Spooner, ed., *Population Growth.* Cambridge, MA: MIT Press.

Lee, Richard B. 1979. *The !Kung San: Men, Women, and Work in a Foraging Society.* Cambridge: Cambridge University Press.

Lees, Susan H., and Daniel G. Bates. 1974. "The Origins of Specialized Nomadic Pastoralism: A Systemic Model." *American Antiquity,* 39: 187–93.

Leibowitz, Lila. 1978. *Females, Males, Families: A Biosocial Approach.* North Scituate, MA: Duxbury.

Lenski, Gerhard. 1984 [1966]. *Power and Privilege: A Theory of Social Stratification.* Chapel Hill: University of North Carolina Press.

Leonard, William R. 2002. "Food for Thought: Dietary Change Was a Driving Force in Human Evolution." *Scientific American* (December): 108–15.

Lepowsky, Maria. 1990. "Big Men, Big Women and Cultural Autonomy." *Ethnology,* 29: 35–50.

Leslie, C. 1976. "Introduction." In C. Leslie, ed., *Asian Medical Systems: A Comparative Study.* Los Angeles: University of California Press.

Lett, James. 1996. "Scientific Anthropology." In D. Levinson and M. Ember, eds., *Encyclopedia of Cultural Anthropology.* New York: Henry Holt.

Levine, James A., Robert Weisell, Simon Chevassus, Claudio D. Martinez, and Barbara Burlingame. 2002. "The Distribution of Work Tasks for Male and Female Children and Adults Separated by Gender" in "Looking at Child Labor." *Science,* 296 (May 10): 1025.

Levine, Nancy E. 1988. "Women's Work and Infant Feeding: A Case from Rural Nepal." *Ethnology,* 27: 231–51.

Levinson, David. 1989. *Family Violence in Cross-Cultural Perspective.* Newbury Park, CA: Sage.

Levinson, David, and Melvin Ember, eds. 1997. *American Immigrant Cultures: Builders of a Nation,* 2 vol. New York: Macmillan Reference.

Lévi-Strauss, Claude. 1963a. "The Sorcerer and His Magic." In C. Lévi-Strauss, *Structural Anthropology.* New York: Basic Books.

Lévi-Strauss, Claude. 1963b. *Structural Anthropology.* Trans. Claire Jacobson and Brooke Grundfest Schoepf. New York: Basic Books.

Lewin, Roger. 1983a. "Is the Orangutan a Living Fossil?" *Science,* 222 (December 16): 1222–23.

Lewin, Roger. 1983b. "Fossil Lucy Grows Younger, Again." *Science,* 219 (January 7): 43–44.

Lewin, Tamar. 1994. "Sex in America: Faithfulness in Marriage Is Overwhelming." *New York Times National,* October 7, pp. A1, A18.

Lewis, Oscar. 1951. *Life in a Mexican Village: Tepoztlan Revisited.* Urbana: University of Illinois Press.

Lewis, Oscar (with the assistance of Victor Barnouw). 1958. *Village Life in Northern India.* Urbana: University of Illinois Press.

Lichter, Daniel T., Diane K. McLaughlin, George Kephart, and David J. Landry. 1992. "Race and the Retreat from Marriage: A Shortage of Marriageable Men?" *American Sociological Review,* 57: 781–99.

Lieberman, Daniel E. 1995. "Testing Hypotheses about Recent Human Evolution from Skulls: Integrating Morphology, Function, Development, and Phylogeny." *Current Anthropology,* 36: 159–97.

Lieberman, Leonard. 1999. "Scientific Insignificance," *Anthropology Newsletter,* 40: 11–12.

Lingenfelter, Sherwood G. 2004. "Yap: Changing Roles of Men and Women." In *Portraits of Culture,* in C. R. Ember, M. Ember, and P. N. Peregrine, eds., *New Directions in Anthropology.* Upper Saddle River, NJ: Prentice Hall, CD-ROM.

Linton, Ralph. 1936. *The Study of Man.* New York: Appleton-Century-Crofts.

Linton, Ralph. 1945. *The Cultural Background of Personality.* New York: Appleton-Century-Crofts.

Loftin, Colin K. 1971. "Warfare and Societal Complexity: A Cross-Cultural Study of Organized Fighting in Preindustrial Societies." Ph.D. dissertation, University of North Carolina at Chapel Hill.

Loftin, Colin, David McDowall, and James Boudouris. 1989. "Economic Change and Homicide in Detroit, 1926–1979." In T. R. Gurr, ed., *Violence in America, Volume 1: The History of Crime.* Newbury Park, CA: Sage.

Loomis, W. Farnsworth. 1967. "Skin-Pigment Regulation of Vitamin-D Biosynthesis in Man." *Science,* 157 (August 4): 501–506.

Loustaunau, Martha O., and Elisa J. Sobo. 1997. *The Cultural Context of Health, Illness, and Medicine.* Westport, CT: Bergin & Garvey.

Lovejoy, Arthur O. 1964. *The Great Chain of Being: A Study of the History of an Idea.* Cambridge, MA: Harvard University Press.

Lovejoy, C. Owen. 1981. "The Origin of Man." *Science,* 211 (January 23): 341–50.

Lovejoy, C. Owen. 1988. "Evolution of Human Walking." *Scientific American* (November): 118–25.

Low, Bobbi S. 1990. "Marriage Systems and Pathogen Stress in Human Societies." *American Zoologist,* 30: 325–39.

Low, Bobbi S. 2004. "Behavioral Ecology, 'Sociobiology,' and Human Behavior." In *Research Frontiers,* in C. R. Ember, M. Ember, and P. N. Peregrine, eds., *New Directions in Anthropology.* Upper Saddle River, NJ: Prentice Hall, CD-ROM.

Lumbreras, Luis. 1974. *The Peoples and Cultures of Ancient Peru.* Washington, D.C.: Smithsonian Institution Press.

Lyttleton, Chris. 2000. *Endangered Relations: Negotiating Sex and AIDS in Thailand.* Bangkok: White Lotus Press.

MacArthur, R. H., and E. O. Wilson. 1967. *Theory of Island Biogeography.* Princeton, NJ: Princeton University Press.

Maccoby, Eleanor E., and Carol N. Jacklin. 1974. *The Psychology of Sex Differences.* Stanford, CA: Stanford University Press.

Macdonald, Douglas H. and Barry S. Hewlett. 1999. "Reproductive Interests and Forager Mobility." *Current Anthropology,* 40: 501–23.

MacKinnon, John, and Kathy MacKinnon. 1980. "The Behavior of Wild Spectral Tarsiers." *International Journal of Primatology,* 1: 361–79.

MacNeish, Richard S. 1991. *The Origins of Agriculture and Settled Life.* Norman: University of Oklahoma Press.

Madigral, Lorena. 1989. "Hemoglobin Genotype, Fertility, and the Malaria Hypothesis." *Human Biology,* 61: 311–25.

Magner, L. 1992. *A History of Medicine.* New York: Marcel Dekker.

Mahony, Frank Joseph. 1971. *A Trukese Theory of Medicine.* Ann Arbor, MI: University Microfilms, 1070, as seen in eHRAF World Cultures on the Web.

Malefijt, Annemarie De Waal. 1968. *Religion and Culture: An Introduction to Anthropology of Religion.* New York: Macmillan.

Mangin, William. 1967. "Latin American Squatter Settlements: A Problem and a Solution." *Latin American Research Review,* 2: 65–98.

Manhein, Mary H. 1999. *The Bone Lady: Life as a Forensic Anthropologist.* Baton Rouge: Louisiana State University Press.

Marano, Louis A. 1973. "A Macrohistoric Trend toward World Government." *Behavior Science Notes,* 8: 35–40.

Marcus, Joyce, and Kent V. Flannery. 1996. *Zapotec Civilization.* London: Thames and Hudson.

Marks, Jonathan. 1994. "Black, White, Other: Racial Categories Are Cultural Constructs Masquerading as Biology." *Natural History* (December): 32–35.

Marshall, Eliot. 2000. "Rival Genome Sequencers Celebrate a Milestone Together." *Science,* 288 (June 30): 2294–95.

Marshall, Larry G. 1984. "Who Killed Cock Robin? An Investigation of the Extinction Controversy." In P. Martin and R. Klein, eds., *Quaternary Extinctions.* Tucson: University of Arizona Press.

Marshall, Lorna. 1961. "Sharing, Talking, and Giving: Relief of Social Tensions among !Kung Bushmen." *Africa,* 31: 239–42.

Martin, M. Kay, and Barbara Voorhies. 1975. *Female of the Species.* New York: Columbia University Press.

Martin, Paul S. 1973. "The Discovery of America." *Science,* 179 (March 9): 969–74.

Martin, Paul S., and H. E. Wright, eds. 1967. *Pleistocene Extinctions: The Search for a Cause.* New Haven, CT: Yale University Press.

Martin, Robert D. 1990. *Primate Origins and Evolution: A Phylogenetic Reconstruction.* Princeton, NJ: Princeton University Press.

Martorell, Reynaldo. 1980. "Interrelationships between Diet, Infectious Disease, and Nutritional Status." In L. Greene and F. Johnston, eds., *Social and Biological Predictors of Nutritional Status, Physical Growth, and Neurological Development*. New York: Academic Press.

Martorell, Reynaldo, Juan Rivera, Haley Kaplowitz, and Ernesto Pollitt. 1991. "Long-Term Consequences of Growth Retardation during Early Childhood." Paper presented at the Sixth International Congress of Auxology, September 15–19, Madrid.

Mascie-Taylor, C. G. Nicholas. 1990. "The Biology of Social Class." In C. G. N. Mascie-Taylor, ed., *Biosocial Aspects of Social Class*. Oxford: Oxford University Press, pp. 117–42.

Masumura, Wilfred T. 1977. "Law and Violence: A Cross-Cultural Study." *Journal of Anthropological Research*, 33: 388–99.

Mathiassen, Therkel. 1928. *Material Culture of Iglulik Eskimos*. Copenhagen: Glydendalske.

Matossian, Mary K. 1982. "Ergot and the Salem Witchcraft Affair." *American Scientist*, 70: 355–57.

Matossian, Mary K. 1989. *Poisons of the Past: Molds, Epidemics, and History*. New Haven, CT: Yale University Press.

Mayr, Ernst. 1982. *The Growth of Biological Thought: Diversity, Evolution, and Inheritance*. Cambridge, MA: Belknap Press of Harvard University Press.

Mazess, Richard B. 1975. "Human Adaptation to High Altitude." In A. Damon, ed., *Physiological Anthropology*. New York: Oxford University Press.

McCain, Garvin, and Erwin M. Segal. 1988. *The Game of Science*, 5th ed. Monterey, CA: Brooks/Cole.

McCarthy, Frederick D., and Margaret McArthur. 1960. "The Food Quest and the Time Factor in Aboriginal Economic Life." In C. P. Mountford, ed., *Records of the Australian-American Scientific Expedition to Arnhem Land, Volume 2: Anthropology and Nutrition*. Melbourne: Melbourne University Press.

McCorriston, Joy, and Frank Hole. 1991. "The Ecology of Seasonal Stress and the Origins of Agriculture in the Near East." *American Anthropologist*, 93: 46–69.

McCracken, Robert D. 1971. "Lactase Deficiency: An Example of Dietary Evolution." *Current Anthropology*, 12: 479–500.

McDonald, Kim A. 1998. "New Evidence Challenges Traditional Model of How the New World Was Settled." *Chronicle of Higher Education* (March 13): A22.

McElroy, Ann, and Patricia Townsend. 2002. *Medical Anthropology in Ecological Perspective*, 4th ed. Boulder, CO: Westview.

McGarvey, Stephen T. 1994. "The Thrifty Gene Concept and Adiposity Studies in Biological Anthropology." *Journal of the Polynesian Society*, 103: 29–42.

McHenry, Henry M. 1982. "The Pattern of Human Evolution: Studies on Bipedalism, Mastication, and Encephalization." *Annual Review of Anthropology*, 11: 151–73.

McHenry, Henry M. 1988. "New Estimates of Body Weight in Early Hominids and Their Significance to Encephalization and Megadontia in 'Robust' Australopithecines." In F. E. Grine, ed., *Evolutionary History of the "Robust" Australopithecines*. New York: Aldine.

McHenry, Henry M. 2002. "'Robust' Australopithecines: Our Family Tree and Homoplasy." In P. N. Peregrine, C. R. Ember, and M. Ember, eds., *Physical Anthropology: Original Readings in Method and Practice*. Upper Saddle River, NJ: Prentice Hall.

McKee, Lauris. 1984. "Sex Differentials in Survivorship and the Customary Treatment of Infants and Children." *Medical Anthropology*, 8: 91–108.

McMullin, Ernan. 2001. "Plantinga's Defense of Special Creation." In R. Pennock, ed., *Intelligent Design Creationism and Its Critics*. Boston: MIT Press, p. 174.

McNeill, William H. 1967. *A World History*. New York: Oxford University Press.

McNeill, William H. 1976. *Plagues and Peoples*. Garden City, NY: Doubleday/Anchor.

Mead, Margaret. 1950 [1935]. *Sex and Temperament in Three Primitive Societies*. New York: Mentor.

Mead, Margaret. 1961 [1928]. *Coming of Age in Samoa*, 3rd ed. New York: Morrow.

Mead, Margaret. 1978. "The Evolving Ethics of Applied Anthropology." In E. M. Eddy and W. L. Partridge, eds., *Applied Anthropology in America*. New York: Columbia University Press.

Meek, C. K. 1940. *Land Law and Custom in the Colonies*. London: Oxford University Press.

Meggitt, Mervyn J. 1977. *Blood Is Their Argument: Warfare among the Mae Enga Tribesmen of the New Guinea Highlands*. Palo Alto, CA: Mayfield.

Mellaart, James. 1961. "Roots in the Soil." In S. Piggott, ed., *The Dawn of Civilization*. London: Thomas & Hudson.

Mellars, Paul. 1994. "The Upper Paleolithic Revolution." In B. Cunliffe, ed., *The Oxford Illustrated Prehistory of Europe*. Oxford: Oxford University Press, pp. 42–78.

Mellars, Paul. 1996. *The Neanderthal Legacy*. Princeton, NJ: Princeton University Press.

Mellars, Paul. 1998. "The Fate of the Neaderthals." *Nature*, 395 (October 8): 539–40.

Mellor, John W., and Sarah Gavian. 1987. "Famine: Causes, Prevention, and Relief." *Science*, 235 (January 30): 539–44.

Meltzer, David J. 1993. "Pleistocene Peopling of the Americas." *Evolutionary Anthropology*, 1: 157–69.

Merbs, Charles F. 1992. "A New World of Infectious Disease." *Yearbook of Physical Anthropology*, 35: 3–42.

Messer, Ellen. 1996. "Hunger Vulnerability from an Anthropologist's Food System Perspective." In E. F. Moran, ed., *Transforming Societies, Transforming Anthropology*. Ann Arbor: University of Michigan Press.

Michel, R. H., McGovern, P. E., and Badler, V. R. 1993. "The First Wine and Beer: Chemical Detection of Ancient Fermented Beverages." *Analytical Chemistry*, 65: 408A–13A.

Middleton, John. 1971. "The Cult of the Dead: Ancestors and Ghosts." In W. A. Lessa and E. Z. Vogt, eds., *Reader in Comparative Religion*, 3rd ed. New York: Harper & Row.

Middleton, Russell. 1962. "Brother-Sister and Father-Daughter Marriage in Ancient Egypt." *American Sociological Review*, 27: 603–11.

Milanovic, Branko. 2002. "True World Income Distribution, 1988 and 1993: First Calculation Based on Household Surveys Alone." *The Economic Journal*, 112: 51–92.

Miller, Greg. 2004. "Listen, Baby." *Science*, 306 (November 12): 1127.

Miller, Naomi F. 1992. "The Origins of Plant Cultivation in the Near East." In C. W. Cowan and P. J. Watson, eds., *The Origins of Agriculture*. Washington, D.C.: Smithsonian Institution Press.

Millon, René. 1967. "Teotihuacán." *Scientific American* (June): 38–48.

Millon, René. 1976. "Social Relations in Ancient Teotihuacán." In E. Wolf, ed., *The Valley of Mexico*. Albuquerque: University of New Mexico Press.

Miner, Horace. 1956. "Body Rituals among the Nacirema." *American Anthropologist*, 58: 504–505.

Minturn, Leigh, and Jerry Stashak. 1982. "Infanticide as a Terminal Abortion Procedure." *Behavior Science Research*, 17: 70–85.

Miracle, Andrew W. 2004. "A Shaman to Organizations." In *Research Frontiers*, in C. R. Ember, M. Ember, and P. N. Peregrine, eds., *New Directions in Anthropology*. Upper Saddle River, NJ: Prentice Hall, CD-ROM.

Mitchell, Donald. 2004. "Nimpkish: Complex Foragers on the Northwest Coast of North America." In *Portraits of Culture*, in C. R. Ember, M. Ember, and P. N. Peregrine, eds., *New Directions in Anthropology*. Upper Saddle River, NJ: Prentice Hall, CD-ROM.

Moerman, Daniel E. 1997. "Physiology and Symbols: The Anthropological Implications of the Placebo Effect." In L. Romanucci-Ross, D. E. Moerman, and L. R. Tancredi, eds., *The Anthropology of Medicine*, 3rd ed. Westport, CT: Bergin & Garvey, pp. 240–53.

Molnar, Stephen. 1998. *Human Variation: Races, Types, and Ethnic Groups*, 4th ed. Upper Saddle River, NJ: Prentice Hall.

Mooney, Kathleen A. 1978. "The Effects of Rank and Wealth on Exchange among the Coast Salish." *Ethnology*, 17: 391–406.

Moore, Carmella Caracci. 1988. "An Optimal Scaling of Murdock's Theories of Illness Data—An Approach to the Problem of Interdependence." *Behavior Science Research*, 22: 161–79.

Moore, John H., and Janis E. Campbell. 2002. "Confirming Unilocal Residence in Native North America." *Ethnology*, 41: 175–88.

Moore, Omar Khayyam. 1957. "Divination: A New Perspective." *American Anthropologist*, 59: 69–74.

Morell, Virginia. 1995. "The Earliest Art Becomes Older—And More Common." *Science*, 267 (March 31): 1908–909.

Morris, John. 1938. *Living with Lepchas: A Book about the Sikkim Himalayas*. London: Heinemann.

Morwood, M. J., R. Soejono, R. Roberts, T. Sutikna, C. Turney, K. Westaway, W. Rink, J. Zhao, G. van den Bergh, R. Due, D. Hobbs, M. Moore, M. Bird, and L. Fifield. 2004. "Archaeology and Age of a New Hominin from Flores in Eastern Indonesia." *Nature*, 431 (October 28): 1087–91.

Moser, Stephanie. 1998. *Ancestral Images: The Iconography of Human Origins*. Ithaca, NY: Cornell University Press.

Motulsky, Arno. 1971. "Metabolic Polymorphisms and the Role of Infectious Diseases in Human Evolution." In L. N. Morris, ed., *Human Populations, Genetic Variation, and Evolution.* San Francisco: Chandler.

Moyà-solà, Salvador, et al. 2004. "*Pierolapithecus catalaunicus*: A New Middle Miocene Great Ape from Spain." *Science,* 306 (November 19): 1339–44.

Mukerjee, Madhusree. 1996. "Field Notes: Interview with a Parrot." *Scientific American* (April): 28.

Mukhopadhyay, Carol C., and Patricia J. Higgins. 1988. "Anthropological Studies of Women's Status Revisited: 1977–1987." *Annual Review of Anthropology,* 17: 461–95.

Müller-Haye, B. 1984. "Guinea Pig or Cuy." In I. Mason, *Evolution of Domesticated Animals.* New York: Longman.

Munroe, Robert L., Robert Hulefeld, James M. Rodgers, Damon L. Tomeo, Steven K. Yamazaki. 2000. "Aggression Among Children in Four Cultures." *Cross-Cultural Research,* 34: 3–25.

Munroe, Robert L., Ruth H. Munroe, and Stephen Winters. 1996. "Cross-Cultural Correlates of the Consonant-Vowel (CV) Syllable." *Cross-Cultural Research,* 30: 60–83.

Murdock, George P. 1949. *Social Structure.* New York: Macmillan.

Murdock, George P. 1967. "Ethnographic Atlas: A Summary." *Ethnology,* 6: 109–236.

Murdock, George P., and Caterina Provost. 1973. "Factors in the Division of Labor by Sex: A Cross-Cultural Analysis." *Ethnology,* 12: 203–25.

Murdock, George P. 1980. *Theories of Illness: A World Survey.* Pittsburgh: University of Pittsburgh Press.

Murdock, George P., and Douglas R. White. 1969. "Standard Cross Cultural Sample." *Ethnology,* 8: 329–69.

Murphy, Robert F. 1960. *Headhunter's Heritage: Social and Economic Change among the Mundurucú.* Berkeley: University of California Press.

Murphy, Robert F., and Julian H. Steward. 1956. "Tappers and Trappers: Parallel Process in Acculturation." *Economic Development and Cultural Change,* 4 (July): 335–55.

Myers, Fred R. 1988. "Critical Trends in the Study of Hunter-Gatherers." *Annual Review of Anthropology,* 17: 261–82.

Nadel, S. F. 1942. *A Black Byzantium: The Kingdom of Nupe in Nigeria.* London: Oxford University Press.

Nag, Moni, Benjamin N. F. White, and R. Creighton Peet. 1978. "An Anthropological Approach to the Study of the Economic Value of Children in Java and Nepal." *Current Anthropology,* 19: 293–301.

Nagata, Judith. 2001. "Beyond Theology: Toward an Anthropology of 'Fundamentalism'." *American Anthropologist,* 103: 481–98.

Nagel, Ernest. 1961. *The Structure of Science: Problems in the Logic of Scientific Explanation.* New York: Harcourt, Brace & World.

Napier, J. R. 1970. "Paleoecology and Catarrhine Evolution." In J. R. Napier and P. H. Napier, eds., *Old World Monkeys: Evolution, Systematics, and Behavior.* New York: Academic Press.

Napier, J. R., and P. H. Napier. 1967. *A Handbook of Living Primates.* New York: Academic Press.

Naroll, Raoul. 1961. "Two Solutions to Galton's Problem." *Philosophy of Science,* 28 (January): 15–39.

Naroll, Raoul. 1967. "Imperial Cycles and World Order." *Peace Research Society: Papers,* 7: 83–101.

Nash, Manning. 1989. *The Cauldron of Ethnicity in the Modern World.* Chicago: University of Chicago Press.

Neel, James V., Willard R. Centerwall, Napoleon A. Chagnon, and Helen L. Casey. 1970. "Notes on the Effect of Measles and Measles Vaccine in a Virgin-Soil Population of South American Indians." *American Journal of Epidemiology,* 91: 418–29.

Nerlove, Sara B. 1974. "Women's Workload and Infant Feeding Practices: A Relationship with Demographic Implications." *Ethnology,* 13: 207–14.

Neumann, Katharina. 2003. "New Guinea: A Cradle of Agriculture." *Science,* 301 (July 11): 180–81.

Nevins, Allan. 1927. *The American States during and after the Revolution.* New York: Macmillan.

Newman, K. S. 1988. *Falling From Grace: The Experience of Downward Mobility in the American Middle Class.* New York: The Free Press.

Newman, Katherine S. 1983. *Law and Economic Organization: A Comparative Study of Preindustrial Societies.* Cambridge, MA: Cambridge University Press.

Niehoff, Arthur H. 1966. *A Casebook of Social Change.* Chicago: Aldine.

Nimkoff, M. F., and Russell Middleton. 1960. "Types of Family and Types of Economy." *American Journal of Sociology,* 66: 215–25.

Nissen, Henry W. 1958. "Axes of Behavioral Comparison." In A. Roe and G. G. Simpson, eds., *Behavior and Evolution.* New Haven, CT: Yale University Press.

Noll, Richard. 1987. "The Presence of Spirits in Magic and Madness." In S. Nicholson, comp., *Shamanism.* Wheaton, IL: Theosophical Publishing House, pp. 47–61.

Noss, Andrew J., and Barry S. Hewlett. 2001. "The Contexts of Female Hunting in Central Africa." *American Anthropologist,* 103: 1024–40.

Nussbaum, Martha C. 1995. "Introduction." In M. C. Nussbaum and J. Glover, *Women, Culture, and Development: A Study of Human Capabilities.* Oxford: Clarendon Press.

Oakley, Kenneth. 1964. "On Man's Use of Fire, with Comments on Tool-Making and Hunting." In S. L. Washburn, ed., *Social Life of Early Man.* Chicago: Aldine.

O'Brian, Robin. 1999. "Who Weaves and Why? Weaving, Loom Complexity, and Trade." *Cross-Cultural Research,* 33: 30–42.

Ogburn, William F. 1922. *Social Change.* New York: Huebsch.

Oliver, Douglas L. 1955. *A Solomon Island Society.* Cambridge, MA: Harvard University Press.

Olsen, Steve. 2002. "Seeking the Signs of Selection." *Science,* 298 (November 15): 1324–25.

Olszewski, Deborah I. 1991. "Social Complexity in the Natufian? Assessing the Relationship of Ideas and Data." In G. Clark, ed. *Perspectives on the Past.* Philadelphia: University of Pennsylvania Press.

Ortiz de Montellano, B. R., and C. H. Browner. 1985. "Chemical Bases for Medicinal Plant Use in Oaxaca, Mexico." *Journal of Ethnopharmacology,* 13: 57–88.

Osti, Roberto. 1994. "The Eloquent Bones of Abu Hureyra." *Scientific American* (August): 1.

Otterbein, Keith. 1968. "Internal War: A Cross-Cultural Study." *American Anthropologist,* 70: 277–89.

Otterbein, Keith. 1970. *The Evolution of War.* New Haven, CT: HRAF Press.

Otterbein, Keith. 1986. *The Ultimate Coercive Sanction: A Cross-Cultural Study of Capital Punishment.* New Haven, CT: HRAF Press.

Otterbein, Keith, and Charlotte Swanson Otterbein. 1965. "An Eye for an Eye, a Tooth for a Tooth: A Cross-Cultural Study of Feuding." *American Anthropologist,* 67: 1470–82.

Ovchinnikov, Igor V., et al. 2000. "Molecular Analysis of Neanderthal DNA from the Northern Caucasus." *Nature,* 404 (March 30): 490–94.

Paige, Jeffery M. 1975. *Agrarian Revolution: Social Movements and Export Agriculture in the Underdeveloped World.* New York: Free Press.

Paine, Robert. 1994. *Herds of the Tundra.* Washington, D.C.: Smithsonian Institution Press.

Paley, William. 1810. *Natural Theology.* Boston: Joshua Belcher.

Palsson, Gisli. 1988. "Hunters and Gatherers of the Sea." In T. Ingold, D. Riches, and J. Woodburn, eds., *Hunters and Gatherers, Volume 1: History, Evolution, and Social Change.* New York: St. Martin's Press.

Parry, William J. 2002. "When and How Did Humans Populate the New World?" In P. N. Peregrine, C. R. Ember, and M. Ember, eds., *Archaeology: Original Readings in Method and Practice.* Upper Saddle River, NJ: Prentice Hall.

Pasternak, Burton. 1976. *Introduction to Kinship and Social Organization.* Upper Saddle River, NJ: Prentice Hall.

Pasternak, Burton, Carol R. Ember, and Melvin Ember. 1976. "On the Conditions Favoring Extended Family Households." *Journal of Anthropological Research,* 32: 109–23.

Patterson, Leland. 1983. "Criteria for Determining the Attributes of Man-Made Lithics." *Journal of Field Archaeology,* 10: 297–307.

Patterson, Orlando. 1982. *Slavery and Social Death: A Comparative Study.* Cambridge, MA: Harvard University Press.

Patterson, Orlando. 2000. Review of *One Drop of Blood: The American Misadventure of Race* by Scott L. Malcomson. *New York Times Book Review,* October 22, pp. 15–16.

Patterson, Thomas C. 1971. "Central Peru: Its Population and Economy." *Archaeology,* 24: 316–21.

Patterson, Thomas C. 1981. *The Evolution of Ancient Societies: A World Archaeology.* Upper Saddle River, NJ: Prentice Hall.

Peacock, James L. 1986. *The Anthropological Lens: Harsh Light, Soft Focus.* Cambridge: Cambridge University Press.

Pearsall, Deborah. 1992. "The Origins of Plant Cultivation in South America." In C. Cowan and P. Watson, eds., *The Origins of Agriculture.* Washington, D.C.: Smithsonian Institution Press.

Pearson, J. D., Gary D. James, and Daniel E. Brown. 1993. "Stress and Changing Lifestyles in the Pacific: Physiological Stress Responses of Samoans in Rural and Urban Settings." *American Journal of Human Biology,* 5: 49–60.

Pelto, Pertti J., and Ludger Müller-Wille. 1987. "Snowmobiles: Technological Revolution in the Arctic." In H. R. Bernard and P. J. Pelto, eds., *Technology and Social Change,* 2nd ed. Prospect Heights, IL: Waveland Press.

Pelto, Pertti J., and Gretel H. Pelto. 1975. "Intra-Cultural Diversity: Some Theoretical Issues." *American Ethnologist,* 2: 1–18.

Pennisi, Elizabeth. 2000. "Finally, the Book of Life and Instructions for Navigating It." *Science,* 288 (June 30): 2304–307.

Pennisi, Elizabeth. 2001a. "Malaria's Beginnings: On the Heels of Hoes?" *Science,* 293 (July 20): 416–17.

Pennisi, Elizabeth. 2001b. "Genetic Change Wards Off Malaria." *Science,* 294 (November 16): 1439.

Pepperberg, Irene Maxine. 1999. *The Alex Studies: Cognitive and Communicative Abilities of Grey Parrots.* Cambridge, MA: Harvard University Press.

Peregrine, Peter N. 1992. "Social Change in the Woodland-Mississippian Transition: A Study of Household and Community Patterns in the American Bottom." *North American Archaeologist,* 13: 131–47.

Peregrine, Peter N. 1996. "The Birth of the Gods Revisited: A Partial Replication of Guy Swanson's (1960) Cross-Cultural Study of Religion." *Cross-Cultural Research,* 30: 84–112.

Peregrine, Peter N., and Peter Bellwood. 2001. "Southeast Asia Upper Paleolithic." In P. N. Peregrine and M. Ember, eds., *Encyclopedia of Prehistory, Volume 3: East Asia and Oceania.* New York: Kluwer Academic/Plenum, pp. 307–309.

Peregrine, Peter N., Carol R. Ember, and Melvin Ember. 2000. "Teaching Critical Evaluation of Rushton." *Anthropology Newsletter,* 41 (February): 29–30.

Peregrine, Peter N., Carol R. Ember, and Melvin Ember. 2003. "Cross-Cultural Evaluation of Predicted Associations between Race and Behavior." *Evolution and Human Behavior* 24: 357–64.

Peregrine, Peter N., Melvin Ember, and Carol R. Ember. 2004. "Predicting the Future State of the World Using Archaeological Data: An Exercise in Archaeomancy." *Cross-Cultural Research,* 38: 133–46.

Petersen, Erik B. 1973. "A Survey of the Late Paleolithic and the Mesolithic of Denmark." In S. K. Kozlowski, ed., *The Mesolithic in Europe.* Warsaw: Warsaw University Press.

Petersen, L. R., G. R. Lee, and G. J. Ellis. 1982. "Social Structure, Socialization Values, and Disciplinary Techniques: A Cross-Cultural Analysis." *Journal of Marriage and the Family,* 44: 131–42.

Pfaff, C. 1979. "Constraints on Language Mixing." *Language,* 55: 291–318, as cited in Wardhaugh, *An Introduction to Sociolinguistics,* 2nd ed. Oxford: Blackwell.

Phillipson, D. W. 1976. "Archaeology and Bantu Linguistics." *World Archaeology,* 8: 65–82.

Phillipson, David W. 1993. *African Archaeology,* 2nd ed. New York: Cambridge University Press.

Picchi, Debra. 1991. "The Impact of an Industrial Agricultural Project on the Bakairí Indians of Central Brazil." *Human Organization,* 50: 26–38.

Picchi, Debra. 2004. "Bakairí: The Death of an Indian." In *Portraits of Culture,* in C. R. Ember, M. Ember, and P. N. Peregrine, eds., *New Directions in Anthropology.* Upper Saddle River, NJ: Prentice Hall, CD-ROM.

Pickford, Martin, Brigette Senut, Dominique Gommercy, and Jacques Treil. 2002. "Bipedalism in *Orrorin tugenensis* Revealed by Its Femora." *Comptes Rendu de l'Académie de Science des Paris,* 1: 1–13.

Pilbeam, David. 1972. *The Ascent of Man.* New York: Macmillan.

Pilbeam, David, and Stephen Jay Gould. 1974. "Size and Scaling in Human Evolution." *Science,* 186 (December 6): 892–900.

Piperno, Dolores, and Karen Stothert. 2003. "Phytolith Evidence for Early Holocene Cucurbita Domestication in Southwest Ecuador." *Science,* 299 (February 14): 1054–57.

Plattner, Stuart, ed. 1985. *Markets and Marketing.* Monographs in Economic Anthropology, no. 4. Lanham, MD: University Press of America.

Plattner, Stuart. 1989. "Marxism." In S. Plattner, ed., *Economic Anthropology.* Stanford, CA: Stanford University Press.

"Plundering Earth Is Nothing New." 1994. *Los Angeles Times* News Service, as reported in the *New Haven Register,* June 12, pp. A18–19.

Poggie, John J., Jr., and Richard B. Pollnac. 1988. "Danger and Rituals of Avoidance among New England Fishermen." *MAST: Maritime Anthropological Studies,* 1: 66–78.

Poggie, John J., Jr., Richard B. Pollnac, and Carl Gersuny. 1976. "Risk as a Basis for Taboos among Fishermen in Southern New England." *Journal for the Scientific Study of Religion,* 15: 257–62.

Polanyi, Karl. 1957. "The Economy as Instituted Process." In K. Polanyi, C. M. Arensberg, and H. W. Pearson, eds., *Trade and Market in the Early Empires.* New York: Free Press.

Polanyi, Karl, Conrad M. Arensberg, and Harry W. Pearson, eds. 1957. *Trade and Market in the Early Empires.* New York: Free Press.

Polednak, Anthony P. 1974. "Connective Tissue Responses in Negroes in Relation to Disease." *American Journal of Physical Anthropology,* 41: 49–57.

Popenoe, David. 1988. *Disturbing the Nest: Family Change and Decline in Modern Societies.* New York: Aldine.

Popenoe, Rebecca. 2004. *Feeding Desire: Fatness, Beauty, and Sexuality among a Saharan People.* London: Routledge.

Pospisil, Leopold. 1963. *The Kapauku Papuans of West New Guinea.* New York: Holt, Rinehart & Winston.

Post, Peter W., Farrington Daniels, Jr., and Robert T. Binford, Jr. 1975. "Cold Injury and the Evolution of 'White' Skin." *Human Biology,* 47: 65–80.

Potts, Richard. 1984. "Home Bases and Early Hominids." *American Scientist,* 72: 338–47.

Potts, Richard. 1988. *Early Hominid Activities at Olduvai.* New York: Aldine.

Prag, John, and Richard Neave. 1997. *Making Faces: Using Forensic and Archaeological Evidence.* College Station: Texas A&M University Press.

Preuschoft, Holger, David J. Chivers, Warren Y. Brockelman, and Norman Creel, eds. 1984. *The Lesser Apes: Evolutionary and Behavioural Biology.* Edinburgh: Edinburgh University Press.

"Prevalence, Incidence, and Consequences of Violence against Women: Findings from the National Violence against Women Survey." 1988. Washington, D.C.: U.S. Department of Justice.

Pryor, Frederic L. 1977. *The Origins of the Economy: A Comparative Study of Distribution in Primitive and Peasant Economies.* New York: Academic Press.

Pryor, Frederic L. 2005. *Economic Systems of Foraging, Agricultural, and Industrial Societies.* Cambridge: Cambridge University Press.

Quandt, Sara A. 1996. "Nutrition in Anthropology." In C. F. Sargent and T. M. Johnson, eds., *Handbook of Medical Anthropology,* rev. ed. Westport, CT: Greenwood Press, pp. 272–89.

Quinn, Naomi. 1977. "Anthropological Studies on Women's Status." *Annual Review of Anthropology,* 6: 181–225.

Radcliffe-Brown, A. R. 1922. *The Andaman Islanders: A Study in Social Anthropology.* Cambridge: Cambridge University Press.

Radinsky, Leonard. 1967. "The Oldest Primate Endocast." *American Journal of Physical Anthropology,* 27: 358–88.

Rasmussen, D. Tab. 1990. "Primate Origins: Lessons from a Neotropical Marsupial." *American Journal of Primatology,* 22: 263–77.

Rathje, William L. 1971. "The Origin and Development of Lowland Classic Maya Civilization." *American Antiquity,* 36: 275–85.

Ravesloot, John. 1997. "Changing Native American Perceptions of Archaeology and Archaeologists." In N. Swidler et al., eds., *Native Americans and Archaeologists.* Walnut Creek, CA: AltaMira Press.

Ray, Verne F. 1954. *The Sanpoil and Nespelem: Salishan Peoples of Northeastern Washington.* New Haven, CT: Human Relations Area Files.

Raybeck, Douglas. 1998. "Toward More Holistic Explanations: Cross-Cultural Research and Cross-Level Analysis." *Cross-Cultural Research,* 32: 123–42.

Raybeck, Douglas, J. Shoobe, and J. Grauberger. 1989. "Women, Stress and Participation in Possession Cults: A Reexamination of the Calcium Deficiency Hypothesis." *Medical Anthropology Quarterly,* 3: 139–61.

Reed, David, V. Smith, S. Hammond, A. Rogers, and D. Clayton. 2004. "Genetic Analysis of Lice Supports Direct Contact between Modern and Archaic Humans." *PLoS Biology,* 2 (November): 1972–83.

Relethford, John. 1990. *The Human Species: An Introduction to Biological Anthropology.* Mountain View, CA: Mayfield.

Renfrew, Colin. 1969. "Trade and Culture Process in European History." *Current Anthropology,* 10: 156–69.

Rennie, John. 2002. "15 Answers to Creationist Nonsense." *Scientific American* (July): 78–85.

Revkin, Andrew C. 2005. "Tracking the Imperiled Bluefin from Ocean to Sushi Platter." *The New York Times,* May 3, pp. F1, F4.

Rice, Patricia C., and Ann L. Paterson. 1985. "Cave Art and Bones: Exploring the Interrelationships." *American Anthropologist,* 87: 94–100.

Richard, Alison F. 1985. *Primates in Nature.* New York: W. H. Freeman.

Richard, Alison F. 1987. "Malagasy Prosimians: Female Dominance." In B. Smuts et al., eds., *Primate Societies.* Chicago: University of Chicago Press.

Riesenfeld, Alphonse. 1973. "The Effect of Extreme Temperatures and Starvation on the Body Proportions of the Rat." *American Journal of Physical Anthropology,* 39: 427–59.

Rightmire, G. Philip. 1984. "*Homo sapiens* in Sub-Saharan Africa." In F. H. Smith and F. Spencer, eds., *The Origins of Modern Humans.* New York: Alan R. Liss.

Rightmire, G. Philip. 1990. *The Evolution of* Homo erectus: *Comparative Anatomical Studies of an Extinct Human Species.* Cambridge: Cambridge University Press.

Rightmire, G. Philip. 1997. "Human Evolution in the Middle Pleistocene: The Role of *Homo heidelbergensis*." *Evolutionary Anthropology,* 6: 218–27.

Rightmire, G. Philip. 2000. "*Homo erectus*." In I. Tattersall, E. Delson, and J. van Couvering, eds., *Encyclopedia of Human Evolution and Prehistory.* New York: Garland.

Rijksen, H. D. 1978. *A Fieldstudy on Sumatran Orang Utans* (Pongo Pygmaeus Abelii Lesson 1827): *Ecology, Behaviour and Conservation.* Wageningen, The Netherlands: H. Veenman and Zonen.

Rivers, W. H. R. 1967 [1906]. *The Todas.* Oosterhout, N.B., The Netherlands: Anthropological Publications.

Roberts, D. F. 1953. "Body Weight, Race, and Climate." *American Journal of Physical Anthropology,* 533–58.

Roberts, D. F. 1978. *Climate and Human Variability,* 2nd ed. Menlo Park, CA: Cummings.

Roberts, John M. 1967. "Oaths, Autonomic Ordeals, and Power." In C. S. Ford, ed., *Cross-Cultural Approaches.* New Haven, CT: HRAF Press.

Robins, Ashley H. 1999. *Biological Perspectives on Human Pigmentation.* Cambridge: Cambridge University Press.

Robinson, John G., and Charles H. Janson. 1987. "Capuchins, Squirrel Monkeys, and Atelines: Socioecological Convergence with Old World Primates." In B. Smuts et al., eds., *Primate Societies.* Chicago: University of Chicago Press.

Robinson, John G., Patricia C. Wright, and Warren G. Kinzey. 1987. "Monogamous Cebids and Their Relatives: Intergroup Calls and Spacing." In B. Smuts et al., eds., *Primate Societies.* Chicago: University of Chicago Press.

Rodwin, Lloyd, and Bishwapriya Sanyal. 1987. "Shelter, Settlement, and Development: An Overview." In L. Rodwin, ed., *Shelter, Settlement, and Development.* Boston: Allen & Unwin.

Rogers, Everett M. 1983. *Diffusion of Innovations,* 3rd ed. New York: Free Press.

Rohner, Ronald P. 1975. *They Love Me, They Love Me Not: A Worldwide Study of the Effects of Parental Acceptance and Rejection.* New Haven, CT: HRAF Press.

Rohner, Ronald P. 1976. "Sex Differences in Aggression: Phylogenetic and Enculturation Perspectives." *Ethos,* 4: 57–72.

Romney, A. Kimball, Susan C. Weller, and William H. Batchelder. 1986. "Culture as Consensus: A Theory of Culture and Informant Accuracy." *American Anthropologist,* 88: 313–38.

Roosens, Eugeen E. 1989. *Creating Ethnicity: The Process of Ethnogenesis.* Newbury Park, CA: Sage Publications.

Roosevelt, Anna Curtenius. 1984. "Population, Health, and the Evolution of Subsistence: Conclusions from the Conference." In M. N. Cohen and G. Armelagos, eds., *Paleopathology at the Origins of Agriculture.* Orlando, FL: Academic Press.

Roosevelt, Anna Curtenius. 1992. "Secrets of the Forest." *The Sciences* (November/December): 22–28.

Roscoe, Paul. 2002. "The Hunters and Gatherers of New Guinea." *Current Anthropology,* 43: 153–62.

Rose, M. D. 1984. "Food Acquisition and the Evolution of Positional Behaviour: The Case of Bipedalism." In D. Chivers, B. Wood, and A. Bilsborough, eds., *Food Acquisition and Processing in Primates.* New York: Plenum.

Rosenberger, A. L. 1979. "Cranial Anatomy and Implications of *Dolichocebus,* a Late Oligocene Ceboid Primate." *Nature,* 279 (May 31): 416–18.

Rosenblatt, Paul C., R. Patricia Walsh, and Douglas A. Jackson. 1976. *Grief and Mourning in Cross-Cultural Perspective.* New Haven, CT: HRAF Press.

Ross, Marc Howard. 1981. "Socioeconomic Complexity, Socialization, and Political Differentiation: A Cross-Cultural Study." *Ethos,* 9: 217–47.

Ross, Marc Howard. 1985. "Internal and External Conflict and Violence." *Journal of Conflict Resolution,* 29: 547–79.

Ross, Marc Howard. 1988. "Political Organization and Political Participation: Exit, Voice, and Loyalty in Preindustrial Societies." *Comparative Politics,* 21: 73–89.

Ross, Marc Howard. 2004a. "Ethnocentrism and Ethnic Conflict." In *Research Frontiers,* in C. R. Ember, M. Ember, and P. N. Peregrine, eds., *New Directions in Anthropology.* Upper Saddle River, NJ: Prentice Hall, CD-ROM.

Ross, Marc Howard. 2004b. "Political Participation." In *Cross-Cultural Research for Social Science,* in C. R. Ember, M. Ember, and P. N. Peregrine, eds., *New Directions in Anthropology.* Upper Saddle River, NJ: Prentice Hall, CD-ROM.

Rubel, Arthur J., and Michael R. Hass. 1996. "Ethnomedicine." In C. F. Sargent and T. M. Johnson, *Medical Anthropology,* rev. ed. Westport, CT: Praeger.

Rubel, Arthur J., Carl O. Nell, and Rolando Collado-Ardón (with the assistance of John Krejci and Jean Krejci). 1984. *Susto: A Folk Illness.* Berkeley: University of California Press.

Rubin, J. Z., F. J. Provenzano, and R. F. Haskett. 1974. "The Eye of the Beholder: Parents' Views on the Sex of New Borns." *American Journal of Orthopsychiatry,* 44: 512–19.

Rudmin, Floyd Webster. 1988. "Dominance, Social Control, and Ownership: A History and a Cross-Cultural Study of Motivations for Private Property." *Behavior Science Research,* 22: 130–60.

Ruff, Christopher B., and Alan Walker. 1993. "Body Size and Body Shape." In A. Walker and R. Leakey, eds., *The Nariokotome* Homo erectus *Skeleton.* Cambridge, MA: Harvard University Press.

Rumbaugh, Duane M. 1970. "Learning Skills of Anthropoids." In L. Rosenblum, ed., *Primate Behavior,* vol. 1. New York: Academic Press.

Rummel, R. J. 2002a. "Death by Government," chapter 1. Accessed at http://www.hawaii.edu/powerkills/DBG.CHAP1.HTM.

Rummel, R. J. 2002b. "Democracies Are Less Warlike Than Other Regimes." Accessed at http://www.hawaii.edu/powerkills/DP95.HTM.

Rummel, R. J. 2002c. "Statistics of Democide," chapter 17. Accessed at http://www.hawaii.edu/powerkills/SOD.CHAP17.HTM.

Rummel, R. J. 2002d. "Statistics of Democide," chapter 21. Accessed at http://www.hawaii.edu/powerkills/SOD.CHAP21.HTM.

Ruskin, John. 1963. "Of King's Treasures." In J. D. Rosenberg, ed., *The Genius of John Ruskin.* New York: Braziller.

Russell, Elbert W. 1972. "Factors of Human Aggression." *Behavior Science Notes,* 7: 275–312.

Russett, Bruce (with the collaboration of William Antholis, Carol R. Ember, Melvin Ember, and Zeev Maoz). 1993. *Grasping the Democratic Peace: Principles for a Post–Cold War World.* Princeton, NJ: Princeton University Press.

Russett, Bruce, and John R. Oneal. 2001. *Triangulating Peace: Democracy, Interdependence, and International Organizations.* New York: Norton.

Sagan, Carl. 1975. "A Cosmic Calendar." *Natural History* (December): 70–73.

Sahlins, Marshall. 1983. "Other Times, Other Customs: The Anthropology of History." *American Anthropologist,* 85: 517–44.

Sahlins, Marshall D. 1958. *Social Stratification in Polynesia.* Seattle: University of Washington Press.

Sahlins, Marshall D. 1961. "The Segmentary Lineage: An Organization of Predatory Expansion." *American Anthropologist,* 63: 332–45.

Sahlins, Marshall D. 1962. *Moala: Culture and Nature on a Fijian Island.* Ann Arbor: University of Michigan Press.

Sahlins, Marshall D. 1963. "Poor Man, Rich Man, Big-Man, Chief: Political Types in Melanesia and Polynesia." *Comparative Studies in Society and History,* 5: 285–303.

Sahlins, Marshall D. 1972. *Stone Age Economics.* Chicago: Aldine.

Salzman, Philip Carl. 1996. "Pastoralism." In D. Levinson and M. Ember, eds., *Encyclopedia of Cultural Anthropology,* vol. 3. New York: Henry Holt, pp. 899–905.

Salzman, Philip Carl. 2002. "Pastoral Nomads: Some General Observations Based on Research in Iran." *Journal of Anthropological Research,* 58: 245–64.

Sanday, Peggy R. 1973. "Toward a Theory of the Status of Women." *American Anthropologist,* 75: 1682–700.

Sanday, Peggy R. 1974. "Female Status in the Public Domain." In M. Z. Rosaldo and L. Lamphere, eds., *Woman, Culture, and Society.* Stanford, CA: Stanford University Press.

Sanders, William T., and Barbara J. Price. 1968. *Mesoamerica.* New York: Random House.

Sanders, William T., Jeffrey R. Parsons, and Robert S. Santley. 1979. *The Basin of Mexico: Ecological Processes in the Evolution of a Civilization.* New York: Academic Press.

Sapir, Edward. 1931. "Conceptual Categories in Primitive Languages." Paper presented at the autumn meeting of the National Academy of Sciences, New Haven, CT. Published in *Science,* 74.

Sapir, Edward. 1938. "Why Cultural Anthropology Needs the Psychiatrist." *Psychiatry,* 1: 7–12.

Sapir, Edward, and M. Swadesh. 1964. "American Indian Grammatical Categories." In D. Hymes, ed., *Language in Culture and Society.* New York: Harper & Row.

Sarich, Vincent M. 1968. "The Origin of Hominids: An Immunological Approach." In S. L. Washburn and P. C. Jay, eds., *Perspectives on Human Evolution,* vol. 1. New York: Holt, Rinehart & Winston.

Sarich, Vincent M., and Allan C. Wilson. 1966. "Quantitative Immunochemistry and the Evolution of Primate Albumins: Micro-Component Fixations." *Science,* 154 (December 23): 1563–66.

Sassaman, Kenneth. 1996. "Early Archaic Settlement in the South Carolina Coastal Plain." In D. G. Anderson and K. E. Sassaman, eds., *The Paleoindian and Early Archaic Southeast.* Tuscaloosa: University of Alabama Press, pp. 58–83.

Sattler, Richard A. 1996. "Remnants, Renegades, and Runaways: Seminole Ethnogenesis Reconsidered." In J. D. Hill, ed., *Ethnogenesis in the Americas.* Iowa City: University of Iowa Press, pp. 36–69.

Savage-Rumbaugh, E. S. 1992. "Language Training of Apes." In S. Jones, R. Martin, and D. Pilbeam, eds., *The Cambridge Encyclopedia of Human Evolution.* New York: Cambridge University Press.

Savage-Rumbaugh, E. S. 1994. "Hominid Evolution: Looking to Modern Apes for Clues." In D. Quiatt and J. Itani, eds., *Hominid Culture in Primate Perspective.* Niwot: University Press of Colorado.

Scaglion, Richard. 2004. "Law and Society." In *Cross-Cultural Research for Social Science,* in C. R. Ember, M. Ember, and P. N. Peregrine, eds., *New Directions in Anthropology.* Upper Saddle River, NJ: Prentice Hall, CD-ROM.

Schaller, George. 1963. *The Mountain Gorilla: Ecology and Behavior.* Chicago: University of Chicago Press.

Schaller, George. 1964. *The Year of the Gorilla.* Chicago: University of Chicago Press.

Schaller, George. 1972. *The Serengeti Lion: A Study of Predator-Prey Relations.* Chicago: University of Chicago Press.

Schick, Kathy D., and Nicholas Toth. 1993. *Making Silent Stones Speak.* New York: Simon & Schuster.

Schiffer, Michael B., ed. 1984. *Advances in Archaeological Method and Theory,* vol. 7. Orlando, FL: Academic Press.

Schiffer, Michael B. 1987. *Formation Processes of the Archaeological Record.* Albuquerque, NM: University of New Mexico Press.

Schlegel, Alice. 1989. "Gender Issues and Cross-Cultural Research." *Behavior Science Research,* 23: 265–80.

Schlegel, Alice. 1991. "Status, Property, and the Value on Virginity." *American Ethnologist,* 18: 719–34.

Schlegel, Alice, and Herbert Barry, III. 1986. "The Cultural Consequences of Female Contribution to Subsistence." *American Anthropologist,* 88: 142–50.

Schlegel, Alice, and Rohn Eloul. 1987. "A New Coding of Marriage Transactions." *Behavior Science Research,* 21: 118–40.

Schlegel, Alice, and Rohn Eloul. 1988. "Marriage Transactions: Labor, Property, and Status." *American Anthropologist,* 90: 291–309.

Schneider, David M. 1961a. "Introduction: The Distinctive Features of Matrilineal Descent Groups." In D. M. Schneider and K. Gough, eds., *Matrilineal Kinship.* Berkeley: University of California Press, pp. 1–29.

Schneider, David M. 1961b. "Truk." In D. M. Schneider and K. Gough, eds., *Matrilineal Kinship.* Berkeley: University of California Press, pp. 202–33.

Schoepf, B. 1988. "Women, AIDS and Economic Crisis in Central Africa." *Canadian Journal of African Studies,* 22: 625–44.

Schrauf, Robert W. 1999. "Mother Tongue Maintenance Among North American Ethnic Groups." *Cross-Cultural Research,* 33: 175–92.

Schrire, Carmel, ed. 1984a. *Past and Present in Hunter-Gatherer Studies.* Orlando, FL: Academic Press.

Schrire, Carmel. 1984b. "Wild Surmises on Savage Thoughts." In C. Schrire, ed., *Past and Present in Hunter-Gatherer Studies.* Orlando, FL: Academic Press.

Schwarcz, Henry P. ed. 1993. *The Origin of Modern Humans and the Impact of Chronometric Dating.* Princeton, NJ: Princeton University Press.

Scott, Janny, and David Leonhardt. 2005. "Class in America: Shadowy Lines That Still Divide." *New York Times National,* May 15, pp. 1, 26.

Scudder, Thayer. 1978. "Opportunities, Issues, and Achievements in Development Anthropology since the Mid-1960s: A Personal View." In E. M. Eddy and W. L. Partridge, eds., *Applied Anthropology in America,* 2nd ed. New York: Columbia University Press.

Segal, Edwin S. 2004. "Cultural Constructions of Gender." In C. R. Ember and M. Ember, eds., *Encyclopedia of Sex and Gender: Men and Women in the World's Cultures,* vol. 1. New York: Kluwer Academic/Plenum Publishers, pp. 3–10.

Sellen, Daniel W. and Daniel J. Hruschka. 2004. "Extracted-Food Resource-Defense Polygyny in Native Western North American Societies at Contact." *Current Anthropology,* 45: 707–14.

Semenov, S. A. 1970. *Prehistoric Technology.* Trans. M. W. Thompson. Bath, England: Adams & Dart.

Sengupta, Somini. 2002. "Money from Kin Abroad Helps Bengalis Get By." *The New York Times,* June 24, p. A3.

Senner, Wayne M. 1989. "Theories and Myths on the Origins of Writing: A Historical Overview." In W. M. Senner, ed., *The Origins of Writing.* Lincoln: University of Nebraska Press.

Service, Elman R. 1962. *Primitive Social Organization: An Evolutionary Perspective.* New York: Random House.

Service, Elman R. 1975. *Origins of the State and Civilization: The Process of Cultural Evolution.* New York: Norton.

Service, Elman R. 1978. *Profiles in Ethnology,* 3rd ed. New York: Harper & Row.

Service, Elman R. 1979. *The Hunters,* 2nd ed. Upper Saddle River, NJ: Prentice Hall.

Seyfarth, Robert M., and Dorothy L. Cheney. 1982. "How Monkeys See the World: A Review of Recent Research on East African Vervet Monkeys." In C. T. Snowdon, C. H. Brown, and M. R. Petersen, eds., *Primate Communication.* New York: Cambridge University Press.

Seyfarth, Robert M., Dorothy L. Cheney, and Peter Marler. 1980. "Monkey Response to Three Different Alarm Calls: Evidence of Predator Classification and Semantic Communication." *Science,* 210 (November 14): 801–803.

Shanklin, Eugenia. 1993. *Anthropology and Race.* Belmont, CA: Wadsworth.

Shankman, Paul. 1991. "Culture Contact, Cultural Ecology, and Dani Warfare." *Man,* 26: 299–321.

Sheils, Dean. 1975. "Toward a Unified Theory of Ancestor Worship: A Cross-Cultural Study." *Social Forces,* 54: 427–40.

Sheils, Dean. 1980. "A Comparative Study of Human Sacrifice." *Behavior Science Research,* 15: 245–62.

Shibamoto, Janet S. 1987. "The Womanly Woman: Japanese Female Speech." In S. U. Philips, S. Steele, and C. Tanz, eds., *Language, Gender, and Sex in Comparative Perspective.* Cambridge: Cambridge University Press.

Shipman, Pat. 1986. "Scavenging or Hunting in Early Hominids: Theoretical Framework and Tests." *American Anthropologist,* 88: 27–43.

Silver, Harry R. 1981. "Calculating Risks: The Socioeconomic Foundations of Aesthetic Innovation in an Ashanti Carving Community." *Ethnology,* 20: 101–14.

Simcha Lev-Yadun, Avi Gopher, and Shahal Abbo. 2000. "The Cradle of Agriculture." *Science,* 288 (June 2): 1602–603.

Simmons, Janie, Paul Farmer, and Brooke G. Schoepf. 1996. "A Global Perspective." In P. Farmer, M. Connors, and J. Simmons, eds., *Women, Poverty, and AIDS: Sex, Drugs, and Structural Violence.* Monroe, ME: Common Courage Press, pp. 39–90.

Simons, Elwyn L. 1992. "The Primate Fossil Record." In S. Jones, R. Martin, and D. Pilbeam, eds., *The Cambridge Encyclopedia of Human Evolution.* New York: Cambridge University Press.

Simons, Elwyn L. 1995. "Skulls and Anterior Teeth of *Catopithecus* (Primates: Anthropoidea) from the Eocene Shed Light on Anthropoidean Origins." *Science,* 268 (June 30): 1885–88.

Simons, Elwyn L., and D. T. Rassmussen. 1996. "Skull of *Catopithecus browni,* an Early Tertiary Catarrhine." *American Journal of Physical Anthropology,* 100: 261–92.

Simpson, George Gaylord. 1971. *The Meaning of Evolution.* New York: Bantam.

Simpson, S. P., and Ruth Field. 1946. "Law and the Social Sciences." *Virginia Law Review,* 32: 858.

Simpson, Scott W. 2002. "*Australopithecus afarensis* and Human Evolution." In P. N. Peregrine, C. R. Ember, and M. Ember, eds., *Physical Anthropology: Original Readings in Method and Practice.* Upper Saddle River, NJ: Prentice Hall.

Singer, Ronald, and John Wymer. 1982. *The Middle Stone Age at Klasies River Mouth in South Africa.* Chicago: University of Chicago Press.

Sinopoli, Carla. 2002. "Learning about the Past through Archaeological Ceramics: An Example from Yijayanagara, India." In P. N. Peregrine, C. R. Ember, and M. Ember, eds., *Archaeology: Original Readings in Method and Practice.* Upper Saddle River, NJ: Prentice Hall.

Sipes, Richard G. 1973. "War, Sports, and Aggression: An Empirical Test of Two Rival Theories." *American Anthropologist,* 75: 64–86.

Smith, B. Holly. 1986. "Dental Development in *Australopithecus* and Early *Homo.*" *Nature,* 323 (September 25): 327–30.

Smith, Bruce D. 1992a. "Prehistoric Plant Husbandry in Eastern North America." In C. Cowan and P. Watson, eds., *The Origins of Agriculture.* Washington, D.C.: Smithsonian Institution Press.

Smith, Bruce D. 1992b. *Rivers of Change.* Washington, D.C.: Smithsonian Institution Press.

Smith, Fred H., and Frank Spencer, eds. 1984. *The Origins of Modern Humans: A World Survey of the Fossil Evidence.* New York: Alan R. Liss.

Smith, John Maynard. 1989. *Evolutionary Genetics.* New York: Oxford University Press.

Smith, M. W. 1974. "Alfred Binet's Remarkable Questions: A Cross-National and Cross-Temporal Analysis of the Cultural Biases Built into the Stanford-Binet Intelligence Scale and Other Binet Tests." *Genetic Psychology Monographs,* 89: 307–34.

Smith, Michael G. 1966. "Pre-Industrial Stratification Systems." In N. J. Smelser and S. M. Lipset, eds., *Social Structure and Mobility in Economic Development.* Chicago: Aldine.

Smuts, Barbara B., Dorothy L. Cheney, Robert M. Seyfarth, Richard W. Wrangham, and Thomas T. Struhsaker, eds. 1987. *Primate Societies.* Chicago: University of Chicago Press.

Snowdon, Charles T. 1999. "An Empiricist View of Language Evolution and Development." In B. J. King, ed., *The Origins of Language.* Santa Fe, NM: School of American Research Press, pp. 79–114.

Soffer, Olga. 1993. "Upper Paleolithic Adaptations in Central and Eastern Europe and Man-Mammoth Interactions." In O. Soffer and N. D. Praslov, eds., *From Kostenki to Clovis.* New York: Plenum.

Solis, Ruth Shady, Jonathan Haas, and Winifred Creamer. 2001. "Dating Caral: A Preceramic Site in the Supe Valley of the Central Coast of Peru." *Science,* 292 (April 27): 723–26.

Southworth, Franklin C., and Chandler J. Daswani. 1974. *Foundations of Linguistics.* New York: Free Press.

Spanos, Nicholas P. 1983. "Ergotism and the Salem Witch Panic: A Critical Analysis and an Alternative Conceptualization." *Journal of the History of the Behavioral Sciences,* 19: 358–69.

Spencer, Frank. 1984. "The Neandertals and Their Evolutionary Significance: A Brief Historical Survey." In F. H. Smith and F. Spencer, eds., *The Origins of Modern Humans.* New York: Alan R. Liss.

Speth, John D. 2002. "Were Our Ancestors Hunters or Scavengers?" In P. N. Peregrine, C. R. Ember, and M. Ember, eds., *Physical Anthropology: Original Readings in Method and Practice.* Upper Saddle River, NJ: Prentice Hall.

Speth, John D., and Dave D. Davis. 1976. "Seasonal Variability in Early Hominid Predation." *Science,* 192 (April 30): 441–45.

Speth, John D., and Katherine A. Spielmann. 1983. "Energy Source, Protein Metabolism, and Hunter-Gatherer Subsistence Strategies." *Journal of Anthropological Archaeology,* 2: 1–31.

Spiro, Melford E., and Roy G. D'Andrade. 1958. "A Cross-Cultural Study of Some Supernatural Beliefs." *American Anthropologist,* 60: 456–66.

Stanford, Craig. 2002. "Chimpanzee Hunting Behavior and Human Evolution." In P. N. Peregrine, C. R. Ember, and M. Ember, eds., *Physical Anthropology: Original Readings in Method and Practice.* Upper Saddle River, NJ: Prentice Hall.

Stark, Rodney. 1985. *The Future of Religion: Secularization, Revival, and Cult Formation.* Berkeley: University of California Press.

State of the World: A Worldwatch Institute Report on Progress toward a Sustainable Society. 1994. New York: Norton.

Stedman, Hansell, B. Kozyak, A. Nelson, D. Thesier, L. Su, D. Low, C. Bridges, J. Shrager, N. Minugh-Purvis, and M. Mitchell. 2004. "Myosin Gene Mutation Correlates with Anatomical Changes in the Human Lineage." *Nature,* 428 (March 25): 415–18.

Steegman, A. T., Jr. 1975. "Human Adaptation to Cold." In A. Damon, ed., *Physiological Anthropology.* New York: Oxford University Press.

Stephens, William N. 1963. *The Family in Cross-Cultural Perspective.* New York: Holt, Rinehart & Winston.

Stephens, William N. 1972. "A Cross-Cultural Study of Modesty." *Behavior Science Research,* 7: 1–28.

Steward, Julian H., and Louis C. Faron. 1959. *Native Peoples of South America.* New York: McGraw-Hill.

Stewart, T. D. 1950. "Deformity, Trephanating, and Mutilation in South American Indian Skeletal Remains." In J. A. Steward, ed., *Handbook of South American Indians, Volume 6: Physical Anthropology, Linguistics, and Cultural Geography.* Bureau of American Ethnology Bulletin 143. Washington, D.C.: Smithsonian Institution.

Stille, Alexander. 2001. "Grounded by an Income Gap." *The New York Times,* Arts & Ideas, December 15.

Stini, William A. 1971. "Evolutionary Implications of Changing Nutritional Patterns in Human Populations." *American Anthropologist,* 73: 1019–30.

Stini, William A. 1975. *Ecology and Human Adaptation.* Dubuque, IA: Wm. C. Brown.

Stogdill, Ralph M. 1974. *Handbook of Leadership: A Survey of Theory and Research.* New York: Macmillan.

Stoneking, Mark. 1997. "Recent African Origin of Human Mitochondrial DNA." In P. Donnelly and S. Tavaré, eds., *Progress in Population Genetics and Human Evolution.* New York: Springer, pp. 1–13.

Straus, Murray A. 1991. "Physical Violence in American Families: Incidence Rates, Causes, and Trends." In D. D. Knudsen and J. L. Miller, eds., *Abused and Battered.* New York: Aldine.

Straus, Murray A. 1995. "Trends in Cultural Norms and Rates of Partner Violence: An Update to 1992." In S. M. Stith and M. A. Straus, eds., *Understanding Partner Violence: Prevalence, Causes, Consequences, and Solutions.* Minneapolis, MN: National Council on Family Relations, pp. 30–33, accessed at http://pubpages.unh.edu/mas2/v56.pdf/, August 2002.

Straus, Murray A. 2001. "Physical Aggression in the Family: Prevalence Rates, Links to Non-Family Violence, and Implications for Primary Prevention of Societal Violence." In M. Martinez, ed., *Prevention and Control of Aggression and the Impact on Its Victims.* New York: Kluwer Academic/Plenum, pp. 181–200.

Straus, Murray A., and Glenda Kaufman Kantor. 1994. "Change in Spouse Assault Rates from 1975 to 1992: A Comparison of Three National Surveys in the United States." Paper presented at the 13th World Congress of Sociology, Bielefeld, Germany, July, as seen at http://pubpages.unh.edu/mas2/v55.pdf/, August 2002.

Straus, Murray A., and Glenda Kaufman Kantor. 1995. "Trends in Physical Abuse by Parents From 1975 to 1992: A Comparison of Three National Surveys." Paper presented at the annual meeting of the American Society of Criminology, Boston, November 18, accessed at http://pubpages.unh.edu/mas2/V57.pdf/, August 2002.

Straus, Murray A., and Carrie L. Yodanis. 1996. "Corporal Punishment in Adolescence and Physical Assaults on Spouses in Later Life: What Accounts for the Link?" *Journal of Marriage and the Family,* 58: 825–41.

Strauss, Lawrence Guy. 1982. "Comment on White." *Current Anthropology,* 23: 185–86.

Strauss, Lawrence Guy. 1989. "On Early Hominid Use of Fire." *Current Anthropology,* 30: 488–91.

Stringer, Christopher B. 1985. "Evolution of a Species." *Geographical Magazine,* 57: 601–607.

Stringer, Christopher B. 2000. "Neandertals." In I. Tattersall, E. Delson, and J. van Couvering, eds., *Encyclopedia of Human Evolution and Prehistory.* New York: Garland.

Stringer, Christopher B., J. J. Hublin, and B. Vandermeersch. 1984. "The Origin of Anatomically Modern Humans in Western Europe." In F. H. Smith and F. Spencer, eds., *The Origins of Modern Humans.* New York: Alan R. Liss.

Suárez-Orozco, Marcelo. 1992. "A Grammar of Terror: Psychocultural Responses to State Terrorism in Dirty War and Post-Dirty War Argentina." In C. Nordstrom and J. Martin, eds., *The Paths to Domination, Resistance, and Terror.* Berkeley, CA: University of California Press, pp. 219–59.

Susman, Randall L., ed. 1984. *The Pygmy Chimpanzee: Evolutionary Biology and Behavior.* New York: Plenum.

Susman, Randall L. 1994. "Fossil Evidence for Early Hominid Tool Use." *Science,* 265 (September 9): 1570–73.

Susman, Randall L., Jack T. Stern, Jr., and William L. Jungers. 1985. "Locomotor Adaptations in the Hadar Hominids." In E. Delson, ed., *Ancestors: The Hard Evidence.* New York: Alan R. Liss, pp. 184–92.

Sussman, Robert W. 1972. "Child Transport, Family Size, and the Increase in Human Population Size during the Neolithic." *Current Anthropology*, 13: 258–67.

Sussman, Robert W. 1991. "Primate Origins and the Evolution of Angiosperms." *American Journal of Primatology*, 23: 209–23.

Sussman, Robert W., and W. G. Kinzey. 1984. "The Ecological Role of the Callitrichidae: A Review." *American Journal of Physical Anthropology*, 64: 419–49.

Sussman, Robert W., and Peter H. Raven. 1978. "Pollination by Lemurs and Marsupials: An Archaic Coevolutionary System." *Science*, 200 (May 19): 734–35.

Swanson, Guy E. 1969. *The Birth of the Gods: The Origin of Primitive Beliefs.* Ann Arbor: University of Michigan Press.

Swisher, C. C., III, G. H. Curtis, T. Jacob, A. G. Getty, A. Suprijo, and Widiasmoro. 1994. "Age of the Earliest Known Hominids in Java, Indonesia." *Science*, 263 (February 25): 1118–21.

Szalay, Frederick S. 1968. "The Beginnings of Primates." *Evolution* 22: 32–33.

Szalay, Frederick S. 1972. "Paleobiology of the Earliest Primates." In R. Tuttle, ed., *The Functional and Evolutionary Biology of the Primates.* Chicago: University of Chicago Press, pp. 3–35.

Szalay, Frederick S. 1975. "Hunting-Scavenging Protohominids: A Model for Hominid Origins." *Man*, 10: 420–29.

Szalay, Frederick S., and Eric Delson. 1979. *Evolutionary History of the Primates.* New York: Academic Press.

Szalay, Frederick S., I. Tattersall, and R. Decker. 1975. "Phylogenetic Relationships of *Plesiadipis*—Postcranial Evidence." *Contributions to Primatology*, 5: 136–66.

Szklut, Jay, and Robert Roy Reed. 1991. "Community Anonymity in Anthropological Research: A Reassessment." In C. Fluehr-Lobban, ed., *Ethics and the Profession of Anthropology: Dialogue for a New Era.* Philadelphia: University of Pennsylvania Press, pp. 97–116.

Tannen, Deborah. 1990. *You Just Don't Understand: Women and Men in Conversation.* New York: William Morrow and Company.

Tattersall, Ian. 1982. *The Primates of Madagascar.* New York: Columbia University Press.

Tattersall, Ian. 1999. *The Last Neanderthal.* Boulder, CO: Westview, pp. 115–16.

Tattersall, Ian. 2002. "Paleoanthropology and Evolutionary Theory." In P. N. Peregrine, C. R. Ember, and M. Ember, eds., *Physical Anthropology: Original Readings in Method and Practice.* Upper Saddle River, NJ: Prentice Hall.

Tattersall, Ian, and Jeffrey Schwartz. 2000. *Extinct Humans.* Boulder, CO: Westview.

Tattersall, Ian, Eric Delson, and John Van Couvering, eds. 2000. *Encyclopedia of Human Evolution and Prehistory.* New York: Garland.

Taylor, R. E., and M. J. Aitken, eds. 1997. *Chronometric Dating in Archaeology.* New York: Plenum.

Teleki, Geza. 1973. "The Omnivorous Chimpanzee." *Scientific American* (January): 32–42.

Templeton, Alan R. 1993. "The 'Eve' Hypotheses: A Genetic Critique and Reanalysis." *American Anthropologist*, 95: 51–72.

Templeton, Alan R. 1996. "Gene Lineages and Human Evolution." *Science*, 272 (May 31): 1363.

Textor, Robert B., comp. 1967. *A Cross-Cultural Summary.* New Haven, CT: HRAF Press.

Thomas, David H. 1986. *Refiguring Anthropology: First Principles of Probability and Statistics.* Prospect Heights, IL: Waveland.

Thomas, Wesley. 1993. "A Traditional Navajo's Perspectives on the Cultural Construction of Gender in the Navajo World." Paper presented at the University of Frankfurt, Germany. As referred to in Lang 1999.

Thomason, Sarah Grey, and Terrence Kaufman. 1988. *Language Contact, Creolization, and Genetic Linguistics.* Berkeley: University of California Press.

Thompson, Ginger. 2002. "Mexico Is Attracting a Better Class of Factory in Its South." *The New York Times*, June 29, p. A3.

Thompson, Seth. 1965. "Star Husband Tale." In A. Dundes, ed., *The Study of Folklore.* Upper Saddle River, NJ: Prentice Hall.

Thompson-Handler, Nancy, Richard K. Malenky, and Noel Badrian. 1984. "Sexual Behavior of *Pan paniscus* under Natural Conditions in the Lomako Forest, Equateur, Zaire." In R. Susman, ed., *The Pygmy Chimpanzee.* New York: Plenum.

Tierney, Patrick. 2000. *Darkness in El Dorado.* New York: Norton.

Tobias, Philip V. 1994. "The Craniocerebral Interface in Early Hominids: Cerebral Impressions, Cranial Thickening, Paleoneurobiology, and a New Hypothesis on Encephalization." In R. Corruccini and R. Ciochon, eds., *Integrative Paths to the Past.* Upper Saddle River, NJ: Prentice Hall.

Tollefson, Kenneth D. 2004. "Tlingit: Chiefs Past and Present." In *Portraits of Culture*, in C. R. Ember, M. Ember, and P. N. Peregrine, eds., *New Directions in Anthropology.* Upper Saddle River, NJ: Prentice Hall, CD-ROM.

Torrey, E. Fuller. 1972. *The Mind Game: Witchdoctors and Psychiatrists.* New York: Emerson Hall.

Torry, William I. 1986. "Morality and Harm: Hindu Peasant Adjustments to Famines." *Social Science Information*, 25: 125–60.

Traphagan, John W., and L. Keith Brown. 2002. "Fast Food and Intergenerational Commensality in Japan: New Styles and Old Patterns." *Ethnology*, 41: 119–34.

Travis, John. 2000. "Human Genome Work Reaches Milestone." *Science News* (July 1): 4–5.

Treiman, Donald J., and Harry B. G. Ganzeboom. 1990. "Cross-National Comparative Status-Attainment Research." *Research in Social Stratification and Mobility*, 9: 117.

Trevor-Roper, H. R. 1971. "The European Witch-Craze of the Sixteenth and Seventeenth Centuries." In W. A. Lessa and E. Z. Vogt, eds., *Reader in Comparative Religion*, 3rd ed. New York: Harper & Row.

Trigger, Bruce G. 1989. *A History of Archaeological Thought.* Cambridge: Cambridge University Press.

Trinkaus, Erik. 1985. "Pathology and the Posture of the La Chapelle-aux-Saints Neandertal." *American Journal of Physical Anthropology*, 67: 19–41.

Trinkaus, Erik. 1986. "The Neandertals and Modern Human Origins." *Annual Review of Anthropology*, 15: 193–218.

Trinkaus, Erik. 1987. "Bodies, Brawn, Brains, and Noses: Human Ancestors and Human Predation." In M. Nitecki and D. Nitecki, eds., *The Evolution of Human Hunting.* New York: Plenum.

Trinkaus, Erik, and William W. Howells. 1979. "The Neanderthals." *Scientific American* (December): 118–33.

Trinkaus, Erik, and Pat Shipman. 1993a. *The Neandertals: Changing the Image of Mankind.* New York: Knopf.

Trinkaus, Erik, and Pat Shipman. 1993b. "Neandertals: Images of Ourselves." *Evolutionary Anthropology*, 1: 194–201.

Trouillot, Michel-Rolph. 2001. "The Anthropology of the State in the Age of Globalization: Close Encounters of the Deceptive Kind." *Current Anthropology*, 42: 125–38.

Trudgill, Peter. 1983. *Sociolinguistics: An Introduction to Language and Society*, rev. ed. New York: Penguin.

Turner, Christy G., II. 1987. "Telltale Teeth." *Natural History* (January): 6–9.

Turner, Christy G., II. 1989. "Teeth and Prehistory in Asia." *Scientific American* (February): 88–95.

Tuttle, Russell H. 1986. *Apes of the World: Their Social Behavior, Communication, Mentality, and Ecology.* Park Ridge, NJ: Noyes.

Ucko, Peter J., and Andrée Rosenfeld. 1967. *Paleolithic Cave Art.* New York: McGraw-Hill.

Underhill, Anne. 2002. "Investigating Craft Specialization during the Longshan Period of China." In P. N. Peregrine, C. R. Ember, and M. Ember, eds., *Archaeology: Original Readings in Method and Practice.* Upper Saddle River, NJ: Prentice Hall.

Underhill, Ralph. 1975. "Economic and Political Antecedents of Monotheism: A Cross-Cultural Study." *American Journal of Sociology*, 80: 841–61.

Underhill, Ruth M. 1938. *Social Organization of the Papago Indians.* New York: Columbia University Press.

Urban Institute. 2000. "America's Homeless II: Populations and Services." Washington, D.C.: Urban Institute. Accessed at http://www.urban.org/housing/homeless/numbers/index.htm.

U.S. Department of Housing and Urban Development. 2007. "HUD Releases Landmark Homeless Study." http://www.hud.gov/news/release.cfm?CONTENT=pr07-220.cfm.

Valente, Thomas W. 1995. *Network Models of the Diffusion of Innovations.* Cresskill, NJ: Hampton Press.

Valladas, H., J. L. Joron, G. Valladas, O. Bar-Yosef, and B. Vandermeersch. 1988. "Thermoluminescence Dating of Mousterian 'Proto-Cro-Magnon' Remains from Israel and the Origin of Modern Man." *Nature*, 337 (February 18): 614–16.

Van der Merwe, N. J. 1992. "Reconstructing Prehistoric Diet." In S. Jones, R. Martin, and D. Pilbeam, eds., *The Cambridge Encyclopedia of Human Evolution.* New York: Cambridge University Press.

Van Lawick-Goodall, Jane. 1971. *In the Shadow of Man.* Boston: Houghton Mifflin.

Vekua, Abesalom, et al. 2002. "A New Skull of Early *Homo* from Dmanisi, Georgia." *Science,* 297 (July 5): 85–89.

Vigilant, Linda, Mark Stoneking, Henry Harpending, Kristen Hawkes, and Allan C. Wilson. 1991. "African Populations and the Evolution of Human Mitochrondrial DNA." *Science,* 253 (September 27): 1503–507.

"Violent Crime." 1994. NCJ-147486, Washington, D.C.: U.S. Department of Justice.

Vogel, Joseph O. 2002. "De-Mystifying the Past: Great Zimbabwe, King Solomon's Mines, and Other Tales of Old Africa." In P. N. Peregrine, C. R. Ember, and M. Ember, eds., *Archaeology: Original Readings in Method and Practice.* Upper Saddle River, NJ: Prentice Hall.

von Frisch, Karl. 1962. "Dialects in the Language of the Bees." *Scientific American* (August): 78–87.

Wadley, Reed L. 2003. "Lethal Treachery and the Imbalance of Power in Warfare and Feuding." *Journal of Anthropological Research,* 59: 531–54.

Wagley, Charles. 1974. "Cultural Influences on Population: A Comparison of Two Tupi Tribes." In P. J. Lyon, ed., *Native South Americans.* Boston: Little, Brown.

Wald, Matthew L. 2000. "Hybrid Cars Show Up in M.I.T.'s Crystal Ball." *The New York Times,* November 3, p. Fl; and the special advertisement produced by energy companies, "Energy: Investing for a New Century," *The New York Times,* October 30, pp. EN1–8.

Waldbaum, Jane C. 2005. "Helping Hand for China." *Archaeology,* 58: 6.

Walker, Alan, and R. Leakey. 1988. "The Evolution of *Australopithecus boisei.*" In F. Grine, ed., *Evolutionary History of the "Robust" Australopithecines.* New York: Aldine, pp. 247–58.

Wallace, Anthony. 1966. *Religion: An Anthropological View.* New York: Random House.

Wallace, Anthony. 1970. *The Death and Rebirth of the Seneca.* New York: Knopf.

Wanner, Eric, and Lila R. Gleitman, eds. 1982. *Language Acquisition: The State of the Art.* Cambridge: Cambridge University Press.

Ward, Peter M., ed. 1982. *Self-Help Housing: A Critique.* London: Mansell.

Ward, Steve. 1997. "The Taxonomy and Phylogenetic Relationships of *Sivapithecus* Revisited." In D. R. Begun, C. V. Ward, and M. D. Rose, eds., *Function, Phylogeny, and Fossils: Miocene Hominoid Evolution and Adaptation.* New York: Plenum, pp. 269–90.

Ward, Steve, B. Brown, A. Hill, J. Kelley, and W. Downs. 1999. "*Equatorius:* A New Hominoid Genus from the Middle Miocene of Kenya." *Science,* 285 (August 27): 1382–86.

Wardhaugh, Ronald. 2002. *An Introduction to Sociolinguistics,* 4th ed. Oxford: Blackwell.

Washburn, Sherwood. 1960. "Tools and Human Evolution." *Scientific American* (September): 62–75.

Weaver, Muriel Porter. 1993. *The Aztecs, Maya, and Their Predecessors,* 3rd ed. San Diego: Academic Press.

Webb, Karen E. 1977. "An Evolutionary Aspect of Social Structure and a Verb 'Have.'" *American Anthropologist,* 79: 42–49.

Weber, Max. 1947. *The Theory of Social and Economic Organization.* Trans. A. M. Henderson and Talcott Parsons. New York: Oxford University Press.

Weiner, J. S. 1954. "Nose Shape and Climate." *Journal of Physical Anthropology,* 4: 615–18.

Weiner, Jonathan. 1994. *Beak of the Finch.* New York: Vintage.

Weiner, Steve, Q. Xi, P. Goldberg, J. Liu, and O. Bar-Yousef. 1998. "Evidence for the Use of Fire at Zhoukoudian, China." *Science,* 281 (July 10): 251–53.

Weinreich, Uriel. 1968. *Languages in Contact.* The Hague: Mouton.

Weisner, Thomas S., and Ronald Gallimore. 1977. "My Brother's Keeper: Child and Sibling Caretaking." *Current Anthropology,* 18: 169–90.

Weiss, Harvey, M. A. Courty, W. Wetterstrom, F. Guichard, L. Senior, R. Meadow, and A. Curnow. 1993. "The Genesis and Collapse of Third Millennium North Mesopotamian Civilization." *Science,* 261 (August 20): 995–1004.

Wenke, Robert J. 1984. *Patterns in Prehistory: Humankind's First Three Million Years,* 2nd ed. New York: Oxford University Press.

Wenke, Robert. 1990. *Patterns in Prehistory: Humankind's First Three Million Years,* 3rd ed. New York: Oxford University Press.

Werner, Dennis. 1975. "On the Societal Acceptance or Rejection of Male Homosexuality." M. A. thesis, Hunter College of the City University of New York.

Werner, Dennis. 1978. "Trekking in the Amazon Forest." *Natural History* (November): 42–54.

Werner, Dennis. 1979. "A Cross-Cultural Perspective on Theory and Research on Male Homosexuality." *Journal of Homosexuality,* 4: 345–62.

Werner, Dennis. 1982. "Chiefs and Presidents: A Comparison of Leadership Traits in the United States and among the Mekranoti-Kayapo of Central Brazil." *Ethos,* 10: 136–48.

Wheat, Joe B. 1967. "A Paleo-Indian Bison Kill." *Scientific American* (January): 44–52.

Wheatley, Paul. 1971. *The Pivot of the Four Quarters.* Chicago: Aldine.

Wheeler, Peter. 1984. "The Evolution of Bipedality and Loss of Functional Body Hair in Hominids." *Journal of Human Evolution,* 13: 91–98.

Wheeler, Peter. 1991. "The Influence of Bipedalism in the Energy and Water Budgets of Early Hominids." *Journal of Human Evolution,* 23: 379–88.

Whitaker, Ian. 1955. *Social Relations in a Nomadic Lappish Community.* Oslo: Utgitt av Norsk Folksmuseum.

White, Benjamin. 1973. "Demand for Labor and Population Growth in Colonial Java." *Human Ecology,* 1, no. 3 (March): 217–36.

White, Douglas R. 1988. "Rethinking Polygyny: Co-Wives, Codes, and Cultural Systems." *Current Anthropology,* 29: 529–88.

White, Douglas R., and Michael L. Burton. 1988. "Causes of Polygyny: Ecology, Economy, Kinship, and Warfare." *American Anthropologist,* 90: 871–87.

White, Douglas R., Michael L. Burton, and Lilyan A. Brudner. 1977. "Entailment Theory and Method: A Cross-Cultural Analysis of the Sexual Division of Labor." *Behavior Science Research,* 12: 1–24.

White, Frances J. 1996. "*Pan paniscus* 1973 to 1996: Twenty-three Years of Field Research." *Evolutionary Anthropology,* 5: 11–17.

White, Randall. 1982. "Rethinking the Middle/Upper Paleolithic Transition." *Current Anthropology,* 23: 169–75.

White, Tim D., Donald C. Johanson, and William H. Kimbel. 1981. "*Australopithecus africanus:* Its Phyletic Position Reconsidered." *South African Journal of Science,* 77: 445–70.

White, Timothy D., G. Suwa, and B. Asfaw. 1994. "*Australopithecus ramidus,* a New Species of Early Hominid from Aramis, Ethiopia." *Nature,* 371 (September 22): 306–33.

White, Timothy D., G. Suwa, and B. Asfaw. 1995. "Corrigendum: *Australopithecus ramidus,* a New Species of Early Hominid from Aramis, Ethiopia." *Nature,* 375 (May 4): 88.

Whiten, A., et al. 1999. "Cultures in Chimpanzees." *Nature,* 399 (June 17): 682–85.

Whiting, Beatrice Blyth. 1950. *Paiute Sorcery.* Viking Fund Publications in Anthropology No. 15. New York: Wenner-Gren Foundation.

Whiting, Beatrice Blyth. 1965. "Sex Identity Conflict and Physical Violence." *American Anthropologist,* 67: 123–40.

Whiting, Beatrice Blyth, and Carolyn Pope Edwards. 1973. "A Cross-Cultural Analysis of Sex Differences in the Behavior of Children Aged Three through Eleven." *Journal of Social Psychology,* 91: 171–88.

Whiting, Beatrice Blyth, and John W. M. Whiting (in collaboration with Richard Longabaugh). 1975. *Children of Six Cultures: A Psycho-Cultural Analysis.* Cambridge, MA: Harvard University Press.

Whiting, Beatrice Blyth, and Carolyn Pope Edwards (in collaboration with Carol R. Ember, Gerald M. Erchak, Sara Harkness, Robert L. Munroe, Ruth H. Munroe, Sara B. Nerlove, Susan Seymour, Charles M. Super, Thomas S. Weisner, and Martha Wenger). 1988. *Children of Different Worlds: The Formation of Social Behavior.* Cambridge, MA: Harvard University Press.

Whiting, John W. M. 1964. "Effects of Climate on Certain Cultural Practices." In W. Goodenough, ed., *Explorations in Cultural Anthropology.* New York: McGraw-Hill.

Whittaker, John C. 1994. *Flintknapping: Making and Understanding Stone Tools.* Austin: University of Texas Press.

Whyte, Martin K. 1978a. "Cross-Cultural Codes Dealing with the Relative Status of Women." *Ethnology,* 17: 211–37.

Whyte, Martin K. 1978b. *The Status of Women in Preindustrial Societies.* Princeton, NJ: Princeton University Press.

Wiberg, Hakan. 1983. "Self-Determination as an International Issue." In I. M. Lewis, ed., *Nationalism and Self-Determination in the Horn of Africa.* London: Ithaca Press.

Wikan, Unni. 1982. *Beyond the Veil in Arabia.* Baltimore: The Johns Hopkins University Press.

Wilford, John Noble. 1995. "The Transforming Leap, from 4 Legs to 2." *The New York Times,* September 5, pp. C1ff.

Wilford, John Noble. 1997. "Ancient German Spears Tell of Mighty Hunters of Stone Age." *The New York Times,* March 4, p. C6.

Williams, George C. 1992. *Natural Selection: Domains, Levels, and Challenges.* New York: Oxford University Press.

Williams, Melvin D. 2004. "Racism: The Production, Reproduction, and Obsolescence of Social Inferiority." In *Research Frontiers,* in C. R. Ember, M. Ember, and P. N. Peregrine, eds., *New Directions in Anthropology.* Upper Saddle River, NJ: Prentice Hall, CD-ROM.

Williams, Walter L. 1992. *The Spirit and the Flesh.* Boston: Beacon Press.

Wilmsen, Edwin N., ed. 1989. *We Are Here: Politics of Aboriginal Land Tenure.* Berkeley: University of California Press.

Wilson, Edward O. 1975. *Sociobiology: The New Synthesis.* Cambridge, MA: Belknap Press of Harvard University Press.

Winkelman, Michael. 1986a. "Magico-Religious Practitioner Types and Socioeconomic Conditions." *Behavior Science Research,* 20: 17–46.

Winkelman, Michael. 1986b. "Trance States: A Theoretical Model and Cross-Cultural Analysis." *Ethos,* 14: 174–203.

Winkelman, Michael, and Philip M. Peck, eds. 2004. *Divination and Healing: Potent Vision.* Tucson: University of Arizona Press.

Winterhalder, Bruce. 1990. "Open Field, Common Pot: Harvest Variability and Risk Avoidance in Agricultural and Foraging Societies." In E. Cashdan, ed., *Risk and Uncertainty in Tribal and Peasant Economies.* Boulder, CO: Westview.

Witkowski, Stanley R. 1975. "Polygyny, Age of Marriage, and Female Status." Paper presented at the annual meeting of the American Anthropological Association, San Francisco.

Witkowski, Stanley R., and Cecil H. Brown. 1978. "Lexical Universals." *Annual Review of Anthropology,* 7: 427–51.

Witkowski, Stanley R., and Harold W. Burris. 1981. "Societal Complexity and Lexical Growth." *Behavior Science Research,* 16: 143–59.

Wittfogel, Karl. 1957. *Oriental Despotism: A Comparative Study of Total Power.* New Haven, CT: Yale University Press.

Wolf, Eric. 1966. *Peasants.* Upper Saddle River, NJ: Prentice Hall.

Wolf, Naomi. 1991. *The Beauty Myth: How Images of Beauty Are Used against Women.* New York: Morrow.

Wolff, Ronald G. 1991. *Functional Chordate Anatomy.* Lexington, MA: D. C. Heath.

Wolpoff, Milford H. 1971. "Competitive Exclusion among Lower Pleistocene Hominids: The Single Species Hypothesis." *Man,* 6: 601–13.

Wolpoff, Milford H. 1983. "*Ramapithecus* and Human Origins: An Anthropologist's Perspective of Changing Interpretations." In R. Ciochon and R. Corruccini, eds., *New Interpretations of Ape and Human Ancestry.* New York: Plenum.

Wolpoff, Milford H., and Abel Nikini. 1985. "Early and Early Middle Pleistocene Hominids from Asia and Africa." In E. Delson, ed., *Ancestors: The Hard Evidence.* New York: Alan R. Liss, pp. 202–205.

Wolpoff, Milford H. 1999. *Paleoanthropology,* 2nd ed. Boston: McGraw-Hill.

Wong, Kate. 2003. "An Ancestor to Call Our Own." *Scientific American* (January): 54–63.

Wong, Kate. 2005. "The Littlest Human." *Scientific American* (February): 56–65.

Wood, Bernard A. 1992. "Evolution of Australopithecines." In S. Jones, R. Martin, and D. Pilbeam, eds., *The Cambridge Encyclopedia of Human Evolution.* New York: Cambridge University Press.

Wood, Bernard A. 1994. "Hominid Paleobiology: Recent Achievements and Challenges." In R. Corruccini and R. Ciochon, eds., *Integrative Paths to the Past.* Upper Saddle River, NJ: Prentice Hall.

Wood, Gordon S. 1992. *The Radicalism of the American Revolution.* New York: Knopf.

Wood, James W., George R. Milner, Henry C. Harpending, and Kenneth M. Weiss. 1992. "The Osteological Paradox: Problems of Inferring Prehistoric Health from Skeletal Samples." *Current Anthropology,* 33 (1992): 343–70.

Woodburn, James. 1968. "An Introduction to Hadza Ecology." In R. B. Lee and I. DeVore, eds., *Man the Hunter.* Chicago: Aldine.

World Bank. 1995. *World Development Report 1995. Workers in an Integrating World.* Oxford: Oxford University Press.

World Bank. 2001. *2001 World Development Indicators.* Washington, D.C.: World Bank.

Wright, Gary A. 1971. "Origins of Food Production in Southwestern Asia: A Survey of Ideas." *Current Anthropology,* 12: 447–78.

Wright, Henry T. 1986. "The Evolution of Civilizations." In D. Meltzer, D. Fowler, and J. Sabloff, eds., *American Archaeology Past and Future.* Washington, D.C.: Smithsonian Institution Press.

Wright, Henry T., and Gregory A. Johnson. 1975. "Population, Exchange, and Early State Formation in Southwestern Iran." *American Anthropologist,* 77: 267–77.

Wynn, Thomas. 1979. "The Intelligence of Later Acheulean Hominids." *Man,* 14: 371–91.

Yamei, Hou, et al. 2000. "Mid-Pleistocene Acheulean-like Stone Technology of the Bose Basin, South China." *Science,* 287 (March 3): 1622–26.

Yergin, Daniel. 2002. "Giving Aid to World Trade." *The New York Times,* June 27, p. A29.

Yinger, J. Milton. 1994. "*Ethnicity: Source of Strength? Source of Conflict?*" Albany: State University Press.

Young, T. Cuyler, Jr. 1972. "Population Densities and Early Mesopotamian Urbanism." In Ucko, Tringham, and Dimbleby, eds., *Man, Settlement, and Urbanism.* Cambridge, MA: Scherkman.

Zeder, Melinda A. 1991. *Feeding Cities: Specialized Animal Economy in the Ancient Near East.* Washington, D.C.: Smithsonian Institution Press.

Zeder, Melinda A. 1997. *The American Archaeologist: A Profile.* Walnut Creek, CA: AltaMira Press.

Zihlman, Adrienne L. 1992. "The Emergence of Human Locomotion: The Evolutionary Background and Environmental Context." In T. Nishida et al., eds., *Topics in Primatology,* vol. 1.

Zimmer, Carl. 1999. "Kenyan Skeleton Shakes Ape Family Tree." *Science,* 285 (August 27): 1335–37.

Zimmer, Carl. 2004. "Faster Than a Hyena? Running May Make Humans Special." *Science,* 306 (November 19): 1283.

Zohary, Daniel. 1969. "The Progenitors of Wheat and Barley in Relation to Domestication and Agriculture Dispersal in the Old World." In P. J. Ucko and G. W. Dimbleby, eds., *The Domestication and Exploitation of Plants and Animals.* Chicago: Aldine.

PHOTO CREDITS

State Historic Site, painting by Michael Hampshire; page 208: Paul Harris/Getty Images Inc.-Stone Allstock; page 209: Wolfgang Kaehler/Corbis/Bettmann.

CHAPTER 9

Page 212: © Mark A. Johnson/CORBIS, All Rights Reserved; page 215: © Cameron/CORBIS, All Rights Reserved; page 217 (left): N. Martin Haudrich/Photo Researchers, Inc.; page 217 (right): James L. Stanfield/National Geographic Image Collection; page 220 (left): © Ariel Skelley/CORBIS, All Rights Reserved; page 220 (right): © Rolf Bruderer/CORBIS, All Rights Reserved; page 222 (left): Jeremy Horner/Corbis/Bettmann; page 222 (right): Jonathan Blair/Corbis/Bettmann; page 226: © Christel Gerstenberg/CORBIS, All Rights Reserved; page 228: Dagli Orti/The Art Archive/Musée Lapérouse Albi.

CHAPTER 10

Page 233: © Anthony Bannister/Gallo Images/CORBIS, All Rights Reserved; page 236 (left): © Peter Steiner/CORBIS, All Rights Reserved; page 236 (right): Susan Kuklin/Science Source/Photo Researchers, Inc.; page 239: Roy Morsch/Corbis/Bettmann; page 245: © Philip Spruyt/Stapleton Collection/CORBIS, All Rights Reserved; page 249: Vince Streano/Corbis/Bettmann; page 251 (left): Rhoda Sidney; page 251 (right): Renate Hiller; page 255: © Caroline Penn/CORBIS, All Rights Reserved.

CHAPTER 11

Page 258: © Keren Su/CORBIS, All Rights Reserved; page 263: Victor Englebert/Photo Researchers, Inc.; page 265: © Keren Su/CORBIS, All Rights Reserved; page 267: Tiziana Baldizzone/Corbis/Bettmann; page 268: © Richard Hamilton Smith/CORBIS, All Rights Reserved; page 272: James P. Blair/NGS Image Collection; page 274: © Jeremy Horner/CORBIS, All Rights Reserved; page 275: © Bernard Annebicque/Corbis Sygma; page 276: John Roberts/Corbis/Stock Market; page 279: John Eastcott/Yva Momatiuk/Woodfin Camp & Associates, Inc.

CHAPTER 12

Page 284: © Andrew Holbrooke; page 287: Wendy Stone/CORBIS–NY; page 289: Wendy Stone/Odyssey/Chicago/Odyssey Productions, Inc.; page 290: Mike Dobel/Masterfile Corporation; page 293: © Sherwin Crasto/Reuters/Corbis; page 297: Photograph provided courtesy of Syracuse University, All rights reserved; page 300 (left): © Kevin Fleming/CORBIS, All Rights Reserved; page 300 (right): David de Lossy, Ghislain & Marie/Getty Images Inc.-Image Bank.

CHAPTER 13

Page 305: Marc Romanelli/Getty Images Inc.-Image Bank; page 307: Pete Saloutos/Corbis/Stock Market; page 310: Jorgen Shytte/Peter Arnold, Inc.; page 312: Laurence Fordyce/Corbis/Bettmann; page 316: Ann Mohs/Bruce Miller; page 317: © Setboun/CORBIS, All Rights Reserved; page 320 (left): © Kevin Cozad/O'Brien Productions/CORBIS, All Rights Reserved; page 320 (right): © Michael Newman/PhotoEdit, Inc.; page 322: Charles Lenars/Corbis/Bettmann.

CHAPTER 14

Page 327: Don Mason/Corbis/Stock Market; page 328: © Lindsay Hebberd/CORBIS, All Rights Reserved; page 330: © Punch/Rothco; page 332: © Caroline Penn/CORBIS, All Rights Reserved; page 334: © Lindsay Hebberd/CORBIS, All Rights Reserved; page 336: Nik Wheeler/Corbis/Bettmann; page 339: © Hamid Sardar/CORBIS, All Rights Reserved; page 342: Toshifumi Kiramura/Agence France Presse/Getty Images; page 347: Harvey Lloyd/Getty Images, Inc.–Taxi; page 352: Eric Smith/Art Directors & Trip Photo Library.

CHAPTER 15

Page 355: Lionel Bonaventure/Corbis/Sygma; page 360: Katz/Anthro-Photo File; page 363: Peter Andrews/Reuters/Corbis/Reuters America LLC; page 365: © European Commission/Handout/Reuters/CORBIS, All Rights Reserved; page 367: Maria Lepowsky; page 371: David Austen/Woodfin Camp & Associates, Inc.

CHAPTER 16

Page 377: © Dallas and John Heaton/Free Agents Limited/CORBIS, All Rights Reserved; page 380: ScienceCartoonsPlus.com; page 381: © Reuters/Jorge Silva/Corbis; page 384: Mike Yamashita/Woodfin Camp & Associates, Inc.; page 387: © Catherine Karnow/CORBIS, All Rights Reserved; page 391: Ogallala Sioux performing the Ghost Dance at the Pine Ridge Indian Agency, South Dakota, Illustration by Frederic Remington, 1890, The Granger Collection.

CHAPTER 17

Page 396: Greg Girard/Contact Press Images Inc.; page 399: Getty Images, Inc.; page 401: © Bettmann/CORBIS, All Rights Reserved; page 403: Currier & Ives, "Give Me Liberty or Give Me Death!" 1775, Lithograph, 1876, © The Granger Collection, New York; page 406: Peter Bowater/Photo Researchers, Inc.; page 409: Wolfgang Kaehler Photography; page 411: AP Wide World Photos; page 412: Peter Turnley/Corbis/Bettmann.

CHAPTER 18

Page 417: David Greedy/Getty Images, Inc.–Liaison; page 419: Rick Wilking/Corbis/Reuters America LLC; page 421: Sucheta Das/Corbis/Reuters America LLC; page 427: Edouard Berne/Getty Images Inc.–Stone Allstock; page 428: Peter Glass/Peter Glass Photography; page 431: Peter Chen/The Image Works; page 432: © Dusko Despotovic/Bettmann/CORBIS, All Rights Reserved.

CHAPTER 19

Page 435: Richard Lord/The Image Works; page 436: © Reuters/Diario El Pais/Corbis; page 440: Kamal Kishore/Corbis/Reuters America LLC; page 442: © Yannis Kontos/Corbis Sygma; page 445: Jeffrey Aaronson/Still Media; page 446: Henning Christoph/DAS FOTOARCHIV/Peter Arnold, Inc.; page 449: Martha Cooper/Peter Arnold, Inc.; page 451: © Gideon Mendel for The International HIV/AIDS Alliance/CORBIS, All Rights Reserved; page 454: Michael J. Balick/Peter Arnold, Inc.

INDEX

Page numbers followed by *t* indicate tables. Page numbers followed by *f* indicate figures. Page numbers in bold type indicate glossary entries.